INDEX to
American
Reference
Books
Annual

1995–1999
A Cumulative Index to Subjects, Authors, and Titles

INDEX to
American
Reference
Books
Annual

1995–1999
A Cumulative Index to Subjects, Authors, and Titles

COMPILED BY **Susan D. Strickland
and Shannon M. Graff**

1999
LIBRARIES UNLIMITED, INC.
Englewood, Colorado

Copyright © 1999 Libraries Unlimited, Inc.
All Rights Reserved
Printed in the United States of America

No part of this publication may be reproduced, stored in a retrieval system, or transmitted, in any form or by any means, electronic, mechanical, photocopying, recording, or otherwise, without the prior written permission of the publisher.

LIBRARIES UNLIMITED, INC.
P.O. Box 6633
Englewood, CO 80155-6633
1-800-237-6124
www.lu.com

ISBN 1-56308-492-9   ISSN 0192-6969

CONTENTS

Preface vii

AUTHOR/TITLE INDEX. 1

SUBJECT INDEX. 143

PREFACE

American Reference Books Annual (ARBA) is well established as a comprehensive source of reviews for all types of reference books and CD-ROMs published or distributed in the United States and Canada. The 30 annual volumes of ARBA, which began in 1970, contain more than 50,000 reviews of reference books. These titles include books and CD-ROMs on almost any topic in a variety of reference formats (e.g., almanacs, bibliographies, catalogs, dictionaries, encyclopedias, handbooks, indexes).

Access to each annual volume is provided through that volume's indexes of authors, titles, and subjects. Offering comprehensive access, the cumulative index brings together five years of ARBA. Joseph Sprug prepared the first 5-year volume, *Index to American Reference Books Annual 1970-1974*, Christine Gehrt-Wynar, *Index to American Reference Books Annual 1975-1979*; Ruth Blackmore, *Index to American Reference Books Annual 1980-1984;* and Anna Grace Patterson, *Index to American Reference Books Annual 1985-1989* and *Index to American Reference Books Annual 1990-1994*. Although each cumulative index volume contains author, title, and subject indexes, some variations in style and organization showing the unique hand of each volume's individual compiler exists among the volumes.

This cumulative index merges five years of information on published reference materials that have appeared in ARBA from 1995 to 1999. Each entry in ARBA presents full bibliographic information, an evaluative review, and citations to professional journals containing other published reviews. The index is more than a location devise; it is a critical tool for the scholar, librarian, and reader seeking to tap ARBA's wealth of information.

Index to American Reference Books Annual 1995-1999 covers 8,372 books and CD-ROMs reviewed during the 1995-1999 period. In order to offer a reasonable-sized book, short titles and abbreviated words within titles are used.

AUTHORS AND TITLES

The author/title index is arranged alphabetically word by word (when a word is abbreviated, it is filed as if it were spelled out). Multiple volumes of the same title are arranged numerically. Books with the same title published in different years are arranged chronologically. Acronyms are filed alphabetically as they appear.

Author entries in the 1995-1999 index contain author's name with year and entry number.

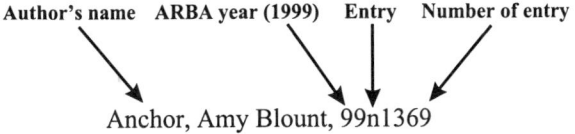

Authors, editors, and compilers appear in the index as their names are shown on the title page; therefore, if authors have written books under their full names, initials, or parts of both, they will appear under all forms in the index.

> Smith, J. L.
> Smith, John
> Smith, John L.

All single, joint, and corporate authors are individually indexed.

Titles appear in a shortened form in title entries. Ordinarily, subtitles are deleted. Usually, abbreviated words are filed as if they were spelled out. Entries show title, year of ARBA, and entry number.

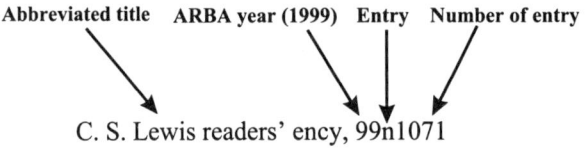

SUBJECTS

The subject index, with a few variations, uses terms that are based upon the 19th edition of *Library of Congress Subject Headings*. This format allows easy access to titles from different years of ARBA. The subject terms are arranged alphabetically and ignore punctuation; therefore, one may find the following alphabetical arrangement:

> EUROPE
> EUROPE, EASTERN
> EUROPE—HISTORY
> EUROPE—POLITICS & GOVERNMENT

Each of these entries will have titles with year and entry number appearing beneath them:

> EUROPE
> Bibliography of European economic & social hist, 2d ed, 95n552
> Birds of Europe with N Africa & the Middle East, 95n1568
> Book of European forecasts, 2d ed, 97n238

Cross-references, both *see* and *see also*, facilitate use of the index.

ACKNOWLEDGMENTS

Although many people have been involved in the preparation of this index, special appreciation goes to Mark Greider for developing the computer program, Pamela J. Getchell for her typesetting, and Bohdan S. Wynar for his encouragement and advice. Comments or suggestions for improvement of this index are encouraged.

Susan D. Strickland and Shannon M. Graff

Author/Title Index

Reference is to entry number.

A&E entertainment almanac, 1997, 98n1264
A. Samarsinghe, S. W. R. de, 99n484
A-Z of cat diseases & health problems, 99n1386
A-Z of contract clauses, 98n531
A-Z of creative photography, 99n860
A-Z of horror films, 98n1297
A to Z of Native American women, 99n386
A-to-Z of pregnancy & childbirth, 95n1645
A to zoo: subject access to children's picture bks, 99n1008
A's & B's of academic scholarships, 95n378
AACC membership dir 1994, 95n358
AACC who's who in community colleges 1993, 95n359
AACTE dir of members, 1994, 95n338
Aaker, Everett, 98n1276
AALL ref bk, 96n593
Aaseng, Nathan, 96n410
AB Bookman's yrbk, 1993-94, 95n970
ABA official American Bar Assn gd to approved law schools, 1999 ed, 99n558
Abate, Frank R., 95n82, 95n500, 98n993, 99n900
Abate, Randall S., 98n558
Abbey, Cherie D., 98n21
Abbott, James, 96n1887
Abbott, R. Tucker, 96n1595
Abbott, Tony, 95n1703
Abbreviations dict, 9th ed, 96n2
ADC for bk collectors, 7th ed, 96n1001
ABC of bkbinding, 99n855
ABC-CLIO world hist companion to capitalism, 99n158
ABC-CLIO world hist companion to utopian movements, 99n1253
ABC-CLIO companion to ...
    American reconstruction, 1862-77, 97n420
    the American labor movement, 95n294
    the civil rights movement, 95n627
    the disability rights movement, 98n776
    the environmental movement, 96n1869
    the media in America, 96n964
    the Native American rights movement, 97n341
    the 1960s counterculture in America, 98n437
    transportation in America, 97n1437
    women in the workplace, 95n913
    women's progress in America, 95n914
Aboba, Bernard, 95n1701
Abortion, 1996 ed, 98n754
Abortion, 2d ed, 97n666
Abortion & reproductive rights [CD-ROM], 98n755
Abortion policies, v.3, 97n665
Abridged Dewey decimal classification & relative index, 13th ed, 98n579
Abstract expressionist women painters, 97n808
AbuKhalil, As'ad, 99n507
Abuov, Zhoumagaly, 97n876

Aby, Stephen H., 98n753
Academic advising: an annot bibliog, 95n357
Academic American ency, 95n41, 98n36
Academic focus Japan: programs & resources in N America, 96n423
Academic lib of the 90s, 96n620
Academic libs in the UK & the Republic of Ireland 1994, 3d ed, 96n635
Academic yr abroad 1995/96, 96n368
Academy awards index, 95n1400
Accent on living buyer's gd, 1994-95 ed, 96n853
ACCESS: the supplementary index to pers, 96n78
ACCESS gd to ethnic conflicts in Europe & the former Soviet Union, 95n146
ACCESS gd to intl affairs internships in the Washington, DC, area, 95n762
ACCESS travel USA: a dir for people with disabilities, 96n856
Accessing US govt info, rev ed, 97n54
Accounting research dir, 3d ed, 95n217
Accredited insts of postsecondary educ, 1997-98, 99n316
Acevedo, Margaret, 99n192, 99n195, 99n213, 99n214
Achar, Rajani, 98n178
Achenbaum, W. Andrew, 96n846
Achor, Amy Blount, 99n1369
Acquaintance & date rape: an annot bibliog, 95n634
Acronyms, initialisms, & abbrevs dict 1997, 21st ed, 97n1
ACS style gd, 2d ed, 98n872
Action! the action movie A-Z, 98n1293
Acton, Edward, 98n481
Acts of the Apostles, 98n1370
Ad men & women, 95n320
Adam, Nicky, 95n1283
Adamec, Ludwig W., 97n106, 98n110
Adams, A. E., 95n1724
Adams, Brian, 95n580
Adams, Bruce, 98n731
Adams electronic job search almanac 1998, 99n264
Adams, Jerome R., 96n938
Adams job almanac 1995, 96n265
Adams jobs almanac 1998, 99n265
Adams, K. Gary, 99n1127
Adams, McCrea, 98n1059, 99n1102
Adams Publishing, editors of, 96n265
Adams, Ramon F., 95n1041
Adamson, Hugh C., 99n1272
Adamson, Lynda G., 95n1161, 99n449, 99n450, 99n512, 99n513, 99n797
Aday, Kathryn L., 98n758
Aday, Ronald H., 98n758
Addison-Wesley sci hndbk, 98n1412
Address bk for German genealogy, 6th ed, 98n363
Address bk for Germanic genealogy, 5th ed, 95n452
Adelman, Alan, 97n310

Adelman, Irving, 98n1108
Adkins, Lesley, 95n586, 96n547, 99n500
Adkins, Roy A., 95n586, 96n547, 99n500
Adler, Bill, Jr., 95n1728, 96n1767
Adler, Daryl, 95n798
Adler, Eve, 96n1128
Adler, Laura, 97n693
Adler, Leonore Loeb, 95n871
Adloff, Richard, 97n95
Adolescence: the survival gd for parents & teenagers, 98n802
Adolescents at risk, 95n1134
Adoption, 99n755
Adoption dir, 2d ed, 96n860
Adrian Bloom's yr-round garden, 99n1347
Advanced composites world ref dict, 99n1410
Adventure heroes, 95n930
Adventure holidays 1995, 18th ed, 96n460
Adventure vacations, 96n473
Adventures in video, 97n314
Advisory Committee for the Co-ordination of Information Systems (ACCIS), 96n769, 96n1783
AEA dir, 1993-94, 95n1609
AFB dir of servs for blind & visually impaired persons in the US & Canada, 99n748
AFB dir of servs for blind & visually impaired persons in the US & Canada [CD-ROM], 99n749
Affirmative action, 97n484
Africa, 98n103
Africa: Africa World Press gd to educ resources from & about Africa, 99n94
Africa, Asia, & S America since 1800, 96n555
Africa in figures 1996, 98n102
Africa in lit for children & YAs, 96n1166
Africa on file, 96n108
Africa S of the Sahara 1997, 26th ed, 98n108
African acronyms & abbrevs, 98n104
African America, 95n406
African American almanac, 98n346
African American almanac, 7th ed, 98n335
African American biog, 95n403
African American biogs, 2, 95n407
African American breakthroughs, 96n397
African American chronology, 95n408
African American criminologists, 1970-96, 99n575
African American ency suppl, 98n336
African American films through 1959, 99n1234
African American genealogical sourcebk, 96n429
African American historic places, 95n410
African American hist in the press 1851-99, 97n412
African American quotations, 99n80
African American theatre dir, 1816-1960, 98n1328
African American voices, 97n328
African art, 98n956
African biog, 99n373
African biogl dict, 96n109
African bks in print, 4th ed, 95n22
African ethnonyms, 97n315
African hist on file, 96n529
African intl relations, 2d ed, 98n699
African placenames, 95n502

African studies companion, 2d ed, 98n105
African traditional religion in South Africa, 98n1344
African writers, 98n1167
African-American address bk, 96n52
African-American almanac, 6th ed, 95n404
African-American baby name bk, 99n407
African-American business leaders, 95n181
African-American firsts, 95n409
African-American inventors, 96n1488
African-American orators, 98n337
African-American scientists, 96n1489
African-American sports greats, 96n792
African-American woman: social & economic conditions, 95n901
African-American yellow pages, 97n329
AGELINE on SilverPlatter: 1978-August 1994 [CD-ROM], 95n831
Ager, David J., 96n1792
Aggression & conflict, 96n835
Aghion, Irene, 98n1257
Aging sourcebk, 99n744
Aging well, 96n838
Agricultural entomology, 96n1625
Agriculture in Britain & America 1660-1820, 95n1512
Agriculture, mining, & construction USA, 99n187
Agrochemicals desk ref: environmental data, 95n1510
AIA gd to the architecture of Washington, DC, 3d ed, 96n1049
Aicher, Peter J., 96n1046
AIDS, 1996 ed, 98n1559
AIDS: a multimedia sourcebk, 95n1675
AIDS crisis, 99n1468
AIDS dict, 99n1470
AIDS funding, 4th ed, 97n683
Aird, Forbes, 96n1883
Airlie, Maree, 96n1123
Airlines worldwide, 99n1573
Aitchison, Jean, 97n705
Akiyama, Carol, 97n859
Akiyama, Nobuo, 97n859
Al Jolson: a bio-bibliog, 95n1345
ALA fingertip gd to natl health-info resources 1995-96, ref desk ed, 96n1684
Alabama hist, 99n451
Alali, A. Odasuo, 95n616
Alampi, Gary, 95n895, 97n279
Alampi, Mary, 99n602
Alaska A to Z, 95n100
Albala, Elie, 96n249
Albala, Leila, 96n249
Alban Berg: a gd to research, 97n1045
Albania, rev ed, 99n118
Albanian etymological dict, 99n921
Albaugh, Gaylord P., 96n1447
Albert, Daniel M., 96n846
Albert, George, 95n1291, 96n1312
Albert, Richard N., 97n944
Alcohol in the British Isles from Roman times to 1996, 97n441
Alcoholism & aging, 96n897
Aldcroft, Derek H., 95n552
Alderton, David, 96n67, 96n70

Aldighieri, Ann Marie, 97n3, 99n2
Aldred, Heather E., 98n1561, 99n1438
Aldrich, Richard, 99n289
Alexander, Harriet Semmes, 97n1015
Alexander, William, 95n1630
Algeria, rev ed, 97n93
Ali, Javed, 99n644
Aliens, robots, & spaceships, 96n1360
All music bk of hit albums, 97n1066
All music bk of hit singles, 95n1293
All music bk of hit singles, 97n1067
All music gd, 2d ed, 95n1256
All music gd, 3d ed, 98n1228
All music gd to country, 98n1230
All music gd to jazz, 95n1304
All music gd to rock, 96n1330
All music gd to rock, 2d ed, 98n1238
All music gd to the blues, 97n1072
All over the map, 95n470
All the best contests for kids 1994-95, 95n1324
Allaby, Michael, 96n1497, 96n1854, 99n1525, 99n1526, 99n1527, 99n1528, 99n1529, 99n1530
Allen, Chris, 98n106
Allen, Dell K., 96n1670
Allen, Gerald R., 96n1633
Allen, Larry, 99n158
Allen, Marilyn O'Connell, 99n953, 99n987
Allen, Rick, 96n1384
Allen, Ruth, 99n989
Allen Sapp: a bio-bibliog, 97n1038
Allergies A-Z, 95n1677
Allin, Craig W., 99n1571
Allison, A. F., 95n1463
Allison, Jonathan, 98n1174
Allison, Kathleen Cahill, 98n1564
Allison, Robert J., 99n467, 99n469
Allison, Stephen, 98n1401
Alloy finder [CD-ROM], 96n1660
Allsopp, Richard, 97n834
Almanac of ...
    American employers 1996-97, 97n259
    American employers 1998-99, 99n266
    business & industrial financial ratios 1996, 27th ed, 98n177
    European pols 1995, 97n605
    famous people, 6th ed, 99n17
    intl jobs & careers, 95n314
    state legislatures, 95n710
    the executive branch 1997/98, 98n642
    the unelected, 98n649
    the unelected 1994, 95n713
Alphabet: a hndbk of ABC bks, 2d ed, 96n328
Alphabetical gd to the lang of name studies, 97n824
Alpines, 96n1590
Altamiranda, Daniel, 99n1098
Altbach, Philip G., 95n666, 96n370
Alternative advisor: the complete gd to natural therapies & alternative treatments, 98n1544
Alternative healing, 95n1671
Alternative health & medicine ency, 96n1716
Alternative health & medicine ency, 2d ed, 99n1457

Alternative medicine: the definitive gd, 95n1669
Alternative medicine resource gd, 98n1547
Alternative paths to teaching, 95n360
Alternative press index, 97n58
Alternative publishers of bks in N America, 2d ed, 96n668
Alternative realities, 96n785
Alternative travel dir 1998, 4th ed, 99n439
Alternatives to the Peace Corps, 96n868
Altherr, Thomas L., 99n711
Alting, Leo, 96n1670
Altitude-rated places, v.1, 2d ed, 95n1664
Altman, Roberta, 95n1580
Altman, Susan, 98n338
Altner, Patricia, 99n1035
Aluminum & aluminum alloys, 95n1622
Alvino, Paola, 96n170
Alyson almanac, 1994-95 ed, 95n852
AMA style gd for business writing, 98n873
Aman, Michael G., 95n1687
Amateur radio ency, 95n960
Amazing animals of the world, 96n1603
Amell, Samuel, 97n1014
America: hist & life on disc [CD-ROM], 96n512
America at the polls, 95n737
America in histl fiction, 98n1114
America in so many words, 98n1000
America in the 20th century, 96n499
America preserved, 96n1047
America votes 21, 96n735
America votes 22, 99n677
American Academy of Pediatrics gd to your child's symptoms, 99n1464
American & British poetry, 97n1015
American Animal Hospital Assn ency of cat health & care, 96n1618
American Animal Hospital Assn ency of dog health & care, 96n1619
American Animal Hospital Assn, 96n1618, 96n1619
American art colonies, 1850-1930, 97n800
American art dir 1997-98, 56th ed, 99n871
American artists of Italian heritage, 1776-1945, 95n1002
American assn: yr-by-yr stats for the baseball minor league, 1902-52, 98n738
American Assn of Colleges for Teacher Educ dir of members 1995, 96n316
American attitudes, 2d ed, 99n90
American bibliog of Slavic & E European studies for 1993, 97n114
American Bird Conservancy's field gd to all the birds of N America, 98n1459
American black women in the arts & social scis, 3d ed, 95n416
American bk & mag illustrators to 1920, v.188, 99n884
American bk collectors & bibliographers, 2d series, 99n591
American bk of the dead: the definitive Grateful Dead ency, 99n1175
American bk publishing record, cum 1993, 95n17
American bk publishing record, cum 1997, 99n9
American bk trade dir 1997-98, 98n596
American bk-collectors & bibliographers, 1st series, 95n971

American business climate & economic profiles, 95n207
American business disc, 1995 ed [CD-ROM], 96n181
American business locations dir, 97n157
American Camping Assn, 96n811
American casino gd, 1997 ed, 98n411
American chemists & chemical engineers, v.2, 95n1718
American choral music since 1920, 95n1280
American Civil War, 96n504, 97n421
American community colleges, 10th ed, 96n362
American cost of living survey, 95n205
American decades 1900-09, 97n422
American decades 1910-19, 97n423
American decades 1920-29, 97n424
American decades 1930-39, 96n513
American decades 1940-49, 96n514
American decades 1950-59, 95n544
American decades 1960-69, 96n515
American decades 1970-79, 96n516
American decades 1980-89, 97n425
American decades on CD [CD-ROM], 99n457
American Diabetes Assn complete gd to diabetes, 98n1562
American dir of job & labor market info, 95n298
American diversity, American identity, 96n1198
American drama criticism: suppl 4 to the 2d ed, 97n1146
American dream: the 50s, 99n466
American electricians' hndbk, 13th ed, 98n1485
American elves, 98n1255
American eras: Civil War & reconstruction, 1850-77, 98n444
American eras: dvlpmt of a nation 1783-1815, 99n467
American eras: dvlpmt of the industrial US, 1878-99, 98n445
American eras: the reform era & E US dvlpmt, 99n468
American eras: the revolutionary era 1754-83, 99n469
American evangelicalism 2: 1st bibliogl suppl, 1990-96, 98n1383
American expatriate writers, 98n1127
American export register 1995, 96n286
American Film Inst cat of motion pictures produced in the US: feature films, 1931-40, 95n1367
American Film Inst cat, within our gates: ethnicity in American feature films, 1911-60, 98n1288
American film personnel & co credits, 1908-20, 97n1142
American first ladies, 97n407
American folklore, 97n1088
American forecaster almanac 1994, business ed, 95n3
American foreign policy during the French Revolution-Napoleonic period 1789-1815, 95n712
American foreign policy index 1995, v.3, no.2, 96n743
American fuging-tunes, 1770-1820, 95n1281
American govt & pols, 98n646
American health care in transition, 98n1503
American Heritage children's dict, 96n1086
American Heritage children's thesaurus, 98n1016
American Heritage Dictionaries, editors of, 95n1046, 96n1086, 96n1095
American Heritage dict of American quotations, 99n75
American Heritage dict of idioms, 98n1006
American Heritage ency of American hist, 99n458
American Heritage 1st dict, 95n1046
American Heritage Stedman's medical dict, 96n1697
American Heritage student dict, 95n1047

American Heritage talking dict [CD-ROM], 98n997
American Heritage talking dict, 3d ed [CD-ROM], 96n1062
American Histl Assn's gd to histl lit, 3d ed, 96n554
American homelessness: a ref hndbk, 2d ed, 95n842
American Horticultural Society A-Z ency of garden plants, 98n1432
American house designs: an index to popular & trade pers, 1850-1915, 96n1050
American humanities index for 1995, v.21, 97n744
American immigrant cultures, 99n365
American Indian: a multimedia ency [CD-ROM], 98n352
American Indian law deskbk, 2d ed, 99n561
American Indian quotations, 97n345
American Indian ref & resource bks for children & YAs, 2d ed, 96n1177
American Indian reservations & trust areas, 97n342
American Indian studies, 96n421
American Jewish Historical Society, 95n449
American Jewish yr bk 1996, v.96, 97n1220
American jobs abroad, 95n313
American leaders 1789-1994, 95n714
American legislative leaders in the West, 1911-94, 98n650
American Lib Assn gd to info access, 95n641
American Lib Assn Reference Bks Bulletin Editorial Board, 95n14, 96n12
American Lib Assn Social Responsibilities Round Table Alternatives in Print Task Force, 96n668
American lib dir 1994-95, 95n638
American lib dir 1996-97, 49th ed, 98n572
American mag journalists, 1900-60: 2d series, 95n955
American marketplace, 3d ed, 98n246
American Medical Assn family medical gd [CD-ROM], 96n1707
American men & women of sci 1995-96, 19th ed, 96n1485
American military hist, 96n678
American music in the 20th century, 99n1124
American musical theatre song ency, 96n1416
American naturalization records 1790-1990, 2d ed, 99n402
American nature writers, 97n965
American novel explication 1991-95, 99n1040
American novelists since WWII, 3d series, 96n1204
American novelists since WWII, 4th series, 96n1203
American novelists since WWII, 5th series, 98n1128
American paintings in the Detroit Institute of Arts, v.2, 99n887
American places dict, 95n500
American playwrights, 1880-1945, 96n1202
American poets since WW II, 5th series, 98n1140
American poets since WW II, 4th series, 98n1141
American pol scientists, 95n705
American pop from minstrel to mojo: on record, 1893-1956, 99n1162
American popular culture, 96n1357
American popular psychology, 95n771
American population before the fed census of 1790, 95n891
American population change annual 1994, 95n885
American presidency [CD-ROM], 98n668
American printmakers 1880-1945, 95n1009
American prisons, 99n574
American proverbs about women, 99n807
American reform & reformers, 97n408

American Revolutionary War sites, memorials, museums, & lib collections, 99n472
American salaries & wages survey, 3d ed, 96n266
American salaries & wages survey, 4th ed, 98n229
American sci fiction TV series of the 1950s, 99n1213
American short-story writers since WW II, 95n1179
American Sign Lang concise dict, rev ed, 96n1132
American Sign Lang dict, rev ed, 96n1133
American Sign Lang dict on CD-ROM [CD-ROM], 96n1130
American Sign Lang, unabridged ed, 99n910
American silent film comedies, 96n1378
American Society for Testing & Materials, 95n1635
American song, 2d ed, 97n1077
American stock exchange, 96n211
American stock exchange 1994 fact bk, 95n218
American studies in China: a dir, 95n109
American synagogue, 97n1221
American theatre, 97n1150
American theatre: a chronicle of comedy & drama, 1869-1914, 95n1418
American travel writers, 1776-1864, 99n1044
American univs & colleges, 15th ed, 99n348
American West: a multicultural ency, 96n505
American women, 98n247
American women historians, 1700s-1990s, 97n411
American women in sci, 96n1486
American women in sci, 1950 to the present, 99n1299
American women writers, v.5, 95n1168
American women's almanac, 98n826
American women's track & field, 97n664
American writers, 99n1043
American writers, retrospective suppl 1, 99n1045
American writers, suppl 4, 97n961
Americana song reader, 99n1125
Americans 55 & older, 99n279
Americans & their homes, 99n783
Americans at play, 98n726
Americans traveling abroad, 95n515
America's best bed & breakfasts, 2d ed, 98n408
America's best beers, 96n1536
America's best genealogy resource centers, 99n399
America's best hotels & restaurants, 98n409
America's corporate families 1995, 97n158
America's 50 fastest growing jobs, 2d ed, 95n308
America's intl trade, 96n239
America's lowest cost colleges, 9th ed, 96n359
America's new fndns 1998, 12th ed, 99n760
America's religions, 98n1364
America's royalty, rev ed, 96n719
America's Standard Gauge electric trains, 99n852
America's top internships, 1998 ed, 98n221
America's top jobs for college graduates, rev ed, 95n309
America's top jobs for people without college degrees, 3d ed, 98n227
America's top medical & human servs jobs, 2d ed, 95n310
America's top office, mgmt, & sales jobs, 2d ed, 95n311
America's top office, mgmt, sales, & professional jobs, 3d ed, 98n228
America's top technical & trade jobs, 2d ed, 95n312
America's top-rated cities 1997, 5th ed, 98n820
America's top-rated smaller cities, 1994-95 ed, 96n926
America's top-rated smaller cities 1996-97, 2d ed, 98n821
Ametsbichler, Elizabeth G., 99n1095
Amey, Lawrence, 99n607
Amico, Eleanor B., 99n796
Amindarov, Aziz, 96n1114
Ammer, Christine, 96n1680, 98n1006
Ammon, Bette D., 98n1090
Amory, Hugh, 97n39
Amos, Kharma, 96n1652, 97n1416, 97n1418
Amphibians & reptiles of Alta., 95n1596
Amphibians & reptiles of Trinidad & Tobago, 98n1474
Amsel, Nachum, 95n1475
Amsterdam, 96n476, 99n135
Amusement parks, 2d ed, 95n796
Anastazievsky, Walter, 95n956, 95n957
Anatomy of wonder 4, 96n1191
Anaya, Alison, 99n316
Ancell, R. Manning, 97n409
Ancestors: a beginner's gd to family hist & genealogy, 98n372
Ancestral trails: the complete gd to British genealogy & family hist, 99n401
Ancient Caribbean, 95n420
Ancient civilizations of the Mediterranean [CD-ROM], 99n490
Ancient Egypt, 98n486
Ancient Greece & Rome, 99n491
Ancient Greeks, 98n472
Ancient Peruvian art, 97n794
Ancient Romans, 99n518
Ancient Rome chronology, 264-27 BC, 99n523
Ancient world lists & nos, 96n41
And Adam knew Eve: a dict of sex in the Bible, 96n1452
Andacht, Sandra, 98n890
Anders CD-ROM gd, 2d ed, 97n15
Anders, Susan B., 95n330
Andersen, Charles J., 99n349
Anderson, Bruce H., 95n1575
Anderson, Byron, 96n668
Anderson, David S., 96n1667
Anderson, Erland, 96n1245
Anderson, Gerald H., 99n1281
Anderson, Gordon T., 99n201
Anderson, Ian E., 96n980
Anderson, James D., 98n1142, 98n1185, 99n1100
Anderson, Kenneth N., 95n1514
Anderson, Lois E., 95n1514
Anderson, Lorin W., 97n298
Anderson, Sarah, 97n383
Anderson, Sean, 96n597
Anderson, Vicki, 95n1116, 95n1117, 95n1118, 99n1010
Anderson's travel companion: a gd to the best non-fiction & fiction for travelling, 97n383
Andorra, 95n148
Andre Malraux, 96n1253
Andres, Linda R., 99n953, 99n987
Andrew M. Greeley: an annot bibliog, 95n1191
Andrews, Barry, 96n1248
Andrews, Joyce, 98n1038

Andrews, Robert, 95n88, 98n80
Andrews, Shelly, 98n1061, 98n1062, 98n1063
Andrews, Tamra, 99n1184
Andrews, William L., 98n1129
Angels A to Z, 97n1176
Anglim, Christopher, 97n480
Anglim, Christopher Thomas, 98n515
Animal health yrbk 1993, 96n1553
Animal life, 96n1604
Animal rights, 96n1435
Animal rights, 2d ed, 99n1369
Animal rights movement in the US, 1975-90, 96n1424
Animals on screen & radio, 96n1366
Annimated film collector's gd, 99n1222
Animation, caricature, & gag & pol cartoons in the US & Canada, 95n1331
Anjo, Ikuko, 95n1084
Ankrapp, Betty, 97n1324, 98n1520
Ann Radcliffe, 97n998
Ann Sheridan: a bio-bibliog, 98n1274
Annales historiography & theory, 95n573
Anne Tyler: a critical companion, 99n1051
Annenberg, Maurice, 96n666
Annotated art, 96n1052
Annotated bibliog of Canada's major authors, v.8, 95n1227
Annotated bibliog of Jane Austen studies 1984-94, 97n988
Annotated bibliog of jazz fiction & jazz fiction criticism, 97n944
Annotated bibliog of N America doctoral dissertations on old Norse-Icelandic, 99n892
Annotated bibliog on leprosy, 99n1472
Annotated catalog, S Texas College of law, special collections, 97n480
Annotated catalogue of early eds of Erasmus, 96n1250
Annotated catalogue of types of the Univ of Ill. mycological collections (ILL), 98n1451
Annotated dict of technical, histl, & stylistic terms relating to Theatre & Drama, 96n1417
Annotated gd to adoption research 1986-97, 99n754
Annotations: a dir of pers listed in the Alternative Press Index, 1996 ed, 97n63
Annual bibliog of modern art, 1995, 98n939
Annual bulletin for transport stats for Europe, 1995, v.45, 96n1877
Annual bulletin of ...
    coal stats for Europe & N America, 1994, 96n1838
    electric energy stats for Europe & N America, 1994, v.38, 96n1839
    gas stats for Europe & N America 1994, v.38, 96n1840
    housing & bldg stats for Europe & N America 1996, 98n822
    stats of world trade in steel 1993, 96n287
    steel stats for Europe, v.21: 1991-94, 97n1307
    trade in chemical products, 97n1384
    transport stats for Europe & N America 1996, v.46, 98n1644
Annual gd to graduate nursing educ 1997, 99n1474
Annual obituary 1993, 95n23
Annual register 1995, 97n581
Annual register 1997, 99n657

Annual report of the USA 1998, 99n673
Annual review of info sci & tech, v.28, 95n642
Annual review of info sci & tech, v.29, 1994, 96n622
Ansell, Janis, 99n999
Anson, Chris M., 95n333
Answer atlas, 98n380
Anthony Eden, 1897-1977, 96n759
Anthony, Michael, 98n484
Anthropological lit on disc [CD-ROM], 95n391, 98n317
Anthropology bibliog on disc [CD-ROM], 99n362
Anthropology of religion, 98n1359
Anti-abortion movement, 98n756
Anticancer drugs from animals, plants, & microorganisms, 96n1740
Antiquarian bks, 96n1002
Antiquarian, specialty, & used bk sellers 1997-98, 2d ed, 98n597
Antique & collectible buttons, 98n902
Antique Trader Books antiques & collectibles price gd, 1999 ed, 99n840
Antique trader's gd to games & puzzles, 98n891
Antisemitism, v.3, 95n628
Antokoletz, Elliott, 98n1210
Anton Rubinstein, 99n1144
Antonio Gardano, Venetian Music Printer 1538-69, 99n1112
Antosz, Lynn, 98n1517
Anzovin, Steven, 95n102, 99n46
APELL annot bibliog, 96n777
Apostolos-Cappadona, Diane, 96n1028, 97n797
Appel, Marsha C., 99n876
Apple, Hope, 97n946
Apple, Rima D., 95n904
Applegate, Edd, 95n320, 97n977, 99n1062
Applications in criminal analysis, 96n604
Applied sci & tech index 1996, 98n1418
APT for libs 1995: alternative pr titles for the general reader, 96n79
Apte, Vasudeo Govind, 97n868
Aquarium fish, 95n1586
Aquarium fish of the world, 95n1589
Aquariums of N America, 96n1621
Arab women in ESCWA member states, 96n156
Arab-Israeli dispute, 97n457
Arakin, V. D., 98n1045
Arany, Lynne, 96n1400
Arany-Makkai, Agnes, 98n1043
Arav, Rami, 97n1213
ARBA gd to subject encys & dicts, 2d ed, 98n5
Arceneaux, Elizabeth, 99n213
Archaeology of prehistoric Native America, 99n443
Archaeology of the Mississippian culture, 97n398
Archibald, Chestina Mitchell, 98n1369
Architectural graphic standards, 9th ed, 95n1011
Architecture, 98n976
Architecture & ornament, 99n879
Architecture on screen, 95n1012
Architecture sourcebk, 98n977
ArchivesUSA [CD-ROM], 98n430
ARCO 100 best careers in entertainment, 96n1364
Arctic & Antarctic regions [CD-ROM], 96n127

Arctic exploration & dvlpmt, c.500 B.C. to 1915, 95n495
Arden, Andrea, 99n424
Ardley, Neil, 95n1487, 96n1493
Area bibliog of China, 98n112
Area bibliog of Japan, 99n111
Argenti, Paul A., 95n203
Argentina business, 97n245
Argentina co hndbk, 97n246
Argentine novel, 98n1168
Aristotle's Metaphysics: annot bibliog of the 20th-century lit, 99n1250
Arkansas hist, 96n490
Arkin, William M., 98n617
ARL stats 1994-95, 97n527
Armantrout, Neil B., 99n1501
Armenia, 95n149
Armenian American almanac, 96n391
Armenian (Eastern)-English dict, 97n844
Armenian folklore bibliog, 96n1340
Armenian ref bks, 95n150
Armenians & Iran, 2d ed, 95n151
Armitage, Peter, 99n1418
Armored forces: hist & sourcebk, 96n702
Arms, Thomas S., 95n577
Armstrong, C. J., 96n225, 96n453, 96n587, 96n1788, 97n78, 97n172, 97n1241, 97n1247, 97n1383, 98n849
Armstrong, Mary Willems, 95n1389
Armstrong, Megan C., 95n553
Armstrong, Neil, 98n45
Armstrong, Richard B., 95n1389
Army Times bk of great land battles, 96n698
Arnest, Lauren Krohn, 99n551
Arnold, Claude Graveley, 98n1225
Arnold, Corliss Richard, 96n1289
Arnold, Guy, 95n143, 97n568, 97n615, 98n120
Arnold, H. J. P., 98n1604
Arnold, John, 96n39, 97n112
Arnold Schoenberg companion, 99n1128
Arntzen, Charles J., 95n1507
Aromatherapy oils, 98n1551
Aronson, Marc, 96n503
Around the world: an atlas of maps & pictures, 96n443
Arps, Louisa Ward, 95n501
Art: a world hist, 99n874
Art & architecture in the poetry of Robert Browning, appendix A, 98n1154
Art & architecture thesaurus, 2d ed, 95n650
Art & artists of 20th-century China, 98n967
Art & design scholarships, 96n1036
Art bks, 2d ed, 98n940
Art business ency, 95n1004, 96n1039
Art diary 97/98, 98n953
Art directors in cinema, 99n1210
Art for hist's sake, 95n1008
Art index, Nov 1995 to Oct 1996, 98n968
Art mktg sourcebk for the fine artist, 2d ed, 96n1035
Art mktg sourcebk for the fine artist, 3d ed, 99n872
Art nouveau, 99n862
Art of children's picture bks, 2d ed, 96n1183
Art of the ancient Mediterranean world, 98n957

Art on screen on CD-ROM [CD-ROM], 96n1037
Art, truth, & high pols: a bibliographic study of the official lives of Queen Victoria's ministers in Cabinet, 1843-1969, 97n608
ARTbibliographies modern on disc, fall 1993 [CD-ROM], 95n991
Arthur Andersen N American business sourcebk, 96n288
Arthur Bliss: a source bk, 98n1211
Arthurian hndbk, 2d ed, 99n1066
Articles describing archives & ms collections in the US, 98n577
Artists: from Michelangelo to Maya Lin, 96n1024
Artist's & graphic designer's market, 1995, 96n1038
Artist's & graphic designers market, 1998, 99n875
Artists & writers colonies, 97n745
Artists communities, 98n954
Artist's complete health & safety gd, 2d ed, 96n1042
Artist's resource hndbk, 95n1007, 96n1040
Artist's resource hndbk, rev ed, 98n964
ArtNetwork yellow pages, 96n1033
Artworks: a glossary of contemporary art theory, 98n951
Artz, Joan W., 96n978, 98n76
Artz, John C., 99n566
Arweck, Elisabeth, 98n1343
A's & B's of academic scholarships 1997/98, 19th ed, 98n285
Asante, Clement E., 98n850
Ash, Irene, 95n1712, 95n1714, 96n1533, 97n1385
Ash, Michael, 95n1712, 95n1714, 96n1533, 97n1385
Ash, Russell, 96n61, 99n63
Ashby, Bonnie, 99n1445
Ashe, Geoffrey, 99n1066
Asher, R. E., 95n1024, 95n1030
Ashley, Mike, 96n1194
Ashment, Catherine, 99n650, 99n651
Asia, 2d ed, 99n240
Asia Pacific securities hndbk 1993, 95n259
Asian & Australasian companies, 95n240
Asian American almanac, 96n392
Asian American biog, 96n393
Asian American chronology, 97n326
Asian American ency, 96n394
Asian American genealogical sourcebk, 96n430
Asian American woman, 99n795
Asian Americans: social, economic, & pol aspects, 97n327
Asian higher educ, 98n295
Asian hist on file, 96n533
Asian markets, 4th ed, 97n234
Asian states' relations with the Middle East & N Africa, 95n763
Asia-Pacific in figures, 10th ed, 98n811
Asia-Pacific petroleum dir 1998, 14th ed, 99n195
ASIS thesaurus of info sci & librarianship, 95n636
ASIS thesaurus of info sci & librarianship, 2d ed, 99n598
ASM engineered materials ref bk, 2d ed, 95n1623
ASM hndbk, v.5, 96n1661
ASM hndbk, v.6, 95n1626
ASM hndbk: comprehensive index, 95n1624
ASM hndbk: comprehensive index [CD-ROM], 95n1625
ASM Intl Handbook Committee, 95n1624, 96n1661, 96n1665
ASM metals ref bk, 95n1627

ASM ready ref properties & units for engineering alloys, 99n1408
ASM specialty hndbk: stainless steels, 96n1662
ASM specialty hndbk: tool materials, 96n1678
Aspen, Kristan, 98n1218
ASSIA plus [CD-ROM], 96n97
Assistantships & graduate fellowships in the math scis, 1993-94, 95n1738
Assistantships & graduate fellowships in the math scis, 1996-97, 98n1624
Assistantships & graduate fellowships in the math scis, 1997-98, 99n1540
Associated Press, 96n485
Associated Press lib of disasters, 99n64
Associated Press stylebk & libel manual, 6th ed, 98n874
Association for Library Service to Children, 96n661
Association for Population/Family Planning Libs & Info Centers—Intl (AFPLIC-I) union list of serials, 96n861
Association for Population/Family Planning Libs & Info CentersIntl (AFPLIC-I) union list of serials, 96n861
Association of American Univ Prs dir 1996-97, 98n598
Association of Desk & Derrick Clubs, 96n1832
Asteroid name ency, 96n790
ASTM dir of scientific & tech consultants & expert witnesses, 1994 ed, 95n1498
ASTM dir of scientific & tech consultants & expert witnesses, 1997-98 ed, 99n1320
ASTM intl dir of testing laboratories, 1998 ed, 99n1321
ASTM standards in bldg codes, 34th ed, 99n1401
ASTM standards source [CD-ROM], 96n1663
Aston, Mick, 99n444
Astrology ency, 95n790
Astronomy, 96n1800
Astrup, Arne, 95n1303
Athena: classical mythology on CD-ROM [CD-ROM], 95n1318
Athletes, 96n410
Athletic scholarships, 95n795, 96n799
Atkins, Beryl T., 98n1024
Atkins, G. Pope, 98n695
Atkinson, David J., 97n1209
Atkinson, Toby D., 95n253
Atkinson, W. Patrick, 97n1155
Atlas & survey of S Asian hist, 96n534
Atlas of ...
 American agriculture, 97n1246
 American hist, updated ed, 95n524
 American migration, 99n780
 anatomy, English ed, 98n1499
 apartheid, 95n395
 archaeology, 99n444
 British hist, 2d ed, 95n557
 contemporary America, 95n890
 English dialects, 97n839
 global change, 99n1550
 histl county boundaries: Iowa, 99n447
 histl county boundaries: N.C., 99n448
 holy places & sacred sites, 97n1167
 human hist, 97n458
 Indians of N America, 96n413
 industrial protest in Britain, 1750-1990, 97n146
 Jewish hist, 95n446
 Mesozoic & Cenozoic coastlines, 96n1807
 Micronesia, 2d ed, 95n490
 Neptune, 95n1722
 religious change in America, 1952-90, 96n1437
 Russia & the Independent Republics, 96n445
 Russian hist, 2d ed, 95n562
 sacred places, 95n1434
 shipwrecks & treasure, 96n1896
 the Arab-Israeli conflict, 6th ed, 95n759
 the Civil War, 96n486
 the environment, 95n1756
 the Holocaust, 95n569
 the human body, 96n1694
 the langs & ethnic communities of S Asia, 99n101
 the mysterious in N America, 96n786
 the world's langs, 95n1030
 threatened cultures, 98n318
 US economy, tech, & growth, 97n714
 Western art hist, 95n990
 westward expansion, 96n488
 wild places, 95n1558
 world dvlpmt, 96n444
 WW I, 2d ed, 96n675
Attenborough, David, 99n1372
Atterbury, Paul, 95n968
Attitudes toward the outdoors: an annot bibliog, 95n1759
Attwater, Donald, 97n1174
Atwater, Kevin G., 98n650
Atwell, Robert H., 96n362
Atwood, Thomas C., 99n701
Auchter, Dorothy, 99n40
Auchterlonie, Paul, 99n139
Audi, Robert, 97n1159
Audio bk breakthrough, 95n664
Audiovisual resources for family programming, 97n313
Auditions & scenes from Shakespeare, 95n1216
Audouze, Jean, 95n1719
Audrey Hepburn: a bio-bibliog, 95n1347
Auerbach, Alan J., 97n627
Auerbach, Rena R., 96n425
Aufderheide, Arthur C., 99n1439
Auger, C. P., 95n10
Augsburger, Jeff, 98n921
August Wilson: a research & production sourcebk, 99n1249
August, Eugene R., 96n866
Aurbach, Susan, 95n396
Austin, Jan, 95n732
Austin, Mary C., 97n142
Australasia & S Pacific Islands bibliog, 98n144
Australia, 99n436
Australia: a reader's gd, 97n112
Australia business, 97n237
Australian bks in print 1995, 96n22
Australian film, 99n1206
Authentic Jane Williams' home school market gd, 97n280
Authentic Jane Williams' home school market gd, 99n305
Authoritative gd to self-help bks, 95n774

Authors & artists for YAs, v.13, 95n1144
Authors & artists for YAs, v.14, 96n1171
Authors & artists for YAs, v.20, 98n1100
Authors & artists for YAs, v.21, 98n1101
Author's gd to biomedical jls, 95n1661
Autobiographies by Americans of color 1980-94, 98n347
Automobile, 98n1647
AV market place 1994, 95n965
AV market place 1997, 98n884
Avakian, Anne M., 96n1340
Avallone, Susan, 97n767, 99n1219
Avato, Rose M., 95n1471, 97n1203
Aversa, Elizabeth, 95n921
Avery index to architectural pers at Columbia Univ [CD-ROM], 98n970, 95n1013
Avery index to architectural pers, 13th suppl, 95n1014
Avery, Christine, 98n241
Avery's choice: 5 centuries of great architectural bks, 98n971
Aviation: a Smithsonian gd, 96n1882
Aviation & aerospace almanac 1995, 96n1879
Avisson bk of contests & prize competitions for poets, 98n864
Awad, Elias M., 97n1340
Award winning films, 95n1398
Award-winning quilts & their makers, v.1-4, 95n977
Awards alamanac 1996, 97n701
Awards dir 1993-94, 95n1226
Awards, honors, & prizes 1997, 13th ed, 98n49
Awe, Susan C., 98n5
Awesome almanac—N.Y., 97n85
Awesome almanac—Ohio, 97n86
Awesome almanac—Tex., 97n89
Axelrod, Alan, 96n705, 97n415, 97n504, 98n764, 99n538
Axford, Elizabeth C., 99n1148
Axsom, Richard H., 99n867
Ayala, Marta Stiefel, 96n621
Ayala, Reynaldo, 96n621
Aycock, Wendell M., 96n1195, 98n1118
Ayers, Kenneth W., 95n1775
Ayre, Jim, 96n1751
Azemoun, Youssef, 97n876
Azikiwe, Uche, 97n725

B* student's (or lower) complete scholarship bk, 99n338
Babiel, Nikolai, 98n1044
Baca, Murtha, 95n995
Bachtler, John, 97n243
Backstrom, Gayle, 96n854
Bacon, Donald C., 96n720
Bacon's business media dir 1994, 95n933
Bacon's business media dir 1998, 99n821
Bacon's dirs on disc 1995 update [CD-ROM], 96n974
Bacon's Information Inc., 95n933, 95n950, 95n951, 95n961, 95n962
Bacon's intl media dir 1996, 97n760
Bacon's mag dir 1994, 95n950
Bacon's mag dir 1998, 46th ed, 98n876
Bacon's newspaper dir 1994, 95n951
Bacon's newspaper dir 1998, 46th ed, 98n877
Bacon's radio dir 1994, 95n961

Bacon's radio dir 1998, 12th ed, 98n885
Bacon's TV/cable dir 1994, 95n962
Bacon's TV/cable dir 1998, 12th ed, 98n886
Bad boys: legends of hockey's toughest, meanest, most-feared players, 96n826
Baer, Beverly, 95n514, 99n68
Baer, D. Richard, 95n1368
Baerg, Harry J., 96n1611
Baetjer, Katherine, 97n804
Bagby, Meredith, 99n673
Baghdasarian, Louisa, 97n844
Baguley, David, 95n1229
Bahamas hndbk & businessman's annual 1995, 35th ed, 96n170
Bahamonde, Ramon, 99n697
Bahjat, Andrew, 99n643
Bahm, Archie J., 95n1430, 98n1340
Bahn, Paul, 95n520
Bahorsky, Russ, 99n1489
Bail, Paul, 99n1051
Bailey, Brooke, 96n939, 96n940, 96n941
Bailey, Jill, 96n1604
Bailey, Joseph A., 99n552
Bailey, Martha J., 96n1486, 99n1299
Bailey, Walter B., 99n1128
Bailey, William G., 95n73, 95n987, 96n599
Bain, Robert, 96n1199
Baker, Barbara E., 95n302
Baker, Charles F., III, 98n472, 99n518
Baker, Christopher, 97n796
Baker, Daniel B., 96n259, 96n454, 99n418
Baker, David, 95n1787, 97n1300
Baker, Derck, 96n813
Baker ency of Bible places, 96n1450
Baker, Janet, 97n112
Baker, Mark Allen, 97n775, 99n851
Baker, Mona, 99n896
Baker, Philip, 96n111
Baker, Richard, 96n1269
Baker, Rosalie F., 98n472, 99n518
Baker, Theodore, 96n1271
Baker, William, 97n880, 99n592
Baker's biogl dict of 20th-century classical musicians, 98n1197
Baker's dict of music, 99n1123
Bakich, Michael E., 96n1798
Balachandran, M., 95n277
Balachandran, Sarojini, 95n1757
Balay, Robert, 97n8
Balch, James F., 98n1508
Balch, Phyllis A., 98n1508
Bald, Margaret, 99n604
Baldwin, Carl R., 98n702
Baldwin, David, 97n663
Baldwin, Dean, 95n1165, 96n1228
Baldwin, Louis, 97n733
Bales, Barbara A., 97n55
Bales, Jack, 99n1053
Ball, J., 95n1061, 98n1015
Ball, John, 95n1404

Ball perennial manual, 97n1275
Ball pest & disease manual, 99n1360
Ball redbk, 99n1346
Ball, Robert W. D., 98n630, 99n848
Ball, Vic, 99n1346
Ballard, Ednalou C., 98n791
Ballast, David Kent, 95n1602
Ballendorf, Dirk Anthony, 96n168
Ballinger, Erich, 95n1323, 96n598
Baltic states, 95n154
Baltics info sources dir 1996, 98n124
Bamberger, Michelle, 97n1261
Bamberger, W. C., 96n1209
Bambrick, Susan, 95n138
Bangs, David H., Jr., 95n211
Banham, Joanna, 98n935
Banham, Martin, 95n1420, 96n1415
Bank profitability: financial statements of banks 1983-92, 95n227
Banks, Peter, 99n1471
Banks, Robert, 98n1385
Bankston, Carl L., III, 96n138
Banned bks: lit suppressed on pol grounds, 99n603
Banned bks: lit suppressed on rel grounds, 99n604
Banned bks: lit suppressed on sexual grounds, 99n605
Banned bks: lit suppressed on social grounds, 99n606
Banned in the media, 99n825
Banned in the USA, 95n658
Bantas, Andrei, 97n865
Barbanell, Edward, 99n1252
Barber, David W., 99n1119
Barber, Katherine, 99n41
Barbier, Karen, 98n185
Barbillon, Claire, 98n1257
Barbour, Roger W., 96n1636
Barbuto, Domenica M., 96n230
Bardwell, Rebecca, 97n735
Barile, Michele A., 99n142
Barish, Eileen, 98n402
Barker, Nicolas, 96n1001
Barker, Robert L., 96n890
Barlow, Clive, 99n1373
Barlow, Deborah L., 95n101
Barlowe, Wayne Douglas, 98n979
Barlowe's gd to fantasy, 98n979
Barnard, Alan, 97n317
Barnard, Timothy, 97n1124
Barnes, Dana Ramel, 99n1082, 99n1083
Barnes, Jay, 99n1531
Barnes, John A., 96n422
Barnes, Judy, 99n427
Barnes, Rik, 97n385, 98n410
Barnes-Svarney, Patricia, 96n1512, 99n1484
Barnett, Colleen A., 99n1030
Barnhardt, Clarence L., 95n1053
Barnhardt, Phillip, 96n267
Barnhart abbrevs dict, 96n1
Barnhart, Clarence L., 98n1009
Barnhart concise dict of etymology, 97n825
Barnhart, David K., 95n1025, 98n1000, 98n1010

Barnhart dict companion, v.10, no.1, summer 1997, 98n1010
Barnhart new-words concordance, 95n1025
Barnhart, Phillip A., 98n313
Barnhart, Richard M., 99n888
Barnhart, Robert K., 96n1, 97n825, 98n996
Baron, Deborah G., 97n326
Baron, Scott, 99n623
Barondess, Jeremiah A., 96n1702
Barone, Michael, 99n674
Baroque art, 97n798
Barovick, Barry M., 95n206
Barr, Catherine, 95n644, 96n623, 99n993
Barranger, Milly S., 95n1340
Barrera, Rosalinda B., 98n1087
Barrett, Buckley Barry, 95n565
Barrett, David V., 98n1360
Barron, Neil, 95n1158, 96n1191, 99n1036
Barron's best buys in college educ, 3d ed, 96n331
Barron's best buys in college educ, 5th ed, 99n317
Barron's business thesaurus, 97n178
Barron's compact gd to colleges, 9th ed, 95n361
Barron's educl series, college division, 95n361
Barron's ency of cat breeds, 99n1382
Barron's gd to graduate business schools, 99n318
Barron's gd to law schools, 11th ed, 96n581
Barron's jr illus dict: French-English, 95n1072
Barron's Russian dict, 98n1044
Barrow, Steve, 99n1171
Barrows, Robert G., 96n929
Barry, Bob, 95n4
Barry, Ines, 97n206
Barson, Michael, 96n1367
Barstow, Barbara, 96n1180
Barstow, Jane Missner, 98n1124
Barteau, Harry C., 97n119
Barterian, Gerald R., 99n973, 99n974
Barthelmas, Della Gray, 98n434
Bartis, Peter T., 96n1341
Bartlett, Johnathan, 97n1248
Bartlett, Laurence, 97n991
Bartnett, Joy E., 99n1447
Barton, Barbara J., 95n1525
Barton, Wayne, 99n1028
Basch, Elizabeth, 95n345, 95n622, 95n863
Baseball: a comprehensive bibliog, suppl 2, 99n717
Baseball & American culture, 96n806
Baseball by the nos, 97n650
Baseball ency update, 1995, 96n803
Baseball pioneers: ratings of 19th century players, 98n730
Baseball ratings, 2d ed, 96n804
Baseball records registry, 98n728
Basic business lib: core resources, 3d ed, 96n173
Basic laboratory & industrial chemicals, 95n1717
Basic music lib, 3d ed, 98n1186
Basic Newbury House dict of American English, 99n898
Basic word list, 3d ed, 98n992
Baskin, Ellen, 97n1104
Bassett, Jane, 98n983
Bassett, John E., 97n976
Bastian, Dawn E., 99n98

Bataille, Gretchen M., 97n322
Batalden, Sandra L., 95n163, 98n125
Batalden, Stephen K., 95n163, 98n125
Batchelor, R. E., 95n1073
Bates, Dawn, 96n1119
Bates, Timothy, 95n178
Batho, V. A., 95n564
Bati, Anwar, 96n1351
Batson, Raymond, 98n1609
Batten, Donna, 98n49, 99n670
Battles of the Somme, 1916, 97n561
Battleships: US battleships, 1935-92, rev ed, 96n700
Battleships of the world, 98n626
Battley, Nick, 95n221
Bauccio, Michael, 95n1623, 95n1627
Bauer, Aaron M., 95n1596, 96n1634
Bauer, David G., 97n684
Baughman, Judith S., 95n1177, 97n424
Baum, Harald, 99n546
Bauman, Richard W., 97n492
Baumgartner, James, 97n683
Baumgartner, James E., 96n896, 96n952, 97n300, 97n531, 97n697, 97n698, 97n1184
Baumgartner, Walter, 96n1455, 97n1198
Bauml, Betty J., 98n711
Bauml, Franz H., 98n711
Baumohl, Jim, 98n766
Baxter, Angus, 95n453, 95n454, 95n455
Baxter, Colin F., 97n460
Baxter, Craig, 98n460
Baxter, Joan, 98n1301
Baxter, Mark, 98n562
Bayers, Albert F., III, 96n1781
BBC Music Mag top 1000 CDs gd, 97n1055
BBI dict of English word combinations, rev ed, 99n913
Be reasonable, 95n1433
Beach, Cecilia, 95n1405, 97n943
Bead dir, 2d ed, 95n978
Bead dir, 3d ed, 96n1011
Beadle, David, 96n1613
Beadle, Richard, 95n1419
Beal, George, 95n1051, 96n1088
Beall, Julianne, 97n535, 98n579
Beam, Joan, 97n958
Beaman, Mark, 99n1374
Beanie family album & collectors gd, 99n853
Bear, John, 96n363, 99n302
Bear, Mariah, 96n363, 99n302
Bearden, William O., 95n321
Beasley, Heather, 98n272
Beat generation, 99n1042
Beatles memorabilia price gd, 3d ed, 98n921
Beatles: the ultimate recording gd, 3d ed, 96n1338
Beaton, K. B., 98n1029
Beaty, Wayne, 99n1546
Beaumont, J. Graham, 97n626
Beauregard, Estelle, 95n621
Beaver, Bonnie V., 96n1554
Bebbington, Warren, 99n1122
Becher, Anne, 99n1556

Bechtel, Stefan, 95n1647
Beck, John H., 96n1291
Beck, Robert J., 99n1549
Beckel, Lothar, 99n1550
Becker, Udo, 95n1441
Beckett, Wendy, 95n1018
Beckner, Chrisanne, 96n927
Beckson, Karl, 99n1075
Bed & breakfast ency, 98n427
Bee genera of N & Central America (Hymenoptera: Apoidea), 95n1591
Beede, Benjamin R., 95n685
Beeley, Brian W., 99n134
Beeman, Marsha Lynn, 95n1341
Beene, LynnDianne, 98n1143
Beer lover's rating gd, 96n1537
Beers, G. Kylene, 97n925
Beers, Mark H., 98n1540
Beer-Taster's log, 97n1252
Beethoven ency, 96n1281
Behrens, David W., 97n1295
Beider, Alexander, 98n375
Beim, Howard J., 99n1568
Beinecke Lesser Antilles collection at Hamilton College, 95n171
Beinert, Wolfgang, 96n1475
Beit-Hallahmi, Benjamin, 99n1264
Bel Canto operas of Rossini, Donizetti, & Bellini, 96n1300
Bela Bartok: a gd to research, 2d ed, 98n1210
Belchem, John, 95n578
Bell, Edward L., 95n519
Bell, George H., 95n1562
Bell, Joan Kuder, 95n1216
Bell, Richard O., 95n1216
Bell, Walter F., 95n101
Bellenir, Karen, 99n1271, 99n1452
Belluck, David, 95n1771
Belmonte, Frances R., 98n1501
Benet's reader's ency, 4th ed, 98n843
Benally, AnCita, 99n387
Benamati, Dennis C., 99n547
Benbow-Niemier, Glynis, 99n1201
Benbow-Pfalzgraf, Taryn, 99n1201
Bendall, Sarah, 98n394
Benedictine Monks of St. Augustine's Abbey, 95n1460
Benewick, Robert, 99n655
Benin, 98n106
Benjamin Britten: a gd to research, 97n1040
Benjamin Franklin: a biogl companion, 99n455
Benjamin Rush, M.D.: a bibliographic gd, 97n403
Benjamin, Sally, 95n1771
Benmour, Linda, 95n978, 96n1011
Bennett, Alice, 97n755
Bennett, Bev, 98n1420
Bennett, Fordyce R., 98n1135
Bennett, James R., 96n605
Bennett, Jim, 96n1884
Bennett, John M., 99n573
Bennett, Matthew, 97n557
Bennett, Ruth M., 98n191

Bennett, Suzanne, 98n1106
Benny Goodman: wrappin' it up, 97n1071
Benowitz, June Melby, 99n1265
Bensen, Clark H., 96n733
Benson, Eugene, 95n1102, 99n1088
Benson, Evelyn, 99n913
Benson, Marjorie, 97n86
Benson, Michael, 95n620
Benson, Morton, 99n913
Bent gd to gay/lesbian Canada 1994, 95n853
Bentley, Chantelle, 98n868
Bentley, Elizabeth Petty, 96n428, 96n588, 97n354
Bentley, G. E., Jr., 96n1244
Bentley, Michael, 99n829
Benton, M. J., 97n1405
Benyukh, Oleg P., 96n1122, 98n1047
Benz, Wolfgang, 98n470
Bercot, David W., 99n1285
Bercovitch, Jacob, 98n696
Berens, Ralph, 96n500
Berent, Irwin M., 98n362
Berg, Steven L., 95n880
Berger, James L., 96n376, 99n357
Berger, Klaus, 97n1201
Berger, Laura Standley, 96n1175
Bergstrom, Craig, 95n1324
Bergstrom, Joan M., 95n1324
Berinstein, Paula, 98n1592
Berke, Danielle, 96n1672
Berkman, Bob I., 98n575
Berkman, Robert I., 95n78
Berko, Robert L., 98n703
Berkow, Robert, 98n1540
Berliant, Adam, 96n1885
Berlin, 95n155
Berliner gramophone records, 96n1273
Berlow, Lawrence H., 96n801, 99n1397
Berman, Allen G., 98n915
Berman, Daniel K., 98n1249
Berman, Louis A., 98n1249
Berman, Matt, 96n1162, 98n1076, 99n990
Bermuda, 99n137
Bernal, Rodrigo, 96n1589
Bernard, Leo, 96n1002
Bernard, Philippa, 96n1002
Bernardin, Claude, 96n1331
Berner, Brad K., 99n626
Berney, K. A., 95n1155, 95n1176, 95n1206, 97n468
Bernhard, Elizabeth A., 98n274, 98n765, 98n792
Bernikow, Louise, 98n826
Bernson, Carol, 98n1241
Bernstein, Joanne E., 95n773
Berry, Barbara, 98n279
Berry, David, 96n1370
Berry, Dawn Bradley, 98n513
Berryman-Fink, Cynthia, 97n265
Berthold-Bond, Annie, 98n1425
Bertram, Anne, 96n1093, 97n837, 99n902, 99n914, 99n915
Bertuca, David J., 97n404

Bessette, Alan E., 97n1278
Bessette, Arleen R., 97n1278
Bessette, Joseph M., 99n667
Best bks for children, 5th ed, 95n1130
Best bks for YA readers, 98n1094
Best bks for YAs, 95n1127
Best bulbs for temperate climates, 96n1545
Best dir of recruiters, 4th ed, 97n253
Best dir of recruiters on-line, 97n254
Best distance learning graduate schools, 99n304
Best graduate programs: humanities & social scis, 2d ed, 99n335
Best graduate programs: physical & biological scis, 2d ed, 99n336
Best hospitals in America, 2d ed, 96n1693
Best in sci fiction, 95n1164
Best law schools, 99n560
Best medical schools, 99n1450
Best of health, 99n1437
Best of teams, the worst of teams, 96n807
Best of the Latino heritage, 98n358
Best places to go, 95n505
Best plays of 1996-97, 99n1246
Best private high schools & how to get in, 2d ed, 99n313
Best 75 business schools, 1999 ed, 99n320
Best toys, bks & videos for kids, 96n1010
Best Web sites for teachers, 2d ed, 99n308
Best wines! 1999, 3d ed, 99n1335
Bestseller index, 99n12
Betrus, Michael, 98n218
Better buys for business, 97n187
Better than it sounds: a dict of humorous musical quotations, 99n1119
Bettschart, Roland, 99n1456
Betty Comden & Adolph Green: a bio-bibliog, 95n1352
Bevans, Stephen B., 98n1350
Bever, Edward, 98n103
Bever, Michael B., 95n1632
Bewes, Diccon, 98n500
Beyer, Gerry W., 96n580
Beyond Jennifer & Jason, 95n465
Beyond picture bks, 2d ed, 96n1180
Beyond the hill, 97n598
BFI film & TV hndbk 1995, 96n1401
BHA: bibliog of the hist of art: subject headings/English, 97n790
BHA: bibliog of the hist of art 1996 [CD-ROM], 97n791
BHI plus [CD-ROM], 96n955
Bianchi, R. S., 96n1350
Bianco, David, 99n275
Bianco, David P., 96n194
Bianculli, David, 97n1110
Bible: God's word for the biblically-inept, 99n1280
Bible & the saints, 96n1448
Bible baby names, 97n368
Biblical quotation & allusion in the canata libretti of J. S. Bach, 98n1245
Bibliographic checklist of African American newspapers, 96n971

Bibliographic gd to ...
- anthropology & archaeology 1995, 98n319
- art & architecture 1993, 95n992
- art & architecture 1996, 98n941
- black studies 1994, 96n398
- black studies 1995, 98n339
- business & economics 1994, 96n174
- business & economics 1995, 98n147
- conference pubs 1996, 99n7
- dance 1995, 98n1267
- E Asian studies 1995, 98n109
- educ 1996, 98n265
- Gabriel Garcia Marquez, 1986-1992, 95n1228
- govt pubs—foreign 1994, 96n57
- govt pubs—US 1994, 96n58
- jazz poetry, 99n1099
- Latin American studies 1996, 98n139
- law 1996, 98n509
- maps & atlases 1996, 98n391
- Middle Eastern studies 1996, 98n143
- music 1996, 98n1187
- N American hist 1994, 96n489
- psychology 1996, 98n707
- Slavic, Baltic, & Eurasian studies 1996, 98n126
- tech 1996, 98n1398
- the environment 1996, 98n1629
- the hist of computer applications, 1950-90, 97n1365
- theatre arts 1996, 98n1322

Bibliographic hist of the bk, 96n664
Bibliographic index 1996, 98n6
Bibliographical gd to Spanish music for the violin & viola, 1900-97, 99n1149
Bibliographical gd to the study of Western American lit, 2d ed, 97n959
Bibliographies for African studies, 1987-93, 95n113
Bibliographies of northern & central Calif. Indians, 95n426
Bibliographies on SE Asia, 99n103
Bibliography for hist, hist curatorship, & museums, 98n495
Bibliography of ...
- African lang texts . . . to 1963, 95n1029
- African lits, 97n1001
- American demographic hist, 96n906
- Bertrand Russell, 96n1423
- British hist 1914-89, 98n464
- business/competitive intelligence & benchmarking lit, 96n175
- Canada's peoples, suppl.1, 95n417
- European economic & social hist, 2d ed, 95n552
- Fla., v.1, 95n105
- Fla., v.2: 1846-80, 97n84
- geosci theses of the US & Canada, 95n1723
- human behavior, 95n770
- Jane Austen, new ed, 98n1153
- Latin American & Caribbean bibliogs: annual report 1992-93, 95n168
- McClelland & Stewart imprints, 1909-1985, 95n677
- medical & biomedical biog, 2d ed, 96n1696
- museum studies, 11th ed, 96n82
- sources in Christianity & the arts, 97n1206
- S Asia, 95n128
- Syrian archaeological sites to 1980, 96n484
- the Caribbean, 97n128
- the English novel from the Restoration to the French Revolution, 96n1236
- the Indians of San Diego County, 99n383
- the Indonesian Revolution, 99n481
- the myth of Don Juan in literary hist, 99n944
- the Samaritans, 2d ed, 95n1435
- the Soviet Union, its predecessors & successors, 97n124
- the works of Richard Price, 95n1427
- theatre hist in Canada, 95n1404
- Va. legal hist before 1900, 2d ed, 99n548
- works on Canadian foreign relations 1986-90, 96n748
- works on Canadian foreign relations 1991-95, 99n689

Bibliography on publishing & bk dvlpmt in the Third World, 1980-93, 95n666
Bibliography on writing & written lang, 98n984
Bibo (Pui Bo), Bai, 98n1034
Bidding dict, 98n744
Biddle, Stanton F., 97n329
Bidwell, Robin, 99n508
Bieber's dict of legal abbrevs reversed, 95n592
Bieber's dict of legal citations, Prince's 5th ed, 98n516
Biebuyck, Daniel P., 97n315
Bierley, Paul E., 98n1229
Big bk of America, 95n469
Big bk of lib grant money, 95n643
Big bk of minority opportunities, 6th ed, 96n891
Big bk of minority opportunities, 7th ed, 99n339
Big bk of opportunities for women, 98n269
Big bk of show business awards, 99n1198
Big broadcast, 1920-50, 2d ed, 98n887
Biger, Gideon, 96n455
Biggs, Donald A., 95n775
Biggs, Mary, 97n72
Biggs, Melissa E., 97n1115
Bignaud, Marie-Claude, 99n185
Bigsby, Christopher, 99n1247
Bill Clinton's pre-presidential career, 95n534
Bill James presents: STATS all-time major league hndbk, 99n715
Billboard 1996 music yrbk, 98n1205
Billboard bk of ...
- no.1 albums, 97n1060
- top 40 albums, 3d ed, 97n1061
- top 40 hits, 6th ed, 97n1062

Billboard illus ency of rock, 99n1172
Billboard music yrbk 1993, 95n1289
Billboard music yrbk 1994, 96n1303
Billboard video yrbk 1993, 95n1390
Billboard video yrbk 1994, 96n1402
Billboard's American rock 'n' roll in review, 98n1239
Billboard's hottest hot 100 hits, rev ed, 97n1080
Billiard market place 1994, 95n811
Billips, Connie, 96n1390
Billman, Larry, 98n1268, 98n1272
Billy Murray: the phonograph industry's 1st great recording artist, 98n1198
Bilovsky, Frank, 95n808
Bilstein, Paula, 99n1450

Bimson, John J., 96n1450
Binns, Margaret, 97n97
Binocular stargazer, 96n1801
Biodiversity, 99n1556
Biographical companion to lit in English, rev ed, 98n1066
Biographical dict of ...
    actors, actresses, musicians, dancers, managers...v.15, 95n1411
    actors, actresses, musicians, dancers, managers...v.16, 95n1412
    American & Canadian naturalists & environmentalists, 99n1552
    American newspaper columnists, 96n973
    American sports, 1992-95 suppl, 96n793
    artists, rev ed, 96n1022
    Chinese women, 99n798
    Christian missions, 99n1281
    European labor leaders, 97n151
    modern American educators, 98n266
    N American classicists, 95n1154
    N American & European educationists, 99n289
    professional wrestling, 98n752
    psychology, 98n710
    Saskatchewan artists: [v.2]: men artists, 96n1023
    scientists, 95n1485
    the hist of tech, 97n1236
    the Union, 96n495
    the US Secretaries of the Treasury, 1789-1995, 97n587
    transcendentalism, 97n962
    20th-century philosophers, 97n1158
    WW II, 97n463
    WWII generals & flag officers: the US armed forces, 97n409
Biographical dir of ...
    Native American painters, 97n807
    the American Congress, 1774-1996, 98n651
    the governors of the US 1988-94, 95n717
Biographical ency of scientists, 99n1300
Biographical ency of scientists, 2d ed, 95n1484
Biographical hndbk of Hispanics & US film, 98n1277
Biographies of British women, 95n910
Biographies of scientists, 99n1298
Biographies of Western photographers, 99n861
Biography & genealogy master index 1999, 99n404
Biography index [CD-ROM], 96n24
Biography index, Sept 1995-Aug 1996, 98n20
Biography today, 98n21
Biography today, 1993 annual cum, 96n25
Biological anomalies: humans III, 96n1559
Bionat, Marvin P., 96n395
Biondi, Joann, 96n390
Biotechnology abstracts: agricultural & environmental, 1983-Feb 1997 [CD-ROM], 98n1490
Biotechnology gd USA, 3d ed, 96n1655
Biotechnology in the US pharmaceutical industry 1995, 4th ed, 96n1733
Biotechnology info sources, 96n1658
Bird, Christiane, 96n1321
Birdlife of Fla., 95n1575
Birds of Europe with N Africa & the Middle East, 95n1568
Birds of Ky., 95n1571
Birds of Mich., 95n1570
Birds of N America, 95n1565
Birds of S America, v.2, 95n1573
Birds of the world, 95n1567
Birdwatcher's hndbk, 96n1614
Birren, James E., 97n667
Bischiniotis, George, 96n1769
Bishop, Chris, 97n579
Bishop, Rudine Sims, 96n1182
Bishop, Sherman C., 96n1635
Bisio, Attilio, 96n1830
Biskupic, Joan, 98n526, 98n529
Bissell, Frances, 95n1519
Bisson, Wilfred J., 95n528
Bittence, John C., 95n1628
Bitton, Davis, 95n1464
Bjorklund, Dennis A., 98n1302
Bjorling, Joel, 99n708
Bjorner, Susanne, 96n982
Black African lit in English, 1987-91, 96n1247
Black Americana price gd, 98n892
Black bk, 4th ed, 98n796
Black conductors, 96n1285
Black demographic data, 1790-1860, 98n342
Black firsts, 95n412
Black hndbk, 99n375
Black heritage sites, 97n330
Black in focus, 96n1163
Black, Jeremy, 97n556
Black, John, 98n151
Black student's gd to scholarships, 3d ed, 95n371
Black studies on disc [CD-ROM], 96n399
Black talent resource gd, 1994 ed, 95n1356
Black talk, 95n413
Black/White relations in American hist, 99n454
Black woman's gumbo ya-ya, 95n920
Black writers, 2d ed, 95n1108
Blackburn, G. Meredith, III, 95n1152
Blackburn, S., 96n253
Blackburn, Simon, 95n1428
Blackfoot dict of stems, roots, & affixes, 2d ed, 97n872
Blackhurst, Hector, 97n90
Blacks in black & white, 2d ed, 96n1410
Blacks in opera, 96n1301
Blackwell dict of evangelical biog, 1730-1860, 97n1208
Blackwell dict of neuropsychology, 97n626
Blackwell ency of modern Christian thought, 95n1465
Blackwell ency of writing systems, 97n811
Blackwell gd to soul recordings, 95n1308
Blackwell gd to recorded contemporary music, 98n1221
Blackwell hndbk of educ, 96n325
Blackwell, Kenneth, 96n1423
Blair, John, 96n1332
Blair, Judy, 96n385
Blair, Karen J., 98n828
Blaise, Albert, 96n1115
Blake, Barbara, 96n1181
Blake bks suppl, 96n1244
Blake, David, 95n112

Blalock, Susan E., 97n970
Blanchard, Dallas A., 98n756
Blanchard, Margaret A., 99n820
Blank, Robert H., 97n1330
Blank, Thomas O., 95n832
Blazek, Ron, 95n529, 95n921
Bleaney, C. H., 96n135, 96n163
Bleiler, David, 97n1125
Blevins, Carolyn DeArmond, 97n731
Blewett, Daniel K., 96n678
Bliese, Richard H., 98n1350
Bliss, Marilyn, 97n1026
Blizzards, 99n1525
Blockbuster Entertainment gd to movies & videos 1998, 99n1241
Bloedow, Steve, 98n906
Blom, F., 97n1204
Blom, J., 97n1204
Bloom, Adrian, 99n1347
Bloom, Carole, 96n1523
Bloom, Ken, 96n1275, 97n1077
Bloomberg, Marty, 95n565
Bloomfield, B. C., 98n588
Bloor, David, 96n1664
Blouin, Francis X., Jr., 99n1284
Blueprint for a green school, 96n1870
Blues & gospel records 1890-1943, 99n1160
Blum, George P., 99n694
Blum, Laurie, 95n356, 97n189
Blumberg, Arnold, 96n706, 99n509
Blumenthal, Howard J., 99n1159, 99n1165
Blunden, Caroline, 99n106
Blythe, Hal, 95n944
BNA's dir of state & fed courts, judges, & clerks, 1997 ed, 98n521
Boarding school gd, 97n297
Boatner, Mark M., III, 96n506, 97n463
Boatner, Maxine Tull, 96n1083
Bob Dylan, 96n1334
Boccaccio in English: a bibliog of eds, adaptations, & criticism, 97n1011
Bock, Hanne, 98n517
Bock, Ian, 98n517
Bock, Judy, 99n1005
Bock-Weiss, Catherine C., 97n805
Boczek, Boleslaw Adam, 96n610
Bodart, Joni Richards, 98n1081, 98n1082, 98n1083
Bodell, Heather C., 96n882
Bodenhamer, David J., 96n929
Body, mind & spirit, 95n1477
Bogart, Dave, 97n528, 97n576
Bogdanov, Vladimir, 95n1256, 96n1330, 97n1072, 98n1228, 98n1230
Bogduk, Nikolai, 96n1723
Bognar, Desi K., 96n984
Bogot, Howard I., 95n1080
Bohlman, Philip V., 97n1073
Boice, Daniel, 98n592
Boire, Richard Glen, 98n527
Boland, Maeve A., 96n1804

Boles, Janet K., 97n735
Bollard, John, 96n1087
Bollard, John K., 99n900
Bolles, Richard Nelson, 98n222
Bolozky, Shmuel, 97n854
Bolton, Barry, 95n1590
Bonavita, Mark, 97n656, 97n658, 98n742
Bond markets, 1995 ed, 96n292
Bond, Mary E., 97n19
Bond, W. H., 97n39
Bondanella, Julia Conaway, 97n1010
Bondanella, Peter, 97n1010
Bondi, Victor, 96n513, 96n514, 96n516, 97n425
Bond's franchise gd, 1996, 97n180
Bonk, Mary Rose, 97n1
Bonsai survival manual, 97n1256
Bonta, Bruce D., 95n91
Book industry trends 1994: covering the yrs 1988-98, 95n667
Book of ...
   Amos, 98n1372
   art, rev ed, 96n1029
   Ephesians, 97n1188
   European forecasts, 2d ed, 97n238
   food, 95n1519
   Jeremiah, 97n1194
   lists for regulated hazardous substances, 8th ed, 99n1557
   lists for regulated hazardous substances 1996, 97n1433
   mosts, 99n65
   Psalms: an annot bibliog, 95n1457
   Revelation, 97n1191
   rhododendrons, 96n1573
   rules, 99n713
   Ruth: an annot bibliog, 95n1449
   saints, 99n1263
   saints, 6th ed, 95n1460
   salvias, 98n1434
   world-famous libretti, 95n1406
Book prices: used & rare 1995, 96n1003
Book review digest, Mar 1996 to Feb 1997 inclusive, 98n65
Book review index: 1997 cumulation, 99n68
Booker, M. Keith, 95n1109, 99n1068
Booker-Canfield, Suzanne, 99n1039
Booking Hawaii Five-O: an episode gd & critical hist of the 1968-80 TV detective show, 98n1313
Bookman's gd to archaeology, 96n1005
Bookman's price index, v.50, 96n1004
Books & pers online, 1997 ed, 98n1582
Books for the teen age 1994, 95n1119
Books for you, 98n1095
Books from Chapel Hill 1922-97, 98n595
Books in print 1994-95, 95n18
Books in print 1995-96, 96n15
Books in print 1996-97, 49th ed, 97n18
Books in print 1997-98, 98n15
Books in print with bk reviews plus [CD-ROM], 96n17
Books on the move, 95n509
Books out-of-print plus [CD-ROM], 96n18
Books to help children cope with separation & loss, 4th ed, 95n773

Booktalking the award winners: children's retrospective volume, 98n1081
Booktalking the award winners 3, 98n1082
Boondas, Jennifer, 96n1681
Boorkman, Jo Anne, 95n1644
Booth, Ken, 95n690
Boots, Sharon, 96n1830
Bopp, Mary S., 95n1357
Bopp, Richard E., 96n647
Bor, Victoria L., 99n566
Borcherding, David H., 97n754
Borchert, Donald M., 97n1160
Borck, Jim Springer, 98n7, 99n515, 99n516
Borders, Rebecca, 97n598
Bordman, Gerald, 95n1418, 97n1150
Bordwell, Sally, 96n1619
Boring, M. Eugene, 97n1201
Borins, Sara, 95n347
Boris Pasternak: a ref gd, 95n1239
Boritt, Gabor S., 97n67
Boritt, Jakob B., 97n67
Borman, Jami Lynne, 96n1748
Born this day, 96n30, 97n41
Borne, Barbara Wood, 97n543
BOSC dir: facilities for people with learning disabilities, 95n384
Bosnian-English, English-Bosnian concise dict, 96n1098
Bosnich, Victor W., 96n736
Bosoni, Anthony J., 96n600
Boswell, David M., 99n134
Boswell, Jackson Campbell, 95n556
Bosworth, C. E., 95n1473
Bosworth, Clifford Edmund, 97n135
Botterweck, G. Johannes, 97n1200, 98n1375, 99n1276
Bottorf, Paula, 97n228
Boulos, Loutfy, 96n1582
Bouloukos, Adam C., 99n547
Boultbee, Paul G., 97n131, 99n137
Boulton, Susie, 96n478
Bourbon companion, 99n1337
Bourgoin, Suzanne M., 95n212, 96n1305
Bourie, Steve, 98n411
Bourne, Joyce, 96n1270
Bove, Cheryl, 95n1215
Bowbeer, Anne Aull, 98n1275
Bowes & Church's food values of portions commonly used, 16th ed, 95n1520
Bowker annual lib & bk trade almanac 1994, 95n644
Bowker annual lib & bk trade almanac, 1995, 40th ed, 96n623
Bowker annual lib & bk trade almanac, 1996, 41st ed, 97n528
Bowker annual lib & bk trade almanac 1997, 98n576
Bowker, John, 98n1357, 98n1361
Bowker's complete video dir 1995, 96n986
Bowker's dir of videocassettes for children 1998, 99n10
Bowler, Gail Hellund, 97n745
Bowles, Stephen E., 95n1401
Bowman, Joel P., 96n310
Bowman, John S., 96n35, 99n471
Bown, Deni, 96n1585, 96n1586
Boxing register, 98n743

Boyd, Alex, 98n327
Boyd, Margaret A., 96n1012, 98n931
Boyden, Matthew, 99n1157
Boyer, Rodney, 96n1669
Boylan, Henry, 99n132
Boyle, Bill, 95n472
Boyne, Walter J., 96n698, 97n562
Bracken, James K., 96n1778, 97n553, 98n594
Brackman, Barbara, 95n979
Brackney, William H., 96n867
Bradford, John, 99n750
Bradley, David, 99n588
Bradley, Edwin M., 97n1116
Bradley, J., 99n258
Bradney, Gail, 99n1335
Bradt, Hilary, 95n119
Brady, Clark A., 97n969
Brain ency, 97n1334
Brako, Lois, 96n1593
Branan, Carl R., 96n1650, 99n1400
Branch, Robert Maribe, 99n356
Branchaw, Bernadine P., 96n310
Brand, Juliane, 98n1059
Brandes, Rand, 97n1008
Brandon, James R., 95n1414
Brands & their cos suppl, 17th ed, 99n148
Brandt, Randal S., 95n426
Branstad, Barbara, 97n958
Branton, Ann, 97n1033
Brass music of black composers, 97n1041
Brass, Ken, 97n392
Brassey's ency of military hist & biog, 96n682
Brassey's world aircraft & systems dir 1996/97, 97n1438
Bratman, Fred, 95n11
Braun, Elisabeth, 96n1596
Braun, Eric, 95n1702
Braun, Erin E., 99n1495
Braun, Marina, 99n553
Braunrot, Bruno, 95n1230
Brawarsky, Sandee, 99n396
Brawer, Moshe, 96n445
Bray, Charles, 97n787
Bray, Dorothy, 99n936
Brazil, rev ed, 98n140
Brazil co hndbk, 1994/95 ed, 95n286
Brazouski, Antoinette, 95n1319
Breakup of Yugoslavia & the war in Bosnia, 99n116
Brecher, Deborah, 95n915
Brecka, Shawn, 98n893, 99n853
Breining, Greg, 98n412
Breitsprecher, Roland, 99n928
Brelin, Christa, 97n703
Bremer, Francis J., 95n530
Bremer, Ronald A., 96n431, 98n364, 99n399
Bremer-David, Charissa, 95n966, 98n946
Bremness, Lesley, 95n1544
Brennan, J. H., 95n1477
Brennan, Shawn, 95n916, 97n1131
Brennan, Thomas H., 95n940
Brent, Bill, 98n796

Brent, Ruth, 97n1094
Brereton, Mary M., 97n529
Bressett, K. E., 97n778
Bressett, Kenneth, 96n1008, 98n910
Breton, Roland J.-L., 99n101
Brett-Surman, M. K., 98n1617
Breuilly, Elizabeth, 98n1348
Brewer, Annie M., 96n975
Brewer, Jeutonne P., 96n966
Brewer's cinema, 96n1373
Brewer's pols, 95n707
Brewer's theater, 96n1414
Brewster, Nancy Peterson, 97n1285
Brian Friel, 96n1257
Bricault, Giselle C., 97n233
Brickell, Christopher, 98n1432
Bricker's intl dir 1998, 99n358
Bridgham, Fred, 97n849
Bridgman, Roger, 96n1508
Bridson, Gavin, 95n1556
Brier, Bob, 99n445
Briggs, Derek E. G., 96n1813
Briggs, Virginia L., 97n252
Briggs, Ward W., Jr., 95n1154
Bright, William, 97n816, 99n420
Brindley, Keith, 95n1617
Bristow, M. J., 95n1260
Britain 1993, 95n156
Britannica atlas, 95n474
Britannica bk of the yr, 1994, 95n63
Britannica CD version 1.01 [CD-ROM], 95n64
Britannica electronic index [CD-ROM], 95n43
British & Irish archaeology, 95n521
British archives, 3d ed, 97n440
British Army campaign medals, 98n630
British children's writers, 1800-1880, 97n934
British children's writers, 1880-1914, 95n1205
British children's writers, 1914-1960, 97n935
British children's writers since 1960, 1st series, 97n936
British cinema sheet music, 98n1195
British cinema source bk, 97n1109
British co-operative movement film catalogue, 98n1289
British dirs, 2d ed, 98n132
British economic & social hist, 3d ed, 97n443
British empire, 97n444
British film studios, 97n1139
British imprints relating to N America, 1621-1760, 97n40
British literary bk trade, 1475-1700, 98n594
British literary bk trade, 1700-1820, 97n553
British novel 1680-1832, 98n1146
British playwrights, 1880-1956, 97n985
British playwrights, 1956-95, 97n986
British pol facts 1900-94, 7th ed, 96n758
British prose writers of the early 17th century, 96n1232
British reform writers, 1789-1832, 97n977
British sci fiction paperbacks & mags 1949-56, 96n1234
British secret servs, 98n686
British short-fiction writers, 1880-80, 97n978
British short-fiction writers, 1880-1914, 97n979, 95n1209
British short-fiction writers, 1915-45, 97n980
British short-fiction writers, 1945-80, 96n1228
British travel writers, 1837-75, 97n981
British women writers, 1700-1850, 98n1144
British women's hist, 97n726
British writers, suppl 3, 97n982
British writers, suppl 4, 98n1149
Britton, John A., 98n697
Broadcast news [CD-ROM], 96n991
Broadcast news manual of style, 2d ed, 96n992
Broadcasting it, 95n858
Broadway, movie, TV, & studio cast musicals on record, 97n1030
Broadway sheet music, 97n1069
Broadway song companion, 99n1170
Brobeck, Stephen, 99n176
Brocardo, G., 95n1729
Brochstein, Martin, 97n165
Brockenbrough, Roger L., 95n1603
Brockman, Norbert C., 96n109, 98n1349
Brockman, Terra Castiglia, 97n363
Brod, Joanna, 98n1080
Broderick, Dorothy M., 99n1012
Brodersen, Martha, 99n617
Brodie, Carolyn S., 95n1120
Brody, Aaron L., 98n1493
Brogan, T. V. F., 95n1248, 97n1019
Brogdon, Jennie, 96n1522
Bromley, Debra J., 96n1419, 97n1153
Bronoel, Stacey, 99n142
Bronson, Fred, 97n1080
Brook, Barry S., 98n1188
Brook, Stephen, 96n479
Brookes, John, 95n1526
Brookesmith, Peter, 99n709
Brooklyn Public Library Business Library Staff, 96n197
Brookman US, UN, & Canada stamps & postal collectibles, 98n928
Brooks & Olmo register of fruit & nut varieties, 99n1330
Brooks, Joan, 98n878
Brooks, Lori, 96n1654
Brooks, Stephen, 96n71
Brosman, Catharine Savage, 96n545
Brostrom, Jennifer, 97n901
Brostrom, Jennifer Allison, 97n902, 97n903, 97n904
Brothers, Barbara, 97n981
Broude, Gwen J., 96n862, 97n708
Broussard, Mark, 98n741, 98n742
Brown, Archie, 95n152
Brown, Chris W., III, 99n430
Brown, David S., 99n660
Brown, George E., 96n1588
Brown, George, Jr., 96n1463
Brown, Harry L., 98n1494
Brown, Jean E., 96n1170, 99n453
Brown, Kathleen, 97n147
Brown, Kyle D., 99n883
Brown, Lawrence D., 95n217
Brown, Lorene Byron, 96n626
Brown, Lynda W., 99n451
Brown, Mary Ellen, 99n962

Brown, Mervyn, 95n119
Brown, Neil L., 98n273
Brown, Risa W., 98n1099
Brown, S. Kent, 96n1461
Brown, Stuart, 97n1158
Brown, Thomas J., 98n444
Brown, Travis, 96n1509
Browne, Peter, 97n112
Brownell, F. William, 99n1558
Browning, W. R. F., 97n1195
Brownmiller, Sara, 98n841
Brownstein, Samuel C., 98n992
Brownstone, David, 95n24, 95n918, 95n925, 96n945, 97n640, 98n803
Brownstone, David M., 99n802
Browsing in info systems, 96n644
Bruccoli, Arlyn, 95n1199
Bruccoli, Matthew J., 98n1127, 99n971
Bruce, Anthony, 99n639
Bruce, Colin R., 99n844
Bruce, Samuel W., 99n970
Bruce-Young, Doris Marie, 97n302
Bruijn, Ria Koopmans-de, 99n111
Brumble, H. David, 99n1017
Brune, Lester H., 97n431
Bruning, Nancy, 98n1548
Brunk, Gregory G., 98n635
Bruno, Leonard C., 95n1786, 98n1402, 99n1308
Bruntjen, Scott, 95n21, 98n17, 99n13
Brunvand, Jan Harold, 97n1088
Brush up your Bible! 95n1454
Bryan, George B., 95n1221, 96n760, 96n1215, 98n1157, 98n1254
Bryan, John, 97n1276
Bryan, Mary Lynn McCree, 97n706
Bryson, William Hamilton, 99n548
Bua, Robert N., 99n1475
Buchanan, Anne L., 96n330
Buchanan, Robert J., 96n855
Bucher, Ward, 97n801
Buckley, John F., 96n268, 96n269, 97n257, 99n559
Buckley, Jonathan, 99n1157
Buckner, Michael E., 95n1199
Bud Collins' modern ency of tennis, 95n825
Bud Collins' tennis ency, 3d ed, 98n750
Bud, Robert, 99n1312
Budapest, 98n133
Buddy DeFranco: a biographical portrait & discography, 95n1303
Budlong, Tom, 98n878
Buening, Alice P., 96n1038, 98n936, 99n828
Bugaboos, chimeras & Achilles' heels, 95n1037
Bugajski, Janusz, 95n749
Building a new South, 96n98
Building a popular sci lib collection for high school & adult learners, 96n660
Building construction cost data 1997, 55th ed, 98n1480
Building design & construction hndbk, 5th ed, 95n1604
Buildings of the District of Columbia, 95n1017
Bulanda, Susan, 95n1581

Bulbs, 99n1348
Bulbs for the rock garden, 97n1255
Bulfinch illus ency of antiques, 95n968
Bulliet, Richard W., 97n136
Bullough, Bonnie, 95n872
Bullough, Vern L., 95n872
Bull's birds of N.Y. state, 99n1375
Bulmer, Martin, 95n97
Bunch, Bryan, 97n1242, 98n1557
Bunis, David M., 95n1026
Bunson, Margaret, 99n1261
Bunson, Margaret R., 97n453
Bunson, Matthew, 95n579, 95n1325, 96n1472, 99n1261
Bunson, Matthew E., 95n1211, 96n565
Bunson, Stephen, 99n1261
Bunson, Stephen M., 97n453
Bunting, Jane, 96n43
Burack, Sylvia K., 99n832
Burak, Sara, 96n1779
Burbank, Richard D., 95n1265
Burchfield, R. W., 97n756
Burden, Ernest, 99n880
Bureau of Economic & Business Research, College of Business Admin, Univ of Fla., 96n916
Burek, Deborah M., 95n68
Burels, Ned, 99n55
Burg, David F., 99n653
Burger, Robert H., 95n162, 96n140
Burger's medicinal chemistry & drug discovery, 5th ed, 98n1565
Burgess, Guy M., 99n554
Burgess, Heidi, 99n554
Burgess, Philip M., 97n248
Burgess, William E., 95n342, 98n280
Burke, David, 99n924
Burke, John Gordon, 96n78, 96n90
Burkholder, Robert E., 95n1187
Burkina Faso, 95n114
Burn, Hilary, 95n1569
Burnie, David, 95n1557, 96n1608
Burnim, Kalman A., 95n1411, 95n1412
Burns, John T., 95n1478, 98n1441
Burras, J. K., 96n1575
Burrelle's index of broadcast transcripts, 1993 ed, 96n998
Burrelle's media dir, June 1994 [CD-ROM], 95n934
Burrelle's media dir, 1998 ed, 99n837
Burroughs cyclopaedia, 97n969
Burroughs, Hugh, 95n1671
Burrows, Andrew S., 95n702
Burrows, Elaine, 97n1109
Bursac, Kristine M., 96n841
Burt, Bernard, 98n405
Burt, Daniel S., 99n1034
Burton Goldberg Group, 95n1669
Burton, Alan, 98n1289
Burton, T. L., 98n1156
Burton, Virgil L., III, 97n160
Burwell dir of info brokers 1994, 96n646
Burwell, Helen, 98n1596
Burwell, Helen P., 96n646, 99n595

Burwell world dir of info brokers, 13th ed, 99n595
Bus, James S., 96n1875
Buse, Dieter K., 99n129
Bush, Betsy Hills, 98n539
Bushell, Chris, 95n1792
Business: name & business type index [CD-ROM], 98n158
Business A to Z source finder, 97n147
Business & economic research dir, 97n159
Business & industry [CD-ROM], 98n189
Business & legal forms for authors & self-publishers, 98n605
Business & legal forms for crafts, 99n854
Business & legal forms for photographers, rev ed, 99n859
Business hist of the world, 95n242
Business info sources, 95n179
Business lib & how to use it, 6th ed, 97n530
Business multimedia explained, 98n242
Business One Irwin intl almanac 1993, 95n247
Business orgs, agencies, & pubns dir, 8th ed, 97n160
Business pers index, v.38: Aug 1995-July 1996, 98n167
Business rankings annual, 1995, 96n197
Business sales leads, 1997 ed [CD-ROM], 98n248
Business stats of the US, 99n159
Business stats of the US, 1995 ed, 97n176
Business traveler's world gd, 99n441
Business Week, editors of, 96n332
Business Week gd to the best business schools, 4th ed, 96n332
Bussmann, Hadumod, 97n812
Bustros, Gabriel M., 96n161, 96n165
Butcher, Debbie, 96n1451
Butcher, Devereux, 96n470
Butcher, Russell D., 96n470
Bute, E. L., 99n375
Butler, David, 96n758
Butler, Diane, 97n220, 97n244
Butler, Gareth, 96n758
Butler, Gregory S., 95n339
Butler, J. Douglas, 98n755
Butler, Marian, 98n18
Butler, Robert Brown, 99n881
Butt, John, 98n1050, 99n938
Butterflies of Delmarva, 95n1579
Butterflies of the W Indies & S Fla., 95n1578
Butterflies of the world, 99n1390
Buttlar, Lois J., 97n522
Buttolph, Ken, 99n1577
Button, John, 96n766
Buttress's world gd to abbrevs of orgs, 11th ed, 98n1
Buxton, Frank, 98n887
By the numbers: emerging industries, 99n188
By the numbers: nonprofit orgs, 99n48
By the numbers: publishing, 99n620
Byars, Mel, 95n982
Bybee, Howard C., 96n484
Byers, Clive, 97n1288
Byers, Paula K., 96n429, 96n430, 96n432, 96n433, 97n367
Bykerk, Loree, 96n216
Bynagle, Hans E., 98n1330
Bynum, W. F., 95n1654
Byrd, Gary W., 95n616
Byrne, John A., 96n332

C. S. Lewis readers' ency, 99n1071
Cabell, David W. E., 96n669, 96n670
Cabell's dir of publishing opportunities in accounting, economics & finance, 6th ed, 96n669
Cabell's dir of publishing opportunities in mgmt & mktg, 6th ed, 96n670
Cackett, Alan, 95n1298
Cacti & succulents, 95n1548
Cahn, Robert W., 95n1631, 95n1632
Caldwell, John Michael, 96n440
Calhoun, Milburn, 98n100
California, 98n413
Calimano, Ivan E., 95n1241
Callaghan, Jane, 96n1751
Callaham, John R., 97n1237
Callaham, Ludmilla Ignatiev, 97n1237
Callaham's Russian-English dict of sci & tech, 4th ed, 97n1237
Callaway, Dorothy J., 95n1551
Callendar, John Hancock, 99n882
Callinan, Paul, 97n1342
Calloway, Colin G., 96n414
Calvert, Stephen J., 98n1094
Cambodia, 99n105
Cambon, Glauco, 95n1233, 95n1234
Cambridge astronomy dict, 97n1392
Cambridge atlas of astronomy, 3d ed, 95n1719
Cambridge Australian English style gd, 96n1090
Cambridge biogl dict, 97n20
Cambridge biogl ency, 95n25
Cambridge biogl ency, 2d ed, 99n18
Cambridge companion to medieval English theatre, 95n1419
Cambridge companion to the Bible, 98n1377
Cambridge dict of ...
    American biog, 96n35
    philosophy, 97n1159
    scientists, 98n1399
    stats in the medical scis, 96n1699
Cambridge ency, 2d ed, 96n44
Cambridge ency, 3d ed, 98n37
Cambridge ency of ...
    Australia, 95n138
    human growth & dvlpmt, 99n1465
    human paleopathology, 99n1439
    lang, 2d ed, 98n989
    Russia & the former Soviet Union, 2d ed, 95n152
    the English lang, 96n1061
Cambridge factfinder, 2d ed, 98n38
Cambridge French-English thesaurus, 99n925
Cambridge gazetteer of the US & Canada, 97n381
Cambridge gd to ...
    African & Caribbean theatre, 95n1420
    American theatre, updated ed, 97n1151
    Asian theatre, 95n1414
    lit in English, 95n1103
    stars & planets, 2d ed, 98n1605
    the constellations, 96n1798
    theatre, new ed, 96n1415
Cambridge hist of American theatre, v.1, 99n1247

Cambridge hist of the native peoples of the Americas, v.1: N America, pt.1, 99n392
Cambridge illus atlas of warfare: Renaissance to Revolution, 1492-1792, 97n556
Cambridge illus atlas of warfare: the Middle Ages, 768-1487, 97n557
Cambridge illus hist of British theatre, 96n1422
Cambridge intl dict of English, 96n1063
Cambridge paperback ency, updated ed, 95n45
Cambridge paperback gd to lit in English, 97n894
Cambridge star atlas, 2d ed, 97n1393
Cambridge thesaurus of American English, 95n1065
Cambridge world hist of human disease, 95n1662
Cameron, Nigel M. de S., 95n1466
Camp, Roderic Ai, 96n763
Campaign & election reform, 98n679
Campbell, Alta, 96n191
Campbell, Barbara D., 95n774
Campbell, Donal, 98n134
Campbell, Eileen, 95n1477
Campbell, George L., 97n813
Campbell, Gordon, 95n923
Campbell, Karlyn Kohrs, 95n905
Campbell, Peter, 98n1214
Campbell, Robert Jean, 98n1556
Campbell, Robert L., 96n1322
Campe, Petra, 96n1057
Campus-free college degrees, 6th ed, 95n376
Campus-free college degrees, 7th ed, 97n292
Canada: a reader's gd, 1991-92 suppl, 95n15
Canadian address bk, 96n54
Canadian almanac & dir 1997, 97n3
Canadian almanac & dir 1999, 152d ed, 99n2
Canadian bed & breakfast gd, 12th ed, 97n393
Canadian bk review annual 1994: children's lit, 96n1176
Canadian bk review annual 1997, 99n16
Canadian bks in print 1997, 98n18
Canadian co hists, v.1, 98n208
Canadian dict of abbrevs, 95n1
Canadian ency plus, 1997 [CD-ROM], 97n42
Canadian film & video, 98n1271
Canadian Football League facts, figures, & records, 1994 ed, 95n819
Canadian gd to clinical preventive health care, 96n1708
Canadian Histl Review index, vs.52-71, 95n551
Canadian insurance claims dir 1997, 99n246
Canadian medical dir 1994, 95n1658
Canadian medical dir on CD-ROM, 1996 [CD-ROM], 97n1320
Canadian music & music educ, 98n1194
Canadian newsmakers 1997, 98n33
Canadian oil industry dir, 1994, 95n1746
Canadian Oxford dict, 99n41
Canadian parliamentary, 98n683
Canadian professional schools factsheets, 95n348
Canadian profile: alcohol, tobacco, & other drugs 1995, 96n898
Canadian ref sources, 97n19
Canadian representatives abroad, 96n749
Canadian sourcebk, 1997, 32d ed, 97n4
Canadian sourcebk 1998, 33d ed, 99n3
Canadian who's who 1996: v.31, 97n37
Canadian who's who 1997, v.32, 99n38
Canadian writers & their works: fiction series, v.12, 97n1003
Canadian writers & their works: poetry series, v.11, 97n1004
Canadiana in US repositories: a preliminary gd, 96n136
Cane, Paul W., Jr., 98n530
Canfield, Christopher J., 95n1581
Canfield Reisman, Rosemary M., 99n1039
Canine source bk, 4th ed, 95n1581
Cannon, Donald Q., 96n1461
Cannon, Garland, 95n1036
Cannon, John, 99n503
Cantarella, Gina Marie, 98n787
Cantor, George, 97n386, 97n387, 97n645
Cantor, Nathan L., 99n57, 99n157
Capela, John J., 97n203
Capital punishment, 95n623
Carabillo, Toni, 95n917
Caras, Roger A., 95n1535
Cardarelli, Francois, 98n1597
Cardim, Ismael, 95n1092
Career connection for college educ, 2d ed, 95n318
Career connection for tech educ, 2d ed, 95n319
Career discovery ency, 98n213
Career opportunities for bilinguals & multilinguals, 2d ed, 95n1031
Career opportunities for writers, 3d ed, 96n967
Career opportunities in ...
   art, rev ed, 96n1041
   health care, 98n1513
   the food & beverage industry, 96n1538
   the music industry, 3d ed, 96n1276
   travel & tourism, 96n461
Career perspectives software series [CD-ROM], 98n223
Career Xroads, 3d ed, 99n267
Careers in intl affairs, 6th ed, 98n698
Caribbean lit, 99n1089
Carl H. Pforzheimer Lib, English lit, 1475-1700, 1997 ed, 98n1148
Carl Ruggles, 96n1280
Carland, Maria Pinto, 98n698
Carley, James A., 95n1601
Carley, Rachel, 96n1044
Carlos Chavez: a gd to research, 99n1141
Carlson, Barbara, 98n414
Carlson, Barbara W., 95n1338
Carlson, Betty, 95n1311
Carlton, R. Scott, 98n909
Carmichael, Cathie, 97n122
Carnes, Mark C., 97n402
Carney, Faye, 96n1102
Caron, Martine M., 97n19
Carpenter, Allan, 95n108, 98n823, 99n89
Carpenter, Charles A., 98n1105
Carpenter, Dora, 95n1078
Carpenter, Edwin, 95n1078
Carpenter, Kathryn Hammell, 96n899
Carpenter, Ronald H., 99n1282
Carper, James C., 95n351, 97n301

Carr, Brian, 99n1254
Carr, Fred K., 96n589
Carr, Ian, 97n1076
Carr, James A., 95n712
Carr-Gomm, Sarah, 96n1030
Carranza, Miguel A., 97n322
Carrington, Vee Friesner, 97n8
Carroll, Bob, 98n747
Carroll, Frances Laverne, 98n574
Carroll, Stephen, 97n1326
Carroll's county dir, 96n721
Carroll's environmental dir 1995, 96n1863
Carroll's fed advisory dir 1995, 96n722
Carroll's fed assistance dir, 96n892
Carroll's fed dir, 96n723
Carroll's fed regional dir, 96n724
Carroll's military facilities dir, 96n686
Carroll's municipal dir, 96n725
Carroll's state dir, 96n726
Carruth, Gordon, 95n46
Carruthers, Margaret W., 99n1535
Carson, D. A., 96n1458
Carter, April, 96n536
Carter, Betty, 95n1127
Carter, Craig, 95n809, 96n828, 97n648, 97n655, 97n657, 98n741, 99n718
Carter, David E., 95n322
Carter, John, 96n1001
Cartographic satellite atlas of the world, 99n410
Carty, Dick, 98n1198
Carty, T. J., 96n1229
Caruba, Alan, 96n988
Caruso, Luisa, 99n919
Carvajal, Carol Styles, 98n1051, 99n941
Carwardine, Mark, 96n1629
Casati, Roberto, 98n1331
Case, Christopher, 98n1303
Case, Frederick W., Jr., 98n1448
Case, Roberta B., 98n1448
Case, semantic roles, & grammatical relations, 96n1057
Casey, Marion R., 97n346
Cash Box charts for the post-modern age, 96n1312
Cash Box pop singles charts 1950-93, 95n1291
Cash constituents of Congress, 2d ed, 95n735
Cashmore, Ellis, 95n394, 99n366
Casino gaming in the US, 98n724
Caspi, Mishael Maswari, 95n1449
Cass & Birnbaum's gd to American colleges, 16th ed, 95n362
Cass, Melissa, 95n362
Cass-Liepmann, Julia, 95n362
Cassell cluefinder, 97n832
Cassell companion to quotations, 99n76
Cassell, Dana K., 95n1678
Cassell dict of ...
    appropriate adjectives, 95n1034
    cliches, 98n1018
    cynical quotations, 96n89
    Norse myth & legend, 98n1259
Cassell English-Japanese business dict, 95n260
Cassell multilingual dict of local govt & bus, 95n750
Cassell sex & sexuality, 95n873
Cassell student English dict, 95n1054
Cassell's queer companion, 96n864
Cassidy, Daniel J., 96n333, 96n334
Cassidy, Frederic G., 97n833
Cassin, Barbara, 98n1553
Cassin-Scott, Jack, 95n986
Castagno, John, 98n980
Castagno, Joseph M., 99n1317
Castello, Elena Romero, 96n424
Castello-Cortes, Ian, 95n480
Castro, Emilio G. Muniz, 99n146
Castronova, Frank V., 98n25, 99n17
Cat owner's question & answer bk, 99n1387
Cat World, 98n1465
Catala, Rafael, 98n1142, 98n1185, 99n1100
Catalan dict, 95n1071
Catalog of catalogs 3, 95n226
Catalog of catalogs 5, 98n183
Catalog of music for the cornett, 97n1051
Catalog of teratogenic agents, 8th ed, 96n1720
Catalog of the Cooper-Hewitt Museum of Design lib of the Smithsonian Inst libs, 95n924
Cataloging nonbook materials with AACR2R & MARC, 96n631
Cataloging Policy & Support Office, 95n651
Catalogue of ...
    American silver, 96n999
    Canadian catalogues, 96n249
    choral music arranged in biblical order, 2d ed, 97n1053
    forbidden German feature & short film productions held in Zonal Film Archives..., English lang ed, 97n764
    medieval & Renaissance mss in the Houghton Lib, Harvard Univ, v.1, 97n546
    paintings in the Folger Shakespeare lib, 95n1021
    the 15th-century printed bks in the Harvard Univ lib, v.3, 96n42
    the 15th-century printed bks in the Harvard Univ Lib, v.4, 97n547
    the 15th-century printed bks in the Harvard Univ Lib, v.5, 99n614
Catalogue Russian films 1991-94, 95n1369
Catanese, Lynn Ann, 99n801
Cate, Thomas, 98n152
Cates, Jo A., 98n851
Catholic almanac, 1994, 95n1471
Catholic Internet, USA ed, 98n1390
Catholicism on the Web, 98n1391
Catling, Christopher, 96n476, 96n478
Caton, Hiram, 95n770
Caulfield, Anna Breiner, 95n1157
Cavazos-Gaither, Alma E., 98n82, 99n1328
Cavelle, Simon, 95n967
Cavendish, J. M., 95n655
Cavendish, Richard, 96n784, 96n1348
Cawkell, A. E., 95n1689
Caygill, Howard, 96n1428
Cayman Islands, 97n131
Cazoria, Angelina, 96n1862

CCCC bibliog of composition & rhetoric 1992, 96n1058
CCH Tax Law Editors, , 95n332
CD estimator, 1998 [CD-ROM], 99n1402
CD-ROM bk index, 96n80
CD-ROM dir, 14th ed [CD-ROM], 96n1768
CD-ROM dir 95 with multimedia CDs, 13th ed, 96n1769
CD-ROM finder, 96n8
CD-ROMs for librarians & educators, 2d ed, 98n282
CD-ROMs in print 1995 [CD-ROM], 97n16
CD-ROMs in print 1996, 97n17
CD-ROMs in print, 12th ed, 99n8
CD-ROMs rated, 96n10
CDs, super glue, & salsa: how everyday products are made, 96n221
CDs, super glue, & salsa, series 2, 97n193
Ceausescu's Romania: an annot bibliog, 95n160
Cello music since 1960, 96n1286
Celluloid couch, 99n1233
Celtic baby names, 98n378
Cemeteries of the US, 95n68
Censorship, 99n607, 99n608
Center: a gd to genealogical research in the natl capital area, 97n358
Central & E European info, 2d 3d, 95n280
Central Cambridge, 95n374
Central European folk music, 97n1073
Central Office of Information, 95n156
Centre for Development of Instructional Technology (CENDIT), 96n243
Centre for Human Rights, 95n630
Century of design, 99n878
Century of musicals in black & white, 95n1416
Cernea, Ruth Fredman, 97n307
Cerrito, Joann, 96n1158, 96n1159, 96n1160, 97n795, 97n908
Certification & accreditation programs dir, 98n270
Cerutti, Steve, 99n732
Cevasco, George A., 99n1552
Chabran, Rafael, 97n337
Chabran, Richard, 97n337
Chad, 96n115
Chadwick, Bruce A., 97n718
Chadwick, Ruth, 99n1251
Chai, Alan, 97n182
Chaliand, Gerard, 98n807
Chalip, Laurence, 98n725
Chalker, Sylvia, 96n1080
Challenge of urbanization, 97n722
Challoner, Jack, 96n1819
Chalmers, Irena, 95n1521
Chaloner, W. H., 97n443
Chamber music for solo voice & instruments 1960-89, 96n1299
Chambers, Ann, 96n1672
Chambers dict on CD-ROM [CD-ROM], 96n1064
Chambers, Frances, 95n169, 99n127
Chambers, Steven D., 98n606
Chambers 21st century dict, 99n42
Chambliss, J. J., 97n287
Champagne companion, 96n1354
Champagne, Duane, 95n433, 95n438, 95n439, 95n443, 96n415

Champion, Dean J., 99n576
Chan, Karen Y., 99n142
Chan, Lois Mai, 96n627
Chandler, David G., 95n686
Chandler, Karen, 99n1470
Chandler, Ralph C., 96n606, 99n555
Channel Islands, 99n130
Chao, Sheau-Yueh J., 95n1790
Chaplin, Lois Trigg, 95n1527
Chapman, Antony J., 98n710
Chapman, Charles F., 95n1656
Chapman, Jeff, 98n1068
Chapman, Robert L., 95n1069
Characters in 20th-century lit, bk 2, 96n1155
Characters in YA lit, 98n1103
Charismatic movement, pts.1-4, 97n1205
Charles Burchfield, 99n889
Charles Dickens A to Z, 99n1072
Charles Dickens on the screen, 97n1121
Charles, Jill, 96n1419, 97n1152, 97n1153, 98n1325
Charles Wuorinen: a bio-bibliog, 95n1265
Charles-Maurice de Talleyrand 1754-1838, 97n447
Charlesworth, Andrew, 97n146
Charlton price gd to Canadian clocks, 97n777
Charlton standard catalogue of Canadian govt paper money, 11th ed, 99n843
Charlton standard catalogue of chintz, 2d ed, 98n924
Charlton standard catalogue of Royal Doulton beswick figurines, 5th ed, 98n925
Charlton standard catalogue of Royal Doulton beswick jugs, 4th ed, 98n926
Charmed circle: 20-game-winning pitchers in baseball's 20th century, 98n732
Charosh, Paul, 96n1273
Charteris, Richard, 97n1034
Chase, A. R., 98n1446
Chase, Henry, 95n506
Chase, Jayni, 96n1870
Chase, Simon, 96n1351
Chase's calendar of events 1997, 40th ed, 97n5
Chase's calendar of events 1998, 99n4
Chase's sports calendar of events 1997, 97n639
Chatfield, Michael, 97n179
Chaucer's Miller's, Reeve's, & Cook's Tales, 98n1156
Chaucer's pilgrims, 97n989
Checklist of American imprints for 1844, 95n21
Checklist of American imprints for 1845, 98n17
Checklist of American imprints for 1846, 99n13
Checklist of painters c1200-1994, 2d ed, 96n652
Chemical & biological warfare, 98n607
Chemical gd to the Internet, 97n1382
Chemical industry in 1993, 96n222
Chemical research faculties, 97n1380
Chemical scis graduate school finder 1994-95, 96n1791
Chemicals on the Internet, v.1, 98n1478
Chemistry citation index [CD-ROM], 97n1390
ChemLab series, 99n1507
Chemotherapy hndbk, 95n1681
Chenes, Betz Des, 99n522
Cheremisinoff, Paul N., 96n1857, 96n1858, 96n1859

Cherniaev, Vladimir Iu., 98n481
Chernofsky, Jacob L., 95n970
Chernow, Barbara A., 95n49
Cherry, R. L., 98n784
Chesler, Andrew, 96n437, 98n79
Chessick, Richard D., 95n776
Chestochowski, Ben, 98n745
Chevalier, Tracy, 98n1107
Chevallier, Andrew, 97n1343
Chevrefils, Marlys, 96n658, 96n1249, 97n1005
Chicago Bulls ency, 99n726
Chickasaw: an analytical dict, 96n1099
Chidester, David, 98n1344, 98n1345, 98n1382
Chief executives of Tex., 96n718
Child abuse, 1997 ed, 98n568
Child abuse & neglect [CD-ROM], 96n616
Child, Greg, 96n829
Child sexual abuse custody dispute annot bibliog, 96n900
Childers, Joseph, 96n960
CHILDES/BIB: an annot bibliog of child lang & lang disorders, 1994 suppl, 95n334
Childhood & children, 99n779
Childhood sexual abuse, 96n618
Children in foster care & adoption, 99n756
Children of separation, 95n851
Children, YAs, & the law, 99n551
Children's atlas of ...
  civilizations, 95n572
  natural wonders, 96n1806
  the 20th century, 96n553
Children's authors & illustrators, 5th ed, 96n1178
Children's bk awards annual 1998, 99n990
Children's bk prizes, 99n989
Children's bks: awards & prizes, 1996 ed, 97n932
Children's bks & their creators, 97n939
Children's bks from other countries, 99n991
Children's bks in print 1995, 96n19
Children's bks in print 1998, 99n992
Children's bks on ancient Greek & Roman mythology, 95n1319
Children's Britannica, 95n47
Children's catalog, 17th ed, 98n586
Children's ency [CD-ROM], 98n39
Children's fiction series, 98n1088
Children's illus atlas, 1997 ed, 98n381
Children's jukebox, 96n1278
Children's lit awards & winners, 3d ed, 95n1148
Children's media market place, 4th ed, 96n649
Children's museums, 99n71
Children's nonfiction for adult info needs, 99n996
Children's ref plus [CD-ROM], 96n21
Children's rights, 97n515
Children's song index, 1978-93, 97n1033
Children's TV, 1947-90, 96n1404
Children's visual dict, 96n43
Children's writer's & illustrator's market, 1998, 99n828
Child's 1st Catholic dict, 95n1468
Childs, John, 95n687
Chilton, John, 98n1235

China, new ed, 98n111
China, 7th ed, 99n110
China: a dir & sourcebk, 2d ed, 99n107
China: a provincial atlas, 96n452
China: facts & figures annual hndbk, v.23, 99n108
China bibliog, 96n535
China-Burma-India campaign, 1931-45, 99n517
China business: the portable ency for doing business with China, 95n261
China business dir 1994, 95n267
China environmental report, 97n223
China facts & figures annual hndbk, v.17, 95n129
China hndbk, 99n241
China mktg data & stats, 99n242
Chinese filmography, 98n1296
Chinese 1000, 98n1022
Chinese religion pubs in W langs 1981 through 1990, 95n1438
Chinese synonyms usage dict, 98n1023
Chinese-English-French Kuaisu dict, 99n920
Chiron dict of Greek & Roman mythology, 95n1320
Chironomidae [Diptera] of Japan, 96n1626
Cho, Elisa, 98n783
Choate, Jerry R., 96n1630
Choi, Hyaeweol, 95n666
CHOICE reviews on SilverPlatter [CD-ROM], 96n84
Choices, v.3, 95n1132
Choices for young readers [CD-ROM], 98n1086
Choose the right word, 95n1063
Choosing your children's bks: 5-8 yrs, 2d ed, 95n1142
Choosing your children's bks: 8-12 yrs, 95n1143
Choral arrangements of the African-American spirituals, 99n1152
Choral music by African American composers, 97n1054
Christensen, Karen, 97n470, 98n721
Christian music dirs: printed music 1997-98, 98n1244
Christian music dirs: printed music 1994-95, 95n1309
Christian music dirs: recorded music 1994, 95n1310
Christian music dirs, 1998, 99n1176
Christian music finder [CD-ROM], 99n1177
Christian, Nicole, 99n1097
Christian voluntarism in Britain & N America, 96n867
Christianity in S Africa, 98n1382
Christianson, Stephen G., 97n600
Christopher, A. J., 95n395
Christopher Lee & Peter Cushing & horror cinema, 96n1396
Christophory, Jul, 98n135
Chronicle 2-yr college databk, rev ed, 96n335
Chronicle financial aid gd, rev ed, 96n364
Chronicle of ...
  America, 96n500
  America, rev ed, 98n435
  American music, 1700-1995, 97n1025
  the cinema, 96n1371
  the cinema, rev ed, 98n1282
  the Olympics 1896-1996, 97n660
  the Olympics, 1896-2000, 99n738
  the 20th century, 96n558
  the world, rev ed, 97n464
  the yr 1995, 97n465
Chronicle vocational school manual, rev ed, 96n381

Chronology & glossary of propaganda in the US, 97n595
Chronology of ...
    European hist, 98n462
    Hispanic-American hist, 96n550
    medicine & related scis, 98n1541
    native N American hist, 95n433
    the ancient world, 96n559
    the Cold War at sea 1945-91, 99n643
    the expanding world, 96n560
    the medieval world, 96n561
    the modern world, 2d ed, 96n562
    20th-century E European hist, 95n559
    weather, 99n1526
    women's hist, 95n911
    world hist, compact ed, 96n564
Chumash & their predecessors, 99n381
Cibbarelli, Pamela R., 96n643, 99n609
Cibbarelli, Shawn E., 99n609
Cicarelli, James, 97n150
Cicarelli, Julianne, 97n150
Cigar companion, 2d ed, 96n1351
CIJE on disc, Jan 1969-Jul 1994 [CD-ROM], 95n346
Cilurzo, Mary Jeanne, 97n1313
Cimbala, Paul A., 97n408
Ciment, James, 98n355
Cindric, Susan J., 99n56
Cirn, Cyril, 98n34
Cirn, Kit, 98n34
CITES identification gd—birds, 96n1612
Cities of the biblical world, 98n1378
Cities of the world, 4th ed, 95n514
Citino, Robert M., 96n702
Citizen's companion to US Supreme Court opinions, 1996-97 term, 99n562
City crime rankings, 96n602
City crime rankings, 3d ed, 98n552
City profiles USA 1996, 97n388
Civil law lexicon for lib classification, 99n599
Civil rights decisions of the US Supreme Court, the 19th century, 96n607
Civil rights decisions of the US Supreme Court, the 20th century, 96n608
Civil rights movement, 99n473
Civil serv career starter, 99n272
Civil trial practice deskbook, 98n528
Civil War [CD-ROM], 96n691
Civil War battlefields, 96n517
Civil War bks: a critical bibliog, 98n432
Civil War CD-ROM [CD-ROM], 97n401
Civil War in bks, 98n433
Civil War 100, 99n625
Civil War sites, memorials, museums, & lib collections, 98n448
Civil War Society, 96n504
Civilizations of the ancient Near East, 96n159
Claggett, Hilary D., 99n1371
Claghorn, Charles E., 96n1304
Claghorn, Gene, 97n1035
Clarice Lispector: a bio-bibliog, 95n1225
Clark, Amy, 95n795

Clark, Andrew F., 95n123
Clark, Andy, 95n795
Clark, David Lindsey, 98n1220
Clark, Edward, 98n340
Clark, Jerome, 97n632, 97n638
Clark, John, 95n1491
Clark, Lewis J., 99n1366
Clark, M., 98n1030
Clark, Neil, 96n68
Clark, Paul C., Jr., 99n462
Clark, Sandra, 96n1241, 98n1161
Clark, Stuart, 96n1799
Clark, Suzanne M., 99n452
Clark, Thomas L., 97n841
Clark, Walter A., 99n1129
Clarke, Boden, 96n1209, 96n1218
Clarke, Paul Barry, 97n73
Clarke, Peter B., 98n1343
Clarkson, Christopher, 99n600
Clarkson, J. Shannon, 97n1177
Class FC, a classification for Canadian hist, 2d ed, 96n628
Classic American cars, 98n1650
Classic FM gd to classical music, 98n1222
Classical & medieval lit criticism, v.14, 96n1149
Classical myths & legends in the Middle Ages & Renaissance, 99n1017
Classical singers of the opera & recital stages, 95n1250
Classical studies, 97n461
Classification of chronic pain, 2d ed, 96n1723
Classification plus [CD-ROM], 97n533
Claudio, Virginia S., 98n1422
Clayton, Constance, 95n409
Clayton, Florence E., 95n1784
Clayton, George D., 95n1784
Clayton, Jade, 99n1491
Clean air hndbk, 3d ed, 99n1558
Clebsch, Betsy, 98n1434
Cleere, Nigel, 99n1376
Clemens, Joe, 98n906
Clement, Russell T., 95n996, 95n997, 95n1019, 97n806
Clements, Frank A., 96n166, 97n140, 98n689
Cleveland, William A., 95n474
Clewis, Beth, 95n1528
Cliches, 98n1019
Climbing, 96n829
Cline, Camille N., 99n67
Clinkscale, Martha Novak, 97n1050
ClinPSYC: 1980-Dec 1996 [CD-ROM], 98n712
Clinton 500, 95n744
Clitics, 96n1060
Clive Barker's A-Z of horror, 98n1306
Close, Arthur C., 95n199
Clothier, Galina, 99n553
Clotworthy, William G., 99n428
Cloud nine: a dreamer's dict, 96n781
Clough, David G., 98n791
Clough, Leonard G., 98n791
Clucas, Richard A., 98n657
Clute, John, 96n1192, 98n1116
Clynes, Tom, 96n1352, 97n1029

Coal info 1992, 95n1749
Coastal fishes of SE Australia, 95n1585
Coasting: an expanded gd to the N gulf coast, 3d ed, 99n427
Cochrane, John, 99n636
Cockerham, William C., 98n1524
Cockrill, Pauline, 95n974
Cockroach hall of fame & 101 other off-the-wall museums, 95n84
Cocks, Elijah E., 97n1394
Cocks, Josiah C., 97n1394
Code of medial ethics: current opinons with annots, 1996-97 ed, 98n1537
Codes of professional responsibility, 3d ed, 96n1431
Codex alimentarius, v.5a, 2d ed, 96n1534
Codex alimentarius, v.13, 2d ed, 96n1535
Coffel, Steve, 97n1425
Coffey, Frank, 96n1335
Coffman, Steve, 99n596
Cogan, Neil H., 98n669
Cogar, William, 99n639
Coger, Dalvan, 97n98
Cogger, Harold G., 99n1395
Coggins, Margaret, 99n1002
Cohen, Allen, 99n1207
Cohen, David Harris, 95n980
Cohen, E. Richard, 97n1406
Cohen, Elliot D., 99n826
Cohen, Morris L., 97n493
Cohen, Norm, 95n1302
Cohen, Richard M., 95n820, 98n746
Cohen, Selma Jeanne, 99n1202
Cohen, Susan Sarah, 95n628
Cohl, H. Aaron, 99n65
Cohn, Arthur, 99n1153
Cohn-Sherbok, Dan, 95n446, 97n1222, 99n1291
Cohn-Sherbok, Lavinia, 96n1481, 97n1222, 99n1283
Coined by Shakespeare, 99n1078
Colander, David C., 98n152
Colborn, Candy, 95n1128
Cold War, 99n544
Cold War culture media & the arts 1945-90, 99n1191
Cold War ency, 97n473
Cold War ref gd, 98n508
Cole Porter discography, 97n1068
Cole, Robert, 97n618
Cole, Stephen, 95n1342
Coleman, Charles J., 96n255
Coleman, Gordon J., 98n1412
Coleman, J. A., 97n832
Colin, Wilson, 97n1167
Coll, Susan, 99n873
Collaborative bibliog of women in philosophy, 98n1332
Collapse of communism in the Soviet Union, 99n693
Collected eds histl series & sets & monuments of music, 98n1190
Collecting dolls ref & price gd, 98n917
Collecting in cyberspace, 98n893
Collecting world coins, 7th ed, 99n844
Collector's ency of Depression glass, 11th ed, 96n1013
Collector's gd to celebrity autographs, 97n775

Collector's gd to TV memorabilia, 1960s & 1970s, 98n922
Collectors value gd to Oriental decorative arts, 98n890
College Board gd to jobs & career planning, 2d ed, 95n388
College check mate, 1995-96, 95n379
College chemistry faculties 1996, 10th ed, 97n303
College comparison gd, 95n377
College costs & financial aid hndbk 1998, 99n340
College degrees by mail & modem 1998, 99n302
College degrees by mail 1996, rev ed, 96n363
College.edu: on-line resources for the cyber-savvy, 98n301
College financial aid, 99n341
College football bibliog, 95n821
College hndbk 1998, 99n350
College hndbk for transfer students 1997, 98n296
College majors & careers, 3d ed, 98n316
College media dir 1994, 95n952
College students research companion, 99n610
CollegeSource [CD-ROM], 98n297
Collegeville pastoral dict of biblical theology, 97n1196
Collett, Jonathan, 98n1640
Colletta, John Philip, 95n456, 95n457
Collier, Clifford Duxbury, 97n351
Collier, Frederick J., 96n1813
Collier's ency, 95n48
Collier's ency, 98n40
Collier's ency 1998 [CD-ROM], 98n41
Collin, P. H., 99n145, 99n654, 99n1440, 99n1553
Collin, S. M. H., 98n1574
Collinge, William J., 98n1384
Collings, E. W., 96n1669
Collins, Bud, 95n825, 98n750
Collins concise atlas of the world, rev ed, 98n382
Collins dict of archaeology, 95n520
Collins ency of Scotland, 96n148
Collins German-English, English-German dict, 2d ed, 96n1104
Collins German-English, English-German dict, unabridged 3d ed, 99n928
Collins, James Lawton, Jr., 95n686
Collins, James T., 98n264
Collins, John J., 99n1266
Collins, Louise Mooney, 95n23, 95n33
Collins nations of the world atlas, 97n372
Collins, Raymond L., 96n689
Collins Scottish clan & family ency, 96n435
Collins Spanish-English, English-Spanish dict, unabridged 5th ed, 99n939
Collins, William J., 95n1286
Collinson, Diane, 96n1427, 97n1158
Collins-Robert French-English, English-French dict, 3d ed, 98n1024
Collinwood, Dean W., 99n102
Colloquial Navaho: a dict, 95n1090
Collver, Michael, 97n1051
Colman, Andrew M., 95n777
Colombo, John Robert, 99n77
Colombo's concise Canadian quotations, 99n77
Colonial wars of N America, 1512-1763, 97n413
Color atlas of rocks & minerals in thin section, 95n1724

Color of words: an encyclopaedic dict of ethnic bias in the US, 98n328
Colorado rockhounding, 95n1732
Colpe, Carsten, 97n1201
Colton, Theodore, 99n1418
Columbia chronicles of American life, 1910-92, 96n501
Columbia companion to British hist, 98n465
Columbia dict of modern literary & cultural critcism, 96n960
Columbia dict of quotations, 95n88
Columbia ency, 5th ed, 95n49
Columbia ency [CD-ROM], 98n42
Columbia Granger's gd to poetry anthologies, 2d ed, 96n1263
Columbia Granger's index to poetry, 10th ed, 95n1245
Columbia Granger's index to poetry in collected & selected works, 97n1016
Columbia Granger's world of poetry [CD-ROM], 97n1017
Columbia gd to the Cold War, 99n543
Columbia Univ Dept of Pediatrics children's medical gd, 98n1554
Columbia world of quotations [CD-ROM], 97n68
Comay, Joan, 96n1481
Combined membership list 1995-96, 96n1825
Combined membership list 1996-97, 97n1412
Comedy quotes from the movies, 95n1402
Comedy stars at 78 RMP, 99n1196
Comfort, Nicholas, 95n707
Comic art of Europe, 95n1332
Comic bks & comic strips in the US: an intl bibliog, 95n1333
Comics buyer's gd 1998, 98n908
Comics values annual, 1998 ed, 98n907
Command performance, USA! a discography, 97n772
Commercial air transport bks, 98n1646
Commins, David, 97n141
Commire, Anne, 95n575, 95n576
Committees in the US congress 1947-92, v.2, 96n733
Commodity indexes for the Standard Intl Trade Classification, revision 3, 95n258
Common American birds, 96n1611
Common birds of E Africa, 98n1461
Common medical abbrevs, 96n1695
Commonwealth univs yrbk 1993, 95n363
Communities dir, 1995 ed, 96n852
Commuter airlines of the US, 96n1880
Compact music dict, 97n1026
Compact up-to-date English-Hebrew dict, 97n856
Companies intl [CD-ROM], 97n209
Companies intl, DOS version 1.3 [CD-ROM], 95n245
Companion ency of ...
    anthropology, 95n392
    Asian philosophy, 99n1254
    geography, 98n397
    psychology, 95n777
    the hist & philosophy of the mathematical scis, 95n1740
    the hist of medicine, 95n1654
Companion to ...
    historiography, 99n829
    the characters in the fiction & drama of W. Somerset Maugham, 97n996
    the Greek lyric poets, 99n1018
    the philosophy of mind, 96n1432
    the US Constitution & its amendments, 2d ed, 99n685
    20th-century German lit, 2d ed, 99n1093
Company museums, industry museums & industrial tours, 95n235
Comparative gd to American elem & secondary schools, 99n311
Comparative gd to American suburbs, 98n824
Comparative Russian-English dict of Russian proverbs & sayings, 96n1125
Compendium of ...
    American railroad radio frequencies, 13th ed, 96n1891
    histl sources, rev ed, 96n431
    histl sources, rev ed, 98n364
    human settlements stats 1995, 5th ed, 97n715
    modern instrumental techniques, 95n1273
    social stats & indicators, 4th issue, 99n787
    soil clean-up techs & soil remediation cos, 98n1496
    the Confederate armies: Ky., Md., Mo., Confederate units & Indian units, 96n522
    the Confederate armies: La., 96n523
    the Confederate armies: Miss., 96n524
    the Confederate armies: S.C. & Ga., 96n525
    the Confederate armies: Tex., 96n526
Competitions, 97n299
Compilation of state & fed privacy laws, 1997 ed, 98n543
Complete anime gd, 98n1307
Complete atlas of world hist, 98n491
Complete baby & child care, 96n904
Complete bill of rights, 98n669
Complete book of ...
    cacti & succulents, 95n1549
    Catholic colleges, 1998 ed, 98n288
    colleges, 1998 ed, 98n286
    everyday Christianity, 98n1385
    natural & medicinal cures, 95n1670
    personal legal forms, 2d ed, 98n541
    pet names, 98n1462
    small business legal forms, 2d ed, 98n542
    symptoms & treatments, 99n1456
Complete cat health manual, 98n1464
Complete college financing gd, 4th ed, 99n342
Complete cross-ref gd to the baby buster generations collective unconscious, 99n1187
Complete cyberspace ref & dir, 96n1772
Complete dict of sexology, new expanded ed, 96n885
Complete dinosaur, 98n1617
Complete dir for ...
    people with chronic illness, 1994, 95n1659
    people with chronic illness, 99n1467
    people with disabilities, 1997-98, 98n771
    people with rare disorders, 1998/99, 99n1447
Complete dir of nursing facilities for younger adults with chronic physical disabilities, 1994, 96n855
Complete dir of large print bks & serials 1998, 99n11
Complete dir to sci fiction, fantasy, & horror TV series, 99n1224
Complete ency of natural healing, 99n1459
Complete family gd to healthy living, 97n1326
Complete family gd to natural home remedies, 98n1545
Complete film dict, 98n1285

Complete footwear dict, 95n988
Complete golfer's almanac 1995, 96n821
Complete grants sourcebk for higher educ, 3d ed, 97n684
Complete gd to ...
    American bed & breakfast, 4th ed, 97n385
    American bed & breakfast, 98n410
    America's natl parks, 10th ed, 99n429
    bed & breakfasts, inns & guesthouses in the US & Canada, 11th ed, 95n510
    Canadian univs, 3d ed, 96n320
    citing govt info resources, rev ed, 95n74
    homeopathy, 97n1347
    household chemicals, 96n1795
    sharpening, 96n1679
    special interest videos [CD-ROM], 95n1360
    whiskey, 98n1426
    writers' conferences & workshops, 96n965
Complete hist of our presidents, 98n658
Complete home healer, 95n1674
Complete home health advisor, 97n1344
Complete horse care manual, 96n1556
Complete James Bond movie ency, rev ed, 96n1382
Complete learning disabilities dir, 1995/96, 96n374
Complete learning disabilities dir, 1998, 99n303
Complete Marquis Who's Who on CD-ROM [CD-ROM], 98n28, 99n19
Complete motorcycle bk, 96n1884
Complete "no geek-speak" gd to the Internet, 99n1499
Complete scholarship bk, 98n287
Complete vampire companion, 95n1327
Complete weather resource, 98n1611
Completely queer: the gay & lesbian ency, 99n757
Composites, 2d ed, 95n1629
Comprehensive, annot bibliog on Mahatma Gandhi, 97n430
Comprehensive annot bk of Mormon bibliog, 98n1397
Comprehensive dict of measurement & control, 3d ed, 97n1311
Comprehensive dissertation index, 1996 suppl, 98n844
Comprehensive name index for The American Slave, 98n341
Comprehensive networking glossary & acronym gd, 96n1759
Comprehensive ref manual for signers & interpreters, 4th ed, 96n1131
Compton's ency & fact-index, 1994 ed, 95n50
Compton's interactive ency, version 3.00, 1995 ed [CD-ROM], 95n51
CompuMath citation index 1993, 2d semiannual, 95n1739
CompuServe companion, 95n953
Computer & info sci & tech abbrevs & acronyms dict, 95n1698
Computer desktop ency, 97n1369
Computer dict for kids & their parents, 96n1748
Computer glossary, 7th ed, 96n1757
Computer health hazards, v.2, 95n1694
Computer support dir, 96n1767
Concise atlas of the world, 95n475
Concise atlas of the world, 3d ed, 98n383
Concise Columbia ency, 3d ed, 96n45
Concise compendium of the world's langs, 97n813
Concise conservative ency, 98n691

Concise dict of ...
    American biog, 5th ed, 98n29
    American Jewish biog, 95n447
    biomedicine & molecular biology, 98n1439
    Christian theology, 96n1453
    Christianity in America, 96n1466
    Indian philosophy, rev ed, 98n1336
    lib & info sci, 97n525
    medical-legal terms, 99n552
Concise ency biochemistry & molecular biology, 3d ed, 98n1599
Concise ency biology, 97n1266
Concise ency chemistry, 95n1713
Concise ency of ...
    Christianity, 99n1287
    composite materials, rev ed, 95n1632
    environmental systems, 95n1768
    foods & nutrition, 96n1524
    Hinduism, 99n1290
    Judaism, 99n1291
    measurement & instrumentation, 96n1641
    psychology, 2d ed, 97n627
Concise engineering & tech index 1987-May 1994 [CD-ROM], 95n1479
Concise histl atlas of Canada, 99n409
Concise histl atlas of Eastern Europe, 97n446
Concise metals engineering data bk, 99n1409
Concise Oxford dict of ...
    current English, 9th ed, 96n1065
    ecology, 96n1854
    linguistics, 99n893
    music, 4th ed, 97n1027
    quotations, 99n78
    sociology, 96n834
Concise Oxford Russian dict, 97n866
Concise world atlas, 98n384
Concordance to the complete poems & plays of T. S. Eliot, 97n971
Concordance to the poetry of Robert Frost, 95n1190
Conductors & composers of popular orchestral music, 99n1158
Conductor's gd to choral-orchestral works, 96n1297
Conductor's gd to choral-orchestral works, 20th century, part 2, 99n1151
Cone, Robert J., 99n1484
Confessions of Saint Augustine, 97n1207
Congo, 95n116
Congress & the nation, 1993-96, 99n675
Congress & the nation, v.8, 95n731
Congress at your fingertips: 103d Congress, 2d session, 1994: alpha ed, 95n720
Congress at your fingertips: 103d Congress, 2d session, 1994: condensed ed, 95n721
Congress at your fingertips: 103d Congress, 2d session, 1994: standard ed, 95n722
Congressional dir: 105th congress, 99n669
Congressional elections 1946-96, 99n676
Congressional Quarterly almanac, v.49, 95n732
Congressional Quarterly almanac, v.52, 98n670

Congressional Quarterly's desk ref on American govt, 96n737
Congressional Quarterly's gd to the US Supreme Court, 3d ed, 98n529
Congressional Quarterly's gd to US elections, 3d ed, 95n733
Congressional Quarterly's Political Staff, 96n738
Congressional Quarterly's pols in America 1996, 96n738
Congressional roll call 1996, 98n671
Congressional staff dir fall 1997, 98n652
Congressional voting gd, 5th ed, 96n736
Congressional yrbk 1996, 104th Congress, 2nd session, 98n672
Congressional yellow bk, fall 1994, 95n734
Congressional yrbk 1993, 96n739
Conley, Jill, 96n892
Connecticut, Maine, Mass., [&] R.I.,: atlas of histl county boundaries, 96n438
Connecting cultures, 98n1093
Connell, James E., 97n777
Connoisseurs' hndbk of the wines of Calif. & the Pacific Northwest, 4th ed, 99n1341
Connor, D. Russell, 97n1071
Connors, Martin, 95n1399, 96n1398
Conoley, Jane Close, 95n787
Conolly, L. W., 95n1102
Conroy, Thomas F., 97n276
Conroy, Wendy A., 98n710
Conservation & environmentalism, 97n1426
Conservation & the law, 99n584
Conservation dir, 1994, 95n1769
Considine, Douglas M., 96n1502
Consolidated bibliog of urban hist, 98n825
Consolidated list of products whose consumption and/or sale have been banned...., 5th ed, 96n217
Constitutional law & YAs, 2d ed, 98n540
Constitutional law dict, v.1, 96n606
Constitutional law dict, v.2, suppl 1, 99n555
Constitutions of the world, 96n611
Consultants & consulting orgs dir 1996 suppl, 16th ed, 97n161
Consulting spirits, 99n708
Consumer Asia 1995, 2d ed, 96n242
Consumer Asia 1998, 99n215
Consumer Canada 1996, 97n268
Consumer China 1994, 95n268
Consumer China 1998, 99n216
Consumer E Europe 1996, 96n251
Consumer E Europe 1998/9, 99n248
Consumer Europe 1994, 95n278
Consumer Europe 1998/9, 14th ed, 99n249
Consumer health info source bk, 4th ed, 95n1666
Consumer health info source bk, 5th ed, 99n1416
Consumer health USA, 96n1711
Consumer health USA, v.2, 98n1538
Consumer intl 1997/98, 99n218
Consumer intl 1995, 95n248
Consumer Japan 1993, 95n269
Consumer Latin America 1993, 95n287
Consumer Latin America 1997, 4th ed, 98n209
Consumer Mexico 1996, 97n269
Consumer Middle East 1998, 99n217

Consumer protection & the law, 97n487
Consumer Research study on bk purchasing, 1993, 96n673
Consumer sales leads, 1997 ed [CD-ROM], 98n249
Consumer South Africa 1995, 97n270
Consumer USA 1996, 97n271
Consumer's dict of cosmetic ingredients, 4th ed, 96n1790
Consumer's dict of food additives, 4th ed, 96n1530
Consumer's dict of medicines, 95n1688
Consumers Index, staff of, 95n224
Consumers index to product evaluations & info sources, v.24, no.2, April-June 1996, 97n188
Consumers ref disc [CD-ROM], 96n218
Container gardening through the yr, 96n1544
Contat, Michel, 95n1426
Conte, Francis, 95n561
Conte, Joseph, 98n1140, 98n1141, 99n1059
Contemporary African-American female playwrights, 99n1050
Contemporary African pols & dvlpmt, 96n110
Contemporary American dramatists, 95n1176
Contemporary American folk art, 97n783
Contemporary & histl lit of food sci & human nutrition, 96n1522
Contemporary architects, 3d ed, 96n1043
Contemporary artists, 4th ed, 97n795
Contemporary Australian women 1996/97, 97n734
Contemporary authors, v.158, 99n949
Contemporary authors, v.159, 99n950
Contemporary authors autobiog series, v.25, 98n1061
Contemporary authors autobiog series, v.26, 98n1062
Contemporary authors autobiog series, v.27, 98n1063
Contemporary authors autobiog series, v.28, 99n953
Contemporary authors new revision series, v.43, 96n1150
Contemporary authors new revision series, v.59, 99n947
Contemporary authors new revision series, v.60, 99n948
Contemporary authors on CD [CD-ROM], 98n1064, 95n1110
Contemporary Barbie dolls, 99n847
Contemporary black biog, v.8, 96n400
Contemporary black biog, v.9, 96n401
Contemporary black biog, v.16, 99n376
Contemporary British dramatists, 95n1206
Contemporary Canadian authors, v.1, 98n1169
Contemporary Canadian pols, 1988-94, 96n751
Contemporary democracy, 98n638
Contemporary designers, 99n857
Contemporary diesel spotter's gd, 2d ed, 96n1889
Contemporary fashion, 96n1017
Contemporary Greek artists, 95n1000
Contemporary heroes & heroines, bk 3, 99n20
Contemporary Hollywood's negative Hispanic image, 95n1387
Contemporary Jewish-American novelists, 98n1125
Contemporary Latin American artists, 98n955
Contemporary literary criticism, v.84, 96n1152
Contemporary literary criticism, v.85, 96n1153
Contemporary literary criticism, v.86, 97n895
Contemporary literary criticism, v.87, 97n896
Contemporary literary criticism, v.88, 97n897
Contemporary literary criticism, v.89, 97n898
Contemporary literary criticism, v.90, 98n1068

Contemporary literary criticism, v.100, 99n966
Contemporary literary criticism, v.101, 99n967
Contemporary literary criticism, v.102, 99n968
Contemporary literary criticism, v.103, 99n969
Contemporary literary criticism annual cum index for 1995, 96n1151
Contemporary literary criticism yrbk 1996, v.99, 99n965
Contemporary musicians, v.13, 96n1305
Contemporary musicians, v.19, 99n1115
Contemporary musicians, v.20, 99n1116
Contemporary novel, 2d ed, 98n1108
Contemporary photographers, 3d ed, 96n1018
Contemporary poets, dramatists, essayists, & novelists of the South, 96n1199
Contemporary popular writers, 98n1058
Contemporary printed lit of the English counter-reformation between 1558 & 1640, v.2, 95n1463
Contemporary quotations in black, 98n78
Contemporary S men fiction writers, 99n1039
Contemporary S women fiction writers, 95n1181
Contemporary Spanish novel, 97n1014
Contemporary Spanish-speaking writers & illustrators for children & YAs, 95n1151
Contemporary theatre, film, & TV, v.13, 96n1362
Contemporary theatre, film, & TV, v.17, 99n1195
Contemporary thesaurus of social sci terms & synonyms, 95n94
Contemporary women dramatists, 95n1155
Contemporary women scientists, 95n1486
Contemporary women's issues 1992-July 1997 [CD-ROM], 98n838
Contento, William, 96n1194
Continuing medical educ dir 1996-97, 98n1532
Continuum dict of religion, 95n1440
Continuum ency of symbols, 95n1441
Controller's & treasurer's desk ref, 95n233
Conway, George L., 98n933
Cook, Allan R., 99n1473
Cook, Charles, 96n824
Cook, Chris, 95n558, 95n747, 96n530, 96n711, 98n500, 99n690
Cook, Edward M., 95n1452
Cook, James F., 96n496
Cook, Kevin L., 97n711
Cook, Mary F., 98n224
Cook, Rhodes, 98n673, 99n677
Cook, Samantha, 95n1370
Cooke, Ian, 99n1349
Cooke, Jacob Ernest, 95n540, 99n464
Cook's dict & culinary ref, 97n1248
Cooley, Laurel, 98n6
Cooney, Jerry W., 96n551
Co-op America's natl green pages, 1996 ed, 97n1428
Cooper, Adam Merton, 97n359
Cooper, Andre R., Sr., 97n1434
Cooper, B. Lee, 96n806, 96n1333, 99n1173
Cooper, Barbara T., 99n1092
Cooper, Cheryl, 96n319
Cooper, Gail, 98n281
Cooper, Garry, 98n281

Cooper, Gordon, 96n1353
Cooper, J. C., 97n1210
Cooper, J. I., 95n1552
Cooper, Jerry, 95n682
Cooper, John, 96n1403
Cooper, Kay, 95n1153
Cooper, Robert M., 96n1233, 99n1065
Cooper's comprehensive environmental desk ref, 97n1434
Cooper's comprehensive environmental desk ref [CD-ROM], 99n1559
Copel, Linda Carman, 97n1355
Coplin, William D., 95n153
Coppell, Bill, 97n643
Copper, John F., 95n137
Cops, crooks, & criminologists, 97n504
Copyright hndbk, 2d ed, 96n590
Copyright laws & treaties of the world 1991-95 suppl, 98n566
Coral reef animals of the Indo-Pacific, 97n1295
Coral snakes of the Americas, 98n1475
Cordry, Harold V., 98n1250
Core collection for small libs, 98n1077
Coretta Scott King awards bk, 95n411
Corey, Melinda, 96n1374, 99n525, 99n818, 99n1307
Corke, Bettina, 98n35
Corliss, William R., 96n1559
Cormier, Ramona, 95n1431, 98n1342
Cornell, Charles R., 98n20
Cornett, Lloyd H., Jr., 99n451
Cornfield, Daniel B., 97n250
Cornwell, Neil, 99n1097
Corporate affiliations plus, spring/summer 1995 [CD-ROM], 97n162
Corporate & fndn fundraising manual for Native Americans, 3d ed, 98n793
Corporate & fndn grants 1995, 95n861
Corporate dir of US public cos, 99n149
Corporate dir of US public cos [CD-ROM], 97n163
Corporate dir of US public cos 1996, 97n164
Corporate 500, 13th ed, 97n685
Corporate fndn profiles, 98n785
Corporate giving dir 1999, 20th ed, 99n761
Corporate giving yellow pages 1998, 13th ed, 99n762
CorpTech CD-ROM dir of tech cos [CD-ROM], 98n1570
CorpTech dir of tech cos 1996, 10th US ed, 96n1749
CorpTech explore database [CD-ROM], 98n1571
Corpus admin index, 1994, 95n748
Correard, Marie-Helene, 96n1100, 98n1026, 98n1027
Correctional admin vocab, 95n621
Corriente, F., 99n922
Corrigan, Maureen, 99n1032
Corsica, 98n131
Corsini, Raymond J., 95n779, 97n627
Cortada, James W., 96n284, 97n1364, 97n1365
Corvinus press: a hist & bibliog, 95n675
Corvisier, Andre, 95n687
Corwin, Charles, 95n1085
Cosgrove, Holli, 98n213
Cosloy, Sharon D., 95n1619
Cosman, Madeleine Pelner, 97n838
Cosmic influences on humans, animals, & plants, 98n1441

Cosmopolitan world atlas, 96n446
Cosner, Shaaron, 97n411
Cossolotto, Matthew, 97n605
Costa, Marie, 97n666
Costa, Vincenzo, 96n1814
Costello, Elaine, 99n909
Costello, M. Rita, 95n202
Costello, Tom, 95n1379
Cote d'Ivoire, 97n96
Cotterell, Arthur, 99n526
Cottridge, David, 96n1617
Coulmas, Florian, 97n811, 98n984
Coulson, Jessie, 96n1127
Counseling older persons, 96n843
Counties USA 1997, 98n662
Countries of the world & their leaders yrbk 1995: suppl, 96n710
Countries of the world & their leaders yrbk 1999, 99n658
Country Americana price gd, 98n894
Country music, 98n1234
Country music: 70 yrs of America's favorite music, 95n1300
Country Music Fndn, 95n1296
Country on CD, 95n1296
County & city extra, 1995, 4th ed, 97n712
County courthouse bk, 2d ed, 96n588
County executive dir, 96n727
County locator (LOCUS): ultimate place name & zip code locator, 95n69
Courtroom drama: 120 of the world's most notable trials, 99n556
Courtroom hndbk on fed evidence, 1995 ed, 96n591
Covenants not to compete, 2d ed, 97n494
Covert, Nadine, 95n1012
Coville, Gary, 99n1213
Covington, Melody Mauldin, 96n1755
Covington, Michael A., 96n1755
Cowan, Tom, 95n405
Cowboy dict, 95n1041
Cowboy ency, 96n510
Cowboys & the wild west, 95n541
Cowden, Robert H., 95n1250
Cowgill, Allison A., 98n724
Cowie, Leonard W., 95n751, 97n439
Cowlard, Keith A., 98n467, 99n504
Cowles, C. McKeen, 97n1327
Cowley, Chris, 96n1078
Cowley, Robert, 98n616
Cox, C. Brian, 98n1167
Cox, Elizabeth M., 97n601, 98n829
Cox, Harold E., 97n446
Cox, Mary, 96n1038, 99n875
Cox, Michael, 96n1659
Coy, Cris, 95n383
Coye, Dale F., 99n1076
Coykendall, Ralf, Jr., 98n895
Coykendall's complete gd to sporting collectibles, 98n895
Coyne, Mark S., 99n1571
CPI.Q: Canadian per index [CD-ROM], 98n75
CPT '97: physicians' current procedural terminology, 98n1525
CQ's pocket gd to the lang of Congress, 95n723

CQ's state fact finder 1997, 98n817
Crabtree, Phillip D., 95n1251
Cracking Latin America: a country-by-country gd to doing business..., 95n288
Cracking the corporate closet, 96n259
Craft, Donna, 98n1583, 99n271
Crafts supply source bk, 3d ed, 96n1012
Crafts supply source bk, 4th ed, 98n931
Cragg, Dan, 97n562
Craggs, Stewart R., 96n1279, 98n1211, 99n1130, 99n1131
Craig, Barbara L., 96n653
Craig, Bruce D., 96n1667
Craig, Robert D., 99n459
Craighead's intl bus, travel, & relocation gd to 78 countries, 96n231
Crain, Esther, 96n1263
Crainer, Stuart, 98n148
Cralley, Lester V., 96n1875
Cralley, Lewis J., 96n1875
Cramer, Clayton E., 98n342
Cramer, Eugene Casjen, 99n1132
Crampton, Luke, 97n1081
Cran, Angela, 98n136
Crandell, George W., 96n1220
Crane, J. L., 98n1451
Crane, Janet, 96n171
Crane, Nancy B., 98n875
Crawford, Ann M., 97n990
Crawford, Gary William, 96n1256
Crawford, Mark, 99n1560
Crawford, Tad, 98n605, 99n854, 99n859
Crawford, Walter B., 97n990
Crayton, Tabatha, 96n52
CRC hndbk of chemistry & physics, 75th ed, 95n1711
CRC hndbk of laboratory safety, 4th ed, 97n1386
CRC materials sci & engineering hndbk, 2d ed, 95n1630
CRC standard mathematical tables & formulae, 30th, 97n1413
Creaton, Heather, 97n116
Creber, Geoffrey, 97n1273
Creese, Mary R. S., 99n1301
Creeth, Terry, 99n92
Cremeans, John E., 99n220
Cremona, Candida H., 96n856
Crenshaw, Marshall, 95n1391
Crime & the justice system in America, 98n550
Crime fiction 2, 95n1160
Crime in America, 97n508
Crime in America's top-rated cities, 99n579
Crime state rankings 1994, 95n624
Crime victim compensation programs, 95n625
Crimes & punishment, 96n573
Crimes of perception: an ency of heresies & heretics, 96n1468
Criminal justice abstracts 1968-93 [CD-ROM], 95n626
Criminal justice in Israel, 96n596
Criminal justice info, 99n547
Criminal justice research in libs & on the Internet, 99n581
Criminal quotes, 98n79
Crisostomo, Isabelo T., 97n332
Crispin, Gerry, 99n267

Critical bibliog of French lit, v.5, 95n1229
Critical companion to the Russian revolution 1914-21, 98n481
Critical essays on Laurence Sterne, 99n1074
Critical gd to mgmt training videos & selected multimedia, 1996, 97n266
Critical hist & filmography of Toho's Godzilla series, 98n1294
Critical hist of TVs The Twilight Zone, 1959-64, 99n1232
Critical legal studies, 97n492
Critical review of bks in religion 1997, v.10, 99n1260
Critical survey of drama, rev ed, 95n1156
Crocker, Malcolm J., 98n1619
Croddy, Eric, 98n607
Croft, Terrell, 98n1485
Crompton, Clifford W., 95n1537
Croom, Emily Anne, 95n458
Crosbie, Michael J., 99n882
Cross, F. L., 98n1389
Crossley, Heather, 99n906
Crossword puzzle dict, 6th ed, 96n1085
Crosswy, Tiffany, 98n427
Crow, Laura, 96n722
Crowdus, Gary, 96n1409
Crowley, William R., 97n1415, 98n1478
Crown, Alan David, 95n1435
Crown crime companion, 96n1189
Crows & jays, 95n1569
Cruisers of WW II, 97n574
Cruising gd to N.Y. waterways & Lake Champlain, 99n430
Crum, Howard, 95n1547
Crumbley, D. Larry, 95n330
Crutchfield, Roger S., 99n901
Crystal clear v.2, 96n993
Crystal, David, 95n25, 95n45, 96n44, 96n1061, 97n20, 98n37, 98n38, 98n989, 99n18
Csida, June Bundy, 95n917
Cuba, 97n132
Cuban Americans, 99n397
Cubbage, Sue A., 95n307
Cubberley, Carol W., 96n379
Cubberly, William H., 95n1500
Cuddon, J. A., 99n960
Cueto, Gail, 99n93
Culbertson, Margaret, 96n1050
Culinary schools, 99n1336
Cullen, Tony, 99n646
Cullen-DuPont, Kathryn, 97n736, 98n563
Culligan, Judy, 99n24, 99n143, 99n582, 99n1304
Cultural atlas of ...
    Africa, rev ed, 99n95
    China, rev ed, 99n106
    India, 98n113
    Russia & the Former Soviet Union, rev ed, 99n125
    Spain & Portugal, 96n539
    the Viking world, 95n563
Cultural ency of baseball, 98n733
Culturally diverse lib collections for youth, 98n1099
Culture vulture, 95n928

Cultures of color in America, 99n367
Cultures of the World, 99n84
Cultures outside the US in fiction, 95n1116
Culturgrams, 95n99
Cumming, Robert, 96n1052
Cummings, David, 99n956, 99n1101
Cummings, David M., 96n1267
Cummings, Paul, 95n998
Cummings, Robert, 99n863
Cummins, Alex G., 99n123
Cumulated indexes to the public papers of the presidents of the US: George Bush, 1989-93, 96n744
Cumulated indexes to the public papers of the presidents of the US: Ronald Reagan, 1981-89, 96n745
Cumulative bk index 1995, 98n11
Cumulative index to the biogl dict of American sports, 95n804
Cumulative index to vols. 1-6 of Paul Oskar Kristeller's Iter Italicum, 99n1259
Cunningham, William P., 95n1764
Cupboard love: a dict of culinary curiosities, 98n1423
Curme, Lynn M., 98n1631
Curran, Daniel, 99n1211
Curren-Aquino, Deborah T., 95n1217
Current biog yrbk 1996, 98n22
Current issues sourcefile [CD-ROM], 97n59
Current world leaders almanac, v.38, no.3, June 1995, 96n104
Currie, Philip J., 99n1539
Curson, Jon, 96n1613, 97n1288
Curtis, Anthony R., 95n1720
Curtis, Nancy C., 97n330
Curtiss, Jon, 96n336
Cushion plants for the rock garden, 97n1237
Cusic, Don, 95n541
Cussans, Thomas, 95n555
Custard, Ed, 98n288
Custard, Edward T., 96n357
Custer & the battle of Little Bighorn, 98n441
Custy, Mary C., 98n638
Cuthbertson-Johnson, Beverley, 95n826
Cuticchia, A. Jamie, 96n1656
Cuts in defense jobs in US counties, metropolitan areas, & states, 1992-2003, 96n270
Cutshaw, Charles C., 99n645
Cutten, Mervyn, 98n982
Cutter, Charles, 95n448
Cutting for all! the satorial arts, related crafts, & the commercial paper pattern, 98n934
Cutts, Martin, 96n1075
Cuvalo, Ante, 99n120
Cvancara, Alan M., 96n1803
Cy Young award winners, 96n808
CyberDictionary, 98n1575
CyberHound's gd to ...
    cos on the Internet, 98n1583
    Internet discussion groups, 98n1584
    people on the Internet, 98n1585
CyberHound's Internet gd to the coolest stuff out there, 97n1374

Cyberstocks, 97n182
CyberTools for business, 98n163
Cybriwsky, Roman, 98n461
Cyclamen: a gd for gardeners, horticulturists, & botanists, 98n1449
Cycles in humans & nature, 95n1478
Cyclopedia Anatomicae, 98n978
Cyclopedia of literary characters, rev ed, 99n959
Cyclopedia of world authors, 3d ed, 98n1059
Cyprus, rev ed, 96n130
Czech Republic, 95n517, 99n121
Czerepanov, S. K., 96n1594
Czerwinski, E. J., 95n1237

D & D standard oil abbreviator, 4th ed, 96n1832
D. H. Lawrence: a ref companion, 97n995
Da Capo companion to 20th-century popular music, rev ed, 96n1306
Dabbagh, Maureen, 99n752
Dabrishus, Michael J., 97n1046
D'Agostino, Annette M., 95n1343, 96n1413, 98n1316
Dahl, Anne, 99n931
Dahl, Henry Saint, 96n574, 97n486
Dahl's law dict, 96n574
Dahl's law dict: an annot legal dict, Spanish-English/English-Spanish, 2d ed, 97n486
Dailey, Kazuko, 95n659
Daily celebrity almanac, 7th ed, 95n4
Daily life in ancient Mesopotamia, 99n511
Daily life of the ancient Greeks, 99n501
Daily planetary gd 1997, 98n713
Daintith, John, 95n1484, 96n1072
Dakin, Shaun, 98n204
Dalby, Andrew, 95n126, 99n890
Dale, Jean, 98n925, 98n926
Dale, Leigh, 99n946
Dallman, Peter R., 99n1359
Dalton, Peter, 99n1171
Daly, K. S., 96n142
Dalzell, Tom, 97n842, 99n43
Damon, William, 99n707
Dan Cassidy's worldwide college scholarship dir, 4th ed, 96n333
Dan Cassidy's worldwide graduate scholarship dir, 4th ed, 96n334
Dana's new mineralogy, 99n1537
Dance on camera, 99n1200
Dance on disc [CD-ROM], 98n1269, 95n1358
Dance words, 97n1102
Dancers & choreographers, 97n1100
Dane, Suzanne G., 95n511, 97n390
Danforth, Bryan N., 95n1591
Dangerous sky: resource gd to the Battle of Britain, 96n544
Dani, A. H., 97n479
Daniel, Clifton, 96n558
Daniel, LaNelle, 97n1146
Daniells, Lorna M., 95n179
Daniels, David, 98n1226
Daniels, Judith M., 95n447

Daniels, Morna, 97n96
Daniels, Peter T., 97n816
Danilov, Victor J., 95n83, 97n62, 99n69
Danopoulos, Constantine P., 98n621
Darch, Colin, 97n102
Dardanelles campaign, 1915, 98n494
Darke, Rick, 96n1583
Darnay, Arsen J., 95n204, 95n205, 95n833, 97n197, 97n279, 99n187, 99n1436, 99n1572
Darnay, Brigitte T., 97n161
Darnell, Adrian C., 95n182
Dartmouth atlas of health care, 99n1414
Darton, Mike, 95n1491
Dasch, E. Julius, 97n1391
Dashefsky, H. Steven, 95n1772
Dastrup, Boyd L., 96n703
Data sources for business & market analysis, 4th ed, 96n296
Datapedia of the US, 1790-2000, 95n896
David, Jack, 95n1227, 97n1003, 97n1004
David M. Kennedy Center for International Studies, Brigham Young University, 95n99
David, Rosalie, 95n568, 99n510
Davids, Peter H., 99n1274
Davidson, Cathy N., 96n1200
Davidson, George, 99n42
Davidson, Judith A., 95n798
Davidson, Lance, 95n89
Davidson, Linda Kay, 96n1462
Davidson, Pamela, 98n1181
Davidson, Roger H., 96n720
Davies, Eryl, 96n72
Davies, Owen B., 98n1596
Davies, Paul, 95n1541
Davies, Philip H. J., 98n686
Davies, R. E. G., 96n1880
Davies, Richard, 99n1250
Davies, Robert, 98n1473
Davies, Valerie, 98n1473
Davies, Vitoria, 98n1041
Davis, Craig W., 95n881
Davis, Cynthia J., 97n738
Davis, Donald G., Jr., 95n637
Davis, Elisabeth B., 97n1264, 97n1272
Davis, Geoffrey V., 96n122
Davis, Greg, 98n922
Davis, J. R., 95n1622, 96n1662, 96n1678
Davis, James B., 99n1424
Davis, Jeffery, 96n1404
Davis, John B., 99n161
Davis, Joseph R., 99n1409
Davis, Lloyd, 99n776
Davis, Mary B., 95n434
Davis, Neil M., 98n1526
Davis, Paul, 99n1072
Davis, Paul K., 97n564
Davis, Todd M., 97n311, 99n352
Davis-Kimball, Jeannine, 95n426
Dawson, Dawn P., 99n1443
Dawson, J. L., 97n971
Dawson, Jeff, 97n676, 98n781

Day, Alan, 95n98, 95n157, 97n13, 97n133, 98n146, 99n83
Day, Alan J., 97n581, 99n649, 99n657
Day by day: the 80s, 96n503
Day, David Howard, 98n1290
Day, Lance, 97n1236
Day, Peter D., 95n1467
Day, Robert A., 95n941
Day-Viaud, Valerie, 96n115
D-Day ency, 95n686
De Angelis, Carl, 98n988
de Angury, Maree, 97n706
de Barreto, Lourdes Gavaldon, 95n1151
De Bellis, Jack, 95n1196
De Chiara, Joseph, 96n1048
de Grummond, Nancy Thomson, 97n397
de Jong, P. C., 95n1554
De La Pedraja, Rene, 95n1794
De Laet, S. J., 96n568
de Ley, Gerd, 99n1179
De Lucca, J. L., 96n1808
De Mente, Boye Lafayette, 97n107, 97n109, 97n134, 99n193
de Montano, Martha Kreipe, 95n441
De Sola, Ralph, 96n2
De Stasio, Giovanna Wedel, 95n1233, 95n1234
De Vries, Mary A., 97n178
Dead countries of the 19th & 20th centuries, 99n530
Deaf persons in the arts & scis, 96n857
Deal, Carl, 95n1770
Dean, William G., 99n409
DeAndrea, William L., 95n932
Deane, Bill, 97n1127
DeAngelis, James, 95n861
Deans, Candace, 98n204
Dear, I. C. B., 97n571
Dearling, Robert, 97n1052
Death dict, 95n844
Deaton, Wendy, 96n900
DeBeer, Shane R., 96n575
Debrett's peerage & baronetage, 1995 ed, 96n426
Decalo, Samuel, 95n114, 96n119, 96n124, 97n95, 97n103, 98n453, 98n454
Decca lables: a discography, 97n1031
Decorative arts: an illus summary cat of the collections of the J. Paul Getty Museum, 95n966
DeCoste, F. C., 98n510
Deeck, William F., 95n1159
Dees, Jerome S., 95n1222
Deever, Beverly Ann Deepe, 98n852
Deevey, Brian, 98n1503
Definitive Andy Griffith show ref, 97n1134
Definitive country, 96n1320
DeFrancis, Beth, 96n901
DeFranco, Laurence J., 95n710, 98n329, 99n674
DeGraaf, Richard M., 97n1289
DeHart, Jean, 98n1131
Deivert, Bert, 98n1287
Dejevsky, Nikolai, 99n125
Del Conte, Anna, 97n1280
Del Vecchio, Deborah, 97n1119
Delahunty, Andrew, 96n1076

DeLancey, Mark W., 95n755, 98n699
Delaney, John, 97n963, 99n954, 99n955
Delaware-English/English-Delaware dict, 97n845
DeLeon, David, 95n715
Delgado, James P., 99n446
Delgado, Jane L., 96n409
Delijska, B., 97n1366
Dell Orto, Arthur E., 97n670
Delmar ref manual: essentials for the electronic office, 96n310
Delmar's A-Z NDR-97: nurse's drug ref, 98n1566
Delmar's automotive dict, 98n1477
Delmar's English/Spanish pocket dict for health professionals, 98n1527
Delmar's therapeutic class drug gd for nurses 1997, 98n1567
DeLoach, Charles, 96n1346
DeLong, Janice A., 98n1077
DeLong, Thomas A, 97n762
Delves, Peter J., 99n1419
Delvin, Edgard, 95n1618
Demastes, William W., 96n1202, 97n985, 97n986, 98n1175
Demographic yrbk, 1992, 44th ed, 95n886
Demographic yrbk, 1995, 47th ed, 98n804
Demographic yrbk, special issue: population ageing, 95n834
Demographics USA 1994, city ed, 95n887
Demographics USA 1994, county ed, 95n888
Demographics USA 1994, ZIP ed, 95n889
DenBoer, Gordon, 96n438, 96n439, 97n371, 99n447, 99n448
Denckla, Tanya, 96n1543
Denenberg, Dennis, 96n321
Dennis, Marguerite J., 99n342
Dennis, Peter, 97n565
Denny, Dallas, 95n874
Denoeu, Francois, 97n846
Department for Economic & Social Info & Policy Analysis, Population Division, 96n912
Department for Economic & Social Info & Policy Analysis, Statl Division, 96n1841
Department for Policy Coordination & Sustainable Dvlpmt, 96n217
Department of Military Art & Engineering, US Military Academy, 96n677
Depression, 96n1724
Depression in the elderly, 98n761
Derbyshire, Ian, 97n582
Derbyshire, Ian D., 96n131
Derbyshire, J. Denis, 97n582
Derks, Scott, 96n198
Dervaes, Claudine, 95n504, 96n1082, 97n384, 99n425
DeRyan, Tim, 98n1390
Des Chenes, E. A., 95n1144, 96n1171
Deschamps, Judith, 98n1643
Descriptive catalog of the music printed by Hubert Waelrant & Jan de Laet, 96n1266
Desert Mag subject index, 98n878
Desert wildflowers of N America, 99n1365
Design ency, 95n982
DesJardins, Dawn Conzett, 98n50
Desk ref for organic chemists, 96n1792
Desk ref on the fed budget, 99n687

Desktop ency of telecommunications, 99n1493
Desmond, Ray, 96n1562
DeSousa, Luis R., 96n1695
Destination: Vatican II [CD-ROM], 99n1288
Detecting men: a reader's gd & checklist for mystery series written by men, 99n1031
Detecting women 2, 1996-97 ed, 97n947
Detective dict, rev ed, 96n598
Detrez, Raymond, 99n494
Deutsche Gesellschaft fur Materialkunde e.V., 96n1666
Devaney, Joan, 96n235
Development Centre of the Organisation for Economic Co-operation, 96n909
DeVenney, David P., 95n1280, 99n1170
Dever, John P., 96n680
Dever, Maria C., 96n680
Devereux, Daniel T., 98n1334
Devereux, Paul, 99n709
Devine, Mary Elizabeth, 99n315
Devious derivations, 95n1035
DeVries, LaMoine F., 98n1378
Dewan, John, 99n715
Dewar, David, 98n1412
Dewey decimal classification & relative index, 21st ed, 97n535
Dewey for Windows [CD-ROM], 97n536
Dewey, Patrick R., 95n678
DeWitt, Donald L., 95n523, 98n577
Deyl, Z., 96n1505
Di Lima, Sara Nell, 97n1324
Diabetes A to Z, 3d ed, 99n1471
Diagram Group, 96n529, 96n533, 96n1815
Dial recordings of Charlie Parker, 99n1166
Dial up! Gale's bulletin board locator, 97n1376
Diamant, Anita, 97n368
Diamond, Norma, 95n397
Diana, Joan P., 98n757
Dibner, Mark D., 96n1655
Dickenson, John, 98n140
Dickey, Alison Adams, 98n968
Dickey, Bruce, 97n1051
Dickey, Jerry, 98n1132
Dickey, Norma H., 95n54
Dickinson, Donald C., 99n616
Dickinson, Mary B., 95n485
Dickinson, W. Calvin, 97n435
Dickson, Nancy, 96n83
Dickson, Paul, 96n83, 97n369
Dickstein, Ruth, 98n841
Dictators & tyrants, 96n705
Dictionary catalog of the collection of African American lit in the Mildred F. Sawyer Lib of Suffolk Univ, 98n340
Dictionary for business & finance, 3d ed, 96n180
Dictionary for psychotherapists, 95n776
Dictionary of ...
   accounting, 96n210
   Afghan wars, revolutions, & insurgencies, 97n106
   Afro-American slavery, updated ed, 98n438
   agriculture, 96n1517

   agriculture, 2d ed, 99n1329
   alternative defense, 96n683
   American & English law, 98n520
   American antiquarian bkdealers, 99n616
   American biog [CD-ROM], 99n33
   American biog, comprehensive index, 97n32
   American biog, suppl 9, 1971-75, 95n36
   American biog, suppl 10, 96n36
   American children's fiction, 1990-94, 97n938
   American criminal justice, 99n576
   American food & drink, rev ed, 95n1517
   American hist, 97n419
   American hist suppl, 97n414
   American idioms, 96n1083
   American penology, rev ed, 97n506
   American regional English, v.3: I-O, 97n833
   ancient hist, 95n583
   Andalusi Arabic, 99n922
   animal words & phrases, 96n1073
   art, 98n947
   astronomy, 98n1607
   astronomy, 99n1518
   Australian colloquialisms, 4th ed, 97n829
   automotive engineering, 2d ed, 97n1303
   banking terms, 99n186
   Baptists in America, 96n1467
   beer & brewing, 2d ed, 99n1332
   bibliometrics, 95n649
   British & Irish botanists & horticulturalists, rev ed, 96n1562
   British & Irish travellers in Italy, 1701-1800, 98n476
   British literary characters: 20th-century novels, 95n1199
   bldg preservation, 97n801
   business, 2d ed, 99n145
   business & legal terms: Russian-English/English-Russian, 96n575
   business & mgmt, 95n187
   business, English-Spanish, Spanish-English, repr ed, 99n147
   business terms, 2d ed, 96n178
   Canadian biog, v.13, 95n26
   Canadian place names, 99n423
   canine terms, 97n1292
   Caribbean English usage, 97n834
   catchphrases, 96n1084
   ceramic sci & engineering, 2d ed, 95n1634
   Chicano Spanish, 2d ed, 96n1136
   Christian art, 96n1028
   Christianity, 97n1210
   classical ballet terminology, 99n1204
   Cleveland biog, 97n87
   communication & media studies, 3d ed, 95n939
   communication & media studies, 4th ed, 98n857
   communications tech, 3d ed, 99n1492
   computer terms, 4th ed, 96n1755
   computer words, 95n1691
   computer works, rev ed, 96n1754
   computing, 4th ed, 98n1576
   contemporary American artists, 6th ed, 95n998
   contemporary French connectors, 97n847

contemporary quotations, vol.8, 3d ed, 96n90
contemporary Spain, 99n943
counseling, 95n775
cricket, 2d ed, 96n814
cultural & critical theory, 97n746
cytokines, 96n1558
dvlpmtl psychology, 97n629
dicts & encys, 2d ed, 98n45
early Christian beliefs, 99n1285
E European hist since 1945, 95n560
ecclesiastical Latin, 96n1118
ecology & the environment, 3d ed, 99n1553
econometrics, 95n182
economics, 97n156
economics, 98n151
endocrinology & related biomedical scis, 97n1352
engineering acronyms & abbrevs, 2d ed, 95n1599
English place-names, 2d ed, 99n422
English surnames, 3d ed, 96n427
environment & sustainable dvlpmt, 98n1633
environmental law & sci, 96n1855
environmental sci & tech, 2d ed, 98n1636
epidemiology, 3d ed, 96n1698
ethics, theology, & society, 97n73
euphemisms, 97n827
European hist & pols, 1945-95, 97n438
eye terminology, 3d ed, 98n1553
family therapy, rev ed, 96n1718
feminist theologies, 97n1177
feminist theory, 2d ed, 96n948
film quotations, 96n1374
finance & investment terms, 4th ed, 96n220
fundamental theology, 95n1470
gastronomic terms, French/English, 99n1334
gene tech, 96n1657
generic names of seed plants, 96n1565
geopols, 95n708
glass, 97n787
govt & politics, 2d ed, 99n654
grammatical terms in linguistics, 95n1040
healthful food terms, 98n1420
herbs, spices, seasonings, & natural flavorings, 95n1518
heresy trials in American Christianity, 99n1289
Hispanic biog, 97n334
histl allusions & eponyms, 99n40
human oncology, 96n1726
image tech, 3d ed, 96n985
info tech & computer sci, 2d ed, 95n1693
insurance terms, 3d ed, 97n201
intl biog 1996, 24th ed, 97n21
intl biog 1998, 26th ed, 99n21
intl business terms, 97n203
intl business terms, 99n194
intl human rights law, 97n516
intl trade, 95n244
Irish biog, 3d ed, 99n132
Irish family names, 98n376
Irish lit, rev ed, 97n1007
Irish quotations, 95n445
Islamic architecture, 97n803

Italian cuisine, 99n1331
Italian lit, rev ed, 97n1010
Japanese & English idiomatic equivalents, 95n1085
Japanese financial terms, 96n248
Japanese loanwords, 98n1003
Jewish surnames from the Kingdom of Poland, 98n375
Judaism in the biblical period, 97n1223
La Creole, 99n935
land surveyors & local map-makers of Great Britain & Ireland, 1530-1850, 98n394
law, 3d ed, 96n576
legal terms, 95n604
literary biog: British reform writers, 1832-1914, 99n1062
literary biog, v.191, 99n1063
literary biog, v.192, 99n1092
literary biog, v.193, 99n1059
literary biog, v.194, 99n1064
literary biog documentary series, v.12, 96n1201
literary biog documentary series, v.13, 97n963
literary biog documentary series, v.14, 98n1089
literary biog documentary series, v.16, 99n954
literary biog documentary series, v.17, 99n955
literary biog yrbk: 1995, 97n899
literary biog yrbk: 1996, 99n970
literary biog yrbk: 1997, 99n971
literary pseudonyms in the English lang, 96n1229
literary terms & literary theory, 4th ed, 99n960
mktg & advertising, 96n304
mathematics terms, 2d ed, 96n1826
mechanical engineering, 4th ed, 97n1310
media literacy, 98n856
medical sociology, 98n1524
medical terms, 3d ed, 95n1656
medicine, 2d ed, 99n1440
Mexican rulers, 1325-1997, 98n485
military abbrevs, 95n679
military hist & the art of war, 95n687
mission, 98n1350
modern Arab hist, 99n508
modern biology, 98n1445
modern legal usage, 2d ed, 96n577
multicultural educ, 98n267
multimedia terms & acronyms, 98n1572
natl biog, 1986-90, 97n38
Native American lit, 95n1175
natural products, 98n1569
natural resource mgmt, 98n1632
nature, 95n1557
19th century British bk illustrators & caricaturists, rev ed, 98n944
19th-century world hist, 95n578
N.C. biog, v.5, 95n37
nursing theory & research, 2d ed, 96n1732
occupational terms, 95n297
1000 Dutch proverbs, 99n1179
1000 Jewish proverbs, 98n1251
1000 Polish proverbs, 98n1252
1000 Spanish proverbs with English equivalents, 97n1089
Paul & his letters, 95n1450
personal computing & the Internet, 98n1574

Dictionary of ... (*continued*)
  philosophy, 3d ed, 97n1164
  philosophy & religion, new ed, 98n1337
  phonetics & phonology, 97n819
  plant genetics & molecular biology, 99n1358
  Polish lit, 95n1237
  portrait painters in Britain up to 1920, 98n982
  Portuguese-African civilization, v.1, 96n532
  Portuguese-African civilization, v.2, 97n427
  pseudonyms, 99n408
  public health promotion & educ, 97n1317
  race & ethnic relations, 99n366
  race & ethnic relations, 3d ed, 95n394
  real estate, 98n263
  Russian & Soviet artists 1420-1970, 95n1001
  Russian slang & colloquial expressions, 96n1128
  sci, 95n1490
  sci, 96n1493
  Scottish art & architecture, 96n1025
  Scottish church hist & theology, 95n1466
  Scottish quotations, 98n136
  sexual lang & imagery in Shakespearean & Stuart lit, 96n1243
  Shakespeare's semantic wordplay, 99n1084
  social & market research, 98n253
  South African English on histl principles, 97n830
  sports injuries & disorders, 97n1357
  street alcohol & drug terms, 4th ed, 95n881
  subtances & their effects [CD-ROM], 97n1314
  symbols, 99n886
  symbols in western art, 96n1030
  tax terms, 95n330
  teleliteracy, 97n1110
  TV & audiovisual terminology, 99n838
  the arts, 95n926
  the avant-gardes, 95n1005
  the Bible, 97n1195
  the British Empire & Commonwealth, 97n117
  the Earth, 96n1805
  the English lang [CD-ROM], 98n1020
  the 1st World War, 97n474
  the Holocaust, 99n528
  the later N.T. & its developments, 99n1274
  the Middle East, 97n138
  the modern pols of SE Asia, 96n747
  the modern US military, 97n566
  the NW Semitic inscriptions, 96n1129
  the Turkic langs, 97n876
  traditional S-E Asian theatre, 96n1418
  20th century British bk illustrators, 96n1055
  20th century British business leaders, 95n282
  20th century culture: American culture after WW II, 95n927
  20th century culture: French culture 1900-75, 96n545
  20th century culture: Hispanic culture of Mexico, Central America, & the Caribbean, 97n348
  20th century culture: Hispanic culture of S America, 96n406
  20th-century world hist, 98n504
  Ukrainian composers, 98n1217

  US intelligence servs, 97n597
  universal biog of all ages & of all peoples, 2d ed, 95n28
  wellerisms, 95n1314
  who, what, & where in Shakespeare, 98n1161
  women artists, 98n948
  word origins, 97n826
  world biog, v.1, 99n519
  world biog, v.2, 99n520
  worldwide gestures, 98n711
Die cast price gd, 98n930
Diefenderfer, William M., III, 95n710, 98n329
Diefendorf, Elizabeth, 97n882
Dietrich, Gerhard, 97n1266
Dietz, Hugo Ortiz, 95n172
Diffor, Elaine N., 96n375
Diffor, John C., 96n375
Digby, Joan, 99n331
Diggs, Anita Doreen, 96n96
Digital imaging dict, 97n1368
Diglossia: a comprehensive bibliog 1960-90, 95n1027
DiGregorio, Mario J., 98n1450
Dikel, Margaret Riley, 99n268
Dillard, Philip H., 98n1212
Dillard, Tom W., 96n490
Diller, Daniel, 96n764
Diller, Daniel C., 98n653
Dillon, Kim, 97n12
Dillon, Patrick M., 96n1750
Dillon Press children's atlas, 95n476
Dilworth, David A., 99n1257
DiMartino, Dave, 96n1307
DiMona, Lisa, 96n951
Dimond, Peter, 98n1213
Dinan, Desmond, 99n691
Dines, Nicholas T., 99n883
Dingbo, Wu, 95n1326
Dinosaur hunter [CD-ROM], 97n1403
Dinosaur safari gd, 96n1814
Dinosaur Society's dinosaur ency, 95n1734
Dinosaurs, 98n1618
Dintrone, Charles V., 97n1144
DiNucci, Darcy, 95n1696
Diodato, Virgil, 95n649
Diplomatic, consular, & other representatives in Canada, 96n750
Directories in print, 15th ed, 98n50
Directory for exceptional children, 13th ed, 95n385
Directory of ...
  African American religious bodies, 2d ed, 97n1181
  agencies & orgs serving individuals who are deaf-blind, rev ed, 98n772
  American disc record brands & manufacturers, 1891-1943, 95n1255
  American firms operating in foreign countries, 14th ed, 97n210
  American philosophers 1994-95, 95n1430
  American philosophers 1996-97, 18th ed, 98n1340
  American poetry bks, 95n1198
  American poets & fiction writers, 1995-96 ed, 97n749
  American research & tech 1995, 29th ed, 96n182

American youth orgs 1994-95, 5th ed, 96n902
American youth orgs 1998-99, 7th ed, 99n52
biomedical & health care grants 1995, 9th ed, 96n1685
bldg & equipment grants, 4th ed, 98n1481
business & financial info servs, 9th ed, 95n202
business info resources, 1994, 95n195
business info resources, 1997, 5th ed, 98n250
business per special issues, 96n209
business to business catalogs, 1997, 98n190
Canadian lib & info sci consultants, 96n642
Canadian manufacturers [BOSS 1994], 95n274
Canadian schools, 6th ed, 96n319
chemical producers & products, v.1, pt.1, 2d ed, 97n1381
Chinese agricultural & related orgs, 95n1511
college & univ librarians in Canada, 2d ed, 97n550
college cooperative educ programs, 97n304
college facilities & services for people with disabilities, 4th ed, 98n773
Community legislation in force & other acts of the Community insts, 96n768
cos offering dividend reinvestment plans, 99n163
cos required to file annual reports with the SEC, 96n183
cos required to file annual reports with the SEC, 1997, 99n164
computer & high tech grants, 2d ed, 96n1770
Congressional voting scores & interest group ratings, 2d ed, 98n678
consumer brands & their owners 1998: Eastern Europe, 99n250
consumer brands & their owners 1998: Europe, 99n251
consumer brands & their owners 1998: Latin America, 99n260
corporate affiliations 1998, 99n150
corporate & fndn givers, 1996, 97n686
corporate & fndn givers, 1998, 99n763
corporate name changes, 95n193
designated members, 1996, 97n282
dirs on the Internet, 95n1707
educ grants, 98n271
electronic journals, newsletters, & academic discussion lists, 6th ed, 97n1375
environmental electronic mail users in Eurasia, 4th ed, 97n1429
environmental info sources, 5th ed, 96n1864
environmental law educ opportunities at American law schools, 98n558
European research & dvlpmt 1995, 96n1504
EU info sources 1995-96, 7th, 97n606
family assns, 3d ed, 97n354
fed jobs & employers, 97n258
fed libs, 3d ed, 98n573
financial aids for minorities 1995-97, 96n880
financial aids for women 1995-97, 96n879
financial aids for women 1997-99, 99n773
franchise opportunities, 95n220
graduate student employee bargaining agents & orgs, 96n336
grants for orgs serving people with disabilities, 10th ed, 98n774

grants for orgs serving people with disabilities, 8th ed, 95n846
grants in the humanities 1994/95, 95n931
grants in the humanities 1998/99, 12th ed, 99n812
hazardous waste servs, 1994-95, 5th ed, 96n1654
health care professionals 1995, 96n1686
health grants, 97n1321
hospital personnel 1994, 95n1648
hyphenated techniques, 96n1505
import regimes, pt.1, 96n289
import regimes, pt.2, 96n290
importers in Latin America, 1994 ed, 96n291
Indian film-makers & films, 95n1364
intl business, 96n233
intl corporate giving in America & abroad 1995, 96n869
intl corporate giving in America & abroad 1998, 99n764
intl economic org, 98n161
intl orgs, 97n617
Japanese-affiliated cos in the EU, 1996-97, 97n211
Japanese-affiliated cos in the USA & Canada 1993-94, 95n270
lib automation software, systems, & servs, 96n643
lib automation software, systems, & servs, 99n609
lib technical servs home pages, 98n591
listed derivative contracts 1996/97, 98n171
literary societies & author collections, 95n1106
mail order catalogs, 1995, 9th ed, 96n219
mail order catalogs 98, 99n175
medical & dental schools worldwide, 6th ed, 96n1687
medical health care libs in the UK & Republic of Ireland 1997-8, 10th ed, 99n611
medical rehabilitation facilities 1995, 96n1703
multinationals, 99n197
natl helplines, 1998 ed, 99n49
new & emerging fndns, 3d ed, 96n870
nursing homes, 1995, 96n1731
officials & orgs in China, 95n130
operating grants, 3d ed, 98n786
overseas catalogs, 1997, 97n212
physicians in the US, 35th ed, 98n1533
physicians in the US, 35th ed [CD-ROM], 98n1534
physics, astronomy, & geophysics staff, 1997 biennial ed, 99n1322
poetry publishers, 98n599
population ageing research in Europe, 99n745
power plant equipment & processes, 1996, 97n1416
printers, 1994-95 ed, 96n671
professional & occupational regulation in the US & Canada, 96n730
publishers in religion, 99n619
publishing 1997, 22d ed, 98n600
publishing 1999, 24th ed, 99n618
rare bk & special collections in the UK & the Republic of Ireland, 2d ed, 98n588
research grants 1996, 97n687
retirement facilities 1995, 96n847
safety standards, lit, & servs, 98n1495
schools for alternative & complementary health care, 99n1448
small pr & mag editors & publishers, 24th ed, 95n668

Directory of ... (*continued*)
    small pr/mag editors & publishers 1997-98, 28th ed, 98n601
    social research orgs in the UK, 95n97
    social service grants, 2d ed, 99n765
    social serv grants, 97n688
    special libs & info centers, v.1, 21st ed, 98n589
    special libs & info centers, v.2, 21st ed, 98n590
    the steel industry & the environment, 97n194
    the wood products industry, 1998, 99n1343
    theatre training programs, 5th ed, 96n1419
    theatre training programs 1997-99, 6th ed, 98n1325
    trade & investment related orgs of developing countries & areas in Asia & the Pacific, 7th ed, 97n235
    UN info sources, 5th ed, 96n769
    US labor orgs, 1997 ed, 98n219
    US labor orgs, 1994-95 ed, 96n260
    US military bases worldwide, 96n687
    US military bases worldwide, 3d ed, 99n631
Dirr, Michael A., 98n1456
Dirr's hardy trees & shrubs, 98n1456
DiscLit: world authors [CD-ROM], 96n1154
Discography of 78 rpm era recordings of the horn, 98n1203
Discovering ancient Egypt, 95n568
DISCovering authors, Canadian ed [CD-ROM], 98n1065
DISCovering authors modules [CD-ROM], 97n900
DISCovering biog [CD-ROM], 98n23
DISCovering careers & jobs [CD-ROM], 96n271
Discovering maps: a children's world atlas, 95n477
DISCovering multicultural America [CD-ROM], 97n323
DISCovering nations, states, & cultures [CD-ROM], 99n85
DISCovering sci [CD-ROM], 98n1413
DISCovering US hist [CD-ROM], 98n446
DISCovering world hist [CD-ROM], 98n505
Diseases, 98n1557
Dissertation abstracts [CD-ROM], 97n60
Distance educ, 96n377
Distinguished African American scientists of the 20th century, 97n1230
DiTomaso, Joseph M., 98n1453
Dittmar, Joseph J., 98n728
Divine inspriations: pearls of Bible wisdom from the O. & N.T.s, 98n1369
Divining the future: prognostication from astrology to zoomancy, 96n791
Divorce help sourcebk, 95n847
Divorce yourself, 4th ed, 99n567
Dixon, Robert M. W., 99n1160
Dixon, Ted, 99n165
Dixon-Kennedy, Mike, 99n1185
Dixonia: a bio-discography of Bill Dixon, 99n1146
DK ency of rock stars, 97n1081
DK geography of the world, 97n379
DK illus Oxford dict, 99n44
DK nature ency, 99n1309
DK sci ency, rev ed, 99n1310
DK student atlas, 99n411
DK ultimate visual dict of sci, 99n1311
D'Lugo, Marvin, 99n1237
Dobrin, Adam, 97n507

Dobroslavic, Therese, 95n1
Docherty, James C., 97n251, 99n695
Dockery, C. C., 97n598
Doctor of philosophy degree, 96n330
Doctoral dissertations on China & on inner Asia, 1976-90, 99n15
Doctrine of the Holy Spirit, 97n1193
Documents of Soviet-American relations, v.3, 99n122
Documents of Soviet hist, v.4, 99n123
Dodd, David G., 98n1240
Dodd, Donald B., 95n893, 99n451
Dodd, Janet S., 98n872
Dodd, Mary Ann, 97n1036
Dodd, Peter, 96n759
Dodds de Wolf, Gaelan, 98n1012
Dodge, Richard W., 99n782
Dodgers ency, 99n716
Doerper, John, 98n415
Doerr, Juergen C., 99n129
Dogra, Ramesh Chander, 97n1225
Dogs from A to Z, 99n1385
Doherty, Charles, 98n960
Doherty, P., 98n1604
Doig, Melissa Walsh, 99n389
Doll, Carol A., 95n1121
Doll values antique to modern, 98n918
Dollarhide, William, 99n399
Dolphins & porpoises: a worldwide gd, 95n1595
Domestic violence, 97n675
Dominic, Catherine C., 97n909, 97n910, 97n911, 98n1163, 98n1164
Don Juan theme, 95n922
Donahue, Debra L., 99n584
Donahue, Mildred A., 98n279
Dondurei, Daniil, 95n1378
Doniach, N. S., 97n855
Donio, Michael A., 98n1539
Donnelly, Judy, 95n677
Donovan, Joe, 95n827
Don't do it: a dict of the forbidden, 99n1193
Donzel, E. van, 95n174
Doody's rating serv 1997, 98n1502
Dorf, Richard C., 95n1610, 99n1405
Dorgan, Charity A., 96n905
Dorgan, Charity Anne, 96n922
Dori, John T., 99n219
Dority, G. Kim, 96n9
Dorling Kindersley children's illus dict, 95n1048
Dorling Kindersley ency of fishing, 95n815
Dorling Kindersley hist of the world, 95n587
Dorling Kindersley ultimate visual dict, 95n52
Dorling Kindersley visual ency, 96n46
Dorling Kindersley visual timeline of transportation, 96n1878
Dorling Kindersley world ref atlas, 95n480
Dorling Kindersley world ref atlas, 2d ed, 97n373
Dorn, A. Walter, 95n699
Dornan, Michael, 95n826
Dorsey, Learthen, 95n121
Doss-Quinby, Eglal, 96n1251
Douchant, Michael, 96n809

Douchant, Mike, 98n739
Dougan, Michael B., 96n490
Douglas, Ian, 98n397
Douglas, J. D., 96n1465, 98n1373
Douglas, Krystan V., 97n987
Douglas, Livingston G., 96n292
Dover, Jeffrey S., 97n1333
Dow, James W., 97n318
Dow Jones & Co, editors of, 96n212
Dow Jones averages, 1885-1995, 97n183
Dow Jones gd to the world stock market, 1995-96 ed, 96n212
Dow, Sheila, 99n56
Dower, John W., 96n537
Dowling, Robert J., 99n1221
Downes, John, 96n220
Downey, Dennis B., 95n530
Downey, Douglas W., 95n65
Downey, Pat, 95n1290, 95n1291
Downing, Douglas, 96n1826
Downing, Douglas A., 96n1755
Downs, Buck, 99n57, 99n157
Doyle, Billy H., 96n1368
Doyle, Francis R., 96n569
Doyle, Rodger, 95n890
Dr. Ruth's ency of sex, 95n878
Dr. Tom Linden's gd to online medicine, 96n1709
Drabble, Margaret, 96n1231
Drake, Paul, 95n451
Drama criticism, v.7, 99n1019
Drama criticism, v.8, 99n1020
Drama for students, v.1, 99n1021
Drama for students, v.2, 99n1022
Drama for students, v.3, 99n1023
Drama for students, v.4, 99n1024
Draper, James P., 96n1152
Dream ency, 96n779
Dreiver, Steven L., 95n493
Drescher, Seymour, 99n542
Dressman, Mark, 98n1087
Drew, Bernard A., 97n941, 98n1102
Drew, Wilfred, 96n1518
Driver, Dorothy, 95n1240
Drone, Jeanette Marie, 99n1244
Droste, Kathleen, 95n894
Droughts, 99n1527
Drowne, Kathleen Morgan, 97n890
Drug abuse in society, 95n882
Drug Topics red bk, 1995, 96n1734
Drury, George H., 95n1791, 96n1886
Drury, John, 96n1264
du Noyer, Paul, 96n1336
Duarte, Orlando, 95n822
Dubester's US census bibliog with SuDocs class nos & indexes, 97n711
Dubitskaja, Victoria, 95n1378
DuBoff, Leonard, 95n1004, 96n1039
DuBoff, Leonard D., 98n1265
Duchet-Suchaux, Gaston, 96n1448
Duckles, Vincent H., 95n1252, 98n1189
Due, Andrea, 97n458

Duensing, Edward E., 96n928
Duffy, Paul, 99n502
Dugan, Patrick, 95n1773
Duiker, William J., 99n488
Duke of Newcastle, 1693-1768, & Henry Pelham, 1694-1754, 98n687
Duke, James A., 98n1546
Dulbecco, Renato, 99n1355
Dulin, Robert O., Jr., 96n700
Dumouchel, J. Robert, 97n689
Duncan, Philip D., 96n738
Dunkle, Margaret, 96n1163
Dunlap, Carol, 95n928
Dunn, D. Elwood, 96n1118
Dunn, Jerry, 98n1014
Dunn, Maryjane, 96n1462
Dunnigan, James F., 99n627
Dunning, Joan, 95n1566
Dunster, Julian, 98n1632
Dunster, Katherine, 98n1632
Dupont, Ellen, 99n1538
DuPree, Mary, 98n1200
Dupuis, Diane L., 96n1398
Dupuy, Marigny J., 99n990
Durant, David N, 98n1011
Durham, Jennifer L., 97n508, 99n455
Durham, Michael S., 96n411
Durkan, Michael J., 97n1008
Durusau, Patrick, 99n1269
Duskis, Neil, 98n979
Dusseau, John L., 95n1037
Dutch art, 98n949
Dutch modernism, 97n802
Duval, Alain, 98n1024
DuVall, Audre, 98n898
Duvvuri, Raj, 97n817
Duxbury, John, 97n649
Dwiggins, Boyce H., 98n1477
Dworkin, Rita, 98n1108
Dwyer, Jim, 97n1424
Dwyer, Judith A., 96n1470
Dwyer, Philip G., 97n447
Dyal, Donald H., 99n884
Dyches, Richard W., 95n1468
Dye, Jennifer, 95n894
Dyer, Janyce G., 97n1353
Dyja, Tom, 96n1400
Dynamic nutrition for maximum performance, 98n1514
Dyson, Peter, 96n1756, 96n1761
Dystopian lit, 95n1109
Dziggel, Oliver C., 95n288

Eades, J. S., 98n106
Eagle, Selwyn, 98n1643
Eagleson, Mary, 95n1713
Ear, nose, & throat disorders sourcebk, 99n1452
Earl Mountbatten of Burma, 1900-79, 99n505
Earls, Irene, 97n798

Early modern Russian writers, late 17th & 18th centuries, 96n1261
Early music dict, 96n1272
Early TV, 98n889
Early US-Hispanic relations 1776-1860, 96n776
Earth atlas, 95n1725
Earth online, 99n1516
Earth words, 96n1861
Earth work, 96n1871
Earth works, 97n1424
Earthkeepers, 95n1763
Earthly recordings of Sun Ra, 96n1322
Earthquakes & the built environment index, 1984 - July 1995 [CD-ROM], 97n1399
Earthscape: exploring endangered ecosystems [CD-ROM], 99n1513
Earth-Science educ resource dir, 96n1804
East & NE Africa bibliog, 97n90
East Europe & the republics: a pol risk annual, June 1994, 95n153
East, Michael B., 96n1792
East, Roger, 99n650, 99n651
Eastern Europe, 2d ed, 99n252
Eastern Europe: a bibliographic gd to English lang pubs, 1986-93, 96n140
Eastern Europe: a resource gd, 96n141
Eastern Europe & the Commonwealth of Independent States 1997, 3d ed, 98n127
Eastman, Richard M., 96n845
Eaton, Faith, 95n975
Eberhart, George M., 96n624
Eberle, Linda, 98n924
Eberwein, Jane Donahue, 99n1052
Eble, Mary M., 95n1129
Eblen, Ruth A., 95n1765
Eblen, William R., 95n1765
Eby, Vivienne M., 96n1555
Eccleshall, Robert, 96n704
Ecclesia: a theological ency of the Church, 98n1387
Echeruo, Michael J. C., 99n932
Echeverria, Durand, 95n531
Eck, Marty, 98n921
Eckel, Patricia M., 95n1547
Ecker, Ronald L., 96n1452
Eckersley, Richard, 96n667
Eckes, James, 95n817, 95n818
Eckl, Corina, 99n678
Eckstein, Richard, 95n846
Eckstein, Richard M., 96n1770, 99n765
Ecofeminist theory, 96n935
Economic & social survey of Asia & the Pacific 1995, 96n128
Economic & Social Commission, 99n746, 99n787, 99n808
Economic & Social Commission for Asia & the Pacific, 96n128, 96n295, 96n1842, 96n1843
Economic & Social Commission for Western Asia, 96n129, 96n156, 96n157, 96n158, 96n919
Economic & social progress in Latin America 1995 report: overcoming volatility, 97n127
Economic & social survey of Africa, 1994-95, 97n231
Economic Commission for Africa, 96n113

Economic Commission for Europe, 96n222, 96n287, 96n303, 96n1649, 96n1838, 96n1839, 96n1840, 96n1877, 96n1890, 98n1496, 98n1581
Economic Commission for Latin America & the Caribbean, 96n151, 96n153, 96n154
Economic indicators hndbk, 95n204
Economic integration in Europe & N America, 96n232
Economic panorama of Latin America 1995, 96n151
Economic survey of Europe in 1995-96, 97n239
Economic survey of Latin America & the Caribbean 1995-96, 98n210
Economics, trade, & dvlpmt: English-Spanish general terminology, 97n272
Economist desk companion, rev ed, 95n79
Eddy Arnold discography, 1944-96, 98n1231
Edel, Theodore, 96n1292
Edelheit, Abraham J., 95n588, 96n552
Edelheit, Hershel, 95n588, 96n552
Eden, Philip, 96n76
Eden-Green, Monica, 96n235
Edens, John A., 95n532
Edgar, Kathleen J., 99n1195
Edible plants & animals, 95n1516
Edinburgh ency, 98n137
Editor & Publisher intl yr bk 1994, 96n980
Editor & Publisher market gd 1994, 96n976
Editor & Publisher market gd 1994 [CD-ROM], 96n977
Editor & Publisher yr bk 1994 [CD-ROM], 96n981
Editorial cartooning & caricature, 99n1192
Editorial Staff of Government Institutes, 96n1864
Edmonds, Beverly C., 97n515
Edmund Burke 1729-97: a bibliog, 95n751
Education & the law, 97n491
Education for the Earth, 2d ed, 96n337
Education index, July 1995 to June 1996, 98n279
Education sourcebk, 99n296
Educational media & tech yrbk, 99n356
Educational media & tech yrbk 1993, 95n386
Educational media & tech yrbk 1994, 95n387
Educational media & tech yrbk 1995/96, v.21, 97n312
Educational opportunity gd, 1998, 99n312
Educational rankings annual 1998, 99n297
Educational software preview gd, 1998, 99n306
Educators grade gd to free teaching aids 1995, 41st ed, 96n322
Educators gd to free films, filmstrips, & slides 1995, 55th ed, 96n375
Educator's gd to free multicultural materials 1998, 99n285
Educators gd to free sci materials, 35th ed, 95n1480
Educator's gd to free sci materials 1998-99, 39th ed, 99n286
Educator's gd to free social studies materials 1998-99, 38th ed, 99n287
Educators gd to free videotapes 1995, 42d ed, 96n376
Educator's gd to free videotapes 1998, 45th ed, 99n357
Educators index of free materials 1995, 104th ed, 97n294
Educator's word frequency gd, 97n817
Edwardian fiction, 98n1152
Edwards, Adrian, 97n121
Edwards, Alan F., Jr., 98n289
Edwards, Bill, 97n784, 97n785
Edwards, Elwyn Hartley, 95n1582

Edwards, Jolane, 99n427
Edwards, Michael, 96n1354
Edwards, Paul M., 95n683, 98n1291, 99n514
Edwards, Richard L., 96n893
Eerdmans' hndbk to the world's religions, rev ed, 96n1446
Effects of drugs on the fetus & nursing infant, 97n1358
Effects of neurologic & psychiatric drugs on the fetus & nursing infant, 99n1480
Egan, Christopher, 95n1563
Eggers, Ellen K., 98n455
Ehlich, Konrad, 98n984
Ehr, Catherine M., 96n176, 96n188, 96n189
Ehrens, Cheryl, 98n93
Ehrlich, Eugene, 95n1063, 95n1066, 96n1116, 98n1017, 98n1025
Ehrlich, Paul R., 96n1614
Eicher, David J., 96n517, 98n433
Eighteenth Century, 99n515, 99n516
Eighteenth-Century Anglo-American women novelists, 98n1111
Eighteenth-Century British & American rhetorics & rhetoricians, 95n1113
Eighteenth-Century British literary biographers, 95n1204
Eighteenth Century, n.s.15 for 1989, 98n7
Einstein, Daniel, 98n1304
Einstein dict, 97n1409
Eis, Arlene L., 97n498
Eisaguirre, Lynne, 95n633, 99n563
Eisenberg, Harry K., 99n167
Eisenmann, Linda, 99n803
EJS: discography of the Edward J. Smith recordings, 95n1286
El-Hadidi, M. Nabil, 96n1582
El-Hi textbks & serials in print 1994, 95n350
El-Hi textbks & serials in print 1997, 98n283
El-Shamy, Hasan M., 96n1342
Elazar, Daniel J., 96n712
Elder, George R., 98n1352
Elder, John, 97n965
Eleanor Powell: a bio-bibliog, 95n1353
Eleanor Roosevelt: a comprehensive bibliog, 95n532
Election results dir 1997, 98n663
Electric light & power US electric utility industry dir, 1995, 4th ed, 96n1651
Electric light & power US non-utility power dir, 1995, 96n1652
Electric power in Asia & the Pacific, 1991 & 1992, 97n1420
Electric power industry yrbk, 1996, 97n1421
Electric power stats sourcebk, 97n1422
Electrical & electronics trades dir 1996 [CD-ROM], 98n1486
Electrical engineering hndbk, 99n1405, 95n1610
Electronic & computer industry gd to chemical safety & environmental compliance, 99n1567
Electronic & computer music, 98n1196
Electronic Gieck's engineering formulas [CD-ROM], 96n1642
Electronic materials & processes hndbk, 2d ed, 95n1614
Electronic styles: a hndbk for citing electronic info, 2d ed, 98n875
Electronics & telecommunications vocabulary, 95n1611
Electronics pocket ref, 2d ed, 96n1653
Elementary school lib collection, 19th ed, 95n661

Elementary school lib collection, 19th ed [CD-ROM], 95n662
Elementary school lib collection, 20th ed, 97n544
Elementary school lib collection, 20th ed [CD-ROM], 97n545
Elementary teachers gd to free curriculum materials 1995, 52d ed, 96n323
Elements, 98n1600
Elements explorer [CD-ROM], 99n1509
Elfstrom, Gerard, 99n698
Elgar companion to classical economics, 99n160
Elias, Stephen, 97n520, 98n534
Eliceiri, Ellen M. Enright, 98n856
Elizabeth Gaskell: an annot bibliog of English-lang sources 1976-91, 95n1213
Elkins, Rita, 97n1344
Ellavich, Marie C., 99n1302, 99n1303
Ellet, William, 96n282, 97n266
Elliott, Clark A., 97n1235
Elliott, Deni, 99n826
Elliott, Doreen, 97n704
Elliott, Jack, 97n1255, 98n1435
Elliott, Stuart, 99n636
Elliott, Sydney, 96n761
Ellis, John, 95n691
Elmer Rice: a research & production sourcebk, 98n1326
Elrod, Bruce C., 96n1308
Els, David, 95n1531
Elsevier's dict of ...
  acronyms, initialisms, abbreviations, & symbols, 99n1
  agriculture & food production, 96n1516
  biometry, 96n1557
  climatology & meteorology, 96n1808
  computer sci & math in English, German, French, & Russian, 97n1366
  European Community co/business/financial law in English, Danish, & German, 98n517
  financial & economic terms, 97n153
  financial terms, rev ed, 99n185
  fundamental & applied biology, 97n1267
  industrial tech, 96n1494
  info tech in English, German, & French, 98n581
  plant names, 97n1273
Elsevier's nautical dict, 3d ed, 96n1894
Elste, Martin, 96n1288
Elvers, Barbara, 96n1789
Elvin, Mark, 99n106
Elvis ency, 96n1335
Elwell, Walter A., 95n1461, 97n1197
Elwood, Ann, 99n27
Ely, Donald P., 95n386, 95n387, 97n312
Emanoil, Mary, 95n1564
Emanuel, Muriel, 96n1043
Ember, Melvin, 97n316, 99n365
Emblidge, David, 98n871
Embree, Lester, 98n1335
Emergency Librarian index, vs.1-20: 1973-93, 96n645
Emerson chronology, 95n1188
Emerson, Isabelle, 97n1103
Emerson, William K., 98n624
Emil Brunner: a bibliog, 97n1172
Emily Dickinson ency, 99n1052

Employee benefits desk ency, 97n252
Employee duty of loyalty, 97n495
Employee duty of loyalty, 1996 suppl covering 1994, 97n496
Employment discrimination law, 3d ed, 98n530
Employment of the elderly, 96n842
Employment opportunites, USA, 99n269
Employment/Unemployment & earnings stats, 97n249
Encyclicals of John Paul II on CD-ROM [CD-ROM], 97n1217
Encyclopaedia Africana dict of African biog, v.3, 97n91
Encyclopaedia Judaica, 98n1393
Encyclopaedia Judaica decennial bk 1983-92, 96n1478
Encyclopaedia of ...
   Celtic wisdom, 96n788
   Indian cinema, 96n1381
   Islam, new ed, v.8, fascicules 139-40, 95n1473
   mathematics, v.10, 96n1827
   Middle Eastern mythology & religion, 95n1442
   occupational health & safety, 4th ed [CD-ROM], 99n280
   Sikh religion & culture, 97n1225
Encyclopaedic dict of info tech & systems, 95n1689
Encyclopaedic dict in ...
   the 18th century, v.1, 99n813
   the 18th century, v.2, 99n814
   the 18th century, v.3, 99n815
   the 18th century, v.4, 99n816
   the 18th century, v.5, 99n817
Encyclopedia Americana, 99n45
Encyclopedia Americana [CD-ROM], 97n43
Encyclopedia Americana, 1995 [CD-ROM], 96n47
Encyclopedia Americana, intl ed, 95n53
Encyclopedia mysteriosa, 95n932
Encyclopedia of ...
   acoustics, 98n1619
   adult dvlpmt, 95n781
   advanced materials, 96n1664
   Africa S of the Sahara, 99n100
   African airlines, 99n1574
   African-American culture & hist, 97n331
   African-American educ, 97n285
   African-American heritage, 98n338
   afterlife beliefs & phenomena, 96n1445
   aging, 96n850
   agricultural sci, 95n1507
   allegorical lit, 97n890
   alternative medicine, 97n1345
   American architecture, 2d ed, 96n1045
   American biog, 2d ed, 97n33
   American business hist & biog: iron & steel in the 20th century, 95n238
   American Catholic hist, 99n1286
   American communes, 1663-1963, 99n747
   American educ, 97n288
   American family names, 96n437
   American farm implements & antiques, 98n1419
   American govt, 99n667
   American Indian civil rights, 98n562
   American Indian costume, 95n442
   American Indian wars, 1492-1890, 99n460
   American industries, 95n236
   American pol reform, 98n657
   American prisons, 97n505
   American religious hist, 97n1180
   American women & religion, 99n1265
   analytical sci, 96n1495
   ancient civilizations of the Near East & Mediterranean, 98n487
   ancient Mesoamerica, 97n453
   angels, 98n1355
   apocalyptic lit, 97n893
   apocalypticism, 99n1266
   applied ethics, 99n1251
   applied physics, v.15, 97n1407
   applied physics, v.16, 97n1408
   applique, 95n979
   archetypal symbolism, v.1, 98n1351
   archetypal symbolism, v.2, 98n1352
   assns: natl orgs of the US, 99n50
   assns: natl orgs of the US [CD-ROM], 97n49
   assns: regional, state, & local orgs, 7th ed, 99n51
   Australian art, rev ed, 96n1032
   Australian dolls, 95n976
   beer, 96n1525
   biblical errancy, 96n1456
   bioethics, rev ed, 96n1429
   bioethics, rev ed [CD-ROM], 98n1333
   biog, 99n22
   biostats, 99n1418
   birds, 2d ed, 99n1377
   bodywork, 97n1350
   British humorists, 97n984
   business, 97n155
   business info sources: Europe, 95n277
   business info sources suppl, 10th ed, 97n177
   Canadian rock, pop & folk, 95n1292
   capital punishment, 99n577
   careers & vocational guidance, 10th ed, 98n215
   careers & vocational guidance [CD-ROM], 96n382
   careers & vocational guidance, 2d ed [CD-ROM], 98n214
   chemical processing & design, v.56, 97n1378
   chemical tech suppl vol, 99n1503
   civil rights in America, 99n588
   claims, frauds, & hoaxes of the occult & supernatural, 97n637
   classical philosophy, 98n1334
   Cleveland hist, 2d ed, 97n88
   climate & weather, 97n1396
   college basketball, 96n809
   computer sci & tech, v.34, suppl 19, 97n1367
   conflict resolution, 99n554
   constitutional amendments, proposed amendments, & amending issues, 1789-1995, 97n596
   consumer brands, 95n324
   contemporary French culture, 99n128
   creation myths, 96n1444
   cryptology, 98n855
   cultural anthropology, 97n316
   daytime TV, 99n1212
   decorative paint techniques, 95n967
   democracy, 97n612

dinosaurs, 99n1539
disability & rehabilitation, 97n670
drugs & alcohol, 97n707
early Christianity, 2d ed, 98n1386
earth & physical scis, 99n1514
earthquakes & volcanoes, 95n496
E philosophy & religion, 96n1483
educ info for elementary & secondary school professionals, 1994/95, 95n353
educ info, 1994/95, 96n324
electronic circuits, v.6, 97n1305
empiricism, 99n1252
endangered species, 95n1564
energy tech & the environment, 96n1830
English studies & lang arts, 95n929
environmental biology, 96n1856
environmental control tech, v.7, 96n1857
environmental control tech, v.8, 96n1858
environmental control tech, v.9, 96n1859
environmental info sources, 95n1757
European cinema, 97n1111
family health, 99n1441
famous suicides, 98n768
fantasy, 98n1116
feminist literary theory, 99n961
figure skating, 99n739
film directors in the USA & Europe, v.1, 95n1372
folklore & lit, 99n962
frontier biog, v.4, 95n538
frontier biog on CD-ROM [CD-ROM], 96n497
frontier lit, 98n1130
garbage, 97n1425
geographical treatures in world hist, 98n399
German resistance to the Nazi movement, 98n470
gerontology, 97n667
ghosts & spirits, 95n791
global industries, 97n204
govtl advisory orgs 1997, 11th ed, 99n670
great civilizations, 95n580
healing therapies, 98n1552
herbs & their uses, 96n1585
home care for the elderly, 96n1681
homoeopathy, 2d ed, 95n1673
housing, 99n792
human behavior, 95n778
human biology, 99n1355
human rights, 2d ed, 97n517
hurricanes, typhoons, & cyclones, 99n1532
immunology, 2d ed, 99n1419
Indianapolis, 96n929
infectious diseases, 99n1445
interior design, 98n935
intl boundaries, 96n455
invasions & conquests from ancient times to the present, 97n564
Irish schools, 1500-1800, 96n315
Japanese pop culture, 99n112
keyboard instruments, v.1, 95n1278
Keynesian economics, 98n152
land invertebrate behaviour, 95n1592

lang & linguistics, 95n1024
Latin American hist & culture, 97n349
Latin American lit, 98n1178
lib hist, 95n637
lib & info sci, v.57, 98n569
lib & info sci, v.58, suppl 21, 97n524
lib & info sci, v.59, 98n570
lib & info sci, v.60, suppl 23, 99n593
lib & info sci, v.61, suppl 24, 99n594
life scis, 97n1268
literary epics, 97n889
living artists, 7th ed, 95n999
mammals, 98n1469
mammals, 2d ed, 99n1391
marriage & the family, 96n863
martial arts movies, 96n1380
materials sci & engineering, v.3, 95n1631
medical media & communications, 98n1529
medicinal plants, 97n1343
memory & memory disorders, 96n780
mental health, 95n780
mental health, 99n704
Mexico, 98n141
microcomputers, v.18, 97n1371
Minor League Baseball, 2d ed, 98n729
modern American social issues, 99n742
molecular biology & molecular medicine, v.1, 97n1269
molecular biology & molecular medicine, v.2, 97n1270
molecular biology & molecular medicine, v.3, 97n1271
multiculturalism, 95n396
mummies, 99n445
mythology, 95n1321
Native American biog, 98n350
Native American healing, 97n340
Native American legal tradition, 99n388
natural pet care, 99n1384
Naval hist, 99n639
network blueprints, 99n1490
NYC, 96n107
N American eating & drinking traditions, customs, & rituals, 97n1250
N American Indians, 98n353
N American Indians, 98n354
novels into film, 99n1216
nutrition & good health, 98n1521
nutritional suppls, 97n1349
obesity & eating disorders, 95n1678
occultism & parapsychology, 4th ed, 97n633
percussion, 96n1291
phenomenology, 98n1335
philosophy suppl, 97n1160
plague & pestilence, 96n1725
police sci, 2d ed, 96n599
popular misconceptions, 96n62
post-colonial lits in English, 95n1102
psychiatry, psychology, & psychoanalysis, 97n1356
psychology, 2d ed, 95n779
relationships across the lifespan, 97n631
religion [CD-ROM], 98n1353
religious controversies in the US, 98n1354

Encyclopedia of ... (*continued*)
- reptiles & amphibians, 2d ed, 99n1395
- revolutions & revolutionaries, 97n477
- rhetoric & composition, 97n840
- rural America, 98n98
- sacred places, 98n1349
- satirical lit, 97n892
- sci, 95n1487
- small business, 99n277
- snakes, 96n1637
- social & cultural anthropology, 97n317
- social hist, 95n96
- social work, 19th ed, 96n893
- software engineering, 95n1607
- southern lit, 99n1047
- sports sci, 98n720
- statl scis: update v.1, 98n809
- student & youth movements, 99n653
- TV, 98n888
- TV sci fiction, 98n1283
- the American Constitution [CD-ROM], 98n518
- the American legislative system, 95n742
- the American military, 95n688
- the American presidency, 95n542
- the American Revolution, 3d ed, 96n506
- the American West, 97n415
- the ancient Greek world, 97n450
- the blues, 2d ed, 99n1150
- the bk, 2d ed, 97n554
- the cat, 98n1463
- the Cold War, 95n577
- the consumer movement, 99n176
- the dog, 96n1620
- the Enlightenment, 97n475
- the environment, 95n1765
- the essay, 98n1107
- the EU, 99n691
- the future, 97n44
- the hist of classical archaeology, 97n397
- the horse, 95n1582
- the inter-American system, 98n695
- the McCarthy era, 97n591
- the Middle Ages, 96n565
- the modern Middle East, 97n136
- the motorcycle, 96n1893
- the musical theatre, 95n1415
- the N American colonies, 95n540
- the N American Free Trade Agreement, 96n305
- the novel, 99n963
- the paranormal, 97n634
- the peoples of the world, 95n399
- the Persian Gulf War, 97n454
- the Reagan-Bush yrs, 97n593
- the Republican Party & the ency of the Democratic Party, 98n659
- the Roman Empire, 95n579
- the sayings of the Jewish people, 99n1293
- the sword, 96n816
- the US in the 20th century, 97n416
- the US congress, 96n720
- the Vietnam War, 97n433
- the Vietnam War, 99n527
- the War of 1812, 98n612
- time, 95n58
- toxicology, 99n1504
- traditional epics, 95n1322
- transcendentalism, 97n964
- TV game shows, 2d ed, 97n1113
- 20th century conflict, 98n613
- underwater & maritime archaeology, 99n446
- US Army insignia & uniforms, 98n624
- US biomedical policy, 97n1330
- US foreign relations, 98n660
- urban America, 99n793
- utopian lit, 96n1147
- values & ethics, 97n1163
- vaudeville, 95n1417
- virology, 95n1680
- virology plus [CD-ROM], 98n1442
- vitamins, minerals, & supplements, 97n1265
- war & ethics, 97n1161
- women & sports, 97n644
- women artists of the American west, 99n869
- women in religious art, 97n797
- women's hist in America, 97n736
- words & phrases, legal maxims, 95n603
- world biog, 2d ed, 99n23
- world cultures, v.6: Russia & Eurasia/China, 95n397
- world cultures, v.7: S America, 95n398
- world cultures, v.8: Middle America & the Caribbean, 97n318
- world cultures, v.9: Africa & the Middle East, 97n319
- world cultures, v.10: indexes, 97n320
- World Cup soccer, 95n822
- world facts & dates, 95n46
- world problems & human potential, 4th ed, 95n828
- world sport, 98n721
- world terrorism, 98n551

Encyclopedia plus of world problems & human potential, 4th ed [CD-ROM], 98n86
Encyclopedia Sherlockiana, 95n1211
Encyclopedia USA, suppl v.1, 98n439
Encyclopedia USA, v.25, 99n461
Encyclopedia USA, v.22, 97n417
Encyclopedia USA, v.23, 97n418
Encyclopedia USA, v.24, 98n440
Encyclopedias, atlases, & dicts, 96n48
Encyclopedic dict of conflict & conflict resolution, 1945-96, 99n628
Encyclopedic dict of gears & gearing, 96n1674
Endangered & threatened species [CD-ROM], 95n1534
Endangered English dict, 96n1089
Endangered species, 99n1370
Enderlyn, Allyn, 95n288
Endres, Gunter, 97n1442
Endres, Kathleen L., 95n215, 96n950, 97n743
Energy, 96n1833
Energy analysis of 108 industrial processes, 6th ed, 98n1494
Energy & American society, 95n1752
Energy & environmental industry survey 1997, 98n191

Energy balances & electricity profiles, 1992, 96n1841
Energy balances for countries in transition 1993, 1994-2010, & energy prospects in CIS countries, 98n1627
Energy balances for Europe & N America, 1992, 1993-2010, 97n1423
Energy policies of IEA countries, 95n1750
Energy stats yrbk, 1992, 95n1751
Energy stats yrbk, 1995, 99n1547
Engel, Margaret, 98n731
Engel, Margorie L., 95n847
Engel, Peter H., 99n283
Engelbert, Phillis, 98n1611, 99n1319
Engerman, Stanley L., 99n542
Engholm, Christopher, 97n168
Engineered materials hndbk, 96n1665
Engineering mathematiics hndbk, 99n1544
Engineering plastics & composites, 2d ed, 95n1636
England, 95n157
Engle, Ron, 96n1420, 97n1147
Englefield, Dermot, 96n540
English castles, 97n394
English Catholic bks, 1701-1800, 97n1204
English, Deborah L., 96n669, 96n670
English lang & orientation programs in the US, 11th ed, 98n988
English lang scholarship, 97n809
English novel, 1660-1700, 98n1145
English novel explication, suppl 5, 95n1208
English novel explication, suppl 6, 99n1069
English usage & style for editors, 99n836
English vocabulary quick ref, 99n901
English-Arabic standard dict, 95n1070
English-Azerbaijani/Azerbaijani-English concise dict, 96n1097
English-German dict of materials & process engineering, 96n1666
English-Norwegian, Norwegian-English dict, 99n937
English-Russian comprehensive dict, 96n1122
English-Russian dict of American criminal law, 99n553
English-Russian economics glossary, 97n154
English-Russian, Russian-English dict, rev ed, 96n1124
English-Somali, Somali-English dict, 96n1134
English-Spanish glossary of environmental terms & abbrevs, 96n1862
English-Spanish, Spanish-English electrical & computer engineering dict, 97n1297
English-Ukrainian dict of business, 98n155
English-Yiddish/Yiddish-English practical dict, 95n1100
English-Yiddish, Yiddish-English dict, rev ed, 98n1054
Engquist, Jayson Rod, 97n1036
Enhanced occupational outlook hndbk, 98n226
Enos, Theresa, 97n840
Enslen, Richard A., 96n606, 99n555
Ensminger, Audrey H., 95n1515, 96n1524
Entertainers in British films, 99n1225
Entertainment awards, 97n1099
Environment abstracts 1994, 95n1774
Environment & the law, 97n514
Environment ency & dir 1998, 99n1561
Environment 1: clean water, 95n1760

Environment property & the law, 99n585
Environment 2: clean air, 95n1761
Environmental acronyms, 96n1850
Environmental contaminant ref databk, v.1, 97n1387
Environmental contaminant ref databk, v.2, 97n1388
Environmental ency, 95n1764
Environmental engineering dict, 3d ed, 99n1407
Environmental ethics, 98n1628
Environmental gd to the Internet, 96n1868
Environmental grantmaking fndns 1996, 4th ed, 97n690
Environmental hazards: marine pollution, 95n1778
Environmental justice, 97n1435
Environmental law hndbk, 14th ed, 98n559
Environmental literacy, 95n1772
Environmental racism & the environmental justice movement, 97n513
Environmental sci & tech hndbk, 95n1775
Environmental statutes, 1995 ed, 96n1872
Environmental studies: an annot bibliog, 95n1758
Environmental telephone dir, 97n1430
EPA database bk, 96n1865
Epic lives, 95n909
Epics for students, 98n1069
EPM licensing letter sourcebk, 1997 ed, 97n165
Epps, Roselyn Payne, 97n1341
Epstein, Eric Joseph, 99n528
Epstein, Lee, 95n612, 97n497
Equal educl opportunity for all children, 95n354
Erb, Uwe, 95n1599
Erdman, David V., 97n884
Ergas, G. Aimee, 96n1024
ERIC identifier authority list (IAL) 1995, 96n629
ERIC on CD-ROM [CD-ROM], 97n293
Erickson, Hal, 96n1375
Erickson, John, 97n558
Erickson, Judith B., 96n902, 99n52
Erickson, Ljubica, 97n558
Erickson, Millard J., 96n1453
Ericson, Margaret D., 97n1020
Eritrea, 96n116
Erlewine, Michael, 95n1256, 96n1330, 97n1072, 98n1228, 98n1230, 98n1238
Erlewine, Stephen Thomas, 98n1228, 98n1230
Ernest, James D., 96n1457
Ernst & Young almanac & gd to US business cities, 95n206
Ernst, Carl H., 96n1636
Ernst, Carl R., 98n63, 98n524, 98n525, 98n665, 98n666, 98n706, 99n597
Ernst, Edzard, 99n1456
Ernst, Gordon E., Jr., 96n1207
Errors in English & ways to correct them, 4th ed, 95n1039
Erwin, Douglas H., 96n1813
Esch, Natasha, 95n1355
Eskind, Andrew H., 97n789
Espejo-Saavedra, Rafael, 95n493
Espencheid, Mark, 96n1795
Esposito, John L., 96n1477
Esposito, Vincent J., 96n677
Essay & general lit index 1990-94, 96n81
Essential ASL, 97n871

Essential business buyer's gd, 98n179
Essential French dict, 95n1077
Essential gd to ...
   chronic illness, 98n1558
   prescription drugs 1995, 96n1737
   wilderness camping & backpacking in the US, 96n824
Essential Internet info gd, 96n1784
Essential Matthew Arnold, 95n1210
Essinger, James, 95n228
Esteban, H. Bartolome, 97n1279
Estell, Kenneth, 95n404, 95n406, 99n391, 99n774
Estes, Ellen G., 98n791
Ester Forbes, 99n1053
Estrada, James, 95n659
Ethiopia, 96n117
Ethnic & vernacular music, 1898-1960, 97n1075
Ethnic conflict & human rights in Sri Lanka, v.2, 95n136
Ethnic cuisines, 97n1253
Ethnic cultures of the world, 98n331
Ethnic dress, 96n388
Ethnic groups worldwide, 99n368
Ethnic minority health, 98n1504
Ethnic pols in E Europe, 95n749
Ethnic relations, 96n389
Ethnic studies in the US, 97n322
Ethnohistorical dict of China, 99n370
Ethnohistorical dict of the Russian & Soviet empires, 95n400
Ethridge, James M., 98n597
Ethridge, Karen, 98n597
Etnier, David A., 95n1584
ETS test collection catalog, v.2, 2d ed, 96n314
Ettlinger, Steve, 96n1526
Etulain, Richard W., 97n959
EU Insts' register, 3d ed, 99n692
Eudora Welty: a bibliog of her work, 95n1197
Eurail gd to train travel in the new Europe, 1996, 97n1443
Eurail gd to world train travel, 1996, 26th ed, 97n1444
Eureka! scientific discoveries & inventions, 96n1496
Europa world yrbk 1998, 39th ed, 99n66
Europe on file, 98n121
European art since 1850, 98n958
European art to 1850, 98n959
European dir of retailers & wholesalers, 2d ed, 99n253
European dir of SE Asian studies, 99n319
European drinks mktg dir, 4th ed, 97n240
European employment law, 96n252
European environmental stats hndbk, 95n1783
European food databk 1994, 95n1522
European food mktg dir, 1994, 95n279
European forests & timber, 98n1430
European hist on file, 98n463
European mktg data & stats 1996, 31st ed, 97n273
European mktg data & stats 1998, 33d ed, 99n254
European myth & legend, 99n1185
European oilfield serv, supply, & manufacturers dir, 1996, 2d ed, 97n1417
European paintings in the Metropolitan Museum of Art by artists born before 1865, 97n804
European pharmaceutical technical & regulatory compendium, 96n1742
European pol facts, 1900-96, 99n690
European powers in the 1st World War, 97n467
European private label dir, 97n241
European regional incentives, 1996-97, 97n243
European research & dvlpmt database 1995 [CD-ROM], 96n1510
European Union ency & dir 1996, 2d ed, 97n607
Europe's major cos dir 1997, 2d ed, 99n255
Europe's medium-sized cos dir, 97n242
Europe's medium-sized cos dir, 2d ed, 99n256
Evangelical dict of biblical theology, 97n1197
Evangelical sectarianism in the Russian Empire & the USSR, 97n1173
Evangelista, Nick, 96n816
Evans, Charlotte, 95n590
Evans, Denise, 99n973, 99n974
Evans, Linda, 98n1236
Evans, Martin Marix, 96n1018
Evans, Michael L., 95n206
Evans, Nancy, 95n1645
Evans, Philip R., 96n1323, 98n1236
Evans, Robert C., 98n1119
Evans, Toshie M., 98n1003
Events that changed America in the 18th century, 99n456
Everitt, B. S., 96n1699
Everitt, David, 99n1242
Every manager's gd to business processes, 97n267
Every thing in Dickens, 97n992
Everyone in Dickens, 97n993
Everyone's gd to children's lit, 99n1000
Everthing Civil War, 98n447
Everything you need to know about diseases, 97n1336
Everything you need to know about medical tests, 97n1337
Everything you need to know about medical treatments, 97n1338
Everything you pretend to know & are afraid someone will ask, 97n57
EveryWoman's gd to prescription & noprescription drugs, 98n1564
Evinger, William R., 96n687, 98n573, 99n631
Evriviades, Marios L., 96n130
Ewert, Richard H., 96n1674
Executive order 9066 [CD-ROM], 99n470
Executive's bk of quotations, 95n216
Exegetical bibliog of the N.T., v.4, 97n1185
EXEGY: the source for current world info, 96n49
Exhaustive concordance to the Greek N.T., 97n1199
Experiencing America's past: a travel gd to museum villages, 2d ed, 95n507
Experimental TV, test films, pilots, & trial series, 1925-95, 98n1314
Explorers, 99n417
Explorers & discoverers, 96n454
Explorers & discoverers, v.5, 99n418
Exploring health care careers, 99n1429
Exploring our natl parks & monuments, 9th ed, 96n470
Exploring poetry [CD-ROM], 98n1184
Exploring Shakespeare [CD-ROM], 98n1162
Exploring the Great Lakes states through lit, 95n1123
Exploring the mountain states through lit, 95n1125

Exploring the NE states through lit, 95n1122
Exploring the Pacific states through lit, 95n1121
Exploring the plains states through lit, 95n1120
Exploring the SE states through lit, 95n1126
Exploring the SW states through lit, 95n1124
Exploring your world, rev ed, 95n494
Export financing & insurance vocabulary, 97n206
Exporting to the USA & the dict of intl trade, 1996-97 ed [CD-ROM], 97n205
Exporting to the USA, 1995-96 ed, 96n297
Expositor's bible commentary [CD-ROM], 99n1277
Exter, Thomas G., 98n225
External degrees in the info age, 98n308
External trade bulletin of the ESCWA region, 7th ed, 96n157
External trade monthly stats, 96n293
Extractives, manufacturing, & servs, 98n162
Extraordinary women in support of music, 98n1199
Eyewitness atlas of the world, 96n447
Eyewitness ency of ...
    nature [CD-ROM], 97n1287
    sci [CD-ROM], 98n1403
    space & the universe [CD-ROM], 97n1395
Eyewitness garden hndbk: annuals & biennials, 98n1436
Eyewitness hist of the world [CD-ROM], 96n567
Eyston, Felice, 97n662, 99n740
Eytan, Zeev, 96n695

F. Scott Fitzgerald A to Z, 99n1054
Faber, Charles F., 96n804, 98n730
Faberge & his works, 95n994
Fabre, Michel, 96n1197
Fabry, Heinz-Josef, 97n1200, 98n1375, 99n1276
Facets African-American video gd, 95n1392
Fackler, P. Mark, 96n1441
Fact bk on higher educ, 1997 ed, 99n349
Facts about Canada, its provinces & territories, 96n137
Facts about the American wars, 99n471
Facts about the British prime ministers, 96n540
Facts about the cities, 2d ed, 98n823
Facts about the Congress, 97n600
Facts about the states, 2d ed, 95n102
Facts about the Supreme Court of the US, 98n538
Facts on File Asian political almanac, 95n747
Facts on File bibliog of American fiction through 1865, 95n1177
Facts on File children's atlas, rev ed, 99n412
Facts on File D-Day atlas, 95n680
Facts on File dict of ...
    astronomy, 3d ed, 95n1721
    biotech & genetic engineering, 95n1619
    nautical terms, 95n1795
    TV, cable, & video, 95n959
Facts on File ency of black women in America, 98n343
Facts on File ency of word & phrase origins, rev ed, 98n1001
Facts on File environment atlas, rev ed, 99n1551
Facts on File wildlife atlas, rev ed, 99n1295
Facts on File world news CD-ROM 1997 [CD-ROM], 98n506
Facts on File world pol almanac, 3d ed, 96n711
Faerber, Marc, 98n589, 98n590

Fagan, Brian M., 98n428
Fagan, Thomas K., 97n286
Fage, J. D., 96n531
Failed tech, 96n1511
Fainges, Marjory, 95n976
Fairweather, Digby, 97n1076
Fales, Alexcia, 98n771
Falick, Melanie, 96n1526
Falk, Byron A., Jr., 98n67, 98n68
Falk, Nancy Auer, 96n934
Falk, Peter Hastings, 99n868
Falk, Valerie R., 98n67, 98n68
Falkenstein, Jeffrey A., 98n790
Falkland Islands, S Georgia, & the S Sandwich Islands, 97n133
Famighetti, Robert, 95n6, 96n7
Familia Gekkonidae (Reptilia, Sauria), pt.1, 96n1634
Familiar dinosaurs, 95n1736
Family archive viewer [CD-ROM], 97n355
Family homeopathy, 97n1342
Family planning & reproductive health servs in Ghana, 95n849
Family studies database [CD-ROM], 97n674
Family wisdom, 97n69
Famous 1st facts, 99n46
Famous firsts of black women, 95n908
Famous lines: a Columbia dict of familiar quotations, 98n80
Fandom dir, no.15, 1995-96 ed, 96n1355
Fant, Maureen B., 99n1331
Fantasia, Rick, 95n841
Fantasy lit for children & YAs, 4th ed, 96n1167
FAO/ECE Agriculture & Timber Division of the Economic Commission for Europe, 96n1519, 96n1520
Faoro, Victoria, 95n977
FAQ's of life, 99n67
Far East & Australasia 1995, 26th ed, 96n167
Far East & Australasia 1997, 28th ed, 97n143
Far Eastern art, 98n960
Farace, Joe, 97n1368
Faragher, John Mack, 99n458
Fargnoli, A. Nicholas, 97n1009
Faris, Jocelyn, 95n1344
Farlow, James O., 98n1617
Farmer, Ann Dahlstrom, 99n1056
Farmer, David Hugh, 99n1262
Farndon, John, 96n1805, 98n48
Farquhar, Doug, 96n1866
Farr, David F., 96n1593, 97n1279
Farr, J. Michael, 95n308, 95n309, 95n310, 95n311, 95n312, 98n226, 98n227, 98n228
Farrell, Michael, 96n325
Farry, Mike, 99n619
Farwell, Harold F., Jr., 95n1042
Fashion & costume in American popular culture, 97n1093
Fashion & merchandising fads, 95n987
Fast, Cathy Carroll, 96n933
Fast, Timothy H., 96n933
Father Charles E. Coughlin, 99n1282
Fatigue data bk, 97n1308
Faucett, Bill F., 99n1133

Faulkner, Benjamin, 96n436
Faulkner, Keith, 97n577
Favorite annuals, 96n1568
Favorite flowering shrubs, 96n1569
Favorite hobbies & pastimes, 95n801
Favorite men hymn writers, 95n1311
Favorite perennials, 96n1570
Favorite shade plants, 96n1571
Fawcett, Jan, 95n780
FaxUSA, 1994 ed, 95n189
FaxUSA, 1998, 99n151
FBI: an annot bibliog & research gd, 95n619
Feather, John, 98n571
Feature films, 1940-49: a US filmography, 95n1380
Fechhelm, Janice D., 99n1388
Feczko, Margaret Mary, 95n364, 96n870, 96n871, 96n875, 96n878, 96n961, 99n768
Feder, Jody, 98n274, 98n792
Federal assistance dir, spring 1994, 95n862
Federal chemical regualtion, 99n586
Federal database finder, 4th ed, 96n59
Federal executive dir: May/June 1994, 95n725
Federal grants & funding locator [CD-ROM], 99n766
Federal legislative hists, 96n717
Federal regional executive dir, Mar/Aug 1994, 95n726
Federal regulatory dir, 7th ed, 96n731
Federal regulatory dir, 8th ed, 98n664
Federal support for nonprofits 1994, 95n866
Federal systems of the world, [2d ed], 96n712
Federal wildlife laws hndbk with related laws, 99n587
Federal writers' project, 96n966
Federal Writers' Project of the WPA for the State of Montana, 95n513
Federal yellow bk, fall 1994, 95n727
Fee, Margery, 99n907
Fegan, Sean, 99n1412
Fegley, Randall, 95n116, 95n122, 96n116
Feher, Gyorgy, 98n978
Fehrenbach, R. J., 96n1006
Feinberg, Barbara Silberdick, 95n724
Feinberg, Sandra, 96n903
Feinstein, Sascha, 99n1099
Feldman, Andrew J., 97n1431
Feldman, Douglas A., 99n1468
Feldman, George, 99n539
Feldman, Julie, 99n1226
Feldman, Lynne B., 95n181
Feldman, Susan E., 98n1592
Fellowships in intl affairs, 95n365
Felts, Eva M., 98n166
Female dramatist, 99n1025
Female offenders, 98n549
Feminism & postmodern theory, 97n727
Feminism worldwide, 98n831
Feminist chronicles 1953-93, 95n917
Feminist criticism of American women poets, 96n1222
Feminist ency of Italian lit, 98n1177
Feminist jurisprudence, 97n739
Feminist writers, 97n886
Fenton, John Y., 96n1438

Fenton, R. R., 97n78, 97n172, 97n1241, 98n849
Fenton, Thomas P., 95n144
Fenwick, Elizabeth, 98n802
Fenwick, Gillian, 96n26, 99n1073
Ferbel, Peter J., 95n420
Ferber, Gene, 95n260
Ference, Gregory C., 95n559
Ferguson, Everett, 98n1386
Ferguson, Gary Lynn, 96n1318
Ferguson, J. G., editorial staff, 95n1646
Ferguson, Jacqueline, 95n343
Ferguson, John H., 98n1483
Ferguson, Tom, 97n1328
Ferguson's gd to apprenticeship programs, 2d ed, 99n359
Fergusson, Rosalind, 95n1058, 95n1064
Ferling, John, 95n533
Fernandes, David, 97n1134
Fernandez, Mauro, 95n1027
Fernandez, Ronald, 99n93
Fernekes, William R., 97n515
Ferrara, Miranda H., 95n1107, 97n701, 99n958
Ferrari's places for men, Apr 94-Apr 95, 95n854
Ferrari's places for women, Apr 94-Apr 95, 95n855
Ferrari's places of interest, Apr 94-Apr 95, 95n856
Ferrari, Marianne, 95n854, 95n855, 95n856, 95n857
Ferrell, Robert H., 95n524, 97n414
Ferrier, James A., 99n1406
Ferstler, Howard, 95n1257
Festivals of Europe, 96n1353
Festivals of W Europe, 95n1336
Fetishes, Florentine girdles, & other explorations into the sexual imagination, 96n886
Fetrow, Alan G., 95n1380
Feuer, Bryan, 97n448
Feuerhahn, Ronald R., 97n1168
Feuerman, Francine, 98n1547
Feuerstein, Georg, 98n1338
Few, Roger, 95n1558
Fiala, John L., 96n1567
Ficher, Miguel, 97n1042
Fiction catalog, 13th ed, 97n945
Fiction dict, 96n1185
Fiction of L. Ron Hubbard, 95n1192
Fiction sequels for readers 10 to 16, 2d ed, 99n1010
Field artillery, 96n703
Field, David H., 97n1209
Field gd to ...
    America's historic neighborhoods & museum houses, 99n433
    birds of the Gambia & Senegal, 99n1373
    business terms, 95n185
    common animal poisons, 97n1262
    current training videos, 96n282
    demons, fairies, fallen angels, & other subversive spirits, 99n1181
    nearby nature, 95n1559
    prehistoric life, 96n1815
    sailboats of N America, 95n1796
    shells, 4th ed, 96n1595
    the palms of the Americas, 96n1589

the trees & shrubs of the S Appalachians, 95n1553
trains of N America, 97n1445
venomous animals & poisonous plants, 95n1535
wild flowers of S Europe, 95n1541
Field manual for the amateur geologist, rev ed, 96n1803
Field, Shelly, 96n1276, 96n1364, 98n1513
Fieldhouse, Richard W., 95n702
Fieldwork in the lib, 95n393
Fierro, Alfred, 99n497
Fiess, Stephen C. E., 95n1277
Fiesta, 98n1262
1500 Calif place names, 99n420
50 most influential women in American law, 98n513
50 yrs of events, 98n1331
Fifty-seven saints, 2d ed, 96n1464
Fiji, 96n169
Filby, P. William, 97n367
Fildes, Robert, 96n208
Filipino achievers in the USA & Canada, 97n332
Film actors gd, 1997, 3d ed, 97n1143
Film & TV in-jokes, 99n1239
Film & video finder, 5th ed, 98n310
Film & video on the Internet, 98n1287
Film anthologies index, 95n1401
Film cartoons: a gd to 20th century American animated features & shorts, 99n1231
Film choreographers & dance directors, 98n1268
Film composers gd, 3d ed, 97n1037
Film directors, 11th intl ed, 96n1405
Film distribution gd 1986-1992, v.1, 96n1384
Film ency, 2d ed, 95n1371
Film festival gd, 99n1223
Film index intl 1996 [CD-ROM], 99n1240
Film noir, 96n1383
Film producers, studios, agents, & casting directors gd, 5th ed, 97n766
Film quotations, 95n1403
Film researcher's hndbk, 98n1309
Film superlist: motion pictures in the US public domain, 1894-1939, updated ed, 95n1368
Film writers gd, 6th ed, 97n767
Film writers gd, 7th ed, 99n1219
Film, TV, video in Russia '94, 95n1378
Filmmakers in The Moving Picture World, 98n1316
Films into bks, 96n1394
Financial aid bk, 2d ed, 98n298
Financial aid financer, 98n306
Financial aid for African Americans 1997-99, 99n292
Financial aid for Asian Americans 1997-99, 99n293
Financial aid for Native Americans 1997-99, 99n772
Financial aid for the disabled & their families 1994-96, 96n858
Financial aid for the disabled & their families 1998-2000, 99n294
Financial aid for vets, military personnel, & their dependents 1994-96, 96n690
Financial planner's desk ref, 95n229
Financial resources for intl study, 2d ed, 97n309
Finch, Christopher, 96n1536

Finch, Jim, 98n1112
Find anyone fast, 96n837
Find it fast, 3d ed, 95n78
Find it fast, 4th ed, 98n575
Find public records fast, 98n665
Finding help: a ref gd for personal concerns, 97n55
Finding images online, 98n1592
Finding Italian roots, 95n456
Finding your Hispanic roots, 98n368
Findlay, Allan M., 96n120
Findlay, Anne M., 96n120
Findlay, Michael Shaw, 99n894
Findlay, Scott, 97n1002
Findling, John E., 97n661, 99n456
Finegan, Jack, 99n1278
Fink, Charles B., 97n265
Finkelman, Paul, 99n535
Finkelstein, L., 96n1641
Finland, rev ed, 98n123
Finn, Daniel, 95n1383, 96n1392, 96n1393
Fiordelisi, Livia, 95n1448
Fiorenza, Francis Schussler, 96n1475
First Americans, 96n386
First century of film, 97n1112
First civilizations, 95n571
First dict of cultural literacy, 2d ed, 97n296
First editions, 95n972
First Hollywood musicals, 97n1116
Fischel, Jack R., 99n540
Fischer, Carolyn A., 99n822
Fischer, Clare B., 97n1169
Fischer-Schreiber, Ingrid, 97n1226
Fischler, Stan, 96n826, 96n827
Fish & fisheries worldwide [CD-ROM], 96n1605
Fisher, Helen S., 95n205, 96n266, 96n930, 98n229, 99n48
Fisher, James, 95n1345
Fisher, Janet, 96n1179
Fisher, Louis, 95n542
Fisher, Richard D., Jr., 99n219
Fishes of Tenn., 95n1584
Fishes of the Galapagos Islands, 98n1468
Fishes of the Gulf of Mexico, v.1, 99n1388
Fishes of the tropical E Pacific, 96n1633
Fishes of the world, 95n1587
Fishing tackle source dir, 99n729
Fishkin, Shelley Fisher, 99n588
Fishman, Stephen, 96n590
Fisichella, Rino, 95n1470
Fiske gd to colleges 1994, 95n366
Fiske, Edward B., 95n366
Fiske, John D., 95n129
Fiske, Robert Hartwell, 95n1067, 97n759
Fist, Stewart, 98n1593
Fister, Barbara, 96n946
Fitch, Thomas P., 99n186
Fitt, Stephen D., 99n383
Fitton, Robert A., 98n81
Fitzgerald, Mary Ann, 99n356
Fitzpatrick, Kathleen A., 99n298

Fitzroy Dearborn dir ...
   of the world's futures & options markets, 95n221
   venture capital funds, 96n184
   the world's banks, 11th ed, 97n190
Fitzroy Dearborn ency of banking & finance, 10th ed, 95n230
Fitzroy Dearborn intl dir of venture capital funds, 2d ed, 97n181
Fitzroy Dearborn intl dir of venture capital funds 1998-99, 99n198
Fitzsimmons, Richard, 98n757
501 Hebrew verbs, 97n854
Flackes, W. D., 96n761
Flags of the world, 99n406
Flanagan, Mike, 96n502
Flanders, Stephen A., 99n780
Flannery, Tim, 96n1631, 96n1632
Flappers 2 rappers: American youth slang, 97n842
Flaum, Eric, 95n1321
Flavell, A. J., 95n675
Flavell, Linda, 97n826
Flavell, Roger, 97n826
Flea market trader, 11th ed, 98n896
Fleeger, Carolyn A., 96n1747
Fleming, James Rodger, 95n1727
Fleming, Michael C., 97n716
Fleschar, Manfred H., 95n1620
Fletcher, Andrew J., 98n1540
Fletcher, Beverly R., 98n549
Fletcher, John, 95n1215
Flexner, Doris, 95n1313
Flexner, Stuart, 95n1313
Flexner, Stuart Berg, 98n1002
Flight & flying: a chronology, 95n1787
Floods, 99n1528
Flora Europaea, v. 1, 2d ed., 95n1540
Flora of N America n of Mexico, v.3, 98n1447
Flora, Joseph M., 96n1199
Florence, Gene, 96n1013
Florida, 98n416
Florida: atlas of histl county boundaries, 98n431
Florida almanac 1997-98, 11th ed, 98n99
Florida hndbk 1993-94, 95n104
Florida statl abstract, 1994, 28th ed, 96n916
Florida's hurricane hist, 99n1531
Floring, John, 97n1246
Flowering crabapples, 96n1567
Flowering plants of the world, updated ed, 95n1542
Flows & stocks of fixed capital 1967-92, 96n213
Fluorescence: gems & minerals under ultraviolet light, 96n1812
Fly-fisher's gd to saltwater naturals & their imitation, 96n817
Flynn, James H., Jr., 95n1524
Focus on eating disorders, 95n1679
Focus on relationships, 95n883
Foden, Charles R., 95n1650
Fodor's great American vacations for travelers with disabilities, 96n471
Fodor's ballpark vacations, 98n731
Fodor's exploring Canada, 98n421
Fodor's exploring the Greek Islands, 98n424
Fodor's healthy escapes, 5th ed, 98n405
Fodor's upclose Europe, 99n437
Foerstel, Herbert N., 95n658, 98n584, 99n825
Fogelman, Peggy, 98n983
Fogle, Bruce, 96n1620, 98n1463
Folcarelli, Ralph J., 95n653, 99n601
Foliage plant diseases, 98n1446
Folk traditions of the Arab world, 96n1342
Folklife sourcebk, 2d ed, 96n1341
Folklore: an ency of hist, methods, & theory, 99n1180
Folklore, culture, & aging, 98n762
Following The Fugitive: an episode gd & hndbk to the 1960s TV series, 97n1127
Folsom, W. Davis, 98n153
Folts, W. Edward, 96n838
Foner, Eric, 98n344
Fontana, David, 95n784, 95n785
Food aid in figures, v.11, 96n881
Food & beverage market place, 1996, 97n1249
Food & beverage market place, 1997/98, 99n1339
Food & drink in lit, 97n881
Food chronology, 96n1539
Food festivals, 98n414
Foods & nutrition ency, 2d ed, 95n1515
Fools & jesters in lit, art, & hist, 99n951
Foot & ankle sourcebk, 97n1340
Foot, M. R. D., 97n571
Footage, 99n1220
Foran, Dorothy, 96n853
Ford, A., 99n257
Ford, Simon, 97n792
Foreign descriptions of Muscovy, 96n147
Foreign trade stats for Africa, 96n294
Foreign trade stats of Asia & the Pacific 1988-92, 96n295
Forest & forest industries country fact sheets, 98n1431
Forestiero, Saverio, 99n1390
Forget, Carl, 99n1332
Form & analysis theory, 99n1114
Former major league teams, 97n646
Forms of address, 96n311
Forrester, William H., 99n611
Forshaw, Joseph, 99n1377
Fort, Clancy, 97n1363
Fortner, Diane, M., 95n1758
Fortune ency of economics, 95n184
Forty, George, 98n613
Fosbrook, Deborah, 98n531
Foss, Christopher F., 97n575, 97n576, 99n646
Fossil atlas: fishes, 97n1404
Fossils of the Burgess Shale, 96n1813
Foster, Allan, 95n1783
Foster, David William, 99n1098
Foster, Donald H., 95n1251
Foster, Frances Smith, 98n1129
Foster, Gerald L., 97n1445
Foster, Gwendolyn Audrey, 96n947
Foster, Janet, 97n440
Foster, Race, 98n1464
Foster, Steven, 95n1535

Fostoria, v.2: identification & value gd to etched, carved & cut designs, 98n899
Foulkes, Christopher, 96n1527
Foundation Center, 95n867, 96n883
Foundation dir 1997, 19th ed, 98n787
Foundation dir suppl, 98n788
Foundation dir suppl, 1995 ed, 96n871
Foundation giving, 1997 ed, 98n794
Foundation grants index 1994, 95n867
Foundation grants index 1996, 24th ed, 96n883
Foundation grants to individuals, 9th ed, 96n872
Foundation 1000 1995/96, 96n873
Foundation reporter 1999, 30th ed, 99n767
Foundations of the 1990s, 99n768
Founders of modern nations, 96n556
Four British women novelists, 99n1061
Four centuries of special geography, 95n492
Four French symbolists, 97n806
Fowler, David J., 96n654
Fowler, H. W., 97n756
Fox, Claire G., 97n403
Fox, Franklin W., III, 97n2
Fox, Ken, 98n1311
Fox, Thomas C., 98n1391
Foxwell, Elizabeth, 95n360
Foy, Felician A., 95n1471, 97n1203
Fradkin, Robert A., 97n1056
Frame by frame 2: a filmography of the African American image, 1978-94, 98n1295
Frame, Murray, 96n548
France, Peter, 96n1252
Franceschetti, Donald R., 99n1315
Francillon, Rene J., 96n697, 99n637
Francis, Raymond L, 99n1306
Franck, Irene, 95n24, 95n918, 95n925, 96n945, 97n640, 98n803
Franck, Irene M., 99n802
Franco, Alvaro, 96n1834
Francoeur, Robert T., 96n885, 98n797
Francois Rabelais: a ref gd, 1950-90, 95n1230
Frank, Ben G., 97n436
Frank, Frederick S., 98n1137
Frank, Sam, 98n1273
Frankenhoff, Brent, 98n908
Franklin, D., 97n219
Franklin, Laurel F., 98n700
Franklin Pierce: a bibliog, 95n528
Franklin-Smith, Constance, 95n999
Frankovich, Nicholas, 97n1016
Franks, David D., 95n826
Franks, Don, 97n1099
Frantz, Donald G., 97n872
Frantz, Pollyanne, 97n1033
Fraser, Kristy, 96n1767
Frasier, David K., 97n503
Frayser, Suzanne G., 96n887
Fred Astaire: a bio-bibliog, 98n1272
Fred Waring discography, 97n1049
Freda, Michael D., 98n1231
Fredericks, Anthony D., 99n1006

Frederikse, H. P. R., 95n1711
Frederiksen, Elke P., 99n1095
Fredriksen, John C., 98n608
Free & inexpensive career materials, 96n383
Free expression & censorship in America, 98n584
Free mags for libs, 4th ed, 95n647
Free market environmental bibliog 1995-96, 4th ed, 98n1630
Free money for college, 3d ed, 95n356
Free money from the fed govt for small businesses & entrepreneurs, 2d ed, 97n189
Free or low cost health info, 99n1428
Free stuff from the Internet, 95n1709
Freed, Judith M., 96n1356
Freed, Melvyn N., 95n1663
Freedman, Alan, 96n1757, 97n1369
Freedom of religion decisions of the US Supreme Court, 97n1183
Freedom of speech decisions of the US Supreme Court, 97n541
Freedom of the press: an annot bibliog, 2d suppl: 1978-92, 95n704
Freedom of the press decisions of the US Supreme Court, 97n761
Freedom's lawmakers: a dir of black officeholders during Reconstruction, rev ed, 98n344
Freed's gd to student contests & publishing, 5th ed, 96n1356
Free-floating subdivisions, 6th ed, 95n651
Freelance Editorial Assn yellow pages & code of fair practice, 1997-98, 98n863
Freeman, Carla Conrad, 96n378
Freeman, John Crosby, 96n1016
Freeman, Judy, 96n663
Freeman, Roger L, 95n1612
Freese, Mel R., 98n732
Freeze, Gregory L., 96n247
Freiman, Fran Locher, 96n1511, 98n1530
Freitag, Wolfgang M., 98n940
French critical reception of African-American lit from the beginnings to 1970, 96n1197
French feminist theory 2, 95n902
French feminist theory 3, 98n832
French films, 1945-93, 97n1115
French image of America, 95n531
French tapestries & textiles in the J. Paul Getty Museum, 98n946
French women playwrights before the 20th century, 95n1405
French women playwrights of the 20th century, 97n943
French-English, English-French dict, unabridged ed, 95n1074
French-English, English-French practical dict, 95n1079
Frent, David J., 95n741
Freshwater fishes of the Carolinas, Va., Md., & Dela., 95n1588
Freudenheim, Ellen, 97n1315
Frey, Gisela, 98n517
Frey, Linda, 96n762
Frey, Marsha, 96n762
Frey, P. Diane, 95n1122
Frick, John P., 96n1671
Frick, John W., 95n1410
Frickhinger, Karl Albert, 97n1404

Fried, Stephen B., 95n771
Friedl, Friedrich, 99n885
Friedl, Vicki L., 97n559
Friedman, Howard S., 99n704
Friedman, J. M., 95n1682, 97n1358, 99n1480
Friedman, Jack P., 95n330, 96n178
Friedman, John B., 99n810
Friedman, Mark, 95n919
Friedman, Mickey, 96n1189
Friedman, Norman, 95n701, 98n629, 98n634
Friedmann, Robert R., 96n596
Friedrich, Paul, 95n397
Friendly German-English dict, 97n849
Fritze, Ronald H., 97n442
Froelke, Ruth, 95n463
Frois, Jeanne, 98n100
From Afar to Zulu: a dict of African cultures, 96n390
From Aristotle to Zoroaster: an A to Z companion to the classical world, 99n526
From biog to hist, 99n993
From headline hunter to Superman: a journalism filmography, 98n1298
From metal to Mozart, 96n1298
From silents to sound, 99n1209
From talking drums to the Internet, 98n854
From the beginning to Plato, 99n1255
Fromm, Joy, 98n821
Frommer's comprehensive travel gd: Caribbean '95, 96n483
Frontiers of space exploration, 99n1520
Frost, Lee, 99n860
Frost-Knappman, Elizabeth, 95n550, 95n914, 98n563, 99n556, 99n572
Fry, Eric J., 95n222
Fry, Plantagenet Somerset, 95n587
Fryer, Mary Beacock, 95n692
Fudyma, Janice, 98n1568
Fugitive: a complete episode gd, 1963-67, 96n1403
Fujie-Winter, Kumiko, 97n860
Fujioka, Yasuhiro, 96n1324
Fuld, James J., 95n1406
Fuller, Sue, 96n73
Fulltext sources online, July 1997, 98n51
Fulton, Len, 95n668, 95n669, 98n599, 98n601
Fulton, Roger, 98n1283, 99n774
Fund raiser's gd to religious philanthropy 1996, 9th ed, 97n691
Funding for US study, 2d ed, 97n305
Funding in aging, 98n759
Funding sources for community & economic dvlpmt 1996, 97n692
Funding sources for community & economic dvlpmt 1998, 99n770
Funding sources for K-12 schools & adult basic educ, 99n290
Fund-Raising regulation, 98n539
Fundukian, Laurie, 99n59
Fungi on rhododendron, 97n1279
Funk & Wagnalls new ency, 95n54
Funnell, Brian M., 96n1807
Furia, Philip, 99n1134
Furman, John M., 97n1042
Furness, Raymond, 99n1093

Furniture assns in N America, 96n223
Furr, A. Keith, 97n1386
Furtaw, Julia, 95n1399
Fury, David, 95n1381
Fuss, Charles J., 97n1074

G. A. Henty 1832-1902: a bibliogl study of his British eds..., 98n1159
Gabel, Dorothy L., 95n344
Gabrielsen, Egill Daae, 99n937
Gaccione, Laura, 98n1509
Gaer, Linda, 96n1866
Gaffke, Carol T., 99n1104, 99n1105
Gage Canadian dict, rev ed, 98n1012
Gagne, Kathleen Dunne, 95n773
Gagne, Louise, 98n603, 98n880
Gagnon, Eric, 95n1710
Gailey, Harry A., 99n638
Gaines, Richard V., 99n1537
Gaither, Carl C., 98n82, 99n1328
Galaeno, Gloria, 96n1589
Galante, Steven P., 99n200
Galante's venture capital & private equity dir, 1997 ed [CD-ROM], 99n199
Galante's venture capital & private equity dir, 1998 ed, 99n200
Galazka, Jacek, 98n1253
Galbraith, Stuart, IV, 95n1382, 97n1117
Gale bk of averages, 95n894
Gale business resources [CD-ROM], 96n199
Gale city & metro rankings reporter, 96n930
Gale country & world rankings reporter, 96n905
Gale dir of databases, 99n1495
Gale dir of pubns & broadcast media, 131st ed, 99n822
Gale ency of ...
  business & professional assns, 96n185
  childhood & adolescence, 99n778
  multicultural America, 96n387
  Native American tribes, 99n389
  psychology, 97n628
  sci, 97n1238
Gale environmental almanac, 95n1776
Gale 5 lang finance dict, 95n231
Gale 5 lang tech dict, 95n1488
Gale gd to Internet databases, 96n1779
Gale, Robert L., 96n1212, 99n957
Gale state rankings reporter, 95n895
Gale, Steven H., 97n984
Galens, David, 99n1021, 99n1022, 99n1023, 99n1024
Galens, Judy, 96n387
Galer, Scott W., 99n1090
Gale's career guidance system, expanded ed [CD-ROM], 96n384
Gale's quotations [CD-ROM], 96n91
Gale's ready ref shelf [CD-ROM], 97n50
Gall, Susan, 96n392, 97n628, 98n834, 99n806
Gall, Susan B., 96n393, 96n396, 97n326
Gall, Susan Bevan, 97n79, 98n119
Gall, Tim, 98n834, 99n806

Gall, Timothy L., 97n79, 97n511, 97n512, 98n119, 99n364
Gallagher, Michael G., 97n223
Gallant, Frank K., 99n421
Gallant, R. W., 96n1793
Gallay, Alan, 97n413
Galle, Fred C., 98n1457
Gallery of her own: an annot bibliog of women in Victorian painting, 98n981
Gallup, George, Jr., 95n92, 98n87
Gallup Poll, 98n87
Gallup Poll: public opinion 1993, 95n92
Galvan, Roberto A., 96n1136
Gamache, Murielle E., 95n738
Games & entertainment on CD-ROM, 1994 ed, 95n814
Gamlin, Linda, 96n1608
Gander, Terry J., 97n570, 98n633, 99n645
Ganeri, Anita, 95n1733, 99n1314
Gangs, 97n509
Gangster films, 97n1114
Ganly, John, 96n296
Gann, Kyle, 99n1124
Ganzl, Kurt, 95n1415
Gaquin, Deirdre A., 99n782
Garage sale & flea market annual, 5th ed, 98n897
Garcia, Frank, 98n1286
Garcia, Maria J., 99n943
Garcia, Richard A., 98n349
Garden bulbs for the South, 96n1546
Garden trees, 97n1282
Gardener's gd to ...
  Britain, new ed, 96n1548
  growing irises, 98n1454
  growing ivies, 98n1455
  growing lilies, 96n1572
  growing peonies, 99n1352
  plant diseases, 96n1547
Gardener's index, 95n1528
Gardener's Supply Co passport to gardening, 99n1350
Gardening by mail, 4th ed, 95n1525
Gardening with roses, 96n1549
Gardiner, Juliet, 98n465
Gardiner, Vince, 99n130
Gardinier, David E., 95n118
Gardner, Bonnie, 95n359
Gardner, John C., 95n217
Gardner, John D., 95n603
Gardner, Karen M., 95n603
Gardner read: a bio-bibliog, 97n1036
Gardner, Robert, 98n854
Gardner's chemical synonyms & trade names, 10th ed, 95n1714
Garee, Betty, 96n853
Gariepy, Jennifer, 97n919, 97n920, 97n921, 97n922, 99n980, 99n981, 99n982
Garland ency of world music, v.9, 99n1120
Garland, Henry, 98n1173
Garland, Mary, 98n1173
Garland, Robert, 99n501
Garment & textile dict, 98n933
Garner, Bryan A., 96n577

Garner, Carolyn, 98n1099
Garner, Diane L., 95n74
Garner, Roberta, 98n690
Garnier, Camille, 98n1151
Garoogian, Andrew, 96n926, 96n931, 98n820, 98n821, 99n579
Garoogian, Rhoda, 96n926, 96n931, 98n820, 98n821, 99n579
Garraty, John A., 96n528, 97n33, 97n402
Garrett, Don, 99n1252
Garrett, George, 99n971
Garrett, Heidi M. Siegenthaler, 95n1648
Garrett, Jenkins, 96n657
Garvey, Mark, 95n670
Garwood, Alfred N., 97n1397
Garzke, William H., Jr., 96n700
Gasaway, Laura N., 95n656
Gaschnitz, K. Michael, 98n722
Gaslin, Glenn, 99n1187
Gastelu, Daniel, 98n1514
Gasterias of South Africa, 95n1550
Gastrow, Shelagh, 97n611
Gates, J. E., 96n1083
Gatten, Jeffrey N., 97n1082
Gause, Ken, 96n709
Gauthier, Mark A., 97n529
Gay almanac, 97n677
Gay & lesbian address bk, 96n53
Gay & lesbian biog, 98n782
Gay & lesbian literary heritage, 97n888
Gay & lesbian lit, 95n1111
Gay & lesbian movement, 97n681
Gay & lesbian online, 97n676
Gay & lesbian online, rev ed, 98n781
Gay & lesbian rights: a ref hndbk, 95n859
Gay, Kathlyn, 95n1777, 97n22, 97n1250
Gay, Martin K., 97n22, 97n538, 97n1250
Gay 100, 96n865
Gaze, Delia, 98n948
Gazit, Shlomo, 96n695
Geahigan, Priscilla Cheng, 95n207
Geary, James W., 96n495
Geddes, Joan Bel, 99n779
Geddes, Nicola, 95n1672, 97n1347
Gedridge, Jolen Marya, 95n837
Gee, Robin, 97n753
Geer, Ira W., 98n1612
Gelbart, Marsh, 98n631
Gelbert, Doug, 95n235, 98n448, 99n472
Gelder, Alice A., 95n249
Geller, Kenneth S., 99n569
Gemmette, Elizabeth Villiers, 99n945
Gems, Gerald R., 97n642
Gemstones, 95n1730
Gemstones of the world, rev ed, 98n1615
Gender dysphoria, 95n874
Gender equity in educ, 96n313
Gender gap in higher educ, 95n372
Genealogical & local hist bks in print, 5th ed, 97n350
Genealogical & local hist bks in print: gen ref & world resources v., 5th ed, 98n359

Genealogical & local hist bks in print: US sources & resources v., 5th ed, 98n360
Genealogical research in England's public record office, 97n357
Genealogist's address bk, 3d ed, 96n428
Genealogist's companion & sourcebk, 95n458
Genealogy & local hist to 1900, 97n351
Genealogy annual, 1995, 98n361
General bibliog for music research, 3d ed, 97n1022
General Douglas MacArthur, 1880-1964: historiography & annot bibliog, 95n536
Generals in muddy boots: a concise ency of combat commanders, 97n562
Generation X: the YA market, 98n256
Genetics & cell biology on file, 99n1357
Genreflecting: a gd to reading interests in genre fiction, 4th ed, 96n1186
Genzberger, Christine A., 95n261, 95n262, 95n263, 95n264, 95n265, 95n266
Geographic database for US economy, tech, & growth [CD-ROM], 98n818
Geography on file, 1995 ed, 96n457
Geologists & the hist of geology, suppl 2, v.1, 97n1402
Geopedia [CD-ROM], 95n497
George F. Kennan: an annot bibliog, 98n700
George Gordon, Lord Byron, 98n1155
George Herbert companion, 96n1238
George, John, 95n1433
George, Leonard, 96n785, 96n1468
George Orwell: a bibliog, 99n1073
George Ryga papers, 96n1249
George Sidney: a bio-bibliog, 95n1350
George, Timothy S., 96n537
George Whitefield Chadwick, 99n1133
Georges Bataille: a bibliog, 95n1423
Georges Braque: a bio-bibliog, 95n996
Georgieva, Valentina, 99n495
Gerald, Debra E., 99n299
Gerardi, Pamela, 96n554
Gerard-Sharp, Lisa, 96n481
Gerber, Douglas E., 99n1018
Gergits, Julia, 97n981
Gerhan, David R., 96n906
Gerhard, Peter, 95n567
Geritz, Albert J., 99n1086
Germaine Tailleferre: a bio-bibliog, 95n1271
German Baroque writers, 1580-1660, 97n1006
German Baroque writers, 1661-1730, 98n1172
German-English dict of idioms, 97n852
German loanwords in English, 95n1036
German poetry in song, 97n1032
German theatre, 98n1323
German writers & works of the early Middle Ages, 96n1254
Germany's top 300: a hndbk of Germany's largest corps, 1993/94 ed, 95n281
Gerring, Anthony L., 96n55, 96n339, 96n340, 97n170
Gershman, Michael, 98n737
Gervais, Marty, 96n1443
Gessel, Van C., 99n1096
Getz, Leslie, 97n1100

Gevinson, Alan, 95n1367, 98n1288
Geyer, B., 96n1516
Ghorayshi, Parvin, 95n292
Ghosts & angels in Hollywood films, 95n1386
Giants: a ref gd from hist, the Bible, & recorded legend, 96n1346
Gibbon, Guy, 99n443
Gibbons, Bob, 95n1541
Gibbs, Tyson, 97n1322
Gibilisco, Stan, 95n960, 95n1613, 96n1753, 97n1372, 98n1488
Giblin, Nan J., 97n55
Gibson, Gloria J., 98n1295
Gibson, J., 96n1726, 97n1357
Gibson, John S., 97n516
Giffin, James M., 99n1354
Gifford, C. D., 98n219
Gifford, Courtney D., 96n260
Gifford, Denis, 99n1225
Gifis, Steven H., 95n604
Giglio, James N., 96n491
Gilber, Nedda, 97n169
Gilbert, Harriett, 96n886
Gilbert, Martin, 95n557, 95n562, 95n569, 95n759, 96n675
Gilbert, Nedda, 99n320
Gilbert, Steve, 96n607, 96n608, 97n541, 97n761, 97n1183
Gilchrist, J. Brian, 97n351
Gilden, Julia, 95n919
Giles, James R., 96n1203, 96n1204, 98n1128
Giles, Wanda H., 96n1203, 96n1204, 98n1128
Gill, Frank B., 95n1565
Gill, Kay, 99n151
Gillaspie, Jon A., 98n1220
Gillaspy, Mary L., 97n537
Gillespie, Anna, 96n1293
Gillespie, John, 96n1293
Gillespie, John T., 95n653, 95n1130, 95n1131, 98n1091, 98n1103, 99n601
Gillespie, Michael Patrick, 97n1009
Gillett, Harriet J., 99n1361
Gillon, Margaret, 97n678
Gilpin, Alan, 98n1633
Gilson, David, 98n1153
Ginger, Ann Fagan, 95n629
Ginger Rogers: a bio-bibliog, 95n1344
Ginsberg, Leon, 96n894
Ginsberg, Susan, 97n69
Giovanni Gabrieli (ca.1555-1612): a thematic catalogue of his music...., 97n1034
Gipson, Carolyn R., 95n243
Gira, Catherine, 95n1218
Giroux, Christopher, 96n1153, 97n895, 97n896, 97n897, 97n898, 98n1068
Giuseppe Verdi: a gd to research, 99n1137
Glaister, Geoffrey Ashall, 97n554
Glassman, Bruce S., 97n7
Glatt, Hillary, 96n1341
Glauser, Beat, 95n1028
Glazier, Michael, 95n1469, 99n1286
Glazier, Stephen D., 98n1359

Glenn, Leigh, 99n590
Glenn, William M., 96n1873
Glenz, W., 97n1379
Glick, David M., 98n1443
Glickman, Simon, 97n339
Glickman, Sylvia, 97n1047, 97n1048, 99n1145
Glisson, Peg, 95n1132
Glitsch, Catherine, 99n1040
Global bks in print plus [CD-ROM], 96n13
Global data locator, 98n812
Global dvlpmt, 97n228
Global dir of financial info vendors, 95n228
Global ency of histl writing, 99n529
Global links: a gd to key people & insts worldwide, 99n54
Global refugee crisis, 96n895
Global trends: world almanac of dvlpmt & peace, 96n200
Global village companion, 97n470
Global voices, global visions: a core collection of multi-cultural bks, 97n10
Globe & Mail report on bus: Canada co hndbk 1994, 96n250
Glock, Hans-Johann, 97n1162
Glomski, Jacqueline, 96n1250
Glossary of ...
   aquatic habitat inventory terminology, 99n1501
   biochemistry & molecular biology, rev ed, 98n1443
   biotech terms, 95n1620
   environment stats, 98n1634
   environmental & regulatory terms & phrases, 95n1766
   industrial org economics & competition law, 95n183
   insurance & risk mgmt terms, 6th ed, 97n200
   insurance terms, 5th ed, 96n226
   plastics terminology in 6 langs, 3d ed, 97n1379
   reliability & maintenance terms, 98n1497
   typesetting terms, 96n667
   vital terms for the home gardener, 95n1529
   weather & climate with related oceanic & hydrologic terms, 98n1612
Glover, Denise M., 96n402
Glut, Donald F., 95n1734, 98n1618
Glynn, Jeannette, 95n190, 96n186
Gneuss, Helmut, 97n809
Goalies: legends from the NHL's toughest job, 96n827
Gobbett, Brian, 99n489
Gobbledygook bk: dict of acronyms, abbrevs, initializations, & estoric terminology, 97n2
Gochman, David S., 99n1420
God on the Internet, 98n1365
Goddard, Ives, 98n356
Goddesses, heroes, & shamans, 96n1347
Godin, Seth, 95n1705
Godrich, John, 99n1160
Gods & symbols of ancient Mexico & the Maya, 95n1444
Gods & heroes of classical antiquity, 98n1257
Goehlert, Robert U., 96n715, 97n584, 97n585, 97n586, 98n646
Goerss, John Mark, 98n1369
Goetzel, Claus G., 96n1666
Goetzel, Lilo K., 96n1666
Goetzfridt, Nicholas J., 96n1260
Going out in style: the architecture of eternity, 98n973

Goins, Charles Robert, 96n440
Gold, David L., 99n942
Gold, Paul, 95n1402
Goldberg, Harold J., 99n122
Goldberg, Marian, 96n465
Golden age of Walt Disney records 1933-88, 98n1209
Golden atlas for children, 95n473
Golden horrors: an illus critical filmography of terror cinema, 1931-39, 97n1122
Goldmine price gd to rock 'n' roll memborabilia, 99n851
Goldmine's celebrity vocals, 96n1274
Goldoftas, Lisa, 97n520
Goldschmidt, Arthur, Jr., 96n162
Goldsmith, Gary, 96n1400
Goldstein, Joshua, 95n735, 95n736, 98n675
Goldstein, Norm, 98n874
Golitzin, Alexander, 97n1212
Gomes, Michael, 95n1436
Gonen, Amiram, 95n399, 99n371
Gonyea, James C., 96n272
Gonzalez, Alexander G., 98n1176
Gonzalez, Ann, 96n1258
Gonzalez, Martin L., 99n1434
Gonzalez-Pando, Miguel, 99n397
Good, Gregory A., 99n1517
Good old index: the Sherlock Holmes hndbk, 98n1158
Good skiing & snowboarding gd 1998, 99n740
Good skiing gd 1997, 97n662
Good wine gd 1999, 99n1340
Goodall, Francis, 98n149
Goode, Clement Tyson, Jr., 98n1155
Goode, Steven, 96n591
Goodfellow, William D., 96n1309
Goodin, M. Elspeth, 95n663
Goodloe, Carolyn Lee, 99n427
Goodman, Edward C., 95n1014
Goodman, Jordan Elliot, 96n220
Goodman, Roy E., 95n1727
Goodrick, Edward W., 97n1199
Goodridge, George E., Jr., 96n439
Goodsell, Don, 97n1303
Goodwin, Calvin M., 95n1286
Goodwin, Katherine R., 96n657
Googins, Bradley K., 98n778
Gopaul, V. Mitra, 95n1692
Gorbachev biblog, 1985-91, 98n482
Gorder, Cheryl, 96n317
Gordon, Alan, 96n501
Gordon, Bertram M., 99n498
Gordon, John S., 95n323
Gordon, Karen Elizabeth, 95n945
Gordon, Lois, 96n501
Gordon, Peter, 99n289
Gordon, Rue E., 95n1769
Gordon, Sean, 97n1432
Gordon, Virginia N., 95n357
Gordon, William A., 96n472
Gore, Tom, 99n1354
Goreham, Gary A., 98n98
Goring, Rosemary, 95n31, 95n1105, 95n1443, 96n1145

Gorlach, Manfred, 95n1028
Gorlin, Rena A., 96n1431
Gorman, G. E., 96n169
Gorman, Lyn, 95n1474
Gorman, Martha, 95n1778
Gorman, Robert F., 95n829, 98n564
Gosliner, Terence M., 97n1295
Gosling, William A., 96n136
Goslinga, Marian, 97n128, 99n1089
Gospel of Matthew, 95n1455
Goss, Glenda D., 99n1135
Gotshall, Daniel W., 95n1594
Gottlieb, Nicholas, 98n771
Gottlieb, Richard, 96n219, 96n228, 97n1249, 99n141, 99n175
Gottschalk, Jack A., 96n233
Gottsegen, Mark D., 96n1053
Gough, Jeanne, 99n296
Gough, Robert E., 95n1529
Gould, Dennis E., 98n483
Gould, Edwin, 99n1391
Gould, Elizabeth, 95n1448
Gould, Lewis L., 97n407
Gould, Robert F., 95n1718
Goulding, Phil G., 98n1223
Gourman, Jack, 99n321
Gourman report of undergraduate programs, 99n321
Gourvish, Terry, 98n149
Gove, Thomas P., 97n253, 97n254
Govea, Wenonah Milton, 96n1287
Government affairs yellow bk, v.1, no.1, 96n187
Government assistance almanac 1996-97, 10th ed, 97n689
Government career gds [CD-ROM], 96n256
Government dir of addresses & telephone nos 1995, 3d ed, 96n732
Government financial aid bk, 2d ed, 98n299
Government info on the Internet, 99n61
Government job finder, 98n234
Government job finder, 2d ed, 95n315
Government on file, 99n684
Government online, 96n1776
Government phone bk USA 1997, 5th ed, 98n52
Government ref bks 92/93, 95n75
Governors of Ga., 1754-1995, rev ed, 96n496
Gowing, Lawrence, 96n1022
Gozdecka-Sanford, Adriana, 96n144, 98n479
Graber, Jeffrey, 99n1489
Graber, Steven, 98n220, 99n264, 99n265
Grabowski, John, 97n85
Grabowski, John J., 97n87, 97n88
Grace, Betsy, 99n173
Grading student writing, 99n310
Graduate Group's new internships for 1994-95, 96n261
Graduate Group's new internships for 1997-98, 99n322
Graduate medical educ dir 1997-98, 98n1535
Graduate programs in journalism & mass communications, 98n309
Graduate school funding hndbk, 96n365
Graduate student's complete scholarship bk, 99n343
Graedon, Joe, 97n1359
Graedon, Teresa, 97n1359

Graefen, Gabriele, 98n984
Graf, Rudolf F., 97n1305
Graff, Gary, 97n1084, 98n1233
Graff, Henry F., 97n589
Graham, Ian, 98n1404
Graham, Judith, 98n22
Graham, Robert J., 99n843
Graham Stuart Thomas rose bk, rev ed, 96n1551
Grain market, v.2, 96n1519
Grambs, David, 96n1089
Grammatically correct, 98n1005
Grammatically correct hndbk, 98n1004
Grand, Gail L., 95n340
Grandparents, 98n780
Granoff, Allan, 95n1680, 98n1442
Grant, Carl A., 98n267
Grant, Daniel, 95n1007, 96n1040, 98n865, 98n964
Grant, Edmond, 98n1311
Grant, John, 98n1116
Grant, Peter W., 96n815
Grant seekers gd, 4th ed, 97n693
Grant, Steven A., 95n164
Grant, Tina, 97n214, 97n215, 97n216, 98n208, 99n203, 99n204, 99n206, 99n208
Grants & awards available to American writers, 30th ed, 99n830
Grants & awards available to American writers 1996-97, 19th ed, 97n694
Grants for libs & info servs, 95n639
Grants for teachers, 95n343
Grants for the aging, 95n835
Grants on disc [CD-ROM], 97n695
Grants register 1995-97, 95n367
Grants register 1998, 16th ed, 98n300
Graphic novels, 96n1359
Grassy, John, 99n1392
Grateful Dead & the deadheads, 98n1240
Grattan, K. T. V., 96n1641
Grattan-Guinness, I., 95n1740
Graves, Genevieve, 98n174
Graves, Karen J., 95n1663
Gravesteijn, J., 97n1400
Gravlin, Erika, 96n317
Gray, Richard A., 96n1721
Gray, Sharon A., 97n338
Graying of America: an ency of aging, health, mind, & behavior, 97n668, 98n760
Great admirals, 99n624
Great American trials, 95n613
Great artists, 99n863
Great athletes, suppl 21-23, 96n794
Great Britain, 96n480
Great citrus bk, 98n1428
Great dates in Islamic hist, 97n137
Great dates in Russian & Soviet hist, 95n561
Great dates in US hist, 95n539
Great escapes: the spring breaker's gd to beaches & beyond, 98n417
Great events: the 20th century, suppl, 97n478
Great events from hist: N American series, rev ed, 98n497

Great events from hist 2: business & commerce series, 95n209
Great events from hist 2: ecology & the environment series, 96n1853
Great food almanac, 95n1521
Great leaders, great tyrants?, 96n706
Great lives from hist: American women series, 96n942
Great misadventures, 99n522
Great new nonfiction reads, 96n1184
Great rock discography, 97n1085
Great scientific achievements: the 20th century, 95n1489
Great stage directors, 95n1413
Great thinkers of the E world, 96n1433
Great war: a gd to the serv records of all the worlds fighting men & volunteers, 99n635
Great women writers, 95n906
Great world trials, 98n532
Great Zimbabwe, 95n522
Greece: Athens & the mainland, 98n425
Greek Islands, 98n426
Greek-English lexicon, 97n853
Greeley, Ronald, 98n1609
Green, Alan, 97n1038
Green, Carol Hurd, 95n1168
Green, David E., 99n1276
Green, Don W., 98n1479
Green kitchen hndbk, 98n1425
Green, Jonathon, 96n89
Green, Jonathan D., 96n1280, 96n1297, 99n1151
Green, Joseph, 98n1112
Green, Kelly L., 96n1176
Green pharmacy, 98n1546
Green, Philip, 99n655
Green, Scott E., 97n968
Green, Sharon Weiner, 98n992
Green, Thomas A., 99n1180
Green, Thomas E., 96n226
Greenaway, Theresa, 96n75
Greenberg, Gerald S., 97n747
Greenberg's gd to marbles, 2d ed, 97n786
Greene, Evarts B., 95n891
Greene, Stanley A., 97n1436, 98n1642, 99n1567
Greenfield, George, 98n1462
Greenfield, Gerald Michael, 95n899
Greenfield, Jane, 99n855
Greenfield, John R., 95n1199, 97n978
Greenfieldt, John, 95n1166, 96n81, 97n945, 98n1122
Greening the college curriculum: a gd to environmental teaching in the liberal arts, 98n1640
Greenman, David, 99n1578
Greenpeace gd to anti-environmental orgs, 95n1770
Greensmith, Alan, 95n1567
Greenspon, Joanna, 98n846
Greentree, Rosemary, 98n1156
Greenwald, Douglas, 96n179
Greeson, Janet, 99n1007
Greger, Rene, 98n626
Gregg, Robert J., 98n1012
Gregorovich, Andrew, 95n417
Gregory, Hugh, 95n1276, 95n1297, 96n1339

Gregory, Ross, 96n518
Grehan, Ida, 98n376
Grenville, J. A. S., 95n589
Gressman, Eugene, 99n569
Greve, Bent, 99n777
Grey-Wilson, Christopher, 98n1449
Gribbin, John, 96n1820
Gribbin, Mary, 96n1820
Gridiron greats: a century of Polish Americans in college football, 98n745
Grieve, James, 97n847
Griffin, Kenton G., 95n768
Griffith, Susan, 95n380, 96n273
Griffiths, Mark, 95n1530
Griffiths, W. Scott, 96n1536
Griggs, Jack L., 98n1459
Grigoriev, Igor S., 98n1620
Grimes, John, 98n1336
Grimes, Scott, 97n168
Grinde, Donald A., Jr., 98n350
Griscom, Richard, 96n1294
Grisewood, John, 96n1087
Gritzmacher, Lucy G., 95n1649
Groden, Michael, 95n1104
Groenier, Paul D., 98n72
Grohol, John M., 98n1515
Grolier illus ency, 95n55
Grolier illus lib of the environment, 96n1860
Grolier lib of ...
   environmental concepts & issues, 97n1427
   intl biogs, 97n23
   N American biogs, 96n27
   sci biogs, 98n1400
   women's biogs, 99n799
Grolier lib of WW I, 98n614
Grolier master ency index, 1994 [CD-ROM], 95n44
Grolier multimedia ency, 1998, deluxe ed [CD-ROM], 98n43
Grolier student ency of endangered species, 96n1597
Grolier student ency of sci, tech, & the enviroment, 97n1239
Grolier student lib of explorers & exploration, 99n419
Groseclose, David A., 97n973
Gross, David C., 95n1100, 97n878, 98n1251
Gross, Liza, 97n609
Gross, Melissa, 98n1560
Grossman, Ellie, 98n1004
Grossman, John, 97n755
Grossman, Mark, 95n627, 96n1869, 97n341, 97n454, 99n577
Grossman, Paul, 98n530
Grotpeter, John J., 99n477
Grounds, Roger, 99n1351
Group work with the elderly, 98n758
Grove, Jack Stein, 98n1468
Grove Pr gd to the blues on CD, 95n1294
Growing herbs, 96n1586
Growing up: a cross-cultural ency, 97n708
Grubel, Monika, 98n1394
Gruber, Mayer I., 97n1186
Gruber, Paul, 95n1284
Grumet, Joanne, 96n1087
Grunts, Marita V., 95n154

Gubert, Betty Kaplan, 95n1788
Guernsey, Lisa, 98n301
Guernsey, Otis L., Jr., 99n1246
Guerrilla warfare, 98n620
Guide bk of US coins, 1996, 49th ed, 96n1008
Guide to ...
- accredited camps, 1995/96, 39th ed, 96n811
- American cinema, 1930-65, 99n1217
- American cinema, 1965-95, 99n1211
- American crime films of the 30s, 96n1393
- American crime films of the 40s & 50s, 96n1392
- American educl dirs, 7th ed, 95n341
- American scientific & technical dirs, 3d ed, 95n1499
- American silent crime films, 95n1383
- American studies resources, 1994, 96n338
- America's sex laws, 97n499
- ancient Native American sites, 96n411
- background investigations, 7th ed, 98n640
- bk publishers' archives, 99n617
- bks on AIDS, 96n1719
- British drama explication, v.1, 97n987
- British naval papers in N America, 96n679
- British poetry explication, v.4, 96n1245
- British prose fiction explication: 19th & 20th centuries, 98n1143
- campus & non-profit meeting facilities 95, 7th ed, 95n191
- Canadian English usage, 99n907
- Central American collections in the US, 96n152
- children's bks about Asian Americans, 96n1181
- children's ref works & multimedia material, 99n994
- collections on Paraguay in the US, 96n551
- college programs in hospitalitiy & tourism, 5th ed, 98n314
- engineering materials producers, 95n1628
- ethnic health collections in the US, 97n1322
- executive recruiters, new ed, 98n218
- fed funding for anti-crime programs, 95n622
- fed funding for anti-crime programs, 2d ed, 98n553
- fed funding for educ, 1994, 95n345
- fed funding for educ, 1997, 23d ed, 98n274
- fed funding for govts & nonprofits, 1994, 95n863
- fed funding for govts & nonprofits, 1995, Native American ed, 96n882
- fed funding for govts & nonprofits, 19th ed, 98n792
- fed funding for housing & homeless programs, 3d ed, 98n765
- fed funding for volunteer programs & community serv, 3d ed, 96n874
- films on the Korean War, 98n1291
- flowering plant families, 96n1580
- free computer materials 1995, 13th ed, 96n1771
- free computer materials 1998-99, 16th ed, 99n288
- French lit: beginnings to 1789, 95n1231
- funding for intl & foreign programs, 2d ed, 96n875
- graduate environmental programs, 98n1641
- greater Washington, DC grantmakers 1994-95, 96n876
- Indian mss, 95n131
- info at the UN, 96n770
- info resources in ethnic museum, lib, & archive collections in the US, 97n522
- info sources in the botanical scis, 2d ed, 97n1272
- Internet job searching, 1998-99 ed, 99n268
- Latin American, Caribbean, & US Latino-made films & video, 99n1226
- literary agents, 1997, 98n866
- marine invertebrates, 95n1594
- microforms in print 1997, 98n1580
- mss & docs in the British Isles relating to Africa, v.1, 95n111
- multicultural resources 1997/98, 98n327
- natl professional certification programs, 98n313
- natl professional certification programs, 96n267
- naturalization records of the US, 98n332
- N American steam locomotives, 95n1791
- original sources for precolonial W Africa published in European langs, rev ed, 96n531
- popular music ref bks, 96n1311
- popular US govt pubns, 3d ed, 95n73
- popular US govt pubns 1995/96, 5th ed, 99n60
- private fortunes, v.2, 96n188
- private fortunes, v.3, 96n189
- public policy experts, 1997-98, 99n701
- published Canadian violin music suitable for student performers, 95n1279
- ref bks, 11th ed, 97n8
- ref bks for small & medium-sized libs, 1984-94, 96n9
- ref works for the study of the Spanish lang & lit & Spanish American lit, 98n1183
- religious & inspirational mags, 95n1448
- serial bibliogs for modern lits, 2d ed, 97n885
- South African ref bks, 6th ed, 98n19
- special issues & indexes of pers, 4th ed, 95n86
- summer camps & summer schools 1995/96, 27th ed, 96n326
- technical servs resources, 95n665
- the aqueducts of ancient Rome, 96n1046
- the best products, 1994, 95n224
- the birds of Mexico & N Central America, 96n1615
- the blues, 95n1295
- the cinema of Spain, 99n1237
- the Community initiatives 1994-99, 96n753
- the early reports of the Supreme Court of the US, 97n493
- the evaluation of educl experiences in the armed servs, 1996, v.1: Army, 98n275
- the evaluation of educl experiences in the armed servs, 1996, v.2: Navy, 98n276
- the evaluation of educl experiences in the armed servs, 1996, v.3: Air Force, Coast Guard, Dept of Defense, Marine Corps, 98n277
- the Fonds d'Archives & collections in the holdings of the York Univ Archives, 96n653
- the histl geography of New Spain, rev ed, 95n567
- the hist of Pa., 95n530
- the Indian wars of the West, 99n474
- the most competitive colleges, 99n325
- the presidency, 2d ed, 98n674
- the republics of the former Soviet Union, 95n166
- the secular poetry of T. S. Eliot, 97n970
- the Sol Feinstone collection of the David Lib of the American Revolution, 96n654
- the sources of US military hist, suppl IV, 99n622

the US supreme court, 98n526
the zoological lit: the animal kingdom, 95n1562
tourist railroads & railroad museums, 4th ed, 96n1886
US fndns, their trustees, officers, & donors, 1997 ed, 98n789
useful woods of the world, 95n1524
wildflowers in winter, 96n1584
world lang dicts, 99n890
Guidebook for publishing philosophy, 1997 ed, 98n867
Guidebook to Canadian population studies & stats, 95n141
Guidelines for bias-free writing, 96n968
Guides to ...
 archives & ms collections in the US, 95n523
 collection dvlpmt for children & YA lit, 99n601
 lib collection dvlpmt, 95n653
Guidry, Josee G., 96n385
Guiley, Rosemary Ellen, 95n1327, 96n786, 96n967, 98n1355
Guillemette, Aurel, 95n1164
Guillermo, Artemio R., 99n487
Guinea, 97n97
Guinea pig, 98n1466
Guinness bk of espionage, 95n761
Guinness bk of records 1995, 95n1329
Guinness ency of popular music, 2d ed, 96n1310
Guinness multimedia disc of records, 1994: Windows 2.0 [CD-ROM], 95n1330
Guitar music by women composers, 98n1218
Gulevich, Tanya, 99n1194
Gun control, 97n510
Gun digest, 98n920
Gunston, Bill, 95n1789, 97n1298
Gunter, Kahl, 96n1657
Gunter, Wagner, 97n1185
Gunton, Tony, 95n1693
Gunzenhauser, Margot, 97n1101
Gurvis, Sandra, 95n84
Gustav Mahler's symphonies, 98n1248
Gutek, Gerald, 95n507
Gutek, Patricia, 95n507
Gutman, Bill, 96n818
Guttenplan, Samuel, 96n1432
Guttentag, Roger M., 99n1562
Guttery, Ben R., 99n1574
Gutt-Mostowy, Jan, 97n864
Gutzke, David W., 97n441
Guy, Jonelle, 96n1651, 96n1835, 97n1419
Gyeszly, Suzanne D., 96n141
Gypsies, 96n405

H. L. Mencken: a descriptive bibliog, 99n1027
Haas, Marilyn L., 95n427
Habitats, 96n1598
Hadamitzky, Wolfgang, 97n860
Hadley, Frank-John, 95n1294
Hadro, Jane E., 98n528
Haeberle, Erwin J., 99n775
Hager, Alan, 98n1060
Haggerty, Gary, 96n1311
Hahn, Harley, 96n1775, 98n1594, 99n1496

Haider, Thomas John, 96n322, 96n323
Haig, John H., 99n933
Haines, David W., 98n801
Haines, Lila, 97n132
Haines, Meic F., 97n132
Haines, Miranda, 99n426
Hainsworth, Philip, 99n1272
Haiti, rev ed, 95n169
Hajnal, Peter I., 98n693
Hale, Constance, 97n758
Hale, Linton, 95n629
Hales, Michael Gordon, 95n232
Haley, Barbara A., 98n1503
Halfdanarson, Guomundur, 98n474
Hall, Amy, 99n51
Hall, Cally, 95n1730, 96n69
Hall, Carolyn M., 97n524, 99n593, 99n594
Hall, Charles J., 97n1025
Hall, Clifton, 99n1094
Hall, David E., 98n104
Hall, G. S., 96n1581
Hall, George E., 97n712
Hall, Hal W., 98n1117
Hall, James, 96n1031
Hall, Joan Houston, 97n833
Hall, L. Victoria, 96n872
Hall of fame museums, 99n69
Hall, Rob, 96n617
Hall, Sarah M., 97n917
Hall, Susan, 96n1164
Halliwell, Leslie, 98n1305
Halliwell's film gd 1995, 96n1385
Halliwell's filmgoer's companion, 12th ed, 98n1305
Hallucinogenic & poisonous mushroom field gd, 98n1452
Halper, Evan, 99n431
Halperin, Michael, 95n255, 99n228
Halvorson, Peter L., 96n1437
Hamada, Yoh-ichi, 96n1324
Hamadeh, Samer, 95n303, 98n221, 99n270
Hamel, April Vahle, 96n365
Hamel, Bernard B., 98n1494
Hamel, Raymond, 95n1593, 98n1471
Hamer, Frank, 98n932
Hamer, Janet, 98n932
Hamilton, Ian, 95n1249
Hamilton, Neil A., 96n556, 97n613, 98n437
Hamito-Semitic etymological dict, 96n1107
Hamlet: a gd to the play, 99n1077
Hamlin Garland, 99n1055
Hamm, Rita R., 95n180
Hammer films: an exhaustive filmography, 97n1119
Hammer, Patricia Cahape, 98n272
Hammond atlas of ...
 the 20th century, 97n459
 the world, 99n413
 world hist, 95n570
Hammond Citation world atlas, 97n374
Hammond comparative world atlas, 95n478
Hammond explorer atlas of the world, 98n385
Hammond intl atlas of the world, 95n482

Hammond, Lorne F., 99n1552
Hammond new century world atlas, 97n375
Hammond new headline world atlas, 95n479
Hammond odyssey atlas of N America, 95n466
Hammond odyssey atlas of the world, 95n483
Hammond road atlas America, 96n441
Hammond road atlas & vacation gd, 96n442
Hammond students atlas of the world, 96n448
Hammond US atlas, Gemini ed, 95n467
Hammond US hist atlas, 95n468
Hammud, Zicky, 96n54
Hancock, Lee, 96n1688
Hancock, Susan, 99n994
Hand, Richard A., 96n1005
Handbook for research in American hist, 2d ed, 95n535
Handbook of ...
   African medicinal plants, 95n1546
   American military hist, 97n569
   ancient Greek & Roman coins, 97n778
   Biblical chronology, rev ed, 99n1278
   bird identification for Europe & the W Palearctic, 99n1374
   campaign spending: money in the 1992 Congressional races, 95n738
   Catholic theology, rev ed, 96n1475
   child & adolescent psychology, v.5-7, 99n1466
   child psychology, 5th ed, 99n707
   Chinese popular culture, 95n1326
   Christian Latin, 96n1115
   construction tolerances, 95n1602
   copyright in British publishing practice, 3d ed, 95n655
   corrosion data, 96n1667
   cosmetic & personal care additives, 95n1712
   current sci & tech, 2d ed, 97n1242
   economic methodology, 99n161
   environmental data on organic chemicals, 3d ed, 97n1389
   evangelical theologians, 95n1461
   food additives, 96n1533
   frogs & toads of the US & Canada, 3d ed, 96n1640
   health behavior research, 99n1420
   Hispanic cultures in the US: hist, 95n421
   Hispanic cultures in the US: lit & art, 95n422
   inorganic compounds, 96n1794
   intl financial terms, 98n184
   intl trade & dvlpmt stats 1993, 96n234
   lab health & safety, 2d ed, 96n1796
   Latin American Studies: social scis, no.55, 99n398
   leftist guerrilla grps in Latin America & the Caribbean, 97n609
   literary research, 2d ed, 96n1142
   lizards, 96n1639
   mammals of the S-central states, 96n1630
   mktg scales, 95n321
   N American Indians, v.17: langs, 98n356
   N American industry, 99n220
   N American stock exchanges, 99n168
   oil industry terms & phrases, 5th ed, 96n1676
   persuasive tactics, 95n937
   physical quantities, 98n1620
   plastic & rubber additives, 97n1385
   pol sci research on the Middle East & N Africa, 99n648
   population & housing censuses, pt.4, 98n805
   private schools 1995, 76th ed, 96n327
   research on sci teaching & learning, 95n344
   salamanders, 96n1635
   snakes of the US & Canada, 95n1598
   solid waste mgmt, 95n1780
   the American frontier, 99n393
   the American frontier, v.3, 95n440
   the American frontier, v.4: the far West, 98n357
   the nations, 14th ed, 96n713
   therapeutic interventions, 96n1735
   thermal conductivity, v.1, 96n1821
   thermal conductivity, v.2, 96n1822
   thermal conductivity, v.3, 96n1823
   thermal conductivity, v.4, 98n1622
   transport property data, 96n1824
   US coins, 1998, 55th ed, 98n910
   US labor stats, 98n230
   viscosity, v.4: inorganic compounds & elements, 98n1623
   world mineral trade stats 1990-95, 98n251
   world stock indices, 99n221
Handbook to ...
   Bach's sacred cantata texts, 98n1247
   life in ancient Egypt, 99n510
   life in ancient Greece, 99n500
   life in ancient Rome, 95n586, 96n547
Handbooks & tables in sci & tech, 3d ed, 95n1483
Handel, Marsha J., 98n1547
Hands, D. Wade, 99n161
Handy, D. Antoinette, 96n1285
Handy sci answer bk, 2d ed, 98n1414
Handy weather answer bk, 98n1613
Haney, Wayne S., 99n1173
Hani-English/English-Hani dict, 98n1034
Hannah Arendt 2: a bibliog, 98n636
Hannam, June, 97n726
Hans Holbein the younger: a gd to research, 98n943
Hansan, John E., 97n669
Hansen, Brad, 98n1572
Hansen, Gladys, 97n83
Hansen, Lucia, 96n649
Hanson, Patricia King, 95n1367
Happy trails: a dict of W expressions, 95n1043
Harbottle, Philip, 96n1234
Harcourt Brace student dict, 2d ed, 95n1049
Harcourt Brace student thesaurus, 2d ed, 95n1050
Harcourt, Geoff, 98n152
Hardaway, Roger D., 97n405
Hardin, James, 95n1232, 96n1254, 97n1006, 98n1172
Harding, Les, 99n530
Harduf, David Mendel, 98n1054, 98n1055
Harduf's transliterated English-Hebrew dict, 1st v., 95n1081
Harduf's transliterated English-Hebrew dict, 2d v., 95n1082
Harduf's transliterated English-Hebrew dict, 3d v., H-K, 96n1108
Harduf's transliterated English-Hebrew dict, 4th v., L-M, 98n1035
Harduf's transliterated English-Yiddish, Yiddish-English dict, rev ed, 98n1055
Hardy, Gayle J., 98n60

Hardy, Peter, 97n662, 99n740
Hardy, Phil, 95n1375, 95n1376, 96n1306, 96n1379
Hardy, R. Willson, 99n57, 99n157
Hare, Tony, 96n1598
Harewood, Earl of, 95n1285
Hargreaves, David, 96n235
Harkness, Linda, 97n650
Harland, Mike, 98n1041
Harlem renaissance, 99n378
Harley Hahn's Internet & Web yellow pages 1998, 5th anniversary ed, 99n1496
Harlow, Victoria, 95n313
Harmer, H. J. P., 99n375
Harmon, Robert B., 97n975
Harmond, Richard P., 99n1552
Harmony illus ency of country music, 3d ed, 95n1298
Harmony theory, 98n1193
Harms, Jeanne McLain, 98n284
Harner, James L., 98n1165
Harold Lloyd: a bio-bibliog, 95n1343
Harper, Charles A., 95n1614
Harper, David C., 99n845
Harper, Judith E., 99n800
Harper, Nancy Lee, 99n1136
Harper, Timothy, 95n323
HarperCollins dict of biog, 95n27
HarperCollins ency of Catholicism, 96n1469
HarperCollins Portuguese dict, college ed, 98n1041
HarperCollins Russian dict: Russian-English, English-Russian, college ed, 96n1123
HarperCollins world atlas, 95n484
Harpur, James, 95n1434
Harries, Dan, 98n1287
Harrington, Virginia D., 95n891
Harris, Barbara P., 98n1012
Harris, Brian, 99n897
Harris, Charles W., 99n883
Harris, Christopher, 95n1779
Harris, Dan R., 99n744
Harris, David, 99n642
Harris, Duncan, 95n372
Harris, Elree I., 98n981
Harris, James G., 95n1538
Harris, John M., 98n1227
Harris, Laurie Lanzen, 96n25, 98n21
Harris, Marjorie, 96n1568, 96n1569, 96n1570, 96n1571
Harris, Melinda Woolf, 95n1538
Harris, Nigel G. E., 98n1341
Harris, Robert L., 97n1370
Harris, Trudier, 98n1129
Harris, Wayne, 98n163
Harrison, Ben, 98n546
Harrison, Colin, 95n1567
Harrison, Elizabeth, 95n1191
Harrison, Maureen, 96n607, 96n608, 97n541, 97n761, 97n1183
Harrison, Nigel, 99n1117
Harrison, P. S., 96n1406
Harrison's reports & film reviews, 96n1406
Harrod's librarians' glossary, 8th ed, 97n526

Harrold, Ann, 96n635, 96n637
Hart, James D., 97n966
Hart-Davis, Adam, 99n1188
Hartel, Lynda Jones, 96n888
Hartman, Charles, 99n1090
Hartman, Donald K., 95n1162, 97n404
Hartman, Stephen W., 97n203, 98n263
Harty, Sheila, 95n862
Harvard biogl dict of music, 97n1024
Harvard Business School core collection, 1998, 99n140
Harvard Law Students, 95n608
Harvey, Joan M., 95n98
Harvey, Nancy Lenz, 95n1219
Harvey, Robert, 98n1171
Harvey, Scott A., 95n1779
Harwood, Gregory, 99n1137
Haschak, Paul G., 95n1101
Haskins, Jim, 96n390
Hastedt, Catherine A., 99n884
Hastings' dict of the Bible, 96n1454
Hastings, Elizabeth Hann, 99n81
Hastings, James, 96n1454
Hastings, Philip K., 99n81
Hasty, Will, 96n1254
Hatch, Terry, 96n1545
Hatch, Thom, 98n441
Hatfield, Fred, 98n1514
Hatfield, John T., 98n1364
Hattendorf, Lynn C., 99n297
Haubenstock, Susan H., 96n1041
Haubrich, William S., 98n1528
Hauchler, Ingomar, 96n200
Hauck, Dennis William, 95n788, 95n1346, 97n635
Haught, James A, 98n1347
Haunted places: the natl dir, rev ed, 97n635
Haupt, Clyde V., 95n1393
Hauser, Barbara R., 98n544
Havel, James T., 97n588
Having children: the best resources to help you prepare, 99n753
Havlice, Patricia Pate, 96n1056
Hawisher, Gail, 96n1058
Hawker, Sara, 96n1078
Hawkins, Stephen, 96n1789
Hawkins, Walter L., 95n407
Hawkins-Dady, Mark, 95n1421, 97n915
Hawks, John, 96n371
Hawks, John K., 96n461
Hawley's condensed chemical dict, 13th ed, 99n1505
Hawthorne, Gerald F., 95n1450
Hayakawa, S. I., 95n1063
Hayashi, Tetsumaro, 96n1216
Haycock, Ken, 96n645
Hayden, Gerry, 95n528
Hayes, David, 99n1429
Hayes, James L., 99n837
Hayes, Melissa, 96n336
Hayes, S. V., 95n34
Hayford, Charles W., 98n111
Haynes, Craig, 98n1504

Haynes, Douglas, 96n1439
Haynes, Theodora T., 96n255
Hayslip, Bert, Jr., 96n839
Haythornthwaite, J. A., 95n564
Hayward, Susan, 98n1284
Haywood, John, 98n487
Hazardous chemicals & the right to know, 95n1779
Hazardous chemicals desk ref, 3d ed, 95n1781
Hazardous chemicals desk ref, 4th ed, 98n1635
Hazardous materials hndbk, 97n1436
Hazardous substances resource gd, 2d ed, 98n1642
Hazen, Edith P., 95n1245
Hazen-Hammond, Susan, 98n351
Hazewinkel, Michiel, 96n1827
Heads of states & govts: a worldwide ency, 95n706
Head-Word & rhyme-word concordances to Des Minnesangs Fruhling, 99n1094
Healey, Jon, 98n672
Health: US, 1996-97 & injury chartbk, 99n1430
Health & environment in America's top-rated cities, 96n931
Health & safety manager's A-Z gd to environmental mgmt, 96n1873
Health & British mags in the 19th century, 99n1417
Health & illness, 98n1509
Health & medical yrbk 1997, 98n1516
Health & medicine on the Internet, 99n1424
Health care almanac, 97n1316, 99n1431
Health care bk of lists, 95n1652
Health care crisis in the US, 98n1506
Health care reform terms, 2d ed, 95n1657
Health care software sourcebk 1997, 98n1517
Health care terms, 3d ed, 97n1319
Health care terms, healthy communities ed, 98n1511
Health industry quicksource, 97n1313
Health of native people of N America, 97n338
Health online, 97n1328
Health professions educ dir 1997-98, 98n1512
Health professions educ dir, 1998-99, 99n1425
Health stats, 2d ed, 98n1505
Heathcare resource & ref gd, 95n1653
HealthSpeak, 97n1315
Heard, J. Norman, 95n440, 98n357, 99n393
Hearn, Daniel Allen, 98n554
Heatley, Michael, 95n1305
Heaton, Donald D., 98n1421
Heaton, Tim B., 97n718
Hebrew & Aramaic lexicon of the O.T., v.1, 96n1455
Hebrew & Aramaic lexicon of the O.T., v.2, 97n1198
Hecht, Cheryl S., 96n383
Hecht, Hans, 95n1548
Hedblad, Alan, 99n986, 99n988
Hedman, Bruce A., 98n1494
Heenan, Patrick, 99n198
Heffernan, Eileen, 96n1464
Heffron, Mary J., 95n144
Heggoy, Alf Andrew, 96n114
Heiberger, Mary Morris, 96n365
Heidenreich, Conrad E., 99n409
Heidler, David S., 98n612
Heidler, Jeanne T., 98n612

Heising, Willetta L., 97n947, 99n1031
Heisler, Sanford I., 99n1398
Heitman, Francis B., 95n693
Helander, Brock, 97n1083
Helbig, Alethea, 98n1092
Helbig, Alethea K., 95n1133, 97n938, 98n1084
Held, Gilbert, 96n1772, 99n1492
Held, Joseph, 95n560
Helgren, J. Anne, 99n1382
Hellebust, Lynn, 97n602, 97n622
Hellenistic commentary to the N.T., 97n1201
Heller, Craig, 96n1298
Heller, Jules, 96n1026
Heller, Kurt A., 95n352
Heller, Mark A., 99n634
Heller, Nancy G., 96n1026
Hellweg, Paul, 98n1016
Hellwig, Monika K., 95n1469
Helmer, William, 99n580
Help! the quick gd to first aid for your cat, 97n1261
Helsel, Sandra K., 95n1700
Helterman, Jeffrey, 96n1230
Hemley, Ginette, 96n1599
Hempelman, Kathleen A., 96n592
Hemsworth, Brian, 96n815
Henderson, Andrew, 96n1589
Henderson, Chuck, 99n1486
Henderson, David R., 95n184
Henderson, Helene, 96n1358, 98n1263
Henderson, Kathy, 97n751
Henderson, Lesley, 97n917
Hendricks, Bonnie L., 97n1291
Hendrickson, Kenneth E., Jr., 96n718
Hendrickson, Robert, 95n1043, 97n835, 98n1001, 98n1007, 99n904
Henkes, Robert, 96n1054
Henle, Klaus, 96n1634
Hennessee, Don A., 95n1254
Henning, Bill, 96n259
Henri Matisse: a bio-bibliog, 95n997
Henri Matisse: a gd to research, 97n805
Henriques, Gary, 98n898
Henritze, Barbara K., 96n971
Henry IV pts 1 & 2: an annot bibliog, 95n1218
Henry, Laurie, 96n1185
Henry, Scott D., 97n1308
Henry, Tom, 97n796
Henshaw, Richard, 95n824
Hentzi, Gary, 96n960
Herald, Cherry L., 96n1740
Herald, Diana Tixier, 96n1186, 98n1096
Herbal home remedy bk, 99n1461
Herber, Mark D., 99n401
Herbert, Kevin, 97n779
Herbert, Stephen, 98n1280
Herbote, Burkhard, 96n464, 96n465, 96n466
Herbs, 95n1544
Herbs of choice, 95n1545
Herbst, Philip H., 98n328
Herbst, Sharon Tyler, 98n1429

Heritage ency of band music, suppl v.3, 98n1229
Heritage Fdnn Congressional dir, 99n671
Herlocher, Dawn, 98n916
Herman Melville ency, 96n1212
Herman, Richard A., 95n836
Hermann Sasse: a bibliog, 97n1168
Herndon, Constance, 96n951
Herner & Co, staff of, 95n1649
Heroes & pioneers, 99n24
Heroes of conscience: a biogl dict, 97n22
Herring, Eric, 95n690
Herrmann, Joachim, 98n507
Herrmann, Robert O., 99n176
Herron, Nancy L., 97n76
Herubel, Jean-Pierre V. M., 95n573, 96n330
Herzhaft, Gerard, 99n1150
Heslop, Janet, 98n246
Hess, Catherine, 95n980
Hess, Thom, 96n1119
Hester, Joseph P., 97n1163
Hester, M. L., 98n864
Hester, M. Thomas, 95n1200
Hester, Stanley, 98n1236
Hester, Stephen, 98n1236
Hettinga, Donald R., 97n935
Heuvel, Michael Vanden, 98n1326
Hewett, Janet B., 98n451, 98n452, 99n475
Hewett, Jerry, 96n1218
Hewitt, Terry, 95n1549
Hewson, Colin, 95n112
Hey, David, 97n352
Heyman, Charles, 98n555
Heyman, Neil M., 97n1118, 99n541
Heyn, Udo, 99n492
Hicken, Mandy, 96n1187
Hicks, P. J., 97n1296
Hicks, Roger, 95n469
Hicks, S. David, 96n1644
Hicks, Tyler G., 96n1644
Hiesinger, Kathryn B., 95n983
Higbee, Joan F., 97n437
Higby, Gregory, 96n1736
Higginson, Roy, 95n334
High country names, 95n501
High definition compact disc recordings, 95n1257
High places in cyberspace, 2d ed, 99n1269
High school senior's gd to merit & other no-need funding 1996-98, 98n307
High strangeness: UFOs from 1960 through 1979, 97n632
Higham, Robin, 99n622
High-definition TV, 95n958
Higher educ dir 1995, 95n368
Higher educ money bk for women & minorities, 1997 ed, 97n302
Highfill, Philip H., Jr., 95n1411, 95n1412
Highlander Polish-English/English-Highlander Polish dict, 97n864
Highly selective dict for the extraordinarily literate, 98n1017
Highly selective thesaurus for the extraordinarily literate, 95n1066

Hiking trails, E US, 96n825
Hilbert, Vi, 96n1119
Hile, Kevin, 99n1013
Hile, Kevin S., 95n1144, 96n1172, 96n1173, 96n1174, 97n926, 97n927, 97n928, 97n929, 97n930
Hill, Anne, 95n939, 98n857
Hill, Brad, 98n1206
Hill, Carolinda E., 95n485
Hill, Carolyn N., 96n646
Hill, Dennis S., 96n1625
Hill, Errol, 95n1420
Hill, George R., 98n1190
Hill, Gerald N., 96n578
Hill, Jeremy D., 96n1625
Hill, Kathleen Thompson, 96n578
Hill, Raymond, 99n131
Hillard, James M., 96n1621
Hillerbrand, Hans J., 97n1211
Hillier, Malcolm, 96n1544
Hillila, Ruth-Esther, 99n1121
Hillstrom, Kevin, 95n236, 99n277, 99n1041
Hillstrom, Laurie Collier, 99n277, 99n1041
Hindi-English, English-Hindi practical dict, 95n1083
Hindle, Tim, 95n185
Hine, Andrea, 96n1716, 99n1457
Hine, Darlene Clark, 98n343
Hinegardner, Patricia G., 98n1505
Hinkelman, Edward G., 96n297, 96n298, 97n236, 97n245
Hinnells, John R., 97n1179
Hinrichsen, Don, 95n1756
Hipp, James W., 95n544, 96n515, 97n899
Hipple, Ted, 98n1104
Hippocrene concise Haitian Creole-English, English-Haitian Creole dict, 96n1106
Hippocrene concise Hungarian-English, English-Hungarian dict, 97n857
Hippocrene concise Sanskrit-English dict, 97n868
Hippocrene concise Yoruba-English, English-Yoruba dict, 97n879
Hippocrene practical English-Yiddish, Yiddish-English dict, expanded ed, 97n878
Hippocrene practical Fulani-English dict, 96n1103
Hippocrene standard dict Dutch-English, English-Dutch, 99n923
Hippocrene USA gd to historic Hispanic America, 95n508
Hippocrene USA gd to Irish America, 95n444
Hiro, Dilip, 97n138
Hirsch, E. D., Jr., 97n296
Hirsch, Peter, 99n438
Hirschfelder, Arlene, 95n441
His master's voice/die stimme seines herrn, 95n1258
Hischak, Thomas S., 96n1416, 98n1327
Hispanic American biog, 96n407
Hispanic American chronology, 97n335
Hispanic American genealogical sourcebk, 96n432
Hispanic databk of US cities & counties, 95n423
Hispanic firsts, 98n348
Hispanic lit criticism, 95n1242
Hispanic 100, 96n408
Hispanic resource dir, 3d ed, 97n336

Hispanic surnames & family hist, 97n356
Hispanics in Hollywood, 95n1377
Historic docs index, 1972-95, 98n682
Historic docs of 1997, 99n679
Historic festivals, 97n386
Historic railroad, 97n1446
Historic world leaders, 95n575
Historical abstracts on disc [CD-ROM], 99n545
Historical atlas of ...
- Colo., 95n527
- La., 96n440
- Mormonism, 96n1461
- NYC, 96n487
- SE Asia, 97n429
- the congresses of the Confederate States of America 1861-65, 95n526
- the Holocaust, 98n493
- the Holocaust [CD-ROM], 98n492
- the US, rev ed, 95n525
- the Vietnam War, 97n434
- WW I, 95n681

Historical dict of ...
- Afghanistan, 2d ed, 98n110
- aid & dvlpmt orgs, 97n615
- Albania, 97n113
- Algeria, 2d ed, 96n114
- Bangladesh, 2d ed, 98n460
- Bosnia & Herzegovina, 99n120
- Botswana, 3d ed, 97n94
- Brunei Darussalam, 99n482
- Bulgaria, 99n494
- Burkina Faso, 2d ed, 99n96
- Burundi, 98n455
- Catholicism, 98n1384
- Chad, 3d ed, 98n453
- Congo, 97n95
- Denmark, 99n493
- ecumenical Christianity, 96n1473
- Egypt, 96n162
- Eritrea, 99n479
- Ethiopia & Eritrea, 2d ed, 95n117
- European orgs, 96n139
- feminism, 97n735
- Gabon, 2d ed, 95n118
- Germany, 96n546
- Germany's Weimar Republic, 1918-33, 98n471
- Guam & Micronesia, 96n168
- Hinduism, 98n1392
- Honduras, 2d ed, 95n170
- Honolulu & Hawai'i, 99n459
- human rights & humanitarian orgs, 98n564
- Hungary, 98n473
- Iceland, 98n474
- India, 97n108
- intl orgs in sub-Saharan Africa, 95n755
- intl tribunals, 96n610
- Ireland, 98n475
- Latvia, 98n477
- Lebanon, 99n507
- Libya, 3d ed, 99n480
- Lithuania, 98n478
- Luxembourg, 97n119
- Mali, 3d ed, 97n99
- Mauritania, 2d ed, 97n100
- Methodism, 97n1214
- Mongolia, 97n111
- Mormonism, 95n1464
- Morocco, new ed, 98n458
- multinatl peacekeeping, 97n616
- New Zealand, 97n144
- Niger, 3d ed, 98n454
- North American environmentalism, 98n1638
- organized labor, 97n251
- Palestine, 98n488
- Papua New Guinea, 95n177
- Paris, 99n497
- Poland, 96n144
- refugee & disaster relief orgs, 95n829
- Romania, 97n120
- Russia, 99n502
- Rwanda, 95n121
- Saudi Arabia, 95n176
- school segregation & desegregation, 99n301
- Senegal, 2d ed, 95n123
- socialism, 99n695
- Spain, 97n452
- Sri Lanka, 99n484
- Stockholm, 98n483
- Stuart England, 1603-89, 97n442
- Sweden, 96n150
- Syria, 97n141
- Taiwan, 95n137
- Tanzania, 2d ed, 98n457
- Taoism, 99n1294
- terrorism, 96n597
- the Baha'i faith, 99n1272
- the British Empire, 98n466
- the civil rights movement, 98n565
- the Comoro Islands, 95n115
- the Czech state, 99n496
- the green movement, 99n1554
- the Gulf Arab States, 98n489
- the gypsies (Romanies), 99n380
- the intl food agencies, 96n1529
- the modern Olympic movement, 97n661
- the music & musicians of Finland, 99n1121
- the orthodox church, 97n1212
- the People's Republic of China: 1949-97, 99n483
- the Persian Gulf War 1990-91, 99n630
- the Philippines, 99n487
- the Republic of Croatia, 96n549
- the Republic of Guinea-Bissau, 3d ed, 98n456
- the Republic of Macedonia, 99n495
- the UK, v.1: England & the UK, 98n467
- the UK, v.2, 99n504
- the UNESCO, 98n694
- the US Marine Corps, 99n638
- the US Merchant Marine & shipping industry, 95n1794
- the US-Mexican war, 99n462
- the US Navy, 99n641

the wars of the French Revolution, 99n499
the welfare state, 99n777
the World Bank, 98n186
the world health org, 99n1421
Togo, 3d ed, 97n103
Tokyo, 98n461
trade unions, v.4, 96n264
Trinidad & Tobago, 98n484
Tunisia, 2d ed, 98n459
Uganda, 96n125
Venezuela, 2d ed, 98n142
Vietnam, 99n488
war journalism, 98n881
Warsaw, 98n479
W Sahara, 2d ed, 95n110
women's educ in the US, 99n803
WW I, 99n532
WW II France, 99n498
Zambia, 2d ed, 99n477
Historical ency of school psychology, 97n286
Historical ency of the Arab-Israeli conflict, 97n455, 99n531
Historical figures in fiction, 95n1162
Historical 1st patents, 96n1509
Historical gd to the US govt, 99n668
Historical gd to world slavery, 99n542
Historical register & dict of the US army, 95n693
Historical stats 1960-94, 1996 ed, 97n225
Historical stats of ...
    black America, 96n403
    the states of the US, 95n893
    the US, bicentennial ed [CD-ROM], 98n819
History & annot bibliog of American religious pers & newspapers, 96n1447
History & use of our Earth's chemical elements, 99n1510
History of ...
    accounting, 97n179
    agricultural sci & tech, 95n1508
    American classical music, 97n1059
    art for young people, 5th ed, 98n965
    astronomy, 98n1606
    black business in America, 99n144
    humanity, v.1, 96n568
    humanity, v.2, 97n479
    humanity, v.3, 98n507
    Israel, 99n509
    music for harpsichord or piano & orchestra, 98n1227
    natural hist, 95n1556
    pharmacy, 96n1736
    photography, v.2, 96n1019
    photography, v.3, 98n938
    physical anthropology, 98n320
    sci in the US, 97n1235
    the ancient & medieval world, 98n501
    the Holocaust, 95n588
    the mass media in the US, 99n820
    the world in the 20th century, 95n589
    women & sci, health, & tech, 2d ed, 95n904
Hitchcock, Eloise R., 97n435
Hitchens, Susan Hayes, 97n1039
HIV/AIDS & HIV/AIDS-related terminology, 97n537
HIV/AIDS info for children, 98n1560
HIV/AIDS Internet info sources & resources, 99n1469
Hixon, Don L., 95n1254
HMO/PPO dir 1996, 97n1323
Hobbes dict, 97n1165
Hobbs, Jack, 96n1545
Hobson, Archie, 97n381
Hobson, Constance Tibbs, 95n1266
Hochleitner, Rupert, 95n1731
Hochman, Jiri, 99n496
Hochman, Neil E., 99n665
Hochmuth, George J., 98n1437
Hocking, George Macdonald, 98n1569
Hodges, Daniel, 95n867
Hodges, Harriet, 96n1051
Hodges, Tony, 95n110
Hodgson, Peter J., 97n1040
Hoehner, Jane, 99n578
Hoepelman, J. P., 98n581
Hoeveler, Diane Long, 97n735
Hoff, Joan, 97n414
Hoffman, Cheryl M., 96n1131
Hoffman, Eric, 98n867
Hoffman, Frank, 95n1291
Hoffman, Joseph, 99n1463
Hoffman, Marian, 97n350, 98n359, 98n360
Hoffman, Miles, 98n1202
Hoffman, Preston, 95n664
Hoffman, Verena, 97n581
Hoffmann, David, 96n1714
Hoffmann, Frank, 96n1312, 96n1333, 98n1198
Hoffmann, Frank W., 95n987, 96n1357, 99n60
Hoffos, Signe, 96n1751
Hofling, Charles Andrew, 98n1040
Hofstede, David, 95n1347, 96n1376
Hoftijzer, J., 96n1129
Hogan, Kathleen M., 96n8
Hogan, Robert, 97n1007
Hogan, Steve, 99n757
Hogg, Ian V., 95n700, 98n633, 99n532
Hoke, John Ray, 95n1011
Holberg, Andrea, 96n311
Holden, Amanda, 95n1287, 95n1288
Holder, R. W., 97n827
Holderness-Roddam, Jane, 99n1383
Holiday symbols 1998, 99n1189
Holidays & festivals index, 96n1358
Holidays, festivals, & celebrations dict, 2d ed, 98n1263
Holidays, festivals & celebrations of the world dict, 95n1338
Holiness mss, 95n1458
Holland, Clive, 95n495
Holland, Francis Schmid, 97n739
Holland, P. D., 97n971
Holland, Stephen, 96n1234
Hollander, David Adam, 99n560
Hollander, Jolanda Leemburg-Den, 99n319
Hollander, P. Scott, 96n787
Hollander, Zander, 95n825, 98n749, 98n750
Holley, E. Jens, 96n1442
Hollies, 98n1457

Hollings, Robert L., 98n644, 98n704
Hollis, Daniel Webster, III, 96n964, 99n1253
Hollister, Benjamin, 95n225
Hollywood & the foreign touch, 97n1108
Hollywood blu-book dir 1997, 99n1221
Hollywood heroes, 96n1376
Hollywood novel, 96n1411
Hollywood Reporter bk of box office hits, rev ed, 97n1128
Hollywood rock, 95n1391
Hollywood song, 96n1275
Hollywood war films, 1937-45, 97n1123
Holm, Kirsten, 95n670
Holm, Kirsten C., 98n870
Holm, LeRoy, 99n1368
Holmberg, Erin E., 97n17
Holmes, Kim R., 98n169
Holmes, Marie S., 99n381
Holmes, Robyn, 98n1214
Holmes, Roger, 97n1259
Holocaust, 99n540, 98n502
Holocaust series, 99n533
Holonitch, Lisa, 95n1506
Holsinger, M. Paul, 96n1165
Holston, Kim R., 96n1290, 98n1292
Holtin, Alice Y., 98n1232
Holtje, Steve, 99n1168
Holtstag, Astrid, 95n517
Holtze, Sally Holmes, 97n937
Holye, Russ, 95n1776
Homa, Linda L., 95n661, 97n544
Homberger, Eric, 96n487
Hombs, Mary Ellen, 95n842, 98n799
Home educ resource gd, 3d ed, 96n317
Home health gd to poisons & antidotes, 96n1727
Home herbal, 97n1281
Home improvements & projects index 1990-93, 98n1498
Homelessness: a sourcebk, 95n841
Homelessness in America, 98n766
Homelessness in America, 1893-1992, 95n843
Homicide: a bibliog, 2d ed, 95n617
Homuth, Donald, 96n1286
Honderich, Ted, 97n1166
Hone, E. Wade, 98n365
Hong, Barbara Blanchard, 99n1121
Hong, Julie, 96n1850
Hong Kong business, 95n262
Hook, line, & sinker, 95n816
Hooks, Ed, 95n1407
Hooper, Nicholas, 97n557
Hoopes, David S., 95n246
Hoopes, Laura L. Mays, 99n1356
Hooray for heroes! 96n321
Hooton, Joy, 96n1248
Hoover, Gary, 96n191
Hoover, Herbert T., 95n428, 95n429
Hoover's billion dollar dir, 98n159
Hoover's co & industry database on CD-ROM [CD-ROM], 96n190
Hoover's co capsules on CD-ROM, 98n192
Hoover's co profiles on CD-ROM [CD-ROM], 98n193
Hoover's dir of human resources executives 1996, 97n255
Hoover's global 250, 98n202
Hoover's gd to …
   computer cos, 96n1773
   media cos, 98n859
   private cos 1994-95, 95n192
Hoover's hndbk of ...
   American business 1995, 96n191
   American business 1998, 99n169
   emerging cos 1997, 98n173
   emerging cos 1998, 99n170
   private cos 1997, 98n164
   private cos 1998, 99n171
   world business 1995-96, 3d ed, 96n201
   world business 1998, 99n222
Hoover's hndbks index 1997, 98n168
Hoover's hndbks index 1998, 99n172
Hoover's masterlist of …
   America's top 2,500 employers, 96n192
   major intl cos 1998-99, 99n201
   major Latin American cos 1996-97, 98n211
   major US cos 1996-97, 97n166
Hopi pottery symbols, 96n1015
Hopkins, Bruce R., 96n579
Hopkins, Mariane S., 96n1355
Hopkinson, Barbara, 98n12, 98n13
Hordeski, Michael F., 96n1760
Horn, Barbara Lee, 99n1248
Horn Bk gd to children's & YA bks, v.7, no.2, 98n1078
Horn, Delton T., 98n1487
Horn, Elizabeth L., 99n1362
Horn, Marguerite E., 95n160
Horne, Aaron, 97n1041
Horne, Alan, 96n1055
Horning, S. E., 96n253
Hornsby, Alton, Jr., 95n408
Horowitz, Amy, 98n788
Horror & sci fiction films 4, 98n1300
Horror in silent films, 96n1391
Horse companion, 99n1383
Horse dict, 96n1555
Horse owner's veterinary hndbk, 2d ed, 99n1354
Horton, Carrell Peterson, 96n403
Horton, Tara A., 98n868
Horwitz, Barbara J., 98n1144
Horwood, Jane, 98n1051, 99n941
Hosking, David, 98n1461, 98n1470
Hospice & palliative care, 98n1522
Hostelling N America, 1997, 98n403
Hostelling USA, 1996, 97n389
Hostels USA, 99n431
Hostetter, Edwin C., 97n1187
Hot links: lit links for the middle school curriculum, 99n1001
Houaiss, Antonio, 95n1092
Houck, Susan, 98n574
Houdek, Frank G., 96n593
Houfe, Simon, 98n944
Hough, Penelope R. O., 95n171
Hough, Samuel J., 95n171
Houghton Mifflin dict of geography, 98n395

Houlahan, Micheal, 99n1138
House plant ency, 98n1433
Household chemicals & emergency first aid, 95n1650
Household hints & tips, 98n180
Houseplant ency, 95n1532
Houston, James E., 96n318, 96n629
Houze, Herbert, 96n1009
Hovey, Harold A., 98n817
Hovey, Kendra A., 98n817
How much can I make? 98n174
How products are made, 95n237
How products are made, v.3, 99n189
How the new tech works, 99n1484
How to ...
    be a perfect stranger, 98n1362
    be a perfect stranger, v.2, 98n1363
    find chemical info, 3d ed, 99n1511
    find co intelligence in state docs, 15th ed, 96n202
    find info about divisions, subsidiaries & products, 5th ed, 96n203
    find info about foreign firms, 6th ed, 96n204
    find info about private cos, 6th ed, 96n205
    locate anyone who is or has been in the military, rev ed, 96n688
    research Congress, 97n585
    research the presidency, 97n586
    write & publish a scientific paper, 4th ed, 95n941
Howard, Carol, 97n982, 98n1149
Howard, Dale E., 96n831
Howard, Joyce M., 98n1418
Howard Keel: a bio-bibliog, 97n1078
Howard, N. Jill, 97n959
Howarth, Sarah, 96n553
Howe-Grant, Mary, 99n1503
Howell, Steve N. G., 96n1615
Howes, Keith, 95n858
Howes, Kelly King, 96n1155
Howland, Harris, 96n1572
Howlett, Colin, 96n1127, 97n866
Howsam, Leslie, 99n1297
Hoxie, Frederick E., 98n354
HR words you gotta know!, 96n258
Hrabovsky, Leonid, 95n1099
Hsieh, Chiao-min, 96n452
Hsieh, Jean Kan, 96n452
Hsu, Robert C., 95n273
Hubbard, Benjamin J., 98n1364
Hubbard, Monica M., 95n514
Hubbell, John T., 96n495
Hubbs, Clayton A., 99n439
Hubbs, Don, 96n317
Huber, Jeffrey T., 97n537, 99n1469
Hubin, Allen J., 95n1160
Huckleberry Finn on film, 95n1393
Hudson, Alice, 96n487
Hudson, Christopher, 99n241, 99n963
Hudson, Grace L., 98n131
Hudson, Lee, 99n757
Hudson's subscription newsletter dir, 12th ed, 96n978
Hudson's subscription newsletter dir, 13th ed, 98n76
Hudson's Washington news media contacts dir 1994, 95n935
Hudson's Washington news media contacts dir 1998, 99n823
Huellmantel, Michael B., 96n185
Huettner, Janet S., 96n884
Huffman, James L., 99n486
Huggett, Richard, 98n397
Hughes, Alex, 99n128
Hughes, Ann, 97n726
Hughes, H. G. A., 98n145
Hughes, James, 97n46
Hughes, Marija Matich, 95n1694
Hullfish, Lori, 95n1676
Hulse, David Allen, 95n789, 96n1121
Human choice & climate change, 99n1563
Human dvlpmt report 1994, 95n93
Human environments, 96n1797
Human gene mapping 1994, 96n1656
Human nutrition 1990-Sept 1994 [CD-ROM], 95n1643
Human resources yrbk 1996/97, 98n224
Human rights bibliog, 95n630
Human rights on CD-ROM, 2d ed [CD-ROM], 96n609
Human rights orgs & pers dir 1993, 95n629
Human sexuality, 95n872
Humanities: a selective gd to info sources, 4th ed, 95n921
Humanities abstracts full text [CD-ROM], 98n845
Humanities index, April 1995 to Mar 1996, 98n846
Humble, Malcolm, 99n1093
Humling, Virginia, 97n1215
Humm, Maggie, 96n948
Humor in British lit, from the Middle Ages to the Restoration, 98n1150
Humor in 18th- & 19th-century British lit, 99n1060
Humorous quotations, 96n93
Humphrey, Paul, 96n499
Hungary, 99n131
Hunt, Caroline C., 97n936, 98n1089
Hunt, Garry E., 95n1722
Hunt, Kimberly N., 99n210
Hunt, Thomas C., 95n351, 97n301
Hunter, Brian, 96n102
Hunter, C. Stuart, 95n1222
Hunter, Erica C. D., 95n571
Hunter, John, 96n1082
Hupchick, Dennis P., 97n446
Hupper, William G., 95n1451, 99n1273
Hurh, Won Moo, 99n374
Hurrelmann, Klaus, 98n1518
Hurricanes, 99n1529
Hurt, C. D., 95n1481
Hurt, Mary Ellen, 95n1508
Hurt, R. Douglas, 95n1508
Husband, Janet G., 99n1029
Husband, Jonathan F., 99n1029
Husen, Torsten, 95n337
Husfloen, Kyle, 98n892, 98n894, 98n927, 99n840
Husni, Samir A., 98n882
Huso, Deborah R., 97n67
Hussar, William J., 99n299
Hussey, Mark, 96n1221
Hussey, R., 96n210

Hutcheson, Polly, 97n304
Hutchings, Jonathan F., 99n1403, 99n1404
Hutchings, Noel, 98n1332
Hutchings, Raymond, 97n113
Hutchinson dict of ...
    ancient & medieval warfare, 99n534
    ideas, 95n56
    world hist, 95n581
Hutchinson gd to the world, 3d ed, 99n86
Hutchison, Kevin Don, 95n684, 96n563
Huttner, Harry J. M., 96n99
Huxford, Bob, 98n896, 98n905
Huxford, Sharon, 98n896, 98n905
Huxford's old bk value gd, 8th ed, 97n776
HVAC design data sourcebk, 95n1641
Hyam, R., 96n1563
Hyamson, Albert M., 95n28
Hyatt, Lesley Anne, 99n1025
Hyatt, Wesley, 99n1212
Hyland, Pat, 96n519
Hyman, Paula E., 99n394
Hyman, Robin, 96n94
Hymnology, 98n1246
Hymntune index & related hymn materials, 99n1178

Ibelgaufts, Horst, 96n1558
IBM dict of computing, 95n1695
IBM mainframe programmer's desk ref, 95n1692
Iceland, rev ed, 97n118
Icons of architecture, 99n877
IDEA: intl dir of educl audiovisuals [CD-ROM], 98n311
Identification gd to the ant genera of the world, 95n1590
Identities & issues in lit, 98n1070
Idiom savant: slang as it is slung, 98n1014
Idrogo, Curt, 98n327
Igbo-English dict, 99n932
Iger, Arthur L., 99n1139
Ilko, John "Jake" A., Jr., 97n343
Illiano, Antonio, 95n1233, 95n1234
Illingworth, Valerie, 95n1721
Illinois hist, 96n492
Illustrated almanac of sci, tech, & inventions, 99n1306
Illustrated bk of questions & answers, 97n56
Illustrated bk of world rankings, rev ed, 98n813
Illustrated computer dict for young people, 96n1763
Illustrated dict for building construction, 95n1605
Illustrated dict of ...
    architecture, 99n880
    Bible life & times, 99n1275
    constitutional concepts, 97n594
    dermatologic syndromes, 96n1728
    electronics, 6th ed, 95n1613
    electronics, 7th ed, 98n1488
    little-known words from literary classics, 96n1148
    mythology, 99n1186
    sci, rev ed, 96n1497
    symbols in E & W art, 96n1031
Illustrated discography of surf music, 1961-65, 3d ed, 96n1332
Illustrated ency of ...
    active new religions sects & cults, rev ed, 99n1264
    billiards, 95n813
    camellias, 99n1364
    costume & fashion from 1066 to the present, rev ed, 95n986
    divination, 98n714
    essential oils, 97n1346
    handguns, 97n782
    healing remedies, 99n1460
    musical instruments, 97n1052
    Victoriana, 96n1016
    world hist, 98n503
    world religions, 98n1356
Illustrated glossary of early S architecture & landscape, 95n1016
Illustrated glossary of protoctista, 95n1536
Illustrated gd to the Bible, 96n1459
Illustrated petroleum ref dict, 4th ed, 95n1745
Illustrated sci ency, 98n1405
Illustrated survey of orchid genera, 96n1578
Illustrated who's who of Hollywood directors, v.1, 96n1367
Illustration index 8, 1992-96, 99n876
Ilson, Robert, 99n913
Images in the dark: an ency of gay & lesbian film & video, 95n1374
Imber, Jane Hunter, 99n1002
Immigrant experience in American fiction, 96n1206
Immigrants in the US in fiction, 95n1117
Immigration questions & answers, rev ed, 98n702
Immunization resource gd, 2d ed, 97n1339
Impact of Napoleon, 1800-15, 98n469
Impara, James C., 95n787
Imperato, Pascal James, 97n99
Imperial War Museum film catalog, v.1, 96n557
Importers manual USA, 1995-96 ed, 96n298
Importers manual USA & the dict of intl trade, 1996-97 ed [CD-ROM], 97n274
Imports & exports of the Republic of China on Taiwan 1993, 95n271
In search of ...
    your Canadian roots, 2d ed, 95n453
    your European roots, 2d ed, 95n454
    your German roots, 3d ed, 95n455
In their footsteps, 95n506
Ince, Martin, 98n1607
Inchon landing, Korea, 1950, 95n683
Independent study catalog, 6th ed, 97n290
Index & dir of industry standards, 95n1504
Index digest of state constitutions, 95n745
Index of ...
    American per verse: 1994, 98n1185
    American per verse 1995, 98n1142
    American per verse 1996, 99n1100
    American watercolor exhibitions 1900-45, 95n1022
    economic freedom, 1997, 98n169
    English literary mss, v.4, pt.3, 95n1202
    garden plants, 95n1530
    majors & graduate degrees 1998, 99n326
    songs on children's recordings, 2d ed, 95n1264

Index to ...
American Jewish Histl Quarterly/American Jewish Hist: vs.51-80, 97n347
American photographic collections, 3d ed, 97n789
AV producers & distrs 1997, 10th ed, 98n312
black pers 1995, 98n345
black pers 1997, 99n377
dance pers: 1995, 98n1270
docs of the Natl Security Council, 96n774
English per lit on the O.T. & ancient Near Eastern studies, v.6, 95n1451
English per lit on the O.T. & ancient Near Eastern studies, v.7, 99n1273
fairy tales, 1987-92, 95n1316
histl fiction for children & young people, 96n1179
how to do it info, 1994 suppl, 96n1014
intl public opinion, 1996-97, 99n81
law school theses & dissertations, 96n570
legal citations & abbrevs, 2d ed, 95n593
Marquis who's who pubs 1998, 99n25
poetry for children & young people 1988-92, 95n1152
proceedings of the economic & social council, 96n771
proceedings of the General Assembly: 47th session, 95n756
proceedings of the Security Council, 48th yr, 95n757
pubns of the American Jewish Histl Society, vs.21-50, 95n449
resolutions of the security council, 1946-91, 95n758
short & feature film reviews in the Moving Picture World, 96n1413
Spanish lang short stories in anthologies, 95n1241
the biblical refs, parallels, & allusions in the poetry & prose of John Milton, 95n1214
the Chemical Weapons Convention, 95n699
the House of Commons parliamentary papers on CD-ROM [CD-ROM], 99n571
the Roll of Honor, 96n434
the Wilson authors series, 98n1075
the Wilson bktalking series, 98n1083
translated short fiction by Latin American women in English lang anthologies, 98n1179
US marriage record, 1691-1850 [CD-ROM], 99n405
women's studies anthologies, 98n841
Indexing bks, 95n657
India, rev ed, 96n131
India & S Asia, 3d ed, 99n104
India hndbk, 99n243
Indian slavery, labor, evangelization, & captivity in the Americas, 99n382
Indian social & economic dvlpmt 1993, 96n243
Indian terms of the Americas, 95n436
Indiana: atlas of histl county boundaries, 98n379
Indiana companion to traditional Chinese lit, v.2, 99n1090
Indiana factbk 1998-99, 5th ed, 99n92
Indians of N & S America, 2d suppl, 99n385
Indicators of school quality, 99n298
Indigenous langs of the Americas, 97n810
Indigenous lit of Oceania, 96n1260
Indo-Australian Agaoninae (pollinators of figs), 96n1628
Indonesia, 96n134

Indoor garden bk, 95n1526
Indoor pollution, 99n1565
Industrial commodity stats yrbk 1994, 97n195
Industrial commodity stats yrbk 1995, 29th ed, 99n223
Industrial Relations Center, University of Hawaii at Manoa, 96n257
Informatics glossary, 95n1697
Informatics hndbk, 98n1593
Information graphics, 97n1370
Information industry dir, 1994, 95n1690
Information industry dir 1998, 18th ed, 99n602
Information please almanac, atlas, & yrbk, 1996, 49th ed, 97n6
Information please women's sourcebk, 1995, 96n951
Information sci abstracts, v.29, no.12, 96n619
Information sourcebk of herbal medicine, 96n1714
Information sources 98, 99n202
Information sources in ...
    architecture & construction, 2d ed, 97n1299
    engineering, 3d ed, 97n1296
    environmental protection, 98n1643
    finance & banking, 97n191
    grey lit, 3d ed, 95n10
    law, 2d ed, 98n533
    official pubns, 98n61
    physics, 3d ed, 95n1737
    sci & tech, 2d ed, 95n1481
    urban & regional planning, 96n928
Information-finding & the research process, 95n769
Ingamells, John, 98n476
Ingardia, Richard, 95n1437
Ingham, John N., 95n181
Ingold, Tim, 95n392
Ingraham, Holly, 98n377
Ingraham, Mary I., 99n1143
Ingram, Caroline, 96n460
Inhaber, Herbert, 99n363
Injury prevention for the elderly, 96n844
Injury prevention for young children, 97n710
Inlander, Charles B., 98n1539
Inn places 1994, 95n857
Innes, Brian, 96n1348
Innes, Clive, 96n1590
Inside gd to American nursing homes, 1988-99 ed, 99n1475
Inside Sports Mag college basketball, 2d ed, 98n739
Inside Sports Mag golf, 98n748
Inside Sports Mag hockey, 1997 ed, 98n749
Inside Sports world series factbk, 97n645
Insider's gd to ...
    graduate programs in clinical psychology, 1994/95 ed, 95n786
    law firms, 2d ed, 96n582
    law firms 1993-94, 95n608
    mental health resources online, 98n1515
INSPEC list of jls & other serial sources 1996/7, 97n1306
Instant natl locator gd, 3d ed, 98n53
Instat: intl stats sources, 97n716
Institute for Biotechnology Information, 96n1733
Instruments of sci, 99n1312

Insurance stats yrbk 1983-90, 95n239
Integrated curriculum: bks for reluctant readers, grades 2-5, 2d ed, 99n1006
Integrated pest mgmt glossary, 95n1513
Intellectual freedom manual, 5th ed, 97n542
Interactive sci ency [CD-ROM], 99n1313
Interdisciplinary undergraduate programs, 2d ed, 98n289
Interinstitutional dir: European Union, 96n754
Interior design sourcebk, 99n858
Interlibrary loan policies dir, 5th ed, 96n641
International advertising & mktg info sources, 96n299
International African Institute, 96n111
International Atomic Energy Agency, 95n1755
International authors & writers who's who, 15th ed, 99n956
International bibliog of ...
   business hist, 98n149
   meteorology, 95n1727
   theatre, 97n1148
International biogl dict of computer pioneers, 96n1758
International biogl dir of natl archivists, documentalists, & librarians, 98n574
International bk trade dir 1997, 98n602
International bks in print 1997, 98n12, 98n13
International Boundaries Research Unit, 96n455
International business & trade dirs, 96n228
International business & trade dir, 2d ed, 99n141
International business info, 95n255, 99n228
International children's Bible dict, 98n1376
International conflict, 98n696
International dict of ...
   broadcasting & film, 96n984
   desserts, pastries, & confections, 96n1523
   films & filmmakers, 2d ed, v.5, 95n1370
   food & nutrition, 95n1514
   historic places, v.1, 96n467
   historic places, v.2, 96n468
   historic places, v.3, 96n469
   historic places, v.4, 97n468
   historic places, v.5, 97n469
   modern dance, 99n1201
   psychology, 2d ed, 97n630
   theatre, v.2, 95n1421
   theatre, v.3: actors, directors, & designers, 97n1149
   univ hists, 99n315
International direct investment stats yrbk 1993, 95n250
International dir of ...
   African studies research, 3d ed, 96n111
   arts, 99n811
   arts 1993/94, 95n1006
   business historians, 95n194
   business info sources & servs 1996, 2d ed, 97n213
   co hists, v.8, 95n251
   co hists, v.9, 96n236
   co hists, v.10, 96n237
   co hists, v.11, 96n238
   co hists, v.12, 97n214
   co hists, v.13, 97n215
   co hists, v.14, 97n216
   co hists, v.16, 99n203
   co hists, v.17, 99n204
   co hists, v.18, 99n205
   co hists, v.19, 99n206
   co hists, v.20, 99n207
   co hists, v.21, 99n208
   consumer brands & their owners, 98n200
   govt 1995, 2d ed, 96n707
   Indonesianists, 2d ed, 96n133
   little mags & small prs, 29th ed, 95n669
   philosophy & philosophers 1993-94, 95n1431
   philosophy & philosophers 1997-98, 10th ed, 98n1342
   primatology, 95n1593
   primatology, 3d ed, 98n1471
   Renaissance & Reformation assns (1993), 95n553
   serials specialists, 96n655
International educ quotations ency, 97n289
International electric power ency 1998, 99n1406
International encyclopaedic dict of numismatics, 98n909
International ency of ...
   dance, 99n1202
   educ, 2d ed, 95n337
   horse breeds, 97n1291
   info & lib sci, 98n571
   public policy & admin, 99n702
   secret societies & fraternal orders, 98n764
   sexuality, 98n797
   teaching & teacher educ, 2d ed, 97n298
   the sociology of edu, 98n268
   violin-keyboard sonatas & composer biogs, 2d ed, 97n1043
International ethics, 99n698
International film, TV & video acronyms, 95n1359
International financial stats locator, 96n230
International fndn dir 1994, 95n864
International fndn dir 1996, 7th ed, 97n696
International fndn dir 1998, 8th ed, 99n769
International gd to lit on film, 95n1379
International gd to securities market indices, 98n175
International hndbk of ...
   environmental sociology, 99n1564
   funeral customs, 99n1270
   local & regional govt, 95n709
   medical educ, 95n1667
   public health, 98n1518
   research & dvlpmt of giftedness & talent, 95n352
International hndbk on ...
   gender roles, 95n871
   servs for the elderly, 96n851
   social work educ, 97n704
International histl stats: Africa, Asia, & Oceania, 1750-1988, 96n917
International holidays, 96n1361
International index to music pers 1997:2 [CD-ROM], 98n1208
International info documents, 98n693
International instruments of the UN, 99n696
International intellectual property protection for computer software, 96n638
International investing wth ADRs, 95n222
International labor & employment laws, v.1, 99n564
International league, 99n724
International literary market place 1995, 95n671
International mktg data & stats 1994, 95n252

International mktg data & stats 1998, 99n224
International mktg forecasts, 99n225
International motion picture almanac, 1996, 67th ed, 97n770
International multimedia yrbk 1995-96, 96n1751
International multimedia yrbk 1995-96 on CD-ROM [CD-ROM], 96n1752
International mycological dir, 3d ed, 96n1581
International petroleum ency 1994, 95n1744
International petroleum ency 1998, 99n1399
International petroleum research dir 1994, 95n1747
International policy insts around the Pacific Rim, 99n697
International relations, 5th ed, 97n620
International relations research dir, 97n619
International research centers dir 1996-97, 8th ed, 96n55
International Rugby Information Centre, 96n830
International satellite dir, 1995, 10th ed, 96n1780
International satellite dir 1998, 99n1497
International schools dir, 1993/1994 ed, 95n381
International standards desk ref, 98n206
International student hndbk of US colleges 1998, 99n327
International student's gd to Mexican univs, 97n310
International subscription agents, 6th ed, 95n648
International tax summaries, 1998, 99n226
International TV & video almanac, 1996, 41st ed, 97n771
International thesaurus of refugee terminology, 2d ed, 97n705
International trade fairs & conferences dir 1995, 19th ed, 96n300
International trade sources, 98n199
International trade stats yrbk, 1995, 98n252
International treaties on intellectual property, 2d ed, 98n567
International vital records hndbk, 3d ed, 95n460
International Washington almanac, 1994, 95n760
International who's who 1994-95, 95n29
International who's who in music 1998/99, v.2, 2d ed, 99n1161
International who's who in music & musicians dir, 14th ed, 96n1267
International who's who in music, v.2: popular music, 97n1063
International who's who in poetry & poets' ency, 7th ed, 95n1246
International who's who in poetry & poets' ency 1997, 8th ed, 99n1101
International who's who of women, 99n26
International wildlife trade, 96n1599
International yr bk 1997, 98n44
International yrbk of industrial stats 1996, 97n196
International yrbk of industrial stats 1997, 98n194
Internet: an introductory gd for UN orgs, 96n1783
Internet access providers, 95n1708
Internet & lib & info servs, 98n582
Internet compendium: subject gds to health & sci resources, 96n1774
Internet compendium: subject gds to humanities resources, 96n100
Internet compendium: subject gds to social scis, bus, & law resources, 96n101
Internet complete ref, 2d ed, 98n1594
Internet dir, 95n1702
Internet gd for the legal researcher, 2d ed, 98n535

Internet resource dir for K-12 teachers & librarians, 94/95 ed, 95n1706
Internet resource dir for K-12 teachers & librarians, 96/97 ed, 98n1590
Internet resource dir for K-12 teachers & librarians, 98/99 ed, 99n307
Internet resources & servs for intl business, 99n209
Internet searcher's hndbk, 98n1595
Internet tools of the profession, 2d ed, 98n1586
Internet white pages 1994, 95n1705
Internet World's on Internet 94, 95n1703
Internet yellow pages, 2d ed, 96n1775
Internet-Plus dir of express lib servs, 99n596
Internship bible, 1998 ed, 99n270
Internships 1994, 95n299
Interstate exit authority, 99n432
Introducing Canada, 99n489
Introduction to ref sources in the health scis, 3d ed, 95n1644
Introduction to US govt info sources, 5th ed, 97n53
Invisible wings: an annot bibliog on blacks in aviation, 1916-93, 95n1788
Ionescu, Serban N., 95n30
Iordanskaja, Lidija, 97n867
Iowa state constitution, 99n568
Iraq, 2d ed, 96n135
Ireland, 96n481
Ireland: a dir 1998, 32d ed, 99n133
Ireland: an ency for the bewildered, 96n142
Iris Murdoch: a descriptive primary & annot secondary bibliog, 95n1215
Irish almanac & yrbk of facts 1997, 98n134
Irish bed & breakfast bk, 96n482
Irish experience in NYC, 97n346
Irish playwrights, 1880-1995, 98n1175
Irish-American landmarks, 96n422
Irons-Georges, Tracy, 99n1443
Irvine, Sherry, 95n459
Irving Berlin, 99n1134
Irwin, Robert, 99n489
ISA gd to measurement conversions, 95n1495
ISA hndbk of measurement equations & tables, 95n1500
Isaac Albeniz, 99n1129
Isaac Asimov: an annot bibliog of the Asimov collection at Boston Univ, 97n968
Isaacs, Howard M., 99n1331
Isaacs, Katherine M., 99n900
Isaacs, Robert H., 99n1292
Isaacs, Ronald H., 95n1476, 96n1479
Isely, Duane, 96n1564
Islam, Hinduism, & Judaism in South Africa, 98n1345
Islam in China, 95n1474
Islamic desk ref, 95n174
Islamic economics & finance, 97n232
Isler, Charlotte, 99n1442
Israel & the Jewish world, 1948-93, 96n552
Israel & the W Bank & Gaza Strip, 2d ed, 96n163
Israel, Elaine, 99n6
Israel, Fred L., 95n741, 98n661
Israel, Guy, 95n1719
Israeli, Raphael, 95n1474

Israeli secret servs, 98n689
ISS dir of overseas schools, 1994-95 ed, 96n372
Isserman, Maurice, 95n841
Issue briefs: 1997 annual ed, 99n1432
Italian film: a who's who, 95n1365
Italian horror films of the 1960s, 99n1205
Italian paintings before 1600 in the Art Inst of Chicago, 95n1020
Italian women writers, 95n1235
Italy, 96n143, 97n395
ITP Nelson Canadian dict of the English lang, 98n1013
It's only rock 'n' roll: the ultimate gd to the Rolling Stones, 98n1241
Itzaj Maya-Spanish-English dict, 98n1040
IUCN-The World Conservation Union, 95n1564
Ivens, Stephen H., 97n817
IVP Bible background commentary: Genesis-Deuteronomy, 98n1379
Iwu, Maurice M., 95n1546
Izod, Irene, 98n12, 98n13

J. Sheridan Le Fanu, 96n1256
Jackson, Frank, 97n1292
Jackson, Guida M., 95n1322, 97n889
Jackson, J. R. de J., 95n1247
Jackson, Keith, 97n144
Jackson, Kenneth T., 95n36, 96n36, 96n107, 99n35
Jackson, Michael, 99n1333
Jackson, Pat, 97n1419
Jackson, Paul, 97n1440, 99n1155, 99n1575
Jackson, Richard, 98n696
Jackson, Richard H., 96n1461
Jackson, Rick, 95n1292
Jacob, Merle, 97n946
Jacobs, Arthur, 97n1028
Jacobs, Dale W., 95n66
Jacobs, Eva E., 98n230
Jacobs, Jennifer, 97n1345
Jacobs, Karen, 99n1423
Jacobs, Nancy R., 98n754, 98n1559
Jacobs, Timothy, 96n795
Jacobsen, Lawrence, 95n1593, 98n1471
Jacobson, Arthur Lee, 97n1283
Jacobson, Jeffrey, 95n1700
Jacobson, Ronald L., 96n987
Jacobstein, J. Myron, 95n601
Jacques Derrida (II), 96n956
Jacquet-Francillon, Vincent, 97n1037
Jaegly, Peggy J., 98n1115
Jaffe, Jerome H., 97n707
Jakubiak, Joyce, 96n274, 97n262
James A. Garfield, 98n645
James A. Michener, 96n1213
James A. Michener: a bibliog, 97n973
James, Bill, 99n715
James, David, 96n1020
James, Dick, 95n1766
James, Elizabeth, 99n70
James, Ewart, 99n908

James Joyce A to Z, 97n1009
James, Laylin K., 95n1715
James Madison & the American nation 1751-1836, 96n507
James, Peter D., 96n653
James, W. J., 95n1766
Jandora, John Walter, 98n609
Jane Addams papers, 97n706
Jane Austen ency, 99n1070
Jane's aero-engines, 97n1298
Jane's air traffic control 1996-97, 3d ed, 97n1439
Jane's aircraft upgrades, 1996-97, 4th ed, 97n572
Jane's air-launched weapons image lib [CD-ROM], 98n632
Jane's airports & handling agents, 1995-96, 96n1881
Jane's all the world's aircraft 1996-97, 87th ed, 97n1440
Jane's all the world's aircraft 1998-99, 89th ed, 99n1575
Jane's ammunition hndbk 1996-97, 5th ed, 98n633
Jane's armour & artillery 1995-96, 16th ed, 97n575
Jane's avionics 1996-97, 15th ed, 97n1441
Jane's electro-optic systems 1996-97, 2d ed, 98n619
Jane's fighting ships 1994-95, 95n698
Jane's fighting ships 1996-97, 99th ed, 97n573
Jane's helicopter markets & systems, 97n1442
Jane's infantry weapons 1994-95, 95n700
Jane's infantry weapons 1998-99, 24th ed, 99n645
Jane's intl ABC aerospace dir 1996, 46th ed, 97n217
Jane's intl defence dir 1997, 97n218
Janes, Joseph, 96n100, 96n101, 96n1774, 98n1595
Jane's land-based air defense 1998-99, 11th ed, 99n646
Jane's major warships 1997, 99n640
Jane's merchant ships 1998-99, 3d ed, 99n1578
Janes, Michael, 95n1078
Jane's military aircraft image lib [CD-ROM], 98n623
Jane's military communications 1993-94, 95n694
Janes military communications, 1997-98, 98n618
Jane's NBC protection equipment 1996-97, 9th ed, 97n570
Jane's police & security equipment 1996-97, 9th ed, 98n555
Janes, Robert W., 96n656
Jane's sentinel: Central America & the Caribbean security assessment, 1996 ed, 97n129
Jane's simulation & training systems 1996-97, 9th ed, 98n1573
Jane's space dir 1996-97, 12th ed, 97n1301
Jane's tank & combat vehicle recognition gd, 97n576
Jane's urban transport systems 1994-95, 95n1792
Jane's warship recognition gd, 97n577
Jane's warships image lib [CD-ROM], 98n627
Jane's world railways, 36th ed, 96n1887
Janik, Vicki K., 99n951
Jankowski, Bernard, 97n691
Jankowski, Katherine, 96n262
Jankowski, Katherine E., 96n869, 97n686, 99n760, 99n763, 99n764
Janoulis, Brenda H., 99n1449, 99n1476
Janoulis, Jason F., 99n1449, 99n1476
Janson, Anthony F., 98n965
Janson, H. W., 98n965
Jantra, Ingrid, 98n1433
Japan: exploring your options, 96n373
Japan & the Japanese, 97n110
Japan & the Pacific Rim, 4th ed, 99n102

Japan business: the portable ency for doing business with Japan, 95n263
Japan dir of professional assns, 3d ed, 96n244
Japan ency, 97n109
Japan trade dir 1997-98, 99n244
Japanese automobile industry: an annot bibliog, 95n1790
Japanese business law in W languages, 99n546
Japanese fiction writers since WW II, 99n1096
Japanese filmography, 97n1117
Japanese hist & culture from ancient to modern times, 2d ed, 96n537
Japanese psycholinguistics, 96n1059
Japanese sci fiction, fantasy & horror films, 95n1382
Japanese studies in Canada: the 1990s, 98n115
Japanese women writers: a bio-critical sourcebk, 95n1236
Japanese-English, English-Japanese concise dict, 95n1084
Jarrell, Howard R., 95n193
Jarvis, Helen, 99n105
Jason, Philip K., 99n1102
Jaszczak, Sandra, 97n701, 99n50
Jawed, Mohammed Jawed, 97n81
Jay, Antony, 98n641
Jayawardene, S. A., 97n1227
Jazz: the rough gd, 97n1076
Jazz & blues lover's gd to the US, updated ed, 96n1321
Jazz CD listener's gd, 99n1165
Jazz discography, 99n1167
Jazz discography, v.9, 96n1326
Jazz research & performance materials, 2d ed, 96n1327
Jean Sibelius: a gd to research, 99n1135
Jefferis, David, 98n1645
Jefferson-Brown, Michael, 96n1572
Jefferson's welding ency, 18th ed, 98n1491
Jeffrey, Nan, 95n505
Jehovah's Witness lit, 95n1459
Jenkins, Carol A., 97n142
Jenkins, Esther C., 97n142
Jenkins, Everett, Jr., 97n426, 99n505
Jenkins, Fred W., 97n461
Jenkins, Hugh, 96n1718
Jenkins, Mark, 96n1729
Jensen, Gregory C., 96n1622
Jentleson, Bruce W., 98n660
Jerath, Bal K., 95n617
Jerath, Rajinder, 95n617
Jeremy, David J., 95n194, 95n282
Jerry Lewis films, 96n1397
Jerusalem Center for Public Affairs, staff of, 96n712
Jessamyn West: a descriptive & annot bibliog, 99n1056
Jessup, John E., 95n688, 99n628
Jesus & his world, 97n1213
Jewell, Terri L., 95n920
Jewish alcoholism & drug addiction, 95n880
Jewish ency of moral & ethical issues, 95n1475
Jewish info source bk, 95n1476
"Jewish question" in German-speaking countries, 1848-1914, 96n425
Jewish roots in Poland, 99n400
Jewish sports legends, 2d ed, 98n719
Jewish women in America, 99n394

Jewish writers of Latin America, 98n1180
Jewish yr bk 1997, 98n1395
Jews & Europe, 96n424
Jezic, Diane Peacock, 95n1267
Jimenez, Alfredo, 95n421
JIST's electronic enhanced dict of occupational titles, 2d ed [CD-ROM], 98n216
JIST's electronic gd for occupational exploration [CD-ROM], 96n275
JIST's electronic occupational outlook hndbk, 2d ed [CD-ROM], 98n231
JIST's multimedia occupational outlook hndbk, 2d ed [CD-ROM], 98n232
Joan Baez: a bio-bibliog, 97n1074
Joan Fontaine: a bio-bibliog, 95n1341
Joan Robinson: a bio-bibliog, 97n150
Job hotlines USA, 1994-95 ed, 95n300
Job hunter's sourcebk, 3d ed, 98n233
Job hunter's yellow pages, 1994-95 ed, 95n301
Job seeker's gd to socially responsible cos, 96n262
Job sharing: an annot bibliog, 95n293
JobBank gd to employment servs 1998-99, 98n220
Job-Hunting on the Internet, 98n222
Jobs for people over 50, 96n276
Joel Whitburn presents Billboard's top 10 chart 1958-95, 96n1319
Joel Whitburn's pop hits 1940-54, 96n1313
Joel Whitburn's rock tracks, 96n1337
Joel Whitburn's top country singles 1944-93, 95n1299
Joel Whitburn's top pop albums 1955-96, 97n1070
Joel Whitburn's top pop singles CD gd 1955-79, 96n1316
Joel Whitburn's top pop singles 1955-93, 96n1314
Joel Whitburn's top R&B singles 1942-1995, 97n1079
Joes, Anthony James, 98n620
Joffe, George, 96n115
Johann Baptist Cramer (1771-1858): a thematic cat of his works, 95n1269
Johannes Brahms: an annot bibliog of the lit from 1982 to 1996, 99n1143
Johansen, Bruce E., 98n350
Johansen, Bruce Elliott, 99n388
John Adams: a bibliog, 95n533
John Alden Carpenter: a bio-bibliog, 95n1270
John, Catherine Rachel, 97n1174
John Coltrane, 96n1324
John F. Kennedy, 96n491
John Holmes Library, staff of, 96n748
John Huston a gd to refs & resources, 99n1207
John Max Wulfing collection in Washington Univ, v.3: Roman imperial coins...., 97n779
John Metcalf papers, 97n1005
John Steinbeck, 96n1216
John Steinbeck: an annot gd to biogl sources, 97n975
John Updike: a bibliog, 1967-93, 95n1196
Johnen, M., 96n1894
Johnny Cash discography, 1984-93, 95n1301
Johnny Cash record catalog, 96n1317
Johns Hopkins atlas of human functional anatomy, 99n1415
Johns Hopkins gd to literary theory & criticism, 95n1104
Johns, Robert L., 95n412, 96n404

Johnsen, Ferris, 96n62
Johnson, Anne E., 97n359, 97n360
Johnson, Arthur, 98n725
Johnson, Bryan T., 98n169
Johnson, Chris, 97n1441
Johnson, Curt, 96n959
Johnson, Dale A., 97n1170
Johnson, Dana, 98n929
Johnson, Donald Leslie, 98n972
Johnson, Ellen S., 95n1268
Johnson, George M., 96n1235, 99n1063
Johnson, Gordon, 98n113
Johnson, Hamish, 96n1240
Johnson, Hans, 98n654
Johnson, Jean E., 97n682, 98n783
Johnson, Jeffrey, 96n1277
Johnson, John R., 99n381
Johnson, Karen L., 95n848
Johnson, Lloyd, 98n729
Johnson, Michael G., 95n435
Johnson, N. Peter, 95n881
Johnson, Otto, 97n6
Johnson, Peggy, 95n665
Johnson, Richard S., 96n688, 96n837
Johnson, Robert V., 96n1722
Johnson, Salvatore, 96n820
Johnson, Samuel, 98n1020
Johnson, Steve, 96n1532
Johnson, Thomas D., 95n200, 95n201
Johnson, Tom, 97n1119
Johnson, Willis L., 96n891
Johnson, Yolanda A., 97n51
Johnston, Bernard, 95n48
Johnston, Deborah, 98n107
Johnston, Francis E., 99n1465
Johnston, Phillip M., 96n999
Johnston, Stephen, 99n1312
Johnston, Susanne L., 95n883
Johnston, William M., 98n1346
Johnston-Des Rochers, Janeen, 97n206
Joint FAO/WHO Food Standards Programme Codex Alimentarius Commission, 96n1534, 96n1535
Jolma, Dena Jones, 95n1759
Jonathan Edwards, 96n1440
Jones, Alison, 96n1343
Jones, Almut G., 98n1451
Jones, C. Lee, 95n640
Jones, Charles Edwin, 97n1205
Jones, Clyde, 96n1630
Jones, Constance, 97n702, 98n767
Jones, Daniel, 99n947, 99n948
Jones, David L., 97n1284
Jones, David R., 96n146
Jones, Dawnette, 99n1474, 99n1477
Jones, Diane Brown, 95n1189
Jones, Dolores Blythe, 95n1148, 96n661
Jones, Donald D., 97n646
Jones, Edward, 96n1214
Jones, Francine, 96n873, 98n785
Jones, H. G., 96n493
Jones, Henry Stuart, 97n853
Jones, J. Knox, Jr., 96n1630
Jones, Joy, 95n508
Jones, Marie F., 97n63
Jones, Oscar, 95n508
Jones, P. A. L., 95n1427
Jones, Peter, 99n919
Jones, Stephen, 98n1306
Jones, Tiffany M., 99n665
Jones, W. Landis, 95n1446
Jones-Wilson, Faustine C., 97n285
Jongeling, K., 96n1129
Jonsson, Lars, 95n1568
Jordan, Barbara, 96n903, 97n313
Jordan, Casper L., 95n412
Jordan, Sarah, 95n929
Jordan, William Chester, 97n471
Jorgensen, Janice, 95n324
Jorgenson, John D., 99n947, 99n948
Jose, Colin, 95n823
Joselit, David, 96n1041
Joseph Addison & Richard Steele, 96n1237
Joseph, Andrew, 98n1311
Joseph Chamberlain 1836-1914: a bibliog, 95n752
Joseph, Robert, 99n1340
Jost, Kenneth, 97n603
Jouris, David, 95n470
Journalism, 2d ed, 98n851
Journalism ethics, 99n826
Judaica Americana, 96n1480
Judaica ref sources, 2d ed, 95n448
Judaism, 98n1394
Judicial staff dir, 1997, 98n522
Jules Verne ency, 97n952
Julien, Nadia, 97n636
Julier, Guy, 95n984
Julius, Marshall, 98n1293
Junior chronicle of the 20th century, 98n498
Junior DISCovering authors [CD-ROM], 95n1145
Junior Judaica: ency Judaica for youth, rev ed, 95n450
Junior sci experiments on file, 95n1501
Junior timelines on file, 98n499
Junior Worldmark ency of the Canadian provinces, 98n119
Junior Worldmark ency of the nations, 97n79
Juniper, Tony, 99n1378
Juo, Pei-Show, 98n1439
Jurinski, James John, 99n300
Justice, Keith L., 99n12
Juvenile novels of WW II, 95n1140

K & W gd to colleges for the learning disabled, 1998 ed, 98n290
Kabdebo, Thomas, 98n45
Kadupski, Charlie, 96n805
Kaeppler, Adrienne L., 99n1120
Kagan, Jerome, 99n778
Kaganoff, Nathan M., 96n1480
Kahane, A., 97n855
Kahl, Jonathan D. W., 99n1533

Kahn, Ada P., 95n780, 99n705
Kalasky, Drew, 96n1196, 96n1265, 97n954, 97n955, 97n956, 97n957
Kalasky, Kyung Lim, 97n193
Kalat, David, 98n1294
Kaleidoscope: a multicultural bklst for grades K-8, 96n1182
Kaleidoscope: a multicultural bklist for grades K-8, 98n1087
Kalfatovic, Martin R., 95n993
Kalfatovic, Mary C., 95n1348
Kamalipour, Yahya R., 95n936
Kambarov, Nasir, 97n876
Kamiya, Taeko, 95n1086
Kamm, Antony, 98n1066
Kamp, Jim, 95n1169
Kane, Joseph Nathan, 95n102, 99n46
Kanellos, Nicholas, 97n335
Kanellos, Nicolas, 96n550, 98n348
Kanji dict, 97n860
Kanner, Barbara Penny, 99n39
Kant dict, 96n1428
Kanter, Sanford, 96n719
Kantha, Sachi Sri, 97n1409
Kaplan, Steven M., 95n606, 96n782, 97n1297, 98n157, 98n519, 99n1506
Kapon, Uriel Macias, 96n424
Kaptur, Marcy, 98n833
Karakashian, Stephen, 98n1640
Karasik, Theodore W., 98n128
Karcher, Stephen, 98n714
Kari, Daven Michael, 97n1206
Karlsten, Christopher M., 96n734
Karnbach, James, 98n1241
Karnes, Frances A., 97n299
Karney, Robyn, 96n1371, 98n1282
Karolides, Nicholas J., 99n603
Karolle, Bruce G., 95n490
Karp, Rashelle, 97n940
Karp, Rashelle S., 96n173, 96n620
Karr, Nicholas P., 99n57, 99n157
Karr, Paul, 99n431
Karr, Ronald Dale, 96n1888
Kartesz, John T., 95n1555
Kascus, Marie A., 97n521
Kaser, Michael, 95n152
Kasinec, Denise, 97n918
Kaspi, Andre, 95n539
Kassel, Richard, 99n1123
Kastenbaum, Robert, 95n781
Kastner, Mark, 95n1671
Katharine Cornell: a bio-bibliog, 95n1351
Katz, Bernard S., 97n587
Katz, Bill, 96n85, 99n72
Katz, Doris B., 95n86
Katz, Ephraim, 95n1371
Katz, Linda Sternberg, 96n85, 96n1263, 99n72
Katz, William, 96n1263
Katzner, Kenneth, 96n1124, 97n814
Kaufeld, Jennifer, 99n53
Kaufeld, John, 99n53
Kaufman, Alan S., 95n805

Kaufman, James C., 95n805
Kaufman, Kenn, 98n1460
Kaufman, Stephen A., 95n1452
Kauppila, Jean L., 96n1366
Kausler, Barry C., 97n668, 98n760
Kausler, Donald H., 97n668, 98n760
Kavanagh, Gaynor, 98n495
Kavasch, E. Barrie, 97n366
Kavass, Igor I., 95n592
Kay, Ernest, 95n32
Kaywell, Joan F., 95n1134
Kazzazi, Kerstin, 97n812
Kear, Lynn, 98n715
Kearey, Philip, 97n1401
Kearns, Patricia M., 99n641
Keay, John, 96n148
Keay, Julia, 96n148
Kee, Howard Clark, 98n1377
Keegan, John, 96n681
Keeler, Todd E., 98n649
Keeling, Richard, 98n1191
Keen, Peter G. W., 97n267, 98n242
Keenan, Jerry, 99n460
Keenan, Philip E., 99n1363
Keenan, Sheila, 98n836
Keenan, Stella, 97n525
Keene, Ann T., 95n1763
Keene, Chuck, 99n1392
Keeping score: film & TV music, 1988-97, 99n1140
Kehde, Ned, 96n78, 96n90
Kehler, Dorothea, 99n972
Kehoe, Cynthia A., 99n596
Keirstead, Richard S., 95n605, 96n613
Keister, Douglas, 98n973
Keller, Estela, 98n1277
Keller, Gary D., 98n1277
Keller, Harald, 95n1599
Keller, Michael, 96n970
Keller, Michael A., 95n1252
Keller, Morton, 96n720
Keller, William L., 99n564
Kelley, Gordon E., 95n1394
Kelliher, Susan, 97n315
Kellner, Mark A., 98n1365
Kelly, Alan, 95n1258
Kelly, Anthony, 95n1632
Kelly, Douglas R., 98n930
Kelly, Gary, 97n977, 99n1062
Kelly, Katherine E., 97n985
Kelly, Michael, 97n248
Kelly, W. A., 99n612
Kelson, John F., 97n764
Kelz, Rochelle K., 98n1527
Kemp, Herman C., 99n103
Kemp, Sandra, 98n1152
Kemp, Thomas J., 98n361
Kemp, Thomas Jay, 95n460, 98n366
Kemper, Daniele Renee, 96n283
Kemper, Kurt, 97n504
Kemper, Robert E., 96n283, 98n243

Kenealy, Pamela M., 97n626
Kennedy, Felicitas, 97n1304
Kennedy, Mary Lynch, 99n831
Kennedy, Michael, 96n1270, 97n1027
Kennedy, Paul, 96n200
Kennett, Frances, 96n388
Kenny, Anthony, 96n1434
Kenny, Michael, 96n704
Kenny, Monica L., 96n1648
Kenrick, Donald, 99n380
Kent, Allen, 97n524, 97n1367, 97n1371, 98n569, 98n570, 99n593, 99n594
Kent, Cassandra, 98n180
Kentucky: atlas of histl county boundaries, 97n371
Kenya, rev ed, 97n98
Kenyon, Nicholas, 95n1287, 95n1288
Kenyon, Sherrilyn, 95n944
Kepars, I., 98n118
Kepos, Paula, 95n251, 96n236, 96n237, 96n238
Kerchelich, Karen, 96n2
Kermode, Frank, 97n916
Kern, Kerry V., 95n731
Kern, Robert W., 97n451
Kernfeld, Barry, 96n1328
Kerr, Ann, 98n899
Kerr, Donald, 97n567
Kerr, Susan D., 96n1672
Kerrod, Robin, 99n1295
Kerry, Carolle, 96n325
Kerry, Trevor, 96n325
Kerschen, Lois, 99n807
Kerschner, Helen K., 97n669
Kersey, Tanya, 95n1356
Kerwin, Christine, 99n150
Kesler, Christine A., 99n148
Kess, Joseph F., 96n1059
Kessler, James H., 97n1230
Kester-Shelton, Pamela, 97n886
Keuper, Jerome P., 98n1022
Ke-wen, Wang, 99n109
Key concepts in cinema studies, 98n1284
Key dates in number theory hist, 96n1829
Key gd to ...
    electronic resources: agriculture, 96n1518
    electronic resources: art & art hist, 98n942
    electronic resources: engineering, 96n1643
    electronic resources: health scis, 96n1688
    electronic resources: lang & lit, 98n985
Key indicators of county growth 1970-2025, 1996 ed, 98n806
Key of it all, bk.1, 95n789
Key of it all, bk.2, 96n1121
Keyguide to info sources in museum studies, 2d ed, 95n85
Keyguide to info sources in strategic studies, 95n690
Key-word-in-context concordance to Targum Neofiti, 95n1452
KGB world factbk, v.4, no.1 [CD-ROM], 95n5
Khakimov, Kamran M., 96n1141
Khan, Javed Ahmad, 97n232
Khorana, Meena, 96n1166, 97n934
Kich, Martin, 96n1205
Kidd, Charles, 96n426

Kids' world almanac of football, 96n818
Kiefer, Marie, 96n671
Kiefer, Peter T., 97n1049
Kiell, Norman, 97n881
Kienholz, Michelle L., 96n1709
Kier, Kathleen E., 95n1194
Kightley, Chris, 99n1379
Kikuchi, Mihoko, 96n1626
Killion, Tom, 99n479
Killpatrick, Frances, 95n799, 98n723
Killpatrick, James, 95n799, 98n723
Kilmer, David, 99n1222
Kim, David U., 96n674
Kim, Sun-Jin, 97n659
Kimball, Michelle R., 98n830
Kimmens, Andrew C., 97n887
Kiner, Larry F., 96n1323
King, A. C., 95n521
King, Anita, 98n78
King, Constance, 98n917
King, J. E., 97n148
King John: an annot bibliog, 95n1217
Kingery, Elinor Eppich, 95n501
Kingery, Hugh E., 95n501
Kingfisher 1st ency, 97n45
Kingfisher 1st ency of animals, 96n1608
Kingfisher 1st sci ency, 99n1314
Kingfisher 1st thesaurus, 95n1051
Kingfisher illus children's dict, 96n1087
Kingfisher illus hist of the world, 95n590
Kingfisher illus jr dict, 99n906
Kingfisher illus thesaurus, 96n1088
Kingfisher young people's ency of the US, 95n103
Kingfisher young world ency, 96n50
Kings of medieval England, c. 560-1485, 97n445
Kings of the jungle, 95n1381
Kingsbury, Paul, 95n1296
Kingsbury, Stewart A., 95n1314
Kinnard, Roy, 96n1391, 99n1227
Kinnear, Karen L., 96n603, 96n618, 97n509, 98n839
Kinoshita, Sumie, 99n163
Kipen, David M., 97n766
Kipfer, Barbara Ann, 96n1092
Kiple, Kenneth F., 95n1662
Kipp, Rita Smith, 96n133
Kipps, Harriet Clyde, 98n795
Kirkpatrick, Betty, 95n1054, 98n1019
Kirkpatrick, Melanie, 98n169
Kirsch, George B., 96n798
Kirshon, John W., 96n500
Kister, Kenneth F., 95n57
Kister's best encys, 2d ed, 95n57
Kitromilides, Paschalis M., 96n130
Kittrie, Nicholas N., 99n476
Klatt, Mary J., 95n1319
Klaue, Wolfgang, 95n963
Klaus, Kenneth S., 96n1299
Klawans, Zander H., 97n778
Kleczek, Josip, 96n1645, 96n1646
Kleczkova, Helena, 96n1645, 96n1646

Klein, Barry, 95n341, 95n1499
Klein, Barry T., 96n412
Klein, Bob, 96n1537
Klein, Milton M., 99n464
Klein, William W., 97n1188
Klemp, P. J., 97n997
Klepper, Nancy, 96n462
Klepper, Robert K., 97n1120
Klett's modern German & English dict, 99n929
Klezmer, Deborah, 95n575
Kliatt audiobk gd, 95n12
Klingaman, William K., 97n591
Klingler, Thomas A., 99n935
Klinkner, Kenneth K., 95n109
Klisz, Anjanelle M., 95n673
Kloesel, Christian J. W., 95n1208, 99n1069
Klooster, H. A. J., 99n481
Klostermaier, Klaus K., 99n1290
Klotman, Phyllis R., 98n1295
Klugherz, Laura, 99n1149
Knapp, Brian, 96n1860, 98n1600, 99n1507
Knapp, Ellen M., 97n267
Knapp, Sara D., 95n94
Knapp, Thomas R., 96n1732
Knappert, Jan, 95n1442
Knappman, Edward W., 95n313, 95n613, 98n532, 99n556
Knell, Simon J., 96n82
Kneller, Marianna, 96n1573
Knight, Charles A., 96n1237
Knight, Denise D., 98n1126
Knight, Paul, 97n852
Knight, Virginia Curtin, 99n373
Kniskern, Nancy V., 98n418, 99n781
Knives: military edged tools & weapons, 99n647
Knorr, Margaret, 95n509
Knorr, Susan M., 95n509
Knott's hndbk for vegetable growers, 4th ed, 98n1437
Knowledge Exchange business ency, 98n154
Knowles, Mark, 99n1203
Kochanoff, Peggy, 95n1559
Kocurek, Dianna S., 96n1852
Koda, Cub, 97n1072
Kodansha's furigana Japanese-English dict, 96n1111
Kodansha's pocket kanji gd, 96n1112
Koehler, Ludwig, 96n1455, 97n1198
Koenig, Harold G., 96n840
Koff, Theodore H., 96n841
Kofmel, Kim G., 97n550
Kohlenberger, John R., III, 95n1453, 97n1199
Kohler, Dayton, 97n906
Kohn, George C., 96n1725
Kohut, Joe, 95n1306
Kohut, John J., 95n1306
Kolin, Philip C., 99n1057
Komara, Edward M., 99n1166
Kondek, Joshua, 99n1195
Konechni, Sasha, 99n495
Konigsberg, Ira, 98n1285
Kope, Spencer, 98n447, 99n1519
Kope's outer space dir, 99n1519

Korab, Balthazar, 96n1045
Korch, Rick, 95n820, 98n746
Korea [CD-ROM], 96n692
Korea business: the portable ency for doing business with Korea, 95n264
Korean Americans, 99n374
Korean War, 96n538
Korean War, 97n431
Korean War: an annot bibliog, 99n514
Korshel, Mohamud, 96n1134
Korsten, F., 97n1204
Kort, Michael, 99n124, 99n543
Kosberg, Jordan I., 96n851
Koschnick, Wolfgang J., 98n253
Kosek, Jane Kelly, 96n1265, 96n1490
Kostelanetz, Richard, 95n1005, 96n1268
Kostenko, Dmytro, 98n155
Kostlevy, William, 95n1458
Koszegi, Michael A., 95n875
Kotz, Samuel, 98n809
Kovacs, Beatrice, 96n1684
Kovacs, Diane K., 98n985
Kovacs, Ruth, 95n364, 95n865, 95n867, 96n875, 96n877, 96n878, 96n961
Kovinick, Phil, 99n869
Kowaleski-Wallace, Elizabeth, 99n961
Kowalke, Ron, 98n1648
Kozub, Robert M., 98n264
KR Info OnDisc grants database [CD-ROM], 96n848
Kramer, Jack, 96n1574
Krannich, Caryl Rae, 95n314, 97n258
Krannich, Ronald L., 95n314, 97n258
Krantz, Les, 96n10, 97n74, 97n263
Kranz, Rachel, 99n1005
Krapp, Kristine M., 99n189
Kratz, E. Ulrich, 98n986
Krause, Chester L., 97n780, 98n911, 98n912, 99n846
Krausse, Gerald H., 96n134
Krausse, Sylvia Engelen, 96n134
Krautz, Alfred, 95n1372
Krautz, Hille, 95n1372
Krautz, Joris, 95n1372
Kravets, Marybeth, 98n290
Kreamer, Jean Thibodeaux, 96n994
Krebs, Gary M., 98n1242
Krebs, Robert E., 99n1510
Krech, Shepard, III, 95n430
Kreisel, Martha, 95n981
Kreiswirth, Martin, 95n1104
Kreith, Frank, 95n1780
Krell, Robert, 98n708
Kress, Stephen W., 96n1560
Kricher, John, 96n1591
Krippes, Karl A., 99n934
Kroeger, Karl, 95n1281
Krohn, Lauren, 97n487
Krol, John, 95n837, 96n1782
Kronenwetter, Michael, 95n623, 99n742
Kroschwitz, Jacqueline I., 99n1503
Krouglov, Alexander, 98n155

Krstovic, Jelena, 95n1242
Krstovic, Jelena O., 96n1149, 96n1156, 97n909
Kruegler, Christopher, 98n692
Kruger, Anna, 96n46
Kruger, Ursula, 98n1433
Krumenaker, Lawrence, 98n1591
Krupin, Paul J., 96n1867
Krupin's toll-free environmental dir, 96n1867
Kruschke, Earl R., 97n510
Krutt, Susan D., 95n762
Kubey, Craig, 95n696
Kubitschek, Missy Dehn, 99n1058
Kuchan, Barbara L., 98n1505
Kuehn, John, 95n1303
Kuhl, Victoria A., 95n958
Kuhlthaur, Carol Collier, 95n663
Kuhn, Annette, 95n1373
Kuhn, Laura, 96n1271, 98n1197
Kuipers, Barbara J., 96n1177
Kuiter, Rudie H., 95n1585
Kulisheck, P. J., 98n687
Kuman, Arthur, Jr., 96n276
Kumar, Lisa, 99n1495
Kunoff, Hugo, 95n1238
Kuper, Adam, 97n75
Kuper, Jessica, 97n75
Kurdish-English/English-Kurdish dict, 96n1114
Kurds & Kurdistan, 98n116
Kurian, George, 99n656, 99n1190
Kurian, George Thomas, 95n896, 95n900, 97n44, 98n659, 98n812, 98n813, 98n1529, 99n668
Kurian, Sarah, 95n914
Kuroff, Barbara, 97n753, 98n936
Kurth, Martin, 96n644
Kurylko, Katya, 98n155
Kurz, Heinz D., 99n160
Kurz, Kenneth Franklin, 97n592
Kushner, Michael G., 97n252
Kusick, James, 96n1715
Kutler, Stanley I., 97n416, 97n433
Kutzer, M. Daphne, 97n942
Kuwait, rev ed, 97n140
Kvasnicka, Robert M., 95n545
Kwacz, Jose Daniel, 97n153
Kyker, Keith, 99n1498
Kyrgyz-English/English-Kyrgyz glossary of terms, 99n934
Kyrillidou, Martha, 97n527

La Boda, Sharon, 96n467, 96n468, 96n469
Laaser, Ulrich, 98n1518
Labi, Esther, 96n77
LaBlanc, Michael L., 95n800, 95n824
Labor arbitration, 96n255
Labor, employment, & the law, 98n515
Lacey, A. R., 97n1164
Lackmann, Ron, 97n765
Lacy, Norris J., 99n1066
Ladies in the laboratory? American & British women in sci, 1800-1900, 99n1301

Ladson-Billings, Gloria, 98n267
Ladusaw, William A., 97n815
Laessoe, Thomas, 97n1280
Lafferty, Peter, 95n1490
LaFrance, Ronald, 98n355
Lagowski, Joseph J., 98n1601
Lagua, Rosalinda T., 98n1422
Lahti, N. E., 99n870
Laing, Adrian C., 98n531
Laing, Dave, 96n1306
Laird, Ross, 96n1325, 97n1064
Lake, river, & sea-run fishes of Canada, 96n1624
LaLiberte, Katherine, 99n1350
Lamar, Howard R., 99n463
Lamb, G. F., 96n1239
Lamb, Malcolm, 95n130
Lambdin, Laura C., 97n989
Lambdin, Robert T., 97n989
Lambert, David, 96n1815
Lamontagne, Monique, 99n198
Lampl, Richard, 96n1879
Lamy, Marie-Noelle, 99n925
Lancaster, Roy, 96n1566
Lance, Steven, 97n1129
Land & property research in the US, 98n365
Landes, Alison, 98n568, 98n754
Landgraf, Mark J., 96n1891
Landmark docs in American hist [CD-ROM], 96n498
Landmarks of American presidents, 97n391
Landmarks of 20th-century design, 95n983
Landon, Grelun, 98n1234
Landrum, Sherrye, 99n1471
Landry, Sarah, 95n1560
Lands & peoples, 98n95
Lands & peoples special ed: the changing face of Europe, 98n96
Landscape architecture sourcebk, 98n1438
Landskroner, Ronald A., 98n244
Lane, A. Thomas, 97n151
Lane, Carole A., 98n1596
Lane, James M., 96n821
Lane, Jan-Erik, 98n684
Lane, Megan, 99n875
Lang, George, 96n689
Lang, Harry G., 96n857
Lang, Robert, 98n1169
Langenkamp, R. D., 96n1676
Langenkamp, Robert D., 95n1745
Langer, Adam, 99n1223
Langer, Howard J., 97n345
Langhans, Edward A., 95n1411, 95n1412
Langley, Andrew, 97n56
Langley, Myrtle, 98n1381
Langman, Larry, 95n1383, 95n1402, 96n1392, 96n1393, 99n1228, 99n1229
Langmead, Donald, 97n802, 98n972, 98n974
Langsjoen, Odin, 99n1439
Langston, Diane Jones, 95n647
Langton, Mark, 96n815
Language & communication, 99n894

Language arts & environmental awareness, 99n997
Language of art from A to Z, rev ed, 99n870
Language of banking, 95n232
Language of biotech, 2d ed, 96n1659
Language of Canadian pols, 96n752
Language of real estate, 4th ed, 95n329
Language of small bus, 95n188
Languages of the world, new ed, 97n814
Lanier, Pamela, 95n510
Lankford, John, 98n1606
Lansing, Phyllis S., 98n1505
Lanzerotti, Rachel, 96n336
Lao-English dict, 97n861
Lapin, Lee, 96n775
Larger animals of E Africa, 98n1470
Larkin, Colin, 96n1310, 99n1172
Larocca, Felix E. F., 95n1678
Larousse biogl dict, 95n31
Larousse concise French-English/English-French dict, 95n1075
Larousse concise French/English, English/French dict, rev ed, 99n926
Larousse concise Spanish-English/English-Spanish dict, 95n1095
Larousse concise Spanish-English, English-Spanish dict, rev ed, 99n940
Larousse desk ref, 97n46
Larousse dict of ...
   beliefs & religions, 95n1443
   British hist, 96n541
   literary characters, 95n1105
   N American hist, 96n508
   sci & tech, 97n1240
   scientists, 96n1487
   20th century hist, 96n566
   women, 98n24
   world folklore, 96n1343
   world hist, 95n582
   writers, 96n1145
Larousse ency of wine, 96n1527
Larousse English dict, 99n899
Larousse English-Spanish, Spanish-English dict, new, 97n873
Larousse mini French-English, English-French dict, new ed, 97n848
Larousse mini German-English, English-German dict, new ed, 97n850
Larousse mini Italian-English, English-Italian dict, new ed, 97n858
Larousse mini Spanish-English, English-Spanish dict, new ed, 97n874
Larousse pocket French-English/English-French dict, 95n1076
Larousse pocket Spanish-English/English-Spanish dict, 95n1096
Larry Sitsky: a bio-bibliog, 98n1214
Larson, Randall D., 96n1394
LaRue, C. Steven, 99n243
Lasocki, David, 96n1294
Lassiter, Sybil M., 99n367
Last, John M., 96n1698
Last, P. R., 96n1623

Last word: The New York Times bk of obituaries & farewells, 99n34
Last words: a dict of deathbed quotations, 96n95
Laster, James, 97n1053
Late medieval England (1377-1485), 96n542
Late 19th- & early 20th-century British literary biographers, 96n1225
Late Victorian poetry 1880-99, 96n1246
Latest & greatest read-alouds, 95n1137
Late-Victorian & Edwardian British novelist, 1st series, 96n1235
Latham, A. J. H., 96n555
Lathem, Edward Connery, 95n1190
Lathrop, Norman M., 96n1014
Latin America: a dir & sourcebk, 2d ed, 99n261
Latin America on file, 96n155
Latin America petroleum dir 1995, 14th ed, 96n1834
Latin America petroleum dir 1998, 17th ed, 99n196
Latin American advertising, mktg, & media sourcebk, 96n301
Latin American classical composers, 97n1042
Latin American films, 1932-94, 98n1299
Latin American markets, 1993-94 ed, 95n289
Latin American urbanization, 95n899
Latin American women artists, 97n793
Latin for the illiterati, 98n1039
Latinas in the US, 97n728
Latino ency, 97n337
Latinos in the US: social, economic & pol aspects, 95n424
Latitudes & attitudes, 96n915
Latourelle, Rene, 95n1470
Latrobe, Kathy Howard, 95n1123
Lauber, Daniel, 95n315, 95n316, 95n317, 98n234, 98n235, 99n273
Lauber, Timothy J., 96n223
Lauer-Bader, Michele, 96n903
Laufenberg, Cindy, 95n1263
Laufenburg, Cindy, 98n1207
Laughlin, Kay, 97n1033
Launius, Roger D., 99n1520
Laura Ingalls Wilder: an annot bibliog of critical, biogl, & teaching studies, 98n1139
Laurens, Jeannine, 96n549
Lauria, Angela E., 98n643
Lavenberg, Robert J., 98n1468
Lavin, Michael R., 97n713
Law & legal info dir, 9th ed, 98n523
Law & pols, 97n490
Law, Barbara, 99n3
Law bks & serials in print 1996, 97n481
Law for the layperson, 2d ed, 98n511
Law in lit, 99n945
Law, Joe, 97n284
Law, Jonathan, 96n1373
Law lib ref shelf, 3d ed, 97n482
Law, Nicholas S., 99n28
Law of the sea: a bibliog on the law of the sea, 1968-88, 95n594
Law of the sea: a select bibliog 1993, 95n595
Law, religion, theology, 98n510
Law, values, & the environment, 98n560

Lawal, Ibironke O., 96n1668
Lawless, Julia, 97n1346
Lawless, Richard I., 97n93
Lawlor, William, 99n1042
Lawmen & desperadoes, 96n571
Lawrance, Alan, 96n759
Lawrence, Christine C., 96n738
Lawrence, Robert L., 98n520
Lawson, Alan, 99n946
Lawson, Edward, 97n517
Lawson, Edwin D., 97n370
Lawson, James R., 95n812
Lawton, Harry, 99n1207
Lawyers' law bks, 3d ed, 98n512
Lawyer's research companion, 99n549
Layman, Richard, 95n544, 96n515
Lazich, Robert S., 96n240, 99n188, 99n190, 99n620
Lazzari, Marie, 97n908, 97n909, 97n910, 97n911, 97n912, 98n1069, 99n1016
LC period subdivisions under names of places, 5th ed, 96n630
Le Page, Jean, 95n1633
Lea, Christine, 98n1050
Lea, Peter W., 97n13
Lead poisoning prevention, 96n1866
Leaders from the 1960s, 95n715
Leadership: quotations from the world's greatest motivators, 98n81
Leaffer, Marshall A., 98n567
Leahy, Leo, 95n806
Leal-Khouri, Susana, 96n1728
Lean, Geoffrey, 95n1756
Leana, Frank C., 99n313
Leapman, Michael, 96n480
Learning about...the Civil War, 99n453
Learning about the Holocaust, 96n1170
Learning to behave: a gd to American conduct bks before 1900, 95n1422
Lecker, Robert, 95n1227, 97n1003, 97n1004
Leckie, Gloria J., 97n550
Ledoux, Trish, 98n1307
Lee, Antoinette J., 95n1017
Lee, C. C., 97n1382, 99n1407
Lee, J. A. N., 96n1758
Lee, Kelley, 99n1421
Lee, Lauren K., 95n661
Lee, Leonard, 96n1679
Lee, Lily Xiao Hong, 99n798
Lee, Loyd E., 98n622
Lee, Michelle, 99n1082, 99n1083
Lee, Min, 96n508, 96n541, 96n566
Lee, Nancy Ann, 99n1168
Lee, Thomas B., 95n109
Lee Van Cleef: a bibliog, film, & TV ref, 99n1208
Leed, Richard L., 97n867
Leeds, Marc, 96n1219
Leeman, Richard W., 98n337
Leeming, David Adams, 96n1444, 97n890, 98n1256
Leeming, Margaret Adams, 96n1444
Lees, Stella, 95n1149
Leese, Peter, 95n558
Leeson, Richard M., 95n1193, 98n1136
Leeuwenburgh, Todd, 96n708
Leeves, Juliet, 96n636
Lefranc, Norbert, 99n1380
Left gd: a gd to left-of-center orgs, 97n614
Left index, 97n61
Legal executions in N.Y. state, 98n554
Legal info buyer's gd & ref manual 1997-98, 99n570
Legal research, 5th ed, 98n534
Legal researcher's desk ref 1996-97, 97n498
Legalized gambling, 99n714
Legalized gambling: a ref hndbk, 95n803
Legay, Gilbert, 96n413
Legends of the Earth, sea, & sky, 99n1184
Legislative Drafting Research Fund of Columbia University, 95n745
Lehman, Jeffrey, 99n389
Leiby, Bruce R., 97n1078
Leifer, Michael, 96n747
Lein, Clayton D., 96n1232
Leininger, Phillip W., 97n966
Leistritz, F. Larry, 95n180
Leitch, Jay A., 96n1600
Leiter, Richard A., 99n565
Leiter, Samuel L., 95n1413, 98n1324
Lemerand, Karen E., 99n20
Lemke, Bob, 98n906
Lemke, Robert F., 99n846
Lems-Dworkin, Carol, 97n1145
Lenfestey, Thompson, 95n1795
Lenfestey, Tom, Jr., 95n1795
Lenihan, Ayeliffe, 96n1681
Lenk, John D., 95n1615
Lent, John A., 95n1331, 95n1332, 95n1333
Lent, Max, 96n1776
Lentz, Harris M., 97n1130
Lentz, Harris M., III, 95n706, 95n1395, 97n1097, 97n1098, 98n752, 98n1308
Lenz, Millicent, 95n654
Lenzke, James T., 99n1577
Leo Burnett worldwide advertising & media fact bk, 96n302
Leonard, Bill J., 96n1467, 98n1354
Leonard, David C., 96n1750
Leonard, Jane, 95n558
Leonard, Kathy S., 98n1179
Leonard Maltin's movie & video gd, 95n1361
Leonard Maltin's movie & video gd, 1999 ed, 99n1243
Leonard Maltin's movie ency, 96n1377
Leonard, Patt, 97n114
Leonard, Thomas M., 96n152
Leopold, Donald J., 99n1367
Lerner, Loren, 98n1271
Lero, Donna S., 95n848
Les bon mots: how to amaze tout le monde with everyday French, 98n1025
Les Fauves: a sourcebk, 95n1019
Lesbian almanac, 97n679
Lesbian & gay liberation in Canada, 97n680
Lesbians in print, 97n678
Lesch, Ann M., 99n699

Lesh, Robert W., 96n126
Lesko, Matthew, 96n59, 96n60
Leslie Bassett: a bio-bibliog, 95n1268
Leslie, Rodrigues, 99n644
Lesotho, rev ed, 98n107
Lessem, Don, 95n1734
Lesser, M. X., 96n1440
Lester, David, 98n768
Lester, Patrick D., 97n807
Lester, Ray, 97n191
Letellier, Robert Ignatius, 96n1236, 98n1145
Leto, Joseph, 96n1644
Lettow, Lucille J., 98n284
Leventhal, F. M., 96n543
Lever, Richard, 97n1002
Leverington, Karen, 97n580
Levi, Anthony, 95n1231
Levi, Erik, 97n1055
Levine, Carole, 96n1584
Levine, Caroline, 95n247
Levine, Emanuel, 99n1375
Levine, Jeffrey P., 99n152
Levine, John, 97n1373
Levine, Marc H., 99n194
Levine, Martin G., 99n308
Levine, Stuart R., 99n1481
Levine, Sumner N., 95n247
Levinkind, Susan, 98n534
Levinson, David, 96n389, 96n835, 96n863, 96n1797,
    97n316, 97n320, 97n470, 97n1178, 98n721,
    98n1509, 99n365, 99n368
Levitt, Marcus C., 96n1261
Levy, Barbara R., 98n784
Levy, Cynthia J., 99n54
Levy, Leonard W., 95n542
Levy, Patricia, 99n84
Levy, Peter B., 97n593, 99n473
Lewin, Albert E., 95n1059
Lewin, Esther, 95n1059
Lewin, Paul, 97n1417
Lewis, Amy, 96n48
Lewis, Cathleen S., 96n1647
Lewis, Colin, 97n1256
Lewis, Cynthia A., 99n586
Lewis, Donald M., 97n1208
Lewis, Grace Ross, 95n1716
Lewis, Helene M. A., 98n1024
Lewis, James R., 95n790, 96n779, 96n1445, 97n1176
Lewis, Katie, 98n785
Lewis, Kenneth, 96n855
Lewis, Marjorie, 99n1011
Lewis, Mary S., 99n1112
Lewis, Paul W., 98n1034
Lewis, Richard J., 98n1635, 99n1505
Lewis, Richard J., Sr., 95n1781
Lewis, Scott, 95n11
Lewis, Susan A., 99n858
Lewon, Paul, 98n1584, 99n202
Lexicon of Tamil lit, 96n1255
Leyser, Brady J., 96n1315

L'Heureux, Conrad, 96n484
Li, Xia, 98n875
Libbey, Ted, 95n1282
Liberia, 96n1118
Librarian's companion, 2d ed, 97n532
Librarian's gd to public records, rev ed, 98n666
Librarian's gd to public records, special ed, 96n778
Librarian's legal companion, 95n646
Libraries & copyright, 95n656
Libraries in the UK & Republic of Ireland 1995, 96n637
Libraries Unltd professional collection CD 1995 [CD-ROM],
    97n523
Library bldgs consultant list, 1993, 95n659
Library cat of the Metropolitan Museum of Art, 5th suppl,
    1990-92, 2d ed, 95n1015
Library fax/Ariel dir, 8th ed, 95n640
Library lit 1995, 97n529
Library of Congress subject headings, 3d ed, 96n627
Library of Congress subject headings, 19th ed, 97n534
Library of Lord George Douglas, 99n612
Library of the oceans, 99n1538
Library resources for singers, coaches, & accompanists,
    99n1113
Library servs for off-campus & distance educ, 97n521
Library systems in Europe, 96n636
Lichtblau, Myron I., 98n1168
Lichtenberg, Kara Ellynn, 95n876
Liddell, Henry George, 97n853
Lide, David R., 95n1711, 95n1717
Lie, Suzanne Stiver, 95n372
Liebeck, Helen, 96n1070
Lieberman, Philip A., 97n763
Lieberman, Shari, 98n1548
Liebman, Roy, 97n1105, 99n1209
Liechtenstein, 95n159
Life & death in the US, 98n770
Life is just a bowl of cherries & other delicious sayings,
    99n914
Life of birds, 99n1372
Light, Jonathan Fraser, 98n733
Light, Laura, 97n546
Light 'n lively reads, 98n1057
Lighter, J. E., 95n1061, 98n1015
Lignor, Amy, 95n1659, 96n374, 97n1249, 98n250
Ligotti, Thomas, 99n980, 99n981, 99n982
Lilley, William, 99n674
Lilley, William, III, 95n710, 98n329
Lillian Hellman: a research & production sourcebk, 99n1248
Lillian Russell: a bio-bibliog, 98n1275
Lilly, Teri Ann, 98n778
Lima, Carolyn W., 99n1008
Lima, John A., 99n1008
Limb, Peter, 97n1001
Lin, Alvin C., 96n874, 96n882, 98n274, 98n553, 98n792
Lin, Lin, 98n694
Lincoff, Gary, 97n1280
Lincoln, Berna B., 99n1375
Lincoln lib of sports champions, 6th, 95n793
Lincoln, Stanley R., 99n1375
Lind, Beth Beutler, 97n933

Lindeburg, Michael R., 95n1637
Lindemann, Barbara, 98n530
Linden, Tom, 96n1709
Lindfors, Bernth, 96n1247, 97n1012
Lindquist, Richard K., 99n1360
Lindroth, Colette, 96n1208
Lindroth, James, 96n1208
Lindsay, William, 96n68
Lineback, Richard H., 95n1430, 95n1431, 95n1432, 98n1340, 98n1342
Lingaiah, K., 95n1638
Linguistic cultures of the world, 98n990
Linton, David, 96n972
Linzey, Andrew, 97n73
Linzey, Donald W., 99n1393
Lione, Armand, 96n1712
Lipinski, Miroslaw, 98n1252
Lipkowitz, Myron A., 95n1677, 97n1265
Lippincott, Kristen, 96n1800
Lippitt, Jill, 95n915
Lippy, Charles H., 96n1441, 97n1171
Lipset, Seymour Martin, 97n612, 98n639
Lipton, Kathryn L., 96n1517
Lisa, Laurie, 97n322
LISA plus [CD-ROM], 96n625
Lisella, Frank S., 95n1767
Liska, Theresa I., 97n250
Lissarrague, Francois, 98n1257
Lissauer, Robert, 97n1065
Lissauer's ency of popular music in America, 97n1065
List, Barbara A., 95n1503
List of serials indexed for online users 1994, 95n1668
Literally entitled, 97n891
Literary almanac, 98n1071
Literary critical approaches to the Bible, 97n1190
Literary criticism index, 2d ed, 95n1114
Literary gd & companion to N England, 96n1233
Literary gd & companion to S England, rev ed, 99n1065
Literary index to American mags, 1850-1900, 97n960
Literary lifelines, 99n952
Literary market place 1995, 95n672
Literature & gerontology, 96n845
Literature & its times, 98n1072
Literature connections to American hist, K-6, 99n449
Literature connections to American hist, 7-12, 99n450
Literature connections to world hist, K-6, 99n512
Literature connections to world hist, 7-12, 99n513
Literature criticism from 1400 to 1800, v.27, 96n1156
Literature criticism from 1400 to 1800, v.28, 97n901
Literature criticism from 1400 to 1800, v.29, 97n902
Literature criticism from 1400 to 1800, v.30, 97n903
Literature criticism from 1400 to 1800, v.31, 97n904
Literature for children & YAs about Oceania, 97n142
Literature of ...
 American music 3, 1983-92, 97n1021
 animal sci & health, 95n1533
 chamber music, 99n1153
 rock, 3, 96n1333
 soil sci, 95n1509
 the nonprofit sector, v.5, 95n860
 the nonprofit sector, v.7, 97n682
 the nonprofit sector, v.8, 98n783
Lithuanian dict, 97n862
Lithuanian-English/English-Lithuanian concise dict, 95n1088
Little, Anne C., 98n1119
Little Oxford dict of current English, 7th ed, 95n1032
Little Oxford dict of quotations, 96n92
Little Oxford gd to English usage, 96n1076
Littlejohn, Alice C., 96n211
Littman, Barbara, 95n208
Littman, Mark S., 99n791
Liturgical dict of E Christianity, 95n1467
Litz, A. Walton, 97n961, 99n1043, 99n1045, 99n1110
Liu, Lewis-Guodo, 98n582, 99n209
Livas, Haris, 95n1000
Live better/live longer resourcebk, 95n836
Lives & works in the arts from the renaissance to the 20th century, 98n847
Lives of N American birds, 98n1460
Lives of the great composers, 3d ed, 98n1216
Livesey, Anthony, 95n681
Living logos, 95n322
Living with low vision, 97n671
Livingston, A. D., 95n1516
Livingston, Helen, 95n1516
Livingstone, E. A., 98n1389
Ljungquist, Kent P., 95n1177
Llewellyn, Claire, 99n1003
Llompart, Ana Cristina, 98n1051
Lloyd, Christopher, 95n1020
Lloyd, Mark, 95n761
Lobban, Richard Andrew, Jr., 98n456
Lobbying, PACs, & campaign finance, 96n740
Lobenstine, Joy C., 95n838
Local hist collections in libs, 96n659
Lockhart, Charles, 95n705
Lockhart, Darrell B., 98n1180
Lockie, Andrew, 95n1672, 97n1347
Loescher, Ann Dull, 96n895
Loescher, Gil, 96n895
Lofman, Ron, 96n1274
Logue, Calvin McLeod, 98n1131, 99n975
Lomeli, Francisco, 95n422
Lomer, Cecile, 97n552, 98n105
London, 97n116
London Philharmonic discography, 98n1204
Londre, Felicia Hardison, 96n1420
Long, James W., 96n1737, 98n1558
Long, Janet Alice, 99n959
Long, John H., 96n438, 96n439, 97n371, 98n379, 98n431, 99n447, 99n448
Long, Kim, 95n3, 97n1293, 99n1521
Long, Robert Emmet, 99n369
Long term care, 96n841
Longe, Jacqueline L., 99n189
Longman biogl dir of decision-makers in Russia & the successor states, 96n145
Longman companion to America in the era of the 2 world wars, 1910-45, 98n449
Longman, Tremper, 97n1189

Longshore, David, 99n1532
Lonier, Terri, 96n263
Look of the century, 97n788
Looking at European ceramics, 95n980
Looking at European sculpture, 98n983
Loos, John L., 98n497
Lopez, Billie Ann, 99n438
Lopez, Donald S., 96n1882
Lord, John, 96n1787
Lord, Mary E., 97n700
Lord Palmerston 1784-1865: a bibliog, 95n753
Lord, Tom, 96n1326, 99n1167
Lorraine Hansberry: a research & production sourcebk, 98n1136
Los Angeles A to Z, 99n91
Losada, Jose Manuel, 99n944
Louden, Delroy, 99n1474, 99n1477
Loughlin, John, 95n147
Louisiana almanac, 1997-98 ed, 98n100
Lounsbury, Carl R., 95n1016
LoVaglio, Frank, 99n174
Love, Catherine E., 99n940
Love, J. W., 99n1120
Lovejoy's college counselor [CD-ROM], 95n373
Lovejoy's college gd, 24th ed, 99n351
Lovich, Jeffrey E., 96n1636
Lowe, Allen, 99n1162
Lowe, Duncan, 97n1257
Lowenstein, Barbara, 98n703
Lowenthal, Mark M., 96n716
Lubin, Bernard, 95n843, 97n623, 98n709
Lucanio, Patrick, 96n1395, 99n1213
Lucas, Daniel M., 97n511, 97n512
Lucas, Phillip Charles, 98n1366
Lucchesi, Tony, 98n959
Luce, Bernard, 99n1334
Luchinsky, Ellen, 99n1126
Luck, Steve, 98n47
Ludden, LaVerne, 95n220
Ludden, LaVerne L., 98n226
Ludwig, Herbert R., Jr., 96n1600
Luebking, Sandra Hargreaves, 98n370
Lueck, Therese L., 96n950, 97n743
Luey, Beth, 99n617
Luis, William, 96n1258
LuKanic, Steven A., 97n1143
Luker, Ralph E., 98n565
Lull, Janis, 95n1224
Lumbee Indians: an annot bibliog, 95n431
Lumber men: nontraditional statl measurements of the batting careers...., 95n806
Lumley, Elizabeth, 97n37, 99n38
Lumpkin, Betty S., 98n282
Lund, Herbert F., 95n1782
Lundin, Anne H., 96n379
Lundquist, Gunnar, 97n1142
Lunt, Susie, 98n122
Luo, Wei, 95n614
Lushootseed dict, 96n1119
Lutz, William D., 95n1065

Lux presents Hollywood, 96n1390
Luxembourg, rev ed, 98n135
Lyman, Darryl, 96n1073
Lynch, Dennis, 95n544
Lynch, Richard Chigley, 95n1408, 97n1030
Lynching & vigilantism in the US, 98n547
Lynn, Ruth Nadelman, 96n1167
Lyon, William S., 97n340
Lyons, Dianne J. B., 98n1549
Lyons, Walter A., 98n1613
Lyrics of the Trouveres, 96n1251

Mabunda, L. Mpho, 96n400, 96n401, 97n334, 98n335
Mabunda, Lorna Mpho, 95n23
Macabre, J. B., 95n1327
MacAuslan, Janna, 98n1218
MacCary, W. Thomas, 99n1077
MacDonald, Calum, 97n1055
MacDonald, Ron, 96n992
MacDonald-Haig, Caroline, 96n388
Macey, Samuel L., 95n58
MacGregor, Alexander P., 99n891
MacHale, Des, 96n93, 99n79
Machann, Clinton, 95n1210
Machine design data hndbk, 95n1638
Machinists' ready ref, 8th ed, 96n1675
Machovec, George S., 95n1704
Macintosh bible, 5th ed, 95n1696
Macintyre, Pam, 95n1149
Mack, Carol K., 99n1181
Mack, Dinah, 99n1181
Mack, Kibibi Voloria, 98n336
Mack, William C., 97n1309
Mackenzie, Harry, 97n772
Mackenzie, Leslie, 95n195, 95n353, 95n1659, 96n324, 96n374, 98n250, 98n771, 99n1467
MacKenzie, W. S., 95n1724
MacLeod, Don, 98n535
Macmillan centennial atlas of the world, 98n386
Macmillan color atlas of the states, 97n82
Macmillan dict of measurement, 95n1491
Macmillan ency of chemistry, 98n1601
Macmillan ency of earth scis, 97n1391
Macmillan ency of physics, 97n1410
Macmillan ency of sci, rev ed, 98n1406
Macmillan ency of world slavery, 99n535
Macmillan visual dict: multilingual ed, 95n59
MacNee, Marie J., 95n1337, 96n1193, 99n578
Macoboy, Stirling, 99n1364
MacPherson, Lillian, 98n510
Macrone, Michael, 95n1454
MacWhinney, Brian, 95n334
Madagascar, 95n119
Madden, Debra L., 99n1447
Madden, W. C., 98n734
Maddex, Robert L., 96n611, 97n594
Maddox, George L., 96n850
Madge, Steve, 95n1569, 99n1374, 99n1379
Madigan, Carol Orsag, 99n27

Madrid, 98n138
Madsen, Deborah, 95n923
Magazines for kids & teens, 96n86
Magazines for kids & teens, rev ed, 98n879
Magazines for libs, 8th ed, 96n85
Magazines for libs, 9th ed, 99n72
Magee, Bryan, 99n1256
Magee, Stan, 95n1608
Maggio, Rosalie, 97n70, 99n895
Maghreb, 99n97
Magida, Arthur J., 98n1362, 98n1363
Magill, Frank N., 95n209, 95n782, 95n906, 95n1150, 95n1156, 95n1170, 95n1171, 95n1172, 95n1178, 95n1243, 95n1396, 96n741, 96n836, 96n942, 96n949, 96n1853, 97n905, 97n906, 97n953, 97n1302, 98n497, 98n1059, 98n1085, 98n1123, 99n519, 99n520, 99n663, 99n706
Magill index to critical surveys, rev ed, 96n1161
Magill index to Masterplots: cum indexes, 1963-93, 95n1115
Magill's cinema annual 1994: a survey of the films of 1993, 95n1396
Magill's cinema annual 1995, 14th ed, 97n1131
Magill's gd to sci fiction & fantasy lit, 97n948
Magill's literary annual 1994, 95n1172
Magill's medical gd, 96n1700
Magill's medical gd, 1998 rev ed, 99n1443
Magill's survey of sci: earth sci series, 99n1515
Magill's survey of sci: life sci series suppl, 99n1356
Magill's survey of sci: physical sci series suppl, 99n1502
Magill's survey of sci, v.7, 99n1315
Magill's survey of sci [CD-ROM], 95n1502
Magill's survey of sci CD-ROM [CD-ROM], 99n1324
Magill's survey of world lit, 97n905
Magistrale, Anthony, 98n1137
Magnaghi, Russell M., 99n382
Magnuson, Norris A., 98n1383
Magnusson, Magnus, 95n31
Magoulias, Michael, 96n1156, 96n1242, 97n901
Maguire, Jack, 95n405
Mahadevan, Vijitha, 96n110
Mahalingam, Indira, 99n1254
Mahar, Mary, 97n1216
Mahatma Gandhi, 96n536
Mahler, Gregory, 96n751
Mahoney, M. H., 95n907
Mahoney, Paul F., 95n527
Maier, Ernest L., 97n530
Main economic indicators: histl stats: prices, labour & wages 1962-91, 95n210
Maizell, Robert E., 99n1511
Major authors on CD-ROM: Virgina Woolf [CD-ROM], 99n1087
Major business orgs of E Europe & the Commonwealth of Independent States 1995/96, 5th ed, 97n244
Major characters in American fiction, 95n1182
Major cos of ...
   Africa S of the Sahara 1996, 97n219
   Central & E Europe & the Commonwealth of Independent States 1996/97, 6th ed, 97n220
   Central & E Europe & the Commonwealth of Independent States 1998, 99n257
   Europe 1994/5, 96n253
   Europe 1998, 99n258
   Latin America & the Caribbean 1998, 99n262
   Latin America 1996, 97n247
   the Arab world 1996/97, 20th ed, 97n233
   the Arab world 1998, 99n239
   the Far East & Australasia 1995/96, 96n245
   the Far East & Australasia 1998, 99n245
Major state health care policies, 99n1433
Major state health care policies, 5th ed, 98n1519
Major studies of minority business, 95n178
Major Tudor authors, 98n1060
Mak, Grace C. L., 98n295
Makers of the piano, 1700-1820, 97n1050
Makers of 20th century modern architecture, 98n972
Maki, Kathleen E., 98n233, 99n263, 99n361
Maki, Uskali, 99n161
Making of modern Africa: a gd to archives, 96n530
Making wise medical decisions, 99n1453
Makino, Yasuko, 95n132, 97n110
Makinson, Larry, 95n735, 95n736, 98n675
Makkai, Adam, 96n1083
Makowski, Colleen Lahan, 99n889
Makowski, Silk, 99n1012
Malawi, 2d ed, 96n119
Malbin, Michael J., 98n676
Malburg, Christopher R., 95n233
Malcolm Arnold, 99n1130
Maleson, Sandra, 98n305
Mali, 99n98
Malik, Lynda, 95n372
Malinin, Eugene D., 96n246
Malinowski, Sharon, 95n1108, 95n1111, 96n416, 97n339, 99n389
Malinowsky, H. Robert, 95n1482
Maliszewski-Pickart, Margaret, 99n879
Malkani, Sheila V., 96n582
Malkin, Gary Scott, 96n1759
Malless, Stanley, 99n1078
Mallett, Daryl F., 96n1209, 96n1218
Mallory, Susan Bayliss, 96n1728
Malloy, Alex G., 98n907, 98n915
Malloy, Mike, 99n1208
Malloy, Nancy, 98n958
Malmkjer, Kirsten, 99n896
Malo, Jean-Jacques, 95n1384
Malone, Elizabeth L., 99n1563
Malone, John, 98n88, 99n739
Malone, Russ, 95n444
Maloney, David J., Jr., 95n969, 99n841
Maloney, James O., 98n1479
Maloney's antiques & collectibles resource dir, 99n841
Maloney's antiques & collectibles resource dir, 2d ed, 95n969
Maloni, Kelly, 96n813, 96n1781
Malsberger, Brian M., 97n494, 97n495, 97n496
Malta, rev ed, 99n134
Maltin, Leonard, 95n1361, 96n1377, 99n1243
Maman, Marie, 97n1245

Mamedov, Seville, 96n1097
Mammals of New Guinea, rev ed, 96n1631
Mammals of the SW Pacific & Moluccan Islands, 96n1632
Mammels of Va., 99n1393
Mammoth dict of symbols, English lang ed, 97n636
Man, John, 95n680, 99n440
Man, myth & magic, new ed, 96n1348
Managed health care dict, 98n1510
Management consulting [CD-ROM], 98n245
Manager's desk ref, 2d ed, 97n265
Managing the publishing process, 96n665
Managing your city or town, 95n768
Mancoff, Debra N., 99n1066
Mandated benefits, 98n236
Mandel, Miriam B., 96n1211
Mandler, Crystal, 98n794, 99n771
Manela, Stewart S., 97n495
Maney, Ardith, 96n216
Manger, Jason J., 96n1784
Mangin, Paul, 98n226
Mangrum, Charles T., II, 96n341
Manheimer, Ronald J., 95n839
Maniguet, Xavier, 96n812
Mankiller, Wilma, 99n804
Manley, Bill, 98n490
Manly movie gd, 99n1242
Mann, David D., 98n1151
Mann, Michael, 95n1029
Mann, Susan Garland, 98n1151
Mann, Thomas E., 98n676
Man's gd to coping with disability, 98n775
Mansfield, Brian, 98n1233
Mansingh, Surjit, 97n108
Mansukhani, Gobind Singh, 97n1225
Mantran, Robert, 97n137
Manual for writers of term papers, theses, & dissertations, 6th ed, 97n755
Manual of ...
   bulbs, 97n1276
   climbers & wall plants, 96n1575
   grasses, 96n1583
   orchids, 96n1576
Manuel de Falla, 99n1136
Manufactures phone bk USA 1997, 98n195
Manufacturing processes ref gd, 96n1670
Manufacturing worldwide, 97n197
Manuscript material, correspondence, & graphic material in the Fiske Icelandic Collection, 95n158
Manzo, Bettina, 96n1424
Maples of the world, 95n1554
Mapping America's past, 97n402
Mapping Specialists, Ltd., 96n108
Mapping the territory, 96n658
Maps & mapping of Africa, 98n392
Maps of the world, 98n387
Maps on file, 99n414
Marantz, Kenneth, 95n1135
Marantz, Kenneth A., 96n1183
Marantz, Sylvia, 95n1135
Marantz, Sylvia S., 96n1183

March, Francis Andrew, 95n1068
March, Francis Andrew, Jr., 95n1068
March, John, 95n1185
Marching band hndbk, 2d ed, 96n1290
Marchington, James, 99n647
Marciniak, John J., 95n1607
Marco, Guy A., 97n1021
Marcus, George H., 95n983
Marcus, Jacob Rader, 95n447
Marder, Louis, 95n1220
Margaret Webster: a bio-bibliog, 95n1340
Margiotta, Franklin D., 96n682
Margiotta, Jennifer, 98n642
Margolit, Evgenji, 95n1369
Marguerite Duras: a bio-bibliog, 98n1171
Margulis, Lynn, 95n1536
Mariani, John, 95n1517
Marijuana law, 2d ed, 98n527
Marill, Alvin H., 99n1140
Marinelli, Robert P., 97n670
Marion, Donald J., 98n1296
Marjorie Kinnan Rawlings: a descriptive bibliog, 97n974
Mark, Claudia, 99n600
Mark, Deborah, 99n396
Mark Twain A to Z, 96n1217
Markel, Howard, 97n1354
Market gd for young writers, 5th ed, 97n751
Market info 1995/96, 97n275
Market share & business rankings worldwide [CD-ROM], 98n254
Market share reporter 1998, 8th ed, 99n190
Market trends for selected chemical products 1985-90 & prospects to 1995, 96n303
Markets of the US for business planners, 97n276
Markoe, Arnold, 95n36, 96n36, 99n35
Markoe, Karen, 99n35
Markoe, Karen E., 95n36, 96n36
Markowitz, Harvey, 96n417
Markus, John, 95n1616, 98n1489
Marley, David F., 96n1344, 99n629
Maroney, James F., 98n1219
Marra, Jean M., 98n70
Marre, Louis A., 96n1889
Marriage, family, & relationships, 96n862
Marsh, Arthur, 96n264
Marsh, Kenneth S., 98n1493
Marsh, Lori, 99n165
Marsh, Sue, 99n140
Marshall Cavendish ency of health, rev ed, 96n1682
Marshall, Gordon, 96n834
Marshall, Margaret M., 99n935
Martello, Mary Ann, 96n60
Marth, Del, 98n99
Marth, Martha J., 98n99
Marti, James, 96n1716, 99n1457
Martin, Christine, 95n943
Martin, Constance R., 97n1352
Martin, Deborah L., 99n754
Martin, Dolores Moyano, 99n398
Martin, Fenton S., 96n715, 97n584, 97n585, 97n586, 98n646

Martin, Garrett D., 95n302
Martin Heidegger (2): a bibliog, 97n1156
Martin, Len D., 99n1230
Martin, Murray S., 97n8
Martin, Ralph P., 95n1450, 99n1274
Martin, Richard, 96n1017
Martin, Samuel E., 96n1113
Martin, Susan Boyles, 96n177
Martin, Suzanne, 97n89
Martindale, Carolyn, 98n852
Martindale-Hubbell dispute resolution dir, 96n583
Martindale-Hubbell law dir on CD-ROM [CD-ROM], 96n584
Martinez, Joseph G. R., 96n1245
Martinez, Nancy C., 96n1245
Marting, Diane E., 95n1225
Martinich, A. P., 97n1165
Martinique, 96n171
Martin's concise Japanese dict, 96n1113
Martis, Kenneth C., 95n526
Martsinkyavitshute, Victoria, 95n1088
Marzollo, Jean, 96n28
Masks from antiquity to the modern era, 99n363
Mason, Antony, 95n572
Mason, Jane, 99n919
Mason, Mary Grimley, 95n1168
Mason, Paul, 98n318
Mason, Steve, 99n1489
Mason, Wendy H., 97n204, 98n1583
Mass media in the Middle East, 95n936
Massil, Stephen W., 98n1395
Mast, Jennifer Arnold, 95n213, 96n196
Master bk of Irish surnames, 95n464
Master hndbk of IC circuits, 3d ed, 98n1487
Master index to more summaries of children's bks, 1980-90, 99n1009
Mastering Spanish vocabulary, 97n875
Masterpieces of American lit, 95n1170
Masterpieces of Latino lit, 95n1243
Masterplots, 2d ed, 97n906
Masterplots fiction CD-ROM, rev ed [CD-ROM], 95n1112
Masterplots 2: African-American lit series, 95n1171
Masterplots 2: American fiction series suppl, 95n1178
Masterplots 2: juvenile & YA biog series, 95n1150
Masterplots 2: juvenile & YA lit series suppl, 98n1085
Masterplots 2: poetry series suppl, v.9, 99n1102
Masterplots 2: short story series suppl, 97n953
Masterplots 2: women's lit series, 96n949
Masterworks of man & nature, 2d ed, 96n458
Matchbox toys 1947-96, 2d ed, 98n929
Materials properties hndbk: titanium alloys, 96n1669
Mathematical scis professional dir 1995, 96n1828
Mathematical scis professional dir 1997, 98n1625
Mathematically speaking, 99n1328
MathSci disc [CD-ROM], 97n1414
Matlins, Stuart M., 98n1363
Matsunami, Kodo, 99n1270
Mattar, Philip, 97n136
Matter of fact: statements containing stats on current social, economics, & pol issues, v.24, 98n814
Matthews, Alison, 98n913
Matthews, Caitlin, 96n788
Matthews, Elizabeth W., 97n482
Matthews, John, 96n788
Matthews, P. H., 99n893
Matthews, Victor H., 98n1379
Matthews, Winton E., Jr., 97n535, 98n579
Mattia, Fioretta Benedetto, 99n1
Mattison, Chris, 96n1637
Mattix, Rick, 99n580
Mattson, Mark T., 97n82
Matulka, Denise I., 98n1097
Maturi, Richard J., 97n226
Matuz, Roger, 98n748, 99n865
Matz, David, 96n41, 99n523
Maurer, John G., 97n155
Mautz, Carl, 99n861
Maxford, Howard, 98n1297
Maximov, Andrei, 97n610, 98n688
Maximov's companion to who governs Moscow, 98n688
Maximov's companion to who governs the Russian Federation, summer 96, v.2, no.1, 97n610
Maxwell Anderson on the European stage 1929-92, 97n1147
Maxwell, Bruce, 96n1785, 96n1786
Maxwell Espinosa shareholder dir, 95n285
Maxwell, Kimberley A., 97n527
May, James F., 99n562
Mayadas, Nazneen S., 97n704
Mayer, R., 98n581
Mayer, Robert N., 99n176
Maynard, Donald N., 98n1437
Mayne, Tracy J., 95n786
Mayo Clinic complete bk of pregnancy & baby's 1st yr, 96n1722
Mayo-Jefferies, Deborah, 95n354
Mays, Terry M., 95n755, 97n616
Mazurek, Joseph P., 99n561
Mazza, Debora, 98n1036, 98n1037
Mazzeno, Laurence W., 97n906, 97n1000, 98n1146
McAleer, Dave, 95n1293, 97n1066, 97n1067
McAlester, Lee, 99n433
McAlester, Virginia, 99n433
McAlpine, Janice, 99n907
McArt, Pat, 98n134
McBeth, Amy, 98n1203
McBride, Francis R., 97n118
McBride, James S., 95n1705
McBrien, Richard P., 96n1469
McBurney, Melissa, 96n1643
McCall, Douglas L., 99n1231
McCall, Mary Reilly, 96n1496, 98n827
McCallum, Lawrence, 99n1205
McCanless, Christel Ludewig, 95n994
McCann, Gary, 99n549
McCarter, Joan, 97n123
McCarthy, J. Thomas, 97n519
McCarthy, Ronald M., 98n496, 98n692
McCarthy's desk ency of intellectual property, 2d ed, 97n519
McCauley, Martin, 96n145
McClellan, Gail, 96n1384
McCloud, Barry, 96n1320

McClure, Paul, 96n734
McColm, Ian J., 95n1634
McComb, Gordon, 99n1487
McComb, William C., 99n1367
McConnell, Elizabeth Huffmaster, 99n574
McConnell, Stacy A., 99n1115, 99n1116
McCormick, Jim, 97n74
McCoy, Ralph E., 95n704
McCracken, Penny, 99n864
McCready, Sam, 98n1166
McCroskey, Marilyn, 96n631
McCue, Margi Laird, 97n675
McCulloch, Alan, 96n1032
McCulloch, Susan, 96n1032
McCutcheon, Mark, 99n916
McDaniel, George, 95n1695
McDermott, Anne, 98n1020
McDermott, John D., 99n474
McDonald, Lee M., 97n1192
McDonald, Peter, 95n1509
McDonald, Steve, 98n729
McDonald's collectibles, 98n898
McEachran, John D., 99n1388
McElmeel, Sharron L., 95n1137, 96n1184
McElroy, Lorie Jenkins, 98n840, 99n536
McEvedy, Colin, 97n428
McEwan, Peter J. M., 96n1025
McFadden, Margaret, 98n837
McFarland, Daniel Miles, 99n96
McFarland, Ruth, 99n821
McGaughey, Ryan T., 96n963
McGee, Marty, 99n1232
McGillivray, Alice V., 95n737, 96n735, 98n673, 99n677
McGinley, Ronald J., 95n1591
McGinn, Bernard, 99n1266
McGovern, Bernie, 98n99
McGovern, Edythe M., 95n1138
McGrath, Alister E., 95n1465
McGrath, Anne F., 96n1004
McGrath, Kimberley A., 96n1492
McGraw-Hill circuit ency & troubleshooting gd, v.2, 95n1615
McGraw-Hill concise ency of sci & tech, 3d ed, 95n1492
McGraw-Hill dict of ...
   astronomy, 98n1608
   biosci, 98n1440
   chemistry, 98n1602
   earth sci, 98n1603
   engineering, 98n1476
   geology & mineralogy, 98n1614
   intl trade & finance, 95n243
   mathematics, 98n1626
   physics, 2d ed, 98n1621
   scientific & technical terms, 5th ed, 95n1493
McGraw-Hill electronics dict, 5th ed, 95n1616
McGraw-Hill electronics dict, 6th ed, 98n1489
McGraw-Hill ency of ...
   economics, 96n179
   personal computing, 97n1372
   quality terms & concepts, 96n284
   sci & tech, 8th ed, 98n1407

McGraw-Hill illus dict of personal computers, 4th ed, 96n1760
McGraw-Hill illus ency of robotics & artificial intelligence, 96n1753
McGraw-Hill illus telecom dict, 99n1491
McGraw-Hill machining & metalworking hndbk, 95n1639
McGraw-Hill machining & metalworking hndbk, 2d ed, 99n1413
McGraw-Hill multimedia ency of sci & tech [CD-ROM], 95n1494, 99n1316
McGraw-Hill recycling hndbk, 95n1782
McGraw-Hill yrbk of sci & tech 1996, 97n1243
McGraw-Hill yrbk of sci & tech 1999, 99n1325
McGreal, Ian P., 96n1433
McGregor, Andrew, 99n689
McGuckin, Frank, 98n557, 99n583
McGuiness, Colleen, 95n714, 95n731
McHugh, Michael P., 98n1386
McIlwain, John, 95n1048, 95n1052
McIlwaine, John, 97n92, 98n392
McIlwraith, Thomas F., 99n409
McIntire, Dennis, 98n1197
McIntire, Dennis K., 99n956, 99n1101
McKay, David, 98n684
McKay, George, 99n1391
McKay, Ian, 98n903
McKeever, Jane, 95n14
McKeever, Susan, 96n64
McKenna, Erin, 97n365
McKenna, Ted, 98n1497
McKenty, Elizabeth J., 95n860, 97n682
McKenzie, Carol A., 99n637
McKenzie, Diane, 96n898
McKenzie, Kirsty, 97n392
McKernan, Luke, 96n1399, 98n1280
McKetta, John J., 97n1378
McKhann, Heather I., 95n1536
McKim, Donald K., 98n1358
McKim, Mark G., 97n1172
McKinsey, C. Dennis, 96n1456
McKinzey, Rima, 99n900
McKissack, Frederick, 96n1488, 96n1489
McKissack, Patricia, 96n1488, 96n1489
McKitterick, D. J., 97n971
McKnew & Parker's buyer's gd to sportfishing boats, 1995 ed, 96n810
McKnew, Ed, 96n810
McKnight, Jean Sinclair, 98n511
McLaughlin, Arthur J., Jr., 99n1481
McLaughlin, Ben, 96n877
McLeish, Kenneth, 97n1091
McLelland, Y., 99n239
McLeod, Denise, 96n883
McLeod, Donald W., 97n680
McLerran, Jennifer, 98n951
McLoskey, Lansing D., 99n1154
McMahon, Thomas, 98n1100, 98n1101
McMenemy, John, 96n752
McMullen, William Wallace, 95n1275
McMurray, Emily J., 96n1490
McMurtry, Jo, 95n1397

McNally, Mary Jane, 95n663
McNeil, Alex, 97n1132
McNeil, Ian, 97n1236
McNeil, William F., 99n716
McNeir, Clive Leo, 95n750
McNenly, Jennifer, 99n689
McPeek, Gail A., 95n1570
McPherson, James M., 96n486
McQuain, Jeffrey, 99n1078
McQueen, Barbara, 95n1543
McQueen, Jim, 95n1543
McQuiston, Judith L., 96n651
McRae, Linda, 97n315
McRobie, Alan, 97n144
McShane, Clay, 98n1647
McShane, Marilyn D., 97n505
McTyre, Ruthann Boles, 99n1113
Meacham, Mary, 95n654
Mead, Thomas, 99n701
Meadows, Eddie S., 96n1327
Meanor, Patrick, 95n1179
Means, Spencer, 95n1114
Meath-Lang, Bonnie, 96n857
Mechancal engineering ref manual, 9th ed, 95n1637
Mechanical engineer's ref bk, 12th ed, 96n1673
Mecklermedia's official Internet World Internet yellow pages, 1996 ed, 98n1587
Mecklermedia's official Internet WWW yellow pages, 1996 ed, 98n1588
Meckna, Michael, 95n1274
Medal of honor recipients 1863-1994, 96n689
Media courses UK 1997, 4th ed, 98n860
Media French, 99n927
Media in African & Africa in the media, 98n853
Media in the movies, 99n1228
Media review digest, v. 26, 1996, 97n9
Medical abbrevs, 8th ed, 98n1526
Medical advisor, 97n1348
Medical & health info dir 1998, 9th ed, 99n1426
Medical & psychological effects of concentration camps on Holocaust survivors, v.4: genocide, 98n708
Medical device register 1994: intl v, 95n1660
Medical dict in 6 langs, 97n1331
Medical discoveries, 98n1530
Medical meanings: a glossary of word origins, 98n1528
Medicare made easy, rev ed, 98n1539
Medieval & early modern data bank [CD-ROM], 98n165
Medieval & Renaissance mss in the Walters Art Gallery, 99n600
Medieval art, 97n799
Medieval iconography, 99n810
Medieval wordbk, 97n838
Meek, Kerry Lynne, 97n730
Mehler, Mark, 99n267
Meho, Lokman I., 98n116
Mehta, Mukesh, 96n1739, 99n1422
Meier, Matt S., 98n349
Meier, Regula A., 95n159
Meilikhov, Evgenii Z., 98n1620
Meiners, Phyllis A., 98n793

Mellersh, H. E. L., 96n559, 96n564
Melton, J. Gordon, 95n1328, 95n1445, 97n633, 98n1321, 98n1366, 99n1214
Meltzer, Ellen, 96n503
Meltzer, Tom, 96n358
Melville ency: the novels, 95n1194
Members of Congress, 97n584
Memorabilia mathematica: the philomath's quotation bk, 95n1741
Men of achievement, 15th ed, 95n32
Men of achievement 1997, 17th ed, 99n28
Mender, Mona, 98n1199
Mendez, Serafin Mendez, 99n93
Mendy, Peter Karibe, 98n456
Menon, Elizabeth K., 99n862
Men's Health, editors of, 95n1647
Menser, Gary P., 98n1452
Mercatante, Anthony S., 96n1350
Mercer, Derrick, 97n464
Mercer, E. Ian, 98n1599
Merck manual of medical info, home ed, 98n1540
Mercury labels: a discography, 95n1259
Merriam, Louise A., 97n406
Merriam-Webster's biogl dict, 96n29
Merriam-Webster's collegiate dict, deluxe audio ed, 98n998
Merriam-Webster's collegiate dict deluxe, electronic ed [CD-ROM], 96n1066
Merriam-Webster's concise hndbk for writers, 99n833
Merriam-Webster's crossword puzzle dict, 2d ed, 97n836
Merriam-Webster's dict, home & office ed, 97n820
Merriam-Webster's dict of basic English, 96n1067
Merriam-Webster's dict of law, 97n488
Merriam-Webster's ency of lit, 96n1146
Merriam-Webster's geographical dict, 3d ed, 98n396
Merriam-Webster's gd to intl business communications, 95n253
Merriam-Webster's gd to punctuation & style, 96n969
Merriam-Webster's manual for writers & editors, 99n834
Merriam-Webster's medical desk dict, 95n1655
Merriam-Webster's medical dict, 96n1701
Merriam-Webster's pocket biogl dict, 97n24
Merriam-Webster's pocket geographical dict, 97n380
Merriam-Webster's reader's hndbk, 99n964
Merriam-Webster's secretarial hndbk, 3d, 95n328
Merrick, Janna C., 97n1330
Merritt, Frederick S., 95n1603, 95n1604
Merry, John A., 99n1576
Merskey, Harold, 96n1723
Mersky, Roy M., 95n601
Mertvago, Peter, 96n1125, 97n1089
Meserole, Mike, 98n727
Messengers of God: a Jewish prophets who's who, 99n1292
Metals & alloys in unified numbering system, 6th ed, 95n1635
Metalworking in Africa S of the Sahara, 96n1668
Metaphors dict, 96n1091
Metaphysical poets: a chronology, 95n1224
Metcalf, Allan A., 98n1000
Metropolitan Opera gd to recorded opera, 95n1284
Metter, Ellen, 97n752
Metz, Allan, 95n534, 98n255, 98n800

Meuli, Judith, 95n917
Mews, Siegfried, 95n1232
Mexican, Central, & S American art, 98n961
Mexican pol biogs, 1935-93, 3d ed, 96n763
Mexican-American War of 1846-48, 96n657
Mexico, 95n173
Mexico business: the portable ency for doing business with Mexico, 95n290
Mexico co hndbk, 1995/96 ed, 96n254
Mexico data bank, 95n172
Mexico environmental report, 97n224
Meyer, Carol J., 96n673
Meyer, Harvey K., 95n170
Meyer, Jean-Christophe, 95n1072
Meyer, Jessie H., 95n170
Meyer, Sandra, 96n1844, 97n1422, 99n1548
Meyer, Ulrich, 98n1245
Meyering, Sheryl L., 95n1186
Meyerink, Kory L., 99n403
Meyers, Eric M., 98n429, 98n1377
Meyers, Ric, 96n1380
Meyers, Robert A., 96n1561, 97n1269, 97n1270, 97n1271
MFC investment hndbk 1994, 95n272
Michael, Erika, 98n943
Michael Singer's film directors, 1997, 12th ed, 98n1317
Michaelides, Chris, 97n121
Michaels, Alan, 95n1062
Michaels, Philip J., 95n881
Michaluk, Stephen, Jr., 97n952
Micheli, Lyle J., 96n1729
Michell, Simon, 97n572
Michener, Charles D., 95n1591
Mickolus, Edward F., 98n556
Micronesian religion & lore, 96n1439
Microsoft Bkshelf Internet dir, 1996-97 ed, 98n1589
Microsoft Encarta multimedia ency 1995 [CD-ROM], 95n60
Microsoft press computer dict, 99n1488
Middle Ages, 97n471
Middle & jr high school lib catalog, 7th ed, 96n650
Middle East, 8th ed, 96n764
Middle East & N Africa 1995, 96n160
Middle East & N Africa 1997, 43d ed, 97n139
Middle East & N Africa 1998, 99n87
Middle East & N Africa on file, 96n459
Middle East military balance 1993-94, 96n695
Middle East military balance, 1996, 99n634
Middle innings: a documentary hist of baseball, 1900-48, 99n722
Middle level educ, 97n295
Middleplots 4, 95n1131
Middleton, John, 97n319, 99n100
Mid-Youth market, 98n261
Mieder, Wolfgang, 95n1221, 95n1314, 96n760, 96n1215, 98n1157, 98n1254
Miermont, Jacques, 96n1718
Miglani, Gurbachan S., 99n1358
Migration stats 1994, 96n907
Mihailovich, Vasa D., 96n1262, 99n1091
Mihalkanin, Edward S., 98n564
Miniature empires, 99n537

Mikhail Bakhtin (II): a bibliog, 95n1425
Mikhail, E. H., 95n1034
Miki, Mihoko, 97n110
Mikotowicz, Tom, 95n1349
Mildren, K. W., 97n1296
Milepost: trip planner for Ala. & Western Canada, 49th ed, 98n406
Milepost, editors of, 95n100
Miles, Wyndham D., 95n1718
Milestones in sci & tech, 2d ed, 95n1503
Miletich, John J., 95n1675, 96n1724, 98n761
Militarism in Arab society, 98n609
Military aircraft insignia of the world, 99n636
Military contracts/procurement locator [CD-ROM], 99n632
Military ency of Russia & Eurasia, v.5, 96n146
Military hist of the Third World since 1945, 95n697
Military personnel installations locator CD-ROM [CD-ROM], 99n633
Militia & the Natl Guard in America since colonial times, 95n682
Militias in America, 97n613
Millar, David, 98n1399
Millard, Bob, 95n1300
Millard, Robert T., 97n817
Millennium champagne & sparkling wine gd, 99n1342
Miller, Allan W., 99n852
Miller, Blair, 96n1378
Miller, Christine M., 97n409
Miller, Corki, 99n1182
Miller, David, 99n640
Miller, E. Willard, 95n1752, 96n239, 97n621, 99n1565
Miller, Elizabeth B., 95n1706, 98n1590, 99n307
Miller, Eugene, 99n318
Miller, Gordon L., 9/n403
Miller, Hope H., 97n1278
Miller, J. Michael, 97n1217
Miller, Jacqueline Y., 95n1578
Miller, Jacquelyn C., 97n403
Miller, Jay, 96n414
Miller, Jeanette W., 98n1397
Miller, Joseph, 95n652, 98n580
Miller, Joseph C., 99n535
Miller, Judith, 98n903
Miller, Judith A., 98n521
Miller, Julia Wang, 99n1468
Miller, Lee D., 95n1578
Miller, Mark A., 96n1396
Miller, Mary, 95n1444
Miller, Millie, 95n1576
Miller, Orson K., Jr., 97n1278
Miller, Oscar J., 95n596
Miller, R. H., 96n1142
Miller, Randall M., 97n408, 98n438
Miller, Ruby M., 95n1752, 96n239, 97n621, 99n1565
Miller, Sally E., 98n72
Miller, Steve Z., 98n1554
Miller, Tice L., 97n1151
Miller-Lachmann, Lyn, 97n10
Miller's intl antiques price gd 1997, 18th ed, 98n903
Miller's intl antiques price gd 1999, 99n842

Milligan, Thomas B., 95n1269
Mills, A. D., 99n422
Mills, Carlotta, 95n364, 96n875, 96n878, 96n961
Mills, Carlotta R., 95n196
Mills, Dick, 95n1586
Mills, Gary B., 95n546
Mills, J. J., 96n169
Mills, Jerry Leath, 97n924
Mills, Joyce H., 96n1460
Mills, Watson E., 95n1455, 96n1460, 98n1370, 98n1371
Milne, Rosemary C., 98n1024
Milner, John, 95n1001
Milner-Gulland, Robin, 99n125
Milstead, Jessica L., 95n636, 99n598
Milton, Leanne Wiberg, 96n1804
Milton's sonnets, 96n1214
Mimms, Kenneth A., 98n346
Mina, Robin, 98n185
Minahan, James, 97n583, 99n537
Minakir, Pavel A., 96n247
Minars, David, 95n331
Minderovic, Zoran, 99n1541
Miner, Brad, 98n691
Miner, Jeremy T., 99n770, 99n812
Miner, Lynn E., 99n770, 99n812
Miner, Margaret, 99n75
Mineral investment conditions in selected countries of the Asia-Pacific region, 96n1842
Minerals: identifying, learning about, & collecting..., 95n1731
Minerals & gemstones of the world, rev ed, 95n1729
Minerals industry taxation policies for Asia & the Pacific, 96n1843
Minnesota, 98n412
Minnett, Ann M., 95n774
Minor ballet composers, 98n1215
Minor, Barbara B., 95n386, 95n387, 97n312
Minor, Mark, 97n1190
Minority & women's complete scholarship bk, 99n344
Minority orgs, 5th ed, 98n330
Minter, D. W., 96n1581
Mirkovich, Thomas R., 98n724
Mischler, Clifford, 97n780
Mishler, Clifford, 98n911, 98n912
MIT ency of the Japanese economy, 95n273
Mitchell, B. R., 96n917
Mitchell, Bruce M., 97n283
Mitchell, Charlotte, 98n1152
Mitchell, David A., 97n1351
Mitchell express: the fast track to the top colleges, 95n369
Mitchell, Jerome, 96n1230
Mitchell, Joan S., 97n535, 98n579
Mitchell, Joyce Slayton, 95n369, 95n388
Mitchell Kennerly imprint: a descriptive bibliog, 98n592
Mitchell, Laura, 97n1351
Mitchell, Mary T., 96n733
Mitchell, Robert, 98n302
Mitchell, Susan, 96n908, 97n717, 98n256, 99n90
Mitsis, Phillip T., 98n1334
Mix, Ann Bennett, 98n367

Mixter, Keith E., 97n1022
Miyamoto, Tadao, 96n1059
MLA intl bibliog [CD-ROM], 96n1143
Moanin' low: a discography of female popular vocal recordings, 1920-33, 97n1064
Mobley, Mary F., 95n321
Modern African American writers, 95n1173
Modern America 1914-45, 96n518
Modern American lit, v.6, 4th ed, 99n1048
Modern American popular religion, 97n1171
Modern black writers: suppl, 96n1157
Modern British novel of the left, 99n1068
Modern campaigns, 98n615
Modern Catholic ency, 95n1469
Modern China: an ency of hist, culture, & nationalism, 99n109
Modern classic writers, 95n1180
Modern collectible dolls identification & value gd, 98n919
Modern dict for the legal profession, 1994 suppl, 96n580
Modern drama scholarship & criticism 1981-90, 98n1105
Modern ency of E Slavic, Baltic, & Eurasian lits, v.10, 98n1170
Modern ency of religions in Russia & Eurasia, v.7, 99n1267
Modern Germany, 99n129
Modern harpsichord music, 96n1288
Modern Irish writers, 98n1176
Modern Japan, 99n486
Modern Latin-American fiction writers, 2d series, 96n1258
Modern verse drama, 95n1207
Modern women writers, 95n1174, 97n907
Modeste, Naomi N., 97n1317
Moe, Barbara, 99n755
Moeng, Sao Tern, 97n869
Moffat, Riley, 97n723
Mogelonsky, Marcia, 98n257
Mogge, Dru, 97n1375
Mohen, J. -P., 97n479
Molecular biology & biotech, 96n1561
Moles, Peter, 98n184
Molitor, Graham T. T., 97n44
Moll, Verna Penn, 96n172
Mollenkopf, John H., 95n471
Moller, Bjorn, 96n683
Molloy, Les, 96n1601
Momsen, Janet Henshall, 97n145
Monaghan, Patricia, 98n1258
Monash biogl dict of 20th century Australia, 96n39
Monder, Eric, 95n1350
Money for graduate students in the humanities 1996-98, 98n848
Money for graduate students in the scis 1996-98, 98n1411
Money for graduate students in the social scis 1996-98, 98n91
MoneyFind bkware dir of small business investors, 95n197
Mongolia, 95n135
Monkman, Karen, 99n805
Monks, Franz J., 95n352
Monroe, Burt L., Jr., 95n1571, 95n1572, 95n1574
Monroe, Jacqueline Wasserman, 98n523
Monsell, Thomas, 99n1238

Monster manual: a complete gd to your favorite creatures, 95n1323
Montalvo, Rene J., 98n20
Monteath, Peter, 95n566
Montgomery Clift: a bio-bibliog, 95n1348
Montgomery, John H., 95n1510
Monush, Barry, 97n770, 97n771
Mood, Terry Ann, 96n377
Moodie, Michael, 99n644
Moody, Joan, 96n1871
Moody, Marilyn K., 95n76
Moon, Beverly, 98n1351
Moon bk, rev ed, 99n1521
Moon, Spencer, 98n1278
Mooney, Blake, 95n1664
Mooney, Martha T., 98n65
Moore, Chris, 99n281
Moore, Deborah Dash, 99n394
Moore, Jean M., 96n658, 97n1005
Moore, John L., 95n733
Moore, P., 98n1604
Moore, Patrick, 95n1722, 98n1605
Moore, Robert J., 96n1696, 98n1541
Morad, Deborah, 99n761
Morad, Deborah J., 99n59
Moran, Andrea, 96n1503
Moran, Edward, 98n26
Moran, Michael G., 95n1113
More battlefields of Canada, 95n692
More bks kids will sit still for, 96n663
More kids' favorite bks, 96n1168
More names & naming, 97n370
More opening nights on Broadway: a critical quotebk of the musical theatre 1965-81, 98n1329
Morehead, Joe, 97n53
Morelli, Jim, 98n1563
Morelock, J. D., 96n698
Morena, John J., 99n1410
Morey, Carl, 98n1192
Morgan, Bill, 96n1210, 97n972, 98n922
Morgan, Jenny, 98n1309
Morgan, Kathleen O'Leary, 95n624, 96n602, 98n552
Morgan, Rick L., 99n558
Morgan, Scott, 95n624, 96n602, 98n552
Morgan, William, 95n1089, 95n1090
Mori, Fumitoshi, 95n1589
Moriarty, J. Laura, 99n574
Morin, Isobel V., 95n716, 96n943
Moritz, Robert Edouard, 95n1741
Morkot, Robert, 97n449
Morningstar mutual fund 500, 1997-98 ed, 99n173
Morocco, rev ed, 96n120
Morozov, Vladimir, 96n40
Morris, Allen, 95n104
Morris, Audrey Brichetto, 99n617
Morris, Betty J., 96n651
Morris, Bruce B., 98n1310
Morris, Catherine, 95n597
Morris, Christopher, 95n1049, 95n1050
Morris, Deirdre, 96n39

Morris, Desmond, 98n1465
Morris, Dwight, 95n738
Morris, Gregory L., 95n1165
Morris, James M., 99n641
Morris, James McGrath, 97n693
Morris, Leslie R., 96n641
Morris, Neil, 95n473, 98n1033
Morris, Percy A., 96n1595
Morris, Roswitha, 98n1033
Morris, Wendy V. A., 99n928
Morrison, Elizabeth, 97n112
Morriss, Roger, 96n679
Morrone, John, 99n830
Morrow, Blaine Victor, 97n1376
Morrow, Charlene, 99n1542
Morrow, Ed, 96n30
Morse, David, 98n1575
Mortensen, Sandra, 96n1249
Morton, Alan, 99n1224
Morton, Barry, 97n94
Morton, Brian, 98n1221
Morton, Fred, 97n94
Morton, Leslie T., 96n1696, 98n1541
Morton, Mark, 98n1423
Mortuary sci, 95n845
Morville, Peter, 98n1595
Morwood, James, 95n1087, 96n1117
Mosby's GenRx, 8th ed [CD-ROM], 99n1482
Mosby's primary care medicine rapid ref [CD-ROM], 99n1451
Moseley, Christopher, 95n1030
Moseley, Edward H., 99n462
Moseley, Merritt, 99n1064
Moser, James D., 97n770
Moses, Norton H., 98n547
Moses, Robert, 98n1264
Moshkovitz, Moshe, 99n838
Moskin, J. Robert, 95n216
Moss flora of Mexico, 95n1547
Moss, Joyce, 95n127, 95n537, 96n509, 97n472, 98n1072
Mossman, Jennifer, 95n2, 96n3
Mote, Dave, 98n1058
Motif-index of folk lit, new ed [CD-ROM], 95n1317
Motion picture gd, 98n1311
Mott, Wesley T., 97n962, 97n964
Moulton, Carroll, 99n491
Mound, Laurence, 96n71
Mount, Ellis, 95n1503
Mountain bikers almanac, 1996, 96n815
Mountain range: a dict of expressions from Appalachia to the Ozarks, 98n1007
Mouser, Jeffrey D., 99n1411
Mouzard, Francois, 95n1697
Movie list bk, 95n1389
Moving & relocation sourcebk 1998, 2d ed, 99n781
Mowlana, Hamid, 95n936
Mowrey, Peter C., 95n1398
Moyer, Patsy, 98n918, 98n919
Moys, Elizabeth M., 98n533
Mozart diary, 98n1213

Mrozek, Donald J., 99n622
MSA profile, 1996, 97n724
Mudd, Mollie B., 96n193
Muhr, Jeffrey, 95n1496, 95n1497
Muir, Hazel, 96n1487
Mulder, John M., 98n647
Mulhern, Chieko I., 95n1236
Mulholland, Joan, 95n937
Mullaney, Marie Marmo, 95n717
Mullay, Marilyn, 97n1229
Mullay, Sandy, 98n137
Muller, Helen D., 95n1138
Muller, Karl, 98n1350
Muller, Nathan, 99n1493
Muller, Robert N., 99n1367
Muller, Sheila D., 98n949
Multicultural children's lit, 97n933
Multicultural dict of proverbs, 98n1250
Multicultural educ, 97n283
Multicultural educ dir, 98n273
Multicultural picture bks, 95n1135
Multicultural projects index, 99n856
Multicultural student's gd to colleges, rev, 98n302
Multiculturalism, 99n369
Multiethnic children's lit, 95n1136
Multilateral treaties deposited with the secretary-general, 96n612
Multilevel design, 96n99
Multilingual thesaurus of geosciences, 97n1400
Multimedia: law & practice, 95n615
Multimedia: the complete gd, 97n1362
Multimedia business 500 [CD-ROM], 95n198
Multimedia dir, 4th ed, 97n1363
Multimedia tech from A-Z, 96n1750
Multinational corps & the environment, 96n1851
Multistate gd to benefits law, 99n559
Multistate payroll gd, 97n257
Mulvany, Nancy C., 95n657
Mulvenon, James, 99n108
Mundell, P. Sue, 99n398
Municipal executive dir, 96n728
Municipal yr bk 1998, v.65, 99n680
Munro, Neil, 99n715
Munro, Pamela, 96n1099
Munro-Hay, Stuart, 96n117
Munson, Kenneth, 99n1575
Munson, Robert S., 95n801
Murder cases of the 20th century, 97n503
Murph, Roxane C., 96n1190
Murphy, Bruce, 98n843
Murphy, C. Edward, 96n849, 97n683
Murphy, Christina, 97n284
Murphy, J. L., 99n245
Murphy, Jacquelyn M., 95n1462
Murphy, Jennifer L., 96n245
Murphy, John C., 98n1474
Murphy, Justin D., 97n467
Murphy, Linda L., 95n787
Murphy, Michael J., 97n1262
Murphy, Patrick D., 95n1326

Murray, Jim, 98n1426
Murray, Jocelyn, 99n95
Murray, Linda, 98n950
Murray, Michael T., 97n1349
Murray, Peter, 98n950
Murray, R. Michael, 98n1209
Murray, Raymond, 95n1374
Murray, Thomson C., 97n1447
Muschell, David, 97n823
Muse, Robert L., 97n1191
Museum careers & training, 95n83
Museum premieres, exhibitions, & special events, 98n72
Museums of the world, 98n73
Musgrave, Ruth S., 99n587
Mushroom bk, 97n1280
Mushrooms of N America in color, 97n1278
Music & dance of the world's religions, 97n1087
Music & poetry in the Middle Ages, 96n1296
Music, dance & theater scholarships, 96n1365
Music, David W., 98n1246
Music festivals from Bach to blues, 97n1029
Music for voice & classical guitar, 1945-96, 98n1219
Music in Canada, 98n1192
Music of Francis Poulenc (1899-1963), 97n1044
Music of the golden age, 1900-50 & beyond, 99n1139
Music of the repressed Russian avant-garde, 1900-29, 95n1261
Music ref & research materials, 4th ed, rev ed, 95n1252
Music ref & research materials, 5th ed, 98n1189
Music since 1900, 5th ed, 95n1262
Musical Americans: a biogl dict 1918-26, 98n1200
Musical anthologies for analytical study, 97n1023
Musical resources for the rev common lectionary, 95n1312
Musical theater synopses, 99n1244
Musicals, 2d ed, 95n1408
MusicHound country, 98n1233
MusicHound jazz, 99n1168
MusicHound rock, 97n1084
Musiker, Naomi, 97n101, 98n19, 99n1158
Musiker, Reuben, 97n101, 97n551, 98n19, 99n1158
Muslim almanac, 97n1219
Muslim women throughout the world, 98n830
Mussen, William A., Jr., 99n729
Mustachio, Thomas, 95n1468
Mustazza, Leonard, 99n1118
Mutual Fund Public Co., Ltd., 95n272
MVA/SME machine vision industry dir, 1994, 95n1640
MVR bk: motor servs gd 1994, 95n739
MVR bk: motor servs gd 1997 ed, 98n536
MVR decoder digest 1994, 95n740
MVR decoder digest 1997 ed, 98n537
My 1st atlas, 95n472
My 1st bk of animals from A to Z, 95n1563
My 1st bk of biogs, 96n28
My 1st 100 Hebrew words, 95n1080
My 1st sci dict, 96n1498
Mycenaean civilization, 97n448
Myers, Jane E., 96n843
Myers, Robert A., 99n98
Myerson, Joel, 95n1187

Mystery & suspense writers, 99n1032
Mystery Fancier: an index to vs.1-13, 95n1159
Mystery women, v.1 1860-1979, 99n1030
Myth: myths & legends of the world explored, 97n1091
Myths & hero tales, 98n1084
Myxomycetes: a hndbk of slime molds, 96n1587

Naden, Corinne J., 95n1130, 95n1131, 98n1091, 98n1103
Nadine Gordimer: a bibliog of primary & secondary sources, 1937-92, 95n1240
NAFTA & GATT: environmental & economic issues, 98n705
NAFTA bibliog, 98n255
Nagel, Rob, 95n576, 96n407
Nagy, Andrea, 96n1705, 99n1450
Nakamura, Joyce, 95n1146, 96n1178
Naked in cyberspace: how to find personal info online, 98n1596
Name that bk! questions & answers on outstanding children's bks, 2d ed, 99n1007
Namibia, rev ed, 99n99
Nanji, Azim A., 97n1219
Nantz, Jim, 98n739
Napierkowski, Marie Rose, 99n1014, 99n1106, 99n1107, 99n1108
Napolo, Tony, 95n591
Narins, Brigham, 98n1068
Narrative bibliog of the African American frontier, 97n405
Narwekar, Sanjit, 95n1364
NASA atlas of the solar system, 98n1609
NASA thesaurus, 1994 ed, 95n1600
Nash, Jay Robert, 98n701
Nash, Paul W., 95n675
Nash, Rose, 98n1048
Nash, Stanley D., 95n877
NASIRE dir 1994, 95n728
NASW register of clinical social workers 1993, 95n879
Nathanson, Laura Walthier, 95n1665
National accounts stats, 98n203
National accounts stats 1991, 95n254
National accounts studies of the ESCWA region, 96n158
National anthems of the world, 8th ed, 95n1260
National Audubon Society bird garden, 96n1560
National Audubon Society field gd to N American mammals, rev ed, 97n1294
National Audubon Society 1st field gd: birds, 99n1381
National Audubon Society 1st field gd: insects, 99n1389
National Audubon Society 1st field gd: mammals, 99n1392
National Audubon Society 1st field gd: rocks & minerals, 99n1535
National Audubon Society 1st field gd: weather, 99n1533
National Audubon Society interactive CD-ROM gd to N American birds [CD-ROM], 97n1290
National building codes hndbk, 99n1403
National consumer phone bk USA 1998, 99n153
National cultures of the world, 98n90
National dir of ...
   addresses & telephone nos, 1995 ed, 96n56
   AIDS care 1994-95, 95n1676
   bereavement support grps & servs, 1996, 98n769
   catalogs 1997, 98n181
   churches, synagogues, & other houses of worship, 95n1445
   corporate giving, 98n790
   corporate giving, 3d ed, 95n196
   corporate public affairs 1994, 95n199
   corporate public affairs 1998, 99n154
   educl programs in gerontology, 6th ed, 95n838
   grantmaking public charities, 97n697
   haunted places, 95n788
   internships, 9th ed, 95n302
   minority-owned business firms, 7th ed, 95n200
   minority-owned business firms, 9th ed, 99n155
   newspaper op-ed pages, 96n979
   nonprofit orgs 1995, 96n193
   nonprofit orgs 1998, 99n55
   state business licensing & regulation, 96n194
   woman-owned business firms, 95n201
   woman-owned business firm, 9th ed, 99n156
National e-mail & fax dir 1999, 99n56
National faculty dir 1999, 29th ed, 99n328
National fax dir, 1996, 97n51
National 5-digit zip code & post office dir 1996, 97n52
National Gallery complete illus catalogue, 97n796
National Gardening Assoc dict of horticulture, 95n1531
National Geographic picture atlas of our world, rev ed, 95n485
National gd to ...
   educl credit for training programs, 1997 ed, 98n315
   funding for children, youth, & families, 3d ed, 97n698
   funding for community dvlpmt, 97n699
   funding for elementary & secondary educ, 97n300
   funding for higher educ, 4th ed, 98n291
   funding for info tech, 98n583
   funding for lib & info serv, 97n531
   funding for the economically disadvantaged, 95n865
   funding for the environment & animal welfare, 2d ed, 96n878
   funding for women & girls, 96n952
   funding in aging, 4th ed, 96n849
   funding in arts & culture, 3d ed, 96n961
   funding in health, 5th ed, 99n1427
   funding in higher educ, 3d ed, 95n364
   funding in religion, 97n1184
   funding in substance abuse, 96n896
National health dir, 1996, 97n1324
National healthlines dir 1994, 95n1649
National Hispanic media dir, 1997, 98n861
National Hockey League official gd & record bk 1997-98, 99n733
National Hockey League Stanley Cup playoffs fact gd 1998, 99n734
National job hotline dir, 1995, 95n307
National jobbank 1998, 98n237
National jobline dir, 95n305
National museum of American art [CD-ROM], 98n966
National party conventions 1831-1996, 99n681
National Planning for Special Collections Committee, 96n661
National profile of community colleges 1995-96, 96n366
National road race ency, 98n751
National seashores, rev ed, 96n475

National serv & AmeriCorps, 98n800
National sports politicies, 98n725
National storytelling dir, 1996, 97n549
National survey of state laws, 2d ed, 99n565
National trade & professional assns of the US 1998, 99n157
National Trust gd to historic bed & breakfasts, inns & small hotels, 95n511
National Trust gd to historic bed & breakfasts, inns, & small hotels, 4th ed, 97n390
Nations of Africa, 98n321
Nations without states: a histl dict of contemporary natl movements, 97n583
Native America: portrait of the peoples, 95n438
Native America in the 20th century, 95n434
Native American almanac, 95n441
Native American genealogical sourcebk, 96n433
Native American in long fiction, 97n958
Native American info dir, 2d ed, 99n391
Native American issues, 97n344
Native American painters of the 20th century, 96n1054
Native American sun dance religion & ceremony, 99n384
Native Americans, 99n390
Native Americans in fiction, 95n1118
Native Canadian anthropology & hist, rev ed, 95n430
Native educ dir 1997, 98n272
Native N American almanac, 95n439
Native N American almanac, 95n443
Native N American biog, 97n339
Native N American chronology, 96n415
Native N American firsts, 99n387
Native N American lit, 96n1259
Native studies collection, 95n432
Native tribes of N America, 95n435
Natividad, Irene, 96n392
Natkiel, Richard, 95n524
Natural gas stats sourcebk, 95n1753
Natural gas stats sourcebk, 2d ed, 96n1844
Natural resources, 99n1571
Naturopathic hndbk of herbal formulas, 3d ed, 96n1717
Nau, Jim, 97n1275
Nauffrus, William F., 97n979
Nautical almanac for the year 1996, 96n1895
Navajo-English dict, 95n1089
Naval Institute gd to ...
    the ships & aircraft of the US Fleet, 16th ed, 98n628
    world military aviation 1995, 96n697
    world military aviation 1997-98, 99n637
    world naval weapons systems, 1994 update, 95n701
    world naval weapons systems 1997-98, 98n634
Naval Institute histl atlas of the US Navy, 96n701
Navarra, Tova, 95n1677, 97n1265
Navarro, Jose Maria, 97n875
Navia, Luis E., 96n1425
Nayler, G. H. F., 97n1310
Naylor, Lynne, 97n769
Naylor, Phillip Chiviges, 96n114
Nazzal, Laila A., 98n488
Nazzal, Nafez Y., 98n488
NCAA basketball, 97n652

NCAA basketball: the official 1997 women's college basketball records bk, 98n740
NCAA Final Four, 97n653
NCAA football, 96n819, 99n730
NCEA/Ganley's Catholic schools in America 1995, 23d ed, 97n1216
Neagles, James C., 95n695
Neal, Joseph C., 98n1453
Neal, Valerie, 96n1647
Neal-Schuman index to finger-plays, 95n1153
Nebraska hist, 96n494
Needham, Kate, 95n1077
Neft, David S., 95n820, 98n746
Negotiation lit, 96n283
Nehmer, Kathleen S., 96n322
Nehmer, Kathleen Suttles, 96n1771, 99n285, 99n288
Neibaur, James L., 95n1385, 96n1397
Nellis, Joseph G., 97n716
Nelson almanac, 99n642
Nelson, Bonnie R., 99n581
Nelson, Cyndi, 95n1576
Nelson, David N., 95n128
Nelson, Garrison, 96n733
Nelson, Joseph S., 95n1587
Nelson, Michael, 98n674
Nelson, Richard Alan, 97n595
Nemet-Nejat, Karen Rhea, 99n511
Neotropical migratory birds, 97n1289
Nersessian, Vrej Nerses, 95n149
Nerys Purchon's hndbk of natural healing, 99n1458
Ness, Richard R., 98n1298
Net games, 96n813
Net gd, 96n1781
Net jl dir, vol. 1, no. 2, 98n1591
Netemeyer, Richard G., 95n321
Netherlands Antilles & Aruba, 95n167
Nettl, Paul, 96n1281
Network Dvlpmt & MARC Standards Office, 96n634
Network Pr dict of networking, 96n1761
Netzorg, Morton J., 97n432
Neufeldt, Victoria, 95n1033
Neumeister, Susan M., 97n404
Neusner, Jacob, 97n1223
Never eat more than you can lift, & other food quotes & quips, 98n1429
Nevins, Allan, 98n432
Nevis, Joel A., 96n1060
New A to Z of women's health, 3d ed, 96n1680
New acronyms, initialisms, & abbrevs, v.2, 96n3
New Beacon bk of quotations by women, 97n70
New Bible commentary, 96n1458
New Bible dict, 3d ed, 98n1373
New bibliog of writings on varieties of English 1984-92/93, 95n1028
New bk of ...
    goddesses & heroines, 3d ed, 98n1258
    knowledge, 95n61
    knowledge, 98n46
    popular sci, 1998 ed, 99n1317
New comparative world atlas, 98n388

New complete medical & health ency, 95n1646
New cosmopolitan world atlas, rev ed, 95n486
New Deal fine arts projects, 95n993
New dict of ...
  Catholic social thought, 96n1470
  Christian ethics & pastoral theology, 97n1209
  religions, rev ed, 97n1179
New Ency Britannica, 95n62
New ency of the American west, 99n463
New ency of Zionism & Israel, 96n164
New England in fiction 1787-1990, 95n1183
New England in US govt pubs, 1789-1849, 99n452
New England transcendentalists [CD-ROM], 99n1046
New England's mountain flowers, 98n1450
New fortunes 1994, 96n176
New Fowler's modern English usage, 3d ed, 97n756
New, George R., 97n535
New, Gregory R., 98n579
New Grolier ency of WW II, 96n684
New Grolier multimedia ency [CD-ROM], 95n42
New Grove dict of jazz, 96n1328
New hacker's dict, 3d ed, 98n1578
New Hampshire [&] Vt.: atlas of histl county boundaries, 96n439
New histl dict of the American film industry, 99n1215
New info revolution: a ref hndbk, 97n538
New intl dict of O.T. theology & exegesis, 98n1374
New Interpreter's Bible [CD-ROM], 99n1279
New intl atlas, 25th ed, 96n449
New Islamic dynasties, 97n135
New Kabuki ency, 98n1324
New mktg opportunities, 4th ed, 96n1482
New, Melvyn, 99n1074
New members of Congress almanac, 99n661
New members of Congress almanac: 103rd Congress, 95n718
New members of Congress almanac: 105th US Congress, 98n654
New men's studies, 2d ed, 96n866
New Nelson Japanese-English character dict, rev ed, 99n933
New Oxford companion to lit in French, 96n1252
New parents sourcebk, 97n709
New Penguin dict of geology, 97n1401
New Phillies ency, 95n808
New Princeton hndbk of poetic terms, 95n1248
New religious movements in Western Europe, 98n1343
New research centers, 1996, 96n339
New shorter Oxford English dict [CD-ROM], 98n999
New Sotheby's wine ency, 98n1424
New standard ency, 95n65
New Testament intro, 97n1192
New view almanac, 97n7
New well-tempered sentence, rev ed, 95n945
New Yawk tawk: a dict of NYC expressions, 99n904
New York City in the 1980s, 95n471
New York Public Lib bk of popular Americana, 95n1334
New York Public Lib business desk ref, 99n282
New York Public Lib desk ref, 2d ed, 95n80
New York Public Lib sci desk ref, 96n1512
New York Public Lib student's desk ref, 95n81
New York Public Lib writer's gd to style & usage, 95n946

New York Public Lib's bks of the century, 97n882
New York Stock Exchange fact bk: 1993 data, 95n219
New York, the city in more than 500 memorable quotations, 98n101
New York Times almanac 1998, 98n2
New York Times film reviews, v.19: 1993-94, 97n1133
New York Times theater reviews, v.28: 1993-94, 97n1154
New Zealand, rev ed, 99n114
New Zealand bks in print 1995, 23d ed, 96n23
Newbery & Caldecott awards, 1998 ed, 99n995
Newbery companion, 98n1091
Newbolt, Peter, 98n1159
Newby, Gregory B., 95n1707
Newcomb, Horace, 98n888
Newell, Clayton R., 99n630
Newlin, George, 97n992, 97n993
Newlin, Keith, 99n1055
Newly independent states of Eurasia, 95n163
Newly independent states of Eurasia, 2d ed, 98n125
Newman, Barry M., 96n285
Newman, Graeme R., 99n547
Newman, John, 98n1056
Newman, John J., 99n402
Newman, Marketa, 96n1023
Newman, Oksana, 95n1783
Newman, Patricia E., 97n1237
Newman, Richard, 99n80
Newman, William M., 96n1437
Newnes electronic engineer's pocket bk, 95n1617
News media yellow bk, 96n963
Newsletters in print 1998, 10th ed, 98n880
Newsmakers 1994: the people behind today's headlines, 95n33
Newsmakers 1997, 98n25
Newsome, Chevelle, 98n862
Newspapers online, 1995, 3d ed, 96n982
Newton, David E., 95n859, 96n1874, 97n748, 97n1435, 98n855
Newton, Kenneth, 98n684
Newton, Sarah E., 95n1422
Newton, Scott, 95n752
Ng, Franklin, 96n394
Ng, Man Lun, 99n775
Nguyen, Dinh-hoa, 97n877
Nicholas, J. Karl, 95n1042
Nicholas, Jeremy, 98n1222
Nicholls, C. S., 97n38, 99n22
Nichols, Victoria, 99n1033
Niemi, Richard G., 95n743, 99n683
Nienhauser, William H., Jr., 99n1090
Nierenberg, William A., 96n1856
Nietzsche canon, 97n1157
Niger, 95n120
Nightjars: a gd to the nightjars, nighthawks, & their relatives, 99n1376
Niles, Ann, 96n80
Nill, Kimball R., 95n1620
Nilsen, Don L. F., 98n1150, 99n1060
Nimmo, Dan, 98n862
Nine worlds hosted by Patrick Stewart [CD-ROM], 98n1610

1990-91 Gulf War, 97n456
1998 franchise annual, 99n165
1997-98 hockey annual, 99n737
Nineteenth- & 20th-century harpists, 96n1287
Nineteenth-century American western writers, 99n957
Nineteenth-century American women writers, 98n1126
Nineteenth century baseball, 97n651
Nineteenth-century British bk-collectors & bibliographers, 99n592
Nineteenth-century British literary biographers, 96n1226
Nineteenth-century German writers, 1841-1900, 95n1232
Nineteenth-century lit criticism, v.46, 96n1158
Nineteenth-century lit criticism, v.47, 97n908
Nineteenth-century lit criticism, v.48, 97n909
Nineteenth-century lit criticism, v.49, 97n910
Nineteenth-century lit criticism, v.50, 97n911
Nineteenth-century lit criticism, v.51, 97n912
Nineteenth-century lit criticism, v.52, 97n913
Nineteenth-century lit criticism, v.61, 99n973
Nineteenth-century lit criticism, v.62, 99n974
Nineteenth-century lit criticism annual cum title index for 1996, 97n914
NIV compact concordance, 95n1453
NIV complete Bible lib [CD-ROM], 98n1380
Nixon on stage & screen, 99n1238
NLN gd to undergraduate RD educ, 5th ed, 99n1477
Nobari, Nuchine, 98n1582
Nobel laureates in chemistry, 1901-92, 95n1715
Nobel prize winners 1992-96 suppl, 98n26
Noble, Keith Allan, 97n289
Noble, Scott, 97n483
Noble, William, 96n965
Noble's intl gd to the law reports, 97n483
Noel Coward: a bio-bibliog, 95n1342
Noel, Thomas J., 95n527
Noffsinger, James Philip, 98n610
Nofi, Albert A., 99n627
Nogowski, John, 96n1334
Nohria, Nitin, 99n278
Nohring, Fritz-Jurgen, 99n1444
Nolan, Cathal J., 98n655
Nolan, James L., 95n290, 97n237
Noll, Richard, 96n780
Nonprofit law dict, 96n579
Nonprofit manager's resource dir, 98n244
Nonprofit sector yellow bk, winter 1999 ed, 99n142
Non-profits & educ job finder 1997-2000, 98n235
Non-profit's job finder, 3d ed, 95n316
Nonviolent action, 98n496
Norcross, John C., 95n786
Nordby, Judith, 95n135
Nordin, Jorund B., 96n639, 96n640
Nordquist, Joan, 95n275, 95n424, 95n618, 95n901, 95n902, 95n1423, 95n1424, 95n1425, 95n1760, 95n1761, 95n1762, 96n833, 96n935, 96n936, 96n937, 96n956, 96n957, 96n1851, 97n327, 97n484, 97n513, 97n727, 97n728, 97n729, 97n1156, 98n548, 98n636, 98n637, 98n705, 98n831, 98n832, 98n1506, 99n758, 99n795
Norfolk, Elizabeth, 98n903, 99n842

Norman, Teresa, 99n407
Normandy [CD-ROM], 96n693
Norris, Frederick W., 98n1386
Norris, Joann, 95n796, 97n1446, 99n71
Norris, John, 95n796
Norris, John R., 97n1446
Norris, Robert S., 95n702
North America in colonial times, 99n464
North American art since 1900, 98n962
North American art to 1900, 98n963
North American brewers resource dir 1996-97, 13th ed, 97n1251
North American coins & prices, 99n845
North American facsimile bk [CD-ROM], 95n70
North American factbk, 1994-95, 96n1541
North American furniture standards, 99n1412
North American Indian music, 98n1191
North American industry classification system, 1997, 99n162
North American labor markets, 99n227
North American landscape trees, 97n1283
North American shortwave frequency gd, v.3, 97n768
North American women artists of the 20th century, 96n1026
North Atlantic Treaty Org, 96n773
North Carolina Center for Creative Retirement, University of North Carolina at Asheville, 95n839
North Carolina hist, 96n493
Northcutt, Wayne, 97n115
Northeast gd to saltwater fishing & boating, 95n817
Northern Ireland: a pol dir 1968-93, 96n761
Northwest women: an annot bibliog of sources on the hist of Oreg. & Washington women, 1787-1970, 98n828
Norton, Alan, 95n709
Norton, James H. K., 99n104
Norton, Mary Beth, 96n554
Norwegian dict, 2d ed, 96n1120
Noshpitz, Joseph D., 99n1466
Notable Asian Americans, 96n396
Notable black American women, bk.2, 97n34
Notable corporate chronologies, 96n177
Notable Latin American women, 96n938
Notable Latino Americans, 98n349
Notable mathematicians, 99n1541
Notable Native Americans, 96n416
Notable poets, 99n1103
Notable 20th-century pianists, 96n1293
Notable 20th-century scientists, 96n1490
Notable US Ambassadors since 1775, 98n655
Notable women in math, 99n1542
Notable women in the life sciences, 97n1231
Notable women in the physical scis, 98n1598
Notable women in world hist, 99n797
Notess, Greg R., 95n1708, 99n61
Nottage, Luke R., 99n546
Novalis gd to Canadian shrines, 96n1476
Novallo, Annette, 95n1690
Novas, Himilce, 96n408
Novel & short story writer's market, 1996, 97n753
Novel openers, 96n1188
Novels for students, v.1, 98n1109
Novels for students, v.2, 98n1110

Novels for students, v.3, 99n1013
Novels for students, v.4, 99n1014
Novitsky, Ed, 95n1259
Novum Testamentum, v.36a, 96n1460
Now read on: a gd to contemporary popular fiction, 2d ed, 96n1187
Nowak, Ronald M., 96n1610
Nowlan, Gwendolyn W., 95n1403
Nowlan, Robert A., 95n1403, 97n41
NPD Group, Inc., 96n673
NPR classical music companion, 98n1202
NPR gd to building a classical CD collection, 95n1282
NSFRE fund-raising dict, 98n784
NTC's American idioms dict, 2d ed, 95n1044
NTC's compact Russian & English dict, 95n1093
NTC's compact Swedish & English dict, 98n1053
NTC's dict of ...
   advertising, 2d ed, 95n325
   American English pronunciation, 96n1077
   American slang & colloquial expressions, 2d ed, 95n1060
   British slang & colloquial expressions, 99n908
   China's cultural code words, 97n107
   common mistakes in Spanish, 96n1137
   commonplace words in real-life contexts, 99n915
   easily confused words, 95n1038
   euphemisms, 99n902
   folksy, regional, & rural sayings, 97n837
   Japan's business code words, 99n193
   Latin American Spanish, 98n1049
   Mexican cultural code words, 97n134
   quotations, 96n94
   Spanish cognates thematically organized, 98n1048
   Spanish false cognates, 95n1094
   the USA, 99n1190
NTC's hndbk for writers, 96n970
NTC's multilingual dict of American Sign Lang, 97n870
NTC's new college Russian & English dict, 98n1045
NTC's Romanian & English dict, 97n865
NTC's thematic dict of American idioms, 99n905
NTC's thematic dict of American slang, 99n911
NTC's thesaurus of everyday American English, 96n1093
NTC's Vietnamese-English dict, 97n877
NTIS ordernow [CD-ROM], 98n62
Nuba, Hannah, 95n349
Nuclear test ban: glossary in English, French, & Arabic, 97n578
Nuclear weapons databk, v.5, 95n702
Nuiry, Octavio, 98n861
Null, Gary, 98n1550, 99n1459
Nulman, Macy, 99n1293
Numbers: how many, how far, how long, how much, 98n810
Nunez, Benjamin, 96n532, 97n427
Nurcombe, Valerie J., 97n1299, 98n61
Nurse's clinical gd to psychiatric & mental health care, 97n1355
Nursing diagnosis pocket manual, 97n1353
Nursing home statl yrbk, 1995, 97n1327
Nursing licensure gdlines, 1998, 99n1476
Nursing96 drug hndbk, 97n1360
Nutribase nutrition facts desk ref, 96n1540

Nutrition & diet therapy ref dict, 4th ed, 98n1422
Nutt, Timothy G., 96n490
Nwanna, Gladson I., 95n515
Nyeko, Balam, 96n123, 97n104

Oakes, Elizabeth, 99n339
Oakes, Elizabeth H., 98n330, 99n359, 99n750
Oakley, Stewart P., 99n493
O'Bannon, George W., 95n973
Oberly, James W., 97n406
Obituaries in the performing arts, 1994, 97n1097
Obituaries in the performing arts, 1995, 97n1098
O'Brien, Geoffrey, 98n8
O'Brien, George, 96n1257
O'Brien, Jacqueline Wasserman, 96n923
O'Brien, Joanne, 98n1348
O'Brien, Lois A., 95n592
O'Brien, Philip M., 99n1056
O'Brien, Robert L., 98n1491
Occupational outlook hndbk, 1996-97 ed, 98n238
Occupational safety & health glossary, 95n295
Occupational safety & health law 1997, 99n566
Oceanographic & marine resources: 1960-Jan 1997 [CD-ROM], 98n1616
Oceans atlas, 95n1733
Ochoa, George, 96n1374, 99n525, 99n818, 99n1307
Ochoa, Holly Byers, 95n746
Ocko, Stephanie, 96n473
O'Connor, J., 95n1061, 98n1015
O'Connor, Joan, 95n1270
O'Connor, Patrice M., 98n1522
O'Connor, Sharon Hamby, 97n493
O'Daly, Anne, 97n1268
O'Dell, Richard E., 95n696
O'Donnell, Christopher, 98n1387
Ody, Penelope, 97n1281
OECD health systems, 95n1651
OECD Nuclear Energy Agency, 95n1755
OECD statl compendium 1996/1 [CD-ROM], 97n227
Of spirituality, 97n1169
Of the people, by the people, for the people, & other quotations by Abraham Lincoln, 97n67
Ofcansky, Thomas P., 98n457
Office for Subject Cataloging Policy, 96n630
Official ABMS dir of board certified medical specialists 1996, 96n1704
Official America online yellow pages, 99n53
Official athletic college gd: baseball, 1995 ed, 96n805
Official baseball atlas, 1994 ed, 95n807
Official baseball rules 1997, 98n735
Official celebrity registry 1994-95, 96n796
Official fantasy hockey gd, 99n732
Official gd to ...
   American attitudes, 97n717
   American incomes, 2d ed, 98n225
   household spending, 97n278
   racial & ethnic diversity, 97n324
   the American marketplace, 2d ed, 96n911
   the generations, 96n908

Official Internet dict, 99n1489
Official jl of the European Communities, v.38, English ed, 96n755
Official license plate bk, 97n1447
Official Major League Baseball fact bk 1997, 98n736
Official 1996 NFL record & fact book, 97n654
Official rules of ...
   golf, 99n731
   ice hockey, 99n735
   softball, 99n741
   the Natl Basketball Assoc 1997-98, 99n725
Official US Open almanac, 96n820
Offord, M. H., 95n1073
Ofosu-Appiah, L. H., 97n91
Ogden, Scott, 96n1546
Ogden, Suzanne, 99n110
Ogden, Tom, 98n716
Ogilvie, Marilyn Bailey, 97n730
Ogle, Patrick, 95n1392
O'Halloran, M. Sean, 95n1679
O'Handley, Kathryn, 98n683
O'Hara, Scarlett, 96n69, 98n1458
Oheneba-Sakyi, Yaw, 95n849
Ohles, Frederik, 98n266
Ohles, Shirley M., 98n266
Oil & gas info 1992, 95n1754
Oil & gas jl data bk, 1995 ed, 96n1845
Oil & gas on the Internet, 97n1415
Ojibwa chiefs, 1690-1890, 97n343
Okonski, Walter, 98n480
Okuda, Ted, 96n1397
Ol' blue eyes: a Frank Sinatra ency, 99n1118
O'Laughlin, Michael C., 95n464
Old & Middle English lit, 96n1230
Old farmer's almanac 1995, 96n4
Old masters, 98n980
Old Testament commentary survey, 2d ed, 97n1189
Old Testament intro, 97n1187
Old West: day by day, 96n502
Oldenburg, Philip, 99n243
Older Americans almanac, 95n839
Older Americans info dir, 95n837
Oldman, Mark, 95n303, 98n221, 99n270
O'Leary, A. P., 98n619
O'Leary, Michael K., 95n153
O'Leary, Mick, 96n1777
Olendzenski, Lorraine, 95n1536
Olitzky, Kerry M., 96n1479, 97n1221
Oliver, Evelyn Dorothy, 97n1176
Oliver, Judith H., 99n600
Oliver Smith: a bio-bibliog, 95n1349
Oliver, Valerie Burnham, 97n1093
Oliveres, Raphael A., 98n1049
Oliverson, Ray, 98n1497
Olken, Charles E., 99n1341
O'Loughlin, John, 95n708
Olsen, Kirstin, 95n911
Olsen, Margaret, 98n913
Olsen, Wallace C., 95n1533, 96n1522
Olson, Annette, 96n868

Olson, Elizabeth A., 98n269
Olson, James S., 95n400, 97n321, 98n466, 98n562, 99n370
Olson, Jenni, 97n1126
Olson, Richard, 99n1300
Olson, Roberta A., 95n783
Olson, Stan, 95n865
Olsson, Urban, 97n1288
Olton, Roy, 97n620
Oman, rev ed, 96n166
O'Meara, John, 97n845
Omlid, Steve, 98n796
OMRI annual survey of E Europe & the former Soviet Union 1996, 99n115
On common ground: world religions in America [CD-ROM], 98n1367
On tap, 1995 ed, 96n1532
On the move, 95n1786
On the road with your pet, 99n424
On the trail of the buffalo soldier, 96n699
One hundred & one botanists, 96n1564
100 athletes who shaped sports hist, 96n795
100 best mutual funds you can buy, 1995, 97n185
100 best retirement businesses, 95n211
100 best stocks to own in America, 99n166
100 best stocks to own in America, 3d ed, 95n223
100 drugs that work, 95n1683
150 yrs of America's Smithsonian [CD-ROM], 98n74
105 best investments for the 21st century, 97n226
100 great Africans, 96n112
100 great cities of world hist, 96n927
100 greatest, 98n27
100 greatest athletes of all time, 96n797
100 men who shaped world hist, 96n33
100 most popular YA authors, 97n941
100 most popular YA authors, rev ed, 98n1102
100 natural wonders of the world, 96n1602
101 desktop pub & graphic programs, 95n678
100 research topic gds for students, 97n543
110 Canadian stats on work & family, 95n848
100 women who shaped world hist, 96n32
One hundred yrs of American women writing, 1848-1948, 98n1124
1000 great guitarists, 95n1276
1,001 chemicals in everyday products, 95n1716
1001 free goodies & cheapies, 96n60
O'Neill, Angus, 96n1002
O'Neill, Cynthia, 96n1503
O'Neill, James, 98n1318
O'Neill, Mary, 96n1100, 98n1027
On-line job search companion, 96n272
ONLINE 100, 96n1777
Online user's ency, 95n1701
Onorato, Mary L., 99n973
Onstad, Dianne, 98n1427
Open doors 1994/95, 97n311
Open doors 1996/97: report on intl educl exchange, 99n352
Open secrets, 3d ed, 95n736
Open secrets: the ency of congressional money & pols, 4th ed, 98n675
Opera: the rough gd, 99n1157

Opera cos & houses of the US, 96n1302
Opera on screen, 99n1218
Opera premiere reviews & re-assessments, 99n1156
Operas in 1 act, 98n1224
Operation Desert Shield/Desert Storm, 96n563
Opie, Iona, 99n1004
Opie, Mary-Jane, 95n1023
Opie, Peter, 99n1004
Opler, Paul A., 95n1577
Oppenheim, Joanne, 96n1010
Oppenheim, Micha Falk, 95n448
Oppenheim, Mike, 95n1683
Oppenheim, Stephanie, 96n1010
Opportunities for vocational study, 96n385
Orchard, Andy, 98n1259
Orchestra on record, 1896-1926, 98n1225
Orchestral music, 3d ed, 98n1226
Orchestration theory, 97n1057
Orchids for the South, 96n1574
Orchids of Brazil, 95n1543
Ord, Alan J., 96n1295
Orel, Vladimir, 99n921
Orel, Vladimir E., 96n1107
Orenstein, Glenn S., 95n953
Orenstein, Ruth M., 95n953, 98n51
Organ lit, 3d ed, 96n1289
Organic gardener's home ref, 96n1543
Organization for Economic Cooperation & Dvlpmt, 96n918
Organized crime, 96n594
Orgill, Andrew, 97n456
Oriental rugs: a bibliog, 95n973
Origins & dvlpmt of the Arab-Israeli conflict, 99n699
Orion blue bk, 98n182
Orion blue bk: audio 1997, 99n177
Orion blue bk: camera, 99n178
Orion blue bk: car stereo 1998, 99n1485
Orion blue bk: copier, 99n179
Orion blue bk: guitars & musical instruments, 1998 ed, 99n1147
Orion blue bk: gun 1998, 99n849
Orion blue bk: professional sound 1998, 99n180
Orion blue bk: video & TV, 1998 ed, 99n181
Orion blue bk: vintage guitars & collectibles 1998, summer ed, 99n182
Ornstein, Norman J., 98n676
Orodenker, Richard, 98n883
Orthodox Judaism in America, 97n1224
Ortolani, Benito, 97n1148
Orton, Lavinia, 98n860
Oryx gd to distance learning, 95n342
Oryx gd to distance learning, 98n280
Orzepowski, Lisa G., 96n12
Osborne, Charles, 96n1300
Osborne, Robert, 96n1372
Oscar stars from A-Z, 98n1279
Oscar Wilde ency, 99n1075
Oserman, Steve, 99n268
Osgood, Nancy J., 96n897
OSHA field inspection ref manual, 96n277
OSHA quick gd for residential builders & contractors, 99n1404

O'Shea, Kathleen A., 98n549
Osifchin, Gary P., 95n718, 95n744, 98n642, 98n654
Oski, Frank A., 97n1354
Osteyee, Carol H., 95n664
O'Sullivan, Marie, 97n305, 97n309
Oterdoom, H. J., 95n1554
Otfinoski, Steven, 99n121
Ott, Nicolaus, 99n885
Ottenheimer, Harriet, 95n115
Ottenheimer, Martin, 95n115
Our century, 95n591
Our planet Earth, 99n1003
Our Sunday Visitors Catholic ency, rev ed, 99n1268
Our Sunday Visitor's Catholic ency & Catholic dict [CD-ROM], 96n1471
Our Sunday Visitors ency of Catholic doctrine, 98n1388
Our Sunday Visitor's ency of Catholic hist, 96n1472
Our Sunday Visitor's ency of saints, 99n1261
Our Sunday Visitor's 1997 Catholic almanac, 97n1203
Ousaka, Yumi, 97n1202
Ousby, Ian, 95n1103, 97n894
Out Magazine, editors of, 96n53
"Out of the mouths of mathematicians", 95n1742
Outer space, 99n1522
Outlaws, mobsters, & crooks, 99n578
Outline maps on file, 98n398
Outstanding bks for the college bound, 99n1011
Outstanding women athletes, 2d ed, 99n710
Ovando, Natascha M. L., 96n882
Overlook film ency: horror, 96n1379
Overlook film ency: sci fic, 95n1375
Overlook film ency: the western, 95n1376
Overseas summer jobs 1995, 26th ed, 96n278
Owen, Bill, 98n887
Oxbridge dir of newsletters 1994, 95n954
Oxford atlas of exploration, 99n415
Oxford atlas of the world, 4th ed, 97n376
Oxford children's bk of famous people, 96n31
Oxford color Italian dict, 98n1036
Oxford companion to ...
   African American lit, 98n1129
   American lit, 6th ed, 97n966
   archaeology, 98n428
   Australian children's lit, 95n1149
   Australian lit, 2d ed, 96n1248
   Australian military hist, 97n565
   Australian music, 99n1122
   British hist, 99n503
   Canadian lit, 99n1088
Oxford companion to Christian art & architecture, 98n950
   English lit, rev ed, 96n1231
   German lit, 3d ed, 98n1173
   local & family hist, 97n352
   philosophy, 97n1166
   20th-century lit in English, 98n1073
   20th-century poetry in English, 95n1249
   wine, 96n1528
   women's writing in the US, 96n1200
   WW II, 97n571
Oxford desk dict, American ed, 96n1068

Oxford desk dict & thesaurus, American ed, 98n993
Oxford desk ref atlas, 98n389
Oxford desk thesaurus, American ed, 96n1094
Oxford dict & thesaurus, American ed, 98n994
Oxford dict for the business world, 95n186
Oxford dict of ...
   biochemistry & molecular biology, 98n1444
   computing for learners of English, 98n1577
   current english, 97n821
   English grammar, 96n1080
   foreign words & phrases, 99n903
   humorous quotations, 97n71
   music, 96n1270
   nursery rhymes, 99n1004
   philosophy, 95n1428
   pol quotations, 98n641
   quotations, 4th ed, 98n83
   saints, 99n1262
   the Christian Church, 3d ed, 98n1389
   the Jewish religion, 98n1396
   world religions, 98n1357
Oxford ency of ...
   archaeology in the Near East, 98n429
   the modern Islamic world, 96n1477
   the Reformation, 97n1211
Oxford encyclopedic English dict, 2d ed, 96n1069
Oxford encyclopedic world atlas, 95n481
Oxford encyclopedic world atlas, 3d ed, 97n377
Oxford English dict additions series, 95n1055
Oxford English dict on CD, 2d ed [CD-ROM], 97n843
Oxford English minidict, 4th ed, 96n1070
Oxford English-Hebrew dict, 97n855
Oxford family ency, 98n47
Oxford gd to British women writers, 95n1203
Oxford hndbk of clinical dentistry, 2d ed, 97n1351
Oxford hist of W philosophy, 96n1434
Oxford Italian desk dict, 98n1037
Oxford Italian minidict, 2d ed, 98n1038
Oxford large print dict, 2d ed, 97n818
Oxford Latin minidict, 96n1117
Oxford medical companion, 96n1702
Oxford minireference dict & thesaurus, 96n1078
Oxford paperback French dict, 2d ed, 95n1078
Oxford paperback French dict & grammar, 96n1101
Oxford paperback Portuguese dict, 98n1042
Oxford paperback Spanish dict & grammar, 98n1050
Oxford Russian minidict, 96n1126
Oxford Spanish desk dict, 99n941
Oxford starter French dict, 98n1027
Oxford starter German dict, 98n1033
Oxford starter Russian dict, 98n1046
Oxford starter Spanish dict, 98n1051
Oxford 3-in-1 bilingual dict [CD-ROM], 98n1021
Oxford-Duden German desk dict, new ed, 98n1030
Oxford-Duden German dict [CD-ROM], 98n1032
Oxford-Duden German dict, rev ed, 98n1031
Oxford-Duden pictorial English dict, 2d ed, 96n1096
Oxford-Duden pictorial Hungarian-English dict, 96n1109
Oxford-Duden pictorial Italian & English dict, 96n1110
Oxford-Duden pictorial Thai & English dict, 96n1140

Oxford-Hachette French desk dict, 98n1026
Oxford-Hachette French dict, 96n1100
Oxlade, Chris, 99n1314
Ozone dilemma, 96n1874

Pace, Brian P., 95n1653
Pacific coast crabs & shrimps, 96n1622
Pacific Coast League: statl hist, 1903-57, 97n647
Pacific NW, 98n415
Pacific War atlas 1941-45, 96n676
Pacific War ency, 99n627
Packard, Robert T., 96n1045
Pada index & reverse Pada index to early Jain canons, 97n1202
Paddock, Lisa, 98n538, 99n556
Paddock, Lisa Olson, 97n364
Padgett, G. K. Boyle, 96n1712
Padian, Kevin, 99n1539
Padwa, Lynette, 97n57
Paehlke, Robert, 97n1426
Page, Martin, 99n1352
Pagell, Ruth A., 95n255, 99n228
Paietta, Ann C., 96n1366
Pain sourcebk, 99n1473
Paine, Lincoln P., 98n1651
Painted ladies: butterflies of N America, 95n1576
Painter's hndbk, 96n1053
PAIS select [CD-ROM], 98n89
Palac, Pete R., 99n871
Palder, Edward L., 95n226, 98n183
Palestine question, 95n175
Palidvor-Sonevyts'ka, Nataliia, 98n1217
Palm, Mary E., 97n1279
Palma, Robert J. Sr., 96n1795
Palmatier, Robert A., 96n1074
Palmegiano, E. M., 99n1417
Palmer, Alan, 97n117
Palmer, Beverly Wilson, 95n746
Palmer, Bill, 96n1380
Palmer, Clare, 98n1628
Palmer, Jean B., 95n12
Palmer, Karen, 96n1380
Palmer, Martin, 98n1348
Palmer, Pete, 98n737
Palmieri, Margaret W., 95n1278
Palmieri, Robert, 95n1278
Palmisano, Joseph M., 95n390
Palmowski, Jan, 98n504
Palms throughout the world, 97n1284
Palombo, Fulvio, 98n959
Paludan, Eve, 95n942
Pan-African chronology, 97n426
Pan-African chronology 2, 99n478
Pancza-Graham, Arleen, 98n963
Pandiri, Ananda M., 97n430
Pandy, David, 95n1321
Panero, Julius, 96n1048
Panic, M., 96n232
Pankhurst, R., 96n1563

Pankhurst, Richard, 96n117
Pantel, Gerda, 97n393
Panton, Kenneth J., 98n467, 99n504
Papa, Linda, 95n929
Papadakis, Elim, 99n1554
Paperbound bks in print fall 1994, 95n20
Papercutting: an intl bibliog & selected gd to US collections, 95n981
Paperno, Slava, 97n867
Pappas, Lee Brigance, 95n400
Pappas, Nicholas C. J., 95n400
Paradise Lost: an annot bibliog, 97n997
Paramount in Paris, 99n1236
Pardeck, Jean A., 99n756
Pardeck, John T., 95n772, 99n756
Pare, Michael A., 95n794, 96n415, 97n641, 98n270, 98n718
Parent, Mary P., 97n294
Parenting, 96n903
Parenting A to Z, 2d ed, 98n803
Parent's gd to medical emergencies, 98n1523
Parent's gd to the best children's videos & where to find them, 96n1386
Parents' resource almanac, 96n901
Parham, Iris A., 96n897
Paris, 99n127
Parish, James Robert, 95n1386, 96n1407
Parish, Peter J., 98n442
Park, Amy Lynn, 98n166
Park, Jun S., 95n1630
Park, Thomas K., 98n458
Parker, Derek, 96n783
Parker, Geoffrey, 98n616
Parker, Helen, 97n1274, 97n1277
Parker, Julia, 96n783
Parker, Mark, 96n810
Parker, Mary, 99n1026
Parker, Peter, 97n916
Parker, Philip M., 98n90, 98n331, 98n990, 98n1368
Parker, Robert, 99n1141
Parker, Sybil P., 95n1492, 95n1493, 96n456, 98n1407, 98n1440, 98n1476, 98n1602, 98n1603, 98n1608, 98n1614, 98n1621, 98n1626
Parkers' complete bk of dreams, 96n783
Parks dir of the US, 2d ed, 95n512
Parmley, Robert O., 95n1641
Parr, Mike, 99n1378
Parrinder, Geoffrey, 99n1287
Parrish, Thomas, 97n473
Parrots, 99n1378
Parry, David, 95n1056
Parry, Donald W., 98n1397
Parry, Melanie, 98n24
Parsons, Charles H., 99n1156
Partington, Angela, 98n83, 99n78
Partnow, Elaine, 99n1025
Partridge, Karen E., 95n753
Partridge, Michael S., 95n753
Pas, Julian F., 99n1294
Pasahow, Edward, 96n1653
Pascoe, Robin, 96n476

Passenger & immigration lists index, 1996 suppl, 97n367
Passow, A. Harry, 95n352
Patent, copyright, & trademark, 97n520
Patent law index, 1997, 98n545
Patents hndbk, 96n589
Paterek, Josephine, 95n442
Paterson, Thomas G., 98n660
Pathfinder to US export control laws & regulations, 95n614
Patient's desk ref, 95n1663
Patients gd to ...
    medical terminology, 99n1442
    medical tests, 99n1454
    medical tests, 99n1455
Patin, Thomas, 98n951
Patoureau, Michel, 96n1448
Patricia Smith's doll values, 12th ed, 97n781
Patrick, John J., 95n607
Patrick Kavanagh: a ref gd, 98n1174
Patrick, Ruth, 95n1726, 99n1536
Patrick, Vanessa E., 95n1016
Patt, Carol A., 96n629
Patten, Fred, 98n1307
Patterson, Alex, 96n1015
Patterson, Anna Grace, 95n16, 96n11
Patterson, Brad, 99n114
Patterson, Kathryn, 99n114
Patterson, Lotsee, 95n436, 98n327
Patterson, Michael, 98n1323
Patterson, William L., 97n861
Patton-Hulce, Vicki R., 97n514
Patty's industrial hygiene & toxicology, v.2, 4th ed, 95n1784
Patty's industrial hygiene & toxicology, v.3, pt.B, 3d ed, 96n1875
Patty's industrial hygiene & toxicology CD ROM [CD-ROM], 99n1566
Paul, Barbara Dotts, 95n554
Paul, Ellen, 96n860
Paul, Kevin, 96n320
Pavia, Audrey, 98n1466
Pavlov, A. S., 98n629
Paxton, John, 99n690
Payne, Jennifer, 97n746
Payne, Michael, 97n746
Payne, Wardell J., 97n1181
Pazzanita, Anthony G., 95n110, 97n100, 97n105, 99n97
PC Globe maps'n'facts [CD-ROM], 96n450
PC user's essential accessible pocket dict, 96n1756
PCI: pers contents index [CD-ROM], 98n66
PDR family gd to prescription drugs, 99n1483
PDR generics, 96n1738
PDR gd to drug interactions, side effects, indications, 1995, 49th ed, 96n1739
Peabody, Virginia S., 96n285
Peaceful peoples, 95n91
Peacemaking in medieval Europe, 99n492
Peacock, Lindsay, 99n1575
Peacock, Scot, 99n949, 99n950, 99n980
Pear, Nancy, 97n638, 99n418
Pearlman, Mickey, 96n380
Pearsall, Judy, 96n1069

Pearson, J. D., 95n111
Pearson, Joyce A. McCray, 99n62
Pearson, Richard, 95n1202
Pearson's hndbk desk ed, 98n1492
Pease, David A., 96n1541
Peck, David, 98n1070
Peck, Malcolm C., 98n489
Peck, Terrance W., 99n271
Pederson, Jay P., 96n397, 97n951, 99n205, 99n207, 99n208
Pederson, Lucille M., 95n1351
Pedigo, Alan, 97n1043
Pedowitz, Arnold H., 97n494, 97n495, 97n496, 99n589
Peeva, K., 97n1366
Pehle, Walter H., 98n470
Pelka, Fred, 98n776
Pellam, John L., 95n985, 98n150, 99n113
Pelle, Kimberly D., 97n661
Pelletier, Paul A., 95n1505
Peltier, Leslie C., 96n1801
Peltzman, Barbara Ruth, 99n309
Pendergast, Sara, 99n857
Penguin atlas of African hist, new ed, 97n428
Penguin atlas of Diasporas, 98n807
Penguin dict of music, 6th ed, 97n1028
Penguin dict of saints, 3d ed, 97n1174
Penguin histl atlas of ...
   ancient Egypt, 98n490
   ancient Greece, 97n449
   dinosaurs, 97n1405
Penguins of the world, 96n1616
Peniston-Bird, C. M., 99n119
Penn, James R., 98n399
Pennington, Jean A. T., 95n1520
Penzler, Otto, 96n1189
Peonies, 96n1577
People in the news 1994, 95n24
People of the Holocaust, 99n521
Peoplepedia: the ultimate ref on the American people, 97n74
People's gd to deadly drug interactions, 97n1359
People's names, 98n377
Peoples of ...
   Africa, 97n321
   Central Africa, 98n322
   E Africa, 98n323
   N Africa, 98n324
   S Africa, 98n325
   the world, 99n371
   the world: Asians & Pacific Islanders, 95n127
   W Africa, 98n326
Peregrine, Peter N., 97n398
Perennials, 97n1274
Peretz, Don, 97n457
Perez, Arturo, 99n678
Perez, Cristelia, 96n550
Performers, 96n419
Performing artists, 96n1363
Performing arts: a gd to the ref lit, 95n1339
Performing arts business ency, 98n1265
Perilli, Barry, 98n751
Periodical source index CD-ROM [CD-ROM], 98n373

Periodicals in print: Australia, New Zealand, & the S Pacific 1996, 13th ed, 97n64
Perkins, Agnes, 98n1092
Perkins, Agnes Regan, 95n1133, 97n938, 98n1084
Perkins, Edwin C., Jr., 96n1762
Perkins, Kenneth J., 98n459
Perl, Teri, 99n1542
Perle, E. Gabriel, 99n621
Perlman, Seth, 98n539
Perone, James E., 97n1023, 97n1057, 98n1193, 99n1114
Peroni, Gwen, 99n246
Perrault, Anna H., 95n529
Perry, Dale L., 96n1794
Perry, Mike, 99n1071
Perry, Robert H., 98n1479
Perry, Tim, 96n481
Perry, William, 97n129
Perry's chemical engineers' hndbk, 7th ed, 98n1479
Person, James E., Jr., 96n1156, 97n901, 97n911, 97n913
Personal computer dict, 96n1764
Personal name index to The New York Times Index, v.5, 98n67
Personal name index to The New York Times Index, v.6, 98n68
Pessl, Molly, 99n753
Peter Maxwell Davies, 96n1282
Peters, David, 98n1552
Peters, Diane E., 98n1194
Peters, Pam, 96n1090
Peters, Thomas A., 96n644
Petersen, Andrew, 97n803
Peterson, Bernard L., Jr., 95n1416, 98n1328
Peterson, David A., 95n838
Peterson 1st gd to ...
   butterflies & moths, 95n1577
   forests, 96n1591
   urban wildlife, 95n1560
Peterson, J. E., 95n176
Peterson, Jane T., 98n1106
Peterson, Marilyn B., 96n604
Peterson, Michael D., 97n1212
Peterson's choose a Christian college, 4th ed, 96n1474
Peterson's college money hndbk 1998, 15th ed, 98n303
Peterson's colleges with programs for students with learning disabilities, 96n341
Peterson's colleges with programs for students with learning disabilities or attention deficit disorders, 99n329
Peterson's competitive colleges 1997-98, 16th ed, 98n292
Peterson's contract servs for higher educ, 96n342
Peterson's distance learning 1997, 97n291
Peterson's gd to ...
   colleges in the Midwest 1995, 11th ed, 96n343
   colleges in the South 1995, 10th ed, 96n344
   colleges in the West 1995, 9th ed, 96n345
   4-year colleges 1999, 29th ed, 99n330
   grad & professional programs 1995, 29th ed, 96n349
   grad programs in business, educ, health, & law 1995, 29th ed, 96n350
   grad programs in engineering & applied scis 1995, 29th ed, 96n351

grad programs in the biological & agricultural scis 1995, 29th ed, 96n352
grad programs in the humanities, arts, & social scis 1995, 29th ed, 96n353
grad programs in the physical scis & mathematics 1995, 29th ed, 96n354
MBA programs, 96n355
MBA programs 1998, 98n160
middle Atlantic colleges 1995, 11th ed, 96n346
New England colleges 1995, 11th ed, 96n347
N.Y. colleges 1995, 11th ed, 96n348
nursing programs, 96n356
nursing programs, 4th ed, 99n1478
private secondary schools 1994-95, 95n355
2-yr colleges 1998, 28th ed, 98n293
Peterson's hidden job market 1995, 95n304
Peterson's honors programs, 99n331
Peterson's internships 1996, 16th ed, 97n256
Peterson's internships 1998, 18th ed, 99n291
Peterson's job opportunities in ...
business 1995, 96n280
engineering & tech 1995, 96n1513
health care 1995, 96n1689
the environment 1995, 96n1876
Peterson's paying less for college 1995, 95n370
Peterson's private secondary schools 1998-99, 19th ed, 99n314
Peterson's professional degree programs in the visual & performing arts 1995, 96n962
Peterson's professional degree programs in the visual & peforming arts, 4th ed, 99n1197
Peterson's scholarship almanac, 98n304
Peterson's scholarships for study in the USA & Canada 1998, 98n294
Peterson's scholarships for study in the USA & Canada 1999, 2d ed, 99n345
Peterson's sports scholarships & college athletic programs, 95n797
Peterson's sports scholarships & college athletic programs, 3d ed, 99n346
Peterson's study abroad 1994, 95n382
Peterson's study abroad 1998, 99n353
Peterson's summer opportunities for kids & teenagers 1996, 13th ed, 97n167
Peterson's summer study abroad, 96n367
Peterson's top colleges for sci, 97n306
Peterson's US & Canadian medical schools 1997, 98n1542
Peterson's vocational & technical schools, 95n389
Peterson's vocational & technical schools & programs, 99n360
Petonito, Gina, 98n650
Petranka, James W., 99n1396
Petras, Kathryn, 95n90
Petras, Ross, 95n90
Petren, Suzanne, 97n623
Petretti, Allan, 98n923
Petretti's Coca-Cola collectibles price gd, 10th ed, 98n923
Pettenati, Jeanne, 99n661
Petterchak, Janice A., 96n492
Pettifer, Adrian, 97n394

Pettit, George R., 96n1740
Pettus, Daniel D., Jr., 99n1009
Pettus, Eloise S., 99n1009
Pfaff, Bonnie Shaw, 98n523
Pfalzgraf, Jennifer J., 99n265
Pfeffer, J. Alan, 95n1036
PGA tour, 1995, 96n822
Pham, Gisele, 95n1618
PharmFacts for nurses, 97n1361
Phelps, Shirelle, 95n415, 99n376, 99n379
Phenix, Katharine Joan, 97n741
Phifer, Paul, 98n316
Philanthropic studies index, 1995 cum index, 96n884
Philanthropic studies index, v.3, no.1, 95n868
Philip, Anton S., 95n136
Philip, George D. E., 95n173
Philippines business, 97n236
Philippines in WW II & to independence (Dec. 8, 1941-July 4, 1946), 2d ed, 97n432
Philippsborn, H. E., 96n1494
Phillippe, Kent A., 96n366
Phillips, Charles, 96n705, 97n415, 97n504, 99n538
Phillips, Colin, 96n976
Phillips, Diana, 99n185
Phillips, Faye, 96n659
Phillips, Lucie Colvin, 95n123
Phillips, Mark, 98n1286
Phillips, Robert W., 96n1408
Phillips, Sidney L., 96n1794
Phillips, Vicky, 99n304
Philosopher's index [CD-ROM], 96n1436
Philosopher's index, v.27, 95n1432
Philosopher's phone bk, 1995, 96n1430
Philosophy: a gd to the ref lit, 2d ed, 98n1330
Philosophy of Cynicism, 96n1425
Philosophy of educ, 97n287
Phoenix award of the children's lit assn 1990-94, 98n1092
PhoneDisc powerfinder [CD-ROM], 98n54
Phonetic symbol gd, 2d ed, 97n815
Photo dir of the US Catholic hierarchy, 95n1462
Photographer's market, 1994, 95n989
Photographer's market, 1998, 98n936
Photographers on disc [CD-ROM], 98n937
Photographic atlas of the stars, 98n1604
Photographic gd to the shorebirds of the world, 96n1617
Physical properties of hydrocarbons & other chemicals, v.4, 96n1793
Physician characteristics & distribution in the US, 98n1536
Physician marketplace stats 1997-98, 99n1434
Physicians' desk ref companion gd 1998, 52d ed, 99n1422
Physicians' desk ref for nonprescription drugs, 1994, 15th ed, 96n1741
Physicians' desk ref for ophthalmology 1998, 26th ed, 99n1462
Physicians' desk ref lib, Sept 1994 [CD-ROM], 95n1685
Physicians' desk ref 1995, 49th ed, 95n1684
Physics quick ref gd, 97n1406
Piacente, Steve, 95n713, 98n649
Piano music for 1 hand, 96n1292
Piano works of Serge Prokofiev, 95n1277

Pickard, James D., 97n768
Pickard, Roy, 98n1279
Pickering, David, 97n1149
Pickett, Christopher M., 98n545
Pickford, Nigel, 96n1896
Pictorial ency of Japanese life & events, 95n133
Pictorial gd to the living primates, 98n1472
Picture bks to enhance the curriculum, 98n284
Picture this: picture bks for YAs, 98n1097
Pierce, Anne, 98n1369
Pierce, Connie, 96n1390
Pierce, David, 96n362
Pierce, James R., 98n1369
Pierce, Phyllis S., 97n183
Pierson, Darren, 98n562
Pierson, Fiona Hogan, 96n1740
Piesarskas, Bronius, 97n862
Pietrusza, David, 98n737
Pike-Nase, Christal, 98n704
Piland, Sherry, 96n1021
Pilarski, Michael, 96n1542
Pilger, Mary Anne, 97n1244, 99n856
Pilgrimage to Santiago de Compostela, 96n1462
Pillsbury, Richard, 97n1246
Pingatore, Diana R., 98n1138
Ping-Robbins, Nancy R., 99n1142
Pinkepank, Jerry A., 96n1889
Pioneers of early childhood educ, 99n309
Pioneers of rock & roll, 95n1307
Pious, Richard M., 95n543
Pirates! 96n1345
Pirates & privateers of the Americas, 96n1344
Pirates & seafaring swashbucklers on the Hollywood screen, 96n1407
Pirouet, M. Louise, 96n125
Pitman, L. M., 98n1
Pitman, Lesley, 95n161
Pitt, Dale, 99n91
Pitt, Leonard, 99n91
Pitt-Catsouphes, Marcie, 98n778
Pitts, Michael R., 98n1312
Pittsburgh business dir, 99n152
Place called Peculiar, 99n421
Place-name changes 1900-91, 95n503
Placenames of Russia & the former Soviet Union, 97n382
Placenames of the world, 98n401
Places, towns, & townships 1998, 99n782
Placzek, Adolf K., 98n971
Plain English gd, 96n1075
Plakans, Andrejs, 98n477
Planet Earth: Macmillan world atlas, 98n390
Planning your career in alternative medicine, 98n1549
Plano, Jack C., 97n620
Plant explorer's gd to New England, 96n474
Plant identification terminology, 95n1538
Plant life in the world's Mediterranean climates, 99n1359
Plant, Richard, 95n1404
Plantfinder's gd to ornamental grasses, 99n1351
Plantfinder's gd to tender perennials, 99n1349
Plants & their names, 96n1563

Plants that merit attention, v.2: shrubs, 97n1285
Platinum & palladium buyer's gd, 98n913
Platt, George, 95n1495
Platt, Lyman D., 97n356
Platzker, David, 99n867
Playground industry ref dir 1995, 96n800
Plays for children & YAs, suppl 1, 1989-94, 97n940
Pleasant, Barbara, 96n1547
Pletcher, James R., 99n477
Plowden, Martha Ward, 95n908
Plumb, Donald C., 97n1263
Plunkett, Jack W., 97n259, 97n539, 97n1329, 98n185, 98n259, 99n266, 99n827, 99n1435
Plunkett's entertainment & media industry almanac, 99n827
Plunkett's financial servs industry almanac, 98n185
Plunkett's health care industry almanac, 97n1329
Plunkett's health care industry almanac 1997-98, 99n1435
Plunkett's infotech industry almanac, 97n539
Plunkett's retail industry almanac, 98n259
Pluvier, Jan M., 97n429
Pocket billiard gdbk for pool players, tournament directors, & spectators, 95n812
Pocket factfile of 20th century events, 97n466
Pocket factfile of 20th century people, 97n25
Pocket gd to the birds of Britain & NW Europe, 99n1379
Pocket Oxford Greek dict, 96n1105
Pocket Oxford Latin dict, rev ed, 95n1087
Pocket Oxford Russian dict, 2d ed, 96n1127
Pocket Oxford-Duden German dict, rev ed, 99n930
Pockets: aircraft, 98n1645
Pockets: ancient Egypt, 96n63
Pockets: ancient Rome, 96n64
Pockets: Bible companion, 98n1381
Pockets: birds, 96n65
Pockets: bldgs, 96n66
Pockets: cats, 96n67
Pockets: dinosaurs, 96n68
Pockets: dogs, 98n1467
Pockets: Earth facts, 96n69
Pockets: ency, 98n48
Pockets: English dict A to Z, 98n995
Pockets: French dict, 98n1028
Pockets: horses, 96n70
Pockets: insects, 96n71
Pockets: inventions, 96n72
Pockets: nature facts, 98n1458
Pockets: rocks & minerals, 96n73
Pockets: space facts, 96n74
Pockets: spanish dict, 98n1052
Pockets: trees, 96n75
Pockets: weather facts, 96n76
Pockets: world atlas, 96n77
Podell, Diane K., 95n491
Podell, Janet, 95n102, 99n46
Poe, Elizabeth Ann, 95n883
Poe ency, 98n1137
Poe, Marshall, 96n147
Poem finder 95 [CD-ROM], 97n1018
Poetry criticism, v.10, 96n1265
Poetry criticism, v.18, 99n1104

Poetry criticism, v.19, 99n1105
Poetry dict, 96n1264
Poetry for students, v.1, 99n1106
Poetry for students, v.2, 99n1107
Poetry for students, v.3, 99n1108
Poetry for students, v.4, 99n1109
Poets: American & British, 99n1110
Poets House, 95n1198
Poet's market, 1995, 95n943
Poet's market, 1998, 98n868
Pogonowski, Iwo C., 95n1091
Pohanish, Richard P., 97n1436, 98n1642, 99n1512, 99n1567, 99n1569
Pointer, Michael, 97n1121
Poison! how to handle the hazardous substances in your home, 98n1563
Poisons & antidotes, 95n1686
Pol, Louis G., 95n1652
Policies for publishers, 1995 ed, 96n674
Polifka, Janine E., 95n1682, 97n1358, 99n1480
Polish-English, English-Polish concise dict, 95n1091
Polish-German borderlands: an annot bibliog, 95n554
Political commentators in the US in the 20th century, 98n862
Political companion to American film, 96n1409
Political data hndbk: OECD countries, 2d ed, 98n684
Political geography, 98n393
Political leaders & military figures in the 2d World War, 98n606
Political leaders & peacemakers, 96n418
Political leaders of contemporary W Europe, 96n756
Political parties of E Europe, Russia, & the successor states, 2d ed, 96n757
Political parties of the Middle East & N Africa, 96n765
Political prisoners & trials, 96n605
Political role of the military, 98n621
Political systems of the world, 97n582
Polk, Alicia, 97n623
Polk, Noel, 95n1197
Pollard, Elaine, 96n1070, 97n818
Pollen grains of Canadian honey plants, 95n1537
Polling & survey research methods, 1935-79, 97n77
Pollock, Bruce, 98n1243, 99n1164
Pollock, Leland W., 99n1394
Pollock, Sean R., 96n914, 98n25
Polmar, Norman, 95n679, 98n628, 99n643
Polunin, Nicholas, 98n1631
Pomeranz, William E., 95n164
Ponnuswami, Meenakshi, 97n746
Pool, Kate, 95n655
Poole, Alan F., 95n1565
Poor, Janet Meakin, 97n1285
Pop culture landmarks, 97n387
Popa, Marcel, 97n120
Popa, Opritsa D., 95n160
Pope, Joyce, 96n1806
Pope, Stephen, 97n474
Poplawski, Paul, 97n995, 99n1070
POPLINE: through Dec 1996 [CD-ROM], 98n779
Popova, L. P., 95n1093

Popovich, Charles J., 95n202
Popular American housing, 97n1094
Popular bands & performers, 96n1304
Popular dict of Hinduism, 95n1472
Popular dict of Judaism, 97n1222
Popular music, v.21, 1996, 99n1164
Popular music studies, 99n1163
Popular nonfiction authors for children: a biogl & thematic gd, 99n1002
Popular physics & astronomy, 97n1411
Popular religious mags of the US, 96n1441
Population abstract of the US, 1993 ed, 95n892
Population & dvlpmt: dir of non-govtl org in OECD countries, 96n909
Population hist of western US cities & towns, 1850-1990, 97n723
Portable Baker's biog dict of musicians, 96n1268
Portable Kobbe's opera gd, 95n1285
Portable MBA desk ref, 95n203
Portable MBA desk ref, 2d ed, 99n278
Portable pediatrician for parents, 95n1665
Porteous, Andrew, 98n1636
Porter, Darwin, 96n483
Porter, David L., 95n804, 96n792, 96n793
Porter, Dilwyn, 95n752
Porter, Gerald, 95n775
Porter, Harvey, 95n1070
Porter, J. R., 96n1459
Porter, Lewis, 96n1324
Porter, Malcolm, 95n476
Porter, Ray, 95n1485
Porter, Rick, 99n1187
Porter, Roy, 95n1654
Porter, Stanley E., 97n1192
Portman, Janet, 98n534
Portnoi, Paul, 96n1881
Portraits in conservation: E & S Africa, 96n1596
Portugal with Madeira & the Azores, 98n422
Portuguese lit from its origins to 1990, 95n1238
Portuguese-English, English-Portuguese practical dict, 95n1092
Posadskov, Eugene L., 96n246
Posner, Raphael, 95n450
Posner, Richard A., 97n499
Post-Colonial lits in English, 99n946
Post-Colonial lits in English: Australia, 1970-92, 97n1002
Post-Colonial lits in English: SE Asia, New Zealand, & the Pacific, 1970-92, 97n1013
Post Keynesian economics, 97n148
Post-Biblical saints art index, 95n1010
Postic, Lionel J., 96n281
Postiglione, Gerard A., 98n295
Postlethwaite, T. Neville, 95n337
Post-release assistance programs for prisoners, 2d ed, 96n600
Post-Soviet hndbk, 97n123
Potparic, O., 96n1726, 97n1357
Potter, Alicia, 98n1264
Potter, Joan, 95n409
Potter's dict of materials & techniques, 4th ed, 98n932
Pottery & porcelain ceramics price gd, 98n927

Potts, Deborah, 95n125
Potts, Howard E., 98n341
Potts, Karen, 98n588
Poverty in America: an annot bibliog, 95n869
Poverty Row studios, 1929-40: an illus hist of 53 independent film cos..., 98n1312
Powell, Allan Kent, 96n511
Powell, Charles C., 99n1360
Powell, John, 97n608, 98n462
Powell, Russell H., 95n1483
Powell, William S., 95n37
Power industry abbreviator, 96n1672
Power media selects, 9th ed, 96n988
Powers, Bethel Ann, 96n1732
Powers, Roger S., 98n692
Practical dict of Chinese medicine, 99n1446
Practical dict of German usage, 98n1029
Practical ency of sex & health, 95n1647
Practical gd to planned giving 1998, 98n791
Practical gd to the marine animals of northeastern N America, 99n1394
Practical pediatrician, 97n1354
Practitioner's gd to psychoactive drugs for children & adolescents, 95n1687
Prado, Marcial, 95n1094
Prager, Jan C., 97n1387, 97n1388
Prague, 98n122
Prebish, Charles, 99n1260
Precious Moments children's Bible dict, 96n1451
Predicting the future, 98n88
Preece, Michael A., 99n1465
Pregnancy & birth sourcebk, 98n1561
Prehistoria [CD-ROM], 96n1816
Preimesberger, Jon, 95n733, 96n731
Pre-1900 annuals, 95n139
Pre-1900 Canadian dirs, 95n140
Prentice Hall dir of online business info 1997, 97n168
Prescription for nutritional healing, 98n1508
Preservation yellow pages, rev ed, 98n975
Presidential also-rans & running mates, 1788-1996, 99n662
Presidential elections in the US, 96n742
Presidential elections 1789-1996, 99n682
Presidential libs & museums, 96n519
Presidential Medal of Freedom, 98n30
Presidential sites, 99n428
Presidents, 98n661
Presidents: a ref hist, 2d ed, 97n589
Presidents, first ladies, & vice presidents, 98n653
Presidents of the US—their written measure, 98n648
Presnell, Don, 99n1232
Press freedom & dvlpmt, 98n850
Pressly, William L, 95n1021
Pressman, Steven, 95n869
Preston, C. E., 99n960
Preston-Dunlop, Valerie, 97n1102
Preston-Mafham, Ken, 95n1592
Preston-Mafham, Rod, 95n1592
Prevention, editors of, 95n1647
Prevention Magazine Health Books, editors of, 95n1670
Preventive care sourcebk 1997-98, 98n1520

PRI index, 99n771
Price, Anne, 96n650, 98n586
Price, Helen C., 95n112
Price, Richard, 95n578
Prices & financial stats in the ESCWA region, 97n192
Prices of agricultural products & selected inputs for Europe & N America 1992/93, 96n1520
Pricing stats sourcebk, 99n1548, 96n1846
Pride, John, 96n1137
Priestly, Brian, 97n1076
Primaryplots 2, 95n1141
Prime time network serials, 98n1310
Prime-time religion, 98n1366
Prince, Danforth, 96n483
Prince, Mary Miles, 98n516
Princeton hndbk of multicultural poetries, 97n1019
Princeton Language Institute, 95n949
Princeton Review Hillel gd to Jewish life on campus, 1996 ed, 97n307
Princeton Review student access gd: the big bk of colleges, 96n357
Princeton Review student access gd to ...
 the best business schools, 97n169
 the best law schools, 96n585
 the best medical schools, 96n1705
 the best 309 colleges, 96n358
Princeton Review student advantage gd to visiting college campuses, 1997 ed, 98n305
Pring, J. T., 96n1105
Pringle, David, 97n949, 97n950, 99n976
Printed catalogues of the Harvard College Lib, 1723-90, 97n39
Printed sources, 99n403
Printed stuff: prints, posters, & ephemera by Claes Oldenburg, 99n867
Prisma, Bokforlaget, 96n1138
Prisma's abridged English-Swedish & Swedish-English dict, 96n1138
Prisoners of the Japanese in WW II, 95n549
Pritzker, Barry M., 99n390
Private libs in Renaissance England, v.3: PLRE 67-86, 96n1006
Problems in literary research, 4th ed, 99n972
Pro-choice/pro-life issues in the 1990s, 98n757
Procter, Paul, 96n1063
Proctor, Claude O., 97n870
Produce ref gd to fruits & vegetables from around the world, 98n1421
Professional & occupational licensure in the US, 98n704
Professional & technical careers, 99n274
Professional careers sourcebk, 3d ed, 95n390
Professional careers sourcebk, 5th ed, 99n361
Professional codes of conduct in the UK, 2d ed, 98n1341
Professional hndbk of diagnostic tests, 96n1710
Professional secretary's hndbk, 3d ed, 96n312
Professional sports stats, 98n722
Professional sports team hists, 95n800
Professionals job finder 1997-2000, 99n273
Professional's private sector job finder 1994-95, 95n317
Profile of western N America, 97n248

Profiles in American hist, 95n537, 96n509
Profiles in business & mgmt [CD-ROM], 97n221
Profiles in gerontology, 96n846
Profiles in world hist, 97n472
Profiles of ...
    America, S region, v.4: Ky., N.C., Tenn., 96n910
    American colleges, 99n332
    American labor unions, 99n271
    US hospitals 1995, 4th ed, 96n1690
    worldwide govt leaders 1995, 96n708
    worldwide govt leaders 1998, 4th ed, 99n649
Program for Art on Film, 95n1012
Programs & centers in comparative & intl educ, rev ed, 96n370
Projections of educ stats to 2008, 99n299
Prokopowicz, Gerald J., 99n468
Prokurat, Michael, 97n1212
Prominent scientists: an index to collective biogs, 3d ed, 95n1505
Prominent women of the 20th century, 97n26
Pronouncing dict of proper names, 2d ed, 99n900
Pronouncing Shakespeare's words, 99n1076
Propaganda in 20th century war & pols, 97n618
Proper names master index, 95n82
Prostitution in Great Britain 1485-1901, 95n877
Protest, power, & change, 98n692
Prothero, Stephen R., 97n1180
Protocol: a hndbk for legislative staff, 98n677
Prouty, Chris, 95n117
Provence & the Cote D'Azur, 96n477
Proverb wit & wisdom, 98n1249
Proverbial Bernard Shaw, 95n1221
Proverbial Charles Dickens, 98n1157
Proverbial Eugene O'Neill, 96n1215
Proverbial Winston S. Churchill, 96n760
Proverbs in world lit, 98n1254
Provorse, Carl, 95n108, 98n823, 99n89
Prucha, Francis Paul, 95n535
Prues, Don, 98n870
Prues, Donald M., 98n866
Prunckun, Henry W., Jr., 97n501
Pruning of trees, shrubs, & conifers, rev ed, 96n1588
Pruter, Robert, 95n1308
Prytherch, Ray, 96n1187, 97n526
Psychiatric dict, 7th ed, 98n1556
Psychology: an introductory bibliog, 97n624
Psychology basics, 99n706
Psychology of aging, 96n839
Psychotronic video gd, 97n1140
PsycLit [CD-ROM], 97n625
Public enemies, 99n580
Public interest profiles 1996-97, 97n599
Public lib cat, 95n660
Public records online, 1997 ed, 98n706
Publication Systems Department, 96n20
Publishers dir, 1995, 95n673
Publishers dir, 1998, 18th ed, 98n603
Publishers, distrs, & wholesalers of the US 1994-95, 95n674
Publishers, distrs, & wholesalers of the US 1996-97, 97n555
Publishers' intl ISBN dir 1997/98, 98n604

Publishers' intl ISBN dir, 20th ed, 95n676
Publishing & bk dvlpmt in Sub-Saharan Africa, 97n552
Publishing law hndbk, 2d ed, 99n621
Publishing market ref plus 1994-95, 2d ed [CD-ROM], 96n672
Puckett, Barry, 96n1358
Puerto, Cecilia, 97n793
Puerto Rico past & present, 99n93
Pullum, Geoffrey K., 97n815
Pumroy, Eric L., 97n333
Punctuate it right! 2d ed, 95n948
Puniello, Francoise S., 97n808
Punjab, 97n126
Puotinen, C. J., 99n1384
Purcell, Catherine, 95n348
Purcell, L. Edward, 99n664
Purchon, Nerys, 99n1458
Puro, George, 95n810, 96n828
Purves, Alan C., 95n929
Purvis, Thomas L., 97n399, 97n419
Pybus, Victoria, 96n460
Pye, Michael, 95n1440
Pym, John, 97n1136
Pyne, Sandra, 98n1577

Qiaoqiao, Zhang, 95n1511
Qiu, Minjia, 98n174
Quakers in fiction, 95n1157
Qualitative inquiry: a dict of terms, 99n743
Quality mgmt sourcebk, 98n241
Quality, TQC, TQM: a meta lit study, 98n243
Quantum eos, 96n195
Quaratiello, Arlene Rodda, 99n610
Quastler, I. E., 96n1880
Queen, Edward L., II, 97n1180
Queer theory, 99n758
Quennell, Peter, 96n1240
Questions & answers bk of sci facts, 98n1404
Quick ref dict for occupational therapy, 99n1423
Quick ref glossary of eye care terminology, 99n1463
Quick ref to computer graphics terms, 95n1699
Quick ref to ERISA compliance, 96n285
Quien es quien: a who's who of Spanish-speaking librarians in the US 1994, 4th ed, 96n621
Quigley, Christine, 95n844
Quigley, Ellen, 97n1003, 97n1004
Quigley, Martin S, 97n1112
Quigley, Thomas, 99n1143
Quin, Carolyn L., 97n1046
Quinlan, David, 97n1106
Quinlan's illus dir of film character actors, new ed, 97n1106
Quinn, David, 96n1613
Quinn-Musgrove, Sandra L., 96n719
Quintessential cat, 95n1580
Quiram, Jacquelyn, 98n568
Quitno, Neal, 95n624, 96n602, 98n552
Quotable lawyer, rev ed, 99n572

R. R. Bowker Bibliog Group, 96n20
Rabin, Dan, 99n1332
Rabkin, Leslie Y., 99n1233
Rabkin, Sarah, 96n1498
Race, crime, & the criminal justice system, 98n548
Racer's ency of metals, fibers, & materials, 96n1883
Rachel Crothers, 96n1208
Racial & ethnic diversity, 2d ed, 99n372
Racism in contemporary America, 97n325
Radical ecological theory: a bibliog, 95n1762
Radicalism hndbk, 96n766
Radicalism in Minn. 1900-60, 96n767
Radice, Roberto, 99n1250
Radio amateur callbk, 1995, 73d ed, 96n990
Radio stars, 97n762
Radio's morning show personalities, 97n763
Radloff, Lisa, 96n140
Radovich, Don, 97n1096
Radstone, Susannah, 95n1373
Radzig, A. A., 98n1620
Raffel, Jeffrey A., 99n301
Rageau, Jean-Pierre, 98n807
Rahman, Syedur, 98n460
Rail lines of S New England, 96n1888
Raine, David F., 99n137
Rainforest orgs, 98n1639
Rainforests of the world: a ref hndbk, 95n1777
Raish, Martin, 98n942
Raistrick, Donald, 95n593, 98n512
Raitt, Lia Correia, 98n1042
Rajadhyaksha, Ashish, 96n1381
Rajewski, Brian, 96n710, 99n658
Rake, Alan, 96n112
Rakipov, Nazib G., 96n1516
Ralph Waldo Emerson: an annot bibliog of criticism, 1980-91, 95n1187
Ramachandran, V. S., 95n778
Ramil, Axel J. Navarro, 97n875
Ramirez, Gonzalo, Jr., 95n1136
Ramirez, Jan L., 95n1136
Rampelmann, Katja, 97n333
Ramsay, Craig, 96n1691
Ramsay, Jeff, 97n94
Ramsay, John G., 98n266
Rand McNally 1994 commercial atlas & mktg gd, 95n326
Rand McNally world facts & maps, 95n498
Randall, Lilian M. C., 99n600
Randall, Richard C., 96n206
Randall's practical gd to ISO 9000, 96n206
Randel, Don Michael, 97n1024
Randi, James, 97n637
Randol mining dir 1994/95, 96n1836
Randolph, Lillian, 98n1536
Random House concise ency, 97n47
Random House German-English, English-German dict, 99n931
Random House histl dict of American slang, v.1, 95n1061
Random House histl dict of American slang, v.2: H-O, 98n1015
Random House Latin-American Spanish dict, 99n942

Random House Webster's American Sign Lang dict, rev ed, 99n909
Random House Webster's concise thesaurus, 99n917
Random House Webster's large print thesaurus, 99n918
Rankin, Nigel, 96n1127
Ranking of world stock markets, 99n229
Rann, Rick, 98n921
Ranney, Doug, 98n1307
Ranucci, Karen, 99n1226
Rap whoz who, 98n1237
Rapalje, Stewart, 98n520
Rape in America, 96n617
Raphael, Marc Lee, 97n1221
Rapid gd to ...
   hazardous air pollutants, 99n1568
   hazardous chemicals in the environment, 99n1569
   trade names & synonyms of environmentally regulated chemicals, 99n1512
Rapkin, Lenore, 99n599
Rapp, Barbara A., 96n1658
Rappaport, Karen, 99n1448
Rappaport, Susan S., 99n873
Rappole, John H., 97n1289
Rasch, D., 96n1557
Rasmussen, R. Kent, 96n1217, 99n667
Rasor, Eugene L., 95n536, 97n462, 98n611, 99n505, 99n517
Rassam, Amal, 97n319
Ratcliffe, Susan, 96n92
Rate ref gd to the US treasury market 1984-95, 97n184
Rating gd to life in America's 50 states, 96n924
Ratjar, Steve, 96n825
Raulston, J. C., 96n1592
Rawson, Hugh, 95n1035, 97n828, 99n75
Rawson's dict of euphemisms & other doubletalk, rev ed, 97n828
Ray, Michael, 95n208
Ray, Robert H., 96n1238
Rayburn, Alan, 99n423
Raycraft, Carol, 98n904
Raycraft, Don, 98n904
Rayhawk, Peggie, 98n642, 98n654, 99n661
Raymond, Boris, 99n502
Raymond, Eric S., 98n1578
Rayner, Steve, 99n1563
Re, Joseph M., 98n306
Rea, William R., 98n956
Read, Gardner, 95n1273
Reader, Keith, 99n128
Reader's adviser on CD-ROM [CD-ROM], 97n11
Reader's advisor, 14th ed, 95n13
Reader's catalog, 2d ed, 98n8
Reader's companion, 95n11
Reader's companion to military hist, 98n616
Reader's companion to the fiction of Willa Cather, 95n1185
Reader's companion to US women's hist, 99n804
Reader's Digest atlas of Canada, 96n451
Reader's Digest children's illus dict, 95n1052
Reader's Digest illus great world atlas, 99n416
Readers' gd abstracts full text mega ed [CD-ROM], 98n69
Readers' gd for young people [CD-ROM], 98n77

Reader's gd to ...
    American hist, 98n442
    lit in English, 97n915
    per lit 1995, 98n70
    the short stories of Eudora Welty, 98n1138
    the short stories of Sherwood Anderson, 95n1184
    the short stories of Stephen Crane, 98n1133
    the short stories of Willa Cather, 95n1186
    the short stories of William Faulkner, 95n1189
    20th-century writers, 97n916
    women's studies, 99n796
Reading Hemingway, 96n1211
Ready ref: American Indians, 96n417
Ready ref: American justice, 97n489
Ready ref: ethics, 95n1429
Reagan yrs A to Z, 97n592
Real gd to Canadian univs, 95n347
Real Goods solar living sourcebk, 8th ed, 96n1847
Real Goods, staff of, 96n1847
Real life dict of the law, 96n578
Real vitamin & mineral bk, 98n1548
Realization & suppression of the Situationist Intl, 97n792
Reams, Bernard D., Jr., 96n717
Reamy, Martha, 96n434
Reamy, William, 96n434
Reaney, P. H., 96n427
REA's authoritative gd to law schools, rev ed, 96n586
REA's authoritative gd to medical & dental schools, 96n1706
Recent ref bks in religion, 98n1346
Recent work in critical theory, 1989-95, 97n880
Recommended bks in Spanish for children & YAs, 1991-95, 98n1079
Recommended pubs for legal research 1991, 95n596
Recommended reading: 500 classics reviewed, 97n883
Recommended ref bks 1994, 95n16
Recommended ref bks for small & medium-sized libs & media centers 1995, 96n11
Recommended ref bks for small & medium-sized libs & media centers 1997, 98n9
Record of the Carnegie Institutes intl exhibitions 1896-1996, 99n868
Recorder: a gd to writings about the instrument, 96n1294
Recording industry sourcebk, 99n1199
Recovery of internationally abducted children, 99n752
Recreating the past, 95n1161
Recycling & waste mgmt gd to the Internet, 99n1562
Recycling in America, 99n1570
Red list of threatened plants, 1997, 99n1361
Red Nichols story, 98n1236
Redclift, Michael, 99n1564
Redden, Kenneth R., 96n580
Reddy, Marlita A., 95n425, 96n240, 96n420, 96n921
Redmond, Christopher, 95n1212
Reed, David A., 95n1459
Reed, Gretchen, 96n299
Reed, Ida, 98n1189
Reed, Maxine K., 95n959
Reed, Robert M., 95n959
Reed, W. L., 95n1260
Reed, William Cyrus, 98n699

Reel black talk: a sourcebk of 50 American filmmakers, 98n1278
Reel list, 96n1400
Rees, Alan M., 95n1666, 96n1711, 98n1538, 99n1416
Rees, Dafydd, 97n1081
Rees, Nigel, 96n1084, 98n1018, 99n76
Reese, William L., 98n1337
Reference & info servs, 2d ed, 96n647
Reference & Adult Servs Division of the American Lib Assn, 96n648
Reference assessment manual, 96n648
Reference bks bulletin 1992-93, 95n14
Reference bks bulletin 1993-94, 96n12
Reference bks bulletin 1994-95, 97n12
Reference ency: India 2001, 96n132
Reference ency of the American Indian, 7th ed, 96n412
Reference gd for botany & horticulture, 97n1258
Reference gd to ...
    American lit, 3d ed, 95n1169
    famous engineering landmarks of the world, 99n1397
    Russian lit, 99n1097
    short fiction, 95n1167
    the Bible in Emily Dickinson's poetry, 98n1135
    US military hist: 1945 to the present, 96n520
    US military hist 1919-45, 95n548
    world lit, 2d ed, 97n917
Reference manual for telecommunications engineering, 2d ed, 95n1612
Reference sources hndbk, 4th ed, 97n13
Reference sources in sci, engineering, medicine, & agriculture, 95n1482
Refining stats sourcebk, 96n1849
Refugee & immigrant resource dir, 3d ed, 95n401
Refugees in America in the 1990s, 98n801
Rega, Regina, 95n814
Regan, Gary, 99n1337
Regan, Mardee Haidin, 99n1337
Reggae: the rough gd, 99n1171
Regional theatre dir 1996-97, 97n1152
Regions of France, 97n115
Regions of Spain, 97n451
Rehill, Anne Collier, 98n1281
Rehrig, William H., 98n1229
Reich, Bernard, 95n763, 95n764, 97n455, 99n648
Reich, Warren Thomas, 96n1429
Reid, Daniel G., 95n1450, 96n1466
Reid, Judith Prowse, 97n357
Reid, Rob, 96n1278
Reif, Joe, 98n262
Reill, Peter Hanns, 97n475
Reilly, Catherine W., 96n1246
Reilly, John W., 95n329
Reilly, Pauline, 96n1616
Reincarnation: a selected annot bibliog, 98n715
Reinventing govt, 98n644
Reis, Brian, 99n1206
Reiser, Katie, 96n873
Reisman, Rosemary M. Canfield, 95n1181
Rejected: sketches of the 26 men nominated for the Supreme Court but not confirmed by the Senate, 95n601

Religion: a cross-cultural ency, 97n1178
Religion & the American experience, the 20th century, 96n1442
Religion in postwar China, 95n1439
Religion in the schools, 99n300
Religions of the world, 98n1348
Religious cultures of the world, 98n1368
Religious educ, 1960-93, 96n1463
Religious higher educ in the US, 97n301
Religious holidays & calendars, 99n1271
Religious right, 97n1218
Religious schools in the US K-12, 95n351
Remarkable lives of ...
   100 women artists, 96n939
   100 women healers & scientists, 96n940
   100 women writers & journalists, 96n941
Renewable energy sources stats 1989-91, 96n1848
Renshaw, Patrick, 98n449
Renstrom, Peter G., 96n606, 98n540, 99n555
Renton, Jeanne L., 95n1129
Rentschler, Cathy, 97n529
Renz, Loren, 98n794, 99n771
Reports required by Congress, 1995, v.2, no.1, 96n746
Representative American speeches, 1937-97, 99n975
Representative American speeches 1995-96, 98n1131
Reproductive effects of chemical, physical, & biological agents REPROTOX, 96n1712
Reptile & amphibian keeper's dict, 95n1597
Reptile & amphibian problem solver, 98n1473
Republic pictures checklist, 99n1230
Research & professional resources in children's lit, 96n1169
Research centers dir 1996, 20th ed, 96n340
Research centers dir 1999, 24th ed, 99n333
Research gd to human sexuality, 95n876
Research gd to the Turner movement in the US, 97n333
Research in dance, 95n1357
Research in Japanese sources, 95n134
Research on group treatment methods, 97n623
Research on professional consultation & consultation for organizational change, 98n709
Research on religion & aging, 96n840
Research projects supported by the Canadian Ethnic Studies Program 1973-92, 95n419
Research results of projects funded by the Canadian Ethnic Studies Program 1973-88, 95n418
Research servs dir, 97n170
Researching Canadian markets, industries, & business opportunities, 99n247
Resolving community disputes, 95n597
Resource gd for the disabled, 96n854
Resource gd to travel in sub-Saharan Africa, v.1: E & W Africa, 95n516
Resource gd to travel in sub-Saharan Africa v.2, 98n420
Resourceful woman, 95n916
Resources & refs: hazardous waste & hazardous materials mgmt, 96n1852
Resources for early childhood, 95n349
Resources for elders with disabilities, 3d ed, 97n672
Resources for people with disabilities, 99n750

Resources for people with disabilities & chronic conditions, 3d ed, 97n673
Resources for teaching middle school scis, 99n1296
Resources of the Third World, 98n120
Respiratory care drug ref, 99n1481
Response to Allen Ginsberg 1926-94, 97n972
Restaurant lover's companion, 96n1526
Restoration forestry, 96n1542
Retail trade intl, 1998 ed, 99n230
Return to paradise: a gd to S Sea Island films, 99n1229
Reuss, Jerry, 96n1316
Revealing docs: a gd to African American ms sources..., 95n414
Revenue stats of OECD member countries 1965-93, 96n772
Reverse acronyms, initialisms & abbrevs dict, 18th ed, 95n2
Review of maritime transport 1993, 96n1897
Review of maritime transport 1997, 98n260
Revolutionary America 1763-1800, 97n399
Reyes, Luis, 95n1377
Rhine, C. D., 96n1213
Rhoden, David, 97n85
Rhodes, Anne K., 99n214
Rhodes, Christine P., 96n1525
Rhodes, Diane B., 95n1562
Rhodes, Karen, 98n1313
Rhyne, George N., 97n476
Ricchiuto, Steven R., 97n184
Ricciuti, Edward, 99n1535
Rice, Dan, 99n1385
Rich, Elizabeth H., 96n871, 97n699, 98n291, 98n583, 98n759, 98n789, 99n1427
Richard, Alfred Charles, Jr., 95n1387
Richard Baker's companion to music, 96n1269
Richards, Chris, 98n1356
Richards, Larry, 99n1234, 99n1280
Richardson, Andy, 99n264
Richardson, David A., 95n1201, 97n983, 98n1147
Richardson, Deborra A., 95n1266
Richardson, Paul E., 95n283
Richardson, R. C., 97n443
Richter, William L., 97n420, 97n1437
Ricketts, Jonathan T., 95n1604
Rickson, Richard, 95n240
Riddick, John F., 95n131, 99n485
Riddle, Gay, 99n852
Riddle, Peter H., 99n852
Rideout, Philip M., 99n898
Rider, David F., 97n1439
Ridgely, Robert S., 95n1573
Ridinger, Robert B. Marks, 97n681
Ridpath, Ian, 99n1518, 99n1523
Riechel, Rosemarie, 99n996
Rife, John C., 96n842
Riffle, Robert Lee, 99n1344
Rigden, John S., 97n1410
Riggle, Judith, 96n1180
Riggs, Quentin, 98n1198
Riggs, Thomas, 98n945
Rijckaert, Arseen, 99n923
Rijsberman, Marijke, 99n963

Riley, Gail Blasser, 99n608
Riley, Sam G., 95n955, 96n973
Riley, Tracy L., 97n299
Rimler, Walter, 97n1068
Rinderknecht, Carol, 95n21, 98n17, 99n13
Ring, Trudy, 96n467, 96n468, 96n469, 97n468
Ringgren, Helmer, 97n1200, 98n1375, 99n1276
Rinker, Harry L., 98n891
Rinzler, Carol Ann, 97n1318
R.I.P.: the complete bk of death & dying, 98n767
Rise of fascism in Europe, 99n694
Rist, Peter, 97n1124
Ritchey, Ferris J., 98n1524
Ritchie, Adrian C., 99n927
Ritchie, David, 95n496, 96n789, 97n1448
Ritchie, Roy, 99n850
Rittenhouse, Jo-Anne, 99n165
Ritter, Ellen M., 95n1507
Ritter, Michael E., 99n1516
Rivers of the US, 99n1536
Rivers of the US. v.1: estuaries, 95n1726
RKO features, 95n1385
Robb, H. Amanda, 96n437, 98n79
Robbins, Keith, 98n464
Robbins, Manuel, 96n1812
Robbins, Robert A., 98n528
Robert Benchley, 96n1207
Robert, Maguy, 97n206
Roberto, Deborah, 98n703
Roberts' dict of industrial relations, 4th ed, 95n296, 96n257
Roberts, F. X., 96n1213
Roberts, George V., Jr., 96n817
Roberts, Harold S., 95n296, 96n257
Roberts, James B., 98n743
Roberts, Patricia L., 96n328, 99n997, 99n998
Robert's rules in plain English, 98n681
Robertson, D. Ross, 96n1633
Robertson, Jack S., 98n969
Robertson, James, 98n136
Robertson, James D., 97n1252
Robertson, James I., Jr., 98n432
Robertson, Lawrence R., 98n129, 99n126
Robertson, Malcolm J., 98n171
Robertson, Stephen L., 98n653
Robinson, Alice M., 95n1352
Robinson, Dale, 97n1134
Robinson, Diane, 96n1034
Robinson, Jancis, 96n1528
Robinson, Jo Ann, 98n315
Robinson, Judith Schiek, 98n60
Robinson, Lillian S., 97n907
Robinson, Mairi, 99n42
Robinson, Mike, 98n397
Robinson, Richard, 95n242
Robison, William B., 97n442
Robl, Gregory, 97n362
Roby, Norman S., 99n1341
Rochelle, Mercedes, 95n1010
Rock & roll reader's gd, 98n1242
Rock garden plants, 99n1353

Rock music in American popular culture 2, 99n1173
Rock music scholarship, 97n1082
Rock song index, 98n1243
Rock stars/pop stars, 96n1315
Rock talk, 95n1306
Rock who's who, 2d ed, 97n1083
Rocket man: the ency of Elton John, 96n1331
Rodenhouse, Mary Pat, 95n368
Rodger, Richard, 95n552, 98n825
Rodgers, Marie E., 99n378
Rodgers, Nigel, 99n440
Rodriguez, Junius P., 99n531
Rodriquez-Martin, Conrado, 99n1439
Roehm, Frances, 99n268
Roes, Nicholas A., 96n359
Rogak, Lisa Angowski, 95n211
Rogal, Samuel J., 95n1214, 95n1512, 97n996, 97n1086, 98n1160
Rogel, Carole, 99n116
Roger Eberts video companion, 98n1319
Roger Ebert's video companion, 1994 ed, 95n1362
Rogers, Allan, 96n1577
Rogers, D. M., 95n1463
Rogers, Deborah D., 97n998
Rogers, Helen, 96n642
Rogers, Joan C., 98n528
Rogers, John, 95n1199
Rogers, John H., 97n980
Rogers, Marcus J. C., 97n626
Rogers, Pat, 97n994
Rogerson, John, 98n1377
Roget A to Z, 95n1069
Roget's superthesaurus, 2d ed, 99n916
Roget's 2: the new thesaurus, 3d ed, 96n1095
Rogg, Carla S., 97n297
Rogg, Oskar H., 97n297
Rognehaugh, Richard, 98n1510
Rogozinski, Jan, 96n1345
Rohde, Fred C., 95n1588
Rohrs, Roger, 99n180
Roitt, Ivan M., 99n1419
Roland Barthes: a bibliog, 95n1424
Rolka, Gail Meyer, 96n32
Roll of honor: names of soldiers who died in defense of the American Union..., 95n547
Rollberg, Peter, 98n1170
Rollyson, Carl Sokolnicki, 97n364
Romaine-Davis, Ada, 96n1681
Roman de Renart: a gd to scholarly work, 99n1183
Romance writer's pink pages, 95n942
Romance writer's sourcebk, 97n754
Romania, rev ed, 99n136
Romaniuk, Bohdan, 95n861
Romans, 98n1371
Romantic hearts: a personal ref for romance readers, 3d ed, 98n1115
Romantic movement, 97n884
Romantic poetry by women: a bibliog, 1770-1835, 95n1247
Romeiser, John B., 96n1253
Ronald Colman: a bio-bibliog, 98n1273

Ronan, Colin A., 96n1802
Rondina, Marisa, 95n850
Rony, A. Kohar, 98n114
Ronzio, Robert A., 98n1521
Rood, Karen L., 95n927, 96n1201
Room, Adrian, 95n502, 95n503, 97n382, 97n824, 97n891, 98n401, 98n1260, 99n408
Rooney, Terrie M., 96n1362, 99n20
Roosens, Laurent, 96n1019, 98n938
Roots of Afrocentric thought, 99n985
Roots of the Republic, 97n410
Roper, Fred W., 95n1644
Rosa Luxemburg & Emma Goldman: a bibliog, 98n637
Rosair, David, 96n1617
Rosaler, Robert C., 96n1677
Roscoe "Fatty" Arbuckle: a bio-bibliog, 95n1354
Roscoe, Lorraine, 96n321
Rose, Carol, 97n1090
Rose, Cynthia, 95n443
Rose, Peter Q., 98n1455
Rose, Sharon, 96n221, 96n407
Rosen, Craig, 97n1060
Rosen, Joseph, 95n228
Rosen, Philip, 99n528
Rosenak, Chuck, 97n783
Rosenak, Jan, 97n783
Rosenbaum, Barbara, 95n1202
Rosenberg, Bruce A., 99n962
Rosenberg, Jerry M., 95n187, 95n244, 96n304, 96n305
Rosenberg, Kenneth A., 95n1785
Rosenberg, Ronald H., 99n585
Rosenberg, William G., 98n481
Rosenblum, Joseph, 95n971, 96n664, 99n591, 99n1079
Rosenfeld, Eugene, 95n117
Rosenfeld, Louis, 96n100, 96n101, 96n1774, 98n1595
Rosenkrantz, Linda, 95n465
Rosenthal, Bernard M., 98n578
Rosenthal Collection of printed bks with ms annots, 98n578
Rosenthal, Joel T., 96n542
Roses, 97n1277
Rosow, La Vergne, 98n1057
Ross, Carl, 96n767
Ross, Donald, 99n1044
Ross, John M., 97n249
Ross, Lee E., 99n575
Ross Lee Finney: a bio-bibliog, 97n1039
Ross, Leon T., 98n346
Ross, Leslie, 97n799
Ross, Marilyn, 96n979
Ross register of Siberian industry 1995, 96n246
Ross, Robert E., 96n246
Ross, Steven T., 99n499
Ross, Thomas W., 98n1158
Rossi, John V., 96n1638
Rossi, Renzo, 97n458
Rossi, Roxanne, 96n1638
Rossi, William A., 95n988
Rossman, Amy Y., 96n1593
Rossol, Monona, 96n1042
Rosteck, Mary Kay, 99n521

Roster of Confederate soldiers 1861-65, 98n451
Roster of Union soldiers 1861-65: US colored troops, 98n452
Roth, Barry, 97n988
Roth, John E., 98n1255
Roth, John K., 96n1198
Roth, Klaus, 95n1315
Roth, Mitchel P., 98n881
Rothenberg, Mikel A., 95n1656
Rothschild, D. Aviva, 96n1359
Rottet, Kevin J., 99n935
Rountree, Bob, 96n1713, 98n1523
Rousseau, John J., 97n1213
Routh, Rebecca, 97n114
Routledge dict of lang & linguistics, 97n812
Routledge dict of 20th-century pol thinkers, 2d ed, 99n655
Routledge ency of translation studies, 99n896
Routldege French dict of environmental technology, 98n1637
Routledge French dict of telecommunications, 99n1494
Routledge French technical dict, 96n1499
Routledge German dict of ...
   business commerce & finance, 98n156
   chemistry & chemical tech, v.2, 99n1508
   construction, 98n1482
   environmental tech, 99n1555
   info tech, 98n1579
   medicine, v.1, 99n1444
Routledge German technical dict, 97n851
Routledge Spanish dict of business, commerce, & finance, 99n146
Routledge Spanish technical dict, 98n1408
Rovin, Jeff, 95n930, 96n1360
Rowan, Bonnie G., 95n938
Rowan, Davina, 99n843
Rowe, Fred A., 95n318, 95n319
Rowe, Julian, 95n1490
Rowe, Noel, 98n1472
Rowe, Sara, 98n589, 98n590
Rowen, Beth, 98n1264
Rowland, William G., Jr., 97n296
Rowlands, John, 95n461, 97n353
Rowlands, Shane, 99n946
Rowlands, Sheila, 97n353
Rowlinson, William, 96n1101
Roy, Geoffrey, 99n440
Roy, Michelle, 98n237
Roy Rogers, 96n1408
Rozario, Diane, 97n1339
Roze, Janis A., 98n1475
Rubel, David, 96n521, 98n436, 98n443
Rubie, Peter, 95n1377
Rubin, Harvey W., 97n201
Rubin, Janet E., 96n1170
Rubin, Louis D., Jr., 97n924
Rubin, Melvin L., 98n1553
Rubin, Stephen Jay, 96n1382
Ruby, Mary K., 95n236, 99n1106, 99n1107, 99n1108, 99n1109
Rudin, Norah, 98n1445
Rudman, Masha Kabakow, 95n773
Rudman, Theo, 99n183, 99n184

Rudman's cigar buying gd, 99n183
Rudman's complete gd to cigars, 99n184
Rudolph, Donna Keyse, 98n142
Rudolph, G. A., 98n142
Rudolph, Joseph R., Jr., 96n1833
Rudolph, Lloyd I., 99n243
Rudolph, Susanne Hoeber, 99n243
Ruffin, Albert, 95n725, 96n723
Ruffin, C. Bernard, 96n95
Ruffin, M. Holt, 97n123
Rufus, Anneli, 95n1335
Rugby catalogue of info sources, 96n830
Rugg, Frederick E., 99n334
Rugg's recommendation on the colleges, 99n334
Ruhling, Nancy, 96n1016
Ruja, Harry, 96n1423
Rulau, Russell, 98n914
Rules of thumb for chemical engineers, 96n1650
Rules of thumb for chemical engineers, 2d ed, 99n1400
Rummel, Erika, 96n1250
Rumsey, William D., 98n1332
Rundell, Michael, 96n814
Running for president, 95n741
Rupesinghe, Kumar, 95n136
Rupley, Lawrence A., 99n96
Rupp, Robert O., 98n645
Ruppli, Michel, 95n1259, 97n1031
Rural economic dvlpmt, 1975-93: an annot bibliog, 95n180
Rusak, Halina R., 97n808
Russel, Randall P., 96n1719
Russell, Anthony P., 95n1596
Russell, Cheryl, 96n911, 97n324, 98n261, 99n372, 99n783
Russell, Letty M., 97n1177
Russell, Norma Jean, 97n872
Russell, Paul, 96n865
Russell, Rinaldina, 95n1235, 98n1177
Russell, Terence M., 99n813, 99n814, 99n815, 99n816, 99n817
Russell, Thyra K., 95n293
Russell, Timothy O., 98n419
Russey, William, 96n1789
Russia, rev ed, 99n124
Russia & Eurasia facts & figures, v.24, 99n126
Russia & Eurasia facts & figures annual, v.21, 98n128
Russia & Eurasia facts & figures annual, v.22, 98n129
Russia & the former Soviet Union: a bibliographic gd to English lang pubs, 1986-91, 95n162
Russia survival gd, 5th ed, 95n283
Russia/USSR, 2d ed, 95n161
Russian defense business dir 1993, 95n284
Russian far east: an economic hndbk, 96n247
Russian idioms, 98n1043
Russian revolution, 1905-21, 96n548
Russian-English collocational dict of the human body, 97n867
Russian-English comprehensive dict, 98n1047
Rust, E. Gardner, 97n1087
Ruthchild, Rochelle Goldberg, 95n903
Rutland, Robert A., 96n507
Rutten, Peter, 96n1781
Ruttle, Jack, 95n1531

Rwanda, 95n122
Ryan, Bryan, 97n335
Ryan, Marleigh, 95n134
Ryan, Patrick J., 96n594
Ryan, Steve, 97n1113
Ryan, Tracey A., 95n726
Ryan, Tracey A., 722 724, 96n721, 96n725, 96n726, 96n727, 96n728, 96n729
Ryan, Victoria, 96n264
Rybacki, James J., 96n1737
Rybalka, Michel, 95n1426
Rye, Howard, 99n1160
Ryman, Rhonda, 99n1204
Ryskamp, George R., 98n368

Saar, Doreen Alvarez, 98n1111
Saari, Peggy, 96n454, 97n26, 98n834, 98n1401, 99n522, 99n806
Sabin Collection catalog [CD-ROM], 98n10
Sachare, Alex, 95n809, 95n810, 99n726
Sackett, Susan, 97n1128
Sacks, David, 97n450
Sacred celebrations: a Jewish holiday hndbk, 96n1479
Sacred dramas of J. S. Bach, 96n1284
Sader, Marion, 95n13, 96n48
Safety & health on the Internet, 98n239
Safety & health on the Internet, 2d ed, 99n281
Safire, William, 95n729
Safire's new political dict, 95n729
Saha, Lawrence J., 98n268
Sailors, Jean R., 95n843
St. Helena, Ascension, & Tristan da Cunha, 98n146
St. James gd to ...
    black artists, 98n945
    fantasy writers, 97n950
    horror, ghost, & gothic writers, 99n976
    native N American artists, 99n865
    sci fiction writers, 4th ed, 97n951
St. James Press gay & lesbian almanac, 99n759
St. John, Leonard, 96n1476
St. John, Ronald Bruce, 99n480
St. Kitts-Nevis, 96n172
St. Lucia, 97n145
St. Martin's gd to sources in contemporary British hist, v.2, 95n558
Saito, Masaei, 95n132
Sajid, Abdul W., 95n1667
Sakach, Deborah Edwards, 98n427
Sakamoto, Yohei, 95n1589
Sakelliou-Schultz, Liana, 96n1222
Sakurai, Atsushi, 95n1589
Salamanders of the US & Canada, 99n1396
Salazar, Sylvia Ortega, 97n310
Salda, Anne C. M., 98n186
Saldana, Richard H., 95n625
Saldarini, Anthony J., 98n1377
Salem Press, editors of, 96n1700
Sales, Georgia, 95n830
Salkeld, Audrey, 99n442

Salkin, Robert M., 96n467, 96n468, 96n469, 97n469
Salluzzo, Sharon, 95n1132
Salmon, Richard D., 96n276
Salokar, Rebecca Mae, 97n485
Salsbury, Robert E., 97n283
Salter, Frank K., 95n770
Salu, Luc, 96n1019, 98n938
Salvadori, Neri, 99n160
Salzman, Jack, 95n1182, 97n331
Samarsinghe, Vidyamali, 99n484
Same time ... same station: an A-Z gd to radio from Jack Benny to Howard Stern, 97n765
Samir Husni's gd to new consumer mags, 1997 ed, 98n882
Samoa (American Samoa, Western Samoa, Samoans abroad), 98n145
Sampson, Henry T., 96n1410, 99n1235
Sampson, Ronald N., 95n1614
Samsel, Jon, 97n1363
Samuel Johnson ency, 97n994
Samuel Taylor Coleridge: an annot bibliog of criticism & scholarship, v.3, 97n990
Samuels, Barbara G., 97n925
San Francisco almanac, rev ed, 97n83
San Marino, 97n121
Sander, Reinhard, 97n1012
Sanders, Alan J. K., 97n111
Sanders, Valerie, 95n1029
Sandler, Stanley, 96n538
Sanford, George, 96n144
Sanjurjo, Annick, 98n955
Sankey, Michael, 98n63, 98n419, 98n536, 98n537, 98n665, 98n706
Sankey, Michael L., 98n524, 98n525, 98n666, 99n597
Sansfacon, Roland, 99n920
Santrock, John W., 95n774
Santucci, James A., 98n1364
Sao Tome & Principe, 96n121
Sapp, Gregg, 95n1162, 96n660
Saraceno, Dan, 98n288
Sarasohn-Kahn, Jane, 99n847
Saretsky, Cecile L., 96n651
Sarjeant, William A. S., 97n1402
Sarkozi, Matyas, 98n133
Sarnoff, Irving, 99n696
Sartre: bibliog 1980-92, 95n1426
Sasa, Manabu, 96n1626
Sasson, Jack M., 96n159
Satran, Pamela Redmond, 95n465
Sattler, Richard A., 96n414
Savage, Beth L., 95n410
Savage, Kathleen M., 95n390, 99n263, 99n361
Savings & loan crisis: an annot bibliog, 95n234
Savitt, William, 97n228
Sawers, Robin, 96n1104
Sawinski, Diane M., 96n224, 97n204
Saxe, Stephen O., 96n666
Sayette, Michael A., 95n786
Sayler, James, 98n648
Sayre, John R., 97n584
Sbordoni, Valerio, 99n1390

Scalzo, Richard, 96n1717
Scammon, Richard M., 95n737, 96n735, 99n677
Scams, shams, & flimflams, 95n1337
Scanlon, Jennifer, 97n411
Scardellato, Gabriele, 95n417
Scargill, Matthew H., 98n1012
Schaberg, William H., 97n1157
Schaefer, Christina K., 97n358, 98n332, 99n635
Schaefer, Michael W., 98n1133
Schaeffer, John, 96n1847
Schaffner, Bradley L., 97n124
Schandorff, Esther Dech, 97n1193
Schechter, Harold, 99n1242
Scheindlin, Raymond P., 99n395
Schell, Terri Kessler, 96n996
Schellinger, Jennifer, 99n198
Schellinger, Paul, 99n963
Schellinger, Paul E., 97n469
Schemann, Hans, 97n852
Schenk, Trudy, 95n463
Schenkenberg, Amy, 98n676
Scheven, Yvette, 95n113
Schick, Frank L., 95n840
Schick, Renee, 95n840
Schiff, Donald, 99n1464
Schilit, W. Keith, 97n181
Schiller, Carol, 98n1551
Schiller, David, 98n1551
Schilling, Mark, 99n112
Schimke, Ann, 98n285, 98n417
Schinabeck, Michael J., 97n252
Schirmer pronouncing pocket manual of musical terms, 5th ed, 96n1271
Schlachter, Gail Ann, 96n690, 96n858, 96n879, 96n880, 98n91, 98n307, 98n848, 98n1411, 99n292, 99n293, 99n294, 99n772, 99n773
Schlager, Neil, 95n237, 95n1642, 96n221, 96n1511, 97n193, 99n759
Schleifer, Jay, 98n369
Schleifer, Martha Furman, 97n1042, 97n1047, 97n1048, 99n1145
Schlesinger, Arthur M., Jr., 95n741
Schlessinger, Bernard A., 96n173
Schlessinger, Bernard S., 97n30, 97n940
Schlessinger, June H., 97n30, 97n940
Schlicke, Priscilla, 97n1229
Schlueter, June, 98n1067
Schlueter, Paul, 98n1067
Schmalleger, Frank, 98n550
Schmalz, Rosemary, 95n1742
Schmidt, Carl B., 97n1044
Schmidt, Diane, 97n1264, 97n1272
Schmidt, Gary D., 97n935
Schmidt, George W., 95n1107
Schmidt, H. Joachim, 97n1319, 98n1511
Schmidt, Karl J., 96n534
Schmidt, Nancy J., 95n1363
Schmidt, Robert, 95n305
Schmitt, Deborah A., 99n968, 99n969

Schmittroth, Linda, 95n884, 96n953, 96n1496, 98n827, 99n521
Schmitz, Cecilia M., 96n1721
Schneider, Carl J., 95n913
Schneider, Dorothy, 95n913
Schneider, Edgar W., 95n1028
Schneider, Stephen H., 97n1396
Schnorr, Veronika, 99n928
Schobinger, Juan, 96n386
Schoeman, Elna, 99n99
Schoeman, Stanley, 99n99
Schoenenberger, Lori, 99n761
Schoenhals, Kai, 95n167
Schofield, Mary Anne, 98n1111
Scholars' gd to ...
   humanities & social scis in the Soviet successor states, 95n165
   Washington, DC, for peace & intl security studies, 96n656
   Washington, DC, for Russian, Central Eurasian, & Baltic studies, 95n164
   Washington, DC, media collections, 95n938
Scholarships & loans for nursing educ 1997-98, 99n1479
Scholastic children's dict, rev ed, 98n1008
Scholastic children's gd to dinosaurs & other prehistoric animals, 95n1735
Scholastic dict of spelling, 99n912
Scholastic ency of ...
   the N American Indian, 98n355
   the presidents & their times, 96n521
   the presidents & their times, updated ed, 98n443
   the US, 99n1005
   women in the US, 98n836
Scholastic rhyming dict, 95n1057
Scholze-Stubenrecht, Werner, 98n1031
Schomberg Center gd to black lit from the 18th century to the present, 97n918
Schon, Isabel, 95n1151, 98n358, 98n1079
Schonberg, Harold C., 98n1216
School lib media annual 1993, v.11, 95n663
School lib media annual 1995, v.13, 96n651
School violence, 98n278
Schorr, Alan Edward, 95n401, 97n336
Schrader, Richard J., 99n1027
Schraepler, Hans-Albrecht, 97n617, 98n161
Schraff, Anne, 96n944
Schramer, James, 99n1044
Schrank, Bernice, 98n1175
Schreck, Ann L., 97n544
Schreiber, Mae N., 98n199
Schreier, Konrad F., 95n703
Schroeder's antiques price gd, 15th ed, 98n905
Schroy, Ellen T., 99n839
Schubert, Frank N., 96n699
Schuenenman, Bruce R., 98n1215
Schuh, Randall T., 96n1627
Schuhmacher, Stephen, 96n1483
Schuler, Chris, 99n440
Schultz, Jeffrey D., 98n659, 99n54, 99n1071
Schultz, Jon S., 96n638
Schultz, Margie, 95n1353, 98n1274

Schultze, Phyllis A., 99n547
Schumann, Walter, 98n1615
Schupp, Jonathan F., 96n1868
Schwandt, Thomas A., 99n743
Schwartz, Alan M., 98n1638
Schwartz, David, 97n1113
Schwartz, Donald Ray, 98n1275
Schwartz, Jacob, 96n790
Schwartz, Marilyn, 96n968
Schwartz, Mortimer D., 95n596
Schwartz, Richard A., 99n1191
Schwartz, Richard Alan, 98n508
Schwartzman, Steven, 95n1743
Schwarz, Benyamin, 97n1094
Schwarzkopf, LeRoy C., 95n75
Schwedt, Rachel E., 98n1077
Schweizer, Karl W., 95n754
Schwerzel, Marleen, 95n97
Schwiebert, John E., 95n333
Schwiebert, Valerie L., 96n843
Schwing, Ned, 96n1009
Scialli, Anthony R., 96n1712
Science & tech: a purchase gd for libs 1995, 97n1234
Science & tech breakthroughs, 99n1308
Science & tech firsts, 98n1402
Science dict, 96n1501
Science experiments & projects index, 95n1506
Science experiments index for young people, 2d ed, 97n1244
Science fiction: the illus ency, 96n1192
Science fiction & fantasy reference index 1992-95, 98n1117
Science fiction, fantasy, & horror film sequels, series, & remakes, 98n1292
Science fiction, fantasy, & horror writers, 96n1193
Science fiction, horror & fantasy film & TV credits, suppl.2, 95n1395
Science fiction serials, 99n1227
Science fiction TV series, 98n1286
Science navigator [CD-ROM], 96n1500
Science on file [CD-ROM], 98n1415
Science projects for all students, 99n1326
Science, tech, & society in the Third World, 96n138
Science yr 1997, 98n1416
Science yr 1998, 98n1417
Sciences of the earth, 99n1517
Scientific & common names of 7,000 vascular plants in the US, 96n1593
Scientific & technical bks & serials in print 1995, 22d ed, 96n1484
Scientific instruments 1500-1900, 99n1318
Scientific revolution, 97n1227
Scientific style & format, 6th ed, 95n947
Scientific unit conversion, 98n1597
Scientists, 98n1401
Scientists: their lives & works, v.4, 99n1302
Scientists: their lives & works, v.5, 99n1303
Scientists & inventors, 99n1304
Scientists since 1660, 99n1297
Sci-Fi on tape, 98n1318
SciTech ref plus 1995-96 [CD-ROM], 97n1228
Sclater, Neil, 95n1616, 98n1489

Scobbie, Irene, 96n150
Scotland in the 19th century, 95n564
Scott, David L., 98n170
Scott, G., 97n1204
Scott, John F., 98n961
Scott, John S., 95n1606
Scott Joplin: a gd to research, 99n1142
Scott, Julie, 95n280
Scott, Michael D., 95n615
Scott, Pamela, 95n1017
Scott, Robert, 97n853
Scott, Shirley R., 98n981
Scott, Susan, 98n924
Scott, Thomas A., 97n1266, 98n1599
Scott, William, 97n1223
Scottish family hist, 95n462
Scott-Kilvert, Ian, 99n1110
Scouton, William O., 97n230
Scrambled word & anagram finder, 96n1072
Screen, J. E. O., 98n123
Scribner ency of American lives, v.1, 99n35
Scribner's American hist & culture [CD-ROM], 99n465
Scribner's writers series master index, 99n984
Scribner's writers series on CD-ROM: comprehensive ed [CD-ROM], 99n978
Scribner's writers series, selected authors ed [CD-ROM], 99n977
Scroggins, Daniel C., 98n1182
Sculpture, 95n1023
Seabourne, Joan, 98n789
Seaman, Gary, 95n1438
Seamus Heaney: a ref gd, 97n1008
Search for economics as a sci, 97n149
Search for security: fndns in intl affairs, 97n700
Searching the law: the states, 2d ed, 96n569
Sears, Jean L., 95n76
Sears list of subject headings, 15th ed, 95n652
Sears list of subject headings, 16th ed, 98n580
Searson, Michael, 95n349
Seaton, Janet, 96n540
Second bibliographic gd to the hist of computing, computers, & the info processing industry, 97n1364
Secrest, William B., 96n571
Secret lang of dreams, 95n784
Secret lang of symbols, 95n785
Secrets of the nest, 95n1566
Secrist-Schmedes, Barbera, 97n1058
Sects, 'cults,' & alternative religions, 98n1360
Seeds in the wilderness: profiles of world religious leaders, 96n1443
Seeff, Adele, 95n1218
Seely, Bruce E., 95n238
Segal, Jeffrey A., 97n497
Segen, Joseph C., 99n1455
Segida, Miroslava, 95n1369
Sehnert, William F., Jr., 95n1652
Selby, David, 96n1892
Selden, Holly M., 97n160
Seldin, Ruth R., 97n1220
Seldon, Philip, 99n441

Select index to Svoboda, v.3, 95n956
Select index to Svoboda, v.4, 95n957
Selective inventory of social sci info & documentation 1993, 95n95
Self-help dir, 95n827
Seligman, Kevin L., 98n934
Seller, Maxine Schwartz, 95n335
Semmes, Clovis E., 99n985
Sendero Luminoso: an annot bibliog of the Shining Path guerrilla movement, 1980-93, 97n502
Sendero Luminoso in context, 99n573
Sendich, Munir, 95n1239
Sendor, Virginia F., 98n1522
Seneca & Tuscarora Indians: an annot bibliog, 95n427
Senecal, J. A., 95n15
Senick, Gerard J., 98n1080
Senior high school lib catalog, 15th ed, 98n587
Senior PGA tour, 1995, 96n823
Senn, Bryan, 97n1122
Sennitt, Andrew G., 97n773
Sequels: an annot gd to novels in series, 99n1029
Serafin, Steven, 95n1204, 96n1225, 96n1226, 96n1227
Serafin, Steven R., 96n1157
Serge Chaloff, 99n1169
Serials on British TV 1950-94, 97n1104
Serio, John N., 95n1195
Serious about series, 99n1012
Serri, Conchita Franco, 98n349
Servaty, Heather L., 96n839
Services: stats on intl transactions 1970/92, 96n918
Services—the export of the 21st century: a gdbk of US serv exporters, 98n262
Servies, James A., 95n105, 97n84
Servies, Lana D., 95n105, 97n84
Seventeenth-century British nondramatic poets, 3d series, 95n1238
7th annual Graduate Group's internships in fed govt, 99n323
Seventh bk of jr authors & illustrators, 97n937
Severson, Molly, 96n1363
Severson, Richard, 97n1207
Sex & age distribution of the world populations, 99n784
Sex & age distribution of world populations: 1994 revision, 96n912
Sex & love quotations, 96n889
Sexton, Donal J., Jr., 97n560
Sexual behavior in modern China, English-lang ed, 99n775
Sexual harassment, 96n888, 97n702
Sexual harassment, 2d ed, 99n563
Sexual harassment: a ref hndbk, 95n633
Sexuality & gender in the English Renaissance, 99n776
Sexuality & the elderly, 98n798
Sexuality, religion & magic, 95n875
Seymore, Bruce, II, 95n146, 95n762, 97n700
Seymour-Smith, Martin, 97n887
Sfeir de Gonzalez, Nelly, 95n1228
Sgroi, Renee, 99n3
Shackelford, James F., 95n1630
Shadle, Robert, 98n466
Shadow of death: an analytic bibliog on pol violence, terrorism, & low-intensity conflict, 97n501

Shafer, Yvonne, 99n1249
Shafritz, Jay M., 99n702
Shakespeare, 99n1079
Shakespeare cos & festivals, 96n1420
Shakespeare dict, 96n1241
Shakespeare films in the classroom, 95n1397
Shakespeare for students, bk 2, 98n1163
Shakespeare interactive [CD-ROM], 99n1080, 99n1081
Shakespeare quotations, 96n1239
Shakespearean criticism, v.26, 96n1242
Shakespearean criticism, v.38, 99n1082
Shakespearean criticism yrbk 1996, v.37, 99n1083
Shakespeare's characters for students, 98n1164
Shakespeare's lang, 97n999
Shakhmayev, Sergey, 96n1139
Shale, Richard, 95n1400
Shaman, William, 95n1286
Shambhala dict of Taoism, 97n1226
Shambhala ency of yoga, 98n1338
Shamos, Mike, 95n813
Shand, Patricia Martin, 95n1279
Shan-English dict, 97n869
Shapir, Yiftah, 99n634
Shapiro, Robert, 95n1271
Shapiro, Stephen M., 99n569
Shapiro, William E., 95n103
Sharks & rays of Australia, 96n1623
Sharma, R. S., 95n1083
Sharp, Aaron J., 95n1547
Sharp, Gene, 98n496
Sharp, J. Michael, 98n678
Sharp, James Roger, 98n650
Sharp, John, 96n1742
Sharp, Nancy Weatherly, 98n650
Sharp, Pat Tipton, 95n1124
Sharp, Richard M., 99n308
Sharp, Vicki F., 99n308
Sharpe, Richard, 95n698, 97n573
Shattock, Joanne, 95n1203
Shattuck, Gardiner H., Jr., 97n1180
Shatzky, Joel, 98n1125
Shave, D., 97n247
Shave, David, 99n262
Shaw, Caroline S., 96n121
Shaw, Dennis F., 95n1737
Shaw, Eva, 96n791
Shaw, Gareth, 98n132
Shaw, Harry, 95n948, 95n1039
Shaw, Michael, 96n1710
Shaw, Patricia, 98n1214
Shaw, Russell, 98n1388
She, Colleen, 97n361
Shea, Ann M., 97n346
Shealy, C. Norman, 99n1460
Shearer, Barbara S., 95n499, 97n1231, 98n1598
Shearer, Benjamin F., 95n499, 97n1231, 98n1598
Sheehan, Marion, 96n1578
Sheehan, Sean, 95n445
Sheehan, Tom, 96n1578
Sheehy, Noel, 98n710

Sheets, Anna, 96n387, 99n389
Sheets, Anna J., 99n1037, 99n1038
Sheets, Tara E., 99n50
Sheets, William, 97n1305
Sheiman, Deborah Lovitky, 95n349
Shelley, Thomas J., 99n1286
Shelov, Steven P., 99n1464
Shelton, James H., 96n8
Shepard, Thomas H., 96n1720
Shepard's/McGraw-Hill tax dict for business, 95n331
Shepherd, John, 99n1163
Sheppard, Julia, 97n440
Sheppard, Roger, 95n1106
Sherlock Holmes: screen & sound gd, 95n1394
Sherlock Holmes hndbk, 95n1212
Sherman, Gale W., 98n1090
Sherman, Marc I., 98n708
Sherman, Moshe D., 97n1224
Sherrick, Julie, 99n1085
Sherrin, Ned, 97n71
Sherrow, Victoria, 96n418, 97n563, 97n644
Sherry, Clifford J., 96n1435, 99n1370
Sherwood, Richard M., 95n1796
Sherwood, Steve, 97n284
Sheward, David, 99n1198
Shewmaker, Eugene F., 97n999
Shiel, Suzanne, 95n141
Shields, Graham, 98n138
Shields, Graham J., 96n149
Shields, M. J., 95n1246
Shields, Nancy E., 95n297, 99n835
Shiers, George, 98n889
Shiers, May, 98n889
Shifflett, Crandall, 97n400
Shiffman, Jody Robin, 97n1010
Shilling, Henry, 98n175
Shim, Jae K., 97n156, 98n263, 99n194
Shin, Linda M., 99n1452
Shinoda, Gretchen, 96n423
Shipp, Steve, 97n800, 98n1639
Shippey, Karla C., 96n241
Shippey, T. A., 97n948
Ships of the world, 98n1651
Shipwrecks, 97n1448
Shirk, Martha, 96n462
Shlyakhov, Vladimir, 96n1128
Shopping for a better world, 95n225
Shopping with a conscience, 98n178
Short fiction: a criticial companion, 98n1119
Short hist of the Jewish people, 99n395
Short, K. R. M., 97n764
Short, Kathy G., 96n1169
Short stories for students, v.1, 98n1120
Short stories for students, v.2, 98n1121
Short stories for students, v.3, 99n1015
Short stories for students, v.4, 99n1016
Short stories in English: Britain & N America, 95n1165
Short story criticism, v.17, 96n1196
Short story criticism, v.18, 97n954
Short story criticism, v.19, 97n955

Short story criticism, v.20, 97n956
Short story criticism, v.21, 97n957
Short story criticism, v.26, 99n1037
Short story criticism, v.27, 99n1038
Short story index 1989-93, 95n1166
Short story index 1995, 98n1122
Short story writers, 98n1123
Short-title catalogue of bks printed in England, Scotland, Ireland, Wales, & British America..., v.1, 2d ed, 96n14
Short-title catalogue of Hungarian bks printed before 1851 in the British Lib, 97n14
Shortelle, Dennis, 98n854
Shorter dict of catch phrases, 95n1064
Shorter slang dict, 95n1058
Shortwave listening on the road, 97n774
Shot on this site, 96n472
Shou-hsin, Teng, 98n1023
Shrader, Charles Reginald, 95n548, 96n520
Shrager, David S., 99n572
Shrikes: a gd to the shrikes of the world, 99n1380
Shriver, Andrew, 95n1700
Shriver, George H., 98n1354, 99n1289
Shrubs & climbers, 97n1286
Shrum, Wesley, 96n138
Shuldiner, David P., 98n762
Shull, Michael S., 97n1123
Shulman, Frank Joseph, 99n15
Shulman, William L., 99n533
Shumsky, Neil Larry, 99n793
Siani-Davies, Mary, 99n136
Siani-Davies, Peter, 99n136
Sibley, Charles G., 95n1572, 95n1574
Sibley, Katherine A. S., 99n544
Sices, David, 97n846
Sices, Jacqueline B., 97n846
Sidhu, Jatswan S., 99n482
Siebert, Lee, 96n1818
Siegel, Brian V., 99n477
Siegel, David S., 96n1007
Siegel, Joel G., 97n156, 98n263, 99n194
Siegel, Mark A., 98n754, 98n1559
Siegel, Marvin, 99n34
Siegel, Susan, 96n1007
Siegman, Joseph, 98n719
Sienkewicz, Thomas J., 97n1092, 98n1261
Sierra Club green gd, 97n1431
Sierra, Judy, 98n378
Sierra Nev. Wildflowers, 99n1362
Sievers, Maurice L., 96n993
Sifakis, Stewart, 96n522, 96n523, 96n524, 96n525, 96n526
Sight & Sound film review v.: Jan. 1994 to Dec. 1994, 97n1135
Sign-off for the old Met, 99n1155
Signals intelligence in WW II, 97n560
Signers of the Declaration of Independence, 98n434
Signs of the zodiac, 98n717
Sigurdardottir, Dorunn, 95n158
Sikkel, Robert W., 97n494, 97n496, 99n589
Silbaugh, Katharine B., 97n499

Silbey, Joel H., 95n742
Silent film necrology, 96n1369
Silent film performers, 97n1105
Silent films on video, 97n1120
Silk stalkings: more women write of murder, 99n1033
Silva, Penny, 97n830
Silver, A. David, 96n184, 96n195
Silver, Joel, 97n553, 98n594
Silverblatt, Art, 98n856
Silverburg, Sanford R., 95n763, 95n764, 96n570
Silverman, David P., 98n486
Silverman, Helaine, 97n794
Silverstein, Bernard, 96n1077
Silvester, Robert, 95n1409
Silvey, Anita, 97n939
Simkin, Tom, 96n1818
Simmons, R. C., 97n40
Simmons, Susan L., 98n556
Simms, Bryan R., 97n1045
Simon & Schuster D-Day ency: a multimedia exploration! [CD-ROM], 95n689
Simon, Reeva S., 97n136
Simon, Ronald G., 97n1258
Simon, Seymour, 96n1501, 96n1861
Simone Weil, 96n957
Simone, Roberta, 96n1206
Simons, Linda Keir, 95n1339
Simpson, Anthony E, 95n769
Simpson, Beverly K., 96n1216
Simpson, James B., 98n84
Simpson, John, 95n1055
Simpson's contemporary quotations, rev ed, 98n84
Sims-Bell, Barbara, 96n1538
Sing glory & hallelujah! histl & biogl gd to Gospel Hymns nos.1-6 complete, 97n1086
Singapore business: the portable ency for doing business with Singapore, 95n265
Singer, Armand E., 95n922
Singer, David, 97n1220
Singer, Michael, 96n1405, 98n1317
Singer's gd to the American art song 1870-1980, 95n1272
Singerman, Robert, 97n810
Singers of the century, 98n1201
Singer-songwriters, 96n1307
Singh, D. Ranjit, 99n482
Single, Eric, 96n898
Singleton, Carl, 98n117
Sinko, Peggy Tuck, 98n379, 98n431
Siochain, Etain O, 98n45
Sioux & other Native American cultures of the Dakotas, 95n428
SIPRI yrbk 1993, 95n766
Sir Arthur Sullivan: a resource bk, 98n1212
Sir Philip Sidney: an annot bibliog of texts & criticism (1554-1984), 95n1222
Sir Robert Peel 1788-1850: a bibliog, 97n439
Sir Thomas More in the English Renaissance, 95n556
Sirotof, Gene, 96n1419, 97n1153
Sisson, A. F., 96n1092
Sisson's word & expression locater, 2d ed, 96n1092

Sisung, Kelle S., 97n1176
Sitarz, Daniel, 98n541, 98n542, 99n567
Sitsky, Larry, 95n1261, 99n1144
Sixteenth-century British nondramatic writers, 1st series, 95n1201
Sixteenth-century British nondramatic writers, 3d series, 97n983
Sixteenth-century British nondramatic writers, 4th series, 98n1147
6th annual Graduate Group's internships in state govt, 99n324
Sixth bi-annual natl dir of arts internships, 1995/96, 96n1034
Sixties [CD-ROM], 98n450
65 yrs of the Oscar, rev ed, 96n1372
Sizes: the illus ency, 96n1787
Sizesaurus, 96n1514
Skelly, Carole J., 95n1518
Skelly, Elizabeth M. T., 98n1495
Skelly, Kenneth J., 98n1495
Skin deep: an A-Z of skin disorders, treatments, & health, 97n1333
Skole, Robert, 96n83
Skutt, Alexander G., 98n743
Slack, James D., 95n339
Slade, Alexander L., 97n521
Slang of sin, 99n43
Slater, Courtenay M., 97n176, 97n712, 99n159
Slater, James A., 96n1627
Slatta, Richard W., 96n510
Slavens, Thomas P., 95n574
Slavin, Sarah, 97n737
Slee, Debora A., 95n1657, 97n1319, 98n1511
Slee, Vergil N., 95n1657, 97n1319, 98n1511
Sleuths, sidekicks, & stooges, 98n1112
Slide, Anthony, 95n1417, 96n1411, 97n1107, 99n1215
Sloan, Dave, 97n648, 97n655
Sloan, Stephen, 96n597
Slocombe, D. Scott, 95n276
Slocum, Robert B., 95n1183
Slonimsky, Nicholas, 96n1268
Slonimsky, Nicolas, 95n1262, 98n1197, 99n1123
Slote, Nancy, 97n706
Slovak, Irene, 95n384
Slovenia, 97n122
Small business profiles, v.1, 95n212
Small business profiles, v.2, 96n196
Small business sourcebk, 10th ed, 98n166
Small, Judy Jo, 95n1184
Smaller perennials, 98n1435
Smallwood, Carol, 99n1428
Smart medicine for a healthier child, 96n1713
Smethurst, John B., 96n264
Smirnov, A. N., 97n1267
Smirnov, N. N., 97n1267
Smith, A. D., 98n1444
Smith, Adeline Mercer, 95n647
Smith, Alan G., 96n1807
Smith, Angel, 97n452
Smith, Carolyn J., 96n1282
Smith, Clay, 99n561
Smith, Colin, 99n939

Smith, Constance, 96n1033, 96n1035, 99n872
Smith, Dan, 99n700
Smith, Darren L., 95n189, 95n512, 97n1377, 98n418, 99n151, 99n712
Smith, David G., 96n1807
Smith, David Lionel, 97n331
Smith, David Spencer, 95n1578
Smith, Diane H., 95n74
Smith, Edward H., 96n1673
Smith, Eric Ledell, 96n1301
Smith, Gerald S., 95n152
Smith, Henrietta M., 95n411
Smith, Hobart M., 96n1639
Smith, Inese A., 95n154
Smith, Jane Stuart, 95n1311
Smith, Jennifer A., 99n873
Smith, Jessie Carney, 95n412, 95n909, 96n397, 96n403, 96n404, 97n34
Smith, John David, 98n438
Smith, John L., 95n1301, 96n1317
Smith, Linda C., 96n647
Smith, Marty, 98n1464
Smith, Myron J., Jr., 95n821, 99n717
Smith, Patricia, 97n781
Smith, Robert Ellis, 98n543
Smith, Roger, 97n1411, 99n1298, 99n1515, 99n1524
Smith, Ron, 95n802, 98n736, 99n719
Smith, Ronald L., 99n1196
Smith, Shanea L., 99n665
Smith, Sharyl G., 95n1125
Smith, Steven E., 99n884
Smith, Tony, 97n1326, 98n802
Smith, Trevor, 95n1673
Smith, Verity, 98n1178
Smither, Roger, 96n557
Smitherman, Geneva, 95n413
Smith-Peters, Lise, 96n730
Smithsonian on disc [CD-ROM], 95n635
Smithsonian on disc, 4th ed [CD-ROM], 99n613
Smoking: the health consequences of tobacco use, 96n1721
Smoky Mountain voices: a lexicon of S Appalachian speech, 95n1042
Smoley, Lewis M., 98n1248
Smurthwaite, David, 96n676
Smyth, Angela, 95n1674
Snakes of the US & Canada, v.2, 96n1638
Snelling, Dennis, 97n647
Snodgrass, Mary Ellen, 95n436, 96n1147, 96n1148, 96n1349, 97n892, 98n717, 98n1130, 99n1047, 99n1182
Snow, Barbara, 95n1264
Snyder, Keith D., 95n696
Snyder, Kurt, 99n558
Snyder, Lawrence D., 97n1032
Sobczak, A. J., 97n948, 99n959
Soccer stars, 96n831
Social indicators of dvlpmt 1994, 95n870
Social issues in contemporary sport, 95n792
Social movement theory & research, 98n690
Social panorama of Latin America, 1994 ed, 96n153
Social sci ency, 2d ed, 97n75

Social scis, 2d ed, 97n76
Social scis abstracts full text [CD-ROM], 98n92
Social scis index, April 1995 to Mar 1996, 98n93
Social work almanac, 2d ed, 96n894
Social work dict, 3d ed, 96n890
Society of Automotive Engineers, 95n1635
Sociofile: 1974-Dec 1996 [CD-ROM], 98n94
Sociology: a gd to ref & info sources, 98n753
Sociology of emotions: an annot bibliog, 95n826
Sociology of law, 95n598
Sofer, Morry, 98n991
Software engineering standards & specifications, 95n1608
SOHO desk ref, 99n283
Sokoloff, Michael, 95n1452
Solar system, 99n1524
Sollberger, Martha Park, 98n1185
Soloistic English horn lit from 1736-1984, 95n1275
Solomon Islands campaign, Guadalcanal to Rabaul, 98n611
Solomon, Sheila A. B., 98n1553
Solorzano, Lucia, 96n331, 99n317
Soltis, Katherine, 96n1071
Some Joe you don't know: an American biogl gd to 100 British TV personalities, 97n1107
Somers, Paul P., Jr., 99n1192
Somerville, James, 95n47
Something about the author, v.78, 96n1172
Something about the author, v.79, 96n1173
Something about the author, v.80, 96n1174
Something about the author, v.81, 97n926
Something about the author, v.82, 97n927
Something about the author, v.83, 97n928
Something about the author, v.84, 97n929
Something about the author, v.85, 97n930
Something about the author, v.94, 99n988
Something about the author, v.95, 99n986
Something about the author autobiog series, v.18, 95n1146
Something about the author autobiog series, v.24, 98n1080
Something about the author autobiog series, v.25, 99n987
Sommer, Elyse, 96n1091
Sonevyts'kyi, Ihor, 98n1217
Song finder, 96n1318
Song index of the Enoch Pratt Free Lib, 99n1126
Song writers market, 1998, 98n1207
SongCite: an index to popular songs, 96n1309
Songs for bass voice, 96n1295
Songwriters: a biogl dict with discographies, 99n1117
Songwriter's market, 1994, 95n1263
Sonneborn, Liz, 96n419, 99n386
Sonnier, Austin, Jr., 95n1295
Sonntag Blay, Iliana L., 99n1111
Sophie Treadwell: a research & production sourcebk, 98n1132
Soria, Regina, 95n1002
Sorrow, Barbara Head, 98n282
Soucie, Gary, 95n816
Soukhanov, Anne H., 98n1002
Soul music A-Z, rev ed, 96n1339
Soule, George, 99n1061
Soundtracks: an intl dict of composers of music for film, 99n1131
Source: a gdbk of American genealogy, 98n370

Source bk on ageing, 99n746
Sourcebook for Jewish genealogies & family hists, 98n362
Sourcebook for modern Japanese philosophy, 99n1257
Sourcebook for research in music, 95n1251
Sourcebook of ...
   county court records, 95n609
   county court records, 3d ed, 98n524
   county demographics, 11th ed, 99n785
   federal courts, 2d ed, 97n500
   federal courts: US district & bankruptcy, 95n610
   local court & county records retrievers, 95n611
   local court & county record retrievers, 3d ed, 98n525
   local court & county record retrievers 1998, 99n597
   online public record experts, 97n540
   pediatric psychology, 95n783
   public record providers, 95n71
   state public records, 95n730
   state public records, 2d ed, 96n714
   zip code demographics, 10th ed, 96n913
   zip code demographics, 13th ed, 99n786
Sourcebook on parenting & child care, 96n899
Sources & methods: labour stats, v.2, 97n260
Sources of info for histl research, 95n574
Sources of London English, 97n831
South Africa, rev ed, 96n122
South Africa as apartheid ends: an annot bibliog..., 95n124
South African bibliog, 3d ed, 97n551
South America, Central America, & the Caribbean 1997, 6th ed, 97n130
South America, Central America, & the Caribbean 1999, 7th ed, 99n138
South American cinema, 97n1124
South Asian religions in the Americas, 96n1438
South Dakota hist, 95n429
South, David W., 95n1698, 96n1674, 98n1477
South East Asia: a gd to ref material, 95n126
South Slavic folk culture, 95n1315
South Slavic writers before WW II, 96n1262
South Slavic writers since WW II, 99n1091
Southeast Asian langs & lits, 98n986
Southeast gd to saltwater fishing & boating, 95n818
Southern Africa bibliog, 97n101
Southern European studies gd, 95n147
Southern gardener's bk of lists, 95n1527
Southern loyalists in the Civil War, 95n546
Southern mountaineers in silent films, 95n1388
Southerton, Alan, 96n1762
Southwest Pacific campaign, 1941-45, 97n462
Southwick, Leslie H., 99n662
Sova, Dawn B., 99n605, 99n606
Soviet armed forces, 1918-92, 97n558
Space satellite hndbk, 3d ed, 95n1720
Space scis dict 2, 96n1645
Space scis dict 3, 96n1646
Spaceflight: a Smithsonian gd, 96n1647
Spaceflight & rocketry, 97n1300
Spadoni, Carl, 95n677
Spaeth, Harold J., 97n497
Spahn, Mark, 97n860
Spaihts, Jonathan, 99n335, 99n336

Spain, 97n396
Spain, 2d ed, 96n149
Spain, Louise, 99n1200
Spain, Patrick J., 96n191, 96n201
Spaminato, Lynn M., 96n1362
Spampinato, Lynn, 99n1021, 99n1022
Spanish American lit, 99n1098
Spanish artists from the 4th to the 20th century, 98n952
Spanish Civil War in lit, film, & art, 95n566
Spanish dramatists of the golden age, 99n1026
Spanish verbs, 99n938
Spanish-American war, 99n626
Spanish/English dict of human & physical geography, 95n493
Spanish-English, English-Spanish concise dict (Latin America), 95n1098
Spanish-English/English-Spanish dict, unabridged ed, 95n1097
Sparano, Vin T., 95n817, 95n818
Sparke, Penny, 99n878
Sparks, Sheila M., 97n1353
Sparrows & buntings, 97n1288
Spaulding, Seth, 98n694
SPDCD 1995: the standard per dir [CD-ROM], 96n87
Speace, Geri, 99n404
Speak the speech, 95n1220
Speake, Graham, 95n583
Speake, Jennifer, 99n903
Speaking freely, 98n1002
Speaking of animals, 96n1074
Spears, Richard A., 95n1044, 95n1060, 97n837, 99n905, 99n911
Special collections in children's lit, 96n661
Special edition: a gd to network TV documentary series & special news reports, 1980-89, 98n1304
Special-needs reading list, 99n751
Specialty occupational outlook, 96n274
Specialty occupational outlook: trade & technical, 97n262
Species info lib [CD-ROM], 96n1606
Speck, Bruce W., 96n665, 99n310
Spehr, Paul C., 97n1142
Spencer, Anne, 95n791
Spencer, Donald D., 96n1763, 96n1764, 96n1765, 96n1829
Spencer, Frank, 98n320
Spencer, James R., 99n1245
Spencer, Janet, 98n305
Spencer, John, 95n791
Spencer, Jonathan, 97n317
Spencer, Pam, 95n1139, 98n1098, 99n999
Spencer's complete gd to special interest videos, 4th ed, 99n1245
Spencer's illus computer dict, 96n1765
Spero, Jennifer, 99n1568
Spice trade, 96n308
Spicer, Dorothy Gladys, 95n1336
Spicq, Ceslas, 96n1457
Spies, 98n701
Spies: the secret agents who changed the course of hist, 95n765
Spilker, Bert, 97n1331
Spille, Henry A., 98n308
Spirits, fairies, gnomes, & goblins, 97n1090
Spjut, Richard W., 95n1539

Spomer, Cynthia Russell, 95n866
Sponholz, Joseph, 99n347
Sponza, Lucio, 96n143
Sport lawyer's gd to legal pers, 95n599
Sport lawyer's gd to legal pers, 1995 suppl, 96n615
Sport on film & video, 95n798
Sport thesaurus, 1994 ed, 96n802
Sporting News baseball gd, 1996 ed, 97n648
Sporting News complete baseball record bk, 1997 ed, 99n718
Sporting News complete hockey bk, 1995-96 ed, 96n828
Sporting News hockey gd, 1996-97 ed, 97n657
Sporting News hockey register, 1996-97 ed, 97n658
Sporting News official baseball register, 1996 ed, 97n649
Sporting News official NBA gd, 95n809
Sporting News official NBA gd, 1997-98 ed, 98n741
Sporting News official NBA register, 95n810, 98n742
Sporting News pro football gd, 1996 ed, 97n655
Sporting News pro football register, 1996 ed, 97n656
Sporting News selects baseball's greatest players, 99n719
Sporting News this day in sports, 95n802
Sports ency: pro football, 98n746
Sports ency: pro football, 12th ed, 95n820
Sports ethics, 96n801
Sports in N America, v.1, 99n711
Sports in N America, v.4, 96n798
Sports in N America, v.5, 97n642
Sports medicine bible, 96n1729
Sports people in the news 1996, 97n640
Sports phone bk USA , 1998, 99n712
Sports stars, 95n794
Sports stars: series 2, 97n641
Sports stars: series 3, 98n718
Sports style gd & ref manual, 97n757
Sportspeak: an ency of sport, 97n643
Sposato, Jeffrey S., 96n1283
Spratto, George R., 98n1566, 98n1567
Springfield armory: shoulder weapons 1795-1968, 99n848
Sprug, Joseph W., 95n1316
Spurge, Lorraine, 98n154
Spyke, Rebecca, 98n699
Square dance & contra dance hndbk, 97n1101
Square foot costs 1997, 18th ed, 98n1483
Squire, Romilly, 96n435
Squirrels, 97n1293
Squyres, Suzanne B., 98n568, 98n1559
Stachura, Lisa, 98n725
Stackpole, Noreen, 97n313
Stade, George, 97n982, 98n1149, 99n1110
Staff dirs on CD-ROM [CD-ROM], 99n672
Stafford, Pauline, 97n726
Stahl, Dean, 96n2
Stalin: an annot gd to bks in English, 95n565
Stalker, Geoffrey, 99n919
Stallaerts, Robert, 96n549
Stambler, Irwin, 98n1234
Stamm, Andrea L., 96n126, 99n98
Stamm, Johann Jakob, 96n1455, 97n1198
Stancell, Steven, 98n1237
Standard & Poor's 500 gd, 1995 ed, 96n214
Standard & Poor's insurance co ratings gd, 1995 ed, 97n202

Standard & Poor's midcap 400 gd, 1995 ed, 96n215
Standard & Poor's smallcap 600 gd, 1996 ed, 97n171
Standard & Poor's stock & bond gd, 1998 ed, 99n174
Standard carnival glass price gd, 10th ed, 97n784
Standard catalog of ...
    American cars, 1946-75, 98n1648
    baseball cards, 1998, 98n906
    basketball cards, 1998 ed, 99n727
    firearms, 5th ed, 96n1009
    football cards, 98n900
    US paper money, 99n846
    US tokens 1700-1900, 98n914
    world coins 1601-1700, 97n780
    world coins, 18th century 1701-1800, 98n911
    world coins, 1998, 98n912
Standard ency of carnival glass, 5th ed, 97n785
Standard French-English, English-French dict, 96n1102
Standard gd to US WW II tanks & artillery, 95n703
Standard gd to cars & prices, 99n1577
Standard hndbk of ...
    architectural engineering, 99n881
    engineering calculations, 3d ed, 96n1644
    plant engineering, 2d ed, 96n1677
Standard knife collector's gd, 3d ed, 99n850
Standard math interactive [CD-ROM], 99n1543
Standard per dir, 1997, 20th ed, 97n65
Standard per dir, 1998, 99n73
Standish, Peter, 96n406, 97n348
Standley, Laura Berger, 95n1147
Stanford, Michael, 97n296
Stang, Mark, 97n650
Stanley, David E., 96n1335
Stanley, Deborah A., 99n965, 99n966, 99n967
Stanley, Harold W., 95n743, 99n683
Stansfield, Geoffrey, 95n85
Stanton, Greta W., 95n851
Stanton, Tom, 96n1331
Star gd, 1997-98, 98n1266
Stark, Jack, 99n568
Stark, Richard W., 96n802
Stark, Sandra M., 96n492
Starnes, Wayne C., 95n1584
Starr, Glenn Ellen, 95n431
Stars & atoms, 96n1799
Stars & planets, 99n1523
Stars in blue: movie actors in America's sea servs, 98n1281
Start, Hannah, 96n279
StartSmart small business advisor [CD-ROM], 96n207
State & local taxation answer bk, 98n264
State & regional assns of the US 1998, 99n57
State atlas of pol & cultural diversity, 98n329
State budget actions 1997, 99n678
State by state gd to human resources law, 1994, 96n268
State by state gd to human resources law, 1994: midyear suppl & workers' compensation laws, 96n269
State Capital Law Firm Group, 96n740
State executive dir, 96n729
State groundwater regulation, 95n1771
State legislative elections: voting patterns & demographics, 99n674

State legislative sourcebk 1996, 97n602
State legislative summary, 1994, 96n595
State medical licensure gdlines 1998, 99n1449
State names, seals, flags, & symbols, rev ed, 95n499
State occupational outlook hndbk, 99n275
State of war & peace atlas, 99n700
State staff dir, summer 1997, 98n667
State tax actions 1997, 99n284
State-by-state biotech dir, 3d ed, 96n1506
Statesman's yrbk, 132d ed, 96n102
Statesman's yrbk 1998-99, 135th ed, 99n82
Statistical abstract of ...
    the ESCWA region 1983-92, 14th ed, 96n919
    the US 1995, 115th ed, 96n920
    the world, 96n921
Statistical forecasts of the US, 2d ed, 96n914
Statistical hndbk of social & economic indicators for the former Soviet Union, 97n125
Statistical hndbk of working America, 96n922
Statistical hndbk on ...
    adolescents in America, 97n718
    aging Americans, 1994 ed, 95n840
    violence in America, 97n507
    women in America, 2d ed, 97n740
Statistical indicators for Asia & the Pacific, v.23, 95n897
Statistical indicators for Asia & the Pacific, v.27, no.2, June 1997, 99n788
Statistical portrait of the US, 99n791
Statistical record of ...
    black America, 3d ed, 96n404
    children, 95n884
    health & medicine, 99n1436
    Hispanic Americans, 95n425
    native N Americans, 2d ed, 96n420
    older Americans, 95n833
    women worldwide, 96n953
Statistical Service Center, 95n667
Statistical survey of insurance & reinsurance operations in developing countries 1983-90, 96n227
Statistical yrbk for Asia & the Pacific 1996, 98n815
Statistical yrbk for Latin America & the Caribbean, 1994 ed, 96n154
Statistical yrbk, 1992, 95n898
Statistical yrbk 1994, 41st ed, 98n816
Statistically speaking: a dict of quotations, 98n82
Statistics of road traffic accidents in Europe & N America 1995, 96n1890
Statistics on crime & punishment, 97n511
Statistics on occupational wages & hours of work & on food prices 1997, 99n231
Statistics on weapons & violence, 97n512
Statistics sources 1996, 19th ed, 96n923
Statler Brothers discography, 98n1232
STATS hockey hndbk 1997-98, 99n736
STATS minor league hndbk 1998, 99n720
STATS player profiles 1998, 99n721
STATS pro basketball hndbk 1997-98, 99n728
Stauffer, Joseph, 99n1455
Steading, Alma D., 99n451
Steane, J. B., 98n1201

Stearns, Peter N., 95n96
Stebbings, Geoff, 98n1454
Steedman, Scott, 96n63
Steel market in 1995 & prospects for 1996, 97n198
Steele, Apollonia, 96n658, 96n1249, 97n1005
Steele, J. Valerie, 95n199, 99n665
Steele, Sandy, 96n796
Steele, Valerie J., 99n154
Steen, Peter, 98n699
Steen, Sara J., 96n368, 96n369, 97n305, 97n309, 98n988, 99n355
Steer, John, 95n990
Steeves, Paul D., 99n1267
Stefanowska, A. D., 99n798
Stein, Barbara, 96n649
Stein, Barry Jason, 98n625
Stein, Bernard, 99n885
Stein, Gordon, 95n1337, 97n634
Stein, Stephen J., 99n1266
Steinberg, Mark L., 95n1619
Steinfeldt, Cecilia, 95n1008
Steinmann, Martin, 96n970
Stellman, Jeanne Mager, 99n280
Stelten, Leo F., 96n1118
Stempen, Henry, 96n1587
Stepchuk, Roman, 95n956, 95n957
Stephen Crane ency, 98n1134
Stephens, Aarti, 99n1083
Stephens, Alan, 99n1329
Stephens, Elaine C., 96n1170, 99n453
Stephens, John, 95n1427
Stephens, John F., 96n338
Stephens, Michael L., 96n1383, 97n1114, 99n1210
Stephens, Norris L., 98n1190
Stephenson, Steven L., 96n1587
Sterling, Christopher H., 96n1778, 98n1646
Sterling, Keir B., 99n1552
Stern, Peter A., 97n502
Stern, Robert L., 99n569
Stern, Robert N., 97n250
Stern, Steven B., 97n1449
Sternberg, Martin L. A., 96n1132, 96n1133, 97n871, 99n910
Stern's gd to the cruise vacation, 6th ed, 97n1449
Sternstein, Jerome L., 97n33
Sterry, Paul, 98n1404
Stettenheim, Peter, 95n1565
Stevens, J. D., 96n1623
Stevens, Kenneth R., 99n659
Stevens, Matthew, 95n1359
Stevens, Muriel, 96n1531
Stevens, R. Paul, 98n1385
Stevens, Richard E., 95n527
Stevens, Roger T., 95n1699
Stevenson, Barbara, 96n378
Stevenson, Henry M., 95n1575
Stevenson, Neil, 98n976
Stevenson, Tom, 98n1424, 99n1342
Stewart, Barbara, 98n591
Stewart, Brian, 98n982
Stewart, David W., 98n308
Stewart, John, 95n1365, 97n444
Stewart, Joyce, 96n1576
Stewart, Ron, 99n850
Stewart, Sean, 97n649, 97n656, 97n658, 98n742
Stewart, Susan Cobb, 97n1341
Stewart, William, 96n864
Stidworthy, John, 99n1295
Still, Judith Anne, 97n1046
Stillerman, Elaine, 97n1350
Stilman, Anne, 98n1005
Stilwell, Steven A., 98n1113
Stitt, Beverly A., 96n313
Stocker, Friedrich W., 97n1266
Stockwell, Foster, 99n747
Stolbova, Olga V., 96n1107
Stoll, Donald R., 96n86, 98n879
Stone, Jon R., 98n1039, 98n1366
Stoneham, Marshall, 98n1220
Stoppard, Miriam, 96n904, 96n1692
Storey, John W., 97n1218
Storey, R. L., 96n561
Story of painting, 95n1018
Story of philosophy, 99n1256
Story of rock'n'roll, 96n1336
Storytellers: a biogl dir of 120 English-speaking performers worldwide, 99n1182
Storytelling ency, 98n1256
Stott, Carole, 96n74
Stout, Rick, 96n1775
Stover, Lois T., 98n1095
Strachan, Ian W., 98n1573
Stradling, R. A., 96n539
Strahle, Graham, 96n1272
Straighten up & fly right: a chronology & discography of Nat "King" Cole, 96n1329
Straley, Phillip D., 95n760
Strange & unexplained happenings, 97n638
Straub, Deborah Gillan, 95n408, 97n328, 97n967
Straughn, Barbarasue Lovejoy, 99n351
Straughn, Charles T., II, 99n351
Strauss, Carol Ann, 98n780
Strauss, Stephen, 96n1514
Stravinskas, Peter M. J., 99n1268
Street French slang dict & thesaurus, 99n924
Strength in numbers: a lesbian, gay, & bisexual resource, 97n703
Stress A-Z, 99n705
Strichart, Stephen S., 96n341
Strickland, Ruth Ann, 98n679
Strickler, Dave, 97n1095
Stricoff, R. Scott, 96n1796
Stringer, Jenny, 98n1073
Striplin, Deborah, 95n954
Strojny, Duane A., 95n592
Stromquist, Nelly P., 99n805
Strong, Debra L., 99n1570
Strong, M. C., 97n1085
Stroud, Elaine, 96n1736
Strouthes, Daniel P., 97n490
Strub, Sean O'Brien, 96n259

Struble, John Warthen, 97n1059
Structural & ownership changes in the chemical industry of countries in transition, 99n232
Structural steel designer's hndbk, 2d ed, 95n1603
Stuart, Margaret, 95n462
Stuart, Philip, 98n1204
Stuart, Ralph B., III, 98n239, 99n281
Stuart-Hamilton, Ian, 97n629
Stubblebine, Donald J., 97n1069, 98n1195
Stubbs, Jean, 97n132
Stubbs, Kendon, 97n527
Stuckey, Maggie, 95n1532
Student access gd to America's top 100 internships, 1995 ed, 95n303
Student Conservation Association, 96n1871
Student gd to Japanese sources in the humanities, 95n132
Student sci opportunities, 95n340
Student Servs, L. L. C., 99n338, 99n343, 99n344
Student's dict of lang & linguistics, 98n987
Student's gd to ...
   African American genealogy, 97n359
   British American genealogy, 97n360
   Chinese American genealogy, 97n361
   German American genealogy, 97n362
   Italian American genealogy, 97n363
   Scaninavian American genealogy, 97n364
   Irish American genealogy, 97n365
   Jewish American genealogy, 98n369
   Native American genealogy, 97n366
   playwriting opportunities, 96n1421
Studies in human sexuality, 2d ed, 96n887
Studwell, William E., 98n1215, 99n1125
Study abroad 1998-99, 30th ed, 99n354
Stuhlmueller, Carroll, 97n1196
Stuhr-Rommereim, Rebecca, 98n347
Stultz, Newell M., 95n124
Stump, Donald V., 95n1222
Sturges, Paul, 98n571
Sturgill, Claude C., 95n697
Sturm, Gary L., 96n1891
Stutzman, Michael, 96n1268
Stych, F. S., 97n1011
Style Manual Committee, Council of Biology Editors, 95n947
Subject gd to ...
   bks in print 1994-95, 95n19
   bks in print 1995-96, 96n16
   bks in print 1997-98, 98n16
   children's bks in print 1995, 96n20
   US govt ref sources, 2d ed, 98n60
   women of the world, 97n741
Subject headings for African American materials, 96n626
Subject headings for children 1994, 96n632
Subramanian, Jane M., 98n1139
Sub-Saharan African films & filmmakers, 1987-92, 95n1363
Suchowski, Amy R., 99n8
Sudalnik, James E., 95n958
Suderow, Bryce A., 99n475
Suffix obsession, 95n1062
Sugar, Bert Randolph, 96n797
Sukhwal, B. L., 98n393
Sukhwal, Lilawati, 98n393
Sullivan, Bruce M., 98n1392
Sullivan, Dean A., 99n722
Sullivan, Eugene, 98n308
Sullivan, Fran, 96n482
Sullivan, Frank, 96n482
Sullivan, Helen F., 95n162, 96n140
Sullivan, Karen, 98n1545
Sullivan, Lawrence R., 99n483
Sullivan, Michael, 98n967
Sullivan, Thomas F. P., 96n1864, 98n559
Sultenfuss, Sherry Wilson, 96n1743
Sultenfuss, Thomas J., 96n1743
Summer jobs Britain 1995, 26th ed, 96n279
Summer jobs 1994, 43d ed, 95n306
Summer on campus, 2d ed, 96n360
Summer theatre dir 1996, 97n1153
Summerfield, Carol, 99n315
Summers, Claude J., 97n888
Summers, Harry G., Jr., 97n434
Summers, W. Franklin, 98n1224
Summers, Wilford I., 98n1485
Sumner, David E., 98n309
Sumpf, D., 96n1557
Sumrall, Harry, 95n1307
Sundermeier, Theo, 98n1350
Sunshine, Andrew, 95n1026
Sunshine, Linda, 96n1693
Super family vacations, 3d ed, 96n462
SUPER LCCS CD [CD-ROM], 96n633
Supernatural index, 96n1194
Supplement to distribution & taxonomy of birds of the world, 95n1574
Supplement to The Modern Ency of Russian, Soviet, & Eurasian Hist, v.1, 97n476
Supplement to the official records of the Union & Confederate armies, 99n475
Supplementing lit programs, 95n1129
Supreme Court compendium, 95n612
Supreme Court compendium, 2d ed, 97n497
Supreme Court justices, 96n572
Supreme Court rules: the 1997 revisions, 99n569
Supreme Court yrbk 1995-96, 97n603
Surgeons' ref for minimally invasive surgery products, 96n1730
Surnames of Wales, 97n353
Survey of ...
   economic & social conditions in Africa, 1991-92, 96n113
   economic & social dvlpmts in the ESCWA region 1993, 96n129
   English dialects, 95n1056
   social sci: govt & pols series, 96n741
   social sci: psychology series, 95n782
   social sci: sociology series, 96n836
Survival, 96n812
Susan B. Anthony: a biogl companion, 99n800
Suskin, Steven, 98n1329
Susser, Allen, 98n1428
Sussman, Les, 96n1618
Sutcliffe, Andrea, 98n810

Sutcliffe, Andrea J., 95n946
Sutherland, Caroline, 98n683
Sutherland, Stuart, 97n630
Sutnick, Barbara P., 99n371
Sutton, Allan, 95n1255
Sutton, Margaret, 95n47
Sutton, Walter, 97n442
Suziedelis, Saulius, 98n478
Svecevicius, Bronius, 97n862
Svengalis, Kendall F., 99n570
Swan, Jennifer, 97n757
Swanfeldt, Andrew, 96n1085
Swanson, James A., 97n1199
Swanson, Robert E., 95n1553
Swaziland, rev ed, 96n123
Sweeney, Jerry K., 97n569
Sweeney, Patricia E., 95n910
Sweeney, Wilma K., 99n751
Sweet, Charlie, 95n944
Sweetman, Jack, 99n624
Swinerton, E. Nelson, 98n315
Swisher, Karen Gayton, 99n387
Switten, Margaret L., 96n1296
Switzer, Teri R., 98n212
Sydney, 97n392
Sykes, J. B., 98n1031
Sykes, Wendy, 95n97
Sylvestre, Jean-Pierre, 95n1595
Symbols of American libs, 14th ed, 95n645
Symbols of nationhood, 95n142
Symonds, Craig L., 96n701
Syndicated comic strips & artists, 1924-95, 97n1095
SYNERJY, 96n1831
Synonymized checklist of the vascular flora of the US, Canada, & Greenland, 95n1555
Systematic treatment of fruit types, 95n1539
Szabo, John F., 95n845
Szajkowski, Bogdan, 96n757
Szucs, Loretto Dennis, 98n370
Szycher, Michael, 97n1332
Szycher's dict of medical devices, 97n1332

Taber's cyclopedic medical dict, 18th ed, 98n1531
Tabloid journalism, 97n747
Tachau, Frank, 96n765
Tacka, Philip, 99n1138
Taeuber, Cynthia M., 97n740
Taft Group, 95n643
Taiwan business: the portable ency for doing business with Taiwan, 95n266
Takacs, Geza, 97n857
Taking humor seriously in children's lit, 99n998
Talbot, Ian, 97n126
Talbot, James R., 96n201
Talbot, Ross B., 96n1529
Talbott, James N., 95n615
Talevski, Nick, 99n1174
Talk show selects, 1995 ed, 96n989
Talk shows & hosts on radio, 3d ed, 96n975

Talking about people: a gd to fair & accurate lang, 99n895
Talking drums: an African-American quote collection, 96n96
Talley, Pat L., 95n234
Tallia, Rob, 99n560
Tambini, Michael, 97n788
Tamborlane, William V., 98n1555
Taming of the Shrew: an annot bibliog, 95n1219
Tan, Eng Thye Jason, 96n370
Tandy, Ian, 97n217
Tanks, 98n631
Tantalizing tingles: a discography of early ragtime, jazz..., 96n1325
Tanzania, rev ed, 97n102
Tap dance dict, 99n1203
Tapster, C., 99n257
Tardiff, Joseph C., 97n334, 99n602
Tarila, Sophia, 96n1482
Tarot for beginners, 96n787
Tarr, Rodger L., 97n974
Tarrago, Rafael E., 96n776
Task Force on Bias-Free Lang of the Assn of American Univ Presses, 96n968
Task Force on Taxonomy of the IASP, 96n1723
Tasmania, 98n118
Tatar-English/English-Tatar dict, 96n1139
Tate, Mary Jo, 99n1054
Tate, Michael L., 96n494
Tate, Thelma H., 97n1245
Tatla, Darshan Singh, 97n126
Taub, Michael, 98n1125
Taube, Karl, 95n1444
Taunton's fine homebuilding index, issues 1-85, 96n1051
Taussig, Louis, 95n516, 98n420
Taves, Brian, 97n952
Taxonomy of human servs, 3d ed, 95n830
Taylor, Ann C. M., 96n361
Taylor, Barbara, 96n65
Taylor, Barry, 95n148
Taylor, Bonnie B., 97n491
Taylor, C. C. W., 99n1255
Taylor, Cynthia M., 97n1353
Taylor, David, 98n1467
Taylor, Desmond, 95n1140
Taylor, Ed, 99n1490
Taylor, F. W., 96n1103
Taylor, John W. R., 99n1575
Taylor, Kevin, 95n374
Taylor, Michael, 97n1438
Taylor, Patrick, 96n1548, 96n1549
Taylor, Paul F., 95n294
Taylor, Ronald J., 99n1365
Taylor, Tim, 99n444
Taylor's dict for gardeners, 99n1345
Taylor's gd to fruits & berries, 97n1259
Taylor's gd to heirloom vegetables, 97n1260
Taylor's master gd to gardening, 96n1550
Te Matatiki: contemporary Maori words, 97n863
Teacher educ policy in the states, 95n375, 96n329
Teaching children's lit, 96n379

Teaching English abroad, 2d ed, 95n380
Technological capacity-bldg & tech partnership, 96n1515
Technology, 96n1508
Technology opportunities, 2d ed, 96n1507
Teddy bear ency, 95n974
Teen genreflecting, 98n1096
Teen legal rights, 96n592
Teichroew, Jean Kaplan, 95n485
Telecommunications: key contacts & info sources, 99n1500
Telecommunications dir 1995-96, 7th ed, 96n1782
Telecommunications, networking & Internet glossary, 95n1704
Telecommunications research resources, 96n1778
Telecommuters, the workforce of the 21st century, 98n212
Television & cable factbk, 1994 ed, 95n964
Television cartoon shows, 96n1375
Television guest stars, 95n1366
Television musicals, 98n1301
Television program master index, 97n1144
Television research, 96n987
Television specials, 96n1412
Television western players of the 50s, 98n1276
Television westerns episode gd, 98n1308
Television writers gd, 4th ed, 97n769
Telgen, Diane, 98n1109, 98n1110, 99n1013
Templeton, N. G., 95n1155, 95n1176, 95n1206
Ten yrs of classicists: dissertations & outcomes 1988-97, 99n891
Tenenbaum, Barbara A., 97n349
Tenenbaum, Frances, 96n1550, 99n1345
Tennessee Williams, 96n1220, 99n1057
Tenuto, John, 98n690
Teratogenic effects of drugs, 95n1682
Terban, Marvin, 99n912
Terrace, Vincent, 96n1412, 98n1314
Terrell, Peter, 96n1104, 99n928
Terris, Olwen, 96n1399
Terrorism, 1992-95, 98n556
Terrorism & the news media, 95n616
Terrorism in the US, 98n557
Terrorist group profiles [CD-ROM], 96n601
Terry, John V., 96n180
Terry, Nicholas, 98n184
Tesar, Jenny, 97n7
Teschner, Richard V., 96n1136
Test Collection, Educational Testing Serv, 96n314
Tests in print IV, 95n787
Tesucun, Felix Fernando, 98n1040
Tetzloff, Jason M., 98n562
Teubig, Klaus, 96n1329
Texas ref sources, 4th ed, 95n101
Thackeray, Frank W., 99n456
Thaddeus Stevens papers, 95n746
Thailand, 99n435
Thames & Hudson ency of 20th century design & designers, 95n984
Tharp, Lars, 95n968
Thatcher, Virginia S., 99n836
That's enough folks: black images in animated cartoons, 99n1235

Thawley, John, 98n144
Theatregoer's almanac, 98n1327
Theatrical design in the 20th century, 97n1155
Theatrical directors, 95n1410
Thematic atlases for public, academic, & high school libs, 95n491
Thematic catalogues in music, 2d ed, 98n1188
Theodor Adorno (II), 96n833
Theodore, Charmant, 96n1106
Theodore, Louis, 99n1568
Theoharis, Athan, 95n619
Theological dict of ...
 the O.T., 99n1276
 the O.T., v.7, 97n1200
 the O.T., v.8, 98n1375
Theological lexicon of the N.T., 96n1457
Theories of myth, 98n1261
Theories of pol processes, 98n635
Theorizing composition, 99n831
Theosophy in the 19th century, 95n1436
Thesaurus dict of the English lang, 95n1068
Thesaurus of ...
 abstract musical properties, 96n1277
 alternatives to worn-out words & phrases, 95n1067
 ERIC descriptors, 13th ed, 96n318
 slang, rev ed, 95n1059
 traditional English metaphors, 95n1045
Theses on Africa, 1976-88, 95n112
Thesing, William B., 95n1209
They also served: military bios of uncommon Americans, 99n623
They came in ships, 2d ed, 95n457
They made hist, 95n35
They're never too young for bks, 95n1138
Thiel-Siling, Sabine, 99n877
Think tank dir, 97n622
Thinking from A to Z, 98n1339
Third World atlas, 2d ed, 95n145
Third World hndbk, 2d ed, 95n143
Third World resource dir 1994-95, 95n144
Third World women's lits, 96n946
Third World worker in the multinatl corp, 95n275
Thirty-Five Oriental philosophers, 96n1427
32nd annual steam passenger serv dir, 98n1649
This is a Thriller: an episode gd, hist, & analysis of the classic 1960s TV series, 97n1138
This land is our land: a gd to multicultural lit for children & YAs, 95n1133
Thode, Ernest, 95n452, 98n363
Thody, Philip, 99n1193
Thoma, Emile, 98n135
Thomas Aquinas: intl bibliog 1977-90, 95n1437
Thomas Cook intl air travel hndbk 1997, 98n407
Thomas Hardy's major novels, 99n1085
Thomas Jefferson: a biogl companion, 99n660
Thomas More: an annot bibliog of criticism, 1935-97, 99n1086
Thomas register of American manufacturers, 1997, 87th ed, 98n196
Thomas register on CD-ROM, 1997 [CD-ROM], 98n197
Thomas Wolfe: an annot critical bibliog, 97n976

Thomas, Alan, 95n145
Thomas, Alastair H., 99n493
Thomas, Avril, 98n475
Thomas, Brian J., 99n1327
Thomas, Charles Flint, 98n1154
Thomas, Clayton L., 98n1531
Thomas, Colin, 98n475
Thomas, D. O., 95n1427
Thomas, G. Scott, 96n924
Thomas, Graham Stuart, 96n1551
Thomas, Nick, 96n1401
Thomas, Rebecca L., 95n1141, 98n1093
Thomas, Richard K., 95n1652
Thompson, Clifford, 98n26
Thompson, Della, 96n1065, 96n1126, 96n1127, 97n821, 98n1046
Thompson, Henry O., 97n1194, 98n1372
Thompson, Juliet S., 96n546
Thompson, Kathleen, 98n343
Thompson, Laurence G., 95n1438
Thompson, Maggie, 98n908
Thompson, Stith, 95n1317
Thompson, Sue Ellen, 95n1338, 98n1263, 99n1189
Thompson, Susan, 99n1033
Thompson, Susan L., 96n546
Thompson, Verlinda D., 98n1087
Thompson, Virginia, 97n95
Thompson, Wayne C., 96n546
Thompson, William N., 95n803, 97n344, 99n714
Thomsett, Jean Freestone, 96n889, 98n85
Thomsett, Michael C., 96n889, 98n85
Thomson, Sandra A., 96n781
Thorn, John, 98n737
Thorndike, E. L., 95n1053, 98n1009
Thorndike-Barnhardt student dict, updated ed, 95n1053
Thorndike-Barnhart jr dict, 98n1009
Thorne, Kathryn Ford, 98n431
Thorne, Sandra A., 98n1397
Thorowgood, Sarah, 99n426
Thorson, Marcie Kisner, 95n376, 97n292
Thrapp, Dan L., 95n538
365 ways...retirees' resource gd for productive lifestyles, 97n669
3,000 years of Chinese painting, 99n888
Thunder, flush, & Thomas Cooper, 99n1188
Thunder, James M., 99n586
Thunderbird gd to intl business resources on the WWW, 98n204
Thurmond, Molly E., 97n207
Thyen, O., 98n1030
Tibbetts, John C., 99n1216
Ticket to the opera, 98n1223
Tiffin, Helen, 99n946
Tigges, Julie A., 98n544
Tiku, M. L., 96n1557
Tilleman, William A., 96n1855
Tiller, Veronica E. Velarde, 97n342
Tillman, Hope N., 98n1586
Timbrell, Martin C., 99n197
Time & space, 96n1820

Time out film gd, 5th ed, 97n1136
Timelines of ...
    African-American hist, 95n405
    Native American hist, 98n351
    the arts & lit, 95n925
    world hist, 99n524
Times atlas of European hist, 95n555
Times atlas of the world, 9th ed, 95n487
Time-saver standards for architectural design data, 7th ed, 99n882
Time-saver standards for housing & residential dvlpmt, 96n1048
Time-saver standards for landscape architecture design & construction data, 99n883
Tipper, Allison, 98n132
Tirion, Wil, 97n1393, 98n1605
Tischauser, Leslie V., 99n454
Tiwari, R. C., 95n1083
TLA film & video gd 1996-97, 97n1125
To be continued: an annot gd to sequels, 97n946
Toasting Cheers: an episode gd to the 1982-93 comedy series..., 98n1302
Tobacco & health network dir 1996, 4th ed, 97n1325
Tobias, Russell R., 97n1302
Tobiasen, Linda, 96n870
Tobiasen, Linda G., 96n883
Tobler, Judy, 98n1345, 98n1382
Today's world: a new world atlas, rev ed, 95n488
Todd, Robert H., 96n1670
Togo, 96n124
Toll-free phone bk USA 1997, 98n55
Tolliday, Steven, 98n149
Tomaino, Robert P., 99n1447
Tomajczyk, S. F., 97n566
Tomas Luis de Victoria: a gd to research, 99n1132
Tomaselli-Moschovitis, Valerie, 96n155, 98n499, 99n684
Tomassini, Christine, 96n1398
Tombrello, Thomas A., Jr., 99n1502
Tomlinson, Carl M., 99n991
Tompkins, Vincent, 97n422, 97n423, 98n445
Tong, Diane, 96n405
Toni Morrison, 99n1058
Tony Richardson: a bio-bibliog, 97n1096
Top 40 music on compact disc, 1955-81, 95n1290
Top 100: the fastest growing careers for the 21st century, rev ed, 99n276
Top 10 of everything, 96n61
Top 10 of everything 1999, 99n63
Topics in gerontology, 95n832
Topline ency of histl charts, Mar 1997 ed, 98n176
Topp, Chester W., 96n1223, 96n1224
Tornadoes, 99n1530
Total baseball, 98n737
Total football, 98n747
Total TV, 4th ed, 97n1132
Toth, Georgetta, 96n873, 98n785
Totten, Herman L., 98n1099
Totten, Samuel, 97n295
Toucan Valley Publications, research staff of, 95n423, 95n885

Touchstones: a gd to records, rights, & resources for families of American WW II casualties, 98n367
Townsend, Kiliaen V. R., 95n377, 97n297
Townsend, Murray, 99n737
Townshend, Alan, 96n1495
Toxic waste sites, 99n1560
Toye, William, 99n1088
Tozzer Library, Harvard University, 95n391
Tracey, William R., 96n258
Track & field record holders, 97n663
Tracy, Deborah, 98n1585
Trade data elements dir: UNTDED 1993, v.1, 96n306
Trade data elements dir v.3, 97n277
Trade, industrial, & professional pers of the US, 95n215
Trade secrets: a state-by-state survey, 99n589
Trade shows worldwide 1998, 12th ed, 99n210
Traditional Anglo-American folk music, 95n1302
Traditional world music influences in contemporary solo piano lit, 99n1148
Trager, James, 95n912, 96n1539
Trager, Oliver, 99n1175
Traister, John E., 95n1605
Tram: the Frank Trumbauer story, 96n1323
Trammell, Jeffrey B., 95n713, 95n718, 95n744, 95n760, 98n654
Tran, Hoai Huong, 97n278
Tran, Trinh C., 98n794
Translation & interpreting schools, 99n897
Translator's hndbk 1997, 98n991
Trans-Mississippi west 1804-1912, pt.1, 95n545
Transnational corps: a selective bibliog 1991-92, 95n241
Transportation & public utilities USA, 99n1572
Trask, R. L., 95n1040, 97n819, 98n987
Trauth, Gregory, 97n812
Trautmann, Carl O., 95n188
Travel & vacation phone bk USA, 98n404
Travel dict, 95n504
Travel dict, new ed, 97n384, 99n425
Travel gd to Jewish Europe, 2d ed, 97n436
Traveler's atlas, 99n440
Traveler's gd to art museum exhibitions, 10th ed, 99n873
Traveler's gd to Jewish Germany, 99n438
Traveler's hndbk, 7th ed, 99n426
Traveler's sourcebk 1997, 98n418
Travers, Bridget, 95n1496, 95n1497, 96n1496, 97n1238, 98n1530, 99n1426
Travis, William G., 98n1383
Treasure, Geoffrey, 99n506
Treasure hard to attain: images of archaeology in popular film, 98n1290
Treasury of natural 1st aid remedies from A-Z, 96n1715
Treasury of Polish aphorisms, 98n1253
Treaties of the War of the Spanish Succession, 96n762
Tree of liberty: a documentary hist of rebellion & pol crime in America, rev ed, 99n476
Trees of the central hardwood forests of N America, 99n1367
Treharne, Elaine, 96n958
Treiber, Rikard, 99n771
Trejo, Arnulfo D., 96n621
Trelawny, John G., 99n1366

Tremaine, M. David, 97n1340
Trends in Europe & N America 1995, 97n719
Trenz, Brandon, 96n1362
Treptow, Kurt W., 97n120
Tressider, Jack, 99n886
Trevino, A. Javier, 95n598
Tricard, Louise Mead, 97n664
Trice, Patricia Johnson, 99n1152
Trigg, George L., 97n1407, 97n1408
Trigger, Bruce G., 99n392
Trilingual vocabulary of road transport vehicles, 97n229
Trilliums, 98n1448
Tripp, Kim E., 96n1592
Tripp, Leonard L., 95n1608
Trogdon, Robert W., 98n1127
Tromble, Katherine R., 96n656
Tropical look: an ency of dramatic landscape plants, 99n1344
Trosky, Susan M., 96n1150
Trotter, David, 98n1152
Trowers & Hamlin, 96n252
Troy, Leo, 98n177
Trucano, Michael, 98n698
Trudeau, Lawrence J., 99n1019, 99n1020
Trudeau, Noah Andre, 99n475
True bugs of the world (Hemiptera: Heteroptera), 96n1627
True crime narratives, 98n546
Trujillo, Rosanne, 99n617
Trumbauer, William, 96n1323
Trumble, Bill, 96n1069
Trumbull, Priscilla, 98n198
Truscott, Alan, 98n744
Truscott, Sandra, 99n943
Trussler, Simon, 96n1422
Tryon, Jonathan S., 95n646
TSCA hndbk, 3d ed, 98n561
Tschirgi, Dan, 99n699
Tuck, Allene, 98n1577
Tucker, Spencer C., 97n467, 99n527
Tudor, Guy, 95n1573
Tudor music: a research & info gd, 95n1253
Tuleja, Tad, 95n1334
Tull, Pamela M., 99n62
Tuller, Michael N., 98n787, 98n788
Tuma, Jan J., 99n1544
Tun-Atz, Hilary Henri, 98n793
Tunstall, Daniel B., 97n1432
Turabian, Kate L., 97n755
Turbet, Richard, 95n1253
Turck, Mary C., 96n1386
Turgeon, Lynn, 97n149
Turkington, Carol, 95n1686, 96n780, 96n1727, 97n1334, 99n1445
Turkington, Carol A., 97n1333
Turner, Ann, 95n177
Turner, Barry, 99n82
Turner, C. M. E. P., 98n962
Turner, Gerard L'E, 99n1318
Turner, Jane, 98n947
Turner, Jeffrey S., 97n631
Turner, John R., 98n593

Turtles of the US & Canada, 96n1636
Tutin, T. G., 95n1540
Tuttle dict of ...
    legal terms: English-Japanese, Japanese-English, 95n605
    legal terms: English-Japanese, Japanese-English, rev ed, 96n613
    the martial arts of Korea, China, & Japan, 97n659
Tuttle new dict of loanwords in Japanese, 95n1086
Twayne's English authors on CD-ROM [CD-ROM], 99n1067
Twayne's masterwork studies on CD-ROM [CD-ROM], 98n1074
Twayne's US authors on CD-ROM [CD-ROM], 99n1049
Twayne's world authors [CD-ROM], 99n979
Tweedale, Geoffrey, 95n282
Tweedie, Diana L., 99n197
Twentieth century Danish music, 99n1154
Twentieth-century America, 96n485
Twentieth-century American music for the dance, 97n1103
Twentieth-century American sportswriters, 98n883
Twentieth-century artists on art, 2d ed, 98n969
Twentieth-century brass soloists, 95n1274
Twentieth-century Britain, 96n543
Twentieth-century British literary biographers, 96n1227
Twentieth-century Caribbean & black African writers, 3d series, 97n1012
Twentieth-century children's writers, 4th ed, 96n1175
Twentieth-century dict of Christian biog, 96n1465
Twentieth-century hist of US population, 98n808
Twentieth-century Italian poets, 1st series, 95n1233
Twentieth-century Italian poets, 2d series, 95n1234
Twentieth-century literary criticism, v.56, 96n1159
Twentieth-century literary criticism, v.57, 96n1160
Twentieth-century literary criticism, v.58, 97n919
Twentieth-century literary criticism, v.59, 97n920
Twentieth-century literary criticism, v.60, 97n921
Twentieth-century literary criticism, v.61, 97n922
Twnetieth-century literary criticism, v.71, 99n981
Twentieth-century literary criticism, v.72, 99n982
Twentieth-century literary criticism annual cumulative title index for 1996, 97n923
Twentieth-century literary criticism topics volume, v.70, 99n980
Twentieth-century newspaper pr in Britain, 96n972
Twentieth-century poetry from Spanish America, 99n1111
Twentieth-century Radicalism in Minnesota Project, 96n767
Twentieth-century romance & histl writers, 3d ed, 95n1163
Twentieth-century short story explication, v.2, 96n1195
Twentieth-century short story explication: new series, v.3: 1993-94, 98n1118
Twentieth-century Spanish poets: 2d series, 95n1244
Twentieth-century YA writers, 95n1147
21st century manual of style, 95n949
20,000 Spanish American pseudonyms, 98n1182
Twining, David T., 95n166
Twist, Clint, 96n74, 96n76
Twiston-Davies, Suzanne, 96n170
200 best aviation Web sites, 99n1576
200 yrs of dolls, 98n916
Two Jews, 3 opinions: a collection of 20th-century American Jewish quotations, 99n396
2001 French & English idioms, 2d ed, 97n846

2001 Japanese & English idioms, 97n859
2000 yrs of disbelief: famous people with the courage to doubt, 98n1347
Tycoons & entrepreneurs, 99n143
Tyler, Sean, 97n1063, 99n1161
Tyler, Varro E., 95n1545
Type foundaries of America & their catalogs, rev ed, 96n666
Typography, 99n885
Tyrkus, Michael J., 98n782
Tyson, Jacqueline, 98n783

UFO: the definitive gd to unidentified flying objects & related phenomena, 96n789
UFOs & ufology, 99n709
Uganda, rev ed, 97n104
Uhlan, Miriam, 95n86
Uhle, Mary E., 99n835
Ukrainian-English, English-Ukrainian practical dict, 95n1099
Ulane, Art, 96n1540
Ulijaszek, Stanley J., 99n1465
Ullmann's ency of industrial chemistry, v.a25, 5th ed, 96n1789
Ulrich's intl pers dir 1994-95, 95n87
Ulrich's intl pers dir 1996, 96n88
Ulrich's intl pers dir 1997, 35th ed, 97n66
Ulrich's intl pers dir 1998, 36th ed, 99n74
Ultimate beer, 99n1333
Ultimate bk of sports lists 1998, 98n727
Ultimate business lib, 98n148
Ultimate classic car bk, 96n1892
Ultimate dir of the silent screen performers, 96n1368
Ultimate dolls' house bk, 95n975
Ultimate ency of rock, 95n1305
Ultimate family tree deluxe [CD-ROM], 98n1371
Ultimate gd to lesbian & gay film & video, 97n1126
Ultimate gd to sci fiction, 2d ed, 97n949
Ultimate human body version 2.0 [CD-ROM], 98n1500
Ultimate motorcycle bk, 95n1793
Ultimate movie thesaurus, 98n1303
Ultimate pocket: flags of the world, 98n374
Ultimate ref bk, 95n89
Ultimate scene & monologue sourcebk, 95n1407
Ultimate visual dict, 99n919
Ulysses Kay: a bio-bibliog, 95n1266
UNCTAD commodity yrbk 1994, 96n1521
UNCTAD Secretariat, 96n227
UNCTAD statl pocket bk, 96n925
Understanding American business jargon, 98n153
Understanding everyday Sesotho, 96n1135
Understanding the census, library ed, 97n713
Understanding the Holocaust, 99n539
UNESCO intl dir of new & renewable energy info sources & research centres, 95n1748
UNESCO Social & Human Scis Documentation Centre, 95n95, 95n600
Unger, Harlow G., 97n288
Unger, Leonard, 99n1043, 99n1110
Unger, Melvin P., 98n1247
Union list of artist names, 95n995
Union of Intl Assns, 95n828

UK to USA dict, 96n1082
United Nations Commission on Intl Trade Law yrbk, v.24, 1993, 96n307
United Nations Conference on Trade & Dvlpmt, 96n234, 96n289, 96n290, 96n925, 96n1515, 96n1521, 96n1897
United Nations Dvlpmt Programme, 96n1842, 96n1843
United Nations dir of agencies & insts in public admin & finance, 99n703
United Nations disarmament yrbk, v.18: 1993, 95n767
United Nations Library, Geneva, 95n630
United Nations ref gd in the field of human rights, 95n631
US & Asia statl hndbk, 1997-98 ed, 99n219
United States & Latin America, 98n697
United States & World Cup soccer competition, 95n823
U.S. Army patches, 98n625
U.S. Catholic sources, 97n1215
US chemical-biological defense guidebk, 99n644
U.S. Central Intelligence Agency, 96n713
United States Congress, 96n715
United States constitution, 99n686
U.S. consumer interest groups, 96n216
U.S. Dept of Commerce, 95n220
United States Dept of Labor, Occupational Safety & Health Admin, 96n277
U.S. educl policy interest groups, 95n339
U.S. electric industry phone & fax dir, 1996, 97n1418
US electric utility industry dir 1998, 7th ed, 99n1546
U.S. employment opportunities, 98n240
U.S. foreign relations with the Middle East & N Africa, 95n764
US govt dirs, 1982-95, 99n62
US govt leaders, 99n663
United States govt manual 1996/97, 97n604
U.S. govt pers index, v.1, no.1 [CD-ROM], 95n77
U.S. health policy groups, 96n1691
United States hist, 97n406
United States hist: a selective gd to info sources, 95n529
U.S. homes [CD-ROM], 98n56
U.S. homes & business [CD-ROM], 98n57
United States immigration, 97n621
United States in the 1st world war, 96n685
Unites States in the 19th century, 98n436
US industry & trade outlook '98, 99n191
U.S. industry profiles, 96n224
US intelligence community, 96n716
U.S. labor movement, 97n250
U.S. master tax gd, 1994, 95n332
U.S.-Mexican treaties, 98n680
U.S. military online, 98n617
U.S. military records, 95n695
U.S. news coverage of racial minorities, 98n852
USA & Canada 1994, 95n106
USA & Canada 1998, 99n88
USA business: the portable ency for doing business with the US, 96n241
USA in space, 97n1302
USA oil industry dir 1998, 37th ed, 99n192
USA state factbk [CD-ROM], 95n107
U.S. presidential candidates & the elections, 97n588

U.S. presidents [CD-ROM], 96n527
US primary elections 1995-96, 98n673
U.S. religious interest groups, 95n1446
United States theatre: a bibliog from the beginning to 1990, 95n1409
U.S. women's interest groups, 97n737
United States-European Community trade resources, 95n323
United States-Russia Business Dvlpmt Committee Defense Conversion Subcommittee, 95n284
Universal almanac 1995, 96n5
Universe explained, 96n1802
University & college museums, galleries, & related facilities, 97n62
University of London Lib catalogue of the Goldsmiths' Lib of Economic Lit, v.5, 96n662
UNIX & X command compendium, 96n1762
UNIX dict of commands, terms, & acronyms, 97n1373
Unofficial ency of the rock & roll hall of fame, 99n1174
Unofficial gd to ethnic cuisine & dining in America, 96n1531
Untener, Deborah J., 99n210
Unterberger, Amy L., 95n402
Unterburger, Amy L., 96n409
Unveiling Indonesia, 98n114
Unwin, Tim, 96n444
Upholsterer's pocket ref bk, 96n1020
Upjohn, Richard, 97n123
Upton, Clive, 95n1056, 97n839
Uranium: resources, production & demand, 1993, 95n1755
Urdang, Laurence, 96n1068, 96n1094
Uriona, Martha, 97n153
Urofsky, Melvin I., 96n572
Urrutia, Manuel R., 99n147
Urwin, Derek W., 96n139, 97n438
USA Today baseball weekly almanac, 1997, 99n723
USA Today weather almanac 1995, 96n1809
Used bk lover's gd to the Midwest, 96n1007
Used car reliability & safety gd, 96n1885
Usilton, Larry W., 97n445
Using bibliotherapy in clinical practice, 95n772
Using French synonyms, 95n1073
Using govt info sources, 2d ed, 95n76
Using picture storybks to teach literary devices. v.2, 96n1164
Using public records to find & investigate anyone, 98n703
Using the biological lit, 2d ed, 97n1264
USMARC format for bibliographic data, 1994 ed, 96n634
USP DI 1995, v.1, 96n1744
USP DI 1995, v.2, 96n1745
USP DI 1995, v.3, 96n1746
USP dict of USAN & intl drug names, 96n1747
USSR population census, 1989 [CD-ROM], 98n130
Utah hist ency, 96n511
Utah state constitution, 99n688
Utopian/dystopian lit, 95n1101
Utter, Glenn H., 95n705, 97n1218, 98n679
Uva, Richard H., 98n1453
U*X*L biogs [CD-ROM], 97n27
U*X*L multicultural CD [CD-ROM], 98n333
U*X*L sci fact finder, 99n1319
Uzbek-English, English-Uzbek concise dict, 96n1141
Uzicanin, Nikolina S., 96n1098

Vacation study abroad, 99n355
Vacation study abroad 1995/96, 96n369
Vacationing with your pet, 98n402
Vacic, Aleksandar M., 96n232
Valade, Roger M., III, 96n1490, 97n918
Valder, Peter, 96n1579
Valdman, Albert, 99n935
Vallasi, George A., 95n49
Vallillo, Stephen M., 95n1410
Valman, Bernard, 98n1554
Value of a dollar, 1860-1989, 96n198
Vampire bk: the ency of the undead, 95n1328
Vampire ency, 95n1325
Vampire gallery: a who's who of the undead, 99n1214
Vampire readings, 99n1035
van Creveld, Martin, 97n477
van den Eeden, Pieter, 96n99
Van der Bent, Ans Joachim, 96n1473
van der Dennen, J. M. G., 95n770
Van Dijk, Kees, 99n319
van Gelderen, D. M., 95n1554
van Hartesveldt, Fred R., 97n561, 98n494
van Heel, K. Donker, 98n503
Van Heerden, Bill, 99n1239
van Jaarsveld, Ernst J., 95n1550
Van Kemper, Robert, 97n318
van Niekerk, W. A. C., 95n34
Van Nostrand's scientific ency, 8th ed, 96n1502
van Os, Andre, 99n135
van Rose, Susanna, 95n1725
Van Tassel, David D., 97n87, 97n88
Van Tuyl, Ian, 96n585
van Vliet, Willem, 99n792
Van Vynckt, Virginia, 98n1420
Van Whitlock, Rod, 95n843
van Wyk, J. J., 98n638
Vandenberghe, J. -P., 96n1894
Vander Kolk, Martha, 96n100, 96n101, 96n1774
Vanderstel, David G., 96n929
Vandivier, Elizabeth Louise, 97n147
VanGemeren, Willem A., 98n1374
Vangermeersch, Richard, 97n179
VanMeter, Vandelia L., 98n1114
Vardy, Steven Bela, 98n473
Variety & Daily Variety TV reviews, v.18: 1993-94, 98n1315
Variety's film reviews, v.23, 96n1387
Variety's video dir plus [CD-ROM], 96n1388
Varty, Kenneth, 99n1183
Varzi, Achille C., 98n1331
Vasarhelyi, Miklos A., 95n217
Vascular plants of Russia & adjacent states (the former USSR), 96n1594
Vasquez, Milton, 96n1862
Vassilian, Hamo B., 95n150, 95n151, 96n391, 97n1253
Vasudevan, Aruna, 95n1163
Vatican archives: an inventory & gd to histl docs of the Holy See, 99n1284
Vazquez-Gomez, Juana, 98n485
Vazzana, Eugene Michael, 96n1369
Vedder, Polly, 99n983

Vegetarian Journal's gd to natural foods restaurants in the US & Canada, 3d ed, 99n434
Veltrop, Kyle, 95n810, 96n828, 97n649
Veltze, Linda, 95n1126
Vencill, C. Daniel, 97n587
Venger, Natalia, 95n1378
Veni, vidi, vici, 96n1116
Venice & the Veneto, 96n478
Vennebusch, Eva, 96n1104
Venolia, Jan, 96n1081
Venzon, Anne Cipriano, 96n685
Verene, Molly Black, 96n1426
Verify those credentials: do you know who you're dealing with? 98n63
Verkler, Linda A., 96n1003
Vermilyea, Peter C., 97n67
Vermont, Terrell, 96n1531
Vernon, Paul, 97n1075
Verschueren, Karel, 97n1389
Verstappen, Berth, 95n136
Vestiges of mortality & remembrance, 95n519
Veterans benefits: the complete gd, 95n696
Veterinarian's ency of animal behavior, 96n1554
Veterinary drug hndbk, 2d ed, 97n1263
Veutro, Martina, 97n458
VGM's careers ency, 4th ed, 98n217
Viacheslav Ivanov: a ref gd, 98n1181
Viano, Richard, 98n1188
Vice presidents, 97n590, 99n664
Vick, Julia Miller, 96n365
Vico: a bibliog of works in English from 1884-1984, 96n1426
Victims rights, 99n590
Victoria & Albert Museum, 99n70
Victorian America, 1876 to 1913, 97n400
Victorian database on CD-ROM, 1970-95 [CD-ROM], 98n468
Victorian poetry, 97n1000
Victorian yellowbacks & paperbacks, 1849-1905, v.1, 96n1223
Victorian yellowbacks & paperbacks, 1849-1905, v.2, 96n1224
Video annual 1994, 96n994
Video rating gd for libs on CD-ROM 1990-94 [CD-ROM], 96n995
Video source bk 1996, 17th ed, 96n996
VideoHound multimedia [CD-ROM], 96n1389
VideoHound's complete gd to cult flicks & trash pics, 97n1137
VideoHound's golden movie retriever 1994, 95n1399
VideoHound's sci-fi experience, 98n1320
VideoHound's that's amore! 96n1398
VideoHound's vampires on video, 98n1321
Videos of African & African-related performance, 97n1145
Vienna, 96n479, 99n119
Vietnam [CD-ROM], 96n694
Vietnam experience, 99n1041
Vietnam studies, 98n117
Vietnam War films, 95n1384
Vietnam War lit, 3d ed, 98n1056
Viglielmo, Valdo H., 99n1257

Vigliotta, Joan M., 96n285
Vikal, Krishna, 95n1083
Viking opera gd, 95n1287
Viking opera gd on CD-ROM [CD-ROM], 95n1288
Vile, John R., 97n596, 99n685, 99n686
Villains & outlaws, 99n582
Villamil, Victoria Etnier, 95n1272
Vincendeau, Ginette, 97n1111
Vincent, C. Paul, 98n471
Vincent, Charles, 95n1513
Vincent, Mary, 96n539
Vincent, Patrick, 95n1709
Viner, Bradley, 99n1386, 99n1387
Violence & the media, 97n748
Violence in American society, 95n618, 99n583
Violent children, 96n603
Virginia Woolf A to Z, 96n1221
Virtual body [CD-ROM], 97n1312
Virtual field trips, 98n281
Virtual musician, 98n1206
Virtual Reality World's virtual reality market place 1994, 95n1700
Virtual roots: a gd to genealogy & local hist on the WWW, 98n366
Virus diseases of trees & shrubs, 2d ed, 95n1552
Visual dict of ...
   American domestic architecture, 96n1044
   ancient civilizations, 95n584
   physics, 96n1819
   prehistoric life, 96n1817
   the horse, 95n1583
   the skeleton, 96n1683
Visual ency of sci, 96n1503
Visual resources dir, 96n378
Vital gd to combat guns & infantry weapons, 97n579
Vital gd to fighting aircraft of WW II, 97n580
Vital stats on American pols, 4th ed, 95n743
Vital stats on American pols 1997-98, 6th ed, 99n683
Vital stats on Congress 1995-96, 98n676
Vitullo-Martin, Julia, 95n216
Vladimir, Simosko, 99n1169
VNR dict of civil engineering, 4th ed, 95n1606
VNR dict of environmental health & safety, 95n1767
Vocabulary of ...
   computer security & viruses, 96n1766
   enzyme engineering, 95n1618
   family violence, 95n850
   packaging, 95n1633
Vocational careers sourcebk, 99n263
Vogel, Colin, 96n1556
Vogel, Frederick G., 96n696
Vogel, Joseph O., 95n522
Vogele, William B., 98n692
Vogelsong, Diana, 98n1438
Voices of multicultural America, 97n967
Voices of the Holocaust, 99n536
Voices of the spirit, 96n402
Volat, Helene, 98n1171
Volcanoes of the world, 2d ed, 96n1818
Volcansek, Mary L., 97n485

Volet, Jean-Marie, 97n1001
Volkman, Ernest, 95n765
Volunteer America, 4th ed, 98n795
Volvo gd to halls of fame, 96n83
von Frank, Albert J., 95n1188
von Salis, Susan J., 95n414
von Schlegell, Barbara R., 98n830
Vonnegut ency, 96n1219
VonVille, Helena M., 96n888
Voss, D. Stephen, 96n138
Voyages in classical mythology, 96n1349
Voynick, Stephen M., 95n1732
Vyse, Ruth, 96n662

Wacher, Tim, 99n1373
Wading the World Wide Web, 99n1498
Wagman, Richard J., 95n1646
Wagman, Robert J., 98n643
Wagner, Hilory, 97n709
Wagner, J., 98n581
Wagner, Ronald L., 95n1728
Wagner-Martin, Linda, 96n1200
Waier, Phillip R., 98n1480
Waite, Maurice, 95n1032
Walden, Gene, 95n223, 99n166
Walden, Graham R., 97n77
Walden Publishing Ltd., 95n256
Waldman, Carl, 95n437
Waldman, Harry, 97n1108, 99n1236
Waldorf, Sara Tal, 95n837
Waldrup, Carole Chandler, 97n590
Wales & cinema, 96n1370
Walford's gd to ...
   ref material, v.1: sci & tech, 7th ed, 97n1229
   ref material, v.2, 99n83
   ref material, v.2: social & histl scis, 6th ed, 95n98
Walker, Bonnie L., 96n844, 97n710, 98n798
Walker, Donald E., 96n806
Walker, John, 96n1385, 98n1305
Walker, John M., 96n1659
Walker, Juliet E. K., 99n144
Walker, Peter M. B., 97n1240
Walker, Richard, 96n1683
Walker, Ron, 95n797
Walker, Thomas G., 97n497
Walker's bats of the world, 96n1610
Walker's manual of community bank stocks, 98n187
Walker's manual of penny stocks, 99n167
Walker's manual of unlisted stocks, 98n172
Walking shadows, 96n1399
Wall, C. Edward, 97n9, 97n188
Wall, Leon, 95n1089
Wall Street words, 98n170
Wallace, Ian, 95n155
Wallace, Joseph, 95n1736
Wallace Stevens: an annot secondary bibliog, 95n1195
Wallace-Homestead price gd to American country antiques, 98n904
Waller, Lynn, 98n1376

Waller, Philip, 96n562
Wallner, Jeff, 98n1450
Walsh, D., 99n245
Walsh, Gretchen, 98n853
Walsh, James E., 96n42, 97n547, 99n614
Walsh, Michael, 99n83
Walsh, Michael F., 96n582
Walsh, Ronald A., 95n1639, 99n1413, 99n1544
Walsh, Stephen, 95n1287, 95n1288
Walter, John, 97n782
Walter, Kerry S., 99n1361
Walter Scott Publishing Co., 98n593
Walter, Virginia A., 98n1560
Walters, Douglas B., 96n1796
Walton, John, 96n1702
Walton, John H., 98n1379
Walton, Juanita, 96n1249
Walton, Rachel, 96n1713, 98n1523
Wang, Richard T., 98n112
Wanted to buy, 6th ed, 98n901
War & conflict quotations, 98n85
War in N Africa, 1940-43, 97n460
War of 1898 & US interventions 1898-1934, 95n685
War of 1812 eyewitness accounts, 98n608
War of the Spanish Succession, 1702-13, 97n435
Warblers of the Americas, 96n1613
Warburton, Nigel, 98n1339
Ward, Amie S., 96n839
Ward, Jack, 95n1366
Ward, K. Anthony, 95n972
Ward, Robert E, 96n315
Ward, Sally K., 95n634
Warden, Paul G., 97n286
Wardin, Albert W., Jr., 97n1173
Ward's private co profiles, 95n213
Wardwell, Joyce A., 99n1461
Wareham, David C., 95n1597
Warkentin, John, 99n409
Warman's antiques & collectibles price gd, 29th ed, 96n1000
Warman's Americana & collectibles, 99n839
Warman's coins & currency, 2d ed, 98n915
Warmath, Dee Anne, 97n250
Warmenhoven, Henri J., 99n117
Warner, Deborah Jean, 99n1312
Warner, Ila, 95n1098
Warner, Jay, 98n1239
Warner, Ken, 98n920
Warren, Alan, 97n1138
Warren, Albert, 95n964
Warren, Mark, 95n679
Warren, Patricia, 97n1139
Warrick, Susan E., 97n1214
Wars in the Third World since 1945, 2d ed, 97n568
Wars of the Americas, 99n629
Wars of the roses in fiction, 96n1190
Warsaw, 98n423
Warships of the USSR & Russia, 1945-95, 98n629
Wartime Poland, 1939-45, 98n480
Washburn, David E., 98n273
Washburn, Wilcomb E., 99n392

Washington almanac of intl trade & business, 1995/96, 97n230
Washington info dir, 96n734
Washington '97, 14th ed, 98n58
Washington online: how to access the fed govt on the Internet 1995, 96n1785
Washington online: how to access the govt's electronic bulletin boards, 96n1786
Washington representatives 1998, 22d ed, 99n665
Washington Researchers, 96n175, 96n1507
Washington Researchers Publishing, 95n289
Wassall, J., 99n239
Wasserman, Steven, 98n523
Wasserman, Steven R., 96n923
Wasson, D. DeWitt, 99n1178
Waterford, Van, 95n549
Watermeier, Daniel J., 96n1420
Watson, Ben, 99n1350
Watson, Benjamin, 97n1260
Watson, Bruce, 99n643
Watson, Cynthia, 98n621
Watson, Donald, 99n882
Watson, James, 95n939, 98n857
Watson, Lia M., 97n157
Watson, Noelle, 95n1167
Watson, William E., 99n693
Watstein, Sarah Barbara, 99n1470
Watts, Alan, 96n1810
Watts, Phyllis C., 96n1442
Watts, Thomas D., 97n704
Wax, Imy, 98n290
Way, Frederick, Jr., 96n1898
Way, George, 96n435
Wayne, Kathryn M., 98n977
Ways of war: the era of WW II in children's & YA fiction, 96n1165
Way's packet dir, 1848-1994, rev ed, 96n1898
Weate, Jeremy, 99n1258
Weather almanac, 99n1534
Weather America, 97n1397
Weather hndbk, 96n1810
Weather of US cities, 5th ed, 97n1398
Weather sourcebk, 95n1728
Weaver, Bruce L., 96n1188
Weaver, Robert Lee, 96n1266
Weaver, Robert S., 96n1361
Web programming lang sourcebk, 99n1487
Web site source bk 1996, 97n1377
Web site source bk 1998, 99n58
Webb, Dennis, 97n786
Webb, Herschel, 95n134
Webb, Sophie, 96n1615
Weber, David R., 99n292
Weber, Hilary, 95n673
Weber, Paul J., 95n1446
Weber, R. David, 96n690, 96n858, 96n880, 98n91, 98n307, 98n848, 98n1411, 99n293, 99n294, 99n772
Webster, L. F., 98n1484
Webster, L. Kay, 99n970
Webster, Robert G., 95n1680, 98n1442
Webster, Valerie J., 97n157

Webster's new American dict, 97n822
Webster's new world dict of American English, 3d college ed, 95n1033
Webster's new world dict of media & communications, rev ed, 98n858
Webster's new world vest pocket dict, 2d ed, 96n1071
Webster's 2: new college dict, 96n1079
Weddell, Jack L., 95n1650
Weddington, Michael, 98n751
Wedlock, Eldon D., Jr., 99n476
Weed flora of Egypt, rev ed, 96n1582
Weeds of the NE, 98n1453
Weeks, Christopher, 96n1049
Weeks, John M., 95n420
WEFA industrial monitor 1997, 98n198
Wegmann, Jessica M., 99n810
Weidensaul, Scott, 99n1381
Weigel, Molly, 97n961, 99n1045
Weinberg, Meyer, 97n325
Weiner, Alan R., 95n1114
Weiner, E. S. C., 96n1076
Weiner, Edmund, 95n1055, 96n1080
Weiner, Miriam, 99n400
Weiner, Mitchel, 98n992
Weiner, Richard, 98n858
Weiner, Robert G., 98n1240
Weingart, Patrice Walsh, 98n820
Weingartner, Clarence, 96n1675
Weis, Erich, 99n929
Weisbard, Phyllis Holman, 95n904
Weisberg, Gabriel P., 99n862
Weise, Frieda O., 98n1505
Weismantel, Guy E., 97n1378
Weiss, Dorrie, 96n1091
Weiss, Michael J., 96n915
Weissmann, Arnie, 95n518
Weissmann travel planner for W & E Europe 1994-95, 95n518
Welch, Jeanie, 96n308
Welding codes standards & specifications, 99n1411
Weldon, Michael J., 97n1140
Welfare reform, 98n799
Wellborn, Olin Guy, III, 96n591
Weller, Carolyn R., 96n629
Wellner, Alison, 99n1437
Wellner, Alison S., 98n726
Wellner, Alison Stein, 98n258
Wells, Daniel A., 97n960
Wells, Donald A., 97n1161
Wells, Edward R., 98n1638
Wells, Robert N., Jr., 98n560
Wells, Stuart, III, 98n907
Well-tempered announcer: a pronunciation gd to classical music, 97n1056
Welsch, Gerhard, 96n1669
Welsh family hist, 95n461
Welsh, James M., 99n1216
Wemhoff, Rich, 99n753
Wenborn, Neil, 98n465
Wendel, C. H., 98n1419

Wendland, Michael, 99n1499
Wendling, Patricia A., 97n314
Wendt, Pamela F., 95n838
Wenk, Arthur, 95n1312
Werblowsky, R. J. Zwi, 98n1396
Werner, Karel, 95n1472
Werner, Michael S., 98n141
Werry, John S., 95n1687
Wertheim, Eric, 95n679, 99n643
Wertheim, Stanley, 98n1134
Wertsman, Vladimir F., 95n1031, 97n532, 97n1254, 98n101
West, Cornel, 97n331
West, Gilian, 99n1084
West, Jim, 95n1744
West, John G., Jr., 99n1071
West, Kathryn, 97n738
West, Mark I., 99n1000
West Point atlas of American wars, v.1, 96n677
Westcott, Rich, 95n808
Westerman, R. C., 95n393
Western American novelists, 96n1205
Western & frontier film & TV credits 1903-95, 97n1130
Western Apache-English dict, 99n936
Western civilization: a critical gd to documentary films, 97n1118
Western Europe, 5th ed, 99n117
Western Europe since 1945, 97n437
Western garden [CD-ROM], 96n1552
Western lore & lang, 97n841
Western political thought, 96n704
Western Sahara, 97n105
Westheimer, Ruth K., 95n878
Westin, Richard A., 95n331, 98n680
Westminster dict of theological terms, 98n1358
Weston, Mary Ann, 98n852
Weston, Ronald, 96n686
West's ency of American law, 99n557
Wetland economics, 1989-93, 96n1600
Wetlands in danger, 95n1773
Wetterau, Bruce, 95n585, 96n737, 98n30, 99n687
Wetzel, Bethann, 96n1405, 98n1317
Wexler, Alan, 96n488
Wexler, Debra L., 95n378, 95n379
Wexler, Philip, 99n1504
Weyant, Nancy S., 95n1213
Whales, dolphins, & porpoises, 96n1629
Whaley, Leigh Ann, 98n469
What did they mean by that? 95n451
What do children read next? 95n1128
What do children read next? v.2, 99n999
What do I read next? 1994, 95n1158
What do I take? a consumer's gd to nonprescription drugs, 98n1568
What do YAs read next? 95n1139
What do YAs read next? v.2, 98n1098
What else should I read? 96n1162
What else should I read? guiding kids to good bks, v.2, 98n1076
What everyone should know about the 20th century, 99n538
What fantastic fiction do I read next? 99n1036

What happened where, 98n500
What histl novel do I read next? 99n1034
What in the word? origins of words dealing with people & places, 97n823
What mystery do I read next? a reader's gd to recent mystery fiction, 98n1113
What plant where, 96n156 6
What to name your African-American baby, 96n436
What to read, 96n380
What Western do I read next? 99n1028
What works, 95n276
What's cooking in multicultural America, 97n1254
What's in a name, 97n369
What's on the Internet, winter 1994/95 ed, 95n1710
Wheal, Elizabeth-Anne, 97n474
Wheeler, Helen Rippier, 98n763
Wheeless, Carl, 97n391
When tech fails, 95n1642
When they were kids: over 400 sketches of famous childhoods, 99n27
Where credit is due: a gd to proper citing of sources—print & nonprint, 2d ed, 99n835
Where Queen Elizabeth slept & what the butler saw, 98n1011
Where to play in the USA: the gaming gd, 98n419
Whiffin, Jean I., 96n655
Whigham, Thomas, 96n551
Whisenhunt, Donald W., 97n417, 97n418, 98n439, 98n440, 99n461
Whisler, Kirk, 98n861
Whissen, Thomas, 99n1217
Whitaker, John O., Jr., 97n1294
Whitaker's almanack 1995, 95n9
Whitaker's almanack 1996, 128th ed, 96n6
Whitaker's almanack 1999, 131st ed, 99n5
Whitaker's almanack world heads of govt 1998, 99n650
Whitaker's almanack world heads of state 1998, 99n651
Whitaker's Bks in Print 1997, 98n14
Whitburn, Joel, 95n1289, 95n1390, 96n1303, 96n1314, 96n1319, 96n1337, 96n1402, 97n1061, 97n1062, 97n1070, 97n1079, 98n1205
Whitby, Thomas J., 96n887
Whitcut, Janet, 96n1076
White, Antony, 95n990
White, Ernest M., 98n647
White, Ethel S., 98n647
White, Evelyn Davidson, 97n1054
White, Gerard F., 96n689
White, Isobel, 96n540
White, Jean Bickmore, 99n688
White, Paul, 99n723
White, Phillip M., 96n421, 99n383, 99n384
White, R. Kerry, 96n1417
White, Valerie, 95n1142, 95n1143
Whitelegge, Angela, 96n662
Whiteley, Sandy, 95n14, 95n641, 96n12, 97n12
Whiteside, Lesley, 99n1263
Whitfield, Philip, 95n1735
Whiting, Ernestine, 95n371
Whitlam, John, 98n1041, 98n1042
Whitley, M. J., 97n574

Whitney, Ellen M., 96n492
Whitten, Bessie E., 98n162
Whitten, David O., 98n162
Whittington's dict of plastics, 3d ed, 95n1601
Who get grants/who gives grants, 96n877
Who knows who, 5th ed, 95n190
Who knows who 1996, 96n186
Who was who in America with world notables, v.10, 95n38
Who was who in British India, 99n485
Who was who in 20th century Romania, 95n30
Who was who v.9: who was who 1991-95, 97n28
Who's buying food & drink, 98n257
Who's buying for the home, 98n258
Who's wealthy in America, 1998, 99n59
Who's who among African Americans, 1998/99, 99n379
Who's who among Asian Americans 1994/95, 95n402
Who's who among black Americans 1994/95, 95n415
Who's who among Hispanic Americans 1994-95, 3d ed, 96n409
Who's who in ...
    America 1996, 96n37
    American art 1995-96, 21st ed, 96n1027
    American art 1997-98, 99n866
    American educ 1994-95, 95n336
    American law 1994-95, 95n602
    American law 1996-97, 98n514
    American law 1998-99, 10th ed, 99n550
    American pols 1993-94, 95n719
    American pols 1997-98, 99n666
    art, 26th ed, 95n1003
    Asian banking & finance, 98n150
    Australasia & the Pacific nations, 3d ed, 99n29
    biblical studies & archaeology, 2d ed, 95n1456
    British hist, 99n506
    British opera, 95n1283
    Christianity, 99n1283
    classical mythology, 98n1260
    Congress 1997, 98n656
    country music, 95n1297
    democracy, 98n639
    Egyptian mythology, 2d ed, 96n1350
    European pols, 3d ed, 98n685
    European research & dvlpmt 1995, 96n1491
    finance & industry, 1996-97, 97n152
    interior design, 1994-95 ed, 95n985
    intl affairs 1998, 2d ed, 99n652
    Jewish hist, 2d ed, 96n1481
    Latin America, 4th ed, 98n35
    Lebanon 1995-96, 13th ed, 96n165
    medicine & healthcare 1997-98, 98n1507
    Polish America, 1996-1997 ed, 97n35
    Russia & the CIS Republics, 96n40
    sci & engineering 1996-97, 3d ed, 97n1232
    sci & engineering 1998-99, 99n1305
    sci in Europe, 9th ed, 97n1233
    Shakespeare, 96n1240
    South African pols, no.5, 97n611
    tech, 7th ed, 96n1492
    the Arab world 1995-96, 12th ed, 96n161
    the Asian-American community 1994-95, 96n395

Who's who in ... (*continued*)
   the Bible, 96n1449
   the East 1997-98, 26th ed, 98n31
   the European info world 95/96, 2d ed, 96n639
   the JFK assassination, 95n620
   the media & communications 1998-99, 99n819
   the midwest 1994-95, 95n39
   the midwest 1998-99, 26th ed, 99n36
   the South & Southwest 1995-96, 97n36
   the South & Southwest 1999-2000, 26th ed, 99n37
   the UK info world 95/96, 5th ed, 96n640
   the West 1994-95, 95n40
   the West 1998-99, 26th ed, 98n32
   the world 1996, 13th ed, 97n29
   the world 1998, 99n30
   theology & sci, 1996 ed, 97n1175
   Vietnam, 99n113
   Washington nonprofit groups 1994, 95n72
   WW II, 96n681
   writers, editors, & poets, 5th ed, 96n959
Who's who 1995, 96n34
Who's who 1998, 99n31
Who's who of ...
   American women 1995-96, 19th ed, 96n38
   Australian children's writers, 2d ed, 97n931
   British jazz, 98n1235
   Nobel prize winners 1901-95, 3d ed, 97n30
   southern Africa, 95n34
   Victorian cinema, 98n1280
Who's who on the moon, 97n1394
Whole foods companion, 98n1427
Whole lib hndbk 2, 96n624
Whole spy catalog, 96n775
Whole world bk of quotations, 95n90
Wholesale & retail trade USA, 97n279
Why Eve doesn't have an Adam's apple: a dict of sex differences, 97n1318
Wiant, Sarah K., 95n656
Wice, Nathaniel, 96n813
Wick, Robert L., 98n1196
Widder, William J., 95n1192
Widdows, Richard, 95n481
Widdowson, J. D. A., 95n1056, 97n839
Wiebes, J. T., 96n1628
Wiechmann, Jack G., 95n325
Wieczynski, Joseph L., 98n482
Wiedemann, Barbara, 98n1119
Wiedensohler, Pat, 99n596
Wiegand, Wayne A., 95n637
Wiehs, Jean, 96n137
Wieland, James, 97n1002
Wielgorskaya, Tatiana, 96n1565
Wiener, Allen J., 96n1338
Wiener, Michael C., 97n1447
Wierzbianski, Boleslaw, 97n35
Wiget, Andrew, 95n1175
Wiggers, Raymond, 96n474
Wiggins, Kayla McKinney, 95n1207
Wigoder, Geoffrey, 95n35, 96n164, 96n1478, 98n502, 98n1396

Wilbert, Johannes, 95n398
Wilcox, Derk Arend, 97n614
Wilcox, Laird, 95n1433
Wild flowers of the Pacific NW, 99n1366
Wild New Zealand, 96n1601
Wild orchids across N America, 99n1363
Wild planet! 96n1352
Wilde, T. Jesse, 95n599, 96n615
Wilde, William H., 96n1248
Wilderness preservation: a ref hndbk, 95n1785
Wildlife conservation, 99n1371
Wildlife of the world, 95n1561
Wildlife worldwide [CD-ROM], 96n1607
Wiley, Bell I., 98n432
Wiley dict of civil engineering & construction, 98n1484
Wiley dict of civil engineering & construction: English-Spanish/Spanish-English, 97n1304
Wiley ency of packaging tech, 2d ed, 98n1493
Wiley engineer's desk ref, 2d ed, 99n1398
Wiley's English-Spanish, Spanish-English business dict, 98n157
Wiley's English-Spanish, Spanish-English dict, 99n1506
Wiley's English-Spanish, Spanish-English dict of psychology & psychiatry, 96n782
Wiley's English/Spanish & Spanish/English legal dict, 95n606
Wiley's English-Spanish, Spanish-English legal dict, 2d ed, 98n519
Wilhelmina's modeling & acting dict, 95n1355
Wilhite, Robert E., 99n846
Wilkas, Lenore Rae, 95n648
Wilken, Pam, 96n1135
Wilkes, G. A., 97n829
Wilkie, Everett C., Jr., 95n531
Wilkinson, P. R., 95n1045
Wilkinson, Pamela, 95n1182
Wilkinson, Philip, 96n66, 99n1186
Wilkinson, Robert, 96n1427, 97n1158
Wilkirson, Hayward, 96n98
Willard, Jim, 98n372
Willard, Terry, 98n372
Willem Marinus Dudok, a Dutch modernist, 98n974
Willemen, Paul, 96n1381
Willett, Charles, 96n79
William Butler Yeats ency, 98n1166
William Congreve: an annot bibliog, 1978-94, 97n991
William Grant Still: a bio-bibliog, 97n1046
William Henry Harrison: a bibliog, 99n659
William Inge: a research & production sourcebk, 95n1193
William Mathias, 96n1279
William Pitt, Earl of Chatham 1708-78: a bibliog, 95n754
William Schuman: a bio-bibliog, 99n1127
William Shatner: a bio-bibliog, 95n1346
William Somerset Maugham ency, 98n1160
William Thomas McKinley, 96n1283
Williams, Bob, 99n196
Williams, Brian, 95n55
Williams, Dana A., 99n1050
Williams, Dawn Bastian, 96n126
Williams, Deborah K., 95n1038
Williams, Dominic, 96n248

Williams, Frank P., III, 97n505
Williams, Gary C., 97n1295
Williams, Gayle Ann, 95n168
Williams, Gordon, 96n1243
Williams, Jack, 96n1809
Williams, James G., 97n1367, 97n1371
Williams, Jane, 99n305
Williams, Jane A., 97n280
Williams, John Taylor, 99n621
Williams, Lisa, 95n367
Williams, Lynn Barstis, 95n1009
Williams, Marcia P., 95n307
Williams, Mark, 97n1013
Williams, Martha E., 95n642, 96n622
Williams, Neville, 96n560, 96n562
Williams, Ora, 95n416
Williams, Patrick, 97n402
Williams, Phil, 96n773
Williams, Roger, 96n477
Williams, Rosalind, 95n1079
Williams, Tony, 95n1384
Williams, Vergil L., 97n506
Williamson, David, 96n426
Williamson, Gordon K., 97n185
Williamson, J. W., 95n1388
Williamson, John, 95n694, 98n618
Williamson, Michael M., 95n333
Willig, John T., 97n181
Willings press gd 1998, 124th ed, 99n824
Willins, Michael, 95n989, 98n936
Willis, Donald C., 98n1300
Willmond, Catherine, 96n1099
Willson, Quentin, 96n1892, 98n1650
Wilmeth, Don B., 97n1151, 99n1247
Wilsdon, Christina, 99n1389
Wilsford, David, 96n756
Wilson, A., 96n253
Wilson, Andrew, 97n1301
Wilson, Anthony, 96n1878
Wilson author biogs on disc 1995 [CD-ROM], 96n1144
Wilson, Bernice, 98n957
Wilson, Beverly, 95n629
Wilson, C. Dwayne, 97n623, 98n709
Wilson chronology of ideas, 99n525
Wilson chronology of sci & tech, 99n1307
Wilson chronology of the arts, 99n818
Wilson chronology of women's achievements, 99n802
Wilson, Craig A., 96n674
Wilson, Ellen Judy, 97n475
Wilson, Eunice, 96n544
Wilson, George, 95n127, 95n537, 96n509, 97n472, 98n1072
Wilson, Hugo, 95n1793, 96n1893
Wilson, Jane, 98n372
Wilson, John, 99n1102
Wilson, Joyce M., 96n1176, 99n16
Wilson, Katharina M., 98n1067
Wilson, Kathleen, 98n1120, 98n1121, 99n1015, 99n1016
Wilson, Laurel, 99n427
Wilson, N. C., 95n564
Wilson, R. M., 96n427

Wilson, Raymond L., 95n1022
Wilson, William, 97n597
Wilson, William H., Jr., 99n1500
Wilt, David Edward, 97n1123
Wimsatt, Mary Ann, 96n1201
Win, May Kyi, 99n487
Winchester, Tom, 98n1292
Wind chamber music, 97n1058
Wind ensemble sourcebk & biogl gd, 98n1220
Windsor, Steven, 96n638
Wine Spectator Mag's gd to great wine values, 99n1338
Winfield, Jerry Phillips, 95n1244
Wing, Donald, 96n14
Wingard, Helene F., 95n935, 99n823
Winig, Laura, 96n282, 97n266
Winkel, Lois, 96n632
Winklepleck, Julie, 95n916
Winks, Robin W., 99n1032
Winning athletic scholarships, 1998 ed, 99n347
Winning edge: the student-athlete's gd to college sports, 5th ed, 98n723
Winning edge, 3d ed, 95n799
Winter, Frank H., 96n1647
Winter, Ruth, 95n1688, 96n1530, 96n1790
Winterton, Jules, 98n533
Wired style, 97n758
Wise, James E., 98n1281
Wise, Suzanne, 95n792
Wise words & wives' tales, 95n1313
Wiseman, Nigel, 99n1446
Wishlade, Fiona, 97n243
Wisner-Broyles, Laura, 99n762
Wisner-Broyles, Laura A., 99n767, 99n774
Wisniewski, Debra J., 98n902
Wisterias, 96n1579
Wit: humorous quotations from Woody Allen to Oscar Wilde, 99n79
Witalec, Janet, 96n1259
With fire & sword: Italian spectacles on American screens 1958-68, 96n1395
Withers, Martin B., 98n1461, 98n1470
Witman, Kathleen L., 97n193
Witt, Elder, 98n526, 98n529
Wittgenstein dict, 97n1162
Wittstruck, Thorne, 95n1457
Wizansky, Richard, 96n1871
Wizards & sorcerers, 98n716
Wlaschin, Ken, 99n1218
WLN interlibrary loan policies dir, 5th ed, 98n585
Woelfel, Charles J., 95n230
Woerner, Gert, 96n1483
Woishnis, William Andrew, 95n1636
Wojtas, Walter A., 95n1537
Wolden, Kathy, 95n1676
Woldman's engineering alloys, 8th ed, 96n1671
Wolf, Carolyn, 99n385
Wolf, Gabriele, 95n1315
Wolf, Kirsten, 99n892
Wolff, Manfred E., 98n1565
Wolff, Miles, 98n729

Wolfson, Paulette S., 97n224
Wolman, Benjamin B., 97n1356
Wolverton, Ruthe, 96n475
Wolverton, Walt, 96n475
Womack, Carol Z., 96n211
Womack, Kenneth, 97n880, 99n592
Woman to woman, 95n919
Woman's body, 96n1692
Woman's ency of natural healing, 98n1550
Woman's gd to ...
    coping with disability, 96n859
    coping with disability, 2d ed, 98n777
    vitamins & minerals, 96n1743
Women & aging, 96n936
Women & aging, 98n763
Women & health, 98n1501
Women & men in Europe & N America 1995, 97n720
Women & music, 97n1020
Women & religion in Britain & Ireland, 97n1170
Women & religion in India, 96n934
Women & sci, 97n730
Women & the Dict of Natl Biog, 96n26
Women & the military, 96n680
Women & the military, 97n563
Women & work in developing countries, 95n292
Women artists & designers in Europe since 1800, 99n864
Women artists, 2d ed, 96n1021
Women composers, 2d ed, 95n1267
Women composers, v.1, 97n1047
Women composers, v.2, 97n1048
Women composers, v.3, 99n1145
Women composers & songwriters, 97n1035
Women educators in the US, 1820-1993: a bio-bibliog sourcebk, 95n335
Women film directors, 96n947
Women in ...
    agriculture, 97n1245
    China, 99n808
    Christian hist, 97n731
    context, 99n39
    espionage, 95n907
    Intl Security, 95n365
    law, 97n485
    modern American pols, 98n829
    music, 2d ed, 95n1254
    Nigeria, 97n725
    Russia & the Soviet Union, 95n903
    the biblical world, v.1, 97n1186
    the Third World, 98n839
    the Third World, 99n805
    the US: economic conditions, 96n937
    the US military, 1901-95, 97n559
Women of color: feminist theory, 97n729
Women of Congress, 98n833
Women of Ireland, 98n34
Women of peace: Nobel peace prize winners, 96n944
Women of strength, 97n733
Women of the All-American Girls Professional Baseball League, 98n734
Women of the US congress, 95n716
Women playwrights in England, Ireland, & Scotland 1660-1823, 98n1151
Women playwrights of diversity, 98n1106
Women public speakers in the US, 1925-93, 95n905
Women state & territorial legislators, 1895-1995, 97n601
Women who reformed pols, 96n943
Women workers, 97n732
Women writers in German-speaking countries, 99n1095
Women writers in the US, 97n738
Women writers of Great Britain & Europe, 98n1067
Women's almanac, 98n827
Women's atlas of the US, rev ed, 96n933
Womens' business resource gd, 95n208
Women's chronology, 95n912
Women's chronology, 98n834
Women's companion to intl film, 95n1373
Women's complete healthbk, 97n1341
Women's desk ref, 95n918
Women's firsts, 98n835, 99n806
Women's gd to homeopathy, 95n1672
Women's health concerns sourcebk, 99n1438
Women's hist, 99n801
Women's info exchange natl dir, 95n915
Women's issues, 98n837
Women's legal gd, 98n544
Women's per in the US, 97n743
Women's pers in the US: consumer mags, 96n950
Women's rights on trial, 98n563
Women's studies index 1995, 98n842
Women's studies on disc [CD-ROM], 97n742
Women's voices, 98n840
Women's words, 97n72
Women's world: a timeline of women in hist, 96n945
Wong, Glenn M., 95n599, 96n615
Wong, Mary M., 98n769
Wong, Nancy C., 98n11
Wood, Corinne Shear, 99n1472
Wood, Cynthia J., 95n938
Wood, D. R. W., 98n1373
Wood, Donna, 99n333
Wood, Elizabeth, 95n1267
Wood, Helen E., 96n897
Wood, Ian, 95n815
Wood, Laura Matysek, 97n467
Wood, Richard A., 97n1398, 99n1534
Wood, Richard J., 99n60
Woodbridge, Hensley C., 98n1183
Woodbury, Elton N., 95n1579
Woodgate, Graham, 99n1564
Woodham, Anne, 98n1552
Woodhead, Peter, 95n85
Wooding, Frederick H., 96n1624
Woodrow Wilson, 98n647
Woods, Adrienne L., 98n1566, 98n1567
Woods, Geraldine, 95n882
Woods, John A., 96n284
Woodside, Gayle, 96n1852
Woodstra, Chris, 95n1256, 96n1330, 97n1072, 98n1228, 98n1230
Woodworth, David, 96n278, 96n279

Woodworth, Steven E., 97n421
Woodyard, George, 95n1420
Woolf, D. R., 99n529
Woolford, Daniel, 95n419
Woolum, Janet, 99n710
Wooster, Robert, 99n625
Word dance: the lang of Native American culture, 95n437
Words in the news, 95n724
Words of mathematics, 95n1743
Words on cassette 1995, 96n983
Words on cassette 1998, 99n14
Wordsworth's reading 1770-99, 95n1223
Work of Jack Vance, 96n1218
Work of William Eastlake, 96n1209
Work your way around the world, 7th ed, 96n273
Work-Family research, 98n778
Working solo sourcebk, 96n263
Working stiffs, union maids, reds, & riffraff: an organized gd to films about labor, 97n1141
Works of Allen Ginsberg 1941-94, 96n1210
World academic database [CD-ROM], 97n308
World Afghanistan to Zimbabwe, 97n378
World alive [CD-ROM], 96n1609
World almanac & bk of facts 1994, 95n6
World almanac & bk of facts 1994 [CD-ROM], 95n7
World almanac & bk of facts 1996, 96n7
World almanac & bk of facts 1997, 98n3
World Almanac, editors of, 95n108
World almanac for kids 1998, 98n4
World almanac for kids 1999, 99n6
World almanac job finders gd 1997, 97n263
World almanac of ...
   presidential quotations, 95n550
  the USA, 95n108
  the USA, rev ed, 99n89
  US pols, 1993-95 ed, 95n711
  US pols, 1997-99 ed, 98n643
World atlas of nations, 95n489
World authors 1900-50, 97n887
World biogl index, 2d ed [CD-ROM], 97n31
World biogl index, 3d ed, 99n32
World bk dict, 98n996
World bk ency, 95n66
World bk ency, 1996 ed, 97n48
World bk ency of sci, 98n1409
World bk health & medical annual 1997, 98n1543
World bk multimedia ency [CD-ROM], 96n51
World bk multimedia ency, 1998 [CD-ROM], 99n47
World bk new illus info finder [CD-ROM], 95n67
World bk Rush-Presbyterian-St. Luke's medical center medical ency, 7th ed, 97n1335
World bk yr bk, 1997, 98n64
World bk's young scientist, 98n1410
World business & economic review 1994, 95n256
World business desk ref, 95n249
World checklist of birds, 95n1572
World country analyst [CD-ROM], 98n205
World database of consumer brands & their owners 1998 [CD-ROM], 99n259

World databases in ...
  agriculture, 97n1247
  bioscis & pharmacology, 97n1241
  chemistry, 97n1383
  co info, 97n172
  geography & geology, 96n453
  humanities, 98n849
  industry, 96n225
  patents, 96n587
  physics & mathematics, 96n1788
  social scis, 97n78
World dir of ...
  business info libs, 97n548
  business info libs, 3d ed, 99n615
  country environmental studies, 3d ed, 97n1432
  defence & security, 97n567
  exhibitions & trade fairs 1995, 96n309
  human rights research & training insts, 3d ed, 97n518
  mktg info sources, 99n211
  mathematicians 1998, 11th ed, 99n1545
  minorities, 98n334
  moving image & sound archives, 95n963
  non-official statl sources, 2d ed, 99n789
  research & training insts in intl law, 3d ed, 95n600
  trade & business assns, 97n173
  trade & business jls, 97n174
World drinks databk, 95n1523
World economic factbk 1993, 95n214
World economic factbk 1997/98, 5th ed, 99n233
World economic outlook, May 1997, 98n188
World ency of ...
  aircraft manufacturers, 95n1789
  cities: N America, 95n900
  parliaments & legislatures, 99n656
  soccer, 95n824
World engineering industries & automation, 97n199
World engineering industries & automation 1993-95, 96n1649
World factbk [CD-ROM], 95n8
World factbk 1996-97, 97n80
World facts & maps, 98n400
World geographical ency, English lang ed, 96n456
World gd 1997/98, 10th ed, 98n97
World gd to ...
  religious & spiritual orgs 1996, 97n1182
  scientific assns & learned societies, 7th ed, 99n1323
  trade assns, 4th ed, 97n175
World hist: a dict of important people, places, & events..., 95n585
World holiday bk, 95n1335
World holiday festival & calendar bks, 99n1194
World index of economic forecasts, 4th ed, 96n208
World index of resources & population, 96n235
World industrial robots 1997, 98n1581
World investment dir, v.4: Latin America & the Caribbean, 95n291
World investment dir 1996, v.5: Africa, 98n201
World investment dir 1996, v.6: West Asia, 98n207
World investment report 1998, 99n234
World labour report 1997-98, 99n235
World leaders: people who shaped the world, 95n576

World list of univs & other insts of higher educ, 96n361
World list of univs & other insts of higher educ, 21st ed, 99n337
World lit criticism suppl, 99n983
World market share reporter 1995-96, 96n240
World mktg data & stats 1996 on CD-ROM, 2d ed [CD-ROM], 97n281
World mktg data & stats on CD-ROM [CD-ROM], 99n236
World mountaineering, 99n442
World music CD listener's gd, 99n1159
World mythology, 97n1092
World of ...
   difference, 3d ed, 95n383
   ghosts & the supernatural, 96n784
   invention, 95n1496
   learning 1999, 49th ed, 99n295
   magnolias, 95n1551
   scientific discovery, 95n1497
World painting index, 2d suppl, 96n1056
World population monitoring 1996, 99n809
World population prospects, 99n790
World radio TV hndbk, 1996 ed, 97n773
World religions, 98n1361
World religions [CD-ROM], 95n1447
World retail dir & sourcebk, 2d ed, 97n222
World retail dir 1997-98, 99n212
World satellite almanac, 1995, 7th ed, 96n1648
World Shakespeare biblog on CD-ROM 1990-93 [CD-ROM], 98n1165
World stats pocketbk, 97n721
World stock exchange fact bk, 97n186
World tables 1994, 95n257
World tourism dir '95/96, pt.1, 3d ed, 96n464
World tourism dir '95/96, pt.2, 3d ed, 96n465
World tourism dir '95/96, pt.3, 3d ed, 96n466
World trade almanac & the dict of intl trade, 1997 ed [CD-ROM], 97n208
World trade almanac 1996-97, 97n207
World trade atlas: US data, Mar 1994 [CD-ROM], 95n327
World trade org dispute settlement decisions, v.1, 99n237
World urbanization prospects, 99n794
World urbanizations prospects: the 1994 revision, 96n932
World War I, 99n541
World War I aviation, rev ed, 98n610
World War I songs, 96n696
World War II: a statistical survey, 95n691
World War II in Europe, Africa, & the Americas, with general sources, 98n622
World War II in the N Pacific, 95n684
World weatherdisc, 1994 ed [CD-ROM], 96n1811
World weeds, 99n1368
World who is who & does what in environment & conservation, 98n1631
World Wide Web for scientists & engineers, 99n1327
Worldmark ency of ...
   cultures & daily life, 99n364
   the nations, 8th ed, 96n105
   the states, 96n106
World's Columbian Exposition, 97n404
World's major cos dir, 96n229
World's women 1995, 2d ed, 96n954
World's writing systems, 97n816
Worldwide branch locations of multinatl cos, 95n246
Worldwide govt dir with intl orgs 1995, 96n709
Worldwide gd to equivalent nonferrous metals & alloys, 3d ed, 97n1309
Worldwide offshore contractors & equipment dir, 1994, 95n1621
Worldwide offshore contractors & equipment dir, 1996, 28th ed, 97n1419
Worldwide offshore petroleum dir 1998, 30th ed, 99n213
Worldwide petrochemical dir, 1995, 33d ed, 96n1835
Worldwide petrochemical dir, 1998, 36th ed, 99n214
Worldwide petroleum industry outlook, 99n1549
Worldwide pipelines & contractors dir, 1995, 15th ed, 96n1837
Worst baseball pitchers of all time, 95n805
Wortabet, John, 95n1070
Worth a 1,000 words: an annot gd to picture bks for older readers, 98n1090
Worthley, Christopher, 95n281
Wortman, William A., 97n885
Wostbrock, Fred, 97n1113
Woy, James, 97n177
WPA gd to 1930s Mont., 95n513
Wratten, Darrel, 98n1345, 98n1382
Wrend, Julie, 99n561
Wright, Albert Hazen, 95n1598, 96n1640
Wright, Anna Allen, 95n1598, 96n1640
Wright, Cora M., 99n1001
Wright, David, 99n412, 99n1551
Wright, Jill, 99n412
Wright, John W., 96n5, 96n1693, 98n2
Wright, Laura, 97n831
Wright, Marshall D., 97n651, 98n738, 99n724
Wright, Michael, 96n1421
Wright, Philip C., 96n385
Wright, Russell O., 96n742, 96n807, 98n770, 98n808
Write right!3d ed, 96n1081
Writer's companion, 97n924
Writer's Digest character naming sourcebk, 95n944
Writer's Digest dict of concise writing, 97n759
Writer's dir 1994-96, 95n1107
Writer's dir 1998-2000, 13th ed, 99n958
Writer's ency, 3d ed, 97n750
Writers for YAs, 98n1104
Writer's hndbk, 99n832
Writer's market, 1995, 95n670
Writer's market, 1998, 98n870
Writer's market, 1998, electronic ed [CD-ROM], 98n869
Writers of multicultural fiction for YAs, 97n942
Writer's resource, 98n871
Writer's resource hndbk, 98n865
Writer's ultimate research gd, 97n752
Writing across the curriculum: an annot bibliog, 95n333
Writing centers, 97n284
Writings in Indian hist, 1985-90, 96n414
Writings on African archives, 97n92
Writings on writing, 95n940
Written out of TV, 97n1129

Wrobel, Murray, 97n1273
Wrongful termination, 96n281
WRTH satellite broadcasting gd, 1995 ed, 96n997
WTA Tour, 96n832
WTA Tour Communications Staff, 96n832
Wu, Duncan, 95n1223
Wuerch, William L., 96n168, 96n1439
Wuerttemberg emigration index, v.6, 95n463
Wyatt, Flora R., 99n1002
Wyckoff, D. Campbell, 96n1463
Wyckoff, Trip, 96n209
Wynar, Bohdan S., 95n16, 96n11, 98n9
Wynar, Lubomyr R., 97n522
Wynn, Ron, 95n1304

Xtravaganza! the essential sourcebk for Macromedia Xtras, 99n1486

Yaakov, Juliette, 95n660, 95n1166, 96n650, 97n945, 98n586, 98n587
Yager, Cindy, 99n304
Yahnke, Robert E., 96n845
Yai, Olabiyi Babalola, 97n879
Yale gd to children's nutrition, 98n1555
Yamashita, Kenneth, 98n327
Yamazaki, Moriichi, 97n1202
Yampolsky, Selma, 98n26
Yang, Hiyol, 98n167
Yankee talk: a dict of New England expressions, 97n835
Yarmoshuk, Lisa, 95n383
Yaws, Carl L., 96n1793, 96n1821, 96n1822, 96n1823, 96n1824, 98n1622, 98n1623
Ye, Feng, 99n1446
Yeager, Rodger, 98n457
Year bk of the Muslim world 1996, 97n81
Year in trees, 96n1592
Yearbook of ...
    experts, authorities & spokespersons, 12th ed, 96n103
    intl orgs 1997/98, 98n71
    labor stats, 1997, 99n238
    labour stats 1995, 54th ed, 97n261
    the Human Rights Committee 1985-86, v.2, 95n632
    the Intl Law Commission 1992, 96n614
    tourism stats, 46th ed, 96n463
Year's work in English studies, v.71, 95n923
Year's work in English studies, v.73, 1992, 96n958
Yemen, rev ed, 99n139
Yenne, Bill, 96n33, 96n1602
Yeoman, R. S., 96n1008, 98n910
Yiddish linguistics, 95n1026
Yntema, Sharon, 99n279
Yoder, Andrew, 97n774
Yoshinki-Kovinick, Marian, 99n869
Young adult lit & nonprint materials, 95n654
Young, Antonia, 99n118
Young, Arthur P., 96n1442
Young, Ben, 99n1146

Young, Claiborne S., 99n430
Young, Ken, 96n808
Young, Mark C., 95n1329
Young Oxford companion to the presidency of the US, 95n543
Young Oxford companion to the Supreme Court of the US, 95n607
Young person's gd to philosophy, 99n1258
Young person's occupational outlook hndbk, 97n264
Young, Peter C., 95n1768
Young, Philip H., 98n1088
Young reader's companion to American hist, 96n528
Young, Robert, Jr., 95n1354
Young, Robert W., 95n1090
Young, Robyn V., 96n387, 99n1541
Young, Sue, 95n1057
Young, W. Murray, 96n1284
Young, William C., 97n302
Yount, Lisa, 95n1486
Your English ancestry, 95n459
Your hit parade & American top 10 hits, 4th ed, 96n1308
Your reading, 1995-96 ed, 97n925
Yousof, Ghulam-Sarwar, 96n1418
Youth exchanges, 96n371
Yrigoyen, Charles, Jr., 97n1214
Yu, David C., 95n1439
Yu, George T., 95n109
Yuill, Douglas, 97n243
Yuly, Rudy, 95n249

Zabel, Diane, 98n241
Zagars, Julie, 98n975
Zaidman, Laura M., 95n1205
Zaire, 96n126
Zakalik, Joanna, 96n1779
Zamponi, Lynda F., 95n120
Zancani, Diego, 96n143
Zand, Janet, 96n1713, 98n1523
Zaniello, Tom, 97n1141
Zavala, Agustin Jacinto, 99n1257
Zawahri, Neda A., 96n1863
Zelio, Judy, 99n284
Zell, Hans M., 95n22, 97n552, 98n105
Zelnik, Martin, 96n1048
Zemljanukhin, Sergej, 95n1369
Zempel, Edward N., 96n1003
Zenker, Stephanie F., 98n1095
Zeno, Susan M., 97n817
Zeyl, Donald J., 98n1334
Zhang, Puling, 99n1434
Zheutlin, Barbara, 98n871
Zhuk, A. B., 97n782
Zia, Helen, 96n393, 96n396
Zibart, Eve, 96n1531
Zich, Joanne, 99n549
Zietz, Karyl Lynn, 96n1302
Zilberman, Shimon, 97n856
Zilboorg, Caroline, 98n835
Zils, Michael, 97n175, 99n1323
Zimbabwe, rev ed, 95n125

Zimbaro, Valerie P., 97n893
Zimmerman, Doris P., 98n681
Zimmerman, Karen P., 95n428, 95n429
Zimmerman, Michael F., 96n861
Zip code finder, 98n59
Zipperer, Lorri A., 95n1653, 97n1316
Ziring, Lawrence, 97n620
Zminda, Don, 99n715
Zoltan Kodaly: a gd to research, 99n1138
Zomlefer, Wendy B., 96n1580
Zorc, R. David, 97n844
Ztopcu, Kurtulus, 97n876

Zubatsky, David S., 98n362
Zuber, Pam, 99n1195
Zuckerman, Amy, 98n206
Zuidema, George D., 99n1415
Zuk, Judith D., 98n1432
Zumerchik, John, 98n720
Zurcher, Erik, 98n507
Zurndorfer, Harriet T., 96n535
Zvelebil, Kamil V., 96n1255
Zweifel, Richard G., 99n1395
Zwillinger, Daniel, 97n1413
Zwirn, Jerrold, 97n54

Subject Index

Reference is to entry number.

ABBREVIATIONS. *See also* **ACRONYMS**
Abbreviations dict, 9th ed, 96n2
Acronyms, initialisms, & abbrevs dict 1997, 21st ed, 97n1
Barnhart abbrevs dict, 96n1
Buttress's world gd to abbrevs of orgs, 11th ed, 98n1
Canadian dict of abbrevs, 95n1
Common medical abbrevs, 96n1695
Elsevier's dict of acronyms, initialisms, abbrevs, & symbols, 99n1
Index to legal citations & abbrevs, 2d ed, 95n593
New acronyms, initialisms, & abbrevs, v.2, 96n3
Reverse acronyms, initialisms & abbrevs dict, 18th ed, 95n2

ABNORMALITIES, HUMAN
Biological anomalies: humans III, 96n1559
Catalog of teratogenic agents, 8th ed, 96n1720

ABORTION
Abortion, 2d ed, 97n666
Abortion, 1996 ed, 98n754
Abortion & reproductive rights [CD-ROM], 98n755
Abortion policies, v.3, 97n665
Anti-abortion movement, 98n756
Pro-choice/pro-life issues in the 1990s, 98n757
World population monitoring 1996, 99n809

ABSTRACT EXPRESSIONISM
Abstract expressionist women painters, 97n808

ABSTRACTS
Information sci abstracts, v.29, no.12, 96n619

ACADEMIC LIBRARIES
Academic lib of the 90s, 96n620
Academic libs in the UK & the republic of Ireland 1994, 3d ed, 96n635

ACADEMY AWARDS (MOTION PICTURES)
Academy awards index, 95n1400
65 yrs of the Oscar, rev ed, 96n1372

ACCIDENTS
APELL annot bibliog, 96n777
Household chemicals & emergency first aid, 95n1650
Injury prevention for the elderly, 96n844
Injury prevention for young children, 97n710
Sports medicine bible, 96n1729

ACCOUNTING
Accounting research dir, 3d ed, 95n217
Cabell's dir of publishing opportunities in accounting, economics & finance, 6th ed, 96n669
Dictionary of accounting, 96n210
History of accounting, 97n179

ACCREDITATION (EDUCATION)
Certification & accreditation programs dir, 98n270

ACHIEVEMENT TESTS
ETS test collection catalog, v.2, 2d ed, 96n314

ACQUISITIONS (LIBRARIES)
Free mags for libs, 4th ed, 95n647
Policies for publishers, 1995 ed, 96n674

ACRONYMS. *See also* **ABBREVIATIONS**
Acronyms, initialisms, & abbrevs dict 1997, 21st ed, 97n1
Buttress's world gd to abbrevs of orgs, 11th ed, 98n1
Canadian dict of abbrevs, 95n1
Comprehensive networking glossary & acronym gd, 96n1759
Elsevier's dict of acronyms, initialisms, abbrevs, & symbols, 99n1
Environmental acronyms, 96n1850
Gobbledygook bk: dict of acronyms, abbrevs, initializations, & esoteric terminology, 97n2
New acronyms, initialisms, & abbrevs, v.2, 96n3
Reverse acronyms, initialisms & abbrevs dict, 18th ed, 95n2

ACTING
Ultimate scene & monologue sourcebk, 95n1407
Wilhelmina's modeling & acting dict, 95n1355

ACTORS & ACTRESSES. *See also* **MOTION PICTURE ACTORS & ACTRESSES; TELEVISION ACTORS & ACTRESSES**
Ann Sheridan: a bio-bibliog, 98n1274
Biographical dict of actors, actresses, musicians, dancers, managers...v.15, 95n1411
Biographical dict of actors, actresses, musicians, dancers, managers...v.16, 95n1412
Entertainers in British films, 99n1225
Guide to American cinema, 1930-65, 99n1217
Guide to American cinema, 1965-95, 99n1211
International dict of theatre-3: actors, directors, & designers, 97n1149
Katharine Cornell: a bio-bibliog, 95n1351
Lee Van Cleef: a bibliog, film, & TV ref, 99n1208
Leonard Maltin's movie ency, 96n1377
Lillian Russell: a bio-bibliog, 98n1275
Noel Coward: a bio-bibliog, 95n1342
Quinlan's illus dir of film character actors, new ed, 97n1106
William Shatner: a bio-bibliog, 95n1346

ADAMS, JOHN
John Adams: a bibliog, 95n533

ADDAMS, JANE
Jane Addams papers, 97n706

ADDISON, JOSEPH
Joseph Addison & Richard Steele, 96n1237

ADJUSTMENT (PSYCHOLOGY)
Woman's gd to coping with disability, 96n859
Woman's gd to coping with disability, 2d ed, 98n777

ADMINISTRATIVE AGENCIES
Business orgs, agencies, & pubns dir, 8th ed, 97n160
Carroll's fed dir, 96n723
Carroll's fed regional dir, 96n724
Corpus admin index, 1994, 95n748
Directory of professional & occupational regulation in the US & Canada, 96n730
Encyclopedia of govtl advisory orgs 1997, 11th ed, 99n670
Federal regulatory dir, 7th ed, 96n731
Federal regulatory dir, 8th ed, 98n664
Federal yellow bk, fall 1994, 95n727
Global links: a gd to key people & insts worldwide, 99n54
Government phone bk USA 1997, 5th ed, 98n52
State staff dir, summer 1997, 98n667
United Nations dir of agencies & insts in public admin & finance, 99n703
US govt dirs, 1982-95, 99n62

ADOLESCENCE
Adolescence: the survival gd for parents & teenagers, 98n802
Gale ency of childhood & adolescence, 99n778
Teen legal rights, 96n592

ADOPTION
Adoption, 99n755
Adoption dir, 2d ed, 96n860
Annotated gd to adoption research 1986-97, 99n754
Children in foster care & adoption, 99n756

ADORNO, THEODOR
Theodor Adorno (II), 96n833

ADULTHOOD
Encyclopedia of adult dvlpmt, 95n781

ADVENTURE FILMS
Hollywood heroes, 96n1376

ADVENTURE STORIES
Burroughs cyclopaedia, 97n969
Huckleberry Finn on film, 95n1393

ADVERTISING
Ad men & women, 95n320
Dictionary of mktg & advertising, 96n304
International advertising & mktg info sources, 96n299
Latin American advertising, mktg, & media sourcebk, 96n301
Leo Burnett worldwide advertising & media fact bk, 96n302
NTC's dict of advertising, 2d ed, 95n325

AERONAUTICS. *See also* AIRPLANES
Airlines worldwide, 99n1573
Aviation: a Smithsonian gd, 96n1882
Aviation & aerospace almanac 1995, 96n1879
Brassey's world aircraft & systems dir 1996/97, 97n1438
Commercial air transport bks, 98n1646
Commuter airlines of the US, 96n1880
Encyclopedia of African airlines, 99n1574
Flight & flying: a chronology, 95n1787
Jane's aero-engines, 97n1298
Jane's airports & handling agents, 1995-96, 96n1881
Jane's all the world's aircraft 1998-99, 89th ed, 99n1575
Jane's avionics 1996-97, 15th ed, 97n1441
Jane's intl ABC aerospace dir 1996, 46th ed, 97n217
Military aircraft insignia of the world, 99n636
Pockets: aircraft, 98n1645
200 best aviation Web sites, 99n1576
World War I aviation, rev ed, 98n610

AERONAUTICS, MILITARY. *See also* AIRPLANES, MILITARY
Military aircraft insignia of the world, 99n636
Naval Institute gd to world military aviation 1997-98, 99n637

AFFIRMATIVE ACTION PROGRAMS
Affirmative action, 97n484

AFFLUENT CONSUMERS
Who's wealthy in America, 1998, 99n59

AFGHANISTAN
Dictionary of Afghan wars, revolutions, & insurgencies, 97n106
Historical dict of Afghanistan, 2d ed, 98n110

AFRICA
Africa, Asia, & S America since 1800, 96n555
Africa in figures 1996, 98n102
Africa on file, 96n108
African intl relations, 2d ed, 98n699
African placenames, 95n502
Black hndbk, 99n375
Cambridge gd to African & Caribbean theatre, 95n1420
Cultural atlas of Africa, rev ed, 99n95
Dictionary of Portuguese-African civilization, v.1, 96n532
Dictionary of Portuguese-African civilization, v.2, 97n427
Economic & social survey of Africa, 1994-95, 97n231
Encyclopedia of African airlines, 99n1574
Encyclopedia of world cultures, v.9: Africa & the Middle East, 97n319
Foreign trade stats for Africa, 96n294
From Afar to Zulu: a dict of African cultures, 96n390
Handbook of African medicinal plants, 95n1546
International dict of historic places, v.4, 97n468
International histl stats: Africa, Asia, & Oceania, 1750-1988, 96n917
Kenya, rev ed, 97n98
Major cos of Africa S of the Sahara 1996, 97n219
Making of modern Africa: a gd to archives, 96n530
Metalworking in Africa S of the Sahara, 96n1668
Nations of Africa, 98n321
Pan-African chronology, 97n426
Sao Tome & Principe, 96n121
Survey of economic & social conditions in Africa, 1991-92, 96n113

Swaziland, rev ed, 96n123
Videos of African & African-related performance, 97n1145
Year bk of the Muslim world 1996, 97n81

AFRICA—ACRONYMS
African acronyms & abbrevs, 98n104

AFRICA—BIBLIOGRAPHY
Africa: Africa world press gd to educ resources from & about Africa, 99n94
African bks in print, 4th ed, 95n22
Bibliographies for African studies, 1987-93, 95n113
Guide to mss & docs in the British Isles relating to Africa, v.1, 95n111
Guide to original sources for precolonial W Africa published in European langs, rev ed, 96n531
Guinea, 97n97
Mali, 99n98
Theses on Africa, 1976-88, 95n112
Writings on African archives, 97n92

AFRICA, CENTRAL
Peoples of Central Africa, 98n322

AFRICA, EAST
Common birds of E Africa, 98n1461
East & NE Africa bibliog, 97n90
Larger animals of E Africa, 98n1470
Peoples of E Africa, 98n323
Portraits in conservation: E & S Africa, 96n1596

AFRICA—HISTORY
African hist on file, 96n529
Historical dict of Botswana, 3d ed, 97n94
Historical dict of Congo, 97n95
Historical dict of Eritrea, 99n479
Historical dict of Libya, 3d ed, 99n480
Historical dict of Mali, 3d ed, 97n99
Historical dict of Togo, 3d ed, 97n103
Historical dict of Zambia, 2d ed, 99n477
Pan-African chronology 2, 99n478
Penguin atlas of African hist, new ed, 97n428

AFRICA IN MASS MEDIA
Media in African & Africa in the media, 98n853

AFRICA—MAPS
Maps & mapping of Africa, 98n392

AFRICAN AMERICANS. See **AFRO-AMERICANS**

AFRICAN LANGUAGES
Bibliography of African lang texts . . . to 1963, 95n1029

AFRICAN LITERATURE
Africa in lit for children & YAs, 96n1166
African writers, 98n1167
Bibliography of African lits, 97n1001
Black African lit in English, 1987-91, 96n1247
Twentieth-Century Caribbean & black African writers, 3d series, 97n1012

AFRICA, NORTH
Algeria, rev ed, 97n93
Encyclopedia of the modern Middle East, 97n136
Middle East & N Africa 1995, 96n160
Middle East & N Africa 1997, 97n139
Middle East & N Africa 1998, 99n87
Middle East & N Africa on file, 96n459
Peoples of N Africa, 98n324
Political parties of the Middle East & N Africa, 96n765
War in N Africa, 1940-43, 97n460
Western Sahara, 97n105

AFRICA, NORTH—ANTIQUITIES
Oxford ency of archaeology in the Near East, 98n429

AFRICA, NORTH—FOREIGN RELATIONS
Asian states' relations with the Middle East & N Africa, 95n763
US foreign relations with the Middle East & N Africa, 95n764

AFRICANS
African biog, 99n373
African biogl dict, 96n109
Black hndbk, 99n375
Encyclopaedia Africana dict of African biog, v.3, 97n91
100 great Africans, 96n112
Peoples of Africa, 97n321

AFRICA—POLITICS & GOVERNMENT
Africa, 98n103
Contemporary African pols & dvlpmt, 96n110

AFRICA, SOUTH
Peoples of Southern Africa, 98n325
Portraits in conservation: E & S Africa, 96n1596
Southern Africa bibliog, 97n101
Who's who of southern Africa, 95n34

AFRICA—STUDY & TEACHING
African studies companion, 2d ed, 98n105
International dir of African studies research, 3d ed, 96n111

AFRICA, SUB-SAHARAN
Africa S of the Sahara 1997, 26th ed, 98n108
Encyclopedia of Africa S of the Sahara, 99n100
Great Zimbabwe, 95n522
Historical dict of intl orgs in sub-Saharan Africa, 95n755
Resource gd to travel in sub-Saharan Africa, v.1: E & W Africa, 95n516
Resource gd to travel in sub-Saharan Africa, v.2, 98n420

AFRICA, WEST
Benin, 98n106
Historical dict of Burkina Faso, 2d ed, 99n96
Historical dict of the Republic of Guinea-Bissau, 3d ed, 98n456
Peoples of W Africa, 98n326

AFRO-AMERICAN ARTS
Harlem renaissance, 99n378

AFRO-AMERICAN ATHLETES
African-American sports greats, 96n792

AFRO-AMERICAN CHURCHES
Directory of African American religious bodies, 2d ed, 97n1181

AFRO-AMERICAN CONDUCTORS
Black conductors, 96n1285

AFRO-AMERICAN DRAMATISTS
Contemporary African-American female playwrights, 99n1050

AFRO-AMERICAN INVENTORS
African-American inventors, 96n1488

AFRO-AMERICAN MUSICIANS
Blacks in opera, 96n1301

AFRO-AMERICAN NEWSPAPERS
Bibliographic checklist of African American newspapers, 96n971

AFRO-AMERICAN—QUOTATIONS
African American quotations, 99n80
Contemporary quotations in black, 98n78
Talking drums: an African-American quote collection, 96n96

AFRO-AMERICANS—BIOGRAPHY
African American biog, 95n403
African American biogs, 2, 95n407
African-American bus leaders, 95n181
African American criminologists, 1970-96, 99n575
African-American orators, 98n337
African American voices, 97n328
Autobiographies by Americans of color 1980-94, 98n347
Contemporary black biog, v.8, 96n400
Contemporary black biog, v.16, 99n376
Freedom's lawmakers: a dir of black officeholders during Reconstruction, rev ed, 98n344
Who's who among African Americans, 1998/99, 99n379
Who's who among black Americans 1994/95, 95n415

AFRO-AMERICAN SCIENTISTS
African-American scientists, 96n1489
Distinguished African American scientists of the 20th century, 97n1230

AFRO-AMERICANS. See also BLACKS
ABC-CLIO companion to the civil rights movement, 95n627
African America, 95n406
African-American address bk, 96n52
African American almanac, 98n346
African-American almanac, 6th ed, 95n404
African American almanac, 7th ed, 98n335
African-American baby name bk, 99n407
African American breakthroughs, 96n397
African American ency suppl, 98n336
African American genealogical sourcebk, 96n429
African American historic places, 95n410
African American hist in the press 1851-99, 97n412
African-American yellow pages, 97n329
Bibliographic gd to black studies 1994, 96n398
Bibliographic gd to black studies 1995, 98n339
Black demographic data, 1790-1860, 98n342
Black student's gd to scholarships, 3d ed, 95n371
Black talk, 95n413
Century of musicals in black & white, 95n1416
Choral music by African American composers, 97n1054
Comprehensive name index for The American Slave, 98n341
Coretta Scott King awards bk, 95n411
Dictionary of Afro-American slavery, updated ed, 98n438
Directory of African American religious bodies, 2d ed, 97n1181
DISCovering multicultural America [CD-ROM], 97n323
Encyclopedia of African-American educ, 97n285
Encyclopedia of African-American heritage, 98n338
Facets African-American video gd, 95n1392
Financial aid for African Americans 1997-99, 99n292
In their footsteps, 95n506
Index to black pers 1997, 99n377
Kaleidoscope: a multicultural bklst for grades K-8, 96n1182
Narrative bibliog of the African American frontier, 97n405
Revealing docs: a gd to African American ms sources..., 95n414
Student's gd to African American genealogy, 97n359
Subject headings for African American materials, 96n626
U*X*L multicultural CD [CD-ROM], 98n333
Voices of the spirit, 96n402
What to name your African-American baby, 96n436

AFRO-AMERICANS—COLLECTIBLES
Black Americana price gd, 98n892

AFRO-AMERICANS—HISTORY
African American chronology, 95n408
African-American firsts, 95n409
Black firsts, 95n412
Black heritage sites, 97n330
Civil rights movement, 99n473
Encyclopedia of African-American culture & hist, 97n331
Historical dict of the civil rights movement, 98n565
Historical stats of black America, 96n403
History of black bus in America, 99n144
Pan-African chronology, 97n426
Pan-African chronology 2, 99n478
Timelines of African-American hist, 95n405

AFRO-AMERICANS IN AERONAUTICS
Invisible wings: an annot bibliog on blacks in aviation, 1916-93, 95n1788

AFRO-AMERICANS IN LITERATURE
Black writers, 2d ed, 95n1108
Lorraine Hansberry: a research & production sourcebk, 98n1136
Masterplots 2: African-American lit series, 95n1171
Modern African American writers, 95n1173
Multiethnic children's lit, 95n1136

Oxford companion to African American lit, 98n1129
Roots of Afrocentric thought, 99n985
Toni Morrison, 99n1058

AFRO-AMERICANS IN MOTION PICTURES
African American films through 1959, 99n1234
Frame by frame 2: a filmography of the African American image, 1978-94, 98n1295
Reel black talk: a sourcebk of 50 American filmmakers, 98n1278
That's enough folks: black images in animated cartoons, 99n1235

AFRO-AMERICAN SOLDIERS
On the trail of the buffalo soldier, 96n699

AFRO-AMERICAN THEATER
African American theatre dir, 1816-1960, 98n1328

AFRO-AMERICAN WOMEN
African-American woman: social & economic conditions, 95n901
American black women in the arts & social scis, 3d ed, 95n416
Black woman's gumbo ya-ya, 95n920
Epic lives, 95n909
Facts on File ency of black women in America, 98n343
Famous firsts of black women, 95n908
Notable black American women, bk.2, 97n34

AGED. *See also* **GERONTOLOGY; RETIREMENT COMMUNITIES; RETIREMENT INCOMES**
AGELINE on SilverPlatter: 1978-August 1994 [CD-ROM], 95n831
Aging sourcebk, 99n744
Aging well, 96n838
Alcoholism & aging, 96n897
Counseling older persons, 96n843
Demographic yrbk, special issue: population ageing, 95n834
Depression in the elderly, 98n761
Directory of population ageing research in Europe, 99n745
Encyclopedia of aging, 96n850
Encyclopedia of home care for the elderly, 96n1681
Folklore, culture, & aging, 98n762
Grants for the aging, 95n835
Graying of America: an ency of aging, health, mind, & behavior, 97n668
Graying of America: an ency of aging, health, mind, & behavior, 98n760
Group work with the elderly, 98n758
Injury prevention for the elderly, 96n844
International hndbk on servs for the elderly, 96n851
Literature & gerontology, 96n845
Live better/live longer resourcebk, 95n836
National gd to funding in aging, 4th ed, 96n849
Older Americans almanac, 95n839
Older Americans info dir, 95n837
Psychology of aging, 96n839
Research on religion & aging, 96n840
Resources for elders with disabilities, 3d ed, 97n672
Sexuality & the elderly, 98n798
Source bk on ageing, 99n746
Statistical hndbk on aging Americans, 1994 ed, 95n840

Statistical record of older Americans, 95n833
365 ways...retirees' resource gd for productive lifestyles, 97n669

AGED—EMPLOYMENT
Employment of the elderly, 96n842
Jobs for people over 50, 96n276

AGE DISTRIBUTION (DEMOGRAPHY)
Sex & age distribution of world populations: 1994 revision, 96n912

AGED—LONG TERM CARE
Long term care, 96n841

AGED—RELIGIOUS LIFE
Research on religion & aging, 96n840

AGED WOMEN
Women & aging, 96n936
Women & aging, 98n763

AGGRESSIVENESS (PSYCHOLOGY)
Aggression & conflict, 96n835
Peaceful peoples, 95n91

AGNOSTICS
2000 yrs of disbelief: famous people with the courage to doubt, 98n1347

AGRICULTURAL CHEMICALS
Agrochemicals desk ref: environmental data, 95n1510

AGRICULTURAL IMPLEMENTS
Encyclopedia of American farm implements & antiques, 98n1419

AGRICULTURAL INDUSTRIES
Prices of agricultural products & selected inputs for Europe & N America 1992/93, 96n1520

AGRICULTURAL PESTS
Agricultural entomology, 96n1625
Integrated pest mgmt glossary, 95n1513

AGRICULTURE
Agriculture in Britain & America 1660-1820, 95n1512
Agriculture, mining, & construction USA, 99n187
Atlas of American agriculture, 97n1246
Dictionary of agriculture, 96n1517
Dictionary of agriculture, 2d ed, 99n1329
Directory of Chinese agricultural & related orgs, 95n1511
Elsevier's dict of agriculture & food production, 96n1516
Encyclopedia of agricultural sci, 95n1507
History of agricultural sci & tech, 95n1508
Key gd to electronic resources: agriculture, 96n1518
Reference sources in sci, engineering, medicine, & agriculture, 95n1482
Who's who in sci in Europe, 9th ed, 97n1233
Women in agriculture, 97n1245
World databases in agriculture, 97n1247

AIDS (DISEASE)
AIDS: a multimedia sourcebk, 95n1675
AIDS, 1996 ed, 98n1559
AIDS crisis, 99n1468
AIDS dict, 99n1470
AIDS funding, 4th ed, 97n683
Guide to bks on AIDS, 96n1719
HIV/AIDS & HIV/AIDS-related terminology, 97n537
HIV/AIDS info for children, 98n1560
HIV/AIDS Internet info sources & resources, 99n1469
National dir of AIDS care 1994-95, 95n1676

AIR CONDITIONING
HVAC design data sourcebk, 95n1641

AIR-ENGINES
Jane's aero-engines, 97n1298

AIR FORCES
Naval Institute gd to world military aviation 1995, 96n697

AIRPLANES. *See also* **AERONAUTICS**
Brassey's world aircraft & systems dir 1996/97, 97n1438
Jane's all the world's aircraft 1996-97, 87th ed, 97n1440
Pockets: aircraft, 98n1645
World ency of aircraft manufacturers, 95n1789

AIRPLANES, MILITARY. *See also* **AERONAUTICS—MILITARY**
Jane's aircraft upgrades, 1996-97, 4th ed, 97n572
Jane's military aircraft image lib [CD-ROM], 98n623
Naval Institute gd to the ships & aircraft of the US Fleet, 16th ed, 98n628
Naval Institute gd to world military aviation 1995, 96n697
Vital gd to fighting aircraft of WW II, 97n580

AIR POLLUTION
Indoor pollution, 99n1565
Rapid gd to hazardous air pollutants, 99n1568

AIRPORTS
Jane's airports & handling agents, 1995-96, 96n1881
Thomas Cook intl air travel hndbk 1997, 98n407

AIR TRAFFIC CONTROL
Jane's air traffic control 1996-97, 3d ed, 97n1439

AIR TRAVEL. *See* **AERONAUTICS**
Thomas Cook intl air travel hndbk 1997, 98n407

AIR WARFARE. *See also* **MILITARY STUDIES**
Military ency of Russia & Eurasia, v.5, 96n146

ALABAMA
Alabama hist, 99n451

ALASKA
Alaska A to Z, 95n100
Exploring the Pacific states through lit, 95n1121
Milepost: trip planner for Ala. & Western Canada, 49th ed, 98n406

ALBANIA
Albania, rev ed, 99n118
Historical dict of Albania, 97n113

ALBANIAN LANGUAGE
Albanian etymological dict, 99n921

ALBENIZ, ISAAC
Isaac Albeniz, 99n1129

ALBERTA
Amphibians & reptiles of Alta., 95n1596

ALCOHOLIC BEVERAGES
Alcohol in the British Isles from Roman times to 1996, 97n441

ALCOHOLISM
Alcoholism & aging, 96n897

ALGAE
Illustrated glossary of protoctista, 95n1536

ALGERIA
Algeria, rev ed, 97n93
Historical dict of Algeria, 2d ed, 96n114

ALL AMERICAN GIRLS PROFESSIONAL BASEBALL LEAGUE
Women of the All-American Girls Professional Baseball League, 98n734

ALLEGORY
Encyclopedia of allegorical lit, 97n890

ALLERGY
Allergies A-Z, 95n1677

ALLOYS
Alloy finder [CD-ROM], 96n1660
ASM ready ref properties & units for engineering alloys, 99n1408
Fatigue data bk, 97n1308
Metals & alloys in unified numbering system, 6th ed, 95n1635
Worldwide gd to equivalent nonferrous metals & alloys, 3d ed, 97n1309

ALL TERRAIN CYCLING
Mountain bikers almanac, 1996, 96n815

ALLUSIONS
Dictionary of histl allusions & eponyms, 99n40

ALMANACS
A&E entertainment almanac, 1997, 98n1264
African American almanac, 98n346
Canadian almanac & dir 1997, 97n3
Canadian almanac & dir 1999, 152d ed, 99n2
Canadian sourcebk, 1997, 32d ed, 97n4
Canadian sourcebk, 1998, 33d ed, 99n3
Chase's calendar of events 1997, 40th ed, 97n5
Chase's calendar of events 1998, 99n4

Daily celebrity almanac, 7th ed, 95n4
Information please almanac, atlas, & yrbk, 1996, 49th ed, 97n6
Irish almanac & yrbk of facts 1997, 98n134
KGB world factbk, v.4, no.1 [CD-ROM], 95n5
Literary almanac, 98n1071
New view almanac, 97n7
New York Times almanac 1998, 98n2
Old farmer's almanac 1995, 96n4
Pre-1900 annuals, 95n139
Universal almanac 1995, 96n5
Whitaker's almanack 1995, 95n9
Whitaker's almanack 1996, 128th ed, 96n6
Whitaker's almanack 1999, 131st ed, 99n5
Whitaker's almanack world heads of govt 1998, 99n650
Whitaker's almanack world heads of state 1998, 99n651
Women's almanac, 98n827
World almanac & bk of facts 1994, 95n6
World almanac & bk of facts 1994 [CD-ROM], 95n7
World almanac & bk of facts 1996, 96n7
World almanac & bk of facts 1997, 98n3
World almanac for kids 1998, 98n4
World almanac for kids 1999, 99n6
World almanac of the USA, rev ed, 99n89
World factbk [CD-ROM], 95n8
World gd 1997/98, 10th ed, 98n97

ALPHABET
Key of it all, bk.1, 95n789

ALPINE FLORA
Alpines, 96n1590
Cushion plants for the rock garden, 97n1257

ALTERNATIVE MEDICINE
Alternative advisor: the complete gd to natural therapies & alternative treatments, 98n1544
Alternative healing, 95n1671
Alternative health & medicine ency, 96n1716
Alternative health & medicine ency, 2d ed, 99n1457
Alternative medicine: the definitive gd, 95n1669
Alternative medicine resource gd, 98n1547
Aromatherapy oils, 98n1551
Complete bk of symptoms & treatments, 99n1456
Complete ency of natural healing, 99n1459
Complete family gd to natural home remedies, 98n1545
Complete gd to homeopathy, 97n1347
Complete home healer, 95n1674
Complete home health advisor, 97n1344
Directory of schools for alternative & complementary health care, 99n1448
Encyclopedia of alternative medicine, 97n1345
Encyclopedia of bodywork, 97n1350
Encyclopedia of healing therapies, 98n1552
Encyclopedia of nutritional suppls, 97n1349
Green pharmacy, 98n1546
Health & illness, 98n1509
Herbal home remedy bk, 99n1461
Illustrated ency of healing remedies, 99n1460
Information sourcebk of herbal medicine, 96n1714
Medical advisor, 97n1348
Naturopathic hndbk of herbal formulas, 3d ed, 96n1717
Nerys Purchon's hndbk of natural healing, 99n1458
Woman's ency of natural healing, 98n1550

ALTERNATIVE MEDICINE—VOCATIONAL GUIDANCE
Planning your career in alternative medicine, 98n1549

ALTERNATIVE PRESS INDEX
Annotations: a dir of pers listed in the Alternative Press Index, 1996 ed, 97n63

ALUMINUM
Aluminum & aluminum alloys, 95n1622

AMATEUR RADIO STATIONS
Amateur radio ency, 95n960
Radio amateur callbk, 1995, 73d ed, 96n990

AMBASSADORS
International Washington almanac, 1994, 95n760
Notable US Ambassadors Since 1775, 98n655

AMERICANA
Black Americana price gd, 98n892
Country Americana price gd, 98n894
New York Public Lib bk of popular Americana, 95n1334
Warman's Americana & collectibles, 99n839

AMERICAN ASSOCIATION (BASEBALL LEAGUE)
American assn: yr-by-yr stats for the baseball minor league, 1902-52, 98n738

AMERICAN ASSOCIATION OF LAW LIBRARIES
AALL ref bk, 96n593

AMERICAN DEPOSITORY RECEIPTS
International investing with ADRs, 95n222

AMERICAN DRAMA
American drama criticism: suppl 4 to the 2d ed, 97n1146
American playwrights, 1880-1945, 96n1202
American theatre, 97n1150
American theatre: a chronicle of comedy & drama, 1869-1914, 95n1418
Cambridge hist of American theatre, v.1, 99n1247
Concordance to the complete poems & plays of T. S. Eliot, 97n971
Contemporary American dramatists, 95n1176
Contemporary women dramatists, 95n1155
Tennessee Williams, 99n1057
Ultimate scene & monologue sourcebk, 95n1407
United States theatre: a bibliog from the beginning to 1990, 95n1409
Women playwrights of diversity, 98n1106

AMERICAN FICTION
American novelists since WWII, 3d series, 96n1204
American novelists since WWII, 4th series, 96n1203
American novelists since WWII, 5th series, 98n1128
Contemporary Jewish-American novelists, 98n1125

Contemporary novel, 2d ed, 98n1108
Contemporary Southern men fiction writers, 99n1039
Contemporary Southern women fiction writers, 95n1181
Eighteenth-Century Anglo-American women novelists, 98n1111
Facts on File bibliog of American fiction through 1865, 95n1177
Hollywood novel, 96n1411
Immigrant experience in American fiction, 96n1206
Major characters in American fiction, 95n1182
Masterplots 2: American fiction series suppl, 95n1178
Modern classic writers, 95n1180
Modern women writers, 95n1174
Native American in long fiction, 97n958
New England in fiction 1787-1990, 95n1183
Writers of multicultural fiction for YAs, 97n942

AMERICAN FILM INDEX
American film personnel & co credits, 1908-20, 97n1142

AMERICANISMS
America in so many words, 98n1000
American Heritage dict of idioms, 98n1006
Black talk, 95n413
Cambridge thesaurus of American English, 95n1065
Cowboy dict, 95n1041
Happy trails: a dict of W expressions, 95n1043
Idiom savant: slang as it is slung, 98n1014
New York Public Lib bk of popular Americana, 95n1334
NTC's dict of commonplace words in real-life contexts, 99n915
NTC's dict of folksy, regional, & rural sayings, 97n837
NTC's dict of the USA, 99n1190
NTC's thematic dict of American idioms, 99n905
Oxford dict & thesaurus, American ed, 98n994
Random House histl dict of American slang, v.1, 95n1061
Smoky Mountain voices: a lexicon of S Appalachian speech, 95n1042
Speaking freely, 98n1002
Western lore & lang, 97n841
Yankee talk: a dict of New England expressions, 97n835

AMERICAN JEWISH HISTORICAL SOCIETY
Index to American Jewish Histl Quarterly/American Jewish Hist: vs.51-80, 97n347
Index to pubns of the American Jewish Histl Society, vs.21-50, 95n449

AMERICAN LITERATURE
American diversity, American identity, 96n1198
American expatriate writers, 98n1127
American nature writers, 97n965
American novel explication 1991-95, 99n1040
American women writers, v.5, 95n1168
American writers, 99n1043
American writers, retrospective suppl 1, 99n1045
American writers, suppl 4, 97n961
Cambridge gd to lit in English, 95n1103
Cambridge pa gd to lit in English, 97n894
Contemporary popular writers, 98n1058
Encyclopedia of frontier lit, 98n1130
Encyclopedia of transcendentalism, 97n964
First eds, 95n972
Identities & issues in lit, 98n1070
James A. Michener: a bibliog, 97n973
Jessamyn West: a descriptive & annot bibliog, 99n1056
Literary criticism index, 2d ed, 95n1114
Literary index to American mags, 1850-1900, 97n960
Magill's literary annual 1994, 95n1172
Masterpieces of American lit, 95n1170
Nineteenth-Century American women writers, 98n1126
One hundred yrs of American women writing, 1848-1948, 98n1124
Oxford companion to American lit, 6th ed, 97n966
Oxford companion to women's writing in the US, 96n1200
Reference gd to American lit, 3d ed, 95n1169

AMERICAN LITERATURE—19TH CENTURY—DICTIONARIES
Literally entitled, 97n891

AMERICAN LITERATURE—20TH CENTURY
Beat generation, 99n1042

AMERICAN LITERATURE—20TH CENTURY—DICTIONARIES
Literally entitled, 97n891

AMERICAN LITERATURE—AFRO-AMERICAN AUTHORS. *See also* **AFRO-AMERICANS IN LITERATURE**
Dictionary catalog of the collection of African American lit in the Mildred F. Sawyer Lib of Suffolk Univ, 98n340
French critical reception of African-American lit from the beginnings to 1970, 96n1197
Modern black writers: suppl, 96n1157
Oxford companion to African American lit, 98n1129

AMERICAN LITERATURE—INDIAN AUTHORS
Native N American lit, 96n1259

AMERICAN LITERATURE—RESEARCH
Handbook of literary research, 2d ed, 96n1142

AMERICAN LITERATURE—SOUTHERN STATES
Contemporary poets, dramatists, essayists, & novelists of the South, 96n1199
Contemporary Southern men fiction writers, 99n1039
Contemporary Southern women fiction writers, 95n1181
Encyclopedia of southern lit, 99n1047

AMERICAN LITERATURE—WEST (US)
Bibliographical gd to the study of Western American lit, 2d ed, 97n959
Western American novelists, 96n1205

AMERICAN PERIODICALS
Trade, industrial, & professional pers of the US, 95n215

AMERICAN POETRY
American poets since WWII, 4th series, 98n1141
American poets since WWII, 5th series, 98n1140
Bibliographic gd to jazz poetry, 99n1099
Concordance to the complete poems & plays of T. S. Eliot, 97n971
Directory of American poetry bks, 95n1198
Directory of American poets & fiction writers, 1995-96 ed, 97n749
Feminist criticism of American women poets, 96n1222
Guide to the secular poetry of T. S. Eliot, 97n970
Oxford companion to 20th-century poetry in English, 95n1249
Poets: American & British, 99n1110
Romantic poetry by women: a bibliog, 1770-1835, 95n1247

AMERICAN PROSE LITERATURE
Voices of multicultural America, 97n967

AMERICAN SIGN LANGUAGE
American Sign Lang concise dict, rev ed, 96n1132
American Sign Lang dict, rev ed, 96n1133
American Sign Lang dict on CD-ROM [CD-ROM], 96n1130
American Sign Lang, unabridged ed, 99n910
Comprehensive ref manual for signers & interpreters, 4th ed, 96n1131
Essential ASL, 97n871
NTC's multilingual dict of American Sign Lang, 97n870
Random House Webster's American Sign Lang dict, rev ed, 99n909

AMERICAN STOCK EXCHANGE
American stock exchange, 96n211
American stock exchange 1994 fact bk, 95n218

AMERICAN STUDENTS—FOREIGN COUNTRIES
Youth exchanges, 96n371

AMERICAN TURNERS
Research gd to the Turner movement in the US, 97n333

AMERICAN WEST
New ency of the American west, 99n463

AMERICA ONLINE
Official America online yellow pages, 99n53

AMERICORPS
National serv & AmeriCorps, 98n800

AMMUNITION
Jane's ammunition hndbk 1996-97, 5th ed, 98n633

AMPHIBIANS
Amphibians & reptiles of Alta., 95n1596
Amphibians & reptiles of Trinidad & Tobago, 98n1474
Encyclopedia of reptiles & amphibians, 2d ed, 99n1395
Reptile & amphibian keeper's dict, 95n1597
Reptile & amphibian problem solver, 98n1473

AMSTERDAM (NETHERLANDS)
Amsterdam, 96n476
Amsterdam, 99n135

AMUSEMENT PARKS
Amusement parks, 2d ed, 95n796

ANAGRAMS
Scrambled word & anagram finder, 96n1072

ANARCHISTS
Rosa Luxemburg & Emma Goldman: a bibliog, 98n637

ANATOMY, HUMAN
Atlas of anatomy, English ed, 98n1499
Atlas of the human body, 96n1694
Johns Hopkins atlas of human functional anatomy, 99n1415
Russian-English collocational dict of the human body, 97n867
Science on file [CD-ROM], 98n1415
Virtual body [CD-ROM], 97n1312
Visual dict of the skeleton, 96n1683

ANDALUSI ARABIC LANGUAGE—DICTIONARIES—ENGLISH
Dictionary of Andalusi Arabic, 99n922

ANDERSON, MAXWELL
Maxwell Anderson on the European stage 1929-92, 97n1147

ANDERSON, SHERWOOD
Reader's gd to the short stories of Sherwood Anderson, 95n1184

ANDORRA
Andorra, 95n148

ANGELS
Angels A to Z, 97n1176
Encyclopedia of angels, 98n1355
Ghosts & angels in Hollywood films, 95n1386

ANGIOSPERMS
Flowering plants of the world, updated ed, 95n1542
Guide to flowering plant families, 96n1580

ANIMAL CULTURE
Literature of animal sci & health, 95n1533

ANIMAL EXPERIMENTATION
Animal rights, 96n1435
Animal rights movement in the US, 1975-90, 96n1424

ANIMAL HEALTH
Animal health yrbk 1993, 96n1553

ANIMAL RIGHTS
Animal rights, 96n1435
Animal rights, 2d ed, 99n1369
Animal rights movement in the US, 1975-90, 96n1424
Endangered species, 99n1370
Federal wildlife laws hndbk with related laws, 99n587

ANIMALS. See also MAMMALS
Amazing animals of the world, 96n1603

Facts on File wildlife atlas, rev ed, 99n1295
Field gd to common animal poisons, 97n1262
International ency of horse breeds, 97n1291
Kingfisher 1st ency of animals, 96n1608
My 1st bk of animals from A to Z, 95n1563
National gd to funding for the environment & animal welfare, 2d ed, 96n878
Speaking of animals, 96n1074
Species info lib [CD-ROM], 96n1606
Wildlife of the world, 95n1561
World alive [CD-ROM], 96n1609

ANIMALS IN THE PERFORMING ARTS
Animals on screen & radio, 96n1366

ANIMATED FILMS
Animated film collector's gd, 99n1222
Complete anime gd, 98n1307
Film cartoons: a gd to 20th century American animated features & shorts, 99n1231
Television cartoon shows, 96n1375
That's enough folks: black images in animated cartoons, 99n1235

ANKLE
Foot & ankle sourcebk, 97n1340

ANNUALS (PLANTS)
Eyewitness garden hndbk: annuals & biennials, 98n1436
Favorite annuals, 96n1568

ANONYMS & PSEUDONYMS
Dictionary of literary pseudonyms in the English lang, 96n1229
Dictionary of pseudonyms, 99n408
20,000 Spanish American pseudonyms, 98n1182

ANTARCTIC REGIONS
Arctic & Antarctic regions [CD-ROM], 96n127

ANTHEMS
Musical resources for the rev common lectionary, 95n1312

ANTHOLOGIES
Film anthologies index, 95n1401

ANTHONY, SUSAN B.
Susan B. Anthony: a biogl companion, 99n800

ANTHROPOLOGY. *See also* **ARCHAEOLOGY**
Anthropological lit on disc [CD-ROM], 95n391
Anthropological lit on disc [CD-ROM], 98n317
Anthropology bibliog on disc [CD-ROM], 99n362
Anthropology of religion, 98n1359
Atlas of threatened cultures, 98n318
Bibliographic gd to anthropology & archaeology 1995, 98n319
Companion ency of anthropology, 95n392
Encyclopedia of cultural anthropology, 97n316
Encyclopedia of social & cultural anthropology, 97n317
Encyclopedia of world cultures, v.8: Middle America & the Caribbean, 97n318

Encyclopedia of world cultures, v.9: Africa & the Middle East, 97n319
Encyclopedia of world cultures, v.10: indexes, 97n320
Fieldwork in the lib, 95n393
History of physical anthropology, 98n320

ANTI-COMMUNIST MOVEMENTS
Encyclopedia of the McCarthy era, 97n591

ANTILLES, LESSER
Beinecke Lesser Antilles collection at Hamilton College, 95n171
Martinique, 96n171

ANTI-NAZI MOVEMENT—GERMANY
Encyclopedia of German resistance to the Nazi movement, 98n470

ANTIQUARIAN BOOKSELLERS
AB Bookman's yrbk, 1993-94, 95n970
Antiquarian, specialty, & used bk sellers 1997-98, 2d ed, 98n597
Used bk lover's gd to the Midwest, 96n1007

ANTIQUE & CLASSIC CARS
Standard gd to cars & prices, 99n1577

ANTIQUES
Antique Trader Books antiques & collectibles price gd, 1999 ed, 99n840
Bulfinch illus ency of antiques, 95n968
Collectors value gd to Oriental decorative arts, 98n890
Maloney's antiques & collectibles resource dir, 2d ed, 95n969
Maloney's antiques & collectibles resource dir, 99n841
Miller's intl antiques price gd 1997, 18th ed, 98n903
Miller's intl antiques price gd 1999, 99n842
Schroeder's antiques price gd, 15th ed, 98n905
Wallace-Homestead price gd to American country antiques, 98n904
Warman's antiques & collectibles price gd, 29th ed, 96n1000

ANTISEMITISM
"Jewish question" in German-speaking countries, 1848-1914, 96n425

ANTS
Identification gd to the ant genera of the world, 95n1590

APARTHEID
Atlas of apartheid, 95n395
South Africa as apartheid ends: an annot bibliog..., 95n124

APHORISMS
Treasury of Polish aphorisms, 98n1253

APOCALYPTICISM
Encyclopedia of apocalypticism, 99n1266

APOCALYTIC LITERATURE
Encyclopedia of apocalyptic lit, 97n893

APOLOGETICS—CHRISTIAN
Dictionary of fundamental theology, 95n1470

APPALACHIAN REGION
Field gd to the trees & shrubs of the S Appalachians, 95n1553
Smoky Mountain voices: a lexicon of S Appalachian speech, 95n1042

APPLIED SCIENCE
Magill's survey of sci, v.7, 99n1315

APPLIQUE
Encyclopedia of applique, 95n979

AQUARIUM FISHES. *See also* **FISHES**
Aquarium fish, 95n1586
Aquarium fish of the world, 95n1589

AQUARIUMS, PUBLIC
Aquariums of N America, 96n1621

AQUEDUCTS
Guide to the aqueducts of ancient Rome, 96n1046

AQUINAS, SAINT THOMAS
Thomas Aquinas: intl bibliog 1977-90, 95n1437

ARAB COUNTRIES
Dictionary of modern Arab hist, 99n508
Major cos of the Arab world 1996/97, 20th ed, 97n233
Militarism in Arab society, 98n609
Who's who in the Arab world 1995-96, 12th ed, 96n161

ARABIC LANGUAGE—DICTIONARIES—ENGLISH
Dictionary of Andalusi Arabic, 99n922
English-Arabic standard dict, 95n1070

ARAB-ISRAELI CONFLICT
Origins & dvlpmt of the Arab-Israeli conflict, 99n699

ARAMAIC LANGUAGE
Hebrew & Aramaic lexicon of the O.T., v.1, 96n1455
Hebrew & Aramaic lexicon of the O.T., v.2, 97n1198

ARBITRATION, INDUSTRIAL
Labor arbitration, 96n255

ARBITRATION, INTERNATIONAL
Historical dict of intl tribunals, 96n610

ARBUCKLE, ROSCOE
Roscoe "Fatty" Arbuckle: a bio-bibliog, 95n1354

ARCHAEOLOGY
Archaeology of prehistoric Native America, 99n443
Archaeology of the Mississippian culture, 97n398
Atlas of archaeology, 99n444
Bibliographic gd to anthropology & archaeology 1995, 98n319
Bibliography of Syrian archaeological sites to 1980, 96n484
Bookman's gd to archaeology, 96n1005
British & Irish archaeology, 95n521
Collins dict of archaeology, 95n520
Encyclopedia of the hist of classical archaeology, 97n397
Encyclopedia of underwater & maritime archaeology, 99n446
High places in cyberspace, 2d ed, 99n1269
Oxford companion to archaeology, 98n428
Vestiges of mortality & remembrance, 95n519

ARCHAEOLOGY IN MOTION PICTURES
Treasure hard to attain: images of archaeology in popular film, 98n1290

ARCHETYPE (PSYCHOLOGY)
Encyclopedia of archetypal symbolism, v.1, 98n1351
Encyclopedia of archetypal symbolism, v.2: the body, 98n1352

ARCHITECTS
Contemporary architects, 3d ed, 96n1043
Makers of 20th century modern architecture, 98n972
Twentieth-Century artists on art, 2d ed, 98n969
Willem Marinus Dudok, a Dutch modernist, 98n974

ARCHITECTURE
AIA gd to the architecture of Washington, DC, 3d ed, 96n1049
America preserved, 96n1047
American house designs: an index to popular & trade pers, 1850-1915, 96n1050
Architecture, 98n976
Architecture & ornament, 99n879
Architecture on screen, 95n1012
Architecture sourcebk, 98n977
Art & architecture thesaurus, 2d ed, 95n650
Avery index to architectural pers, 13th suppl, 95n1014
Avery index to architectural pers at Columbia Univ [CD-ROM], 95n1013
Avery index to architectural pers at Columbia Univ [CD-ROM], 98n970
Avery's choice: 5 centuries of great architectural bks, 98n971
Bibliographic gd to art & architecture 1993, 95n992
Bibliographic gd to art & architecture 1996, 98n941
Buildings of the District of Columbia, 95n1017
Dictionary of bldg preservation, 97n801
Dictionary of Islamic architecture, 97n803
Dictionary of Scottish art & architecture, 96n1025
Encyclopaedic dict in the 18th century, v.1, 99n813
Encyclopaedic dict in the 18th century, v.2, 99n814
Encyclopaedic dict in the 18th century, v.3, 99n815
Encyclopaedic dict in the 18th century, v.4, 99n816
Encyclopaedic dict in the 18th century, v.5, 99n817
Encyclopedia of American architecture, 2d ed, 96n1045
Illustrated dict of architecture, 99n880
Illustrated glossary of early S architecture & landscape, 95n1016
Information sources in architecture & construction, 2d ed, 97n1299
Masterworks of man & nature, 2d ed, 96n458
Oxford companion to Christian art & architecture, 98n950
Standard hndbk of architectural engineering, 99n881
Time-saver standards for architectural design data, 7th ed, 99n882

ARCHITECTURE—20TH CENTURY
Dutch modernism, 97n802
Icons of architecture, 99n877

ARCHITECTURE, DOMESTIC
American house designs: an index to popular & trade pers, 1850-1915, 96n1050
Visual dict of American domestic architecture, 96n1044

ARCHITECTURE, DUTCH
Dutch modernism, 97n802

ARCHITECTURE IN LITERATURE
Art & architecture in the poetry of Robert Browning, appendix A, 98n1154

ARCHIVES
ArchivesUSA [CD-ROM], 98n430
Articles describing archives & ms collections in the US, 98n577
British archives, 3d ed, 97n440
Directory of literary societies & author collections, 95n1106
Guide to Central American collections in the US, 96n152
Guide to collections on Paraguay in the US, 96n551
Guide to info resources in ethnic museum, lib, & archive collections in the US, 97n522
Guide to mss & docs in the British Isles relating to Africa, v.1, 95n111
Guides to archives & ms collections in the US, 95n523
Landmark docs in American hist [CD-ROM], 96n498
Making of modern Africa: a gd to archives, 96n530
Mapping the territory, 96n658
Revealing docs: a gd to African American ms sources..., 95n414
Scholars' gd to Washington, DC, for Russian, Central Eurasian, & Baltic studies, 95n164
Smithsonian on disc, 4th ed [CD-ROM], 99n613
Trans-Mississippi west 1804-1912, pt.1, 95n545
World of learning 1999, 49th ed, 99n295
Writings on African archives, 97n92

ARCHIVISTS
International biog dir of natl archivists, documentalists, & librarians, 98n574

ARCTIC REGIONS
Arctic & Antarctic regions [CD-ROM], 96n127
Arctic exploration & dvlpmt, c.500 B.C. to 1915, 95n495

AREA STUDIES
Current world leaders almanac, v.38, no.3, June 1995, 96n104
International histl stats: Africa, Asia, & Oceania, 1750-1988, 96n917
Statesman's yr-bk, 132d ed, 96n102

ARENDT, HANNAH
Hannah Arendt 2: a bibliog, 98n636

ARGENTINA
Argentina bus, 97n245
Argentina co hndbk, 97n246

ARGENTINE FICTION
Argentine novel, 98n1168

ARISTOTLE
Aristotle's Metaphysics: annot bibliog of the 20th-century lit, 99n1250

ARIZONA
Hopi pottery symbols, 96n1015

ARKANSAS
Arkansas hist, 96n490

ARMENIA
Armenia, 95n149
Armenian folklore bibliog, 96n1340
Armenian ref bks, 95n150
Armenians & Iran, 2d ed, 95n151

ARMENIAN AMERICANS
Armenian American almanac, 96n391

ARMENIAN LANGUAGE—DICTIONARIES—ENGLISH
Armenian (Eastern)-English dict, 97n844

ARMORED VEHICLES, MILITARY. *See also* TANKS; WEAPONS
Armored forces: hist & sourcebk, 96n702
Jane's tank & combat vehicle recognition gd, 97n576

ARMS CONTROL
SIPRI yrbk 1993, 95n766

ARNOLD, EDDY—DISCOGRAPHY
Eddy Arnold discography, 1944-96, 98n1231

ARNOLD, MALCOLM
Malcolm Arnold, 99n1130

ARNOLD, MATTHEW
Essential Matthew Arnold, 95n1210

AROMATHERAPY
Aromatherapy oils, 98n1551

ART
Art: a world hist, 99n874
Art & architecture thesaurus, 2d ed, 95n650
Art & design scholarships, 96n1036
Art bus ency, 95n1004
Art bus ency, 96n1039
Art diary 97/98, 98n953
Art for hist's sake, 95n1008
Art index, Nov 1995 to Oct 1996, 98n968
Art mktg sourcebk for the fine artist, 3d ed, 99n872
Art of the ancient Mediterranean world, 98n957
Art on screen on CD-ROM [CD-ROM], 96n1037
Artist's & graphic designers market, 1998, 99n875
Artist's resource hndbk, 95n1007
Atlas of Western art hist, 95n990

BHA: bibliog of the hist of art: subject headings/English, 97n790
BHA: bibliog of the hist of art 1996 [CD-ROM], 97n791
Bibliographic gd to art & architecture 1993, 95n992
Bibliographic gd to art & architecture 1996, 98n941
Bibliography of sources in Christianity & the arts, 97n1206
Book of art, rev ed, 96n1029
Career opportunities in art, rev ed, 96n1041
Crafts supply source bk, 4th ed, 98n931
Culture vulture, 95n928
Encyclopedia of Australian art, rev ed, 96n1032
European art since 1850, 98n958
European art to 1850, 98n959
Far Eastern art, 98n960
History of art for young people, 5th ed, 98n965
Italian paintings before 1600 in the Art Inst of Chicago, 95n1020
Library cat of the Metropolitan Museum of Art. 5th suppl, 1990-92, 2d ed, 95n1015
Lives & works in the arts from the renaissance to the 20th century, 98n847
Medieval iconography, 99n810
National gd to funding in arts & culture, 3d ed, 96n961
New Deal fine arts projects, 95n993
Post-Biblical saints art index, 95n1010
Reader's adviser on CD-ROM [CD-ROM], 97n11
Sixth bi-annual natl dir of arts internships, 1995/96, 96n1034

ART, AMERICAN
Dictionary of 20th century culture: American culture after WWII, 95n927
National museum of American art [CD-ROM], 98n966
North American art since 1900, 98n962
North American art to 1900, 98n963
Who's who in American art 1995-96, 21st ed, 96n1027

ART, BAROQUE
Baroque art, 97n798

ART—BIBLIOGRAPHY
Art bks, 2d ed, 98n940

ART, BLACK
African art, 98n956
African ethnonyms, 97n315
St. James gd to black artists, 98n945

ART, CHINESE
Art & artists of 20th-century China, 98n967

ART—CHRONOLOGY
Timelines of the arts & lit, 95n925
Wilson chronology of the arts, 99n818

ART—DICTIONARIES
Dictionary of art, 98n947
Dictionary of symbols in western art, 96n1030
Dictionary of the arts, 95n926
Illustrated dict of symbols in E & W art, 96n1031
Language of art from A to Z, rev ed, 99n870

ART—DIRECTORIES
American art dir 1997-98, 56th ed, 99n871
International dir of arts, 99n811
Peterson's professional degree programs in the visual & performing arts 1995, 96n962
Peterson's professional degree programs in the visual & performing arts, 99n1197
Visual resources dir, 96n378

ART, DUTCH
Dutch art, 98n949

ART, FRENCH
Four French symbolists, 97n806

ARTHURIAN ROMANCES
Arthurian hndbk, 2d ed, 99n1066

ARTIFICIAL INTELLIGENCE
McGraw-Hill illus ency of robotics & artificial intelligence, 96n1753

ARTILLERY. *See also* WEAPONS
Field artillery, 96n703
Jane's armour & artillery 1995-96, 16th ed, 97n575
Standard gd to US WW II tanks & artillery, 95n703

ART—INFORMATION SERVICES
Key gd to electronic resources: art & art hist, 98n942

ART IN LITERATURE
Art & architecture in the poetry of Robert Browning, appendix A, 98n1154
Fools & jesters in lit, art, & hist, 99n951

ARTIST COLONIES
American art colonies, 1850-1930, 97n800
Artists & writers colonies, 97n745
Artists communities, 98n954

ARTISTS
American artists of Italian heritage, 1776-1945, 95n1002
American bk & mag illustrators to 1920, v.188, 99n884
Art bks, 2d ed, 98n940
Artists: from Michelangelo to Maya Lin, 96n1024
Artist's resource hndbk, 96n1040
Artist's resource hndbk, 98n964
Authors & artists for YAs, v.14, 96n1171
Biographical dict of artists, rev ed, 96n1022
Biographical dict of Saskatchewan artists: [v.2]: men artists, 96n1023
Contemporary artists, 4th ed, 97n795
Contemporary Greek artists, 95n1000
Dictionary of 19th century British bk illustrators & caricaturists, rev ed, 98n944
Dictionary of contemporary American artists, 6th ed, 95n998
Dictionary of Russian & Soviet artists 1420-1970, 95n1001
Dictionary of Scottish art & architecture, 96n1025
Dictionary of the avant-gardes, 95n1005
Dictionary of women artists, 98n948

Encyclopedia of Australian art, rev ed, 96n1032
Encyclopedia of living artists, 7th ed, 95n999
Encyclopedia of women artists of the American west, 99n869
Georges Braque: a bio-bibliog, 95n996
Great artists, 99n863
Printed stuff: prints, posters, & ephemera by Claes Oldenburg, 99n867
Remarkable lives of 100 women artists, 96n939
Twentieth-Century artists on art, 2d ed, 98n969
Union list of artist names, 95n995
Who's who in American art 1997-98, 99n866
Who's who in art, 26th ed, 95n1003

ARTISTS' MARKS
Old masters, 98n980

ARTISTS' MATERIALS
ArtNetwork yellow pages, 96n1033

ART, LATIN AMERICAN
Contemporary Latin American artists, 98n955
Latin American women artists, 97n793
Mexican, Central, & S American art, 98n961

ART—MARKETING
Art mktg sourcebk for the fine artist, 2d ed, 96n1035
Artist's & graphic designer's market, 1995, 96n1038

ART, MEDIEVAL
Medieval art, 97n799

ART, MODERN
Abstract expressionist women painters, 97n808
American art colonies, 1850-1930, 97n800
Annual bibliog of modern art, 1995, 98n939
Art & artists of 20th-century China, 98n967
ARTbibliographies modern on disc, fall 1993 [CD-ROM], 95n991
Art nouveau, 99n862
Contemporary artists, 4th ed, 97n795
Contemporary Latin American artists, 98n955
Dictionary of contemporary American artists, 6th ed, 95n998
Encyclopedia of living artists, 7th ed, 95n999
Les Fauves: a sourcebk, 95n1019
Realization & suppression of the Situationist Intl, 97n792

ART MUSEUMS
American art dir 1997-98, 56th ed, 99n871
International dir of arts 1993/94, 95n1006
International dir of arts, 99n811
National Gallery complete illus catalogue, 97n796
Papercutting: an intl bibliog & selected gd to US collections, 95n981
Record of the Carnegie Institutes intl exhibitions 1896-1996, 99n868
Traveler's gd to art museum exhibitions, 10th ed, 99n873

ART NOUVEAU
Art nouveau, 99n862

ART OBJECTS
Faberge & his works, 95n994

ART & RELIGION
Encyclopedia of archetypal symbolism, v.1, 98n1351
Encyclopedia of archetypal symbolism, v.2: the body, 98n1352
Encyclopedia of women in religious art, 97n797

ART, SPANISH
Spanish artists from the 4th to the 20th century, 98n952

ART—TERMINOLOGY
Artwords: a glossary of contemporary art theory, 98n951

ARUBA
Netherlands Antilles & Aruba, 95n167

ASCENSION ISLAND
St. Helena, Ascension, & Tristan da Cunha, 98n146

ASIA
Africa, Asia, & S America since 1800, 96n555
Asia, 2d ed, 99n240
Asia-Pacific in figures, 10th ed, 98n811
Asian higher educ, 98n295
Asian hist on file, 96n533
Cambridge gd to Asian theatre, 95n1414
China, 7th ed, 99n110
Compendium of social stats & indicators, 4th issue, 99n787
Cultural atlas of China, rev ed, 99n106
Cultural atlas of India, 98n113
Electric power in Asia & the Pacific, 1991 & 1992, 97n1420
European dir of SE Asian studies, 99n319
Facts on File Asian pol almanac, 95n747
India & S Asia, 3d ed, 99n104
International dict of historic places, v.5, 97n469
International histl stats: Africa, Asia, & Oceania, 1750-1988, 96n917
Japan & the Pacific Rim, 4th ed, 99n102
Peoples of the world: Asians & Pacific Islanders, 95n127
Source bk on ageing, 99n746
Statistical yrbk for Asia & the Pacific 1996, 98n815
Supplement to The Modern Ency of Russian, Soviet, & Eurasian Hist, v.1, 97n476
World investment dir 1996, v.6: West Asia, 98n207
Year bk of the Muslim world 1996, 97n81

ASIA—BIBLIOGRAPHY
Bibliographies on SE Asia, 99n103
Doctoral dissertations on China & on inner Asia, 1976-90, 99n15

ASIA—BUSINESS
Asia-Pacific petroleum dir 1998, 14th ed, 99n195
Asia Pacific securities hndbk 1993, 95n259
Asian & Australasian cos, 95n240
Asian markets, 4th ed, 97n234
Consumer Asia 1998, 99n215

Directory of trade & investment related orgs of developing countries & areas in Asia & the Pacific, 7th ed, 97n235
Economic & social survey of Asia & the Pacific 1995, 96n128
Major cos of the Far East & Australasia 1995/96, 96n245
Prices & financial stats in the ESCWA region, 97n192
Statistical indicators for Asia & the Pacific, v.23, 95n897
Statistical indicators for Asia & the Pacific, v.27, no.2, June 1997, 99n788
US & Asia statl hndbk, 1997-98 ed, 99n219
Statistical yrbk for Asia & the Pacific 1996, 98n815
World investment dir 1996, v.6: West Asia, 98n207

ASIA—ECONOMIC CONDITIONS
Consumer Asia 1995 [2d ed], 96n242

ASIA—FOREIGN RELATIONS
Asian states' relations with the Middle East & N Africa, 95n763

ASIAN AMERICANS
Asian American almanac, 96n392
Asian American biog, 96n393
Asian American chronology, 97n326
Asian American ency, 96n394
Asian American genealogical sourcebk, 96n430
Asian American woman, 99n795
Asian Americans: social, economic, & pol aspects, 97n327
DISCovering multicultural America [CD-ROM], 97n323
Financial aid for Asian Americans 1997-99, 99n293
Guide to children's bks about Asian Americans, 96n1181
Kaleidoscope: a multicultural bklst for grades K-8, 96n1182
Korean Americans, 99n374
Multiethnic children's lit, 95n1136
Notable Asian Americans, 96n396
Student's gd to Chinese American genealogy, 97n361
Who's who among Asian Americans 1994/95, 95n402
Who's who in the Asian-American community 1994-95, 96n395

ASIANS
Peoples of the world: Asians & Pacific Islanders, 95n127
Who's who in Asian banking & finance, 98n150

ASIA—RELIGION
Encyclopedia of E philosophy & religion, 96n1483
Great thinkers of the E world, 96n1433

ASIA, SOUTHEASTERN
Dictionary of the modern pols of SE Asia, 96n747
Dictionary of traditional S-E Asian theatre, 96n1418
Historical atlas of SE Asia, 97n429
South East Asia: a gd to ref material, 95n126

ASIMOV, ISAAC
Isaac Asimov: an annot bibliog of the Asimov collection at Boston Univ, 97n968

ASSOCIATIONS, INSTITUTIONS, ETC. *See also* TRADE & PROFESSIONAL ASSOCIATIONS
American Assn of Colleges for Teacher Educ dir of members 1995, 96n316
Business orgs, agencies, & pubns dir, 8th ed, 97n160
Directory of American youth orgs 1998-99, 7th ed, 99n52
Encyclopedia of assns, 99n50
Encyclopedia of assns: natl orgs of the US [CD-ROM], 97n49
Encyclopedia of assns: regional, state, & local orgs, 7th ed, 99n51
Gale ency of bus & professional assns, 96n185
National trade & professional assns of the US 1998, 99n157
Post-Soviet hndbk, 97n123
World gd to religious & spiritual orgs 1996, 97n1182
World gd to scientific assns & learned societies, 7th ed, 99n1323
World of learning 1999, 49th ed, 99n295

ASTAIRE, FRED
Fred Astaire: a bio-bibliog, 98n1272

ASTEROIDS
Asteroid name ency, 96n790

ASTROLOGY
Asteroid name ency, 96n790
Astrology ency, 95n790
Cosmic influences on humans, animals, & plants, 98n1441
Daily planetary gd 1997, 98n713
Divining the future: prognostication from astrology to zoomancy, 96n791
Signs of the zodiac, 98n717

ASTRONAUTICS
Frontiers of space exploration, 99n1520
Spaceflight & rocketry, 97n1300
USA in space, 97n1302

ASTRONOMERS
Directory of physics, astronomy, & geophysics staff, 1997 biennial ed, 99n1322

ASTRONOMY
Asteroid name ency, 96n790
Astronomy, 96n1800
Binocular stargazer, 96n1801
Cambridge astronomy dict, 97n1392
Cambridge atlas of astronomy, 3d ed, 95n1719
Cambridge gd to the constellations, 96n1798
Cambridge star atlas, 2d ed, 97n1393
Dictionary of astronomy, 98n1607
Dictionary of astronomy, 99n1518
Eyewitness ency of space & the universe [CD-ROM], 97n1395
Facts on File dict of astronomy, 3d ed, 95n1721
History of astronomy, 98n1606
Kope's outer space dir, 99n1519
McGraw-Hill dict of astronomy, 98n1608
Moon bk, rev ed, 99n1521

Nine worlds hosted by Patrick Stewart [CD-ROM], 98n1610
Outer space, 99n1522
Photographic atlas of the stars, 98n1604
Popular physics & astronomy, 97n1411
Solar system, 99n1524
Stars & atoms, 96n1799
Stars & planets, 99n1523
Universe explained, 96n1802
Who's who on the moon, 97n1394

ATHEISTS
2000 yrs of disbelief: famous people with the courage to doubt, 98n1347

ATHLETES
Athletes, 96n410
Biographical dict of American sports, 1992-95 suppl, 96n793
Cumulative index to the biogl dict of American sports, 95n804
Great athletes, suppl 21-23, 96n794
Jewish sports legends, 2d ed, 98n719
Official celebrity registry 1994-95, 96n796
100 athletes who shaped sports hist, 96n795
100 greatest athletes of all time, 96n797
Outstanding women athletes, 2d ed, 99n710
Sporting News selects baseball's greatest players, 99n719
Sports people in the news 1996, 97n640
Sports stars, 95n794
Sports stars: series 2, 97n641
Sports stars, series 3, 98n718

ATHLETICS
Winning athletic scholarships, 1998 ed, 99n347

ATLANTIC OCEAN
Field gd to shells, 4th ed, 96n1595
Northeast gd to saltwater fishing & boating, 95n817

ATLASES
Answer atlas, 98n380
Atlas of archaeology, 99n444
Atlas of Indians of N America, 96n413
Atlas of Micronesia, 2d ed, 95n490
Atlas of the Arab-Israeli conflict, 6th ed, 95n759
Atlas of westward expansion, 96n488
Atlas of WW I, 2d ed, 96n675
Bibliographic gd to maps & atlases 1996, 98n391
Big bk of America, 95n469
Britannica atlas, 95n474
Cambridge illus atlas of warfare: Renaissance to Revolution, 1492-1792, 97n556
Cartographic satellite atlas of the world, 99n410
China: a provincial atlas, 96n452
Collins concise atlas of the world, rev ed, 98n382
Collins nations of the world atlas, 97n372
Complete atlas of world hist, 98n491
Concise atlas of the world, 95n475
Concise histl atlas of Canada, 99n409
Concise world atlas, 98n384
Cosmopolitan world atlas, 96n446
Dillon Press children's atlas, 95n476
Discovering maps: a children's world atlas, 95n477
DK student atlas, 99n411
Dorling Kindersley world ref atlas, 95n480
Dorling Kindersley world ref atlas, 2d ed, 97n373
Earth atlas, 95n1725
Eyewitness atlas of the world, 96n447
Florida: atlas of histl county boundaries, 98n431
Geography on file, 1995 ed, 96n457
Golden atlas for children, 95n473
Hammond atlas of the 20th century, 97n459
Hammond atlas of the world, 99n413
Hammond Citation world atlas, 97n374
Hammond comparative world atlas, 95n478
Hammond explorer atlas of the world, 98n385
Hammond intl atlas of the world, 95n482
Hammond new century world atlas, 97n375
Hammond new headline world atlas, 95n479
Hammond odyssey atlas of the world, 95n483
Hammond students atlas of the world, 96n448
HarperCollins world atlas, 95n484
Historical atlas of La., 96n440
Historical atlas of SE Asia, 97n429
Historical atlas of the Vietnam War, 97n434
Kentucky: atlas of histl county boundaries, 97n371
Macmillan centennial atlas of the world, 98n386
Macmillan color atlas of the states, 97n82
Mapping America's past, 97n402
Maps of the world, 98n387
Middle East & N Africa on file, 96n459
My 1st atlas, 95n472
NASA atlas of the solar system, 98n1609
National Geographic picture atlas of our world, rev ed, 95n485
New comparative world atlas, 98n388
New cosmopolitan world atlas, rev ed, 95n486
New intl atlas, 25th ed, 96n449
Outline maps on file, 98n398
Oxford atlas of the world, 4th ed, 97n376
Oxford desk ref atlas, 98n389
Oxford encyclopedic world atlas, 95n481
Oxford encyclopedic world atlas, 3d ed, 97n377
PC Globe maps'n'facts [CD-ROM], 96n450
Penguin atlas of African hist, new ed, 97n428
Penguin atlas of Diasporas, 98n807
Penguin histl atlas of ancient Greece, 97n449
Penguin histl atlas of dinosaurs, 97n1405
Photographic atlas of the stars, 98n1604
Planet Earth: Macmillan world atlas, 98n390
Reader's digest illus great world atlas, 99n416
State of war & peace atlas, 99n700
Thematic atlases for public, academic, & high school libs, 95n491
Times atlas of the world, 9th ed, 95n487
Today's world: a new world atlas, rev ed, 95n488
Traveler's atlas, 99n440
World Afghanistan to Zimbabwe, 97n378
World atlas of nations, 95n489

ATTITUDE (PSYCHOLOGY)
Official gd to American attitudes, 97n717

ATTORNEYS
Who's who in American law 1998-99, 10th ed, 99n550

AUDIOCASSETTES
Words on cassette 1995, 96n983
Words on cassette 1998, 99n14

AUDIO EQUIPMENT
Orion blue bk: car stereo 1998, 99n1485
Orion blue bk: professional sound 1998, 99n180

AUDIO-VISUAL EDUCATION
IDEA: intl dir of educl AVs [CD-ROM], 98n311

AUDIO-VISUAL EQUIPMENT
Dictionary of image tech, 3d ed, 96n985

AUDIO-VISUAL MATERIALS
Audiovisual resources for family programming, 97n313
AV market place 1994, 95n965
AV market place 1997, 98n884
Elementary school lib collection, 19th ed, 95n661
Elementary school lib collection, 19th ed [CD-ROM], 95n662
Elementary school lib collection, 20th ed, 97n544
Elementary school lib collection, 20th ed [CD-ROM], 97n545
Index to AV producers & distrs 1997, 10th ed, 98n312
World dir of moving image & sound archives, 95n963
Young adult lit & nonprint materials, 95n654

AUGUSTINE, SAINT
Confessions of Saint Augustine, 97n1207

AUREATE TERMS
Endangered English dict, 96n1089

AUSTEN, JANE
Annotated bibliog of Jane Austen studies 1984-94, 97n988
Bibliography of Jane Austen, [new ed], 98n1153
Jane Austen ency, 99n1070

AUSTRALASIA
Asian & Australasian cos, 95n240
Australasia & S Pacific Islands bibliog, 98n144
Who's who in Australasia & the Pacific nations, 3d ed, 99n29

AUSTRALIA
Australasia & S Pacific Islands bibliog, 98n144
Australia, 99n436
Australia: a reader's gd, 97n112
Australia bus, 97n237
Australian bks in print 1995, 96n22
Black in focus, 96n1163
Cambridge ency of Australia, 95n138
Coastal fishes of SE Australia, 95n1585
Contemporary Australian women 1996/97, 97n734
Encyclopedia of Australian art, rev ed, 96n1032
Encyclopedia of Australian dolls, 95n976
Familia Gekkonidae (Reptilia, Sauria), pt.1, 96n1634

Far East & Australasia 1995, 26th ed, 96n167
Far East & Australasia 1997, 28th ed, 97n143
Garland ency of world music, v.9, 99n1120
Monash biogl dict of 20th century Australia, 96n39
Oxford companion to Australian lit, 2d ed, 96n1248
Oxford companion to Australian military hist, 97n565
Oxford companion to Australian music, 99n1122
Periodicals in print: Australia, New Zealand, & the S Pacific 1996, 13th ed, 97n64
Post-Colonial lits in English: Australia, 1970-92, 97n1002
Sharks & rays of Australia, 96n1623

AUSTRALIANISMS
Cambridge Australian English style gd, 96n1090
Dictionary of Australian colloquialisms, 4th ed, 97n829

AUSTRIAN LITERATURE
Companion to 20th-century German lit, 2d ed, 99n1093
Who's who of Australian children's writers, 2d ed, 97n931

AUTHORITY FILES (CATALOGING)
ERIC identifier authority list (IAL) 1995, 96n629

AUTHORS
Authors & artists for YAs, v.13, 95n1144
Authors & artists for YAs, v.14, 96n1171
Authors & artists for YAs, v.20, 98n1100
Authors & artists for YAs, v.21, 98n1101
Benét's reader's ency, 4th ed, 98n843
Biographical companion to lit in English, rev ed, 98n1066
Children's authors & illustrators, 5th ed, 96n1178
Contemporary authors, v.158, 99n949
Contemporary authors, v.159, 99n950
Contemporary authors autobiog series, v.25, 98n1061
Contemporary authors autobiog series, v.26, 98n1062
Contemporary authors autobiog series, v.27, 98n1063
Contemporary authors autobiog series, v.28, 99n953
Contemporary authors new revision series, v.43, 96n1150
Contemporary authors new revision series, v.59, 99n947
Contemporary authors new revision series, v.60, 99n948
Contemporary authors on CD [CD-ROM], 98n1064
Contemporary authors on CD [CD-ROM], 95n1110
Contemporary literary criticism, v.87, 97n896
Contemporary literary criticism, v.88, 97n897
Contemporary literary criticism, v.89, 97n898
Contemporary literary criticism, v.100, 99n966
Contemporary literary criticism, v.101, 99n967
Contemporary literary criticism, v.102, 99n968
Contemporary literary criticism, v.103, 99n969
Contemporary literary criticism yrbk 1996, v.99, 99n965
Contemporary popular writers, 98n1058
Cyclopedia of world authors, 3d ed, 98n1059
Dictionary of literary biog documentary series, v.16, 99n954
Dictionary of literary biog documentary series, v.17, 99n955
Dictionary of literary biog yrbk: 1996, 99n970
DiscLit: world authors [CD-ROM], 96n1154
DISCovering authors modules [CD-ROM], 97n900
Encyclopedia of the novel, 99n963
Feminist writers, 97n886
Index to the Wilson authors series, 98n1075
International authors & writers who's who, 15th ed, 99n956

John Steinbeck: an annot gd to biogl sources, 97n975
Junior DISCovering authors [CD-ROM], 95n1145
Larousse dict of writers, 96n1145
Literary lifelines, 99n952
Literature criticism from 1400 to 1800, v.28, 97n901
Literature criticism from 1400 to 1800, v.30, 97n903
Literature criticism from 1400 to 1800, v.31, 97n904
Magill index to Masterplots: cum indexes, 1963-93, 95n1115
Magill's survey of world lit, 97n905
Masterplots fiction CD-ROM, rev ed [CD-ROM], 95n1112
Mystery & suspense writers, 99n1032
Nineteenth-Century lit criticism, v.47, 97n908
Nineteenth-Century lit criticism, v.48, 97n909
Nineteenth-Century lit criticism, v.49, 97n910
Nineteenth-Century lit criticism, v.50, 97n911
Nineteenth-Century lit criticism, v.51, 97n912
Nineteenth-Century lit criticism, v.52, 97n913
Nineteenth-Century lit criticism annual cum title index for 1996, 97n914
Novels for students, v.1, 98n1109
Novels for students, v.2, 98n1110
100 most popular YA authors, 97n941
100 most popular YA authors, rev ed, 98n1102
Oxford companion to 20th-century lit in English, 98n1073
Popular nonfiction authors for children: a biogl & thematic gd, 99n1002
Reader's gd to lit in English, 97n915
Reader's gd to 20th-century writers, 97n916
St. James gd to horror, ghost, & gothic writers, 99n976
St. James gd to sci fiction writers, 4th ed, 97n951
Science fiction, fantasy, & horror writers, 96n1193
Scribner's writers series, selected authors ed [CD-ROM], 99n977
Scribner's writers series on CD-ROM: comprehensive ed [CD-ROM], 99n978
Scribner's writers series master index, 99n984
Seventh bk of jr authors & illustrators, 97n937
Short stories for students, v.1, 98n1120
Short stories for students, v.2, 98n1121
Short story criticism, v.18, 97n954
Short story criticism, v.19, 97n955
Short story writers, 98n1123
Something about the author, v.78, 96n1172
Something about the author, v.79, 96n1173
Something about the author, v.80, 96n1174
Something about the author, v.81, 97n926
Something about the author, v.82, 97n927
Something about the author, v.83, 97n928
Something about the author, v.84, 97n929
Something about the author, v.85, 97n930
Something about the author autobiog series, v.18, 95n1146
Something about the author autobiog series, v.24, 98n1080
Television writers gd, 4th ed, 97n769
Twayne's world authors [CD-ROM], 99n979
Twentieth-Century children's writers, 4th ed, 96n1175
Twentieth-Century literary criticism, v.59, 97n920
Twentieth-Century literary criticism, v.60, 97n921
Twentieth-Century literary criticism, v.61, 97n922
Twentieth-Century literary criticism, v.70, 99n980
Twentieth-Century literary criticism, v.71, 99n981
Twentieth-Century literary criticism, v.72, 99n982
Twentieth-Century literary criticism annual cum title index for 1996, 97n923
Twentieth-Century romance & histl writers, 3d ed, 95n1163
Who's Who in writers, editors, & poets, 5th ed, 96n959
Who's who of Australian children's writers, 2d ed, 97n931
Wilson author biogs on disc 1995 [CD-ROM], 96n1144
World authors 1900-50, 97n887
Writer's dir 1994-96, 95n1107
Writer's dir 1998-2000, 13th ed, 99n958
Writers for YAs, 98n1104

AUTHORS, AFRICAN
African writers, 98n1167

AUTHORS, AMERICAN
American expatriate writers, 98n1127
American nature writers, 97n965
American short-story writers since WW II, 95n1179
American travel writers, 1776-1864, 99n1044
American writers, 99n1043
American writers, retrospective suppl 1, 99n1045
American writers, suppl 4, 97n961
Biographical dict of transcendentalism, 97n962
Cambridge gd to lit in English, 95n1103
Contemporary poets, dramatists, essayists, & novelists of the South, 96n1199
Dictionary of literary biog, v.193, 99n1059
Dictionary of literary biog documentary series, v.13, 97n963
Dictionary of literary pseudonyms in the English lang, 96n1229
Directory of American poets & fiction writers, 1995-96 ed, 97n749
Emerson chronology, 95n1188
Eudora Welty: a bibliog of her work, 95n1197
Fiction of L. Ron Hubbard, 95n1192
Hamlin Garland, 99n1055
Herman Melville ency, 96n1212
James A. Michener: a bibliog, 97n973
John Updike: a bibliog, 1967-93, 95n1196
Mark Twain A to Z, 96n1217
Melville ency: the novels, 95n1194
Modern American lit, v.6, 4th ed, 99n1048
Nineteenth-Century American western writers, 99n957
Proverbial Eugene O'Neill, 96n1215
Ralph Waldo Emerson: an annot bibliog of criticism, 1980-91, 95n1187
Reader's companion to the fiction of Willa Cather, 95n1185
Reader's gd to the short stories of Sherwood Anderson, 95n1184
Reader's gd to the short stories of Willa Cather, 95n1186
Reader's gd to the short stories of William Faulkner, 95n1189
Reference gd to American lit, 3d ed, 95n1169
Twayne's US authors on CD-ROM [CD-ROM], 99n1049
Western American novelists, 96n1205
Works of Allen Ginsberg 1941-94, 96n1210

AUTHORS, BRAZILIAN
Clarice Lispector: a bio-bibliog, 95n1225

AUTHORS, CANADIAN
Annotated bibliog of Canada's major authors, v.8, 95n1227
Canadian writers & their works: fiction series, v.12, 97n1003
Contemporary Canadian authors, v.1, 98n1169
DISCovering authors, Canadian ed [CD-ROM], 98n1065
John Metcalf papers, 97n1005

AUTHORS, EAST EUROPEAN
South Slavic writers since WW II, 99n1091

AUTHORS, ENGLISH
Annotated bibliog of Jane Austen studies 1984-94, 97n988
British children's writers, 1800-1880, 97n934
British children's writers, 1914-1960, 97n935
British children's writers since 1960, 1st series, 97n936
British short-fiction writers, 1880-80, 97n978
British short-fiction writers, 1880-1914, 95n1209
British short-fiction writers, 1915-45, 97n980
British writers, suppl 3, 97n982
British writers, suppl 4, 98n1149
Cambridge gd to lit in English, 95n1103
Dictionary of literary biog, v.191, 99n1063
Dictionary of literary biog, v.194, 99n1064
Dictionary of literary biog: British reform writers, 1832-1914, 99n1062
Dictionary of literary pseudonyms in the English lang, 96n1229
Elizabeth Gaskell: an annot bibliog of English-lang sources 1976-91, 95n1213
G. A. Henty 1832-1902: a bibliographical study of his British eds...., 98n1159
George Herbert companion, 96n1238
Guide to British prose fiction explication: 19th & 20th centuries, 98n1143
Iris Murdoch: a descriptive primary & annot secondary bibliog, 95n1215
Literary gd & companion to N England, 96n1233
Major Tudor authors, 98n1060
Now read on: a gd to contemporary popular fiction, 2d ed, 96n1187
Proverbial Bernard Shaw, 95n1221
Samuel Johnson ency, 97n994
Sir Philip Sidney: an annot bibliog of texts & criticism (1554-1984), 95n1222
Sixteenth-Century British nondramatic writers, 1st series, 95n1201
Sixteenth-Century British nondramatic writers, 3d series, 97n983
Sixteenth-Century British nondramatic writers, 4th series, 98n1147
Twayne's English authors on CD-ROM [CD-ROM], 99n1067
William Somerset Maugham ency, 98n1160
Women writers of Gt Brit & Europe, 98n1067

AUTHORS, EUROPEAN
Women writers of Gt Brit & Europe, 98n1067

AUTHORS, FRENCH
Dictionary of literary biog, v.192, 99n1092
Marguerite Duras: a bio-bibliog, 98n1171

AUTHORS, GERMAN
German baroque writers, 1580-1660, 97n1006
German baroque writers, 1661-1730, 98n1172
Nietzsche canon, 97n1157
Nineteenth-Century German writers, 1841-1900, 95n1232

AUTHORSHIP. *See also* PUBLISHERS & PUBLISHING
AMA style gd for bus writing, 98n873
Artists & writers colonies, 97n745
Associate Pr stylebk & libel manual, 6th ed, 98n874
Author's gd to biomedical jls, 95n1661
Career opportunities for writers, 3d ed, 96n967
Children's writer's & illustrator's market, 1998, 99n828
Companion to Historiography, 99n829
Complete gd to writers' conferences & workshops, 96n965
Dictionary of literary pseudonyms in the English lang, 96n1229
Freed's gd to student contests & publishing, 5th ed, 96n1356
Freelance Editorial Assn yellow pages & code of fair practice, 1997-98, 98n863
Grants & awards available to American writers 1996-97, 19th ed, 97n694
Guidebook for publishing philosophy, 1997 ed, 98n867
Market gd for young writers, 5th ed, 97n751
Merriam-Webster's concise hndbk for writers, 99n833
Merriam-Webster's manual for writers & editors, 99n834
Novel & short story writer's market, 1996, 97n753
Poet's market, 1995, 95n943
Romance writer's pink pages, 95n942
Romance writer's sourcebk, 97n754
Writer's market, 1995, 95n670
Writer's Digest dict of concise writing, 97n759
Writer's ency, 3d ed, 97n750
Writer's hndbk, 99n832
Writer's resource, 98n871
Writer's resource hndbk, 98n865
Writer's ultimate research gd, 97n752
Writings on writing, 95n940

AUTHORS—HOMES & HAUNTS
Literary gd & companion to S England, rev ed, 99n1065

AUTHORS, INDIAN
Native N American lit, 96n1259

AUTHORS, IRISH
Modern Irish writers, 98n1176
Oscar Wilde ency, 99n1075

AUTHORS, ITALIAN
Boccaccio in English: a bibliog of eds, adaptations, & criticism, 97n1011
Italian women writers, 95n1235

AUTHORS & PUBLISHERS
Business & legal forms for authors & self-publishers, 98n605
Guide to literary agents, 1997, 98n866
Poet's market, 1998, 98n868
Writer's market, 1998, 98n870
Writer's market, 1998, electronic ed [CD-ROM], 98n869

AUTHORS, SPANISH AMERICAN
Contemporary Spanish-speaking writers & illustrators for children & YAs, 95n1151

AUTHORS, TAMIL
Lexicon of Tamil lit, 96n1255

AUTOBIOGRAPHIES
Autobiographies by Americans of color 1980-94, 98n347

AUTOGRAPHS
Collector's gd to celebrity autographs, 97n775

AUTOMATION
World engineering industries & automation 1993-95, 96n1649

AUTOMOBILE DRIVERS' RECORDS
MVR bk motor servs gd, 1994, 95n739
MVR bk motor servs gd, 1997 ed, 98n536
MVR decoder digest 1994, 95n740
MVR decoder digest, 1997 ed, 98n537

AUTOMOBILE INDUSTRY & TRADE
Japanese automobile industry: an annot bibliog, 95n1790

AUTOMOBILES
Automobile, 98n1647
Classic American cars, 98n1650
Delmar's automotive dict, 98n1477
Dictionary of automotive engineering, 2d ed, 97n1303
Orion blue bk: car stereo 1998, 99n1485
Racer's ency of metals, fibers & materials, 96n1883
Standard catalog of American cars, 1946-75, 98n1648
Standard gd to cars & prices, 99n1577
Ultimate classic car bk, 96n1892
Used car reliability & safety gd, 96n1885

AUTOMOBILES—LICENSES
Official license plate bk, 97n1447

AVANT-GARDE
Dictionary of the avant-gardes, 95n1005
Music of the repressed Russian avant-garde, 1900-29, 95n1261
Realization & suppression of the Situationist Intl, 97n792

AVERY LIBRARY
Avery's choice: 5 centuries of great architectural bks, 98n971

AWARDS
Awards, honors, & prizes 1997, 13th ed, 98n49
Children's bks: awards & prizes, 1996 ed, 97n932
Contemporary literary criticism, v.87, 97n896
Entertainment awards, 97n1099
Grants & awards available to American writers 1996-97, 19th ed, 97n694
Literary almanac, 98n1071

AZERBAIJANI LANGUAGE—DICTIONARIES—ENGLISH
English-Azerbaijani/Azerbaijani-English concise dict, 96n1097

BACH, JOHANN SEBASTIAN
Biblical quotation & allusion in the cantata libretti of J. S. Bach, 98n1245
Handbook to Bach's sacred cantata texts, 98n1247
Sacred dramas of J. S. Bach, 96n1284

BACKPACKING
Essential gd to wilderness camping & backpacking in the US, 96n824

BAEZ, JOAN
Joan Baez: a bio-bibliog, 97n1074

BAHA'I FAITH
Historical dict of the Baha'i faith, 99n1272

BAKHTIN, MIKHAIL
Mikhail Bakhtin (II): a bibliog, 95n1425

BALLET
Dancers & choreographers, 97n1100
Dictionary of classical ballet terminology, 99n1204
International ency of dance, 99n1202
Minor ballet composers, 98n1215

BALTIC STATES
Atlas of Russia & the Independent Republics, 96n445
Baltic states, 95n154
Baltics info sources dir 1996, 98n124
Bibliographic gd to Slavic, Baltic, & Eurasian studies 1996, 98n126

BAND MUSIC
Heritage ency of band music, suppl v.3, 98n1229

BANGLADESH
Historical dict of Bangladesh, 2d ed, 98n460

BANKRUPTCY
Sourcebook of fed courts, 2d ed, 97n500

BANKS & BANKING
Bank profitability: financial statements of banks 1983-92, 95n227
Dictionary of banking terms, 99n186
Dictionary of finance & investment terms, 4th ed, 96n220
Fitzroy Dearborn dir of the world's banks, 11th ed, 97n190
Fitzroy Dearborn ency of banking & finance, 10th ed, 95n230
Information sources in finance & banking, 97n191
Language of banking, 95n232
Plunkett's financial servs industry almanac, 98n185
Prices & financial stats in the ESCWA region, 97n192
Who's who in Asian banking & finance, 98n150

BANK STOCKS
Walker's manual of community bank stocks, 98n187

BAPTISTS
Dictionary of Baptists in America, 96n1467

BARBIE DOLLS
Contemporary Barbie dolls, 99n847

BAROQUE LITERATURE
German Baroque writers, 1580-1660, 97n1006
German Baroque writers, 1661-1730, 98n1172

BARTHES, ROLAND
Roland Barthes: a bibliog, 95n1424

BARTOK, BELA
Bela Bartok: a gd to research, 2d ed, 98n1210

BASEBALL
American assn: yr-by-yr stats for the baseball minor league, 1902-52, 98n738
Baseball: a comprehensive bibliog, suppl 2, 99n717
Baseball & American culture, 96n806
Baseball by the nos, 97n650
Baseball ency update, 1995, 96n803
Baseball pioneers: ratings of 19th century players, 98n730
Baseball ratings, 2d ed, 96n804
Baseball records registry, 98n728
Best of teams, the worst of teams, 96n807
Bill James presents: STATS all-time major league hndbk, 99n715
Charmed circle: 20-game-winning pitchers in baseball's 20th century, 98n732
Cultural ency of baseball, 98n733
Dodgers ency, 99n716
Encyclopedia of Minor League Baseball, 2d ed, 98n729
Fodor's ballpark vacations, 98n731
Former major league teams, 97n646
Inside Sports world series factbk, 97n645
International league, 99n724
Lumber men: nontraditional statl measurements of the batting careers...., 95n806
Middle innings: a documentary hist of baseball, 1900-48, 99n722
Nineteenth Century baseball, 97n651
Official athletic college gd: baseball, 1995 ed, 96n805
Official baseball atlas, 1994 ed, 95n807
Official baseball rules 1997, 98n735
Official Major League Baseball fact bk 1997, 98n736
Pacific Coast League: statl hist, 1903-57, 97n647
Professional sports team hists, 95n800
Sporting News baseball gd, 1996 ed, 97n648
Sporting News complete baseball record bk, 1997 ed, 99n718
Sporting News official baseball register, 1996 ed, 97n649
Sporting News selects baseball's greatest players, 99n719
STATS player profiles 1998, 99n721
Total baseball, 98n737
USA Today baseball weekly almanac, 1997, 99n723
Women of the All-American Girls Professional Baseball League, 98n734
Worst baseball pitchers of all time, 95n805

BASEBALL CARDS
Standard catalog of baseball cards, 1998, 98n906

BASKETBALL
Chicago Bulls ency, 99n726
Encyclopedia of college basketball, 96n809
Inside Sports Mag college basketball, 2d ed, 98n739
NCAA basketball, 97n652
NCAA basketball: the official 1997 women's college basketball records bk, 98n740
NCAA Final Four, 97n653
Official rules of the Natl Basketball Assoc 1997-98, 99n725
Professional sports team hists, 95n800
Sporting News official NBA gd, 95n809
Sporting News official NBA gd, 1997-98 ed, 98n741
Sporting News official NBA register, 95n810
Sporting News official NBA register, 98n742
STATS pro basketball hndbk 1997-98, 99n728

BASKETBALL CARDS
Standard catalog of basketball cards, 1998 ed, 99n727

BASSETT, LESLIE
Leslie Bassett: a bio-bibliog, 95n1268

BATAILLE, GEORGES
Georges Bataille: a bibliog, 95n1423

BATS
Walker's bats of the world, 96n1610

BATTLES & BATTLEFIELDS. *See also* **MILITARY STUDIES; WAR**
Army Times bk of great land battles, 96n698
Civil War battlefields, 96n517
Modern campaigns, 98n615
More battlefields of Canada, 95n692

BEADS
Bead dir, 2d ed, 95n978
Bead dir, 3d ed, 96n1011

BEANIE BABIES (TOYS)
Beanie family album & collectors gd, 99n853

BEAT GENERATION
Beat generation, 99n1042

BEATLES, THE
Beatles: the ultimate recording gd, 3d ed, 96n1338
Beatles memorabilia price gd, 3d ed, 98n921

BED & BREAKFAST ACCOMMODATIONS
America's best bed & breakfasts, 2d ed, 98n408
Bed & breakfast ency, 98n427
Canadian bed & breakfast gd, 12th ed, 97n393
Complete gd to American bed & breakfast, 97n385
Complete gd to American bed & breakfast, 98n410
Complete gd to bed & breakfasts, inns & guesthouses in the US & Canada, 11th ed, 95n510
Irish bed & breakfast bk, 96n482
National Trust gd to historic bed & breakfasts, inns & small hotels, 95n511

National Trust gd to historic bed & breakfasts, inns, & small hotels, 4th ed, 97n390

BEER
America's best beers, 96n1536
Beer lover's rating gd, 96n1537
Beer-Taster's log, 97n1252
Dictionary of beer & brewing, 2d ed, 99n1332
Encyclopedia of beer, 96n1525
North American brewers resource dir 1996-97, 13th ed, 97n1251
On tap, 1995 ed, 96n1532
Ultimate beer, 99n1333

BEES
Bee genera of N & Central America (Hymenoptera: Apoidea), 95n1591

BEETHOVEN, LUDWIG VAN
Beethoven ency, 96n1281

BELARUS
Cultures of the World, 99n84

BENCHLEY, ROBERT
Robert Benchley, 96n1207

BENIN
Benin, 98n106

BEREAVEMENT
Books to help children cope with separation & loss, 4th ed, 95n773

BERG, ALBAN
Alban Berg: a gd to research, 97n1045

BERLIN, IRVING
Irving Berlin, 99n1134

BERMUDA
Bermuda, 99n137

BEST BOOKS
Best bks for YA readers, 98n1094
Books for you, 98n1095
Booktalking the award winners 3, 98n1082
Booktalking the award winners: children's retrospective volume, 98n1081
Children's bk awards annual 1998, 99n990
Children's bk prizes, 99n989
Choices for young readers [CD-ROM], 98n1086
Civil War bks: a critical bibliog, 98n432
Dictionary of American children's fiction, 1990-94, 97n938
Doody's rating serv 1997, 98n1502
Earth works, 97n1424
From biog to hist, 99n993
Kaleidoscope: A multicultural bklist for grades K-8, 98n1087
Newbery & Caldecott awards, 1998 ed, 99n995
Reader's catalog, 2d ed, 98n8

Recommended bks in Spanish for children & YAs, 1991-95, 98n1079
Senior high school lib catalog, 15th ed, 98n587
Special-needs reading list, 99n751
Ultimate bus lib, 98n148
Ultimate gd to sci fiction, 2d ed, 97n949

BEST-SELLERS
Bestseller index, 99n12

BEVERAGE INDUSTRY
Career opportunities in the food & beverage industry, 96n1538
Food & beverage market place, 1996, 97n1249
Food & beverage market place, 1997/98, 99n1339

BEVERAGES
Dictionary of American food & drink, rev ed, 95n1517
European drinks mktg dir, 4th ed, 97n240
Who's buying food & drink, 98n257
World drinks databk, 95n1523

BEVERAGES IN LITERATURE
Food & drink in lit, 97n881

BEVERAGES—QUOTATIONS
Never eat more than you can lift, & other food quotes & quips, 98n1429

BIBLE
And Adam knew Eve: a dict of sex in the Bible, 96n1452
Bible: God's word for the biblically-inept, 99n1280
Bible & the saints, 96n1448
Bible baby names, 97n368
Biblical quotation & allusion in the cantata libretti of J. S. Bach, 98n1245
Brush up your Bible!, 95n1454
Cambridge companion to the Bible, 98n1377
Divine inspirations: pearls of Bible wisdom from the O. & N.T.s, 98n1369
Encyclopedia of biblical errancy, 96n1456
Expositor's bible commentary [CD-ROM], 99n1277
Handbook of Biblical chronology, rev ed, 99n1278
Hermann Sasse: a bibliog, 97n1168
High places in cyberspace, 2d ed, 99n1269
Illustrated gd to the Bible, 96n1459
Literary-Critical approaches to the Bible, 97n1190
New Bible commentary, 96n1458
New Interpreter's Bible [CD-ROM], 99n1279
NIV compact concordance, 95n1453
NIV complete Bible lib [CD-ROM], 98n1380
Pockets: Bible companion, 98n1381
Who's who in biblical studies & archaeology, 2d ed, 95n1456
Who's who in the Bible, 96n1449
Women in the biblical world, v.1, 97n1186

BIBLE—ANTIQUITIES
Jesus & his world, 97n1213

BIBLE—DICTIONARIES
Baker ency of Bible places, 96n1450
Collegeville pastoral dict of biblical theology, 97n1196

Dictionary of the Bible, 97n1195
Evangelical dict of biblical theology, 97n1197
Hastings' dict of the Bible, 96n1454
Illustrated dict of Bible life & times, 99n1275
International children's Bible dict, 98n1376
New Bible dict, 3d ed, 98n1373
Precious Moments children's Bible dict, 96n1451
Theological dict of the Old Testament, 99n1276

BIBLE—GEOGRAPHY
Cities of the biblical world, 98n1378

BIBLE IN LITERATURE
Index to English per lit on the O.T. & ancient Near Eastern studies, v.VI, 95n1451
Index to English per lit on the O.T. & ancient Near Eastern studies, v.VII, 99n1273
Index to the biblical refs, parallels, & allusions in the poetry & prose of John Milton, 95n1214
Reference gd to the Bible in Emily Dickinson's poetry, 98n1135

BIBLE—N.T.
Acts of the Apostles, 98n1370
Book of Ephesians, 97n1188
Book of Revelation, 97n1191
Dictionary of Paul & his letters, 95n1450
Dictionary of the later N.T. & its dvlpmts, 99n1274
Exegetical bibliog of the N.T., v.4, 97n1185
Exhaustive concordance to the Greek N.T., 97n1199
Gospel of Matthew, 95n1455
Hellenistic commentary to the N.T., 97n1201
New Testament intro, 97n1192
Novum Testamentum, v.36a, 96n1460
Romans, 98n1371
Theological lexicon of the N.T., 96n1457

BIBLE—O.T.
Book of Amos, 98n1372
Book of Jeremiah, 97n1194
Book of Psalms: an annot bibliog, 95n1457
Book of Ruth: an annot bibliog, 95n1449
Hebrew & Aramaic lexicon of the O.T., v.1, 96n1455
Hebrew & Aramaic lexicon of the O.T., v.2, 97n1198
IVP Bible background commentary: Genesis-Deuteronomy, 98n1379
Key-word-in-context concordance to Targum Neofiti, 95n1452
Messengers of God: a Jewish prophets who's who, 99n1292
New intl dict of O.T. theology & exegesis, 98n1374
Old Testament commentary survey, 2d ed, 97n1189
Old Testament intro, 97n1187
Theological dict of the O.T., v.7, 97n1200
Theological dict of the O.T., v.8, 98n1375
Theological dict of the O.T., 99n1276

BIBLIOGRAPHERS
American bk collectors & bibliographers, 1st series, 95n971
American bk collectors & bibliographers, 2d series, 99n591

BIBLIOGRAPHICAL CITATIONS
Complete gd to citing govt info resources, rev ed, 95n74

Where credit is due: a gd to proper citing of sources—print & nonprint, 2d ed, 99n835

BIBLIOGRAPHY
African bks in print, 4th ed, 95n22
American bk publishing record cum 1993, 95n17
American bk publishing record, cum 1997, 99n9
Anders CD-ROM gd, 2d ed, 97n15
Audiovisual resources for family programming, 97n313
Bibliographic index 1996, 98n6
Bibliography of Fla., v.1, 95n105
Bibliography of sources in Christianity & the arts, 97n1206
Books in print 1994-95, 95n18
Books in print 1995-96, 96n15
Books in print 1996-97, 49th ed, 97n18
Books in print 1997-98, 98n15
Books in print with bk reviews plus [CD-ROM], 96n17
Books out-of-print plus [CD-ROM], 96n18
Business A to Z source finder, 97n147
Canadian bks in print 1997, 98n18
Catalogue of medieval & Renaissance mss in the Houghton Lib, Harvard Univ, v.1, 97n546
Catalogue of the 15th-century printed bks in the Harvard Univ Lib, v.4, 97n547
CD-ROMs in print 1995 [CD-ROM], 97n16
CD-ROMs in print 1996, 97n17
Checklist of American imprints for 1844, 95n21
Checklist of American imprints for 1845, 98n17
Checklist of American imprints for 1846, 99n13
Children's bks in print, 96n19
China bibliog, 96n535
Classical studies, 97n461
Complete dir of large print bks & serials 1998, 99n11
Contemporary printed lit of the English counter-Reformation between 1558 & 1640, v.2, 95n1463
Cumulative bk index 1995, 98n11
Directory of bus info resources, 1997, 5th ed, 98n250
Eighteenth Century, n.s.15 for 1989, 98n7
El-Hi textbks & serials in print 1997, 98n283
English Catholic bks, 1701-1800, 97n1204
General bibliog for music research, 3d ed, 97n1022
Global bks in print plus [CD-ROM], 96n13
Global voices, global visions: a core collection of multi-cultural bks, 97n10
Guide to ref bks, 11th ed, 97n8
Guides to collection dvlpmt for children & YA lit, 99n601
Guides to lib collection dvlpmt, 95n653
Humanities: a selective gd to info sources, 4th ed, 95n921
International bks in print 1997, 98n12
Law bks & serials in print 1996, 97n481
Library of Lord George Douglas, 99n612
MLA intl bibliog [CD-ROM], 96n1143
1990-91 Gulf War, 97n456
Nineteenth-Century British bk collectors & bibliographers, 99n592
Noble's intl gd to the law reports, 97n483
Paperbound bks in print fall 1994, 95n20
Printed catalogues of the Harvard College Lib, 1723-90, 97n39
Reader's adviser on CD-ROM [CD-ROM], 97n11

Reader's advisor, 14th ed, 95n13
Reference sources hndbk, 4th ed, 97n13
Rosenthal Collection of printed bks with ms annots, 98n578
Science & tech: a purchase gd for libs 1995, 97n1234
Short-Title catalogue of Hungarian bks printed before 1851 in the British Lib, 97n14
South African bibliog, 3d ed, 97n551
Soviet armed forces, 1918-92, 97n558
Subject gd to bks in print 1994-95, 95n19
Subject gd to bks in print 1995-96, 96n16
Subject gd to bks in print 1997-98, 98n16
Subject gd to children's bks in print 1995, 96n20
Vampire readings, 99n1035
Women & music, 97n1020
Young adult lit & nonprint materials, 95n654

BIBLIOGRAPHY—BEST BOOKS
Best bks for children, 5th ed, 95n1130
Best bks for YAs, 95n1127
Choosing your children's bks: 5-8 yrs, 2d ed, 95n1142
Choosing your children's bks: 8-12 yrs, 95n1143
Core collection for small libs, 98n1077
Crown crime companion, 96n1189
Kister's best encys, 2d ed, 95n57
More kids' favorite bks, 96n1168
New York Public Lib's bks of the century, 97n882
Newbery companion, 98n1091
Reader's companion, 95n11
Recommended reading: 500 classics reviewed, 97n883

BIBLIOGRAPHY—EARLY PRINTED BOOKS
British imprints relating to N America, 1621-1760, 97n40
Sabin Collection catalog [CD-ROM], 98n10
Short-title catalogue of bks printed in England, Scotland, Ireland, Wales, & British America...., v.1, 2d ed, 96n14

BIBLIOMETRICS
Dictionary of bibliometrics, 95n649

BIBLIOTHERAPY
Children in foster care & adoption, 99n756
Using bibliotherapy in clinical practice, 95n772

BIENNIALS (PLANTS)
Eyewitness garden hndbk: annuals & biennials, 98n1436

BIG BANDS
Command performance, USA! a discography, 97n772

BILLIARDS
Billiard market place 1994, 95n811
Illustrated ency of billiards, 95n813
Pocket billiard gdbk for pool players, tournament directors, & spectators, 95n812

BIOCHEMISTRY
Concise ency biochemistry & molecular biology, 3d ed, 98n1599
Oxford dict of biochemistry & molecular biology, 98n1444
Vocabulary of enzyme engineering, 95n1618

BIODIVERSITY
Biodiversity, 99n1556

BIOETHICS
Encyclopedia of bioethics, rev ed, 96n1429
Encyclopedia of bioethics, rev ed [CD-ROM], 98n1333

BIOGRAPHERS
Eighteenth-Century British literary biographers, 95n1204
Late 19th- & early 20th-century British literary biographers, 96n1225
Nineteenth-Century British literary biographers, 96n1226
Twentieth-Century British literary biographers, 96n1227

BIOGRAPHICAL DICTIONARY OF AMERICAN SPORTS
Cumulative index to the biogl dict of American sports, 95n804

BIOGRAPHY
Almanac of famous people, 6th ed, 99n17
Ancient Romans, 99n518
Annual obituary 1993, 95n23
Art, truth, & high pols: a bibliographic study of the official lives of Queen Victoria's ministers in Cabinet, 1843-1969, 97n608
Asian American biog, 96n393
Athletes, 96n410
Biographical companion to lit in English, rev ed, 98n1066
Biographical dict of American newspaper columnists, 96n973
Biographical dict of artists, rev ed, 96n1022
Biographical dict of Chinese women, 99n798
Biographical dict of European labor leaders, 97n151
Biographical dict of 20th-century philosophers, 97n1158
Biographical dir of Native American painters, 97n807
Biographical ency of scientists, 99n1300
Biography & genealogy master index 1999, 99n404
Biography index [CD-ROM], 96n24
Biography index, Sept 1995-Aug 1996, 98n20
Biography today, 1993 annual cum, 96n25
Biography today: Profiles of People of Interest to Young Readers, 98n21
British children's writers, 1914-1960, 97n935
British children's writers since 1960, 1st series, 97n936
British literary bk trade, 1475-1700, 98n594
British short-fiction writers, 1880-80, 97n978
British short-fiction writers, 1915-45, 97n980
British women's hist, 97n726
Cambridge biogl dict, 97n20
Cambridge biogl ency, 95n25
Cambridge biogl ency, 2d ed, 99n18
Canadian newsmakers 1997, 98n33
Canadian who's who 1996, v.31, 97n37
Canadian who's who 1997, v.32, 99n38
Complete Marquis who's who on CD-ROM [CD-ROM], 98n28
Complete Marquis who's who on CD-ROM [CD-ROM], 99n19
Concise dict of American biog, 5th ed, 98n29
Concise dict of American Jewish biog, 95n447
Contemporary Australian women 1996/97, 97n734
Contemporary heroes & heroines, bk 3, 99n20

Current biog yrbk 1996, 98n22
Cyclopedia of world authors, 3d ed, 98n1059
Deaf persons in the arts & scis, 96n857
Dictionary of American biog [CD-ROM], 99n33
Dictionary of American biog, suppl 9, 1971-75, 95n36
Dictionary of American biog, suppl 10, 96n36
Dictionary of Canadian biog, v.13, 95n26
Dictionary of Hispanic biog, 97n334
Dictionary of intl biog 1996, 24th ed, 97n21
Dictionary of intl biog 1998, 26th ed, 99n21
Dictionary of Irish biog, 3d ed, 99n132
Dictionary of N.C. biog, v.5, 95n37
Dictionary of natl biog, 1986-90, 97n38
Dictionary of universal biog of all ages & of all peoples, 2d ed, 95n28
Dictionary of world biog, v.1, 99n519
Dictionary of world biog, v.2: the middle ages, 99n520
DISCovering biog [CD-ROM], 98n23
Distinguished African American scientists of the 20th century, 97n1230
Encyclopaedia Africana dict of African biog, v.3, 97n91
Encyclopedia of American biog, 2d ed, 97n33
Encyclopedia of biog, 99n22
Encyclopedia of Native American biog, 98n350
Encyclopedia of world biog, 2d ed, 99n23
50 most influential women in American law, 98n513
Gay & lesbian biog, 98n782
Grolier lib of intl biogs, 97n23
Grolier lib of N American biogs, 96n27
Grolier lib of sci biogs, 98n1400
HarperCollins dict of biog, 95n27
Harvard biogl dict of music, 97n1024
Heroes & pioneers, 99n24
Heroes of conscience: a biogl dict, 97n22
Index to Marquis Who's Who pubs 1998, 99n25
International authors & writers who's who, 15th ed, 99n956
International biogl dict of computer pioneers, 96n1758
International who's who 1994-95, 95n29
International who's who in music, v.2: popular music, 97n1063
International who's who of women, 99n26
Larousse biogl dict, 95n31
Larousse dict of women, 98n24
Last word: The New York Times bk of obituaries & farewells, 99n34
Lincoln lib of sports champions, 6th, 95n793
Members of Congress, 97n584
Men of achievement, 15th ed, 95n32
Men of achievement 1997, 17th ed, 99n28
Merriam-Webster's biogl dict, 96n29
Merriam-Webster's pocket biogl dict, 97n24
Mexican pol biogs, 1935-93, 3d ed, 96n763
Monash biogl dict of 20th century Australia, 96n39
My 1st bk of biogs, 96n28
Newsmakers 1994, 95n33
Newsmakers 1997, 98n25
Nobel prize winners 1992-96 suppl, 98n26
Notable black American women, bk.2, 97n34
Notable Latino Americans, 98n349
Notable women in the life scis, 97n1231

Notable women in the physical scis, 98n1598
100 greatest, 98n27
100 men who shaped world hist, 96n33
100 most popular YA authors, rev ed, 98n1102
100 women who shaped world hist, 96n32
Oxford children's bk of famous people, 96n31
People in the news 1994, 95n24
People of the Holocaust, 99n521
Performers, 96n419
Pocket factfile of 20th century people, 97n25
Political leaders & peacemakers, 96n418
Profiles in American hist, 95n537
Profiles in American hist, 96n509
Profiles in world hist, 97n472
Profiles of worldwide govt leaders 1998, 4th ed, 99n649
Prominent women of the 20th century, 97n26
Scholastic ency of women in the US, 98n836
Scientists, 98n1401
Scientists & inventors, 99n1304
Scribner ency of American lives, v.1, 99n35
Singers of the century, 98n1201
Sports people in the news 1996, 97n640
Stars in blue: movie actors in America's sea servs, 98n1281
Subject gd to women of the world, 97n741
They made hist, 95n35
Tycoons & entrepreneurs, 99n143
US govt leaders, 99n663
U*X*L biogs [CD-ROM], 97n27
Villains & outlaws, 99n582
When they were kids: over 400 sketches of famous childhoods, 99n27
Who was who v.9: who was who 1991-95, 97n28
Who was who in 20th century Romania, 95n30
Who was who in America with world notables, v.10, 95n38
Who's who 1995, 96n34
Who's who 1998, 99n31
Who's who among African Americans, 1998/99, 99n379
Who's who in America 1996, 96n37
Who's who in American law 1994-95, 95n602
Who's who in American law 1998-99, 10th ed, 99n550
Who's who in Asian banking & finance, 98n150
Who's who in Australasia & the Pacific nations, 3d ed, 99n29
Who's who in Christianity, 99n1283
Who's who in finance & industry, 1996-97, 97n152
Who's who in intl affairs 1998, 2d ed, 99n652
Who's who in Latin America, 4th ed, 98n35
Who's who in medicine & healthcare 1997-98, 98n1507
Who's who in sci & engineering 1996-97, 3d ed, 97n1232
Who's who in sci & engineering 1998-99, 99n1305
Who's who in sci in Europe, 9th ed, 97n1233
Who's who in South African pols, no.5, 97n611
Who's who in tech, 7th ed, 96n1492
Who's who in the East 1997-98, 26th ed, 98n31
Who's who in the media & communications 1998-99, 99n819
Who's who in the Midwest 1994-95, 95n39
Who's who in the Midwest 1998-99, 26th ed, 99n36
Who's who in the South & Southwest 1995-96, 97n36
Who's who in the South & Southwest 1999-2000, 26th ed, 99n37
Who's who in the West 1994-95, 95n40

Who's who in the West 1998-99, 26th ed, 98n32
Who's who in the world 1996, 13th ed, 97n29
Who's who in the world 1998, 99n30
Who's who in Vietnam, 99n113
Who's who in writers, editors, & poets, 5th ed, 96n959
Who's who of American women 1995-96, 19th ed, 96n38
Who's who of Nobel prize winners 1901-95, 3d ed, 97n30
Wilson author biogs on disc 1995 [CD-ROM], 96n1144
Women & the Dict of Natl Biog, 96n26
Women in context, 99n39
Women of Ireland, 98n34
Women of strength, 97n733
World biogl index, 2d ed [CD-ROM], 97n31
World biogl index, 3d ed, 99n32

BIOLOGICAL LITERATURE
Using the biological lit, 2d ed, 97n1264

BIOLOGICAL SCIENCES
Best graduate programs: physical & biological scis, 2d ed, 99n336

BIOLOGICAL WEAPONS
Chemical & biological warfare, 98n607
Jane's NBC protection equipment 1996-97, 9th ed, 97n570
US chemical-biological defense gdbk, 99n644

BIOLOGY
Concise dict of biomedicine & molecular biology, 98n1439
Concise ency biochemistry & molecular biology, 3d ed, 98n1599
Concise ency biology, 97n1266
Dictionary of modern biology, 98n1445
Dictionary of nature, 95n1557
Elsevier's dict of fundamental & applied biology, 97n1267
Encyclopedia of human biology, 99n1355
Encyclopedia of molecular biology & molecular medicine, v.2, 97n1270
Encyclopedia of molecular biology & molecular medicine, v.3, 97n1271
Genetics & cell biology on file, 99n1357
Glossary of biochemistry & molecular biology, rev ed, 98n1443
Magill's survey of sci: life sci series suppl, 99n1356
McGraw-Hill dict of biosci, 98n1440

BIOMETRY
Elsevier's dict of biometry, 96n1557

BIOTECHNOLOGY
Biotechnology abstracts: agricultural & environmental, 1983-Feb 1997 [CD-ROM], 98n1490
Biotechnology gd USA, 3d ed, 96n1655
Biotechnology in the US pharmaceutical industry 1995, 4th ed, 96n1733
Biotechnology info sources, 96n1658
Encyclopedia of molecular biology & molecular medicine, v.1, 97n1269
Facts on File dict of biotech & genetic engineering, 95n1619
Glossary of biotech terms, 95n1620

Language of biotech, 2d ed, 96n1659
Molecular biology & biotech, 96n1561
State-by-state biotech dir, 3d ed, 96n1506

BIOTIC COMMUNITIES
Atlas of wild places, 95n1558
Habitats, 96n1598

BIRDS
Birds of the world, 95n1567
CITES identification gd: Birds, 96n1612
Encyclopedia of birds, 2d ed, 99n1377
Life of birds, 99n1372
National Audubon Society bird garden, 96n1560
National Audubon Society 1st field gd: birds, 99n1381
Neotropical migratory birds, 97n1289
Nightjars: a gd to the nightjars, nighthawks, & their relatives, 99n1376
Penguins of the world, 96n1616
Photographic gd to the shorebirds of the world, 96n1617
Pockets: birds, 96n65
Shrikes: a gd to the shrikes of the world, 99n1380
Sparrows & buntings, 97n1288
Supplement to distribution & taxonomy of birds of the world, 95n1574
World checklist of birds, 95n1572

BIRDS, AFRICAN
Common birds of E Africa, 98n1461
Field gd to birds of the Gambia & Senegal, 99n1373
Handbook of bird identification for Europe & the W Palearctic, 99n1374

BIRDS, CENTRAL AMERICA
Guide to the birds of Mexico & N Central America, 96n1615

BIRDS, EUROPE
Birds of Europe with N Africa & the Middle East, 95n1568
Birdwatcher's hndbk, 96n1614
Handbook of bird identification for Europe & the W Palearctic, 99n1374
Pocket gd to the birds of Britain & NW Europe, 99n1379

BIRDS, FLORIDA
Birdlife of Fla., 95n1575

BIRDS, KENTUCKY
Birds of Ky., 95n1571

BIRDS, MEXICO
Guide to the birds of Mexico & N Central America, 96n1615

BIRDS, MICHIGAN
Birds of Mich., 95n1570

BIRDS, MIDDLE EAST
Birds of Europe with N Africa & the Middle East, 95n1568
Handbook of bird identification for Europe & the W Palearctic, 99n1374

BIRDS, NEW YORK STATE
Bull's birds of NY state, 99n1375

BIRDS, NORTH AFRICA
Birds of Europe with N Africa & the Middle East, 95n1568

BIRDS, NORTH AMERICA
American Bird Conservancy's field gd to all the birds of N America, 98n1459
Birds of N America, 95n1565
Common American birds, 96n1611
Lives of N American birds, 98n1460
National Audubon Society interactive CD-ROM gd to N American birds [CD-ROM], 97n1290
Secrets of the nest, 95n1566
Warblers of the Americas, 96n1613

BIRDS, SOUTH AMERICA
Birds of S America, v.2, 95n1573

BIRD WATCHING
Birdwatcher's hndbk, 96n1614

BIRTH CONTROL
Abortion policies, v.3, 97n665
Association for Population/Family Planning Libs & Info Centers Intl (AFPLIC-I) union list of serials, 96n861
Family planning & reproductive health servs in Ghana, 95n849
POPLINE: through Dec 1996 [CD-ROM], 98n779

BIRTHDAY BOOKS
Born this day, 96n30
Born this day, 97n41

BISEXUALS. *See also* **GAYS; LESBIANS**
Queer theory, 99n758
Strength in nos: a lesbian, gay, & bisexual resource, 97n703

BLACK ENGLISH
Black talk, 95n413

BLACKS. *See also* **AFRO-AMERICANS**
Bibliographic gd to black studies 1994, 96n398
Black firsts, 95n412
Black studies on disc [CD-ROM], 96n399
Black talent resource gd, 1994 ed, 95n1356
Contemporary black biog, v.8, 96n400
Contemporary black biog, v.9, 96n401

BLACKS IN LITERATURE
Schomberg Center gd to black lit from the 18th century to the present, 97n918

BLACKS IN THE MOTION PICTURE INDUSTRY
Blacks in black & white, 2d ed, 96n1410

BLACKS—MUSIC
Brass music of black composers, 97n1041

BLACKS—QUOTATIONS
Contemporary quotations in black, 98n78

BLACKS—SOUTH AFRICA—RELIGION
African traditional religion in South Africa, 98n1344

BLACKS—STATISTICS
Statistical record of black America, 3d ed, 96n404

BLAKE, WILLIAM
Blake bks suppl, 96n1244

BLIND & DEAF
AFB dir of servs for blind & visually impaired persons in the US & Canada, 99n748
AFB dir of servs for blind & visually impaired persons in the US & Canada [CD-ROM], 99n749
Deaf persons in the arts & scis, 96n857
Directory of agencies & orgs serving individuals who are deaf-blind, rev ed, 98n772
Living with low vision, 97n671

BLIND—REHABILITATION
Living with low vision, 97n671

BLISS, ARTHUR
Arthur Bliss: a source bk, 98n1211

BLUES (MUSIC)
All music gd to the blues, 97n1072
Blues & gospel records 1890-1943, 99n1160
Encyclopedia of the blues, 2d ed, 99n1150
Grove Pr gd to the blues on CD, 95n1294
Guide to the blues, 95n1295

BOARD GAMES
Antique trader's gd to games & puzzles, 98n891

BOARDING SCHOOLS
Boarding school gd, 97n297

BOATS & BOATING
McKnew & Parker's buyer's gd to sport fishing boats, 1995 ed, 96n810
Northeast gd to saltwater fishing & boating, 95n817
Southeast gd to saltwater fishing & boating, 95n818

BOCCACCIO, GIOVANNI
Boccaccio in English: a bibliog of eds, adaptations, & criticism, 97n1011

BODY, HUMAN
Russian-English collocational dict of the human body, 97n867

BONSAI
Bonsai survival manual, 97n1256

BOOKBINDING
ABC of bkbinding, 99n855

BOOK COLLECTING
ABC for bk collectors, 7th ed, 96n1001
American bk collectors & bibliographers, 1st series, 95n971
American bk collectors & bibliographers, 2d series, 99n591
Antiquarian bks, 96n1002
Book prices: used & rare 1995, 96n1003
Bookman's price index, v.50, 96n1004
First eds, 95n972
Huxford's old bk value gd, 8th ed, 97n776
Nineteenth-Century British bk collectors & bibliographers, 99n592

BOOK INDUSTRIES & TRADE
American bk trade dir 1997-98, 98n596
Book industry trends 1994: covering the yrs 1988-98, 95n667
Bowker annual lib & bk trade almanac 1994, 95n644
British literary bk trade, 1475-1700, 98n594
Harrod's librarians' glossary, 8th ed, 97n526
International bk trade dir 1997, 98n602
Librarian's companion, 2d ed, 97n532

BOOK REVIEWS
Book review digest, Mar 1996 to Feb 1997 inclusive, 98n65
Canadian bk review annual 1997, 99n16
Children's ref plus [CD-ROM], 96n21
Critical review of bks in religion 1997, v.10, 99n1260

BOOKS
Bibliographic hist of the bk, 96n664
Encyclopedia of the bk, 2d ed, 97n554
Philosopher's index, v.27, 95n1432

BOOKSELLERS & BOOKSELLING
AB Bookman's yrbk, 1993-94, 95n970
Antiquarian, specialty, & used bk sellers 1997-98, 2d ed, 98n597
Authentic Jane Williams' home school mrkt gd, 97n280
Bookman's price index, v.50, 96n1004
Bowker annual lib & bk trade almanac 1994, 95n644
Bowker annual lib & bk trade almanac, 1996, 97n528
Bowker annual lib & bk trade almanac, 1997, 98n576
Consumer Research study on bk purchasing, 1993, 96n673
Dictionary of American antiquarian bkdealers, 99n616
Publishers, distrs, & wholesalers of the US 1996-97, 97n555
Publishing market ref plus 1994-95, 2d ed [CD-ROM], 96n672
Used bk lover's gd to the Midwest, 96n1007

BOOKS & READING
Private libs in Renaissance England, v.3: PLRE 67-86, 96n1006
Wordsworth's reading 1770-99, 95n1223

BOOK TALKS
Booktalking the award winners 3, 98n1082
Booktalking the award winners: children's retrospective volume, 98n1081
Index to the Wilson bktalking series, 98n1083

BOSNIA & HERZEGOVINA
Breakup of Yugoslavia & the war in Bosnia, 99n116
Historical dict of Bosnia & Herzegovina, 99n120

BOSNIAN LANGUAGE—DICTIONARIES—ENGLISH
Bosnian-English, English-Bosnian concise dict, 96n1098

BOTANISTS
Dictionary of British & Irish botanists & horticulturalists, rev ed, 96n1562
One hundred & one botanists, 96n1564

BOTANY
Dictionary of generic names of seed plants, 96n1565
Elsevier's dict of plant names, 97n1273
Flora Europaea, v. 1, 2d ed., 95n1540
Flora of N America n of Mexico, v.3, 98n1447
Guide to info sources in the botanical scis, 2d ed, 97n1272
Plant explorer's gd to New England, 96n474
Plant identification terminology, 95n1538
Plants & their names, 96n1563
Reference gd for botany & horticulture, 97n1258
Scientific & common names of 7,000 vascular plants in the US, 96n1593
Synonymized checklist of the vascular flora of the US, Canada, & Greenland, 95n1555
What plant where, 96n1566

BOTSWANA
Historical dict of Botswana, 3d ed, 97n94

BOUNDARY DISPUTES
Encyclopedia of intl boundaries, 96n455

BOURBON
Bourbon companion, 99n1337

BOXING
Boxing register, 98n743

BRAHMS, JOHANNES
Johannes Brahms: an annot bibliog of the lit from 1982 to 1996, 99n1143

BRAIN
Brain ency, 97n1334

BRAND NAME PRODUCTS
Brands & their cos suppl, 17th ed, 99n148
Encyclopedia of consumer brands, 95n324
International dir of consumer brands & their owners, 98n200

BRAQUE, GEORGES
Georges Braque: a bio-bibliog, 95n996

BRASS INSTRUMENTS
Brass music of black composers, 97n1041
Twentieth-Century brass soloists, 95n1274

BRAZIL
Brazil, rev ed, 98n140
Brazil co hndbk, 1994/95 ed, 95n286
Orchids of Brazil, 95n1543

BREAST MILK
Effects of drugs on the fetus & nursing infant, 97n1358

BREWERIES
Encyclopedia of beer, 96n1525
North American brewers resource dir 1996-97, 13th ed, 97n1251
On tap, 1995 ed, 96n1532

BRITISH AMERICANS
Student's gd to British American genealogy, 97n360

BRITISH NEWSPAPERS
Twentieth-Century newspaper pr in Britain, 96n972

BRITTEN, BENJAMIN
Benjamin Britten: a gd to research, 97n1040

BROADCASTING
Bacon's bus media dir 1994, 95n933
Broadcast news manual of style, 2d ed, 96n992
Burrelle's index of broadcast transcripts, 1993 ed, 96n998
Burrelle's media dir, June 1994 [CD-ROM], 95n934
Burrelle's media dir, 1998 ed, 99n837
Dictionary of TV & AV terminology, 99n838
Encyclopedia of TV, 98n888
Informatics hndbk, 98n1593
International dict of broadcasting & film, 96n984
Plunkett's entertainment & media industry almanac, 99n827

BROOKNER, ANITA
Four British women novelists, 99n1061

BROWNING, ROBERT
Art & architecture in the poetry of Robert Browning, appendix A, 98n1154

BRUNEI
Historical dict of Brunei Darussalam, 99n482

BRUNNER, EMIL
Emil Brunner: a bibliog, 97n1172

BUDAPEST
Budapest, 98n133

BUDDHISM
Pada index & reverse Pada index to early Jain canons, 97n1202

BUDGET—UNITED STATES
Desk ref on the fed budget, 99n687

BUILDING
Annual bulletin of housing & bldg stats for Europe & N America 1996, 98n822
Architectural graphic standards, 9th ed, 95n1011
ASTM standards in bldg codes, 34th ed, 99n1401
Building construction cost data 1997, 55th ed, 98n1480
Building design & construction hndbk, 5th ed, 95n1604
CD estimator, 1998 [CD-ROM], 99n1402
Dictionary of bldg preservation, 97n801
Directory of bldg & equipment grants, 4th ed, 98n1481
Encyclopaedic dict in the 18th century, v.1, 99n813
Encyclopaedic dict in the 18th century, v.2, 99n814
Encyclopaedic dict in the 18th century, v.3, 99n815
Encyclopaedic dict in the 18th century, v.4, 99n816
Encyclopaedic dict in the 18th century, v.5, 99n817
Illustrated dict for bldg construction, 95n1605
National bldg codes hndbk, 99n1403
OSHA quick gd for residential builders & contractors, 99n1404
Pockets: bldgs, 96n66
Square foot costs 1997, 18th ed, 98n1483
Structural steel designer's hndbk, 2d ed, 95n1603
Time-saver standards for architectural design data, 7th ed, 99n882
Time-saver standards for housing & residential dvlpmt, 96n1048
Time-saver standards for landscape architecture design & construction data, 99n883
Wiley dict of civil engineering & construction, 98n1484

BULBS (FLOWERS)
Best bulbs for temperate climates, 96n1545
Bulbs, 99n1348
Bulbs for the rock garden, 97n1255
Garden bulbs for the South, 96n1546
Manual of bulbs, 97n1276

BULGARIA
Historical dict of Bulgaria, 99n494

BURKE, EDMUND
Edmund Burke 1729-97: a bibliog, 95n751

BURKINA FASO
Burkina Faso, 95n114
Historical dict of Burkina Faso, 2d ed, 99n96

BURLESQUE (THEATER)
Bibliographic gd to dance 1995, 98n1267

BURROUGHS, EDGAR RICE
Burroughs cyclopaedia, 97n969

BURUNDI
Historical dict of Burundi, 98n455

BUSH, GEORGE
Cumulated indexes to the public papers of the presidents of the US: George Bush, 1989-93, 96n744

BUSINESS. *See also* **ACCOUNTING; CORPORATIONS**
America's corp families 1995, 97n158
Art bus ency, 95n1004
Asian & Australasian cos, 95n240

Bahamas hndbk & businessman's annual 1995, 35th ed, 96n170
Barron's bus thesaurus, 97n178
Book of European forecasts, 2d ed, 97n238
Business & industry [CD-ROM], 98n189
Business pers index, v.38: Aug 1995-July 1996, 98n167
Business rankings annual, 1995, 96n197
Business stats of the US, 99n159
Business stats of the US, 1995 ed, 97n176
Central & East European info, 2d 3d, 95n280
Companies intl [CD-ROM], 97n209
Controller's & treasurer's desk ref, 95n233
Economic & social survey of Africa, 1994-95, 97n231
Economic survey of Latin America & the Caribbean 1995-96, 98n210
Every manager's gd to bus processes, 97n267
Executive's bk of quotations, 95n216
Gale bus resources [CD-ROM], 96n199
Great events from hist II: bus & commerce series, 95n209
Handbook of world stock indices, 99n221
Major cos of Central & E Europe & the Commonwealth of Independent States 1998, 99n257
Major cos of Europe 1998, 99n258
Market share & bus rankings worldwide [CD-ROM], 98n254
NAFTA & GATT: environmental & economic issues, 98n705
National accounts stats, 98n203
North American industry classification system, 1997, 99n162
Peterson's job opportunities in bus 1995, 96n280
Portable MBA desk ref, 95n203
Profiles in bus & mgmt [CD-ROM], 97n221
Search for economics as a sci, 97n149
World investment report 1998, 99n234
World trade almanac 1996-97, 97n207

BUSINESS—BIBLIOGRAPHY
Basic bus lib: core resources, 3d ed, 96n173
Bibliographic gd to bus & economics 1994, 96n174
Bibliographic gd to bus & economics 1995, 98n147
Business info sources, 95n179
Business orgs, agencies, & pubns dir, 8th ed, 97n160
Harvard Business School core collection, 1998, 99n140
Information sources in finance & banking, 97n191
International bus info, 95n255
International bus info, 99n228
Trade, industrial, & professional pers of the US, 95n215
Ultimate bus lib, 98n148

BUSINESS—BIOGRAPHY
Nonprofit sector yellow bk, winter 1999 ed, 99n142
Tycoons & entrepreneurs, 99n143

BUSINESS COMMUNICATION
Delmar ref manual: essentials for the electronic office, 96n310

BUSINESS CYCLES
Cycles in humans & nature, 95n1478

BUSINESS—DICTIONARIES & ENCYCLOPEDIAS
Cassell English-Japanese bus dict, 95n260
Dictionary for bus & finance, 3d ed, 96n180
Dictionary of bus & mgmt, 95n187
Dictionary of bus, 2d ed, 99n145
Dictionary of bus & legal terms: Russian-English/English-Russian, 96n575
Dictionary of bus, English-Spanish, Spanish-English, repr ed, 99n147
Dictionary of bus terms, 2d ed, 96n178
Dictionary of intl bus terms, 99n194
Economics, trade, & dvlpmt: English-Spanish general terminology, 97n272
Elsevier's dict of European Community co/bus/financial law in English, Danish, & German, 98n517
Encyclopedia of bus, 97n155
Encyclopedia of global industries, 97n204
Encyclopedia of small bus, 99n277
English-Ukrainian dict of bus, 98n155
Knowledge Exchange bus ency, 98n154
NTC's dict of Japan's bus code words, 99n193
Oxford dict for the bus world, 95n186
Portable MBA desk ref, 2d ed, 99n278
Routledge German dict of bus commerce & finance, 98n156
Shepard's/McGraw-Hill tax dict for bus, 95n331
Understanding American bus jargon, 98n153
USA bus: the portable ency for doing bus with the US, 96n241
Wiley's English-Spanish, Spanish-English bus dict, 98n157
World trade almanac & the dict of intl trade, 1997 ed [CD-ROM], 97n208

BUSINESS—DIRECTORIES
Almanac of American employers 1998-99, 99n266
Asian markets, 4th ed, 97n234
Bacon's bus media dir 1994, 95n933
Bacon's bus media dir 1998, 99n821
Business A to Z source finder, 97n147
Business & economic research dir, 97n159
Corporate dir US public cos, 99n149
Directory of American research & tech 1995, 29th ed, 96n182
Directory of bus & financial info servs, 9th ed, 95n202
Directory of bus info resources, 1997, 5th ed, 98n250
Directory of corp affiliations 1998, 99n150
Eastern Europe, 2d ed, 99n252
Europe's major cos dir 1997, 2d ed, 99n255
Europe's medium-sized cos dir, 2d ed, 99n256
Hoover's masterlist of major intl cos 1998-99, 99n201
Major bus orgs of Eastern Europe & the Commonwealth of Independent States 1995/96, 5th ed, 97n244
National consumer phone bk USA 1998, 99n153
Pittsburgh bus dir, 99n152
World dir of exhibitions & trade fairs 1995, 96n309
World dir of trade & bus assns, 97n173
World retail dir & sourcebk, 2d ed, 97n222

BUSINESS EDUCATION
Peterson's gd to MBA programs, 96n355
Princeton Review student access gd to the best bus schools, 97n169

BUSINESS ENTERPRISES. See also CORPORATIONS
American bus disc, 1995 ed [CD-ROM], 96n181
American bus locations dir, 97n157

Business hist of the world, 95n242
Canadian co hists, v.1, 98n208
Directory of franchise opportunities, 95n220
Encyclopedia of bus info sources suppl, 10th ed, 97n177
Hoover's billion dollar dir, 98n159
Hoover's co & industry database on CD-ROM [CD-ROM], 96n190
Hoover's co capsules on CD-ROM [CD-ROM], 98n192
Hoover's co profiles on CD-ROM [CD-ROM], 98n193
Hoover's global 250, 98n202
Hoover's gd to computer cos, 96n1773
Hoover's gd to media cos, 98n859
Hoover's gd to private cos 1994-95, 95n192
Hoover's hndbk of American bus 1995, 96n191
Hoover's hndbk of American bus 1998, 99n169
Hoover's hndbk of emerging cos 1997, 98n173
Hoover's hndbk of emerging cos 1998, 99n170
Hoover's hndbk of private cos 1997, 98n164
Hoover's hndbk of private cos 1998, 99n171
Hoover's hndbk of world bus 1995-96, 3d ed, 96n201
Hoover's hndbk of world bus 1998, 99n222
Hoover's hndbks index 1997, 98n168
Hoover's hndbks index 1998, 99n172
Hoover's masterlist of major Latin American cos 1996-97, 98n211
Hoover's masterlist of major US cos 1996-97, 97n166
International dir of bus historians, 95n194
International dir of co hists, v.12, 97n214
International dir of co hists, v.13, 97n215
International dir of co hists, v.14, 97n216
International dir of co hists, v.16, 99n203
International dir of co hists, v.17, 99n204
International dir of co hists, v.18, 99n205
International dir of co hists, v.19, 99n206
International dir of co hists, v.20, 99n207
International dir of co hists, v.21, 99n208
National dir of addresses & telephone nos, 1995 ed, 96n56
National dir of minority-owned bus firms, 9th ed, 99n155
National dir of woman-owned bus firm, 9th ed, 99n156
National jobbank 1998, 98n237
Researching Canadian markets, industries, & bus opportunities, 99n247
World retail dir 1997-98, 99n212
Worldwide branch locations of multinatl cos, 95n246

BUSINESS ETHICS
Codes of professional responsibility, 3d ed, 96n1431

BUSINESS—HISTORY
History of black bus in America, 99n144
International bibliog of bus hist, 98n149
Notable corp chronologies, 96n177

BUSINESS INFORMATION SERVICES
Bibliography of bus/competitive intelligence & benchmarking lit, 96n175
Directory of bus info resources, 1994, 95n195
Encyclopedia of bus info sources: Europe, 95n277
Encyclopedia of bus info sources suppl, 10th ed, 97n177
How to find co intelligence in state docs, 15th ed, 96n202

International bus & trade dirs, 96n228
International bus info, 95n255
International dir of bus info sources & servs 1996, 2d ed, 97n213
Internet compendium: subject gds to social scis, bus, & law resources, 96n101
Merriam-Webster's gd to intl bus communications, 95n253
Portable MBA desk ref, 95n203
Prentice Hall dir of online bus info 1997, 97n168
World dir of bus info libs, 97n548

BUSINESS LEADERS
Dictionary of 20th century British bus leaders, 95n282

BUSINESS LIBRARIES
Basic bus lib: core resources, 3d ed, 96n173
Business lib & how to use it, 6th ed, 97n530
World dir of bus info libs, 3d ed, 99n615

BUSINESS METHODS
Business & legal forms for crafts, 99n854
Business & legal forms for photographers, rev ed, 99n859
Portable MBA desk ref, 2d ed, 99n278

BUSINESS NAMES
International dir of consumer brands & their owners, 98n200

BUSINESS—PERIODICALS
Directory of bus per special issues, 96n209
World dir of trade & bus jls, 97n174

BUSINESS RELOCATION
Craighead's intl bus, travel, & relocation gd to 78 countries, 96n231

BUSINESS SCHOOLS
Barron's gd to graduate bus schools, 99n318
Best 75 bus schools, 1999 ed, 99n320
Business Week gd to the best bus schools, 4th ed, 96n332

BUSINESS WRITING
AMA style gd for bus writing, 98n873
Delmar ref manual: essentials for the electronic office, 96n310

BUTTERFLIES
Butterflies of Delmarva, 95n1579
Butterflies of the W Indies & S Fla., 95n1578
Butterflies of the world, 99n1390
Painted ladies: butterflies of N America, 95n1576
Peterson 1st gd to butterflies & moths, 95n1577

BUTTONS
Antique & collectible buttons, 98n902

BYRD, WILLIAM
Tudor music: a research & info gd, 95n1253

BYRON, GEORGE GORDON
George Gordon, Lord Byron, 98n1155

CACTUS
Cacti & succulents, 95n1548
Complete bk of cacti & succulents, 95n1549

CALDECOTT AWARD
Newbery & Caldecott awards, 1998 ed, 99n995

CALENDARS
Chase's calendar of events 1997, 40th ed, 97n5
Daily celebrity almanac, 7th ed, 95n4
World holiday festival & calendar bks, 99n1194

CALIFORNIA
Bibliographies of northern & central Calif. Indians, 95n426
California, 98n413
Chumash & their predecessors, 99n381
Decorative arts: an illus summary cat of the collections of the J. Paul Getty Museum, 95n966
1500 Calif place names, 99n420
Lawmen & desperadoes, 96n571
Los Angeles A to Z, 99n91

CAMBODIA
Cambodia, 99n105

CAMELLIA
Illustrated ency of camellias, 99n1364

CAMERA
Orion blue bk: camera, 99n178

CAMPAIGN FUNDS
Campaign & election reform, 98n679
Cash constituents of Congress, 2d ed, 95n735
Handbook of campaign spending: money in the 1992 Congressional races, 95n738
Lobbying, PACs, & campaign finance, 96n740
Open secrets: the ency of congressional money & pols, 4th ed, 98n675
Open secrets, 3d ed, 95n736

CAMPS
Guide to accredited camps, 1995/96, 39th ed, 96n811
Guide to summer camps & summer schools 1995/96, 27th ed, 96n326

CANADA
Animation, caricature, & gag & pol cartoons in the US & Canada, 95n1331
Canadian almanac & dir 1997, 97n3
Canadian almanac & dir 1999, 152d ed, 99n2
Canadian bed & breakfast gd, 12th ed, 97n393
Canadian film & video, 98n1271
Canadian medical dir 1994, 95n1658
Canadian oil industry dir, 1994, 95n1746
Canadian professional schools factsheets, 95n348
Canadian profile: alcohol, tobacco, & other drugs 1995, 96n898
Canadian sourcebk, 1997, 32d ed, 97n4
Canadian sourcebk 1998, 33d ed, 99n3
Charlton standard catalogue of Canadian govt paper money, 11th ed, 99n843
Class FC, a classification for Canadian hist, 2d ed, 96n628
Colombo's concise Canadian quotations, 99n77
Complete gd to bed & breakfasts, inns & guesthouses in the US & Canada, 11th ed, 95n510
Concise histl atlas of Canada, 99n409
Dinosaur safari gd, 96n1814
Emergency Librarian index, vs.1-20: 1973-93, 96n645
Facts about Canada, its provinces & territories, 96n137
Favorite annuals, 96n1568
Favorite flowering shrubs, 96n1569
Favorite perennials, 96n1570
Favorite shade plants, 96n1571
Field gd to nearby nature, 95n1559
Field gd to venomous animals & poisonous plants, 95n1535
Fodor's exploring Canada, 98n421
Gardening by mail, 4th ed, 95n1525
Guide to N American steam locomotives, 95n1791
Guide to published Canadian violin music suitable for student performers, 95n1279
In search of your Canadian roots, 2d ed, 95n453
Integrated pest mgmt glossary, 95n1513
Lake, river, & sea-run fishes of Canada, 96n1624
Milepost: trip planner for Ala. & Western Canada, 49th ed, 98n406
Native N American almanac: a ref work..., 95n439
Novalis gd to Canadian shrines, 96n1476
110 Canadian stats on work & family, 95n848
Opportunities for vocational study, 96n385
Pollen grains of Canadian honey plants, 95n1537
Profile of western N America, 97n248
Real gd to Canadian univs, 95n347
Research projects supported by the Canadian Ethnic Studies Program 1973-92, 95n419
Research results of projects funded by the Canadian Ethnic Studies Program 1973-88, 95n418
Symbols of nationhood, 95n142
Synonymized checklist of the vascular flora of the US, Canada, & Greenland, 95n1555
Turtles of the US & Canada, 96n1636
USA & Canada 1994, 95n106
USA & Canada 1998, 99n88
World of difference, 3d ed, 95n383

CANADA—BIBLIOGRAPHY
Bibliography of Canada's peoples, suppl.1, 95n417
Bibliography of McClelland & Stewart imprints, 1909-1985, 95n677
Bibliography of theatre hist in Canada, 95n1404
Bibliography of works on Canadian foreign relations 1991-95, 99n689
Canada: a reader's gd, 1991-92 suppl, 95n15
Canadian bks in print 1997, 98n18
Canadian ref sources, 97n19
Catalogue of Canadian catalogues, 96n249

CANADA—BIOGRAPHY
Biographical dict of N American classicists, 95n1154
Canadian newsmakers 1997, 98n33
Canadian who's who 1996: v.31, 97n37
Contemporary Canadian authors, v.1, 98n1169
Dictionary of Canadian biog, v.13, 95n26

CANADA—BUSINESS HANDBOOKS
Arthur Andersen N American bus sourcebk, 96n288
Consumer Canada 1996, 97n268
Directory of Canadian manufacturers [BOSS 1994], 95n274
Directory of Japanese-affiliated cos in the USA & Canada 1993-94, 95n270
Globe & Mail report on bus: Canada co hndbk 1994, 96n250

CANADA—DICTIONARIES & ENCYCLOPEDIAS
Canadian dict of abbrevs, 95n1
Canadian ency plus, 1997 [CD-ROM], 97n42
Canadian Oxford dict, 99n41
Encyclopedia of Canadian rock, pop & folk, 95n1292
Encyclopedia of words & phrases, legal maxims, 95n603
Junior Worldmark ency of the Canadian provinces, 98n119

CANADA—DIRECTORIES
Awards dir 1993-94, 95n1226
Bent gd to gay/lesbian Canada 1994, 95n853
Best hospitals in America, 2d ed, 96n1693
Canadian address bk, 96n54
Canadian medical dir 1994, 95n1658
Canadian oil industry dir, 1994, 95n1746
Directory of Canadian schools, 6th ed, 96n319
Pre-1900 annuals, 95n139
Pre-1900 Canadian dirs, 95n140
Self-help dir, 95n827

CANADA—ECONOMIC CONDITIONS
Economic integration in Europe & N America, 96n232

CANADA—HISTORY
Bibliographic gd to N American hist 1994, 96n489
Canadian Histl Review index, vs.52-71, 95n551
Genealogy & local hist to 1900, 97n351
Great lives from hist: American women series, 96n942
Introducing Canada, 99n489
Larousse dict of N American hist, 96n508
More battlefields of Canada, 95n692

CANADA—LIBRARY RESOURCES
Canadiana in US repositories: a preliminary gd, 96n136

CANADA—MAPS
Hammond road atlas & vacation gd, 96n442
Reader's Digest atlas of Canada, 96n451

CANADA—NATIVE RACES
Native Canadian anthropology & hist, rev ed, 95n430
Native studies collection, 95n432

CANADA—OFFICIALS & EMPLOYEES
Corpus admin index, 1994, 95n748

CANADA—POLITICS & GOVERNMENT
Bibliography of works on Canadian foreign relations 1986-90, 96n748
Canadian parliamentary, 98n683
Contemporary Canadian pols, 1988-94, 96n751
Corpus admin index, 1994, 95n748
Language of Canadian pols, 96n752

CANADA—POPULATION
Guidebook to Canadian population studies & stats, 95n141

CANADIAN FICTION
Canadian writers & their works: fiction series, v.12, 97n1003

CANADIAN FOOTBALL LEAGUE
Canadian Football League facts, figures, & records, 1994 ed, 95n819

CANADIANISMS
Gage Canadian dict, rev ed, 98n1012
Guide to Canadian English usage, 99n907

CANADIAN LITERATURE
Annotated bibliog of Canada's major authors, v.8, 95n1227
George Ryga papers, 96n1249
Identities & issues in lit, 98n1070
Native N American lit, 96n1259
Oxford companion to Canadian lit, 99n1088
Short stories in English: Britain & N America, 95n1165

CANADIAN PERIODICALS
CPI.Q: Canadian per index [CD-ROM], 98n75

CANADIAN POETRY
Canadian writers & their works: poetry series, v.11, 97n1004

CANADIANS
Canadian who's who 1997, v.32, 99n38

CANCER
Anticancer drugs from animals, plants, & microorganisms, 96n1740
Dictionary of human oncology, 96n1726

CANTATAS
Handbook to Bach's sacred cantata texts, 98n1247

CAPITAL INVESTMENTS
Flows & stocks of fixed capital 1967-92, 96n213

CAPITALISM
ABC-CLIO world hist companion to capitalism, 99n158

CAPITAL PUNISHMENT
Capital punishment, 95n623
Encyclopedia of capital punishment, 99n577
Legal executions in N.Y. State, 98n554

CAREERS. See also VOCATIONAL GUIDANCE; JOB HUNTING
Almanac of American employers 1998-99, 99n266
Career discovery ency, 98n213
Career Xroads, 3d ed, 99n267
College majors & careers, 3d ed, 98n316
Dictionary of occupational terms, 95n297
DISCovering careers & jobs [CD-ROM], 96n271
Encyclopedia of careers & vocational guidance, 2d ed [CD-ROM], 98n214
Ferguson's gd to apprenticeship programs, 2d ed, 99n359

Gale's career guidance system, expanded ed [CD-ROM], 96n384
Museum careers & training, 95n83
On-line job search companion, 96n272
Peterson's hidden job market 1995, 95n304
Professional & technical careers, 99n274
Professional careers sourcebk, 3d ed, 95n390
Professional careers sourcebk, 5th ed, 99n361
Professionals job finder 1997-2000, 99n273
Top 100: the fastest growing careers for the 21st century, rev ed, 99n276

CARIBBEAN AREA
Ancient Caribbean, 95n420
Bahamas hndbk & businessman's annual 1995, 35th ed, 96n170
Bermuda, 99n137
Bibliographic gd to Latin American studies 1996, 98n139
Bibliography of Latin American & Caribbean bibliogs: annual report 1992-93, 95n168
Bibliography of the Caribbean, 97n128
Cambridge gd to African & Caribbean theatre, 95n1420
Caribbean lit, 99n1089
Cayman Islands, 97n131
Dictionary of Caribbean English usage, 97n834
Encyclopedia of world cultures, v.8: Middle America & the Caribbean, 97n318
Frommer's comprehensive travel gd: Caribbean '95, 96n483
Jane's sentinel: Central America & the Caribbean security assessment, 1996 ed, 97n129
South America, Central America, & the Caribbean 1999, 7th ed, 99n138
Statistical yrbk for Latin America & the Caribbean, 1994 ed, 96n154

CARIBBEAN AREA—MOTION PICTURES
Guide to Latin American, Caribbean, & US Latino-made films & video, 99n1226

CARIBBEAN LITERATURE
Caribbean lit, 99n1089
Twentieth-Century Caribbean & black African writers, 3d series, 97n1012

CARICATURES & CARTOONS
Animation, caricature, & gag & pol cartoons in the US & Canada, 95n1331
Comic art of Europe, 95n1332
Editorial cartooning & caricature, 99n1192

CARL H. PFORZHEIMER LIBRARY
Carl H. Pforzheimer Lib, English lit, 1475-1700, 1997 ed, 98n1148

CARNIVAL GLASS
Standard carnival glass price gd, 10th ed, 97n784
Standard ency of carnival glass, 5th ed, 97n785

CAROLINA INDIAN VOICE
Lumbee Indians: an annot bibliog, 95n431

CARPENTER, JOHN ALDEN
John Alden Carpenter: a bio-bibliog, 95n1270

CARTOGRAPHERS
Dictionary of land surveyors & local map-makers of Great Britain & Ireland, 1530-1850, 98n394

CARTOGRAPHY
Bibliographic gd to maps & atlases 1996, 98n391
Maps & mapping of Africa, 98n392

CASH, JOHNNY
Johnny Cash discography, 1984-93, 95n1301
Johnny Cash record catalog, 96n1317

CASINOS
American casino gd, 1997 ed, 98n411
Casino gaming in the US, 98n724
Where to play in the USA: the gaming gd, 98n419

CASTLES
English castles, 97n394

CATALAN LANGUAGE—DICTIONARIES—ENGLISH
Catalan dict, 95n1071

CATALOGING
Cataloging nonbk materials with AACR2R & MARC, 96n631
Class FC, a classification for Canadian hist, 2d ed, 96n628
Classification plus [CD-ROM], 97n533
Dewey decimal classification & relative index, 21st ed, 97n535
Dewey for Windows [CD-ROM], 97n536
Free-floating subdivisions, 6th ed, 95n651
Libraries Unltd professional collection CD 1995 [CD-ROM], 97n523
Library of Congress subject headings, 19th ed, 97n534
SUPER LCCS CD [CD-ROM], 96n633
Symbols of American libs, 14th ed, 95n645
USMARC format for bibliographic data, 1994 ed, 96n634

CATALOGS, CLASSIFIED
Dewey decimal classification & relative index, 21st ed, 97n535
Dewey for Windows [CD-ROM], 97n536
Printed catalogues of the Harvard College Lib, 1723-90, 97n39

CATALOGS, COMMERCIAL
Catalog of catalogs 3, 95n226
Catalogue of Canadian catalogues, 96n249
Directory of mail order catalogs 98, 99n175
Directory of overseas catalogs, 1997, 97n212
National dir of catalogs 1997, 98n181

CATALOGS, PUBLISHERS'
Descriptive catalog of the music printed by Hubert Waelrant & Jan de Laet, 96n1266

CATHER, WILLA
Reader's companion to the fiction of Willa Cather, 95n1185
Reader's gd to the short stories of Willa Cather, 95n1186

CATHOLIC CHURCH
Catholic almanac, 1994, 95n1471
Catholic Internet, USA ed, 98n1390
Catholicism on the Web, 98n1391
Child's 1st Catholic dict, 95n1468
Destination: Vatican II [CD-ROM], 99n1288
Ecclesia: a theological ency of the Church, 98n1387
Encyclicals of John Paul II on CD-ROM [CD-ROM], 97n1217
Encyclopedia of American Catholic hist, 99n1286
English Catholic bks, 1701-1800, 97n1204
Father Charles E. Coughlin, 99n1282
Handbook of Catholic theology [rev ed], 96n1475
HarperCollins ency of Catholicism, 96n1469
Historical dict of Catholicism, 98n1384
Liturgical dict of E Christianity, 95n1467
Modern Catholic ency, 95n1469
NCEA/Ganley's Catholic schools in America 1995, 23d ed, 97n1216
New dict of Catholic social thought, 96n1470
Our Sunday Visitor's 1997 Catholic almanac, 97n1203
Our Sunday Visitor's Catholic ency, rev ed, 99n1268
Our Sunday Visitor's Catholic ency & Catholic dict [CD-ROM], 96n1471
Our Sunday Visitor's ency of Catholic doctrine, 98n1388
Our Sunday Visitor's ency of Catholic hist, 96n1472
Photo dir of the US Catholic hierarchy, 95n1462
US Catholic sources, 97n1215
Vatican archives: an inventory & gd to histl docs of the Holy See, 99n1284

CATHOLIC UNIVERSITIES & COLLEGES
Complete bk of Catholic colleges, 1998 ed, 98n288

CATS
A-Z of cat diseases & health problems, 99n1386
American Animal Hospital Assn ency of cat health & care, 96n1618
Barron's ency of cat breeds, 99n1382
Cat owner's question & answer bk, 99n1387
Cat World, 98n1465
Complete cat health manual, 98n1464
Encyclopedia of the cat, 98n1463
Help! the quick gd to first aid for your cat, 97n1261
Pockets: cats, 96n67
Quintessential cat, 95n1580

CAYMAN ISLANDS
Cayman Islands, 97n131

CD-ROM BOOKS
Anders CD-ROM gd, 2d ed, 97n15
CD-ROM bk index, 96n80
CD-ROM dir 95 with multimedia CDs, 13th ed, 96n1769
CD-ROM dir, 14th ed [CD-ROM], 96n1768
CD-ROM finder, 96n8
CD-ROM for librarians & educators, 2d ed, 98n282
CD-ROMs in print 1996, 97n17
CD-ROMs in print, 12th ed, 99n8
CD-ROMs rated, 96n10
Gale dir of databases, 99n1495

Key gd to electronic resources: art & art hist, 98n942
Key gd to electronic resources: lang & lit, 98n985
Media review digest, v. 26, 1996, 97n9
Multimedia dir, 4th ed, 97n1363
United States hist: a selective gd to info sources, 95n529

CD-ROMS
Abortion & reproductive rights [CD-ROM], 98n755
AGELINE on SilverPlatter: 1978-August 1994 [CD-ROM], 95n831
Alloy finder [CD-ROM], 96n1660
America: hist & life on disc [CD-ROM], 96n512
American bus disc, 1995 ed [CD-ROM], 96n181
American Heritage talking dict, 3d ed [CD-ROM], 96n1062
American Heritage talking dict [CD-ROM], 98n997
American Indian: a multimedia ency [CD-ROM], 98n352
American Medical Assn family medical gd [CD-ROM], 96n1707
American presidency [CD-ROM], 98n668
American Sign Lang dict on CD-ROM [CD-ROM], 96n1130
Ancient civilizations of the Mediterranean [CD-ROM], 99n490
Anthropological lit on disc [CD-ROM], 95n391
Anthropological lit on disc [CD-ROM], 98n317
Anthropology bibliog on disc [CD-ROM], 99n362
ArchivesUSA [CD-ROM], 98n430
Arctic & Antarctic regions [CD-ROM], 96n127
Art on screen on CD-ROM [CD-ROM], 96n1037
ARTbibliographies modern on disc, fall 1993 [CD-ROM], 95n991
ASM hndbk: comprehensive index [CD-ROM], 95n1625
ASSIA plus [CD-ROM], 96n97
ASTM standards source [CD-ROM], 96n1663
Athena: classical mythology on CD-ROM [CD-ROM], 95n1318
Avery index to architectural pers at Columbia Univ [CD-ROM], 95n1013
Avery index to architectural pers at Columbia Univ [CD-ROM], 98n970
Bacon's dirs on disc 1995 update [CD-ROM], 96n974
BHA: bibliog of the hist of art 1996 [CD-ROM], 97n791
BHI plus [CD-ROM], 96n955
Biography index [CD-ROM], 96n24
Biotechnology abstracts: agricultural & environmental, 1983-Feb 1997 [CD-ROM], 98n1490
Black studies on disc [CD-ROM], 96n399
Books in print with bk reviews plus [CD-ROM], 96n17
Books out-of-print plus [CD-ROM], 96n18
Britannica CD version 1.01 [CD-ROM], 95n64
Britannica electronic index [CD-ROM], 95n43
Broadcast news [CD-ROM], 96n991
Burrelle's media dir, June 1994 [CD-ROM], 95n934
Business: name & bus type index [CD-ROM], 98n158
Business & industry [CD-ROM], 98n189
Business sales leads, 1997 ed [CD-ROM], 98n248
Canadian ency plus, 1997 [CD-ROM], 97n42
Canadian medical dir on CD-ROM, 1996 [CD-ROM], 97n1320
Career perspectives software series [CD-ROM], 98n223
CD estimator, 1998 [CD-ROM], 99n1402

CD-ROM dir, 14th ed [CD-ROM], 96n1768
CD-ROMs in print 1995 [CD-ROM], 97n16
Chambers dict on CD-ROM [CD-ROM], 96n1064
Chemistry citation index [CD-ROM], 97n1390
Child abuse & neglect [CD-ROM], 96n616
Children's ency [CD-ROM], 98n39
CHOICE reviews on SilverPlatter [CD-ROM], 96n84
Choices for young readers [CD-ROM], 98n1086
Christian music finder [CD-ROM], 99n1177
CIJE on disc, Jan 1969-Jul 1994 [CD-ROM], 95n346
Civil War [CD-ROM], 96n691
Civil War CD-ROM [CD-ROM], 97n401
Classification plus [CD-ROM], 97n533
ClinPSYC: 1980-Dec 1996 [CD-ROM], 98n712
CollegeSource [CD-ROM], 98n297
Collier's ency 1998 [CD-ROM], 98n41
Columbia ency [CD-ROM], 98n42
Columbia Granger's world of poetry [CD-ROM], 97n1017
Columbia world of quotations [CD-ROM], 97n68
Companies intl, DOS version 1.3 [CD-ROM], 95n245
Companies intl [CD-ROM], 97n209
Complete gd to special interest videos [CD-ROM], 95n1360
Complete Marquis who's who on CD-ROM [CD-ROM], 98n28
Complete Marquis who's who on CD-ROM [CD-ROM], 99n19
Compton's interactive ency, version 3.00, 1995 ed [CD-ROM], 95n51
Concise engineering & tech index 1987-May 1994 [CD-ROM], 95n1479
Consumer sales leads, 1997 ed [CD-ROM], 98n249
Consumers ref disc [CD-ROM], 96n218
Contemporary authors on CD [CD-ROM], 95n1110
Contemporary authors on CD [CD-ROM], 98n1064
Contemporary women's issues 1992-July 1997 [CD-ROM], 98n838
Cooper's comprehensive environmental desk ref [CD-ROM], 99n1559
Corporate affiliations plus, spring/summer 1995 [CD-ROM], 97n162
Corporate dir of US public cos [CD-ROM], 97n163
CorpTech CD-ROM dir of tech cos [CD-ROM], 98n1570
CorpTech explore database [CD-ROM], 98n1571
CPI.Q: Canadian per index [CD-ROM], 98n75
Criminal justice abstracts 1968-93 [CD-ROM], 95n626
Current issues sourcefile [CD-ROM], 97n59
Dance on disc [CD-ROM], 95n1358
Dance on disc [CD-ROM], 98n1269
Destination: Vatican II [CD-ROM], 99n1288
Dewey for Windows [CD-ROM], 97n536
Dictionary of American biog [CD-ROM], 99n33
Dictionary of substances & their effects [CD-ROM], 97n1314
Dictionary of the English lang [CD-ROM], 98n1020
Dinosaur hunter [CD-ROM], 97n1403
Directory of physicians in the US, 35th ed [CD-ROM], 98n1534
DiscLit: world authors [CD-ROM], 96n1154
DISCovering authors, Canadian ed [CD-ROM], 98n1065
DISCovering authors modules [CD-ROM], 97n900
DISCovering biog [CD-ROM], 98n23

DISCovering careers & jobs [CD-ROM], 96n271
DISCovering multicultural America [CD-ROM], 97n323
DISCovering nations, states, & cultures [CD-ROM], 99n85
DISCovering sci [CD-ROM], 98n1413
DISCovering US hist [CD-ROM], 98n446
DISCovering world hist [CD-ROM], 98n505
Dissertation abstracts [CD-ROM], 97n60
Earthquakes & the built environment index, 1984—July 1995 [CD-ROM], 97n1399
Earthscape: exploring endangered ecosystems [CD-ROM], 99n1513
Editor & Publisher market gd 1994 [CD-ROM], 96n977
Electrical & electronics trades dir 1996 [CD-ROM], 98n1486
Electronic Gieck's engineering formulas [CD-ROM], 96n1642
Elementary school lib collection, 19th ed [CD-ROM], 95n662
Elementary school lib collection, 20th ed [CD-ROM], 97n545
Elements explorer [CD-ROM], 99n1509
Encyclicals of John Paul II on CD-ROM [CD-ROM], 97n1217
Encyclopaedia Judaica, 98n1393
Encyclopaedia of occupational health & safety, 4th ed [CD-ROM], 99n280
Encyclopedia Americana, 1995 [CD-ROM], 96n47
Encyclopedia Americana [CD-ROM], 97n43
Encyclopedia of assns: natl orgs of the US [CD-ROM], 97n49
Encyclopedia of bioethics, rev ed [CD-ROM], 98n1333
Encyclopedia of careers & vocational guidance, 2d ed [CD-ROM], 98n214
Encyclopedia of frontier biog on CD-ROM [CD-ROM], 96n497
Encyclopedia of religion [CD-ROM], 98n1353
Encyclopedia of the American Constitution [CD-ROM], 98n518
Encyclopedia of virology plus [CD-ROM], 98n1442
Encyclopedia plus of world problems & human potential, 4th ed [CD-ROM], 98n86
Endangered & threatened species [CD-ROM], 95n1534
ERIC on CD-ROM [CD-ROM], 97n293
European research & dvlpmt database 1995 [CD-ROM], 96n1510
Executive order 9066 [CD-ROM], 99n470
EXEGY: the source for current world info [CD-ROM], 96n49
Exploring poetry [CD-ROM], 98n1184
Exploring Shakespeare [CD-ROM], 98n1162
Exporting to the USA & the dict of intl trade, 1996-97 ed [CD-ROM], 97n205
Expositor's bible commentary [CD-ROM], 99n1277
Eyewitness ency of nature [CD-ROM], 97n1287
Eyewitness ency of sci [CD-ROM], 98n1403
Eyewitness ency of space & the universe [CD-ROM], 97n1395
Eyewitness hist of the world [CD-ROM], 96n567
Facts on File world news CD-ROM 1997 [CD-ROM], 98n506
Family archive viewer [CD-ROM], 97n355
Family studies database [CD-ROM], 97n674
Federal grants & funding locator [CD-ROM], 99n766
Film index intl 1996 [CD-ROM], 99n1240
Fish & fisheries worldwide [CD-ROM], 96n1605
Galante's venture capital & private equity dir, 1997 ed [CD-ROM], 99n199

Gale bus resources [CD-ROM], 96n199
Gale's career guidance system, expanded ed [CD-ROM], 96n384
Gale's ready ref shelf [CD-ROM], 97n50
Games & entertainment on CD-ROM, 1994 ed, 95n814
Geographic database for US economy, tech, & growth [CD-ROM], 98n818
Geopedia [CD-ROM], 95n497
Global bks in print plus [CD-ROM], 96n13
Government career gds [CD-ROM], 96n256
Grants on disc [CD-ROM], 97n695
Grolier master ency index, 1994 [CD-ROM], 95n44
Grolier multimedia ency, 1998, deluxe ed [CD-ROM], 98n43
Guinness multimedia disc of records, 1994: Windows 2.0 [CD-ROM], 95n1330
Historical abstracts on disc [CD-ROM], 99n545
Historical atlas of the Holocaust [CD-ROM], 98n492
Hoover's co & industry database on CD-ROM [CD-ROM], 96n190
Hoover's co capsules on CD-ROM [CD-ROM], 98n192
Hoover's co profiles on CD-ROM [CD-ROM], 98n193
Human nutrition 1990-Sept 1994 [CD-ROM], 95n1643
Human rights on CD-ROM, 2d ed [CD-ROM], 96n609
Humanities abstracts full text [CD-ROM], 98n845
IDEA: intl dir of educl AVs [CD-ROM], 98n311
Importers manual USA & the dict of intl trade, 1996-97 ed [CD-ROM], 97n274
Index to US marriage record, 1691-1850 [CD-ROM], 99n405
Interactive sci ency [CD-ROM], 99n1313
International index to music pers 1997:2 [CD-ROM], 98n1208
International multimedia yrbk 1995-96 on CD-ROM [CD-ROM], 96n1752
Jane's air-launched weapons image lib [CD-ROM], 98n632
Jane's military aircraft image lib [CD-ROM], 98n623
Jane's warships image lib [CD-ROM], 98n627
JIST's electronic enhanced dict of occupational titles, 2d ed [CD-ROM], 98n216
JIST's electronic gd for occupational exploration [CD-ROM], 96n275
JIST's electronic occupational outlook hndbk, 2d ed [CD-ROM], 98n231
JIST's multimedia occupational outlook hndbk, 2d ed [CD-ROM], 98n232
Junior DISCovering authors [CD-ROM], 95n1145
KGB world factbk, v.4, no.1 [CD-ROM], 95n5
Korea [CD-ROM], 96n692
KR Info OnDisc grants database [CD-ROM], 96n848
Landmark docs in American hist [CD-ROM], 96n498
Libraries Unltd professional collection CD 1995 [CD-ROM], 97n523
LISA plus [CD-ROM], 96n625
Lovejoy's college counselor [CD-ROM], 95n373
Magill's survey of sci [CD-ROM], 95n1502
Magill's survey of sci CD-ROM [CD-ROM], 99n1324
Major authors on CD-ROM: Virginia Woolf [CD-ROM], 99n1087
Management consulting [CD-ROM], 98n245
Market share & bus rankings worldwide [CD-ROM], 98n254
Martindale-Hubbell law dir on CD-ROM [CD-ROM], 96n584
Masterplots fiction CD-ROM, rev ed [CD-ROM], 95n1112

MathSci disc [CD-ROM], 97n1414
McGraw-Hill multimedia ency of sci & tech [CD-ROM], 95n1494
McGraw-Hill multimedia ency of sci & tech [CD-ROM], 99n1316
Medieval & early modern data bank [CD-ROM], 98n165
Merriam-Webster's collegiate dict, deluxe audio ed, 98n998
Merriam-Webster's collegiate dict deluxe, electronic ed [CD-ROM], 96n1066
Microsoft Encarta multimedia ency 1995 [CD-ROM], 95n60
Military personnel installations locator CD-ROM [CD-ROM], 99n633
MLA intl bibliog [CD-ROM], 96n1143
Mosby's GenRx, 8th ed [CD-ROM], 99n1482
Mosby's primary care medicine rapid ref [CD-ROM], 99n1451
Motif-index of folk lit, new ed [CD-ROM], 95n1317
Multimedia bus 500 [CD-ROM], 95n198
National Audubon Society interactive CD-ROM gd to N American birds [CD-ROM], 97n1290
National museum of American art [CD-ROM], 98n966
New England transcendentalists [CD-ROM], 99n1046
New Grolier multimedia ency [CD-ROM], 95n42
New Interpreter's Bible [CD-ROM], 99n1279
New shorter Oxford English dict [CD-ROM], 98n999
Nine worlds hosted by Patrick Stewart [CD-ROM], 98n1610
NIV complete Bible lib [CD-ROM], 98n1380
Normandy [CD-ROM], 96n693
North American facsimile bk [CD-ROM], 95n70
NTIS ordernow [CD-ROM], 98n62
Oceanographic & marine resources: 1960-Jan 1997 [CD-ROM], 98n1616
OECD statl compendium 1996/1 [CD-ROM], 97n227
On common ground: world religions in America [CD-ROM], 98n1367
150 yrs of America's Smithsonian [CD-ROM], 98n74
Oxford-Duden German dict [CD-ROM], 98n1032
Oxford English dict on CD, 2d ed [CD-ROM], 97n843
Oxford 3-in-1 bilingual dict [CD-ROM], 98n1021
PAIS select [CD-ROM], 98n89
Patty's industrial hygiene & toxicology CD-ROM [CD-ROM], 99n1566
PC Globe maps'n'facts [CD-ROM], 96n450
PCI: pers contents index [CD-ROM], 98n66
Periodical source index CD-ROM [CD-ROM], 98n373
Philosopher's index [CD-ROM], 96n1436
PhoneDisc powerfinder [CD-ROM], 98n54
Photographers on disc [CD-ROM], 98n937
Physicians' desk ref lib, Sept 1994 [CD-ROM], 95n1685
Poem finder 95 [CD-ROM], 97n1018
POPLINE: through Dec 1996 [CD-ROM], 98n779
Prehistoria [CD-ROM], 96n1816
Profiles in bus & mgmt [CD-ROM], 97n221
PsycLit [CD-ROM], 97n625
Reader's adviser on CD-ROM [CD-ROM], 97n11
Readers' gd abstracts full text mega ed [CD-ROM], 98n69
Readers' gd for young people [CD-ROM], 98n77
Sabin Collection catalog [CD-ROM], 98n10
Science navigator [CD-ROM], 96n1500
SciTech ref plus 1995-96 [CD-ROM], 97n1228

Scribner's writers series, selected authors ed [CD-ROM], 99n977
Scribner's writers series on CD-ROM: comprehensive ed [CD-ROM], 99n978
Scribner's American hist & culture [CD-ROM], 99n465
Shakespeare interactive [CD-ROM], 99n1080
Shakespeare interactive [CD-ROM], 99n1081
Simon & Schuster D-Day ency: a multimedia exploration! [CD-ROM], 95n689
Sixties [CD-ROM], 98n450
Smithsonian on disc [CD-ROM], 95n635
Smithsonian on disc, 4th ed [CD-ROM], 99n613
Social scis abstracts full text [CD-ROM], 98n92
Sociofile: 1974-Dec 1996 [CD-ROM], 98n94
SPDCD 1995: the standard per dir [CD-ROM], 96n87
Species info lib [CD-ROM], 96n1606
Staff dirs on CD-ROM [CD-ROM], 99n672
Standard math interactive [CD-ROM], 99n1543
StartSmart small bus advisor [CD-ROM], 96n207
SUPER LCCS CD [CD-ROM], 96n633
Terrorist group profiles [CD-ROM], 96n601
Thomas register on CD-ROM, 1997 [CD-ROM], 98n197
Twayne's English authors on CD-ROM [CD-ROM], 99n1067
Twayne's masterwork studies on CD-ROM [CD-ROM], 98n1074
Twayne's US authors on CD-ROM [CD-ROM], 99n1049
Twayne's world authors [CD-ROM], 99n979
US govt pers index, v.1, no.1 [CD-ROM], 95n77
US presidents [CD-ROM], 96n527
Ultimate family tree deluxe [CD-ROM], 98n371
Ultimate human body version 2.0 [CD-ROM], 98n1500
US homes [CD-ROM], 98n56
US homes & bus [CD-ROM], 98n57
USA state factbk [CD-ROM], 95n107
USSR population census, 1989 [CD-ROM], 98n130
U*X*L biogs [CD-ROM], 97n27
U*X*L multicultural CD [CD-ROM], 98n333
Variety's video dir plus [CD-ROM], 96n1388
Victorian database on CD-ROM, 1970-95 [CD-ROM], 98n468
Video rating gd for libs on CD-ROM 1990-94 [CD-ROM], 96n995
Vietnam [CD-ROM], 96n694
Viking opera gd on CD-ROM [CD-ROM], 95n1288
Virtual body [CD-ROM], 97n1312
Wildlife worldwide [CD-ROM], 96n1607
Wilson author biogs on disc 1995 [CD-ROM], 96n1144
Women's studies on disc [CD-ROM], 97n742
World academic database [CD-ROM], 97n308
World alive [CD-ROM], 96n1609
World almanac & bk of facts 1994 [CD-ROM], 95n7
World biogl index, 2d ed [CD-ROM], 97n31
World bk multimedia ency [CD-ROM], 96n51
World bk new illus info finder [CD-ROM], 95n67
World bk multimedia ency, 1998 [CD-ROM], 99n47
World country analyst [CD-ROM], 98n205
World factbk [CD-ROM], 95n8
World mktg data & stats 1996 on CD-ROM, 2d ed [CD-ROM], 97n281
World mktg data & stats on CD-ROM [CD-ROM], 99n236
World religions [CD-ROM], 95n1447
World Shakespeare biblog on CD-ROM 1990-93 [CD-ROM], 98n1165
World trade almanac & the dict of intl trade, 1997 ed [CD-ROM], 97n208
World trade atlas: US data, Mar 1994 [CD-ROM], 95n327
World weatherdisc, 1994 ed [CD-ROM], 96n1811
Writer's market, 1998, electronic ed [CD-ROM], 98n869

CELEBRITIES
Almanac of famous people, 6th ed, 99n17
Collector's gd to celebrity autographs, 97n775
Daily celebrity almanac, 7th ed, 95n4
Newsmakers 1997, 98n25
People in the news 1994, 95n24
Star gd, 1997-98, 98n1266
They also served: military bios of uncommon Americans, 99n623
When they were kids: over 400 sketches of famous childhoods, 99n27
Writer's dir 1998-2000, 13th ed, 99n958

CELLS
Illustrated glossary of protoctista, 95n1536

CELTIC LITERATURE
Encyclopaedia of Celtic wisdom, 96n788

CELTS
Celtic baby names, 98n378

CEMETERIES
Cemeteries of the US, 95n68
Roll of honor: names of soldiers who died in defense of the American Union..., 95n547
Vestiges of mortality & remembrance, 95n519

CENSORSHIP
Banned bks: lit suppressed on pol grounds, 99n603
Banned bks: lit suppressed on rel grounds, 99n604
Banned bks: lit suppressed on sexual grounds, 99n605
Banned bks: lit suppressed on social grounds, 99n606
Banned in the media, 99n825
Banned in the USA, 95n658
Censorship, 99n607
Censorship, 99n608
Free expression & censorship in America, 98n584
Intellectual freedom manual, 5th ed, 97n542

CENTRAL AMERICA. See also **LATIN AMERICA**
Dictionary of 20th century culture: Hispanic culture of Mexico, Central America, & the Caribbean, 97n348
Directory of consumer brands & their owners 1998: Latin America, 99n260
Encyclopedia of ancient Mesoamerica, 97n453
Encyclopedia of world cultures, v.8: Middle America & the Caribbean, 97n318
Guide to Central American collections in the US, 96n152
Handbook of Latin American Studies: social scis, no.55, 99n398

Jane's sentinel: Central America & the Caribbean security assessment, 1996 ed, 97n129
Latin America: a dir & sourcebk, 2d ed, 99n261
South America, Central America, & the Caribbean 1999, 7th ed, 99n138
Wars of the Americas, 99n629

CERAMIC ENGINEERING
Dictionary of ceramic sci & engineering, 2d ed, 95n1634

CERAMIC MATERIALS
Potter's dict of materials & techniques, 4th ed, 98n932

CHAD
Chad, 96n115
Historical dict of Chad, 3d ed, 98n453

CHADWICK, GEORGE WHITEFIELD
George Whitefield Chadwick, 99n1133

CHALOFF, SERGE
Serge Chaloff, 99n1169

CHAMBERLAIN, JOSEPH
Joseph Chamberlain 1836-1914: a bibliog, 95n752

CHAMBER MUSIC
Cello music since 1960, 96n1286
Chamber music for solo voice & instruments 1960-89, 96n1299
Discography of 78 rpm era recordings of the horn, 98n1203
Soloistic English horn lit from 1736-1984, 95n1275
Wind chamber music, 97n1058

CHAMPAGNE (WINE)
Champagne companion, 96n1354
Millennium champagne & sparkling wine gd, 99n1342

CHAMPLAIN, LAKE
Cruising gd to NY waterways & Lake Champlain, 99n430

CHANNEL ISLANDS (GREAT BRITAIN)
Channel Islands, 99n130

CHARACTERS & CHARACTERISTICS IN LITERATURE
Characters in 20th-century lit, bk 2, 96n1155
Characters in YA lit, 98n1103
Companion to the characters in the fiction & drama of W. Somerset Maugham, 97n996
Cyclopedia of literary characters, rev ed, 99n959
Dictionary of British literary characters: 20th-century novels, 95n1199
Dictionary of who, what, & where in Shakespeare, 98n1161
Historical figures in fiction, 95n1162
Larousse dict of literary characters, 95n1105
Major characters in American fiction, 95n1182
Shakespeare's characters for students, 98n1164
Who's who in Shakespeare, 96n1240
Writer's Digest character naming sourcebk, 95n944

CHARITABLE USES, TRUSTS, & FOUNDATIONS. *See also* **GRANTS-IN-AID**
AIDS funding, 4th ed, 97n683
America's new fndns 1998, 12th ed, 99n760
Awards almanac 1996, 97n701
Complete grants sourcebk for higher educ, 3d ed, 97n684
Corporate 500, 13th ed, 97n685
Corporate giving dir 1999, 20th ed, 99n761
Corporate giving yellow pages 1998, 13th ed, 99n762
Directory of corp & fndn givers, 1998, 99n763
Directory of social serv grants, 97n688
Food aid in figures, v.11, 96n881
Foundation dir 1997, 19th ed, 98n787
Foundation dir suppl, 98n788
Foundation giving, 1997 ed, 98n794
Foundation reporter 1999, 30th ed, 99n767
Fund raiser's gd to human service funding 1997, 99n774
Fund raiser's gd to religious philanthropy 1996, 9th ed, 97n691
Funding in aging, 98n759
Grant seekers gd, 4th ed, 97n693
Guide to private fortunes, v.2, 96n188
Guide to private fortunes, v.3, 96n189
Guide to US fndns, their trustees, officers, & donors, 1997 ed, 98n789
International fndn dir 1996, 7th ed, 97n696
International fndn dir 1998, 8th ed, 99n769
Literature of the nonprofit sector, v.7, 97n682
National dir of grantmaking public charities, 97n697
National gd to funding for community dvlpmt, 97n699
PRI index, 99n771
Search for security: fndns in intl affairs, 97n700
Who knows who [1996], 96n186

CHARTS, DIAGRAMS, ETC.
Information graphics, 97n1370

CHAUCER, GEOFFREY
Chaucer's Miller's, Reeve's, & Cook's Tales, 98n1156
Chaucer's pilgrims, 97n989

CHAVEZ, CARLOS
Carlos Chavez: a gd to research, 99n1141

CHEERS (TELEVISION PROGRAM)
Toasting Cheers: an episode gd to the 1982-93 comedy series...., 98n1302

CHEMICAL ENGINEERING
Chemicals on the Internet, v.1, 98n1478
Perry's chemical engineers' hndbk, 7th ed, 98n1479
Rules of thumb for chemical engineers, 96n1650
Rules of thumb for chemical engineers, 2d ed, 99n1400

CHEMICAL ENGINEERS
American chemists & chemical engineers, v.2, 95n1718

CHEMICAL INDUSTRY. *See also* **PETROCHEMICAL INDUSTRY**
Annual bulletin of trade in chemical products, 97n1384
Chemical industry in 1993, 96n222

Encyclopedia of chemical processing & design, v.56, 97n1378
Market trends for selected chemical products 1985-90 & prospects to 1995, 96n303
Structural & ownership changes in the chemical industry of countries in transition, 99n232

CHEMICAL LABORATORIES
CRC hndbk of lab safety, 4th ed, 97n1386
Handbook of lab health & safety, 2d ed, 96n1796

CHEMICAL LITERATURE—AUTHORSHIP
ACS style gd, 2d ed, 98n872

CHEMICALS
Basic lab & industrial chemicals, 95n1717
Complete gd to household chemicals, 96n1795
Directory of chemical producers & products, v.1, pt.1, 2d ed, 97n1381
Elements explorer [CD-ROM], 99n1509
Encyclopedia of chemical processing & design, v.56, 97n1378
Environmental contaminant ref databk, v.1, 97n1387
Environmental contaminant ref databk, v.2, 97n1388
Federal chemical regulation, 99n586
Gardner's chemical synonyms & trade names, 10th ed, 95n1714
Hazardous chemicals desk ref, 3d ed, 95n1781
Hazardous chemicals desk ref, 4th ed, 98n1635
History & use of our earth's chemical elements, 99n1510
1,001 chemicals in everyday products, 95n1716
Rapid gd to hazardous chemicals in the environment, 99n1569
Rapid gd to trade names & synonyms of environmentally regulated chemicals, 99n1512

CHEMICAL WEAPONS
Chemical & biological warfare, 98n607
Index to the Chemical Weapons Convention, 95n699
Jane's NBC protection equipment 1996-97, 9th ed, 97n570
US chemical-biological defense gdbk, 99n644

CHEMISTRY
Burger's medicinal chemistry & drug discovery, 5th ed, 98n1565
Chemical gd to the Internet, 97n1382
Chemical research faculties, 97n1380
Chemical scis graduate school finder 1994-95, 96n1791
Chemistry citation index [CD-ROM], 97n1390
ChemLab series, 99n1507
College chemistry faculties 1996, 10th ed, 97n303
Concise ency biochemistry & molecular biology, 3d ed, 98n1599
Concise ency chemistry, 95n1713
CRC hndbk of chemistry & physics, 75th ed, 95n1711
Desk ref for organic chemists, 96n1792
Elements, 98n1600
Encyclopedia of chemical tech suppl vol, 99n1503
Glossary of biochemistry & molecular biology, rev ed, 98n1443
Handbook of environmental data on organic chemicals, 3d ed, 97n1389
Hawley's condensed chemical dict, 13th ed, 99n1505
How to find chemical info, 3d ed, 99n1511

Macmillan ency of chemistry, 98n1601
McGraw-Hill dict of chemistry, 98n1602
Routledge German dict of chemistry & chemical tech, v.2, 99n1508
Wiley's English-Spanish, Spanish-English dict, 99n1506
World databases in chemistry, 97n1383

CHEMISTRY—TECHNICAL
Ullmann's ency of industrial chemistry, v.a25, 5th ed, 96n1789

CHEMISTS
American chemists & chemical engineers, v.2, 95n1718
Nobel laureates in chemistry, 1901-92, 95n1715

CHEMOTHERAPY
Chemotherapy hndbk, 95n1681

CHICAGO BULLS (BASKETBALL TEAM)
Chicago Bulls ency, 99n726

CHICANO LANGUAGE
Dictionary of Chicano Spanish, 2d ed, 96n1136

CHICKASAW LANGUAGE—DICTIONARIES—ENGLISH
Chickasaw: an analytical dict, 96n1099

CHILD ABUSE
Child abuse, 1997 ed, 98n568
Child abuse & neglect [CD-ROM], 96n616
Child sexual abuse custody dispute annot bibliog, 96n900
Childhood sexual abuse, 96n618

CHILDBIRTH. See also **PREGNANCY**
Having children: the best resources to help you prepare, 99n753
Mayo Clinic complete bk of pregnancy & baby's 1st yr, 96n1722
Pregnancy & birth sourcebk, 98n1561

CHILD CARE. See also **MEDICINE—PEDIATRICS; PARENTING**
Complete baby & child care, 96n904
Growing up: a cross-cultural ency, 97n708
Parenting, 96n903
Parenting A to Z, 2d ed, 98n803
Parents' resource almanac, 96n901
Portable pediatrician for parents, 95n1665
Smart medicine for a healthier child, 96n1713
Sourcebook on parenting & child care, 96n899

CHILD DEVELOPMENT
Childhood & children, 99n779
Gale ency of childhood & adolescence, 99n778
Growing up: a cross-cultural ency, 97n708
Portable pediatrician for parents, 95n1665
Resources for early childhood, 95n349

CHILD PSYCHIATRY & PSYCHOLOGY
Handbook of child psychology, 5th ed, 99n707
Sourcebook of pediatric psychology, 95n783

CHILDREN
CHILDES/BIB: an annot bibliog of child lang & lang disorders, 1994 suppl, 95n334
Practical pediatrician, 97n1354
State legislative summary, 1994, 96n595
Statistical record of children, 95n884

CHILDREN, ADOPTED
Children of separation, 95n851

CHILDREN—LAW
Children, YAs, & the law, 99n551

CHILDREN—NUTRITION
Yale gd to children's nutrition, 98n1555

CHILDREN OF DIVORCED PARENTS
Children of separation, 95n851

CHILDREN OF PRESIDENTS
America's royalty, rev ed, 96n719

CHILDREN'S ATLASES
Around the world: an atlas of maps & pictures, 96n443
Atlas of human hist, 97n458
Atlas of threatened cultures, 98n318
Children's atlas of natural wonders, 96n1806
Children's atlas of the 20th century, 96n553
Children's illus atlas, 1997 ed, 98n381
Concise atlas of the world, 3d ed, 98n383
Dillon Press children's atlas, 95n476
Discovering maps: a children's world atlas, 95n477
DK student atlas, 99n411
Facts on File children's atlas, rev ed, 99n412
Facts on File environment atlas, rev ed, 99n1551
Facts on File wildlife atlas, rev ed, 99n1295
Golden atlas for children, 95n473
Hammond comparative world atlas, 95n478
Hammond new headline world atlas, 95n479
My 1st atlas, 95n472
Pockets: world atlas, 96n77

CHILDREN'S DICTIONARIES & ENCYCLOPEDIAS
American Civil War, 96n504
American Heritage 1st dict, 95n1046
American Heritage children's dict, 96n1086
American Heritage student dict, 95n1047
Associated Press lib of disasters, 99n64
Atlas of threatened cultures, 98n318
Blizzards, 99n1525
Career discovery ency, 98n213
Children's Britannica, 95n47
Children's ency [CD-ROM], 98n39
Chronology of weather, 99n1526
Compton's ency & fact-index, 1994 ed, 95n50
Computer dict for kids & their parents, 96n1748
Courtroom drama: 120 of the world's most notable trials, 99n556
Cultures of the World, 99n84
Diseases, 98n1557
DK illus Oxford dict, 99n44
DK nature ency, 99n1309
DK sci ency, rev ed, 99n1310
Dorling Kindersley children's illus dict, 95n1048
Dorling Kindersley visual ency, 96n46
Droughts, 99n1527
Elements, 98n1600
Encyclopedia of earth & physical scis, 99n1514
Encyclopedia of life scis, 97n1268
Encyclopedia of mammals, 98n1469
Encyclopedia of N American Indians, 98n353
Encyclopedias, atlases, & dicts, 96n48
Explorers & discoverers, v.5, 99n418
Fiesta, 98n1262
First dict of cultural literacy, 2d ed, 97n296
Flags of the world, 99n406
Floods, 99n1528
Gale ency of sci, 97n1238
Grolier lib of sci biogs, 98n1400
Grolier lib of women's biogs, 99n799
Grolier lib of WW I, 98n614
Grolier student ency of sci, tech, & the environment, 97n1239
Grolier student lib of explorers & exploration, 99n419
Harcourt Brace student dict, 2d ed, 95n1049
Holocaust, 98n502
Hurricanes, 99n1529
Illustrated ency of world hist, 98n503
Illustrated sci ency, 98n1405
International children's Bible dict, 98n1376
Junior chronicle of the 20th century, 98n498
Junior Worldmark ency of the Canadian provinces, 98n119
Junior Worldmark ency of the nations, 97n79
Kingfisher 1st ency, 97n45
Kingfisher 1st sci ency, 99n1314
Kingfisher illus children's dict, 96n1087
Kingfisher illus thesaurus, 96n1088
Kingfisher illus jr dict, 99n906
Kingfisher young people's ency of the US, 95n103
Kingfisher young world ency, 96n50
Lands & peoples, 98n95
Library of the oceans, 99n1538
Literary lifelines, 99n952
Macmillan ency of sci, rev ed, 98n1406
Maps of the world, 98n387
Medical discoveries, 98n1530
Middle Ages, 97n471
Modern campaigns, 98n615
Nations of Africa, 98n321
Peoples of Central Africa, 98n322
Peoples of E Africa, 98n323
Peoples of N Africa, 98n324
Peoples of Southern Africa, 98n325
Peoples of W Africa, 98n326
Native N American biog, 97n339
New bk of knowledge, 95n61
New bk of knowledge, 98n46
100 greatest, 98n27
Outer space, 99n1522
Oxford children's bk of famous people, 96n31
Peoples of the world, 99n371

Presidents, 98n661
Profiles in American hist, 96n509
Profiles in world hist, 97n472
Questions & answers bk of sci facts, 98n1404
Reader's Digest children's illus dict, 95n1052
Religions of the world, 98n1348
Scholastic children's dict, rev ed, 98n1008
Scholastic ency of the N American Indian, 98n355
Scholastic ency of the presidents & their times, updated ed, 98n443
Scholastic ency of the US, 99n1005
Scholastic ency of women in the US, 98n836
Science & tech breakthroughs, 99n1308
Thorndike-Barnhart jr dict, 98n1009
Thorndike-Barnhardt student dict, updated ed, 95n1053
Tornadoes, 99n1530
Unites States in the 19th century, 98n436
Visual dict of physics, 96n1819
Women's firsts, 99n806
Women's voices, 98n840
World Book ency of sci, 98n1409
World Book yr bk, 1997, 98n64
World Book's young scientist, 98n1410
Young person's gd to philosophy, 99n1258

CHILDREN—SERVICES FOR
National gd to funding for children, youth, & families, 3d ed, 97n698
Parents' resource almanac, 96n901

CHILDREN'S LITERATURE
A to zoo: subject access to children's picture bks, 99n1008
Africa in lit for children & YAs, 96n1166
American Indian ref & resource bks for children & YAs, 2d ed, 96n1177
Art of children's picture bks, 2d ed, 96n1183
Best bks for children, 5th ed, 95n1130
Best toys, bks & videos for kids, 96n1010
Beyond picture bks, 2d ed, 96n1180
Black in focus, 96n1163
Booktalking the award winners 3, 98n1082
Booktalking the award winners: children's retrospective volume, 98n1081
British children's writers, 1800-1880, 97n934
British children's writers, 1880-1914, 95n1205
British children's writers, 1914-1960, 97n935
British children's writers since 1960, 1st series, 97n936
Canadian bk review annual 1994: children's lit, 96n1176
Children's authors & illustrators, 5th ed, 96n1178
Children's bk awards annual 1998, 99n990
Children's bk prizes, 99n989
Children's bks & their creators, 97n939
Children's bks from other countries, 99n991
Children's bks in print, 96n19
Children's bks in print 1998, 99n992
Children's catalog, 17th ed, 98n586
Children's fiction series, 98n1088
Children's lit awards & winners, 3d ed, 95n1148
Children's nonfiction for adult info needs, 99n996
Children's ref plus [CD-ROM], 96n21
Children's writer's & illustrator's market, 1998, 99n828
Choices, v.3, 95n1132
Choices for young readers [CD-ROM], 98n1086
Choosing your children's bks: 5-8 yrs, 2d ed, 95n1142
Choosing your children's bks: 8-12 yrs, 95n1143
Connecting cultures, 98n1093
Contemporary Spanish-speaking writers & illustrators for children & YAs, 95n1151
Core collection for small libs, 98n1077
Cultures outside the US in fiction, 95n1116
Dictionary of American children's fiction, 1990-94, 97n938
Dictionary of literary biog documentary series, v.14, 98n1089
Elementary school lib collection, 19th ed, 95n661
Elementary school lib collection, 19th ed [CD-ROM], 95n662
Elementary school lib collection, 20th ed, 97n544
Elementary school lib collection, 20th ed [CD-ROM], 97n545
Everyone's gd to children's lit, 99n1000
Exploring the Great Lakes states through lit, 95n1123
Exploring the mountain states through lit, 95n1125
Exploring the Northeast states through lit, 95n1122
Exploring the Pacific states through lit, 95n1121
Exploring the plains states through lit, 95n1120
Exploring the SE states through lit, 95n1126
Exploring the SW states through lit, 95n1124
Fantasy lit for children & YAs, 4th ed, 96n1167
From biog to hist, 99n993
Great new nonfiction reads, 96n1184
Guide to children's ref works & multimedia material, 99n994
Horn Bk gd to children's & YA bks, v.7, no.2, 98n1078
Hot links: lit links for the middle school curriculum, 99n1001
Immigrants in the US in fiction, 95n1117
Index to histl fiction for children & young people, 96n1179
Index to the Wilson booktalking series, 98n1083
Integrated curriculum: bks for reluctant readers, grades 2-5, 2d ed, 99n1006
Junior DISCovering authors [CD-ROM], 95n1145
Juvenile novels of WW II, 95n1140
Kaleidoscope: A multicultural bklist for grades K-8, 98n1087
Language arts & environmental awareness, 99n997
Latest & greatest read-alouds, 95n1137
Laura Ingalls Wilder: an annot bibliog of critical, biogl, & teaching studies, 98n1139
Learning about...the Civil War, 99n453
Literary lifelines, 99n952
Magazines for kids & teens, 96n86
Market gd for young writers, 5th ed, 97n751
Master index to more summaries of children's bks, 1980-90, 99n1009
Masterplots 2: juvenile & YA lit series suppl, 98n1085
More bks kids will sit still for, 96n663
More kids' favorite bks, 96n1168
Multicultural children's lit, 97n933
Multicultural picture bks, 95n1135
Name that bk! questions & answers on outstanding children's bks, 2d ed, 99n1007
Native Americans in fiction, 95n1118

Newbery & Caldecott awards, 1998 ed, 99n995
Newbery companion, 98n1091
Our planet Earth, 99n1003
Oxford companion to Australian children's lit, 95n1149
Phoenix award of the children's lit assn 1990-94, 98n1092
Popular nonfiction authors for children: a biogl & thematic gd, 99n1002
Primaryplots 2, 95n1141
Recreating the past, 95n1161
Research & professional resources in children's lit, 96n1169
Seventh bk of jr authors & illustrators, 97n937
Something about the author, v.78, 96n1172
Something about the author, v.79, 96n1173
Something about the author, v.80, 96n1174
Something about the author, v.81, 97n926
Something about the author, v.82, 97n927
Something about the author, v.83, 97n928
Something about the author, v.84, 97n929
Something about the author, v.85, 97n930
Something about the author, v.94, 99n988
Something about the author, v.95, 99n986
Something about the author autobiog series, v.18, 95n1146
Something about the author autobiog series, v.24, 98n1080
Something about the author autobiog series, v.25, 99n987
Special collections in children's lit, 96n661
Subject gd to children's bks in print 1995, 96n20
Taking humor seriously in children's lit, 99n998
Teaching children's lit, 96n379
They're never too young for bks, 95n1138
This land is our land: a gd to multicultural lit for children & YAs, 95n1133
Twentieth-Century children's writers, 4th ed, 96n1175
Using picture storybks to teach literary devices. v.2, 96n1164
Ways of war: the era of WW II in children's & YA fiction, 96n1165
What do children read next?, 95n1128
What do children read next? v.2, 99n999
What else should I read? guiding kids to good bks, v.2, 98n1076
Who's who of Australian children's writers, 2d ed, 97n931
World almanac for kids 1999, 99n6
Your reading, 1995-96 ed, 97n925

CHILDREN'S LITERATURE, SPANISH
Recommended bks in Spanish for children & YAs, 1991-95, 98n1079

CHILDREN'S MUSEUMS
Children's museums, 99n71

CHILDREN'S PERIODICALS
Magazines for kids & teens, rev ed, 98n879
Readers' gd for young people [CD-ROM], 98n77

CHILDREN'S PLAYS—INDEXES
Plays for children & YAs, suppl 1, 1989-94, 97n940

CHILDREN'S POETRY
Index to poetry for children & young people 1988-92, 95n1152
This land is our land: a gd to multicultural lit for children & YAs, 95n1133

CHILDREN'S RIGHTS
Children's rights, 97n515

CHILDREN'S SONGS
Children's jukebox, 96n1278
Children's song index, 1978-93, 97n1033

CHILDREN'S VIDEOCASSETTES
Bowker's dir of videocassettes for children 1998, 99n10

CHINA
American studies in China: a dir, 95n109
Area bibliog of China, 98n112
Bibliographic gd to E Asian studies 1995, 98n109
Biographical dict of Chinese women, 99n798
China, new ed, 98n111
China, 7th ed, 99n110
China: a dir & sourcebk, 2d ed, 99n107
China: a provincial atlas, 96n452
China bibliog, 96n535
China bus dir 1994, 95n267
China bus: the portable ency for doing bus with China, 95n261
China environmental report, 97n223
China: facts & figures annual hndbk, v.17, 95n129
China: facts & figures annual hndbk, v.23, 99n108
China hndbk, 99n241
China mktg data & stats, 99n242
Chinese filmography, 98n1296
Chinese religion pubs in W langs 1981 through 1990, 95n1438
Consumer China 1994, 95n268
Consumer China 1998, 99n216
Cultural atlas of China, rev ed, 99n106
Directory of Chinese agricultural & related orgs, 95n1511
Directory of officials & orgs in China, 95n130
Doctoral dissertations on China & on inner Asia, 1976-90, 99n15
Encyclopedia of world cultures, v.6: Russia & Eurasia/China, 95n397
Handbook of Chinese popular culture, 95n1326
Historical dict of the People's Republic of China: 1949-97, 99n483
Islam in China, 95n1474
Modern China: an ency of hist, culture, & nationalism, 99n109
NTC's dict of China's cultural code words, 97n107
Religion in postwar China, 95n1439
Sexual behavior in modern China, English-lang ed, 99n775
Women in China, 99n808

CHINESE CHARACTERS—JAPAN
Kanji dict, 97n860

CHINESE LANGUAGE
NTC's dict of China's cultural code words, 97n107

CHINESE LANGUAGE—DICTIONARIES— ENGLISH
Chinese 1000, 98n1022
Chinese-English-French Kuaisu dict, 99n920
Chinese synonyms usage dict, 98n1023

CHINESE LITERATURE
Indiana companion to traditional Chinese lit, v.2, 99n1090

CHINTZ WARE
Charlton standard catalogue of chintz, 2d ed, 98n924

CHORAL MUSIC
American choral music since 1920, 95n1280
Catalogue of choral music arranged in biblical order, 2d ed, 97n1053
Choral arrangements of the African-American spirituals, 99n1152
Choral music by African American composers, 97n1054
Conductor's gd to choral-orchestral works, 20th century, part 2, 99n1151

CHOREOGRAPHERS
Film choreographers & dance directors, 98n1268

CHOREOGRAPHY
Dancers & choreographers, 97n1100

CHORUSES WITH ORCHESTRA
Conductor's gd to choral-orchestral works, 96n1297

CHRISTIAN ANTIQUITIES
Jesus & his world, 97n1213

CHRISTIAN ART & SYMBOLISM
Dictionary of Christian art, 96n1028
Medieval art, 97n799
Oxford companion to Christian art & architecture, 98n950

CHRISTIAN BIOGRAPHY
Blackwell dict of evangelical biog, 1730-1860, 97n1208
Dictionary of Scottish church hist & theology, 95n1466
Seeds in the wilderness: profiles of world religious leaders, 96n1443
Twentieth-Century dict of Christian biog, 96n1465
Who's who in Christianity, 99n1283

CHRISTIAN EDUCATION
Peterson's choose a Christian college, 4th ed, 96n1474
Religious educ, 1960-93, 96n1463

CHRISTIAN ETHICS
New dict of Christian ethics & pastoral theology, 97n1209

CHRISTIAN LITERATURE
Handbook of Christian Latin, 96n1115

CHRISTIAN PILGRIMS & PILGRIMAGES
Chaucer's pilgrims, 97n989
Pilgrimage to Santiago de Compostela, 96n1462

CHRISTIAN SECTS
Evangelical sectarianism in the Russian Empire & the USSR, 97n1173
Historical dict of the orthodox church, 97n1212

CHRISTIAN SHRINES
Novalis gd to Canadian shrines, 96n1476

CHRISTIANITY. *See also* CATHOLIC CHURCH
Bible: God's word for the biblically-inept, 99n1280
Bibliography of sources in Christianity & the arts, 97n1206
Book of saints, 99n1263
Compete bk of everyday Christianity, 98n1385
Concise dict of Christian theology, 96n1453
Concise dict of Christianity in America, 96n1466
Concise ency of Christianity, 99n1287
Dictionary of Christianity, 97n1210
Dictionary of early Christian beliefs, 99n1285
Encyclopedia of apocalypticism, 99n1266
Historical dict of ecumenical Christianity, 96n1473
Our Sunday Visitor's Catholic ency, rev ed, 99n1268
Oxford dict of the Christian Church, 3d ed, 98n1389
Oxford ency of the Reformation, 97n1211

CHRISTIANITY & POLITICS
Religious right, 97n1218

CHRISTIANITY—SOUTH AFRICA
Christianity in South Africa, 98n1382

CHRONIC DISEASES
Classification of chronic pain, 2d ed, 96n1723
Complete dir for people with chronic illness, 1994, 95n1659
Complete dir for people with chronic illness, 99n1467
Essential gd to chronic illness, 98n1558
Long term care, 96n841
Resource gd for the disabled, 96n854
Resources for people with disabilities & chronic conditions, 3d ed, 97n673

CHRONOLOGY, HISTORICAL
African American hist in the press 1851-99, 97n412
American decades 1900-09, 97n422
American decades 1910-19, 97n423
American decades 1920-29, 97n424
Asian American chronology, 97n326
Chronicle of the 20th century, 96n558
Chronicle of the Olympics 1896-1996, 97n660
Chronicle of the world, rev ed, 97n464
Chronicle of the yr 1995, 97n465
Chronology of world hist, compact ed, 96n564
Columbia chronicles of American life, 1910-92, 96n501
Hispanic American chronology, 97n335
History of sci in the US, 97n1235
Illustrated almanac of sci, tech, & inventions, 99n1306
Junior chronicle of the 20th century, 98n498
Junior timelines on file, 98n499
Lesbian & gay liberation in Canada, 97n680
Pan-African chronology, 97n426
Pocket factfile of 20th century events, 97n466
Timelines of world hist, 99n524

Women writers in the US, 97n738
Women's chronology, 95n912
Women's chronology, 98n834

CHUMASH INDIANS
Chumash & their predecessors, 99n381

CHURCH COLLEGES
Religious higher educ in the US, 97n301

CHURCH CONTROVERSIES
Encyclopedia of religious controversies in the US, 98n1354

CHURCHES
National dir of churches, synagogues, & other houses of worship, 95n1445

CHURCH HISTORY
Encyclopedia of early Christianity, 2d ed, 98n1386
Historical dict of Catholicism, 98n1384
Women in Christian hist, 97n731

CHURCHILL, WINSTON
Proverbial Winston S. Churchill, 96n760

CHURCH MUSIC. *See also* **GOSPEL MUSIC; HYMNS; SACRED MUSIC**
Catalogue of choral music arranged in biblical order, 2d ed, 97n1053
Christian music dirs: printed music 1994-95, 95n1309
Christian music dirs: recorded music 1994, 95n1310
Christian music finder [CD-ROM], 99n1177
Hymnology, 98n1246

CHURCH SCHOOLS
Religious schools in the US K-12, 95n351

CHURCH & STATE
US religious interest groups, 95n1446

CIGARS
Cigar companion, 2d ed, 96n1351
Rudman's cigar buying gd, 99n183
Rudman's complete gd to cigars, 99n184

CITATION OF ELECTRONIC INFORMATION SOURCES
Electronic styles: a hndbk for citing electronic info, 2d ed, 98n875

CITATION OF LEGAL AUTHORITIES
Bieber's dict of legal abbrevs reversed, 95n592
Index to legal citations & abbrevs, 2d ed, 95n593

CITIES & TOWNS
America's top-rated smaller cities, 1994-95 ed, 96n926
America's top-rated smaller cities 1996-97, 2d ed, 98n821
Challenge of urbanization, 97n722
Cities of the world, 4th ed, 95n514
City crime rankings, 96n602
City profiles USA 1996, 97n388
Comparative gd to American suburbs, 98n824
Consolidated bibliog of urban hist, 98n825
County & city extra, 1995, 4th ed, 97n712
Ernst & Young almanac & gd to US bus cities, 95n206
Facts about the cities, 2d ed, 98n823
Gale city & metro rankings reporter, 96n930
Health & environment in America's top-rated cities, 96n931
Hispanic databk of US cities & counties, 95n423
Latin American urbanization, 95n899
MSA profile, 1996, 97n724
100 great cities of world hist, 96n927
Population hist of western US cities & towns, 1850-1990, 97n723
World ency of cities: N America, 95n900

CITIES & TOWNS, ANCIENT
Cities of the biblical world, 98n1378

CITY PLANNING
Challenge of urbanization, 97n722
Information sources in urban & regional planning, 96n928

CIVIL ENGINEERING
ASTM standards in bldg codes, 34th ed, 99n1401
VNR dict of civil engineering, 4th ed, 95n1606
Wiley dict of civil engineering & construction, 98n1484

CIVILIZATION
American bibliog of Slavic & E European studies for 1993, 97n114
Children's atlas of civilizations, 95n572
Dictionary of ancient hist, 95n583
Encyclopedia of ancient civilizations of the Near East & Mediterranean, 98n487
Encyclopedia of great civilizations, 95n580
Global voices, global visions: a core collection of multi-cultural bks, 97n10
High places in cyberspace, 2d ed, 99n1269
Medieval wordbk, 97n838
Our century, 95n591
Visual dict of ancient civilizations, 95n584
Western civilization: a critical gd to documentary films, 97n1118
Wilson chronology of ideas, 99n525

CIVIL PROCEDURE
Civil trial practice deskbk, 98n528

CIVIL RIGHTS. *See also* **HUMAN RIGHTS**
ABC-CLIO companion to the civil rights movement, 95n627
ABC-CLIO companion to the disability rights movement, 98n776
Antisemitism, v.3, 95n628
Atlas of apartheid, 95n395
Civil rights decisions of the US Supreme Court, the 19th century, 96n607
Civil rights decisions of the US Supreme Court, the 20th century, 96n608
Encyclopedia of American Indian civil rights, 98n562
Encyclopedia of human rights, 2d ed, 97n517
Gay & lesbian rights: a ref hndbk, 95n859

Human rights orgs & pers dir 1993, 95n629
World dir of human rights research & training insts, 3d ed, 97n518

CIVIL RIGHTS MOVEMENTS
Civil rights movement, 99n473
Encyclopedia of civil rights in America, 99n588
Historical dict of school segregation & desegregation, 99n301
Historical dict of the civil rights movement, 98n565

CIVIL SERVICE
Civil serv career starter, 99n272
Directory of fed jobs & employers, 97n258
Government job finder, 2d ed, 95n315
Government job finder, 98n234

CIXOUS, HELENE
French feminist theory 3, 98n832

CLANS
Collins Scottish clan & family ency, 96n435

CLASSICAL ANTIQUITIES
Encyclopedia of the hist of classical archaeology, 97n397

CLASSICAL LITERATURE
Ancient world lists & nos, 96n41
Annotated catalogue of early eds of Erasmus, 96n1250
Classical & medieval lit criticism, v.14, 96n1149

CLASSICAL PHILOLOGY
Classical studies, 97n461

CLASSICISTS
Biographical dict of N American classicists, 95n1154

CLASSIFICATION—LIBRARY MATERIALS
Abridged Dewey decimal classification & relative index, 13th ed, 98n579
Libraries Unltd professional collection CD 1995 [CD-ROM], 97n523
Subject headings for children 1994, 96n632

CLEMENT, CATHERINE
French feminist theory (2), 95n902

CLERGY
Seeds in the wilderness: profiles of world religious leaders, 96n1443

CLEVELAND MUSEUM OF ART
Catalogue of American silver, 96n999

CLEVELAND (OHIO)
Dictionary of Cleveland biog, 97n87
Encyclopedia of Cleveland hist, 2d ed, 97n88

CLIFT, MONTGOMERY
Montgomery Clift: a bio-bibliog, 95n1348

CLIMATOLOGY
Complete weather resource, 98n1611
Elsevier's dict of climatology & meteorology, 96n1808
Encyclopedia of climate & weather, 97n1396
Glossary of weather & climate with related oceanic & hydrologic terms, 98n1612
Handy weather answer bk, 98n1613
Weather almanac, 99n1534
Weather America, 97n1397
Weather of US cities, 5th ed, 97n1398

CLIMBING PLANTS
Shrubs & climbers, 97n1286

CLINICAL PSYCHOLOGY
Insider's gd to graduate programs in clinical psychology, 1994/95 ed, 95n786

CLINICAL SOCIOLOGY
NASW register of clinical social workers 1993, 95n879

CLINTON, BILL
Bill Clinton's pre-presidential career, 95n534

CLOCKS
Charlton price gd to Canadian clocks, 97n777

CLOTHING TRADE
Garment & textile dict, 98n933

COAL
Annual bulletin of coal stats for Europe & N America, 1994, 96n1838
Coal info 1992, 95n1749

COASTS
Atlas of Mesozoic & Cenozoic coastlines, 96n1807

COCA-COLA
Petretti's Coca-Cola collectibles price gd, 10th ed, 98n923

COINS. *See also* **MONEY**
Collecting world coins, 7th ed, 99n844
Guide bk of US coins, 1996, 49th ed, 96n1008
Handbook of ancient Greek & Roman coins, 97n778
Handbook of US coins, 1998, 55th ed, 98n910
International encyclopaedic dict of numismatics, 98n909
John Max Wulfing collection in Washington Univ, v.3: Roman imperial coins...., 97n779
North American coins & prices, 99n845
Platinum & palladium buyer's gd, 98n913
Standard catalog of world coins 1601-1700, 97n780
Standard catalog of world coins, Eighteenth Century 1701-1800, 98n911
Standard catalog of world coins, 1998, 98n912
Warman's coins & currency, 2d ed, 98n915

COLD WAR
Chronology of the Cold War at sea 1945-91, 99n643
Cold War, 99n544
Cold War ency, 97n473

Cold War ref gd, 98n508
Columbia gd to the Cold War, 99n543
Encyclopedia of the Cold War, 95n577
George F. Kennan: an annot bibliog, 98n700

COLE, NAT KING
Straighten up & fly right: a chronology & discography of Nat "King" Cole, 96n1329

COLERIDGE, SAMUEL TAYLOR
Samuel Taylor Coleridge: an annot bibliog of criticism & scholarship, v.3, 97n990

COLLECTIBLES
America's Standard Gauge electric trains, 99n852
Antique Trader Books antiques & collectibles price gd, 1999 ed, 99n840
Beatles memorabilia price gd, 3d ed, 98n921
Black Americana price gd, 98n892
Charlton price gd to Canadian clocks, 97n777
Collecting in cyberspace, 98n893
Collector's gd to TV memorabilia, 1960s & 1970s, 98n922
Country Americana price gd, 98n894
Coykendall's complete gd to sporting collectibles, 98n895
Everything Civil War, 98n447
Flea market trader, 11th ed, 98n896
Garage sale & flea market annual, 5th ed, 98n897
Golden age of Walt Disney records 1933-88, 98n1209
Greenberg's gd to marbles, 2d ed, 97n786
Handbook of ancient Greek & Roman coins, 97n778
Huxford's old bk value gd, 8th ed, 97n776
Maloney's antiques & collectibles resource dir, 2d ed, 95n969
Maloney's antiques & collectibles resource dir, 99n841
McDonald's collectibles, 98n898
Miller's intl antiques price gd 1999, 99n842
Patricia Smith's doll values, 12th ed, 97n781
Petretti's Coca-Cola collectibles price gd, 10th ed, 98n923
Schroeder's antiques price gd, 15th ed, 98n905
Standard carnival glass price gd, 10th ed, 97n784
Standard ency of carnival glass, 5th ed, 97n785
Wanted to buy, 6th ed, 98n901
Warman's antiques & collectibles price gd, 29th ed, 96n1000
Warman's Americana & collectibles, 99n839
Warman's coins & currency, 2d ed, 98n915

COLLECTION DEVELOPMENT (LIBRARIES)
Guides to collection dvlpmt for children & YA lit, 99n601
Guides to lib collection dvlpmt, 95n653

COLLEGE GRADUATES—EMPLOYMENT
America's top jobs for college graduates, rev ed, 95n309
Career connection for college educ, 2d ed, 95n318

COLLEGE LIBRARIANS
Academic lib of the 90s, 96n620
Directory of college & univ librarians in Canada, 2d ed, 97n550

COLLEGE MAJORS
Career connection for college educ, 2d ed, 95n318
College majors & careers, 3d ed, 98n316

Education for the Earth, 2d ed, 96n337
Index of majors & graduate degrees 1998, 99n326

COLLEGE MUSEUMS
University & college museums, galleries, & related facilities, 97n62

COLLEGE SPORTS
College football bibliog, 95n821
Encyclopedia of college basketball, 96n809
Gridiron greats: a century of Polish Americans in college football, 98n745
NCAA basketball: the official 1997 women's college basketball records bk, 98n740
NCAA football, 96n819
Peterson's sports scholarships & college athletic programs, 3d ed, 99n346
Sports phone bk USA, 1998, 99n712
Winning edge: the student-athlete's gd to college sports, 5th ed, 98n723

COLLEGE STUDENTS—EMPLOYMENT
Directory of college cooperative educ programs, 97n304

COLMAN, RONALD
Ronald Colman: a bio-bibliog, 98n1273

COLORADO
Colorado rockhounding, 95n1732
Historical atlas of Colo., 95n527

COLTRANE, JOHN
John Coltrane, 96n1324

COLUMBIA UNIVERSITY
Avery index to architectural pers at Columbia Univ [CD-ROM], 95n1013
Avery index to architectural pers, 13th suppl, 95n1014

COMDEN, BETTY
Betty Comden & Adolph Green: a bio-bibliog, 95n1352

COMEDIANS
Al Jolson: a bio-bibliog, 95n1345
American silent film comedies, 96n1378
Comedy stars at 78 RMP, 99n1196
Encyclopedia of film directors in the USA & Europe, v.1, 95n1372
Harold Lloyd: a bio-bibliog, 95n1343
Jerry Lewis films, 96n1397

COMIC BOOKS, STRIPS, ETC.
Comic bks & comic strips in the US: an intl bibliog, 95n1333
Comics buyer's gd 1998, 98n908
Comics values annual, 1998 ed, 98n907
Graphic novels, 96n1359
Syndicated comic strips & artists, 1924-95, 97n1095

COMMAND PERFORMANCE (RADIO SHOW)
Command performance, USA! a discography, 97n772

COMMERCE
Annual bulletin of trade in chemical products, 97n1384
Consumer Europe 1994, 95n278
Data sources for bus & market analysis, 4th ed, 96n296
Directory of import regimes, pt.1, 96n289
Directory of import regimes, pt.2, 96n290
Economics, trade, & dvlpmt: English-Spanish general terminology, 97n272
Encyclopedia of consumer brands, 95n324
Energy balances for Europe & N America, 1992, 1993-2010, 97n1423
External trade monthly stats, 96n293
Great events from hist II: bus & commerce series, 95n209
International bus & trade dirs, 96n228
Review of maritime transport 1997, 98n260
Shopping for a better world, 95n225
Trade, industrial, & professional pers of the US, 95n215
United Nations Commission on Intl Trade Law yrbk, v.24, 1993, 96n307

COMMERCIAL CATALOGS
Catalog of catalogs 5, 98n183
Directory of bus to bus catalogs, 1997, 98n190
Directory of mail order catalogs, 1995, 9th ed, 96n219

COMMERCIAL CORRESPONDENCE
Forms of address, 96n311

COMMERCIAL LAW
A-Z of contract clauses, 98n531

COMMERCIAL TREATIES
Encyclopedia of the N American Free Trade Agreement, 96n305

COMMERICAL PRODUCTS
Manufacturing worldwide, 97n197

COMMONWEALTH COUNTRIES
Dictionary of the British Empire & Commonwealth, 97n117

COMMONWEALTH LITERATURE (ENGLISH)
Encyclopedia of post-colonial lits in English, 95n1102
Post-colonial lit in English, 99n946

COMMONWEALTH OF INDEPENDENT STATES
Energy balances for countries in transition 1993, 1994-2010, & energy prospects in CIS countries, 98n1627

COMMONWEALTH OF NATIONS
Commonwealth univs yrbk 1993, 95n363

COMMUNAL LIVING
Communities dir, 1995 ed, 96n852
Encyclopedia of American communes, 1663-1963, 99n747

COMMUNICABLE DISEASES
Encyclopedia of infectious diseases, 99n1445

COMMUNICATION
Broadcast news [CD-ROM], 96n991
Culturgrams, 95n99
Dictionary of communication & media studies, 3d ed, 95n939
Dictionary of communication & media studies, 4th ed, 98n857
Dictionary of communications tech, 3d ed, 99n1492
Encyclopedia of rhetoric & composition, 97n840
Handbook of persuasive tactics, 95n937
Language & communication, 99n894
Leo Burnett worldwide advertising & media fact bk, 96n302
Media courses UK 1997, 4th ed, 98n860
Power media selects, 9th ed, 96n988
Webster's new world dict of media & communications, rev ed, 98n858
Who's who in the media & communications 1998-99, 99n819

COMMUNICATION IN MEDICINE
Encyclopedia of medical media & communications, 98n1529

COMMUNICATION, MILITARY
Jane's military communications 1993-94, 95n694

COMMUNICATION & TECHNOLOGY
From talking drums to the internet, 98n854

COMMUNITY
Dictionary of ethics, theology, & society, 97n73

COMMUNITY BANKS
Walker's manual of community bank stocks, 98n187

COMMUNITY COLLEGES. See also EDUCATION, HIGHER
AACC membership dir 1994, 95n358
AACC who's who in community colleges 1993, 95n359
Chronicle 2-yr college databk, rev ed, 96n335
National profile of community colleges 1995-96, 96n366
Peterson's gd to 2-yr colleges 1998, 28th ed, 98n293

COMMUNITY DEVELOPMENT
Alternatives to the Peace Corps, 96n868
Funding sources for community & economic dvlpmt 1996, 97n692
Guide to fed funding for volunteer programs & community serv, 3d ed, 96n874

COMOROS
Historical dict of the Comoro Islands, 95n115

COMPACT DISCS (MUSIC)
Country on CD, 95n1296
Grove Pr gd to the blues on CD, 95n1294
High definition CD recordings, 95n1257
NPR gd to bldg a classical CD collection, 95n1282
Top 40 music on CD, 1955-81, 95n1290

COMPARATIVE GOVERNMENT
International hndbk of local & regional govt, 95n709

COMPENSATION MANAGEMENT
Multistate payroll gd, 97n257

COMPETITION (PSYCHOLOGY)
Competitions, 97n299

COMPOSERS
Alban Berg: a gd to research, 97n1045
Allen Sapp: a bio-bibliog, 97n1038
American music in the 20th century, 99n1124
Anton Rubinstein, 99n1144
Arnold Schoenberg companion, 99n1128
Arthur Bliss: a source bk, 98n1211
Baker's biogl dict of 20th-century classical musicians, 98n1197
Baker's dict of music, 99n1123
Beethoven ency, 96n1281
Bela Bartok: a gd to research, 2d ed, 98n1210
Benjamin Britten: a gd to research, 97n1040
Brass music of black composers, 97n1041
Carl Ruggles, 96n1280
Carlos Chavez: a gd to research, 99n1141
Charles Wuorinen: a bio-bibliog, 95n1265
Classic FM gd to classical music, 98n1222
Cole Porter discography, 97n1068
Conductors & composers of popular orchestral music, 99n1158
Contemporary musicians, v.19, 99n1115
Contemporary musicians, v.20, 99n1116
Film composers gd, 3d ed, 97n1037
Gardner Read: a bio-bibliog, 97n1036
George Whitefield Chadwick, 99n1133
Germaine Tailleferre: a bio-bibliog, 95n1271
Giovanni Gabrieli (ca.1555-1612): a thematic catalogue of his music...., 97n1034
Giuseppe Verdi: a gd to research, 99n1137
Harvard biographical dict of music, 97n1024
International ency of violin-keyboard sonatas & composer biogs, 2d ed, 97n1043
Irving Berlin, 99n1134
Isaac Albeniz, 99n1129
Jean Sibelius: a gd to research, 99n1135
Johann Baptist Cramer (1771-1858): a thematic cat of his works, 95n1269
Johannes Brahms: an annot bibliog of the lit from 1982 to 1996, 99n1143
John Alden Carpenter: a bio-bibliog, 95n1270
Keeping score: film & TV music, 1988-97, 99n1140
Larry Sitsky: a bio-bibliog, 98n1214
Latin American classical composers, 97n1042
Leslie Bassett: a bio-bibliog, 95n1268
Lives of the great composers, 3d ed, 98n1216
Malcolm Arnold, 99n1130
Manuel de Falla, 99n1136
Minor ballet composers, 98n1215
Mozart diary, 98n1213
Music of Francis Poulenc (1899-1963), 97n1044
Music of the golden age, 1900-50 & beyond, 99n1139
Peter Maxwell Davies, 96n1282
Piano works of Serge Prokofiev, 95n1277
Ross Lee Finney: a bio-bibliog, 97n1039
Scott Joplin: a gd to research, 99n1142

Sing glory & hallelujah! histl & biogl gd to Gospel Hymns nos.1-6 Complete, 97n1086
Singer's gd to the American art song 1870-1980, 95n1272
Singer-songwriters, 96n1307
Sir Arthur Sullivan: a resource bk, 98n1212
Songwriter's market, 1994, 95n1263
Songwriters: a biogl dict with discographies, 99n1117
Soundtracks: an intl dict of composers of music for film, 99n1131
Tomas Luis de Victoria: a gd to research, 99n1132
Ulysses Kay: a bio-bibliog, 95n1266
William Grant Still: a bio-bibliog, 97n1046
William Mathias, 96n1279
William Thomas McKinley, 96n1283
Women composers & songwriters, 97n1035
Women composers, v.1, 97n1047
Women composers, v.2, 97n1048
Women composers, v.3, 99n1145
Women composers, 2d ed, 95n1267
Zoltan Kodaly: a gd to research, 99n1138

COMPOSITE MATERIALS
Advanced composites world ref dict, 99n1410
ASM hndbk, v.5: surface engineering, 96n1661
Composites, 2d ed, 95n1629
Concise ency of composite materials, rev ed, 95n1632
Engineering plastics & composites, 2d ed, 95n1636

COMPOSITION (LANGUAGE ARTS)
CCCC bibliog of composition & rhetoric 1992, 96n1058

COMPUTER-ASSISTED INSTRUCTION
CD-ROM for librarians & educators, 2d ed, 98n282

COMPUTER BULLETIN BOARDS
Complete cyberspace ref & dir, 96n1772
Gay & lesbian online, 97n676
Online user's ency, 95n1701
Washington online: how to access the govt's electronic bulletin boards, 96n1786

COMPUTER EDUCATION
Guide to free computer materials 1998-99, 16th ed, 99n288

COMPUTER GAMES
Net games, 96n813

COMPUTER GRAPHICS
Information graphics, 97n1370
101 desktop pub & graphic programs, 95n678
Quick ref to computer graphics terms, 95n1699

COMPUTER INDUSTRY
Electronic & computer industry gd to chemical safety & environmental compliance, 99n1567
Hoover's gd to computer cos, 96n1773

COMPUTER MUSIC
Electronic & computer music, 98n1196

COMPUTER NETWORKS
Complete cyberspace ref & dir, 96n1772
Encyclopedia of network blueprints, 99n1490
Internet searcher's hndbk, 98n1595
Net games, 96n813
Network Pr dict of networking, 96n1761
Telecommunications, networking & Internet glossary, 95n1704

COMPUTER SCIENCE
CompuMath citation index 1993. 2d semiannual, 95n1739
Computer & info sci & tech abbrevs & acronyms dict, 95n1698
Dictionary of info tech & computer sci, 2d ed, 95n1693
Elsevier's dict of computer sci & math in English, German, French, & Russian, 97n1366

COMPUTER SECURITY
Vocabulary of computer security & viruses, 96n1766

COMPUTER SIMULATION
Jane's simulation & training systems 1996-97, 9th ed, 98n1573

COMPUTER SOFTWARE
Educational software preview gd, 1998, 99n306
Guide to free computer materials 1995, 13th ed, 96n1771
International intellectual property protection for computer software, 96n638
Multimedia dir, 4th ed, 97n1363

COMPUTERS. *See also* MICROCOMPUTERS
Bibliographic gd to the hist of computer applications, 1950-90, 97n1365
Computer desktop ency, 97n1369
Computer dict for kids & their parents, 96n1748
Computer glossary, 7th ed, 96n1757
Computer health hazards, v.2, 95n1694
Computer support dir, 96n1767
Dictionary of computer terms, 4th ed, 96n1755
Dictionary of computer words, 95n1691
Dictionary of computer works, rev ed, 96n1754
Dictionary of multimedia terms & acronyms, 98n1572
Digital imaging dict, 97n1368
Directory of computer & high tech grants, 2d ed, 96n1770
Encyclopaedic dict of info tech & systems, 95n1689
Encyclopedia of computer sci & tech, v.34, suppl 19, 97n1367
English-Spanish, Spanish-English electrical & computer engineering dict, 97n1297
IBM dict of computing, 95n1695
Illustrated computer dict for young people, 96n1763
International biogl dict of computer pioneers, 96n1758
McGraw-Hill illus dict of personal computers, 4th ed, 96n1760
Microsoft press computer dict, 99n1488
New hacker's dict, 3d ed, 98n1578
Orion blue bk, 98n182
Second bibliographic gd to the hist of computing, computers, & the info processing industry, 97n1364
Spencer's illus computer dict, 96n1765
UNIX dict of commands, terms, & acronyms, 97n1373
Vocabulary of computer security & viruses, 96n1766

Xtravaganza! the essential sourcebk for Macromedia Xtras, 99n1486

COMPUTING
Dictionary of computing, 4th ed, 98n1576
Dictionary of personal computing & the internet, 98n1574
Oxford dict of computing for learners of English, 98n1577
Plunkett's infotech industry almanac, 97n539

CONCEPTS
Hutchinson dict of ideas, 95n56

CONDUCT OF LIFE
Learning to behave: a gd to American conduct bks before 1900, 95n1422

CONDUCTORS (MUSIC)
Conductors & composers of popular orchestral music, 99n1158

CONFEDERATE STATES OF AMERICA. *See also* UNITED STATES—HISTORY—CIVIL WAR, 1861-1865
Compendium of the Confederate armies: Ky., Md., Mo., Confederate units & Indian units, 96n522
Compendium of the Confederate armies: La., 96n523
Compendium of the Confederate armies: Miss., 96n524
Compendium of the Confederate armies: S.C. & Ga., 96n525
Compendium of the Confederate armies: Tex., 96n526
Historical atlas of the congresses of the Confederate States of America 1861-65, 95n526
Roster of Confederate soldiers 1861-65, 98n451
Supplement to the official records of the Union & Confederate armies, 99n475

CONFERENCE PROCEEDINGS
Bibliographic gd to conference pubs 1996, 99n7

CONFLICT MANAGEMENT
Encyclopedia of conflict resolution, 99n554
Negotiation lit, 96n283

CONGO (BRAZZAVILLE)
Congo, 95n116
Historical dict of Congo, 97n95

CONGREVE, WILLIAM
William Congreve: an annot bibliog, 1978-94, 97n991

CONIFERS
Pruning of trees, shrubs, & conifers, [rev ed], 96n1588

CONNECTICUT
Connecticut, Maine, Mass., [&] R.I.,: atlas of histl county boundaries, 96n438

CONSERVATIONISTS
Earthkeepers, 95n1763
World who is who & does what in environment & conservation, 98n1631

CONSERVATION OF NATURAL RESOURCES
Conservation & environmentalism, 97n1426
Encyclopedia of environmental info sources, 95n1757
Portraits in conservation: E & S Africa, 96n1596

CONSERVATISM
Concise conservative ency, 98n691

CONSERVATISM—RELIGIOUS ASPECTS
Religious right, 97n1218

CONSTITUTIONS
Constitutions of the world, 96n611

CONSTITUTIONS, STATE
Index digest of state constitutions, 95n745
Iowa state constitution, 99n568
Utah state constitution, 99n688

CONSTRUCTION EQUIPMENT
Wiley dict of civil engineering & construction, 98n1484

CONSTRUCTION INDUSTRY
Building construction cost data 1997, 55th ed, 98n1480
Information sources in architecture & construction, 2d ed, 97n1299
Routledge German dict of construction, 98n1482
Square foot costs 1997, 18th ed, 98n1483
Wiley dict of civil engineering & construction: English-Spanish/Spanish-English, 97n1304

CONSULTANTS
ASTM dir of scientific & technical consultants & expert witnesses, 1994 ed, 95n1498
ASTM dir of scientific & tech consultants & expert witnesses, 1997-98 ed, 99n1320
Consultants & consulting orgs dir 1996 suppl, 16th ed, 97n161

CONSUMER BEHAVIOR
American marketplace, 3d ed, 98n246
Americans 55 & older, 99n279
Consumer Canada 1996, 97n268
Consumer intl 1997/98, 99n218
Consumer Latin America 1997, 4th ed, 98n209
Consumer Mexico 1996, 97n269
Consumer South Africa 1995, 97n270
Consumer USA 1996, 97n271
Generation X: the YA market, 98n256
Handbook of mktg scales, 95n321
Mid-Youth market, 98n261
Official gd to household spending, 97n278
Who's buying food & drink, 98n257
Who's buying for the home, 98n258

CONSUMER COOPERATIVES
British co-operative movement film catalogue, 98n1289

CONSUMER EDUCATION
Better buys for bus, 97n187
Complete gd to household chemicals, 96n1795
Consolidated list of products whose consumption and/or sale have been banned...., 5th ed, 96n217
Consumer health USA, 96n1711
Consumer protection & the law, 97n487
Consumers index to product evaluations & info sources, v.24, no.2, April-June 1996, 97n188
Consumers ref disc [CD-ROM], 96n218
Encyclopedia of the consumer movement, 99n176
Guide to the best products, 1994, 95n224
Orion blue bk, 98n182
Orion blue bk: professional sound 1998, 99n180
Orion blue bk: video & TV, 1998 ed, 99n181
Orion blue bk: vintage guitars & collectibles 1998, summer ed, 99n182
Shopping with a conscience, 98n178
US consumer interest groups, 96n216

CONSUMERS
Latitudes & attitudes, 96n915

CONTEMPORARY CHRISTIAN MUSIC. *See also* **CHURCH MUSIC**
Christian music dirs, 1998, 99n1176

CONTESTS
All the best contests for kids 1994-95, 95n1324
Competitions, 97n299
Freed's gd to student contests & publishing, 5th ed, 96n1356
Student sci opportunities, 95n340

CONTINUING EDUCATION
Bricker's intl dir 1998, 99n358

CONTRACT BRIDGE
Didding dict, 98n744

CONTRACTING OUT
Peterson's contract servs for higher educ, 96n342

CONTRACTORS
Worldwide offshore contractors & equipment dir, 1996, 28th ed, 97n1419

CONTRACTS
A-Z of contract clauses, 98n531

CONVENTION FACILITIES
Guide to campus & non-profit meeting facilities 95, 7th ed, 95n191
Trade shows worldwide 1998, 12th ed, 99n210

COOKERY
Cook's dict & culinary ref, 97n1248
Cupboard love: a dict of culinary curiosities, 98n1423
Dictionary of American food & drink, rev ed, 95n1517
Dictionary of gastronomic terms, French/English, 99n1334
Dictionary of herbs, spices, seasonings, & natural flavorings, 95n1518
Ethnic cuisines, 97n1253
Food festivals, 98n414
Great food almanac, 95n1521

International dict of food & nutrition, 95n1514
Mushroom bk, 97n1280
What's cooking in multicultural America, 97n1254
Whole foods companion, 98n1427

COOKING SCHOOLS
Culinary schools, 99n1336

COOPER-HEWITT MUSEUM
Catalog of the Cooper-Hewitt Museum of Design lib of the Smithsonian Inst libs, 95n924

COPYING MACHINES
Orion blue bk: copier, 99n179

COPYRIGHT
Copyright hndbk, 2d ed, 96n590
Copyright laws & treaties of the world 1991-95 suppl, 98n566
Handbook of copyright in British publishing practice, 3d ed, 95n655
Libraries & copyright, 95n656
McCarthy's desk ency of intellectual property, 2d ed, 97n519
Patent, copyright, & trademark, 97n520

COPYRIGHT—COMPUTER PROGRAMS
International intellectual property protection for computer software, 96n638

CORAL REEF FAUNA
Coral reef animals of the Indo-Pacific, 97n1295

CORAL SNAKES
Coral snakes of the Americas, 98n1475

CORETTA SCOTT KING AWARD
Coretta Scott King awards bk, 95n411

CORNELL, KATHARINE
Katharine Cornell: a bio-bibliog, 95n1351

CORNETT MUSIC
Catalog of music for the cornet, 97n1051

CORPORATIONS. See also **BUSINESS—ENTERPRISES**
Almanac of American employers 1996-97, 97n259
American bus disc, 1995 ed [CD-ROM], 96n181
America's corp families 1995, 97n158
Big bk of lib grant money, 95n643
Brands & their cos suppl, 17th ed, 99n148
Business: name & bus type index [CD-ROM], 98n158
Business rankings annual, 1995, 96n197
Business sales leads, 1997 ed [CD-ROM], 98n248
By the nos: emerging industries, 99n188
Canadian co hists, v.1, 98n208
Companies intl [CD-ROM], 97n209
Corporate affiliations plus, spring/summer 1995 [CD-ROM], 97n162
Corporate & fndn grants 1995, 95n861
Corporate dir of US public cos 1996, 97n164
Corporate dir of US public cos [CD-ROM], 97n163
Corporate dir of US public cos, 99n149
Corporate 500, 13th ed, 97n685
Corporate giving dir 1999, 20th ed, 99n761
Corporate giving yellow pages 1998, 13th ed, 99n762
CorpTech CD-ROM dir of tech cos [CD-ROM], 98n1570
CorpTech dir of tech cos 1996, 10th US ed, 96n1749
CorpTech explore database [CD-ROM], 98n1571
CyberHound's gd to cos on the Internet, 98n1583
Directory of American firms operating in foreign countries, 14th ed, 97n210
Directory of cos required to file annual reports with the SEC, 96n183
Directory of cos required to file annual reports with the SEC, 1997, 99n164
Directory of corp & fndn givers 1996, 97n686
Directory of corp name changes, 95n193
Directory of Japanese-affiliated cos in the EU, 1996-97, 97n211
Directory of Japanese-affiliated cos in the USA & Canada 1993-94, 95n270
Encyclopedia of global industries, 97n204
European regional incentives, 1996-97, 97n243
Europe's medium-sized cos dir, 97n242
Fitzroy Dearborn dir of the world's banks, 11th ed, 97n190
Globe & Mail report on bus: Canada co hndbk 1994, 96n250
Government affairs yellow bk, v.1, no.1, 96n187
Hoover's billion dollar dir, 98n159
Hoover's co & industry database on CD-ROM [CD-ROM], 96n190
Hoover's co capsules on CD-ROM, 98n192
Hoover's co profiles on CD-ROM [CD-ROM], 98n193
Hoover's global 250, 98n202
Hoover's gd to computer cos, 96n1773
Hoover's gd to media cos, 98n859
Hoover's gd to private cos 1994-95, 95n192
Hoover's hndbk of American bus 1995, 96n191
Hoover's hndbk of American bus 1998, 99n169
Hoover's hndbk of emerging cos 1997, 98n173
Hoover's hndbk of emerging cos 1998, 99n170
Hoover's hndbk of private cos 1997, 98n164
Hoover's hndbk of private cos 1998, 99n171
Hoover's hndbk of world bus 1995-96, 96n201
Hoover's hndbk of world bus 1998, 99n222
Hoover's hndbks index 1997, 98n168
Hoover's hndbks index 1998, 99n172
Hoover's masterlist of America's top 2,500 employers, 96n192
Hoover's masterlist of major Latin American cos 1996-97, 98n211
Hoover's masterlist of major US cos 1996-97, 97n166
How to find info about foreign firms, 6th ed, 96n204
How to find info about private cos, 6th ed, 96n205
International dir of co hists, v.12, 97n214
International dir of co hists, v.13, 97n215
International dir of co hists, v.14, 97n216
International dir of co hists, v.16, 99n203
International dir of co hists, v.17, 99n204
International dir of co hists, v.18, 99n205
International dir of co hists, v.19, 99n206
International dir of co hists, v.20, 99n207
International dir of co hists, v.21, 99n208

International tax summaries, 1998, 99n226
Job seeker's gd to socially responsible cos, 96n262
Literature of the nonprofit sector, v.5, 95n860
Major cos of Africa S of the Sahara 1996, 97n219
Major cos of Central & E Europe & the Commonwealth of Independent States 1998, 99n257
Major cos of Europe 1994/5, 96n253
Major cos of Latin America 1996, 97n247
Major cos of Latin America & the Caribbean 1998, 99n262
Major cos of the Arab world 1996/97, 20th ed, 97n233
Major cos of the Arab world 1998, 99n239
Major cos of the Far East & Australasia 1998, 99n245
Market share reporter 1998, 8th ed, 99n190
Multimedia bus 500 [CD-ROM], 95n198
Multinational corps & the environment, 96n1851
National dir of corp giving, 3d ed, 95n196
National dir of corp public affairs 1994, 95n199
National dir of corp public affairs 1998, 99n154
National jobbank 1998, 98n237
Notable corp chronologies, 96n177
PhoneDisc powerfinder [CD-ROM], 98n54
Quantum cos, 96n195
Standard & Poor's 500 gd, 1995 ed, 96n214
Standard & Poor's midcap 400 gd, 1995 ed, 96n215
Thomas register of American manufacturers, 1997, 87th ed, 98n196
Thomas register on CD-ROM, 1997 [CD-ROM], 98n197
Transnational corps: a selective bibliog 1991-92, 95n241
US electric industry phone & fax dir, 1996, 97n1418
US homes & bus [CD-ROM], 98n57
Who knows who, 5th ed, 95n190
Who knows who [1996], 96n186
World databases in co info, 97n172
World mktg data & stats 1996 on CD-ROM, 2d ed [CD-ROM], 97n281
World's major cos dir, 96n229

CORRECTIONS
Correctional admin vocab, 95n621
Dictionary of American penology, rev ed, 97n506
Guide to fed funding for anti-crime programs, 2d ed, 98n553

CORRESPONDENCE SCHOOLS & COURSES. *See also* DISTANCE EDUCATION
Campus-free college degrees, 6th ed, 95n376
College degrees by mail 1996, rev ed, 96n363
College degrees by mail & modem 1998, 99n302
Independent study catalog, 6th ed, 97n290

CORROSION & ANTI-CORROSIVES
Handbook of corrosion data, 96n1667

CORSICA (FRANCE)
Corsica, 98n131

CORVINUS PRESS
Corvinus press: a hist & bibliog, 95n675

COSMETICS
Consumer's dict of cosmetic ingredients, 4th ed, 96n1790
Handbook of cosmetic & personal care additives, 95n1712

COSMOLOGY
Stars & atoms, 96n1799
Universe explained, 96n1802

COST & STANDARD OF LIVING
American cost of living survey, 95n205
Sources & methods: labour stats, v.2, 97n260

COSTUME
Cutting for all! the satorial arts, related crafts, & the commercial paper pattern, 98n934
Encyclopedia of American Indian costume, 95n442
Ethnic dress, 96n388
Fashion & costume in American popular culture, 97n1093
Illustrated ency of costume & fashion from 1066 to the present, rev ed, 95n986

COTE D'IVOIRE
Cote d'Ivoire, 97n96

COUGHLIN, CHARLES E.
Father Charles E. Coughlin, 99n1282

COUNSELING
Academic advising: an annot bibliog, 95n357
Dictionary of counseling, 95n775
Dictionary of family therapy, rev ed, 96n1718
Directory of natl helplines, 1998 ed, 99n49
Research on group treatment methods, 97n623

COUNTER-REFORMATION
Contemporary printed lit of the English counter-Reformation between 1558 & 1640, v.2, 95n1463

COUNTRY LIFE
NTC's dict of folksy, regional, & rural sayings, 97n837

COUNTRY MUSIC
All music gd to country, 98n1230
Country music, 98n1234
Country music: 70 yrs of America's favorite music, 95n1300
Country on CD, 95n1296
Definitive country, 96n1320
Harmony illus ency of country music, 3d ed, 95n1298
Joel Whitburn's top country singles 1944-93, 95n1299
MusicHound country, 98n1233
Statler Brothers discography, 98n1232
Who's who in country music, 95n1297

COUNTY GOVERNMENT
Carroll's county dir, 96n721
Carroll's municipal dir, 96n725
Counties USA 1997, 98n662
County courthouse bk, 2d ed, 96n588
County executive dir, 96n727
County locator (LOCUS): ultimate place name & zip code locator, 95n69
Sourcebook of county court records, 3d ed, 98n524
Sourcebook of local court & county records retrievers, 95n611
Sourcebook of local court & county record retrievers, 3d ed, 98n525

COURTS
BNA's dir of state & fed courts, judges, & clerks, 1997 ed, 98n521
Congressional Quarterly's gd to the US Supreme Court, 3d ed, 98n529
Great world trials, 98n532
Guide to fed funding for anti-crime programs, 2d ed, 98n553
Judicial staff dir, 1997, 98n522
Sourcebook of county court records, 95n609
Sourcebook of fed courts: US district & bankruptcy, 95n610
Sourcebook of fed courts, 2d ed, 97n500

COVENANTS (LAW)
Covenants not to compete, 2d ed, 97n494

COWARD, NOEL
Noel Coward: a bio-bibliog, 95n1342

COWBOYS
Cowboy dict, 95n1041
Cowboy ency, 96n510
Cowboys & the wild west, 95n541

CRABS
Pacific coast crabs & shrimps, 96n1622

CRAMER, JOHANN BAPTIST
Johann Baptist Cramer (1771-1858): a thematic cat of his works, 95n1269

CRANE, STEPHEN
Reader's gd to the short stories of Stephen Crane, 98n1133
Stephen Crane ency, 98n1134

CREATION
Encyclopedia of creation myths, 96n1444

CREOLE DIALECTS—DICTIONARIES—ENGLISH
Hippocrene concise Haitian Creole-English, English-Haitian Creole dict, 96n1106

CRICKET
Dictionary of cricket, 2d ed, 96n814

CRIME
City crime rankings, 96n602
City crime rankings, 3d ed, 98n552
Crime & the justice system in America, 98n550
Crime fiction II, 95n1160
Crime in America, 97n508
Crime in America's top-rated cities, 99n579
Crime state rankings 1994, 95n624
Crimes & punishment, 96n573
Criminal justice in Israel, 96n596
Detective dict, rev ed, 96n598
Guide to American crime films of the 30s, 96n1393
Guide to American crime films of the 40s & 50s, 96n1392
Guide to fed funding for anti-crime programs, 95n622
Murder cases of the 20th century, 97n503
Organized crime, 96n594
School violence, 98n278
Statistical hndbk on violence in America, 97n507
Statistics on crime & punishment, 97n511
Statistics on weapons & violence, 97n512
True crime narratives, 98n546
Violence in American society, 99n583

CRIMINAL INVESTIGATION
Applications in criminal analysis, 96n604
Detective dict, rev ed, 96n598
True crime narratives, 98n546

CRIMINAL JUSTICE
African American criminologists, 1970-96, 99n575
American prisons, 99n574
Cops, crooks, & criminologists, 97n504
Criminal justice abstracts 1968-93 [CD-ROM], 95n626
Criminal justice in Israel, 96n596
Criminal justice info, 99n547
Criminal justice research in libs & on the Internet, 99n581
Dictionary of American criminal justice, 99n576
Dictionary of American penology, rev ed, 97n506
Encyclopedia of American prisons, 97n505
Encyclopedia of capital punishment, 99n577
Marijuana law, 2d ed, 98n527
Murder cases of the 20th century, 97n503
Post-release assistance programs for prisoners, 2d ed, 96n600
Race, crime, & the criminal justice system, 98n548
Statistics on crime & punishment, 97n511

CRIMINALS
Cops, crooks, & criminologists, 97n504
Criminal quotes, 98n79
Outlaws, mobsters, & crooks, 99n578
Public enemies, 99n580
Sendero Luminoso in context, 99n573
Villains & outlaws, 99n582

CRITICAL THEORY
Dictionary of cultural & critical theory, 97n746

CRITICAL THINKING
Thinking from A to Z, 98n1339

CRITICISM. *See also* LITERATURE
Bibliography of the English novel from the Restoration to the French Revolution, 96n1236
Classical & medieval lit criticism, v.14, 96n1149
Columbia dict of modern literary & cultural criticism, 96n960
Contemporary literary criticism, v.84, 96n1152
Contemporary literary criticism, v.85, 96n1153
Contemporary literary criticism, v.86, 97n895
Contemporary literary criticism, v.87, 97n896
Contemporary literary criticism, v.88, 97n897
Contemporary Spanish novel, 97n1014
Hispanic lit criticism, 95n1242
Jacques Derrida (II), 96n956
Johns Hopkins gd to literary theory & criticism, 95n1104
Literature criticism from 1400 to 1800, v.27, 96n1156
Literature criticism from 1400 to 1800, v.28, 97n901
Literature criticism from 1400 to 1800, v.29, 97n902
Literature criticism from 1400 to 1800, v.30, 97n903

Literature criticism from 1400 to 1800, v.31, 97n904
Modern women writers, 97n907
Nineteenth-Century lit criticism, v.46, 96n1158
Nineteenth-Century lit criticism, v.47, 97n908
Nineteenth-Century lit criticism, v.48, 97n909
Nineteenth-Century lit criticism, v.49, 97n910
Nineteenth-Century lit criticism, v.50, 97n911
Nineteenth-Century lit criticism, v.51, 97n912
Nineteenth-Century lit criticism, v.52, 97n913
Nineteenth-Century lit criticism annual cum title index for 1996, 97n914
Poetry criticism, v.10, 96n1265
Recent work in critical theory, 1989-95, 97n880
Shakespearean criticism, v.26, 96n1242
Short story criticism, v.17, 96n1196
Short story criticism, v.18, 97n954
Short story criticism, v.19, 97n955
Short story criticism, v.20, 97n956
Short story criticism, v.21, 97n957
Twentieth-Century literary criticism, v.56, 96n1159
Twentieth-Century literary criticism, v.57, 96n1160
Twentieth-Century literary criticism, v.58, 97n919
Twentieth-Century literary criticism, v.59, 97n920
Twentieth-Century literary criticism, v.60, 97n921
Twentieth-Century literary criticism, v.61, 97n922
Twentieth-Century literary criticism annual cum title index for 1996, 97n923

CROATIA
Historical dict of the Republic of Croatia, 96n549

CROSS-CULTURAL STUDIES
Aggression & conflict, 96n835
Ethnic relations, 96n389
Marriage, family, & relationships, 96n862

CROSSWORD PUZZLES
Cassell cluefinder, 97n832
Crossword puzzle dict, 6th ed, 96n1085
Merriam-Webster's crossword puzzle dict, 2d ed, 97n836

CROTHERS, RACHEL
Rachel Crothers, 96n1208

CROWS
Crows & jays, 95n1569

CRYPTOGRAPHY
Encyclopedia of cryptology, 98n855

CRYSTALLOGRAPHY
Pearson's hndbk desk ed, 98n1492

CRYSTAL SETS (RADIO)
Crystal clear v.2, 96n993

CUBA
Cuba, 97n132

CUBAN AMERICANS
Cuban Americans, 99n397

CULTS (RELIGIOUS)
New religious movements in Western Europe, 98n1343
Sects, 'cults,' & alternative religions, 98n1360

CULTURE
Atlas of threatened cultures, 98n318
Cultural atlas of Spain & Portugal, 96n539
Culture vulture, 95n928
Dictionary of cultural & critical theory, 97n746
Dictionary of 20th century culture: American culture after WW II, 95n927
Global voices, global visions: a core collection of multi-cultural bks, 97n10
Lands & peoples, 98n95
Wild planet!, 96n1352
World facts & maps, 98n400

CURIOSITIES & WONDERS
Book of mosts, 99n65
Encyclopedia of claims, frauds, & hoaxes of the occult & supernatural, 97n637
Encyclopedia of popular misconceptions, 96n62
Encyclopedia of world facts & dates, 95n46
New York Public Lib student's desk ref, 95n81
Strange & unexplained happenings, 97n638
Top 10 of everything, 96n61
Top 10 of everything 1999, 99n63

CURRICULUM PLANNING
Greening the college curriculum: a gd to environmental teaching in the liberal arts, 98n1640
Resources for teaching middle school scis, 99n1296

CUSHING, PETER
Christopher Lee & Peter Cushing & horror cinema, 96n1396

CUSTER, GEORGE ARMSTRONG
Custer & the battle of Little Bighorn, 98n441

CUSTODY OF CHILDREN
Child sexual abuse custody dispute annot bibliog, 96n900

CYCLAMEN
Cyclamen: a gd for gardeners, horticulturists, & botanists, 98n1449

CYCLES
Cycles in humans & nature, 95n1478
Encyclopedia of world problems & human potential, 4th ed, 95n828

CYCLONES. See also **WEATHER**
Encyclopedia of hurricanes, typhoons, & cyclones, 99n1532

CYNICS (GREEK PHILOSOPHY)
Philosophy of Cynicism, 96n1425

CYPRUS
Cyprus, rev ed, 96n130

CYTOKINES
Dictionary of cytokines, 96n1558

CY YOUNG AWARD
Cy Young award winners, 96n808

CZECH REPUBLIC
Czech Republic, 95n517
Czech Republic, 99n121
Historical dict of the Czech state, 99n496
Prague, 98n122

DAKOTA INDIANS
Sioux & other Native American cultures of the Dakotas, 95n428

DANCE. *See also* MODERN DANCE
Bibliographic gd to dance 1995, 98n1267
Bibliography of sources in Christianity & the arts, 97n1206
Dance on camera, 99n1200
Dance on disc [CD-ROM], 95n1358
Dance on disc [CD-ROM], 98n1269
Dance words, 97n1102
Dictionary of 20th century culture: American culture after WW II, 95n927
Index to dance pers: 1995, 98n1270
International dict of modern dance, 99n1201
International ency of dance, 99n1202
Music & dance of the world's religions, 97n1087
Music, dance & theater scholarships, 96n1365
Research in dance, 95n1357
Square dance & contra dance hndbk, 97n1101
Tap dance dict, 99n1203

DANCE IN MOTION PICTURES
Film choreographers & dance directors, 98n1268

DANCE MUSIC
Twentieth-Century American music for the dance, 97n1103

DANCERS
Dancers & choreographers, 97n1100
Eleanor Powell: a bio-bibliog, 95n1353
Fred Astaire: a bio-bibliog, 98n1272

DANISH LANGUAGE—DICTIONARIES—GERMAN
Elsevier's dict of European Community co/bus/financial law in English, Danish, & German, 98n517

DATABASES
Arctic & Antarctic regions [CD-ROM], 96n127
Chemistry citation index [CD-ROM], 97n1390
Dr. Tom Linden's gd to online medicine, 96n1709
EPA database bk, 96n1865
ERIC on CD-ROM [CD-ROM], 97n293
Federal database finder, 4th ed, 96n59
Fulltext sources online, July 1997, 98n51
Gale dir of databases, 99n1495
Gale's ready ref shelf [CD-ROM], 97n50
Global data locator, 98n812

Health industry quicksource, 97n1313
Internet resource dir for K-12 teachers & librarians, 94/95 ed, 95n1706
Key gd to electronic resources: agriculture, 96n1518
Key gd to electronic resources: engineering, 96n1643
Key gd to electronic resources: health scis, 96n1688
KR Info OnDisc grants database [CD-ROM], 96n848
ONLINE 100, 96n1777
World databases in agriculture, 97n1247
World databases in bioscis & pharmacology, 97n1241
World databases in chemistry, 97n1383
World databases in co info, 97n172
World databases in geography & geology, 96n453
World databases in humanities, 98n849
World databases in industry, 96n225
World databases in patents, 96n587
World databases in physics & mathematics, 96n1788
World databases in social scis, 97n78

DAVIES, PETER MAXWELL
Peter Maxwell Davies, 96n1282

DEADHEADS
Grateful Dead & the deadheads, 98n1240

DEATH
Death dict, 95n844
Encyclopedia of afterlife beliefs & phenomena, 96n1445
Last words: a dict of deathbed quotations, 96n95
Life & death in the US, 98n770
National dir of bereavement support grps & servs, 1996, 98n769
R.I.P.: the complete bk of death & dying, 98n767

DECCA RECORDS (FIRM)
Decca lables: a discography, 97n1031

DECORATIVE ARTS
Collectors value gd to Oriental decorative arts, 98n890
Decorative arts: an illus summary cat of the collections of the J. Paul Getty Museum, 95n966
Encyclopedia of decorative paint techniques, 95n967
Illustrated ency of Victoriana, 96n1016

DE FALLA, MANUEL
Manuel de Falla, 99n1136

DEFENSE INDUSTRIES
Jane's intl defense dir 1997, 97n218
Russian defense bus dir 1993, 95n284

DEFORESTATION
Rainforests of the world: a ref hndbk, 95n1777

DEFRANCO, BUDDY
Buddy DeFranco: a biogl portrait & discography, 95n1303

DEGREES, ACADEMIC
Campus-Free college degrees, 7th ed, 97n292
Doctor of philosophy degree, 96n330

DELAWARE
Butterflies of Delmarva, 95n1579
Freshwater fishes of the Carolinas, Va., Md., & Dela., 95n1588

DELAWARE LANGUAGE—DICTIONARIES—ENGLISH
Delaware-English/English-Delaware dict, 97n845

DEMOCRACY
Contemporary democracy, 98n638
Encyclopedia of democracy, 97n612
Who's who in democracy, 98n639

DEMOCRATIC PARTY
Encyclopedia of the Republican Party & the ency of the Democratic Party, 98n659

DEMOGRAPHY
American marketplace, 3d ed, 98n246
American population before the fed census of 1790, 95n891
American population change annual 1994, 95n885
American women, 98n247
Americans & their homes, 99n783
Americans at play, 98n726
Atlas of American migration, 99n780
Bibliography of American demographic hist, 96n906
Consumer sales leads, 1997 ed [CD-ROM], 98n249
County & city extra, 1995, 4th ed, 97n712
Demographic yrbk, 1992. 44th ed, 95n886
Demographic yrbk, 1995, 47th ed, 98n804
Demographic yrbk, special issue: population ageing, 95n834
Demographics USA 1994, city ed, 95n887
Demographics USA 1994, county ed, 95n888
Demographics USA 1994, ZIP ed, 95n889
Gale country & world rankings reporter, 96n905
Generation X: the YA market, 98n256
Geographic database for US economy, tech, & growth [CD-ROM], 98n818
Key indicators of county growth 1970-2025, 1996 ed, 98n806
Latitudes & attitudes, 96n915
Mid-Youth market, 98n261
Moving & relocation sourcebk 1998, 2d ed, 99n781
Official gd to the American marketplace, 2d ed, 96n911
Official gd to American incomes, 2d ed, 98n225
Official gd to the generations, 96n908
PhoneDisc powerfinder [CD-ROM], 98n54
Places, towns, & townships 1998, 99n782
Population abstract of the US, 1993 ed, 95n892
Population & dvlpmt: dir of non-govtl org in OECD countries, 96n909
Profiles of America, S region, v.4: Ky. * N.C. * Tenn., 96n910
Racial & ethnic diversity, 2d ed, 99n372
Sourcebk of county demographics, 11th ed, 99n785
Sourcebk of ZIP code demographics, 10th ed, 96n913
Sourcebk of ZIP code demographics, 13th ed, 99n786
Statistical forecasts of the US, 2d ed, 96n914
Statistical hndbk on adolescents in America, 97n718
Statistical portrait of the US, 99n791
World urbanization prospects, 99n794

DEMONOLOGY
Field gd to demons, fairies, fallen angels, & other subversive spirits, 99n1181

DENMARK
Historical dict of Denmark, 99n493

DENTISTRY
Directory of medical & dental schools worldwide, 6th ed, 96n1687
Oxford hndbk of clinical dentistry, 2d ed, 97n1351
REA's authoritative gd to medical & dental schools, 96n1706

DEPRESSION GLASS
Collector's ency of Depression glass, 11th ed, 96n1013

DEPRESSION—MENTAL
Depression, 96n1724
Depression in the elderly, 98n761

DERIVATIVE SECURITIES
Directory of listed derivative contracts 1996/97, 98n171

DERMATOLOGY
Skin deep: an A-Z of skin disorders, treatments, & health, 97n1333

DERRIDA, JACQUES
Jacques Derrida (II), 96n956

DESERT MAGAZINE
Desert Mag subject index, 98n878

DESIGN. *See also* ART
Art & design scholarships, 96n1036
ARTbibliographies modern on disc, fall 1993 [CD-ROM], 95n991
Design ency, 95n982
Illustrated ency of Victoriana, 96n1016
Landmarks of 20th-century design, 95n983
Look of the century, 97n788
Thames & Hudson ency of 20th century design & designers, 95n984

DESIGNERS. *See also* ARTISTS
Contemporary designers, 99n857
International dict of theatre-3: actors, directors, & designers, 97n1149
Twentieth-Century artists on art, 2d ed, 98n969

DESKTOP PUBLISHING
101 desktop pub & graphic programs, 95n678

DESSERTS
International dict of desserts, pastries, & confections, 96n1523

DETECTIVE & MYSTERY FILMS
Gangster films, 97n1114
Guide to American crime films of the 30s, 96n1393
Guide to American crime films of the 40s & 50s, 96n1392
Guide to American silent crime films, 95n1383

DETECTIVE & MYSTERY STORIES
Crime fiction II, 95n1160
Crown crime companion, 96n1189
Detecting men: a reader's gd & checklist for mystery series written by men, 99n1031
Detecting women 2, 1996-97 ed, 97n947
Encyclopedia mysteriosa, 95n932
Encyclopedia Sherlockiana, 95n1211
Good old index: the Sherlock Holmes hndbk, 98n1158
J. Sheridan Le Fanu, 96n1256
Mystery & suspense writers, 99n1032
Mystery Fancier: an index to vs.1-13, 95n1159
Mystery women, v.1 1860-1979, 99n1030
Silk stalkings: more women write of murder, 99n1033
Sleuths, sidekicks, & stooges, 98n1112
What do I read next?, 1994, 95n1158
What mystery do I read next? a reader's gd to recent mystery fiction, 98n1113

DETECTIVES
Detective dict, rev ed, 96n598

DEVELOPING COUNTRIES
Bibliography on publishing & bk dvlpmt in the Third World, 1980-93, 95n666
Global dvlpmt, 97n228
Historical dict of aid & dvlpmt orgs, 97n615
Military hist of the Third World since 1945, 95n697
Resources of the Third World, 98n120
Science, tech, & society in the 3d World, 96n138
Technological capacity-bldg & tech partnership, 96n1515
Third World atlas, 2d ed, 95n145
Third World hndbk, 2d ed, 95n143
Third World resource dir 1994-95, 95n144
Third World women's lits, 96n946
Third World worker in the multinatl corp, 95n275
Wars in the Third World since 1945, 2d ed, 97n568
What works, 95n276
Women & work in developing countries, 95n292

DEVELOPMENTAL PSYCHOLOGY
Cambridge ency of human growth & dvlpmt, 99n1465
Dictionary of dvlpmtl psychology, 97n629
Encyclopedia of adult dvlpmt, 95n781
Encyclopedia of relationships across the lifespan, 97n631

DIABETES
American Diabetes Assn complete gd to diabetes, 98n1562
Diabetes A to Z, 3d ed, 99n1471

DIAGNOSIS. See also MEDICAL DIAGNOSIS
Patients gd to medical tests, 99n1455
Professional hndbk of diagnostic tests, 96n1710

DIARIES
Contemporary literary criticism, v.86, 97n895
Nineteenth-Century lit criticism, v.48, 97n909
Nineteenth-Century lit criticism, v.51, 97n912
Nineteenth-Century lit criticism annual cum title index for 1996, 97n914

DICKENS, CHARLES
Charles Dickens A to Z, 99n1072
Charles Dickens on the screen, 97n1121
Every thing in Dickens, 97n992
Everyone in Dickens, 97n993
Proverbial Charles Dickens, 98n1157

DICKINSON, EMILY
Emily Dickinson ency, 99n1052
Reference gd to the Bible in Emily Dickinson's poetry, 98n1135

DICTATORS
Dictators & tyrants, 96n705

DICTIONARIES, MEDICAL
Medical meanings: a glossary of word origins, 98n1528

DICTIONARIES, POLYGLOT
Callaham's Russian-English dict of sci & tech, 4th ed, 97n1237
Cassell multilingual dict of local govt & bus, 95n750
Chinese-English-French Kuaisu dict, 99n920
Dictionary of bus, English-Spanish, Spanish-English, [repr ed], 99n147
Elsevier's dict of biometry, 96n1557
Elsevier's dict of climatology & meteorology, 96n1808
Elsevier's dict of computer sci & math in English, German, French, & Russian, 97n1366
Elsevier's dict of financial terms, rev ed, 99n185
Elsevier's dict of info tech in English, German, & French, 98n581
Elsevier's nautical dict, 3d ed, 96n1894
Export financing & insurance vocabulary, 97n206
Gale 5 lang finance dict, 95n231
Gale 5 lang tech dict, 95n1488
History of the Holocaust, 95n588
Itzaj Maya-Spanish-English dict, 98n1040
Larousse desk ref, 97n46
Macmillan visual dict: multilingual ed, 95n59
Multilingual thesaurus of geoscis, 97n1400
NTC's multilingual dict of American Sign Lang, 97n870
Oxford 3-in-1 bilingual dict [CD-ROM], 98n1021
Space scis dict 2, 96n1645
Space scis dict 3, 96n1646
Te Matatiki: contemporary Maori words, 97n863
Trilingual vocabulary of road transport vehicles, 97n229

DICTIONARY OF AMERICAN BIOGRAPHY
Dictionary of American biog, comprehensive index, 97n32

DIE-CAST TOYS
Die cast price gd, 98n930

DIESEL LOCOMOTIVES
Contemporary diesel spotter's gd, 2d ed, 96n1889

DIET
Dictionary of healthful food terms, 98n1420
Encyclopedia of vitamins, minerals, & suppls, 97n1265
Great food almanac, 95n1521

Nutrition & diet therapy ref dict, 4th ed, 98n1422
Prescription for nutritional healing, 98n1508
Yale gd to children's nutrition, 98n1555

DINNER THEATER
Regional theatre dir 1996-97, 97n1152

DINOSAURS
Complete dinosaur, 98n1617
Dinosaur hunter [CD-ROM], 97n1403
Dinosaur safari gd, 96n1814
Dinosaur Society's dinosaur ency, 95n1734
Dinosaurs, 98n1618
Encyclopedia of dinosaurs, 99n1539
Familiar dinosaurs, 95n1736
Penguin histl atlas of dinosaurs, 97n1405
Pockets: dinosaurs, 96n68
Scholastic children's gd to dinosaurs & other prehistoric animals, 95n1735
Visual dict of prehistoric life, 96n1817

DIPLOMATIC & CONSULAR SERVICE
Diplomatic, consular, & other representatives in Canada, 96n750
International Washington almanac, 1994, 95n760

DIRECTORIES
British dirs, 2d ed, 98n132
Directories in print, 15th ed, 98n50

DISARMAMENT
SIPRI yrbk 1993, 95n766
United Nations disarmament yrbk, v.18: 1993, 95n767

DISASTER RELIEF
Global refugee crisis, 96n895
Historical dict of refugee & disaster relief orgs, 95n829

DISASTERS
Associated Press lib of disasters, 99n64
Failed tech, 96n1511
Great misadventures, 99n522
When tech fails, 95n1642

DISCOVERIES IN GEOGRAPHY
Explorers & discoverers, v.5, 99n418
Grolier student lib of explorers & exploration, 99n419
Oxford atlas of exploration, 99n415

DISCOVERIES IN SCIENCE
Famous 1st facts, 99n46
World of scientific discovery, 95n1497

DISCRIMINATION
Employment discrimination law, 3d ed, 98n530
Equal educl opportunity for all children, 95n354
Guidelines for bias-free writing, 96n968

DISEASES
Cambridge world hist of human disease, 95n1662
Diseases, 98n1557
Preventive care sourcebk 1997-98, 98n1520

DISPUTE RESOLUTIONS (LAW)
Encyclopedia of conflict resolution, 99n554
Martindale-Hubbell dispute resolution dir, 96n583
Resolving community disputes, 95n597

DISSERTATIONS, ACADEMIC
Bibliography of geosci theses of the US & Canada, 95n1723
Canadian music & music educ, 98n1194
Comprehensive dissertation index, 1996 suppl, 98n844
Dissertation abstracts [CD-ROM], 97n60
Doctoral dissertations on China & on inner Asia, 1976-90, 99n15
Index to law school theses & dissertations, 96n570
Indigenous langs of the Americas, 97n810
Manual for writers of term papers, theses, & dissertations, 6th ed, 97n755
Religion & the American experience, the 20th century, 96n1442
Ten yrs of classicists: dissertations & outcomes 1988-97, 99n891
Theses on Africa, 1976-88, 95n112

DISTANCE EDUCATION. *See also* **CORRESPONDENCE SCHOOLS & COURSES**
Best distance learning graduate schools, 99n304
College degrees by mail & modem 1998, 99n302
Distance educ, 96n377
External degrees in the info age, 98n308
Library servs for off-campus & distance educ, 97n521
Oryx gd to distance learning, 95n342
Oryx gd to distance learning, 98n280
Peterson's distance learning 1997, 97n291

DISTRIBUTIVE JUSTICE
Environmental justice, 97n1435

DISTRIBUTORS (COMMERCE)
Trade shows worldwide 1998, 12th ed, 99n210

DIVINATION
Divining the future: prognostication from astrology to zoomancy, 96n791
Illustrated ency of divination, 98n714
Tarot for beginners, 96n787

DIVORCE
Divorce help sourcebk, 95n847
Divorce yourself, 4th ed, 99n567

DIXON, BILL
Dixonia: a bio-discography of Bill Dixon, 99n1146

DOCUMENTARY FILMS & TELEVISION PROGRAMS
Special ed: a gd to network TV documentary series & special news reports, 1980-89, 98n1304
Western civilization: a critical gd to documentary films, 97n1118

DOCUMENT DELIVERY SERVICES. *See also* **INFORMATION SERVICES**
Internet-Plus dir of express lib servs, 99n596

DOGS
American Animal Hospital Assn ency of dog health & care, 96n1619
Canine source bk, 4th ed, 95n1581
Dictionary of canine terms, 97n1292
Dogs from A to Z, 99n1385
Encyclopedia of the dog, 96n1620
Pockets: dogs, 98n1467

DOLLS
Collecting dolls ref & price gd, 98n917
Contemporary Barbie dolls, 99n847
Doll values antique to modern, 98n918
Encyclopedia of Australian dolls, 95n976
Modern collectible dolls identification & value gd, 98n919
Patricia Smith's doll values, 12th ed, 97n781
200 yrs of dolls, 98n916
Ultimate dolls' house bk, 95n975

DOLPHINS
Dolphins & porpoises: a worldwide gd, 95n1595
Whales, dolphins, & porpoises, 96n1629

DOMESTIC RELATIONS
State legislative summary, 1994, 96n595

DON JUAN (LEGENDARY CHARACTER) IN LITERATURE
Bibliography of the myth of Don Juan in literary hist, 99n944
Don Juan theme, 95n922

DOW JONES INTERNATIONAL AVERAGE
Dow Jones averages, 1885-1995, 97n183

DOYLE, ARTHUR CONAN, SIR
Encyclopedia Sherlockiana, 95n1211
Good old index: the Sherlock Holmes hndbk, 98n1158
Sherlock Holmes hndbk, 95n1212

DRABBLE, MARGARET
Four British women novelists, 99n1061

DRAMA & DRAMATISTS
American drama criticism: suppl 4 to the 2d ed, 97n1146
American theatre, 97n1150
August Wilson: a research & production sourcebk, 99n1249
Betty Comden & Adolph Green: a bio-bibliog, 95n1352
Bibliography of sources in Christianity & the arts, 97n1206
British playwrights, 1880-1956, 97n985
British playwrights, 1956-95, 97n986
Contemporary African-American female playwrights, 99n1050
Contemporary American dramatists, 95n1176
Contemporary British dramatists, 95n1206
Contemporary literary criticism, v.88, 97n897
Contemporary women dramatists, 95n1155
Critical survey of drama, rev ed, 95n1156
Dictionary of literary biog, v.192, 99n1092
Dictionary of 20th century culture: American culture after WW II, 95n927
Directory of theatre training programs 1997-99, 6th ed, 98n1325
DISCovering authors modules [CD-ROM], 97n900
Drama criticism, v.7, 99n1019
Drama criticism, v.8, 99n1020
Drama for students, v.1, 99n1021
Drama for students, v.2, 99n1022
Drama for students, v.3, 99n1023
Drama for students, v.4, 99n1024
Elmer Rice: a research & production sourcebk, 98n1326
Female dramatist, 99n1025
Fools & jesters in lit, art, & hist, 99n951
French women playwrights of the 20th century, 97n943
German theatre, 98n1323
Guide to British drama explication, v.1, 97n987
Hamlet: a gd to the play, 99n1077
International dict of theatre, v.2, 95n1421
Irish playwrights, 1880-1995, 98n1175
Literature criticism from 1400 to 1800, v.28, 97n901
Literature criticism from 1400 to 1800, v.30, 97n903
Maxwell Anderson on the European stage 1929-92, 97n1147
Modern drama scholarship & criticism 1981-90, 98n1105
New York Times theater reviews, v.28: 1993-94, 97n1154
Rachel Crothers, 96n1208
Reader's gd to 20th-century writers, 97n916
Shakespeare, 99n1079
Shakespeare cos & festivals, 96n1420
Shakespeare interactive [CD-ROM], 99n1080
Shakespeare interactive [CD-ROM], 99n1081
Sophie Treadwell: a research & production sourcebk, 98n1132
Spanish dramatists of the golden age, 99n1026
Tennessee Williams, 96n1220
Tennessee Williams, 99n1057
Theatregoer's almanac, 98n1327
William Congreve: an annot bibliog, 1978-94, 97n991
William Inge: a research & production sourcebk, 95n1193

DREAMS
Cloud nine: a dreamer's dict, 96n781
Dream ency, 96n779
Parkers' complete bk of dreams, 96n783
Secret lang of dreams, 95n784

DRESS MAKING
Cutting for all! the satorial arts, related crafts, & the commercial paper pattern, 98n934

DRINKING CUSTOMS
Encyclopedia of N American eating & drinking traditions, customs, & rituals, 97n1250

DRINKING OF ALCOHOLIC BEVERAGES
Alcohol in the British Isles from Roman times to 1996, 97n441

DRUGS. *See also* PHARMACOLOGY
Anticancer drugs from animals, plants, & microorganisms, 96n1740
Chemotherapy hndbk, 95n1681
Consumer's dict of medicines, 95n1688
Delmar's A-Z NDR-97: nurse's drug ref, 98n1566

Delmar's therapeutic class drug gd for nurses 1997, 98n1567
Dictionary of natural products, 98n1569
Dictionary of substances & their effects [CD-ROM], 97n1314
Drug Topics red bk, 1995, 96n1734
Effects of drugs on the fetus & nursing infant, 97n1358
Effects of neurologic & psychiatric drugs on the fetus & nursing infant, 99n1480
Essential gd to prescription drugs 1995, 96n1737
EveryWoman's gd to prescription & nonprescription drugs, 98n1564
Mosby's GenRx, 8th ed [CD-ROM], 99n1482
Nursing96 drug hndbk, 97n1360
100 drugs that work, 95n1683
PDR family gd to prescription drugs, 99n1483
PDR generics, 96n1738
PDR gd to drug interactions, side effects, indications, 1995, 49th ed, 96n1739
People's gd to deadly drug interactions, 97n1359
PharmFacts for nurses, 97n1361
Physicians' desk ref 1995, 49th ed, 95n1684
Physicians' desk ref companion gd 1998, 52d ed, 99n1422
Physicians' desk ref for nonprescription drugs, 1994, 15th ed, 96n1741
Physicians' desk ref lib, Sept 1994 [CD-ROM], 95n1685
Practitioner's gd to psychoactive drugs for children & adolescents, 95n1687
Respiratory care drug ref, 99n1481
Teratogenic effects of drugs, 95n1682
USP DI 1995, v.1, 96n1744
USP DI 1995, v.2, 96n1745
USP DI 1995, v.3, 96n1746
USP dict of USAN & intl drug names, 96n1747
What do I take? a consumer's gd to nonprescription drugs, 98n1568

DURAS, MARGUERITE
Marguerite Duras: a bio-bibliog, 98n1171

DUTCH LANGUAGE
Dictionary of 1000 Dutch proverbs, 99n1179

DUTCH LANGUAGE—DICTIONARIES—ENGLISH
Hippocrene standard dict Dutch-English, English-Dutch, 99n923

DWELLINGS
Consumer sales leads, 1997 ed [CD-ROM], 98n249
Home improvements & projects index 1990-93, 98n1498
PhoneDisc powerfinder [CD-ROM], 98n54
Time-saver standards for housing & residential dvlpmt, 96n1048
US homes [CD-ROM], 98n56
US homes & bus [CD-ROM], 98n57

DYLAN, BOB
Bob Dylan, 96n1334

DYSTOPIAS IN LITERATURE
Dystopian lit, 95n1109

EARTHQUAKES
Earthquakes & the built environment index, 1984—July 1995 [CD-ROM], 97n1399
Encyclopedia of earthquakes & volcanoes, 95n496

EARTH SCIENCES. *See also* **GEOGRAPHY; GEOLOGY**
Associated Press lib of disasters, 99n64
Bibliography of geosci theses of the US & Canada, 95n1723
Earth online, 99n1516
Earth-Science educ resource dir, 96n1804
Earthscape: exploring endangered ecosystems [CD-ROM], 99n1513
Encyclopedia of earth & physical scis, 99n1514
Glossary of aquatic habitat inventory terminology, 99n1501
Macmillan ency of earth scis, 97n1391
Magill's survey of sci [CD-ROM], 95n1502
Magill's survey of sci: earth sci series, 99n1515
McGraw-Hill dict of earth sci, 98n1603
Our planet Earth, 99n1003
Pockets: Earth facts, 96n69
Science on file [CD-ROM], 98n1415
Sciences of the earth, 99n1517

EAST ARMENIAN DIALECT
Armenian (Eastern)-English dict, 97n844

EAST ASIA
Bibliographic gd to E Asian studies 1995, 98n109
Chironomidae [Diptera] of Japan, 96n1626
Far East & Australasia 1995, 26th ed, 96n167
Far East & Australasia 1997, 28th ed, 97n143

EASTERN CHURCHES
Liturgical dict of E Christianity, 95n1467

EASTERN EUROPE
Directory of consumer brands & their owners 1998: Eastern Europe, 99n250
Eastern Europe, 2d ed, 99n252
Historical dict of the Republic of Macedonia, 99n495
OMRI annual survey of E Europe & the former Soviet Union 1996, 99n115

EASTLAKE, WILLIAM
Work of William Eastlake, 96n1209

EAST (US)
Field gd to nearby nature, 95n1559

EATING DISORDERS
Encyclopedia of obesity & eating disorders, 95n1678
Focus on eating disorders, 95n1679

ECOFEMINISM
Ecofeminist theory, 96n935

ECOLOGY
Bibliographic gd to the environment 1996, 98n1629
Biodiversity, 99n1556
Concise Oxford dict of ecology, 96n1854

Co-op America's natl green pages, 1996 ed, 97n1428
Dictionary of ecology & the environment, 3d ed, 99n1553
Earth words, 96n1861
Earthscape: exploring endangered ecosystems [CD-ROM], 99n1513
Encyclopedia of environmental biology, 96n1856
Encyclopedia of environmental info sources, 95n1757
Environmental acronyms, 96n1850
Facts on File environment atlas, rev ed, 99n1551
Great events from hist 2: ecology & the environment series, 96n1853
Grolier lib of environmental concepts & issues, 97n1427
Grolier student ency of sci, tech, & the environment, 97n1239
Krupin's toll-free environmental dir, 96n1867
Radical ecological theory: a bibliog, 95n1762

ECONOMETRICS
Dictionary of econometrics, 95n182

ECONOMIC ASSISTANCE
Directory of biomedical & health care grants 1995, 9th ed, 96n1685
Federal assistance dir, spring 1994, 95n862
Government assistance almanac 1996-97, 10th ed, 97n689
Historical dict of aid & dvlpmt orgs, 97n615
What works, 95n276

ECONOMIC DEVELOPMENT
American bus climate & economic profiles, 95n207
Atlas of world dvlpmt, 96n444
Directory of intl economic org, 98n161
Economic & social progress in Latin America 1995 report: overcoming volatility, 97n127
Funding sources for community & economic dvlpmt 1996, 97n692
Global dvlpmt, 97n228
Human dvlpmt report 1994, 95n93
Population & dvlpmt: dir of non-govtl org in OECD countries, 96n909
Revenue stats of OECD member countries 1965-93, 96n772

ECONOMIC FORECASTING
Bond markets, 1995 ed, 96n292
Global trends: world almanac of dvlpmt & peace, 96n200
Illustrated bk of world rankings, rev ed, 98n813
World index of economic forecasts, 4th ed, 96n208

ECONOMIC HISTORY
Business hist of the world, 95n242
Countries of the world & their leaders yrbk 1995: suppl, 96n710
Economic indicators hndbk, 95n204
Global trends: world almanac of dvlpmt & peace, 96n200
Great events from hist II: bus & commerce series, 95n209
Main economic indicators: histl stats: prices, labour & wages 1962-91, 95n210
World tables 1994, 95n257

ECONOMICS. *See also* **BUSINESS; COMMERCE; FINANCE; INDUSTRY**
ABC-CLIO world hist companion to capitalism, 99n158

Bibliographic gd to bus & economics 1994, 96n174
Bibliographic gd to bus & economics 1995, 98n147
Business pers index, v.38: Aug 1995-July 1996, 98n167
Cabell's dir of publishing opportunities in accounting, economics & finance, 6th ed, 96n669
Dictionary of economics, 98n151
Elgar companion to classical economics, 99n160
Encyclopedia of Keynesian economics, 98n152
Fortune ency of economics, 95n184
Glossary of industrial org economics & competition law, 95n183
Handbook of economic methodology, 99n161
Index of economic freedom, 1997, 98n169
Joan Robinson: a bio-bibliog, 97n150
Knowledge Exchange bus ency, 98n154
Main economic indicators: histl stats: prices, labour & wages 1962-91, 95n210
McGraw-Hill ency of economics, 96n179
Mexico bus: the portable ency for doing bus with Mexico, 95n290
NAFTA & GATT: environmental & economic issues, 98n705
National accounts stats, 98n203
Statesman's yrbk 1998-99, 135th ed, 99n82
Value of a dollar, 1860-1989, 96n198
World economic factbk 1993, 95n214
World economic outlook, May 1997, 98n188
Worldmark ency of the nations, 8th ed, 96n105

ECUMENICAL MOVEMENT
Historical dict of ecumenical Christianity, 96n1473

EDEN, ANTHONY, EARL OF AVON
Anthony Eden, 1897-1977, 96n759

EDINBURGH (SCOTLAND)
Edinburgh ency, 98n137

EDITING—HANDBOOKS
English usage & style for editors, 99n836
Freelance Editorial Assn yellow pages & code of fair practice, 1997-98, 98n863

EDITORIAL CARTOONS
Editorial cartooning & caricature, 99n1192

EDUCATION
Adventures in Video, 97n314
Best Web sites for teachers, 2d ed, 99n308
Bibliographic gd to educ 1996, 98n265
Biographical dict of modern American educators, 98n266
Biographical dict of N American & European educationists, 99n289
Campus-Free college degrees, 7th ed, 97n292
CIJE on disc, Jan 1969-Jul 1994 [CD-ROM], 95n346
Directory of college cooperative educ programs, 97n304
Education & the law, 97n491
Education index, July 1995 to June 1996, 98n279
Education sourcebk, 99n296
Educator's gd to free films, filmstrips, & slides 1995, 55th ed, 96n375
Educator's gd to free multicultural materials 1998, 99n285

Educator's gd to free sci materials 1998-99, 39th ed, 99n286
Educator's gd to free social studies materials 1998-99, 38th ed, 99n287
Educator's gd to free videotapes 1995, 42d ed, 96n376
Educator's index of free materials 1995, 104th ed, 97n294
Educator's word frequency gd, 97n817
El-Hi textbks & serials in print 1997, 98n283
Encyclopedia of African-American educ, 97n285
Encyclopedia of American educ, 97n288
Encyclopedia of educ info, 1994/95, 96n324
Encyclopedia of educ info for elem & secondary school professionals, 1994/95, 95n353
ERIC identifier authority list (IAL) 1995, 96n629
ERIC on CD-ROM [CD-ROM], 97n293
Ferguson's gd to apprenticeship programs, 2d ed, 99n359
Guide to American educl dirs, 7th ed, 95n341
Guide to fed funding for educ, 1997, 23d ed, 98n274
Guide to free computer materials 1998-99, 16th ed, 99n288
Handbook of research on sci teaching & learning, 95n344
Historical dict of school segregation & desegregation, 99n301
Historical dict of women's educ in the US, 99n803
Hooray for heroes!, 96n321
Index to AV producers & distrs 1997, 10th ed, 98n312
Indicators of school quality, 99n298
International educ quotations ency, 97n289
International ency of educ, 2d ed, 95n337
International ency of the sociology of edu, 98n268
Multicultural educ dir, 98n273
Native educ dir 1997, 98n272
Philosophy of educ, 97n287
Princeton Review student access gd to the best medical schools, 96n1705
Religious higher educ in the US, 97n301
Thesaurus of ERIC descriptors, 13th ed, 96n318
US educl policy interest groups, 95n339
Who's who in American educ 1994-95, 95n336
Women educators in the US, 1820-1993: a bio-bibliog sourcebk, 95n335
World of learning 1999, 49th ed, 99n295

EDUCATIONAL EQUALIZATION
Gender equity in educ, 96n313

EDUCATIONAL EXCHANGES
International student's gd to Mexican univs, 97n310
Open doors 1994/95, 97n311
World of difference, 3d ed, 95n383

EDUCATIONAL FUND-RAISING
Funding sources for K-12 schools & adult basic educ, 99n290

EDUCATIONAL PSYCHOLOGY
Historical ency of school psychology, 97n286

EDUCATIONAL TECHNOLOGY
Educational media & tech yrbk 1993, 95n386
Educational media & tech yrbk 1994, 95n387
Educational media & tech yrbk 1995/96, v.21, 97n312
Educational media & tech yrbk, 99n356
Educational software preview gd, 1998, 99n306
Educator's gd to free videotapes 1998, 45th ed, 99n357

EDUCATIONAL TESTS & MEASUREMENTS
ETS test collection catalog, v.2, 2d ed, 96n314
Tests in print IV, 95n787

EDUCATION, EARLY CHILDHOOD
Pioneers of early childhood educ, 99n309
Vatican archives: an inventory & gd to histl docs of the Holy See, 99n1284

EDUCATION, ELEMENTARY
Blackwell hndbk of educ, 96n325
Comparative gd to American elem & secondary schools, 99n311
Directory of Canadian schools, 6th ed, 96n319
Educators grade gd to free teaching aids 1995, 41st ed, 96n322
El-Hi textbks & serials in print 1994, 95n350
Elementary teachers gd to free curriculum materials 1995, 52d ed, 96n323
Encyclopedia of educ info for elem & secondary school professionals, 1994/95, 95n353
International ency of teaching & teacher educ, 2d ed, 97n298
Internet resource dir for K-12 teachers & librarians, 94/95 ed, 95n1706
Internet resource dir for K-12 teachers & librarians, 96/97 ed, 98n1590
Internet resource dir for K-12 teachers & librarians, 98/99 ed, 99n307
National gd to funding for elem & secondary educ, 97n300
Picture bks to enhance the curriculum, 98n284

EDUCATION—FINANCIAL AID
A's & B's of academic scholarships, 95n378
A's & B's of academic scholarships 1997/98, 19th ed, 98n285
America's lowest cost colleges, 9th ed, 96n359
Art & design scholarships, 96n1036
Assistantships & graduate fellowships in the mathematical scis, 1993-94, 95n1738
Assistantships & graduate fellowships in the mathematical scis, 1996-97, 98n1624
Assistantships & graduate fellowships in the mathematical scis, 1997-98, 99n1540
Athletic scholarships, 96n799
B* student's (or lower) complete scholarship bk, 99n338
Barron's best buys in college educ, 3d ed, 96n331
Big bk of minority opportunities, 6th ed, 96n891
Big bk of minority opportunities, 7th ed, 99n339
Big bk of opportunities for women, 98n269
Black student's gd to scholarships, 3d ed, 95n371
Chronicle financial aid gd, rev ed, 96n364
College check mate, 1995-96, 95n379
College costs & financial aid hndbk 1998, 99n340
College financial aid, 99n341
Complete college financing gd, 4th ed, 99n342
Complete scholarship bk, 98n287
Dan Cassidy's worldwide college scholarship dir, 4th ed, 96n333
Dan Cassidy's worldwide graduate scholarship dir, 4th ed, 96n334

Directory of financial aids for minorities 1995-97, 96n880
Directory of financial aids for women 1995-97, 96n879
Directory of financial aids for women 1997-99, 99n773
Fellowships in intl affairs, 95n365
Financial aid bk, 2d ed, 98n298
Financial aid financer, 98n306
Financial aid for African Americans 1997-99, 99n292
Financial aid for Asian Americans 1997-99, 99n293
Financial aid for Native Americans 1997-99, 99n772
Financial aid for the disabled & their families 1994-96, 96n858
Financial aid for the disabled & their families 1998-2000, 99n294
Financial aid for vets, military personnel, & their dependents 1994-96, 96n690
Financial resources for intl study, 2d ed, 97n309
Foundation grants to individuals, 9th ed, 96n872
Free money for college, 3d ed, 95n356
Funding for US study, 2d ed, 97n305
Funding sources for K-12 schools & adult basic educ, 99n290
Government assistance almanac 1996-97, 10th ed, 97n689
Government financial aid bk, 2d ed, 98n299
Graduate student's complete scholarship bk, 99n343
Grants for libs & info servs, 95n639
Grants for teachers, 95n343
Grants register 1998, 16th ed, 98n300
High school sr's gd to merit & other no-need funding 1996-98, 98n307
Higher educ money bk for women & minorities, 1997 ed, 97n302
Minority & women's complete scholarship bk, 99n344
Money for graduate students in the scis 1996-98, 98n1411
Money for graduate students in the social scis 1996-98, 98n91
Music, dance & theater scholarships, 96n1365
National gd to funding for children, youth, & families, 3d ed, 97n698
National gd to funding for higher educ, 4th ed, 98n291
National gd to funding for the economically disadvantaged, 95n865
Official athletic college gd: baseball, 1995 ed, 96n805
Peterson's college money hndbk 1998, 15th ed, 98n303
Peterson's paying less for college 1995, 95n370
Peterson's scholarship almanac, 98n304
Peterson's scholarships for study in the USA & Canada 1998, 98n294
Peterson's scholarships for study in the USA & Canada 1999, 2d ed, 99n345
Peterson's sports scholarships & college athletic programs, 95n797
Peterson's sports scholarships & college athletic programs, 3d ed, 99n346
Scholarships & loans for nursing educ 1997-98, 99n1479
Student sci opportunities, 95n340
Winning athletic scholarships, 1998 ed, 99n347
Winning edge, 3d ed, 95n799

EDUCATION, HIGHER
Accredited insts of postsecondary educ, 1997-98, 99n316
Alternative paths to teaching, 95n360
America's lowest cost colleges, 9th ed, 96n359
American art dir 1997-98, 56th ed, 99n871
American community colleges, 10th ed, 96n362
American univs & colleges, 15th ed, 99n348
Annual gd to graduate nursing educ 1997, 99n1474
Asian higher educ, 98n295
Athletic scholarships, 95n795
Barron's compact gd to colleges, 9th ed, 95n361
Barron's best buys in college educ, 5th ed, 99n317
Barron's gd to graduate bus schools, 99n318
Best 75 bus schools, 1999 ed, 99n320
Best distance learning graduate schools, 99n304
Best graduate programs: humanities & social scis, 2d ed, 99n335
Best graduate programs: physical & biological scis, 2d ed, 99n336
Campus-free college degrees, 6th ed, 95n376
Cass & Birnbaum's gd to American colleges, 16th ed, 95n362
College chemistry faculties 1996, 10th ed, 97n303
College comparison gd, 95n377
College costs & financial aid hndbk 1998, 99n340
College.edu: on-line resources for the cyber-savvy, 98n301
College hndbk 1998, 99n350
College hndbk for transfer students 1997, 98n296
College media dir 1994, 95n952
CollegeSource [CD-ROM], 98n297
Commonwealth univs yrbk 1993, 95n363
Complete bk of colleges, 1998 ed, 98n286
Complete gd to Canadian univs, 3d ed, 96n320
Directory of college facilities & servs for people with disabilities, 4th ed, 98n773
Directory of theatre training programs, 5th ed, 96n1419
English lang & orientation programs in the US, 11th ed, 98n988
European dir of SE Asian studies, 99n319
External degrees in the info age, 98n308
Fact bk on higher educ, 1997 ed, 99n349
Fiske gd to colleges 1994, 95n366
Gender gap in higher educ, 95n372
Gourman report of undergraduate programs, 99n321
Greening the college curriculum: a gd to environmental teaching in the liberal arts, 98n1640
Guide to graduate environmental programs, 98n1641
Guide to the evaluation of educl experiences in the armed servs, 1996, v.1: Army, 98n275
Guide to the evaluation of educl experiences in the armed servs, 1996, v.2: Navy, 98n276
Guide to the evaluation of educl experiences in the armed servs, 1996, v.3: Air Force, Coast Guard, Dept of Defense, Marine Corps, 98n277
Guide to the most competitive colleges, 99n325
Higher educ dir 1995, 95n368
Index of majors & graduate degrees 1998, 99n326
Interdisciplinary undergraduate programs, 2d ed, 98n289
International dict of univ hists, 99n315
International student hndbk of US colleges 1998, 99n327
K & W gd to colleges for the learning disabled, 1998 ed, 98n290
Lovejoy's college counselor [CD-ROM], 95n373
Lovejoy's college gd, 24th ed, 99n351
Media courses UK 1997, 4th ed, 98n860

Mitchell express: the fast track to the top colleges, 95n369
Money for graduate students in the humanities 1996-98, 98n848
Multicultural student's gd to colleges, rev, 98n302
National faculty dir 1999, 29th ed, 99n328
National gd to funding in higher educ, 3d ed, 95n364
National gd to funding for higher educ, 4th ed, 98n291
NLN gd to undergraduate RD educ, 5th ed, 99n1477
Peterson's colleges with programs for students with learning disabilities, 96n341
Peterson's colleges with programs for students with learning disabilities or attention deficit disorders, 99n329
Peterson's competitive colleges 1997-98, 16th ed, 98n292
Peterson's contract servs for higher educ, 96n342
Peterson's distance learning 1997, 97n291
Peterson's gd to colleges in the Midwest 1995, 11th ed, 96n343
Peterson's gd to colleges in the South 1995, 10th ed, 96n344
Peterson's gd to colleges in the West 1995, 9th ed, 96n345
Peterson's gd to middle Atlantic colleges 1995, 11th ed, 96n346
Peterson's gd to New England colleges 1995, 11th ed, 96n347
Peterson's gd to NY colleges 1995, 11th ed, 96n348
Peterson's gd to 4-yr colleges 1999, 29th ed, 99n330
Peterson's gd to nursing programs, 4th ed, 99n1478
Peterson's gd to 2-yr colleges 1998, 28th ed, 98n293
Peterson's honors programs, 99n331
Peterson's paying less for college 1995, 95n370
Peterson's top colleges for sci, 97n306
Peterson's US & Canadian medical schools 1997, 98n1542
Princeton Review Hillel gd to Jewish life on campus, 1996 ed, 97n307
Princeton Review student access gd: the big bk of colleges, 96n357
Princeton Review student access gd to the best 309 colleges, 96n358
Princeton Review student access gd to the best bus schools, 97n169
Princeton Review student advantage gd to visiting college campuses, 1997 ed, 98n305
Profiles of American colleges, 99n332
Real gd to Canadian univs, 95n347
Research centers dir 1999, 24th ed, 99n333
Rugg's recommendation on the colleges, 99n334
Students' gd to playwriting opportunities, 96n1421
Summer on campus [2d ed], 96n360
Translation & interpreting schools, 99n897
World academic database [CD-ROM], 97n308
World list of univ & other insts of higher ed, 96n361
World list of univs & other insts of higher educ, 21st ed, 99n337

EDUCATION, HIGHER—GRADUATE WORK
Barron's gd to graduate bus schools, 99n318
Chemical scis graduate school finder 1994-95, 96n1791
Directory of graduate student employee bargaining agents & orgs, 96n336
Graduate school funding hndbk, 96n365
Graduate student's complete scholarship bk, 99n343

Human choice & climate change, 99n1563
Index of majors & graduate degrees 1998, 99n326
Insider's gd to graduate programs in clinical psychology, 1994/95 ed, 95n786
Peterson's gd to grad & professional programs 1995, 29th ed, 96n349
Peterson's gd to grad programs in bus, educ, health, & law 1995, 29th ed, 96n350
Peterson's gd to grad programs in engineering & applied scis 1995, 29th ed, 96n351
Peterson's gd to grad programs in the biological & agricultural scis 1995, 29th ed, 96n352
Peterson's gd to grad programs in the humanities, arts, & social scis 1995, 29th ed, 96n353
Peterson's gd to grad programs in the physical scis & mathematics 1995, 29th ed, 96n354
Peterson's honors programs, 99n331
Peterson's professional degree programs in the visual & performing arts 1995, 96n962

EDUCATION OF GIFTED & TALENTED
Educational opportunity gd, 1998, 99n312

EDUCATION & POLITICS
Encyclopedia of student & youth movements, 99n653
Religion in the schools, 99n300

EDUCATION, PRIMARY
Hooray for heroes!, 96n321

EDUCATION, SECONDARY
Best private high schools & how to get in, 2d ed, 99n313
Blackwell hndbk of educ, 96n325
Boarding school gd, 97n297
Comparative gd to American elem & secondary schools, 99n311
Directory of Canadian schools, 6th ed, 96n319
Educational opportunity gd, 1998, 99n312
El-Hi textbks & serials in print 1994, 95n350
Encyclopedia of educ info for elem & secondary school professionals, 1994/95, 95n353
Handbook of private schools 1995, 76th ed, 96n327
International ency of teaching & teacher educ, 2d ed, 97n298
International schools dir, 1993/1994 ed, 95n381
Internet resource dir for K-12 teachers & librarians, 94/95 ed, 95n1706
Internet resource dir for K-12 teachers & librarians, 96/97 ed, 98n1590
Internet resource dir for K-12 teachers & librarians, 98/99 ed, 99n307
Middle level educ, 97n295
National gd to funding for elem & secondary educ, 97n300
Peterson's gd to private secondary schools 1994-95, 95n355
Peterson's private secondary schools 1998-99, 19th ed, 99n314
Summer on campus [2d ed], 96n360

EDUCATION—STATISTICS
Educational rankings annual 1998, 99n297
Projections of educ stats to 2008, 99n299

EDUCATION, VOCATIONAL
Guide to the evaluation of educl experiences in the armed servs, 1996, v.1: Army, 98n275
Guide to the evaluation of educl experiences in the armed servs, 1996, v.2: Navy, 98n276
Guide to the evaluation of educl experiences in the armed servs, 1996, v.3: Air Force, Coast Guard, Dept of Defense, Marine Corps, 98n277

EDWARDS, JONATHAN
Jonathan Edwards, 96n1440

EGYPT
Ancient Egypt, 98n486
Discovering ancient Egypt, 95n568
Handbook to life in ancient Egypt, 99n510
Historical dict of Egypt, 96n162
Penguin histl atlas of ancient Egypt, 98n490
Pockets: ancient Egypt, 96n63
Weed flora of Egypt, rev ed, 96n1582
Who's who in Egyptian mythology, 2d ed, 96n1350

EINSTEIN, ALBERT
Einstein dict, 97n1409

ELECTIONS
Almanac of state legislatures, 95n710
America at the polls, 95n737
America votes 21, 96n735
America votes 22, 99n677
Campaign & election reform, 98n679
Congressional elections 1946-96, 99n676
Congressional Quarterly's gd to US elections, 3d ed, 95n733
Handbook of campaign spending: money in the 1992 Congressional races, 95n738
State legislative elections: voting patterns & demographics, 99n674
US presidential candidates & the elections, 97n588
US primary elections 1995-96, 98n673

ELECTRIC ENGINEERING
American electricians' hndbk, 13th ed, 98n1485
Electrical & electronics trades dir 1996 [CD-ROM], 98n1486
Electrical engineering hndbk, 95n1610
Electrical engineering hndbk, 99n1405
Electronic & computer industry gd to chemical safety & environmental compliance, 99n1567
International electric power ency 1998, 99n1406

ELECTRIC POWER
Annual bulletin of electric energy stats for Europe & N America, 1994, v.38, 96n1839
Electric light & power US electric utility industry dir, 1995, 4th ed, 96n1651
Electric light & power US non-utility power dir, 1995, 96n1652
Electric power in Asia & the Pacific, 1991 & 1992, 97n1420
Electric power industry yrbk, 1996, 97n1421
Electric power stats sourcebk, 97n1422
Energy balances & electricity profiles, 1992, 96n1841
US electric industry phone & fax dir, 1996, 97n1418
US electric utility industry dir 1998, 7th ed, 99n1546

ELECTRONIC JOURNALS
Books & pers online, 1997 ed, 98n1582
Directory of electronic jls, newsletters, & academic discussion lists, 6th ed, 97n1375
Net jl dir, vol. 1, no. 2, 98n1591

ELECTRONIC MAIL
Complete cyberspace ref & dir, 96n1772
Directory of environmental electronic mail users in Eurasia, 4th ed, 97n1429
National e-mail & fax dir 1999, 99n56

ELECTRONIC MUSIC
Electronic & computer music, 98n1196

ELECTRONIC PUBLISHING
Anders CD-ROM gd, 2d ed, 97n15
Books & pers online, 1997 ed, 98n1582
CD-ROMs in print 1995 [CD-ROM], 97n16
CD-ROMs in print 1996, 97n17
Encyclopedias, atlases, & dicts, 96n48
International multimedia yrbk 1995-96, 96n1751
International multimedia yrbk 1995-96 on CD-ROM [CD-ROM], 96n1752
Internet World's on Internet 94, 95n1703

ELECTRONICS
AEA dir, 1993-94, 95n1609
Electrical & electronics trades dir 1996 [CD-ROM], 98n1486
Electronic materials & processes hndbk, 2d ed, 95n1614
Electronics & telecommunications vocabulary, 95n1611
Electronics pocket ref, 2d ed, 96n1653
Encyclopedia of electronic circuits, v.6, 97n1305
Illustrated dict of electronics, 6th ed, 95n1613
Illustrated dict of electronics, 7th ed, 98n1488
Jane's avionics 1996-97, 15th ed, 97n1441
Jane's electro-optic systems 1996-97, 2d ed, 98n619
Jane's military communications, 1997-98, 98n618
McGraw-Hill circuit ency & troubleshooting gd, v.2, 95n1615
McGraw-Hill electronics dict, 5th ed, 95n1616
McGraw-Hill electronics dict, 6th ed, 98n1489
Newnes electronic engineer's pocket bk, 95n1617

ELEMENTS
Elements, 98n1600

ELIOT, T. S.
Concordance to the complete poems & plays of T. S. Eliot, 97n971
Guide to the secular poetry of T. S. Eliot, 97n970

ELVES
American elves, 98n1255

EMBERIZA
Sparrows & buntings, 97n1288

EMBLEMS
State names, seals, flags, & symbols, rev ed, 95n499
Symbols of nationhood, 95n142

EMERGENCY LIBRARIAN
Emergency Librarian index, vs.1-20: 1973-93, 96n645

EMERSON, RALPH WALDO
Emerson chronology, 95n1188
New England transcendentalists [CD-ROM], 99n1046
Ralph Waldo Emerson: an annot bibliog of criticism, 1980-91, 95n1187

EMIGRATION & IMMIGRATION
American immigrant cultures, 99n365
Atlas of American migration, 99n780
Guide to naturalization records of the US, 98n332
Immigrant experience in American fiction, 96n1206
Immigrants in the US in fiction, 95n1117
Immigration questions & answers, rev ed, 98n702
NAFTA & GATT: environmental & economic issues, 98n705
Passenger & immigration lists index, 1996 suppl, 97n367
Refugee & immigrant resource dir, 3d ed, 95n401
Research projects supported by the Canadian Ethnic Studies Program 1973-92, 95n419
Research results of projects funded by the Canadian Ethnic Studies Program 1973-88, 95n418
Wuerttemberg emigration index, v.6, 95n463

EMOTIONS
Sociology of emotions: an annot bibliog, 95n826

EMPIRICISM
Encyclopedia of empiricism, 99n1252

EMPLOYEE FRINGE BENEFITS
Employee benefits desk ency, 97n252
Mandated benefits, 98n236
Quick ref to ERISA compliance, 96n285

EMPLOYEE LOYALTY
Employee duty of loyalty, 97n495
Employee duty of loyalty, 1996 suppl covering 1994, 97n496

EMPLOYEE SCREENING
Guide to background investigations, 7th ed, 98n640

EMPLOYEES—DISMISSAL OF
Wrongful termination, 96n281

EMPLOYEES—RECRUITING
Best dir of recruiters, 4th ed, 97n253
Best dir of recruiters on-line, 97n254
Guide to executive recruiters, new ed, 98n218

EMPLOYEES—TRAINING OF
Field gd to current training videos, 96n282
Guide to natl professional certification programs, 96n267
Museum careers & training, 95n83

EMPLOYMENT AGENCIES
Job hunter's yellow pages, 1994-95 ed, 95n301
JobBank gd to employment servs 1998-99, 98n220

EMPLOYMENT IN FOREIGN COUNTRIES
Almanac of intl jobs & careers, 95n314
American jobs abroad, 95n313
Overseas summer jobs 1995, 26th ed, 96n278
Work your way around the world, 7th ed, 96n273

ENCYCLICALS
Encyclicals of John Paul II on CD-ROM [CD-ROM], 97n1217

ENCYCLOPEDIAS & DICTIONARIES. *See also* CHILDREN'S ENCYCLOPEDIAS & DICTIONARIES
Academic American ency, 95n41
Academic American ency, 98n36
Angels A to Z, 97n1176
Atlas of English dialects, 97n839
Baroque art, 97n798
Biographical dict of the hist of tech, 97n1236
Blackwell dict of neuropsychology, 97n626
Blackwell ency of writing systems, 97n811
Brain ency, 97n1334
Britannica bk of the yr, 1994, 95n63
Britannica CD version 1.01 [CD-ROM], 95n64
Britannica electronic index [CD-ROM], 95n43
Callaham's Russian-English dict of sci & tech, 4th ed, 97n1237
Cambridge astronomy dict, 97n1392
Cambridge dict of philosophy, 97n1159
Cambridge ency, 2d ed, 96n44
Cambridge ency, 3d ed, 98n37
Cambridge factfinder, 2d ed, 98n38
Cambridge gd to American theatre, updated ed, 97n1151
Cambridge paperback ency, updated ed, 95n45
Cambridge paperback gd to lit in English, 97n894
Canadian ency plus, 1997 [CD-ROM], 97n42
Cold War ency, 97n473
Collegeville pastoral dict of biblical theology, 97n1196
Collier's ency, 95n48
Collier's ency, 98n40
Collier's ency 1998 [CD-ROM], 98n41
Collins ency of Scotland, 96n148
Columbia ency, 5th ed, 95n49
Columbia ency [CD-ROM], 98n42
Compact music dict, 97n1026
Compact up-to-date English-Hebrew dict, 97n856
Compton's ency & fact-index, 1994 ed, 95n50
Compton's interactive ency, version 3.00, 1995 ed [CD-ROM], 95n51
Computer desktop ency, 97n1369
Concise Columbia ency, 3d ed, 96n45
Concise dict of Christianity in America, 96n1466
Concise dict of lib & info sci, 97n525
Concise ency biology, 97n1266
Concise ency of psychology, 2d ed, 97n627
Concise Oxford dict of music, 4th ed, 97n1027
Cook's dict & culinary ref, 97n1248
Cops, crooks, & criminologists, 97n504
Dance words, 97n1102
Dictionary of American hist, 97n419

Dictionary of American hist suppl, 97n414
Dictionary of American penology, rev ed, 97n506
Dictionary of American regional English, v.3: I-O, 97n833
Dictionary of automotive engineering, 2d ed, 97n1303
Dictionary of bldg preservation, 97n801
Dictionary of canine terms, 97n1292
Dictionary of Christianity, 97n1210
Dictionary of dicts & encys, 2d ed, 98n45
Dictionary of economics, 97n156
Dictionary of endocrinology & related biomedical scis, 97n1352
Dictionary of ethics, theology, & society, 97n73
Dictionary of euphemisms, 97n827
Dictionary of feminist theologies, 97n1177
Dictionary of glass, 97n787
Dictionary of intl bus terms, 97n203
Dictionary of intl human rights law, 97n516
Dictionary of Irish lit, rev ed, 97n1007
Dictionary of Islamic architecture, 97n803
Dictionary of Italian lit, rev ed, 97n1010
Dictionary of mechanical engineering, 4th ed, 97n1310
Dictionary of 1000 Spanish proverbs with English equivalents, 97n1089
Dictionary of philosophy, 3d ed, 97n1164
Dictionary of philosophy & religion, new ed, 98n1337
Dictionary of South African English on histl principles, 97n830
Dictionary of sports injuries & disorders, 97n1357
Dictionary of teleliteracy, 97n1110
Dictionary of the British Empire & Commonwealth, 97n117
Dictionary of the Middle East, 97n138
Dictionary of the modern US military, 97n566
Dictionary of 20th century culture: Hispanic culture of Mexico, Central America, & the Caribbean, 97n348
Dictionary of US intelligence servs, 97n597
Dictionary of word origins, 97n826
DK geography of the world, 97n379
Elsevier's dict of financial & economic terms, 97n153
Elsevier's dict of fundamental & applied biology, 97n1267
Elsevier's dict of plant names, 97n1273
Employee benefits desk ency, 97n252
Encyclopaedic dict in the 18th century, v.1, 99n813
Encyclopaedic dict in the 18th century, v.2, 99n814
Encyclopaedic dict in the 18th century, v.3, 99n815
Encyclopaedic dict in the 18th century, v.4, 99n816
Encyclopaedic dict in the 18th century, v.5, 99n817
Encyclopedia Americana, 99n45
Encyclopedia Americana, intl ed, 95n53
Encyclopedia Americana, 1995 [CD-ROM], 96n47
Encyclopedia Americana [CD-ROM], 97n43
Encyclopedia of African-American culture & hist, 97n331
Encyclopedia of African-American educ, 97n285
Encyclopedia of American educ, 97n288
Encyclopedia of American pol reform, 98n657
Encyclopedia of American prisons, 97n505
Encyclopedia of American religious hist, 97n1180
Encyclopedia of applied physics, v.15, 97n1407
Encyclopedia of applied physics, v.16, 97n1408
Encyclopedia of bioethics, rev ed [CD-ROM], 98n1333
Encyclopedia of British humorists, 97n984

Encyclopedia of chemical processing & design, v.56, 97n1378
Encyclopedia of climate & weather, 97n1396
Encyclopedia of computer sci & tech, v.34, suppl 19, 97n1367
Encyclopedia of constitutional amendments, proposed amendments, & amending issues, 1789-1995, 97n596
Encyclopedia of cultural anthropology, 97n316
Encyclopedia of democracy, 97n612
Encyclopedia of disability & rehabilitation, 97n670
Encyclopedia of electronic circuits, v.6, 97n1305
Encyclopedia of European cinema, 97n1111
Encyclopedia of gerontology, 97n667
Encyclopedia of human rights, 2d ed, 97n517
Encyclopedia of Latin American hist & culture, 97n349
Encyclopedia of lib & info sci, v.58, suppl 21, 97n524
Encyclopedia of molecular biology & molecular medicine, v.1, 97n1269
Encyclopedia of molecular biology & molecular medicine, v.2, 97n1270
Encyclopedia of molecular biology & molecular medicine, v.3, 97n1271
Encyclopedia of nutritional suppls, 97n1349
Encyclopedia of occultism & parapsychology, 4th ed, 97n633
Encyclopedia of philosophy suppl, 97n1160
Encyclopedia of revolutions & revolutionaries, 97n477
Encyclopedia of rhetoric & composition, 97n840
Encyclopedia of snakes, 96n1637
Encyclopedia of social & cultural anthropology, 97n317
Encyclopedia of the American West, 97n415
Encyclopedia of the ancient Greek world, 97n450
Encyclopedia of the bk, 2d ed, 97n554
Encyclopedia of the Enlightenment, 97n475
Encyclopedia of the future, 97n44
Encyclopedia of the paranormal, 97n634
Encyclopedia of the Persian Gulf War, 97n454
Encyclopedia of the Reagan-Bush yrs, 97n593
Encyclopedia of the US in the 20th century, 97n416
Encyclopedia of the Vietnam War, 97n433
Encyclopedia of transcendentalism, 97n964
Encyclopedia of TV game shows, 2d ed, 97n1113
Encyclopedia of vitamins, minerals, & suppls, 97n1265
Encyclopedia of war & ethics, 97n1161
Encyclopedia of women in religious art, 97n797
Encyclopedia of world cultures, v.8: Middle America & the Caribbean, 97n318
Encyclopedia of world cultures, v.9: Africa & the Middle East, 97n319
Encyclopedia of world cultures, v.10: indexes, 97n320
Encyclopedia of world facts & dates, 95n46
Encyclopedia USA, v.22, 97n417
Encyclopedia USA, v.23, 97n418
Encyclopedias, atlases, & dicts, 96n48
European powers in the 1st World War, 97n467
European Union ency & dir 1996, 2d ed, 97n607
EXEGY: the source for current world info, 96n49
Eyewitness ency of space & the universe [CD-ROM], 97n1395
Famous 1st facts, 99n46
Funk & Wagnalls new ency, 95n54
Gale ency of psychology, 97n628

Gangster films, 97n1114
German baroque writers, 1580-1660, 97n1006
Gobbledygook bk: dict of acronyms, abbrevs, initializations, & esoteric terminology, 97n2
Graying of America: an ency of aging, health, mind, & behavior, 97n668
Grolier illus ency, 95n55
Grolier lib of environmental concepts & issues, 97n1427
Grolier lib of intl biogs, 97n23
Grolier master ency index, 1994 [CD-ROM], 95n44
Grolier multimedia ency, 1998, deluxe ed [CD-ROM], 98n43
Grolier student ency of endangered species, 96n1597
Growing up: a cross-cultural ency, 97n708
Health care almanac, 97n1316
Health care terms, 3d ed, 97n1319
HealthSpeak, 97n1315
Hebrew & Aramaic lexicon of the O.T., v.2, 97n1198
High strangeness: UFOs from 1960 through 1979, 97n632
Hippocrene concise Yoruba-English, English-Yoruba dict, 97n879
Historical dict of Spain, 97n452
Historical dict of Stuart England, 1603-89, 97n442
Historical ency of school psychology, 97n286
Historical ency of the Arab-Israeli conflict, 97n455
History of accounting, 97n179
Illustrated ency of handguns, 97n782
Illustrated ency of musical instruments, 97n1052
Importers manual USA & the dict of intl trade, 1996-97 ed [CD-ROM], 97n274
Information graphics, 97n1370
International dict of psychology, 2d ed, 97n630
International relations, 5th ed, 97n620
Japan ency, 97n109
Jules Verne ency, 97n952
Kant dict, 96n1428
Kister's best encys, 2d ed, 95n57
Larousse desk ref, 97n46
Larousse dict of sci & tech, 97n1240
Larousse dict of world folklore, 96n1343
Larousse mini French-English, English-French dict, new ed, 97n848
Larousse mini German-English, English-German dict, new ed, 97n850
Larousse mini Italian-English, English-Italian dict, new ed, 97n858
Larousse mini Spanish-English, English-Spanish dict, new ed, 97n874
Latino ency, 97n337
Law & pols, 97n490
Lissauer's ency of popular music in America, 97n1065
Literally entitled, 97n891
Macmillan ency of earth scis, 97n1391
Macmillan ency of physics, 97n1410
McGraw-Hill ency of personal computing, 97n1372
Medieval art, 97n799
Merriam-Webster dict, home & office ed, 97n820
Merriam-Webster's collegiate dict, deluxe audio ed, 98n998
Merriam-Webster's dict of law, 97n488
Merriam-Webster's pocket biogl dict, 97n24
Merriam-Webster's pocket geographical dict, 97n380

Microsoft Encarta multimedia ency 1995 [CD-ROM], 95n60
New bk of knowledge, 95n61
New dict of religions, rev ed, 97n1179
New Ency Britannica, 95n62
New Grolier multimedia ency [CD-ROM], 95n42
New standard ency, 95n65
New York Public Lib desk ref, 2d ed, 95n80
NTC's dict of China's cultural code words, 97n107
NTC's multilingual dict of American Sign Lang, 97n870
Oxford companion to Australian military hist, 97n565
Oxford dict of current English, 97n821
Oxford ency of the Reformation, 97n1211
Oxford encyclopedic world atlas, 3d ed, 97n377
Oxford English-Hebrew dict, 97n855
Oxford family ency, 98n47
Oxford large print dict, 2d ed, 97n818
Peoples of Africa, 97n321
Philosophy of educ, 97n287
Pockets: ency, 98n48
Random House concise ency, 97n47
Rawson's dict of euphemisms & other doubletalk, rev ed, 97n828
Ready ref: American justice, 97n489
Reagan yrs A to Z, 97n592
Reference ency: India 2001, 96n132
Routledge dict of lang & linguistics, 97n812
Routledge German technical dict, 97n851
Russian-English collocational dict of the human body, 97n867
Same time ... same station: an A-Z gd to radio from Jack Benny to Howard Stern, 97n765
Schirmer pronouncing pocket manual of musical terms, 5th ed, 96n1271
Shambhala dict of Taoism, 97n1226
Shipwrecks, 97n1448
Skin deep: an A-Z of skin disorders, treatments, & health, 97n1333
Social sci ency, 2d ed, 97n75
Sportspeak: an ency of sport, 97n643
Supplement to The Modern Ency of Russian, Soviet, & Eurasian Hist, v.1, 97n476
Szycher's dict of medical devices, 97n1332
Travel dict, new ed, 97n384
Tuttle dict of the martial arts of Korea, China, & Japan, 97n659
2001 French & English idioms, 2d ed, 97n846
U*X*L sci fact finder, 99n1319
UNIX dict of commands, terms, & acronyms, 97n1373
What in the word? origins of words dealing with people & places, 97n823
Why Eve doesn't have an Adam's apple: a dict of sex differences, 97n1318
Wiley dict of civil engineering & construction: English-Spanish/Spanish-English, 97n1304
Wittgenstein dict, 97n1162
World Afghanistan to Zimbabwe, 97n378
World Bk ency, 95n66
World Bk ency, [1996 ed], 97n48
World Bk multimedia ency [CD-ROM], 96n51
World Bk multimedia ency, 1998 [CD-ROM], 99n47
World Bk new illus info finder [CD-ROM], 95n67

World Bk Rush-Presbyterian-St. Luke's medical center medical ency, 7th ed, 97n1335
Writer's companion, 97n924

ENCYCLOPEDIAS & DICTIONARIES— BIBLIOGRAPHY
ARBA gd to subject encys & dicts, 2d ed, 98n5

ENDANGERED SPECIES. *See also* **ZOOLOGY**
Earthscape: exploring endangered ecosystems [CD-ROM], 99n1513
Encyclopedia of endangered species, 95n1564
Endangered & threatened species [CD-ROM], 95n1534
Endangered species, 99n1370
Grolier student ency of endangered species, 96n1597
International wildlife trade, 96n1599
Red list of threatened plants, 1997, 99n1361

ENDOCRINOLOGY
Dictionary of endocrinology & related biomedical scis, 97n1352

ENDOWMENTS. *See also* **GRANTS-IN-AID**
Awards almanac 1996, 97n701
Big bk of lib grant money, 95n643
Complete grants sourcebk for higher educ, 3d ed, 97n684
Corporate & fndn grants 1995, 95n861
Directory of corp & fndn givers 1996, 97n686
Directory of grants for orgs serving people with disabilities, 8th ed, 95n846
Directory of intl corp giving in America & abroad 1995, 96n869
Directory of intl corp giving in America & abroad 1998, 99n764
Directory of new & emerging fndns, 3d ed, 96n870
Foundation 1000 1995/96, 96n873
Foundation grants index 1994, 95n867
Foundation grants index 1996, 24th ed, 96n883
Guide to funding for intl & foreign programs, 2d ed, 96n875
International fndn dir 1994, 95n864
International fndn dir 1996, 7th ed, 97n696
Literature of the nonprofit sector, v.5, 95n860
National dir of nonprofit orgs 1995, 96n193
National gd to funding for elem & secondary educ, 97n300
National gd to funding for higher educ, 4th ed, 98n291
National gd to funding for lib & info serv, 97n531
National gd to funding for the economically disadvantaged, 95n865
National gd to funding for the environment & animal welfare, 2d ed, 96n878
National gd to funding for women & girls, 96n952
National gd to funding in higher educ, 3d ed, 95n364
National gd to funding in religion, 97n1184
National gd to funding in substance abuse, 96n896
Philanthropic studies index, v.3, no.1, 95n868
Philanthropic studies index, 1995 cum index, 96n884
Who get grants/who gives grants, 96n877

ENERGY INDUSTRY
Bibliographic gd to the environment 1996, 98n1629
Electric power industry yrbk, 1996, 97n1421
Energy analysis of 108 industrial processes, 6th ed, 98n1494
Energy & environmental industry survey 1997, 98n191
Energy balances for countries in transition 1993, 1994-2010, & energy prospects in CIS countries, 98n1627
Energy balances for Europe & N America, 1992, 1993-2010, 97n1423
Energy policies of IEA countries, 95n1750
Energy stats yrbk, 1995, 99n1547
US electric utility industry dir 1998, 7th ed, 99n1546
World index of resources & population, 96n235

ENGINEERING
ASTM intl dir of testing laboratories, 1998 ed, 99n1321
Bibliographic gd to tech 1996, 98n1398
Callaham's Russian-English dict of sci & tech, 4th ed, 97n1237
Concise ency of measurement & instrumentation, 96n1641
Concise engineering & tech index 1987-May 1994 [CD-ROM], 95n1479
Concise metals engineering data bk, 99n1409
CRC materials sci & engineering hndbk, 2d ed, 95n1630
Dictionary of engineering acronyms & abbrevs, 2d ed, 95n1599
Electronic Gieck's engineering formulas [CD-ROM], 96n1642
Encyclopedia of applied physics, v.15, 97n1407
Encyclopedia of applied physics, v.16, 97n1408
Engineering mathematics hndbk, 99n1544
English-German dict of materials & process engineering, 96n1666
English-Spanish, Spanish-English electrical & computer engineering dict, 97n1297
Information sources in engineering, 3d ed, 97n1296
INSPEC list of jls & other serial sources 1996/7, 97n1306
Key gd to electronic resources: engineering, 96n1643
McGraw-Hill dict of engineering, 98n1476
Milestones in sci & tech, 2d ed, 95n1503
Peterson's job opportunities in engineering & tech 1995, 96n1513
Reference gd to famous engineering landmarks of the world, 99n1397
Reference sources in sci, engineering, medicine, & agriculture, 95n1482
Standard hndbk of architectural engineering, 99n881
Standard hndbk of engineering calculations, 3d ed, 96n1644
Van Nostrand's scientific ency, 8th ed, 96n1502
Who's who in sci & engineering 1998-99, 99n1305
Wiley dict of civil engineering & construction: English-Spanish/Spanish-English, 97n1304
Wiley engineer's desk ref, 2d ed, 99n1398
World engineering industries & automation, 97n199
World engineering industries & automation 1993-95, 96n1649
World Wide Web for scientists & engineers, 99n1327

ENGINEERS
Notable 20th-century scientists, 96n1490
Who's who in sci & engineering 1996-97, 3d ed, 97n1232

ENGLAND
England, 95n157

ENGLAND—CHURCH HISTORY
Contemporary printed lit of the English counter-Reformation between 1558 & 1640, v.2, 95n1463

ENGLAND—CIVILIZATION
Late medieval England (1377-1485), 96n542

ENGLAND—GENEALOGY
Your English ancestry, 95n459

ENGLISH DRAMA
British playwrights, 1880-1956, 97n985
British playwrights, 1956-95, 97n986
Cambridge companion to medieval English theatre, 95n1419
Companion to the characters in the fiction & drama of W. Somerset Maugham, 97n996
Contemporary British dramatists, 95n1206
Dictionary of who, what, & where in Shakespeare, 98n1161
Guide to British drama explication, v.1, 97n987
Irish playwrights, 1880-1995, 98n1175
Modern verse drama, 95n1207
Shakespeare films in the classroom, 95n1397
Women playwrights in England, Ireland, & Scotland 1660-1823, 98n1151

ENGLISH FICTION. *See also* **LITERATURE—ENGLISH—FICTION**
British novel 1680-1832, 98n1146
British short-fiction writers, 1880-1914, 97n979
British short-fiction writers, 1945-80, 96n1228
Companion to the characters in the fiction & drama of W. Somerset Maugham, 97n996
Contemporary novel, 2d ed, 98n1108
Dictionary of British literary characters: 20th-century novels, 95n1199
Edwardian fiction, 98n1152
Eighteenth-Century Anglo-American women novelists, 98n1111
English novel, 1660-1700, 98n1145
English novel explication, suppl 5, 95n1208
English novel explication, suppl 6, 99n1069
Guide to British prose fiction explication: 19th & 20th centuries, 98n1143
Late-Victorian & Edwardian British novelist, 1st series, 96n1235
Sherlock Holmes hndbk, 95n1212
Thomas Hardy's major novels, 99n1085
Virginia Woolf A to Z, 96n1221

ENGLISH—HORN MUSIC
Soloistic English horn lit from 1736-1984, 95n1275

ENGLISH IMPRINTS
Eastern Europe: a bibliographic gd to English lang pubs, 1986-93, 96n140
English Catholic bks, 1701-1800, 97n1204

ENGLISH LANGUAGE—SYNONYMS & ANTONYMS
American Heritage children's thesaurus, 98n1016
ASIS thesaurus of info sci & librarianship, 2d ed, 99n598

Barron's bus thesaurus, 97n178
Civil law lexicon for lib classification, 99n599
Contemporary thesaurus of social sci terms & synonyms, 95n94
Harcourt Brace student thesaurus, 2d ed, 95n1050
Merriam-Webster's collegiate dict, deluxe audio ed, 98n998
Multilingual thesaurus of geoscis, 97n1400
NTC's thesaurus of everyday American English, 96n1093
Oxford desk dict & thesaurus, American ed, 98n993
Oxford desk thesaurus, American ed, 96n1094
Oxford miniref dict & thesaurus, 96n1078
Random House Webster's concise thesaurus, 99n917
Random House Webster's large print thesaurus, 99n918
Roget's superthesaurus, 2d ed, 99n916
Roget's 2: the new thesaurus, 3d ed, 96n1095
Thesaurus of ERIC descriptors, 13th ed, 96n318

ENGLISH LANGUAGE
Cambridge ency of the English lang, 96n1061
New bibliog of writings on varieties of English 1984-92/93, 95n1028
New York Public Lib writer's gd to style & usage, 95n946
Shakespeare's lang, 97n999
Western lore & lang, 97n841
Writing across the curriculum: an annot bibliog, 95n333
Year's work in English studies, v.73, 1992, 96n958

ENGLISH LANGUAGE ADDRESS, FORMS OF
Forms of address, 96n311

ENGLISH LANGUAGE—ADJECTIVE
Cassell dict of appropriate adjectives, 95n1034

ENGLISH LANGUAGE ALPHABET
Alphabet: a hndbk of ABC bks, 2d ed, 96n328

ENGLISH LANGUAGE ARCHAISMS
Illustrated dict of little-known words from literary classics, 96n1148

ENGLISH LANGUAGE—AUSTRALIA
Dictionary of Australian colloquialisms, 4th ed, 97n829

ENGLISH LANGUAGE—BUSINESS ENGLISH
Language of small bus, 95n188

ENGLISH LANGUAGE—CANADA
Gage Canadian dict, rev ed, 98n1012
Guide to Canadian English usage, 99n907
ITP Nelson Canadian dict of the English lang, 98n1013

ENGLISH LANGUAGE—COGNATE WORDS—SPANISH
NTC's dict of Spanish cognates thematically organized, 98n1048

ENGLISH LANGUAGE—COMPOSITION & EXERCISES
Grading student writing, 99n310

ENGLISH LANGUAGE—DIALECTS. *See also* **AMERICANISMS**
Atlas of English dialects, 97n839
Cowboy dict, 95n1041
Happy trails: a dict of W expressions, 95n1043
New bibliog of writings on varieties of English 1984-92/93, 95n1028
NTC's dict of folksy, regional, & rural sayings, 97n837
Smoky Mountain voices: a lexicon of S Appalachian speech, 95n1042
Sources of London English, 97n831
Survey of English dialects, 95n1056
UK to USA dict, 96n1082

ENGLISH LANGUAGE—DICTIONARIES
American Heritage talking dict [CD-ROM], 98n997
American Heritage talking dict, 3d ed [CD-ROM], 96n1062
American Sign Lang, unabridged ed, 99n910
Barnhart dict companion, v.10, no.1, summer 1997, 98n1010
Basic Newbury House dict of American English, 99n898
Cambridge intl dict of English, 96n1063
Canadian Oxford dict, 99n41
Cassell cluefinder, 97n832
Cassell student English dict, 95n1054
Chambers dict on CD-ROM [CD-ROM], 96n1064
Chambers 21st century dict, 99n42
Concise Oxford dict of current English, 9th ed, 96n1065
Dictionary of modern legal usage, 2d ed, 96n577
Dictionary of the English lang [CD-ROM], 98n1020
DK illus Oxford dict, 99n44
DK ultimate visual dict of sci, 99n1311
ITP Nelson Canadian dict of the English lang, 98n1013
Larousse English dict, 99n899
Little Oxford dict of current English, 7th ed, 95n1032
Merriam-Webster dict, home & office ed, 97n820
Merriam-Webster's collegiate dict, deluxe audio ed, 98n998
Merriam-Webster's collegiate dict deluxe, electronic ed [CD-ROM], 96n1066
Merriam-Webster's dict of basic English, 96n1067
Modern dict for the legal profession, 1994 suppl, 96n580
New shorter Oxford English dict [CD-ROM], 98n999
New Yawk tawk: a dict of New York City expressions, 99n904
Oxford desk dict, American ed, 96n1068
Oxford desk dict & thesaurus, American ed, 98n993
Oxford dict & thesaurus, American ed, 98n994
Oxford dict of current English, 97n821
Oxford dict of English grammar, 96n1080
Oxford encyclopedic English dict, 2d ed, 96n1069
Oxford English Dict additions series, 95n1055
Oxford English Dict on CD, 2d ed [CD-ROM], 97n843
Oxford English-Hebrew dict, 97n855
Oxford English minidict, 4th ed, 96n1070
Oxford large print dict, 2d ed, 97n818
Oxford miniref dict & thesaurus, 96n1078
Pockets: English dict A to Z, 98n995
Random House Webster's American Sign Lang dict, rev ed, 99n909
Rawson's dict of euphemisms & other doubletalk, rev ed, 97n828
Roget A to Z, 95n1069
Scholastic dict of spelling, 99n912
Sisson's word & expression locator, 2d ed, 96n1092
Slang of sin, 99n43
Webster's 2: new college dict, 96n1079
Webster's new American dict, 97n822
Webster's new world dict of American English, 3d college ed, 95n1033
Webster's new world vest pocket dict, 2d ed, 96n1071
World Bk dict, 98n996

ENGLISH LANGUAGE—DICTIONARIES—APACHE
Western Apache-English dict, 99n936

ENGLISH LANGUAGE—DICTIONARIES—ARABIC
English-Arabic standard dict, 95n1070

ENGLISH LANGUAGE—DICTIONARIES—AZERBAIJANI
English-Azerbaijani/Azerbaijani-English concise dict, 96n1097

ENGLISH LANGUAGE—DICTIONARIES—BOSNIAN
Bosnian-English, English-Bosnian concise dict, 96n1098

ENGLISH LANGUAGE—DICTIONARIES—CATALAN
Catalan dict, 95n1071

ENGLISH LANGUAGE—DICTIONARIES—CHICKASAW
Chickasaw: an analytical dict, 96n1099

ENGLISH LANGUAGE—DICTIONARIES—CREOLE DIALECTS
Hippocrene concise Haitian Creole-English, English-Haitian Creole dict, 96n1106

ENGLISH LANGUAGE—DICTIONARIES—DANISH
Elsevier's dict of European Community co/bus/financial law in English, Danish, & German, 98n517

ENGLISH LANGUAGE—DICTIONARIES—DELAWARE
Delaware-English/English-Delaware dict, 97n845

ENGLISH LANGUAGE—DICTIONARIES—DUTCH
Hippocrene standard dict Dutch-English, English-Dutch, 99n923

ENGLISH LANGUAGE—DICTIONARIES—FRENCH
Barron's jr illus dict: French-English, 95n1072
Collins-Robert French-English, English-French dict, 3d ed, 98n1024

Correctional admin vocab, 95n621
Dahl's law dict, 96n574
Electronics & telecommunications vocabulary, 95n1611
Essential French dict, 95n1077
French-English, English-French dict, unabridged ed, 95n1074
French-English, English-French practical dict, 95n1079
Informatics glossary, 95n1697
Integrated pest mgmt glossary, 95n1513
Larousse concise French-English/English-French dict, 95n1075
Larousse concise French-English/English-French dict, rev ed, 99n926
Larousse mini French-English, English-French dict, new ed, 97n848
Larousse pocket French-English/English-French dict, 95n1076
Medical dict in 6 langs, 97n1331
Oxford-Hachette French desk dict, 98n1026
Oxford-Hachette French dict, 96n1100
Oxford paperback French dict, 2d ed, 95n1078
Oxford paperback French dict & grammar, 96n1101
Oxford starter French dict, 98n1027
Pockets: French dict, 98n1028
Routldege French dict of environmental tech, 98n1637
Routledge French dict of telecommunications, 99n1494
Routledge French technical dict, 96n1499
Standard French-English, English-French dict, 96n1102
2001 French & English idioms, 2d ed, 97n846
Vocabulary of computer security & viruses, 96n1766
Vocabulary of enzyme engineering, 95n1618
Vocabulary of family violence, 95n850
Vocabulary of packaging, 95n1633

ENGLISH LANGUAGE—DICTIONARIES—GERMAN

Collins German-English, English-German dict, 2d ed, 96n1104
Collins German-English, English-German dict, unabridged 3d ed, 99n928
Elsevier's dict of European Community co/bus/financial law in English, Danish, & German, 98n517
Elsevier's dict of industrial tech, 96n1494
English-German dict of materials & process engineering, 96n1666
Klett's modern German & English dict, 99n929
Larousse mini German-English, English-German dict, new ed, 97n850
Oxford-Duden German desk dict, new ed, 98n1030
Oxford-Duden German dict [CD-ROM], 98n1032
Oxford-Duden German dict, rev ed, 98n1031
Oxford starter German dict, 98n1033
Practical dict of German usage, 98n1029
Random House German-English, English-German dict, 99n931
Routledge German dict of bus commerce and finance, 98n156
Routledge German dict of chemistry & chemical tech, v.2, 99n1508
Routledge German dict of construction, 98n1482
Routledge German dict of environmental tech, 99n1555
Routledge German dict of info tech, 98n1579
Routledge German technical dict, 97n851

ENGLISH LANGUAGE—DICTIONARIES—GREEK

Pocket Oxford Greek dict, 96n1105

ENGLISH LANGUAGE—DICTIONARIES—HANI

Hani-English/English-Hani dict, 98n1034

ENGLISH LANGUAGE—DICTIONARIES—HEBREW

Compact up-to-date English-Hebrew dict, 97n856
Harduf's transliterated English-Hebrew dict, 1st v., 95n1081
Harduf's transliterated English-Hebrew dict, 2d v., 95n1082
Harduf's transliterated English-Hebrew dict, 3d v., 96n1108
Harduf's transliterated English-Hebrew dict, 4th v., 98n1035

ENGLISH LANGUAGE—DICTIONARIES—HINDI

Hindi-English, English-Hindi practical dict, 95n1083

ENGLISH LANGUAGE—DICTIONARIES—HUNGARIAN

Hippocrene concise Hungarian-English, English-Hungarian dict, 97n857
Oxford-Duden pictorial Hungarian-English dict, 96n1109

ENGLISH LANGUAGE—DICTIONARIES—IGBO

Igbo-English dict, 99n932

ENGLISH LANGUAGE—DICTIONARIES—ITALIAN

Larousse mini Italian-English, English-Italian dict, new ed, 97n858
Medical dict in 6 langs, 97n1331
Oxford color Italian dict, 98n1036
Oxford-Duden pictorial Italian & English dict, 96n1110
Oxford Italian desk dict, 98n1037
Oxford Italian minidict, 2d ed, 98n1038

ENGLISH LANGUAGE—DICTIONARIES—JAPANESE

Cassell English-Japanese bus dict, 95n260
Dictionary of Japanese & English idiomatic equivalents, 95n1085
Japanese-English, English-Japanese concise dict, 95n1084
Martin's concise Japanese dict, 96n1113
Tuttle dict of legal terms: English-Japanese, Japanese-English, 95n605
Tuttle dict of legal terms: English-Japanese, Japanese-English, rev ed, 96n613
Tuttle new dict of loanwords in Japanese, 95n1086
2001 Japanese & English idioms, 97n859

ENGLISH LANGUAGE—DICTIONARIES—KURDISH

Kurdish-English/English-Kurdish dict, 96n1114

ENGLISH LANGUAGE—DICTIONARIES—KYRGYZ

Kyrgyz-English/English-Kyrgyz glossary of terms, 99n934

ENGLISH LANGUAGE—DICTIONARIES—LATIN
Latin for the illiterati, 98n1039
Oxford Latin minidict, 96n1117
Pocket Oxford Latin dict, rev ed, 95n1087
Veni, vidi, vici, 96n1116

ENGLISH LANGUAGE—DICTIONARIES—LITHUANIAN
Lithuanian dict, 97n862
Lithuanian-English/English-Lithuanian concise dict, 95n1088

ENGLISH LANGUAGE—DICTIONARIES—NAVAJO
Colloquial Navaho: a dict, 95n1090
Navajo-English dict, 95n1089

ENGLISH LANGUAGE—DICTIONARIES—NORWEGIAN
English-Norwegian, Norwegian-English dict, 99n937
Norwegian dict, 2d ed, 96n1120

ENGLISH LANGUAGE—DICTIONARIES—POLISH
Highlander Polish-English/English-Highlander Polish dict, 97n864
Polish-English, English-Polish concise dict, 95n1091

ENGLISH LANGUAGE—DICTIONARIES—PORTUGUESE
Elsevier's dict of industrial tech, 96n1494
HarperCollins Portuguese dict, college ed, 98n1041
Oxford pa Portuguese dict, 98n1042
Portuguese-English, English-Portuguese practical dict, 95n1092

ENGLISH LANGUAGE—DICTIONARIES—ROMANIAN
NTC's Romanian & English dict, 97n865

ENGLISH LANGUAGE—DICTIONARIES—RUSSIAN
Comparative Russian-English dict of Russian proverbs & sayings, 96n1125
Concise Oxford Russian dict, 97n866
Dictionary of bus & legal terms: Russian-English/English-Russian, 96n575
Dictionary of Russian slang & colloquial expressions, 96n1128
English-Russian comprehensive dict, 96n1122
English-Russian economics glossary, 97n154
English-Russian, Russian-English dict, rev ed, 96n1124
HarperCollins Russian dict: Russian-English, English-Russian, college ed, 96n1123
NTC's compact Russian & English dict, 95n1093
NTC's new college Russian & English dict, 98n1045
Oxford Russian minidict, 96n1126
Oxford starter Russian dict, 98n1046
Pocket Oxford Russian dict, 2d ed, 96n1127
Russian-English collocational dict of the human body, 97n867

ENGLISH LANGUAGE—DICTIONARIES—SHAMITO—SEMITIC
Hamito-Semitic etymological dict, 96n1107

ENGLISH LANGUAGE—DICTIONARIES—SIKSIKA
Blackfoot dict of stems, roots, & affixes, 2d ed, 97n872

ENGLISH LANGUAGE—DICTIONARIES—SLANG
Black talk, 95n413
Flappers 2 rappers: American youth slang, 97n842
Idiom savant: slang as it is slung, 98n1014
New Yawk tawk: a dict of New York City expressions, 99n904
NTC's dict of American slang & colloquial expressions, 2d ed, 95n1060
NTC's dict of British slang & colloquial expressions, 99n908
NTC's thematic dict of American slang, 99n911
Random House histl dict of American slang, v.1, 95n1061
Random House histl dict of American slang, v.2: H-O, 98n1015
Shorter slang dict, 95n1058
Slang of sin, 99n43
Speaking freely, 98n1002
Thesaurus of slang, rev ed, 95n1059

ENGLISH LANGUAGE—DICTIONARIES—SOMALI
English-Somali, Somali-English Dict, 96n1134

ENGLISH LANGUAGE—DICTIONARIES—SOTHO LANGUAGE
Understanding everyday Sesotho, 96n1135

ENGLISH LANGUAGE—DICTIONARIES—SOUTH AFRICAN
Dictionary of South African English on histl principles, 97n830

ENGLISH LANGUAGE—DICTIONARIES—SPANISH
Collins Spanish-English, English-Spanish dict, unabridged 5th ed, 99n939
Dahl's law dict: an annot legal dict, Spanish-English/English-Spanish, 2d ed, 97n486
Delmar's English/Spanish pocket dict for health professionals, 98n1527
Dictionary of bus, English-Spanish, Spanish-English, [repr ed], 99n147
Dictionary of Chicano Spanish, 2d ed, 96n1136
Dictionary of contemporary Spain, 99n943
Elsevier's dict of financial & economic terms, 97n153
English-Spanish, Spanish-English electrical & computer engineering dict, 97n1297
Larousse concise Spanish-English/English-Spanish dict, 95n1095
Larousse concise Spanish-English/English-Spanish dict, rev ed, 99n940
Larousse English-Spanish/Spanish-English dict, new, 97n873
Larousse mini Spanish-English/English-Spanish dict, new ed, 97n874
Larousse pocket Spanish-English/English-Spanish dict, 95n1096
Medical dict in 6 langs, 97n1331
NTC's dict of common mistakes in Spanish, 96n1137

NTC's dict of Latin American Spanish, 98n1049
NTC's dict of Spanish false cognates, 95n1094
Oxford paperback Spanish dict & grammar, 98n1050
Oxford Spanish desk dict, 99n941
Oxford starter Spanish dict, 98n1051
Pockets: Spanish dict, 98n1052
Random House Latin-American Spanish dict, 99n942
Routledge Spanish dict of bus, commerce, & finance, 99n146
Routledge Spanish technical dict, 98n1408
Spanish-English/English-Spanish concise dict (Latin America), 95n1098
Spanish-English/English-Spanish dict, unabridged ed, 95n1097
Wiley dict of civil engineering & construction: English-Spanish, Spanish-English, 97n1304
Wiley's English-Spanish, Spanish-English dict of psychology & psychiatry, 96n782
Wiley's English/Spanish & Spanish/English legal dict, 95n606
Wiley's English-Spanish, Spanish-English bus dict, 98n157
Wiley's English-Spanish, Spanish-English dict, 99n1506
Wiley's English-Spanish, Spanish-English legal dict, 2d ed, 98n519

ENGLISH LANGUAGE—DICTIONARIES—SWEDISH
NTC's compact Swedish & English dict, 98n1053
Prisma's abridged English-Swedish & Swedish-English dict, 96n1138

ENGLISH LANGUAGE—DICTIONARIES—TATAR
Tatar-English/English-Tatar dict, 96n1139

ENGLISH LANGUAGE—DICTIONARIES—THAI
Oxford-Duden pictorial Thai & English dict, 96n1140

ENGLISH LANGUAGE—DICTIONARIES—TURKISH
Dictionary of the Turkic langs, 97n876

ENGLISH LANGUAGE—DICTIONARIES—UKRAINIAN
English-Ukrainian dict of bus, 98n155
Ukrainian-English, English-Ukrainian practical dict, 95n1099

ENGLISH LANGUAGE—DICTIONARIES—UZBEK
Uzbek-English, English-Uzbek concise dict, 96n1141

ENGLISH LANGUAGE—DICTIONARIES—YIDDISH
English-Yiddish/Yiddish-English dict, [rev ed], 98n1054
English-Yiddish/Yiddish-English practical dict, 95n1100
Harduf's transliterated English-Yiddish, Yiddish-English dict, [rev ed], 98n1055
Hippocrene practical English-Yiddish, Yiddish-English dict, expanded ed, 97n878

ENGLISH LANGUAGE—DICTIONARIES—YORUBA
Hippocrene concise Yoruba-English, English-Yoruba dict, 97n879

ENGLISH LANGUAGE—EPONYMS
Dictionary of histl allusions & eponyms, 99n40
What in the word? origins of words dealing with people & places, 97n823

ENGLISH LANGUAGE—ERRORS OF USAGE—DICTIONARIES
Highly selective dict for the extraordinarily literate, 98n1017

ENGLISH LANGUAGE—ETYMOLOGY
America in so many words, 98n1000
Barnhart concise dict of etymology, 97n825
Devious derivations, 95n1035
Dictionary of animal words & phrases, 96n1073
Dictionary of word origins, 97n826
English vocabulary quick ref, 99n901
Facts on File ency of word & phrase origins, rev ed, 98n1001
Medical meanings: a glossary of word origins, 98n1528
Speaking freely, 98n1002
Speaking of animals, 96n1074

ENGLISH LANGUAGE—EUPHEMISMS
Dictionary of euphemisms, 97n827
NTC's dict of euphemisms, 99n902
Rawson's dict of euphemisms & other doubletalk, rev ed, 97n828

ENGLISH LANGUAGE—FOREIGN WORDS & PHRASES
Bugaboos, chimeras & Achilles' heels, 95n1037
Dictionary of Japanese loanwords, 98n1003
German loanwords in English, 95n1036
Oxford dict of foreign words & phrases, 99n903

ENGLISH LANGUAGE—GLOSSARIES, VOCABULARIES, ETC.
Black talk, 95n413

ENGLISH LANGUAGE—GRAMMAR
Grammatically correct, 98n1005
Grammatically correct hndbk, 98n1004
Merriam-Webster's concise hndbk for writers, 99n833
NTC's hndbk for writers, 96n970
Write right!, 3d ed, 96n1081

ENGLISH LANGUAGE—IDIOMS
American Heritage dict of idioms, 98n1006
Dictionary of American idioms, 96n1083
Dictionary of American regional English, v.3: I-O, 97n833
Dictionary of Caribbean English usage, 97n834
Dictionary of catchphrases, 96n1084
NTC's American idioms dict, 2d ed, 95n1044
NTC's thematic dict of American idioms, 99n905
Thesaurus of traditional English metaphors, 95n1045
Yankee talk: a dict of New England expressions, 97n835

ENGLISH LANGUAGE—LEXICOGRAPHY
Encyclopaedic dict in the 18th century, v.1, 99n813

Encyclopaedic dict in the 18th century, v.2, 99n814
Encyclopaedic dict in the 18th century, v.3, 99n815
Encyclopaedic dict in the 18th century, v.4, 99n816
Encyclopaedic dict in the 18th century, v.5, 99n817

ENGLISH LANGUAGE—MIDDLE ENGLISH
Sources of London English, 97n831

ENGLISH LANGUAGE—OBSOLETE WORDS
Endangered English dict, 96n1089
Medieval wordbk, 97n838
Random House histl dict of American slang, v.1, 95n1061
Random House histl dict of American slang, v.2: H-O, 98n1015
Where Queen Elizabeth slept & what the butler saw, 98n1011

ENGLISH LANGUAGE—PRONUNCIATION
NTC's dict of American English pronunciation, 96n1077
Pronouncing dict of proper names, 2d ed, 99n900
Pronouncing Shakespeare's words, 99n1076

ENGLISH LANGUAGE—PROVINCIALISMS
UK to USA dict, 96n1082

ENGLISH LANGUAGE—PUNCTUATION
Merriam-Webster's gd to punctuation & style, 96n969
New well-tempered sentence, rev ed, 95n945
Punctuate it right!, 2d ed, 95n948
Write right!, 3d ed, 96n1081

ENGLISH LANGUAGE—RHETORIC
Eighteenth-Century British & American rhetorics & rhetoricians, 95n1113
Grammatically correct, 98n1005
Merriam-Webster's concise hndbk for writers, 99n833
Theorizing composition, 99n831

ENGLISH LANGUAGE—RHYME
Scholastic rhyming dict, 95n1057

ENGLISH LANGUAGE—STUDY & TEACHING
English lang & orientation programs in the US, 11th ed, 98n988
Teaching English abroad, 2d ed, 95n380

ENGLISH LANGUAGE—STYLE
ACS style gd, 2d ed, 98n872
Plain English gd, 96n1075
21st century manual of style, 95n949
Wired style, 97n758
Write right!, 3d ed, 96n1081

ENGLISH LANGUAGE—SUFFIXES & PREFIXES
Suffix obsession, 95n1062

ENGLISH LANGUAGE—SYNONYMS & ANTONYMS
Cambridge French-English thesaurus, 99n925
Cambridge thesaurus of American English, 95n1065
Choose the right word, 95n1063
Harcourt Brace student thesaurus, 2d ed, 95n1050
Highly selective dict for the extraordinarily literate, 98n1017

Highly selective thesaurus for the extraordinarily literate, 95n1066
Kingfisher 1st thesaurus, 95n1051
Kingfisher illus thesaurus, 96n1088
Oxford desk dict & thesaurus, American ed, 98n993
Roget A to Z, 95n1069
Roget's 2: the new thesaurus, 3d ed, 96n1095
Thesaurus dict of the English lang, 95n1068
Thesaurus of alternatives to worn-out words & phrases, 95n1067
Thesaurus of slang, rev ed, 95n1059
Thesaurus of traditional English metaphors, 95n1045

ENGLISH LANGUAGE—SYNONYMS & ANTONYMS—JUVENILE LITERATURE
American Heritage children's thesaurus, 98n1016

ENGLISH LANGUAGE—TERMS & PHRASES
BBI dict of English word combinations, rev ed, 99n913
Bugaboos, chimeras & Achilles' heels, 95n1037
Cassell dict of cliches, 98n1018
Cliches, 98n1019
Facts on File ency of word & phrase origins, rev ed, 98n1001
Metaphors dict, 96n1091
New York Public Lib bk of popular Americana, 95n1334
NTC's dict of commonplace words in real-life contexts, 99n915
Roget's superthesaurus, 2d ed, 99n916
Shorter dict of catch phrases, 95n1064
Sisson's word & expression locator, 2d ed, 96n1092

ENGLISH LANGUAGE—TEXTBOOKS FOR FOREIGN SPEAKERS
Light 'n lively reads, 98n1057

ENGLISH LANGUAGE—USAGE
Bugaboos, chimeras & Achilles' heels, 95n1037
English usage & style for editors, 99n836
Errors in English & ways to correct them, 4th ed, 95n1039
Guidelines for bias-free writing, 96n968
Little Oxford gd to English usage, 96n1076
NTC's dict of easily confused words, 95n1038
NTC's hndbk for writers, 96n970
Plain English gd, 96n1075
Thesaurus of alternatives to worn-out words & phrases, 95n1067
21st century manual of style, 95n949

ENGLISH LANGUAGE—WORD FREQUENCY
Educator's word frequency gd, 97n817

ENGLISH LITERATURE
Ann Radcliffe, 97n998
Bibliography of the English novel from the Restoration to the French Revolution, 96n1236
Biographical companion to lit in English, rev ed, 98n1066
British children's writers, 1800-1880, 97n934
British children's writers, 1880-1914, 95n1205
British prose writers of the early 17th century, 96n1232
British reform writers, 1789-1832, 97n977
British short-fiction writers, 1880-1914, 95n1209

British travel writers, 1837-75, 97n981
British women writers, 1700-1850, 98n1144
British writers, suppl 4, 98n1149
C. S. Lewis readers' ency, 99n1071
Cambridge gd to lit in English, 95n1103
Cambridge pa gd to lit in English, 97n894
Carl H. Pforzheimer Lib, English lit, 1475-1700, 1997 ed, 98n1148
Charles Dickens A to Z, 99n1072
Chaucer's pilgrims, 97n989
Contemporary popular writers, 98n1058
D. H. Lawrence: a ref companion, 97n995
Dictionary of literary biog: British reform writers, 1832-1914, 99n1062
Eighteenth-Century British literary biographers, 95n1204
Elizabeth Gaskell: an annot bibliog of English-lang sources 1976-91, 95n1213
Essential Matthew Arnold, 95n1210
Every thing in Dickens, 97n992
Everyone in Dickens, 97n993
First eds, 95n972
Four British women novelists, 99n1061
George Gordon, Lord Byron, 98n1155
George Orwell: a bibliog, 99n1073
Handbook of literary research, 2d ed, 96n1142
Humor in British lit, from the Middle Ages to the Restoration, 98n1150
Humor in 18th- & 19th-century British lit, 99n1060
Jane Austen ency, 99n1070
Late 19th- & early 20th-century British literary biographers, 96n1225
Literally entitled, 97n891
Literary criticism index, 2d ed, 95n1114
Literary gd & companion to N England, 96n1233
Literary gd & companion to S England, rev ed, 99n1065
Major authors on CD-ROM: Virginia Woolf [CD-ROM], 99n1087
Major Tudor authors, 98n1060
Modern British novel of the left, 99n1068
Old & Middle English lit, 96n1230
Oxford companion to English lit, rev ed, 96n1231
Oxford gd to British women writers, 95n1203
Paradise Lost: an annot bibliog, 97n997
Pronouncing Shakespeare's words, 99n1076
Reader's gd to lit in English, 97n915
Seventeenth-Century British nondramatic poets, 3d series, 95n1200
Shakespeare for students, bk 2, 98n1163
Shakespeare interactive [CD-ROM], 99n1080
Shakespeare interactive [CD-ROM], 99n1081
Sixteenth-Century British nondramatic writers, 1st series, 95n1201
Sixteenth-Century British nondramatic writers, 3d series, 97n983
Sixteenth-Century British nondramatic writers, 4th series, 98n1147
Thomas More: an annot bibliog of criticism, 1935-97, 99n1086
Twentieth-Century British literary biographers, 96n1227
Victorian yellowbacks & paperbacks, 1849-1905, v.1, 96n1223
Victorian yellowbacks & paperbacks, 1849-1905, v.2, 96n1224
Year's work in English studies, v.71, 95n923
Year's work in English studies, v.73, 1992, 96n958

ENGLISH LITERATURE—IRISH AUTHORS
Modern Irish writers, 98n1176

ENGLISH PHILOLOGY
Encyclopedia of English studies & lang arts, 95n929
English lang scholarship, 97n809
Year's work in English studies, v.71, 95n923

ENGLISH PLACE-NAMES
Dictionary of English place-names, 2d ed, 99n422

ENGLISH POETRY
Blake bks suppl, 96n1244
Columbia Granger's gd to poetry anthologies, 2d ed, 96n1263
Columbia Granger's index to poetry, 10th ed, 95n1245
Guide to British poetry explication, v.4, 96n1245
Late Victorian poetry 1880-99, 96n1246
Metaphysical poets: a chronology, 95n1224
Oxford companion to 20th-century poetry in English, 95n1249
Poets: American & British, 99n1110
Romantic poetry by women: a bibliog, 1770-1835, 95n1247
Victorian poetry, 97n1000
Who's Who in writers, editors, & poets, 5th ed, 96n959

ENGLISH—STUDY AND TEACHING
Oxford dict of computing for learners of English, 98n1577

ENGLISH WIT & HUMOR
Encyclopedia of British humorists, 97n984
Humor in British lit, from the Middle Ages to the Restoration, 98n1150

ENLIGHTENMENT
Encyclopedia of the Enlightenment, 97n475

ENOCH PRATT FREE LIBRARY
Song index of the Enoch Pratt Free Lib, 99n1126

ENTERTAINERS. *See also* **ACTORS & ACTRESSES**
A&E entertainment almanac, 1997, 98n1264
Encyclopedia of vaudeville, 95n1417
Entertainers in British films, 99n1225
Performing artists, 96n1363
Radio stars, 97n762
Roy Rogers, 96n1408

ENTOMOLOGY
Agricultural entomology, 96n1625

ENTREPRENEURSHIP
Free money from the fed govt for small businesses & entrepreneurs, 2d ed, 97n189
Small bus sourcebk, 10th ed, 98n166
Working solo sourcebk, 96n263

ENVIRONMENTAL ECONOMICS
Attitudes toward the outdoors: an annot bibliog, 95n1759
Dictionary of environment & sustainable dvlpmt, 98n1633

ENVIRONMENTAL EDUCATION
Blueprint for a green school, 96n1870
Education for the Earth, 2d ed, 96n337
Gale environmental almanac, 95n1776
Greening the college curriculum: a gd to environmental teaching in the liberal arts, 98n1640
Grolier illus lib of the environment, 96n1860

ENVIRONMENTAL ENGINEERING
Environmental engineering dict, 3d ed, 99n1407
Environmental sci & tech hndbk, 95n1775

ENVIRONMENTAL ETHICS
Environmental ethics, 98n1628

ENVIRONMENTAL HEALTH
Electronic & computer industry gd to chemical safety & environmental compliance, 99n1567
Health & environment in America's top-rated cities, 96n931
Patty's industrial hygiene & toxicology CD-ROM [CD-ROM], 99n1566
VNR dict of environmental health & safety, 95n1767

ENVIRONMENTALISM
ABC-CLIO companion to the environmental movement, 96n1869
Co-op America's natl green pages, 1996 ed, 97n1428
Environmental grantmaking fndns 1996, 4th ed, 97n690
Historical dict of North American environmentalism, 98n1638
International hndbk of environmental sociology, 99n1564

ENVIRONMENTALISTS
Biographical dict of American & Canadian naturalists & environmentalists, 99n1552
Directory of environmental electronic mail users in Eurasia, 4th ed, 97n1429
Peterson's job opportunities in the environment 1995, 96n1876
World who is who & does what in environment & conservation, 98n1631

ENVIRONMENTAL LAW
Conservation & the law, 99n584
Environment & the law, 97n514
Environment property & the law, 99n585
Environmental law hndbk, 14th ed, 98n559
Environmental statutes, 1995 ed, 96n1872
Federal wildlife laws hndbk with related laws, 99n587
Health & safety manager's A-Z gd to environmental mgmt, 96n1873
Law, values, & the environment, 98n560

ENVIRONMENTAL POLICY
Carroll's environmental dir 1995, 96n1863
China environmental report, 97n223
Mexico environmental report, 97n224
English-Spanish glossary of environmental terms & abbrevs, 96n1862
Environment 1: clean water, 95n1760
Environment 2: clean air, 95n1761
Environment abstracts 1994, 95n1774
Environmental ency, 95n1764
Environmental gd to the Internet, 96n1868
Environmental justice, 97n1435
Environmental racism & the environmental justice movement, 97n513
Environmental studies: an annot bibliog, 95n1758
Environmental telephone dir, 97n1430
European environmental stats hndbk, 95n1783
Free market environmental bibliog 1995-96, 4th ed, 98n1630
Gale environmental almanac, 95n1776
Glossary of environmental & regulatory terms & phrases, 95n1766
Greenpeace gd to anti-environmental orgs, 95n1770
Grolier lib of environmental concepts & issues, 97n1427
Human choice & climate change, 99n1563
NAFTA & GATT: environmental & economic issues, 98n705
National gd to funding for the environment & animal welfare, 2d ed, 96n878
World dir of country environmental studies, 3d ed, 97n1432

ENVIRONMENTAL PROTECTION
Atlas of the environment, 95n1756
Book of lists for regulated hazardous substances 1996, 97n1433
Cooper's comprehensive environmental desk ref, 97n1434
Dictionary of natural resource mgmt, 98n1632
Earth work, 96n1871
Encyclopedia of energy tech & the environment, 96n1830
Encyclopedia of environmental info sources, 95n1757
Environment & the law, 97n514
Environmental contaminant ref databk, v.1, 97n1387
Environmental contaminant ref databk, v.2, 97n1388
EPA database bk, 96n1865
Information sources in environmental protection, 98n1643
Multinational corps & the environment, 96n1851
Ozone dilemma, 96n1874
Rainforest orgs, 98n1639
VNR dict of environmental health & safety, 95n1767

ENVIRONMENTAL SCIENCES
Atlas of global change, 99n1550
Clean air hndbk, 3d ed, 99n1558
Companion ency of geography, 98n397
Concise ency of environmental systems, 95n1768
Concise Oxford dict of ecology, 96n1854
Conservation & environmentalism, 97n1426
Cooper's comprehensive environmental desk ref, 97n1434
Cooper's comprehensive environmental desk ref [CD-ROM], 99n1559
Dictionary of ecology & the environment, 3d ed, 99n1553
Dictionary of environmental law & sci, 96n1855
Dictionary of environmental sci & tech, 2d ed, 98n1636
Directory of environmental info sources, 5th ed, 96n1864
Earth work, 96n1871
Earth works, 97n1424
Encyclopedia of the environment, 95n1765
Environment ency & dir 1998, 99n1561

Environmental literacy, 95n1772
Environmental sci & tech hndbk, 95n1775
Facts on File environment atlas, rev ed, 99n1551
Glossary of environment stats, 98n1634
Guide to graduate environmental programs, 98n1641
Historical dict of the green movement, 99n1554
Indoor pollution, 99n1565
Rapid gd to trade names & synonyms of environmentally regulated chemicals, 99n1512
Sierra Club green gd, 97n1431

ENZYMES
Vocabulary of enzyme engineering, 95n1618

EPIC LITERATURE
Encyclopedia of literary epics, 97n889
Encyclopedia of traditional epics, 95n1322
Epics for students, 98n1069

EPIDEMICS
Encyclopedia of plague & pestilence, 96n1725

EPIDEMIOLOGY
Dictionary of epidemiology, 3d ed, 96n1698

ERASMUS
Annotated catalogue of early eds of Erasmus, 96n1250

ERITREA (ETHIOPIA)
Eritrea, 96n116
Historical dict of Eritrea, 99n479
Historical dict of Ethiopia & Eritrea, 2d ed, 95n117

ESPIONAGE
Guinness bk of espionage, 95n761
Spies, 98n701
Spies: the secret agents who changed the course of hist, 95n765
Whole spy catalog, 96n775

ESSAYS
Contemporary literary criticism, v.86, 97n895
Encyclopedia of the essay, 98n1107
Essay & general lit index 1990-94, 96n81
Literature criticism from 1400 to 1800, v.30, 97n903
Nineteenth-Century lit criticism, v.48, 97n909
Nineteenth-Century lit criticism, v.49, 97n910
Nineteenth-Century lit criticism, v.50, 97n911
Nineteenth-Century lit criticism, v.51, 97n912
Nineteenth-Century lit criticism annual cum title index for 1996, 97n914
Twentieth-Century literary criticism, v.59, 97n920
Twentieth-Century literary criticism annual cum title index for 1996, 97n923

ESSENTIAL OILS
Illustrated ency of essential oils, 97n1346

ETHICS
Dictionary of ethics, theology, & society, 97n73
Ency of applied ethics, 99n1251

Encyclopedia of values & ethics, 97n1163
Encyclopedia of war & ethics, 97n1161
International ethics, 99n698
Jewish ency of moral & ethical issues, 95n1475
Ready ref: ethics, 95n1429

ETHIOPIA
Ethiopia, 96n117
Historical dict of Ethiopia & Eritrea, 2d ed, 95n117

ETHNIC FOLKLORE
American elves, 98n1255

ETHNIC FOOD INDUSTRY
Restaurant lover's companion, 96n1526

ETHNIC GROUPS IN LITERATURE
Identities & issues in lit, 98n1070

ETHNIC RELATIONS
ACCESS gd to ethnic conflicts in Europe & the former Soviet Union, 95n146
Aggression & conflict, 96n835
Dictionary of race & ethnic relations, 3d ed, 95n394
Ethnic relations, 96n389
Jews & Europe, 96n424

ETHNOLOGY. *See also* MINORITIES
American immigrant cultures, 99n365
Atlas of the langs & ethnic communities of S Asia, 99n101
Bibliography of Canada's peoples, suppl.1, 95n417
Black hndbk, 99n375
Black/White relations in American hist, 99n454
Cultures of color in America, 99n367
DISCovering nations, states, & cultures [CD-ROM], 99n85
Encyclopedia of cultural anthropology, 97n316
Encyclopedia of multiculturalism, 95n396
Encyclopedia of the peoples of the world, 95n399
Encyclopedia of world cultures, v.6: Russia & Eurasia/China, 95n397
Encyclopedia of world cultures, v.7: S America, 95n398
Encyclopedia of world cultures, v.8: Middle America & the Caribbean, 97n318
Encyclopedia of world cultures, v.9: Africa & the Middle East, 97n319
Encyclopedia of world cultures, v.10: indexes, 97n320
Ethnic cultures of the world, 98n331
Ethnic dress, 96n388
Ethnic groups worldwide, 99n368
Ethnic minority health, 98n1504
Ethnic studies in the US, 97n322
Ethnohistorical dict of China, 99n370
Ethnohistorical dict of the Russian & Soviet empires, 95n400
From Afar to Zulu: a dict of African cultures, 96n390
Gale ency of multicultural America, 96n387
Guide to info resources in ethnic museum, lib, & archive collections in the US, 97n522
Korean Americans, 99n374
Nations of Africa, 98n321

Peaceful peoples, 95n91
Peoples of Africa, 97n321
Peoples of Central Africa, 98n322
Peoples of E Africa, 98n323
Peoples of N Africa, 98n324
Peoples of Southern Africa, 98n325
Peoples of W Africa, 98n326
Peoples of the world, 99n371
Racial & ethnic diversity, 2d ed, 99n372
Voices of multicultural America, 97n967
Worldmark ency of cultures & daily life, 99n364

ETIQUETTE
Learning to behave: a gd to American conduct bks before 1900, 95n1422
Protocol: a hndbk for legislative staff, 98n677

ETYMOLOGY
Alphabetical gd to the lang of name studies, 97n824

EURASIA
Bibliographic gd to Slavic, Baltic, & Eurasian studies 1996, 98n126
Encyclopedia of world cultures, v.6: Russia & Eurasia/China, 95n397
Military ency of Russia & Eurasia, v.5, 96n146
Modern ency of religions in Russia & Eurasia, v.7, 99n1267
Russia & Eurasia facts & figures annual, v.21, 98n128
Russia & Eurasia facts & figures annual, v.22, 98n129
Russia & Eurasia facts & figures, v.24, 99n126

EUROPE
Bibliography of European economic & social hist, 2d ed, 95n552
Birds of Europe with N Africa & the Middle East, 95n1568
Book of European forecasts, 2d ed, 97n238
Directory of population ageing research in Europe, 99n745
Energy balances for Europe & N America, 1992, 1993-2010, 97n1423
Eurail gd to train travel in the new Europe, 1996, 97n1443
Eurail gd to world train travel, 1996, 26th ed, 97n1444
Europe on file, 98n121
Festivals of W Europe, 95n1336
Festivals of Europe, 96n1353
Flora Europaea, v. 1, 2d ed., 95n1540
Fodor's upclose Europe, 99n437
Lands & peoples special ed: the changing face of Europe, 98n96
Library systems in Europe, 96n636
Migration stats 1994, 96n907
New religious movements in Western Europe, 98n1343
Statistics of road traffic accidents in Europe & N America 1995, 96n1890
Trends in Europe & N America 1995, 97n719
Weissmann travel planner for W & E Europe 1994-95, 95n518
Western Europe, 5th ed, 99n117

EUROPEAN—BUSINESS & ECONOMIC CONDITIONS
Annual bulletin of coal stats for Europe & N America, 1994, 96n1838
Annual bulletin of electric energy stats for Europe & N America, 1994, v.38, 96n1839
Bibliography of European economic & social hist, 2d ed, 95n552
Book of European forecasts, 2d ed, 97n238
Consumer Europe 1994, 95n278
Consumer Europe 1998/9, 14th ed, 99n249
Directory of consumer brands & their owners 1998: Eastern Europe, 99n250
Directory of consumer brands & their owners 1998: Europe, 99n251
Directory of chemical producers & products, v.1, pt.1, 2d ed, 97n1381
Directory of European research & dvlpmt 1995, 96n1504
Economic integration in Europe & N America, 96n232
Economic survey of Europe in 1995-96, 97n239
Encyclopedia of bus info sources: Europe, 95n277
European drinks mktg dir, 4th ed, 97n240
European environmental stats hndbk, 95n1783
European forests & timber, 98n1430
European mktg data & stats 1996, 31st ed, 97n273
European mktg data & stats 1998, 33d ed, 99n254
European oilfield serv, supply, & manufacturers dir, 1996, 2d ed, 97n1417
European pharmaceutical technical & regulatory compendium, 96n1742
European private label dir, 97n241
European research & dvlpmt database 1995 [CD-ROM], 96n1510
Europe's medium-sized cos dir, 97n242
Major cos of Central & Eastern Europe & the Commonwealth of Independent States 1996/97, 6th ed, 97n220
Major cos of Europe 1994/5, 96n253
Major cos of Europe 1998, 99n258
Prices of agricultural products & selected inputs for Europe & N America 1995, 96n1520
Who's who in European research & dvlpmt 1995, 96n1491
World database of consumer brands & their owners 1998 [CD-ROM], 99n259
World mktg data & stats 1996 on CD-ROM, 2d ed [CD-ROM], 97n281

EUROPEAN COMMUNITIES
Directory of Community legislation in force & other acts of the Community insts, 96n768
Directory of EU info sources 1995-96, 7th, 97n606
Directory of Japanese-affiliated cos in the EU, 1996-97, 97n211
Elsevier's dict of European Community co/bus/financial law in English, Danish, & German, 98n517
Encyclopedia of the EU, 99n691
EU Insts' register, 3d ed, 99n692
European regional incentives, 1996-97, 97n243
European Union ency & dir 1996, 2d ed, 97n607
Guide to the Community initiatives 1994-99, 96n753
Interinstitutional dir: European Union, 96n754
Official jl of the European Communities, v.38, English ed, 96n755
Political data hndbk: OECD countries, 2d ed, 98n684
United States-European Community trade resources, 95n323

EUROPEAN COOPERATION
Historical dict of European orgs, 96n139

EUROPEAN LITERATURE
Major Tudor authors, 98n1060

EUROPEANS
In search of your European roots, 2d ed, 95n454

EUROPE—BIBLIOGRAPHY
Malta, rev ed, 99n134
Paris, 99n127
Romania, rev ed, 99n136

EUROPE—COLONIES—AMERICA
Encyclopedia of the N American colonies, 95n540

EUROPE, EASTERN
American bibliog of Slavic & E European studies for 1993, 97n114
Central & East European info, 2d 3d, 95n280
Chronology of 20th-century E European hist, 95n559
Concise histl atlas of Eastern Europe, 97n446
Consumer Eastern Europe 1996, 96n251
Dictionary of E European hist since 1945, 95n560
Directory of chemical producers & products, v.1, pt.1, 2d ed, 97n1381
Eastern Europe: a bibliographic gd to English lang pubs, 1986-93, 96n140
Eastern Europe: a resource gd, 96n141
Eastern Europe & the Commonwealth of Independent States 1997, 3d ed, 98n127
East Europe & the republics: a pol risk annual, June 1994, 95n153
Ethnic pols in E Europe, 95n749
Major bus orgs of Eastern Europe & the Commonwealth of Independent States 1995/96, 5th ed, 97n244
Slovenia, 97n122

EUROPE—EDUCATION
European dir of SE Asian studies, 99n319

EUROPE—ENCYCLOPEDIAS
Encyclopedia of contemporary French culture, 99n128

EUROPE, GERMAN-SPEAKING
"Jewish question" in German-speaking countries, 1848-1914, 96n425

EUROPE—HISTORY
Bibliography of European economic & social hist, 2d ed, 95n552
Chronology of European hist, 98n462
Dictionary of European hist & pols, 1945-95, 97n438
European hist on file, 98n463
Historical dict of Denmark, 99n493
Historical dict of the gypsies (Romanies), 99n380
Medieval & early modern data bank [CD-ROM], 98n165
Peacemaking in medieval Europe, 99n492
Rise of fascism in Europe, 99n694

Supplement to The Modern Ency of Russian, Soviet, & Eurasian Hist, v.1, 97n476
Times atlas of European hist, 95n555
Travel gd to Jewish Europe, 2d ed, 97n436
War of the Spanish Succession, 1702-13, 97n435
Western Europe since 1945, 97n437

EUROPE—POLITICS & GOVERNMENT
Almanac of European pols 1995, 97n605
Encyclopedia of the EU, 99n691
European pol facts, 1900-96, 99n690
Political leaders of contemporary W Europe, 96n756
Rise of fascism in Europe, 99n694
Who's who in European pols, 3d ed, 98n685

EUROPE, SOUTHERN
Field gd to wild flowers of S Europe, 95n1541
Southern European studies gd, 95n147

EVANGELICALISM
American evangelicalism 2: 1st bibliographical suppl, 1990-96, 98n1383
Blackwell dict of evangelical biog, 1730-1860, 97n1208
Evangelical dict of biblical theology, 97n1197
Evangelical sectarianism in the Russian Empire & the USSR, 97n1173
Handbook of evangelical theologians, 95n1461

EVENTS (PHILOSOPHY)
50 yrs of events, 98n1331

EVIDENCE, EXPERT
ASTM dir of scientific & technical consultants & expert witnesses, 1994 ed, 95n1498

EVIDENCE (LAW)
Courtroom hndbk on fed evidence, 1995 ed, 96n591

EXCAVATIONS (ARCHAEOLOGY)
Bibliography of Syrian archaeological sites to 1980, 96n484
British & Irish archaeology, 95n521

EXECUTIONS & EXECUTIONERS
Legal executions in N.Y. State, 98n554

EXECUTIVE ADVISORY BODIES
Carroll's fed advisory dir 1995, 96n722

EXECUTIVE DEPARTMENTS, UNITED STATES.
See also **PRESIDENTS—UNITED STATES**
Almanac of the executive branch 1997/98, 98n642
Reports required by Congress, 1995, v.2, no.1, 96n746
US govt dirs, 1982-95, 99n62

EXECUTIVES
Hoover's dir of human resources executives 1996, 97n255

EXECUTIVES—TRAINING OF
Bricker's intl dir 1998, 99n358
Critical gd to mgmt training videos & selected multimedia, 1996, 97n266

EXHIBITIONS
International trade fairs & conferences dir 1995, 19th ed, 96n300
Museum premieres, exhibitions, & special events, 98n72
World dir of exhibitions & trade fairs 1995, 96n309

EXOBIOLOGY
Cosmic influences on humans, animals, & plants, 98n1441

EXPATRIATE ARTISTS
American expatriate writers, 98n1127

EXPERIMENTS
Science experiments index for young people, 2d ed, 97n1244

EXPERTISE
Yearbook of experts, authorities & spokespersons, 12th ed, 96n103

EXPLORERS
Explorers, 99n417
Explorers & discoverers, 96n454
Explorers & discoverers, v.5, 99n418
Literature criticism from 1400 to 1800, v.31, 97n904
Oxford atlas of exploration, 99n415

EXPORTS
American export register 1995, 96n286
Consumer intl 1995, 95n248
Consumer Japan 1993, 95n269
Exporting to the USA, 1995-96 ed, 96n297
International standards desk ref, 98n206
Pathfinder to US export control laws & regulations, 95n614
Services—the export of the 21st century: a gdbk of US serv exporters, 98n262

EX-PRESIDENTS. *See also* PRESIDENTS— UNITED STATES
How to research the presidency, 97n586

EYE
Dictionary of eye terminology, 3d ed, 98n1553
Quick ref glossary of eye care terminology, 99n1463

FABERGE, PETER CARL
Faberge & his works, 95n994

FACSIMILE TRANSMISSION
FaxUSA, 1998, 99n151
FaxUSA, 1994 ed, 95n189
Library fax/Ariel dir, 8th ed, 95n640
National e-mail & fax dir 1999, 99n56
National fax dir, 1996, 97n51
North American facsimile bk [CD-ROM], 95n70

FADS
Fashion & merchandising fads, 95n987

FAIRIES
Field gd to demons, fairies, fallen angels, & other subversive spirits, 99n1181
Spirits, fairies, gnomes, & goblins, 97n1090

FAIRY TALES
Index to fairy tales, 1987-92, 95n1316

FALKLAND ISLANDS
Falkland Islands, S Georgia, & the S Sandwich Islands, 97n133

FAMILY
Audiovisual resources for family programming, 97n313
Dictionary of family therapy, rev ed, 96n1718
Divorce help sourcebk, 95n847
Encyclopedia of marriage & the family, 96n863
Family studies database [CD-ROM], 97n674
Marriage, family, & relationships, 96n862
National gd to funding for children, youth, & families, 3d ed, 97n698
Work-Family research, 98n778

FAMILY RECREATION. *See also* TRAVEL
Best places to go, 95n505
Books on the move, 95n509
Super family vacations, 3d ed, 96n462

FAMILY VIOLENCE
Domestic violence, 97n675
Vocabulary of family violence, 95n850

FANTASTIC FICTION
Encyclopedia of fantasy, 98n1116
Fantasy lit for children & YAs, 4th ed, 96n1167
St. James gd to fantasy writers, 97n950
Science fiction & fantasy ref index 1992-95, 98n1117
Science fiction, fantasy, & horror writers, 96n1193
Supernatural index, 96n1194

FANTASTIC FILMS
Science fiction, horror & fantasy film & TV credits, suppl.2, 95n1395
Sci-Fi on tape, 98n1318

FANTASTIC LITERATURE
Magill's gd to sci fiction & fantasy lit, 97n948
Poe ency, 98n1137

FANTASY IN ART
Barlowe's gd to fantasy, 98n979

FARM EQUIPMENT
Encyclopedia of American farm implements & antiques, 98n1419

FARM PRODUCE
UNCTAD commodity yrbk 1994, 96n1521

FASCISM
Rise of fascism in Europe, 99n694

FASHION
Contemporary fashion, 96n1017
Fashion & merchandising fads, 95n987

Illustrated ency of costume & fashion from 1066 to the present, rev ed, 95n986
Look of the century, 97n788

FAULKNER, WILLIAM
Reader's gd to the short stories of William Faulkner, 95n1189

FEDERAL GOVERNMENT
American govt & pols, 98n646
Congressional Quarterly's desk ref on American govt, 96n737
Directory of fed jobs & employers, 97n258
Federal regulatory dir, 8th ed, 98n664
Federal systems of the world, [2d ed], 96n712
Government dir of addresses & telephone nos 1995, 3d ed, 96n732
Washington online: how to access the fed govt on the Internet 1995, 96n1785

FEDERAL GRANTS
Federal grants & funding locator [CD-ROM], 99n766

FEDERAL REPUBLIC OF YUGOSLAVIA. *See also* FORMER YUGOSLAV REPUBLICS
Breakup of Yugoslavia & the war in Bosnia, 99n116

FEDERAL WRITERS' PROJECT
Federal writers' project, 96n966

FEMALE OFFENDERS
Female offenders, 98n549

FEMINISM
Encyclopedia of women's hist in America, 97n736
Feminism worldwide, 98n831
Feminist chronicles 1953-93, 95n917
Historical dict of feminism, 97n735
Historical dict of women's educ in the US, 99n803
Reader's companion to US women's hist, 99n804
Susan B. Anthony: a biogl companion, 99n800
US women's interest groups, 97n737
Women & music, 97n1020
Women's issues, 98n837

FEMINISM & ART
Women artists, 2d ed, 96n1021

FEMINISM & LITERATURE
Encyclopedia of feminist literary theory, 99n961
Feminist criticism of American women poets, 96n1222
Feminist writers, 97n886
Italian women writers, 95n1235

FEMINISM & MOTION PICTURES
Women's companion to intl film, 95n1373

FEMINIST JURISPRUDENCE
Feminist jurisprudence, 97n739

FEMINIST THEOLOGY
Dictionary of feminist theologies, 97n1177

FEMINIST THEORY
Dictionary of feminist theory, 2d ed, 96n948
Feminism & postmodern theory, 97n727
Feminist jurisprudence, 97n739
French feminist theory (2), 95n902
French feminist theory 3, 98n832
Women of color: feminist theory, 97n729

FESTIVALS. *See also* HOLIDAYS
Festivals of Europe, 96n1353
Festivals of W Europe, 95n1336
Fiesta, 98n1262
Food festivals, 98n414
Historic festivals, 97n386
Holiday symbols 1998, 99n1189
Holidays & festivals index, 96n1358
Holidays, festivals, & celebrations dict, 2d ed, 98n1263
Holidays, festivals & celebrations of the world dict, 95n1338
Music festivals from Bach to blues, 97n1029
Shakespeare cos & festivals, 96n1420
Wild planet!, 96n1352
World holiday bk, 95n1335
World holiday festival & calendar bks, 99n1194

FETUS
Effects of drugs on the fetus & nursing infant, 97n1358

FICTION
American novel explication 1991-95, 99n1040
Annotated bibliog of jazz fiction & jazz fiction criticism, 97n944
Argentine novel, 98n1168
Children's fiction series, 98n1088
Crown crime companion, 96n1189
English novel, 1660-1700, 98n1145
Fiction catalog, 13th ed, 97n945
Fiction dict, 96n1185
Genreflecting: a gd to reading interests in genre fiction, 4th ed, 96n1186
Jules Verne ency, 97n952
Late-Victorian & Edwardian British novelist, 1st series, 96n1235
Masterplots 2: American fiction series suppl, 95n1178
Masterplots 2: short story series suppl, 97n953
Masterplots fiction CD-ROM, rev ed [CD-ROM], 95n1112
Mystery & suspense writers, 99n1032
Mystery women, v.1 1860-1979, 99n1030
Novel openers, 96n1188
Novels for students, v.1, 98n1109
Novels for students, v.2, 98n1110
Novels for students, v.3, 99n1013
Novels for students, v.4, 99n1014
Now read on: a gd to contemporary popular fiction, 2d ed, 96n1187
Sequels: an annot gd to novels in series, 99n1029
Short stories for students, v.3, 99n1015
Short stories for students, v.4, 99n1016
Short story criticism, v.18, 97n954
Short story criticism, v.19, 97n955
Short story criticism, v.20, 97n956
Short story criticism, v.21, 97n957

Supplementing lit programs, 95n1129
Thomas Wolfe: an annot critical bibliog, 97n976
To be continued: an annot gd to sequels, 97n946
What do I read next?, 1994, 95n1158
What fantastic fiction do I read next?, 99n1036
What Western do I read next?, 99n1028

FICTION GENRES
Teen genreflecting, 98n1096

FIGURES OF SPEECH
Life is just a bowl of cherries & other delicious sayings, 99n914
NTC's dict of folksy, regional, & rural sayings, 97n837
NTC's thematic dict of American idioms, 99n905
Sisson's word & expression locator, 2d ed, 96n1092

FIJI
Fiji, 96n169

FILIPINOS
Filipino achievers in the USA & Canada, 97n332

FILM ADAPTATIONS
Encyclopedia of novels into film, 99n1216
Films into bks, 96n1394
International gd to lit on film, 95n1379

FILM CRITICISM
New York Times film reviews, v.19: 1993-94, 97n1133

FILM FESTIVALS
Film festival gd, 99n1223

FILM NOIR. See also **DETECTIVE & MYSTERY FILMS**
Film noir, 96n1383

FINANCE. See also **INVESTMENTS**
Almanac of bus & industrial financial ratios 1996, 27th ed, 98n177
Bibliographic gd to bus & economics 1995, 98n147
Cabell's dir of publishing opportunities in accounting, economics & finance, 6th ed, 96n669
Controller's & treasurer's desk ref, 95n233
Dictionary for bus & finance, 3d ed, 96n180
Dictionary of bus terms, 2d ed, 96n178
Dictionary of finance & investment terms, 4th ed, 96n220
Dictionary of Japanese financial terms, 96n248
Directory of bus & financial info servs, 9th ed, 95n202
Elsevier's dict of European Community co/bus/financial law in English, Danish, & German, 98n517
Elsevier's dict of financial & economic terms, 97n153
Elsevier's dict of financial terms, rev ed, 99n185
Export financing & insurance vocabulary, 97n206
Financial planner's desk ref, 95n229
Fitzroy Dearborn ency of banking & finance, 10th ed, 95n230
Gale 5 lang finance dict, 95n231
Global dir of financial info vendors, 95n228
Handbook of intl financial terms, 98n184
Information sources in finance & banking, 97n191
International financial stats locator, 96n230
Islamic economics & finance, 97n232
Knowledge Exchange bus ency, 98n154
Language of banking, 95n232
Plunkett's financial servs industry almanac, 98n185
Prices & financial stats in the ESCWA region, 97n192
Routledge German dict of bus commerce & finance, 98n156
Search for economics as a sci, 97n149
Who's who in Asian banking & finance, 98n150
Who's who in finance & industry, 1996-97, 97n152

FINANCE, PERSONAL
Numbers: how many, how far, how long, how much, 98n810
Official gd to household spending, 97n278

FINANCIAL MINISTERS
Biographical dict of the US Secretaries of the Treasury, 1789-1995, 97n587

FINGER PLAY
Neal-Schuman index to finger-plays, 95n1153

FINLAND
Finland, rev ed, 98n123

FINNEY, ROSS LEE
Ross Lee Finney: a bio-bibliog, 97n1039

FINN, HUCKLEBERRY (FICTITIOUS CHARACTER)
Huckleberry Finn on film, 95n1393

FIREARMS. See also **WEAPONS**
Gun control, 97n510
Gun digest, 98n920
Illustrated ency of handguns, 97n782
Orion blue bk: gun 1998, 99n849
Springfield armory: shoulder weapons 1795-1968, 99n848
Standard catalog of firearms, 5th ed, 96n1009
Vital gd to combat guns & infantry weapons, 97n579

FIRST AID IN ILLNESS & INJURY
Household chemicals & emergency first aid, 95n1650
Parent's gd to medical emergencies, 98n1523
Treasury of natural 1st aid remedies from A-Z, 96n1715

FISHES. See also **AQUARIUM FISHES**
Coastal fishes of SE Australia, 95n1585
Dorling Kindersley ency of fishing, 95n815
Fish & fisheries worldwide [CD-ROM], 96n1605
Fishes of Tenn., 95n1584
Fishes of the Galapagos Islands, 98n1468
Fishes of the Gulf of Mexico, v.1, 99n1388
Fishes of the tropical E Pacific, 96n1633
Fishes of the world, 95n1587
Fossil atlas: fishes, 97n1404
Freshwater fishes of the Carolinas, Va., Md., & Dela., 95n1588
Lake, river, & sea-run fishes of Canada, 96n1624
Practical gd to the marine animals of northeastern N America, 99n1394
Species info lib [CD-ROM], 96n1606

FISHING. *See also* **SALTWATER FISHING**
Coykendall's complete gd to sporting collectibles, 98n895
Dorling Kindersley ency of fishing, 95n815
Fishing tackle source dir, 99n729
Fly-fisher's gd to saltwater naturals & their imitation, 96n817
Hook, line, & sinker, 95n816
McKnew & Parker's buyer's gd to sport fishing boats, 1995 ed, 96n810

FISKE ICELANDIC COLLECTION
Manuscript material, correspondence, & graphic material in the Fiske Icelandic Collection, 95n158

FITZGERALD, F. SCOTT
F. Scott Fitzgerald A to Z, 99n1054

FLAGS
Flags of the world, 99n406
State names, seals, flags, & symbols, rev ed, 95n499
Ultimate pocket: flags of the world, 98n374

FLEA MARKETS
Flea market trader, 11th ed, 98n896
Garage sale & flea market annual, 5th ed, 98n897

FLIGHT
Flight & flying: a chronology, 95n1787

FLORICULTURE
Ball redbk, 99n1346

FLORIDA
Bibliography of Fla., v.1, 95n105
Bibliography of Fla., v.2: 1846-80, 97n84
Birdlife of Fla., 95n1575
Butterflies of the W Indies & S Fla., 95n1578
Florida, 98n416
Florida: atlas of histl county boundaries, 98n431
Florida almanac 1997-98, 11th ed, 98n99
Florida hndbk 1993-94, 95n104
Florida statl abstract, 1994, 28th ed, 96n916

FLOWERING SHRUBS
Favorite flowering shrubs, 96n1569

FLOWERING TREES
Flowering crabapples, 96n1567
Garden trees, 97n1282

FLOWERS. *See also* **WILD FLOWERS**
Adrian Bloom's yr-round garden, 99n1347
Bulbs, 99n1348
Cyclamen: a gd for gardeners, horticulturists, & botanists, 98n1449
Desert wildflowers of N America, 99n1365
Illustrated ency of camellias, 99n1364
Wild orchids across N America, 99n1363

FLUORESCENCE
Fluorescence: gems & minerals under ultraviolet light, 96n1812

FLY FISHING
Fly-fisher's gd to saltwater naturals & their imitation, 96n817

FOLGER SHAKESPEARE LIBRARY
Catalogue of paintings in the Folger Shakespeare lib, 95n1021

FOLIAGE PLANTS
Foliage plant diseases, 98n1446

FOLK ART
Contemporary American folk art, 97n783

FOLK LITERATURE
Motif-index of folk lit, new ed [CD-ROM], 95n1317
South Slavic folk culture, 95n1315
This land is our land: a gd to multicultural lit for children & YAs, 95n1133

FOLKLORE
American folklore, 97n1088
Armenian folklore bibliog, 96n1340
Atlas of the mysterious in N America, 96n786
Encyclopedia of folklore & lit, 99n962
Field gd to demons, fairies, fallen angels, & other subversive spirits, 99n1181
Folk traditions of the Arab world, 96n1342
Folklife sourcebk, 2d ed, 96n1341
Folklore: an ency of hist, methods, & theory, 99n1180
Index to fairy tales, 1987-92, 95n1316
Larousse dict of world folklore, 96n1343
Micronesian religion & lore, 96n1439
South Slavic folk culture, 95n1315
Wise words & wives' tales, 95n1313

FOLK MUSIC
Central European folk music, 97n1073
Encyclopedia of Canadian rock, pop & folk, 95n1292
Ethnic & vernacular music, 1898-1960, 97n1075
Traditional Anglo-American folk music, 95n1302

FONTAINE, JOAN
Joan Fontaine: a bio-bibliog, 95n1341

FOOD. *See also* **NUTRITION**
Book of food, 95n1519
Bowes & Church's food values of portions commonly used, 16th ed, 95n1520
Codex alimentarius, v.5a, 2d ed, 96n1534
Codex alimentarius, v.13, 2d ed, 96n1535
Concise ency of foods & nutrition, 96n1524
Contemporary & histl lit of food sci & human nutrition, 96n1522
Cook's dict & culinary ref, 97n1248
Dictionary of American food & drink, rev ed, 95n1517
Dictionary of healthful food terms, 98n1420
Dictionary of Italian cuisine, 99n1331
Edible plants & animals, 95n1516
Elsevier's dict of agriculture & food production, 96n1516
European food databk 1994, 95n1522
Food aid in figures, v.11, 96n881
Food chronology, 96n1539

Foods & nutrition ency, 2d ed, 95n1515
Great food almanac, 95n1521
Green kitchen hndbk, 98n1425
International dict of food & nutrition, 95n1514
Nutribase nutrition facts desk ref, 96n1540
Unofficial gd to ethnic cuisine & dining in America, 96n1531
Who's buying food & drink, 98n257

FOOD ADDITIVES
Consumer's dict of food additives, 4th ed, 96n1530
Handbook of food additives, 96n1533

FOOD CONTAMINATION
Home health gd to poisons & antidotes, 96n1727

FOOD HABITS
Encyclopedia of N American eating & drinking traditions, customs, & rituals, 97n1250

FOOD INDUSTRY & TRADE
Bourbon companion, 99n1337
Career opportunities in the food & beverage industry, 96n1538
Elsevier's dict of agriculture & food production, 96n1516
Food & beverage market place, 1996, 97n1249
Food & beverage market place, 1997/98, 99n1339
Historical dict of the intl food agencies, 96n1529
Statistics on occupational wages & hours of work & on food prices 1997, 99n231

FOOD IN LITERATURE
Food & drink in lit, 97n881

FOOD—QUOTATIONS
Never eat more than you can lift, & other food quotes & quips, 98n1429

FOOLS & JESTERS
Fools & jesters in lit, art, & hist, 99n951

FOOT
Foot & ankle sourcebk, 97n1340

FOOTBALL
Canadian Football League facts, figures, & records, 1994 ed, 95n819
College football bibliog, 95n821
Gridiron greats: a century of Polish Americans in college football, 98n745
Kids' world almanac of football, 96n818
NCAA football, 96n819
NCAA football, 99n730
Official 1996 NFL record & fact bk, 97n654
Professional sports team hists, 95n800
Sporting News pro football gd, 1996 ed, 97n655
Sporting News pro football register, 1996 ed, 97n656
Sports ency: pro football, 12th ed, 95n820
Sports ency: pro football, 98n746
Total football, 98n747

FOOTWEAR
Complete footwear dict, 95n988

FORBES, ESTHER
Ester Forbes, 99n1053

FORCE & ENERGY
Energy stats yrbk, 1992, 95n1751
Natural gas stats sourcebk, 95n1753
Natural gas stats sourcebk, 2d ed, 96n1844
Renewable energy sources stats 1989-91, 96n1848
SYNERJY, 96n1831

FORECASTING
American forecaster almanac 1994, bus ed, 95n3
Encyclopedia of the future, 97n44
Predicting the future, 98n88

FOREIGN STUDY
Academic yr abroad 1995/96, 96n368
Alternative travel dir 1998, 4th ed, 99n439
Encyclopedia of Irish schools, 1500-1800, 96n315
Financial resources for intl study, 2d ed, 97n309
International schools dir, 1993/1994 ed, 95n381
ISS dir of overseas schools, 1994-95 ed, 96n372
Japan: exploring your options, 96n373
Open doors 1994/95, 97n311
Open doors 1996/97: report on intl educl exchange, 99n352
Peterson's study abroad 1994, 95n382
Peterson's study abroad 1998, 99n353
Peterson's summer study abroad, 96n367
Programs & centers in comparative & intl educ, rev ed, 96n370
Study abroad 1998-99, 30th ed, 99n354
Vacation study abroad 1995/96, 96n369
Vacation study abroad, 99n355

FORESTS & FORESTRY. *See also* **WOOD PRODUCTS**
Directory of the wood products industry, 1998, 99n1343
European forests & timber, 98n1430
Forest & forest industries country fact sheets, 98n1431
North American factbk, 1994-95, 96n1541
Parks dir of the US, 2d ed, 95n512
Peterson 1st gd to forests, 96n1591
Restoration forestry, 96n1542

FORMER SOVIET REPUBLICS. *See also* **RUSSIA; SOVIET UNION**
Atlas of Russia & the Independent Republics, 96n445
Bibliography of the Soviet Union, it predecessors & successors, 97n124
Cultural atlas of Russia & the Former Soviet Union, rev ed, 99n125
Documents of Soviet-American relations, v.3, 99n122
Documents of Soviet hist, v.4, 99n123
Eastern Europe & the Commonwealth of Independent States 1997, 3d ed, 98n127
Longman biogl dir of decision-makers in Russia & the successor states, 96n145
Major cos of Central & Eastern Europe & the Commonwealth of Independent States 1996/97, 6th ed, 97n220
Miniature empires, 99n537
Newly independent states of Eurasia, 2d ed, 98n125

OMRI annual survey of E Europe & the former Soviet Union 1996, 99n115
Placenames of Russia & the former Soviet Union, 97n382
Political parties of E Europe, Russia, & the successor states, 2d ed, 96n757
Post-Soviet hndbk, 97n123
Russia & Eurasia facts & figures annual, v.21, 98n128
Russia & Eurasia facts & figures annual, v.22, 98n129
Russia & Eurasia facts & figures, v.24, 99n126
Statistical hndbk of social & economic indicators for the former Soviet Union, 97n125
Who's who in Russia & the CIS Republics, 96n40

FORMER YUGOSLAV REPUBLICS. *See also* **FEDERAL REPUBLIC OF YUGOSLAVIA**
Historical dict of the Republic of Macedonia, 99n495

FORMS (LAW)
Complete bk of personal legal forms, 2d ed, 98n541
Complete bk of small bus legal forms, 2d ed, 98n542

FOSSILS. *See also* **PALEONTOLOGY**
Colorado rockhounding, 95n1732
Fossil atlas: fishes, 97n1404
Fossils of the Burgess Shale, 96n1813

FOSTER CARE
Children in foster care & adoption, 99n756
Children of separation, 95n851

FRANCE
Les Fauves: a sourcebk, 95n1019
Regions of France, 97n115

FRANCE—BIBLIOGRAPHY
Paris, 99n127

FRANCE—ENCYCLOPEDIAS
Encyclopedia of contemporary French culture, 99n128

FRANCE—HISTORY. *See also* **EUROPE—HISTORY**
Battles of the Somme, 1916, 97n561
Charles-Maurice de Talleyrand 1754-1838, 97n447
Dictionary of 20th century culture: French culture 1900-75, 96n545
Historical dict of the wars of the French Revolution, 99n499
Historical dict of WW II France, 99n498
Impact of Napoleon, 1800-15, 98n469

FRANCHISES (RETAIL TRADE)
Bond's franchise gd, 1996, 97n180
Directory of franchise opportunities, 95n220
How much can I make?, 98n174
1998 franchise annual, 99n165

FRANKLIN, BENJAMIN
Benjamin Franklin: a biogl companion, 99n455

FRAUD
Scams, shams, & flimflams, 95n1337

FREEDOM OF RELIGION
Freedom of religion decisions of the US Supreme Court, 97n1183

FREEDOM OF SPEECH
Free expression & censorship in America, 98n584
Freedom of speech decisions of the US Supreme Court, 97n541

FREEDOM OF THE PRESS
Press freedom & dvlpmt, 98n850

FREEDOM OF THE PRESS. *See also* **CENSORSHIP**
Freedom of the press: an annot bibliog, 2d suppl: 1978-92, 95n704
Freedom of the press decisions of the US Supreme Court, 97n761

FREE ENTERPRISE
Free market environmental bibliog 1995-96, 4th ed, 98n1630

FREE MATERIAL. *See also* **EDUCATION**
Educators gd to free films, filmstrips, & slides 1995, 55th ed, 96n375
Educators gd to free sci materials, 35th ed, 95n1480
Educators gd to free videotapes 1995, 42d ed, 96n376
Educators grade gd to free teaching aids 1995, 41st ed, 96n322
Educators index of free materials 1995, 104th ed, 97n294
Elementary teachers gd to free curriculum materials 1995, 52d ed, 96n323
Free mags for libs, 4th ed, 95n647
Guide to free computer materials 1995, 13th ed, 96n1771

FREE TRADE
Arthur Andersen N American bus sourcebk, 96n288
Encyclopedia of the N American Free Trade Agreement, 96n305
NAFTA bibliog, 98n255

FRENCH DRAMA
French women playwrights before the 20th century, 95n1405

FRENCH LANGUAGE
Canadian dict of abbrevs, 95n1

FRENCH LANGUAGE—DICTIONARIES— ENGLISH
Barron's jr illus dict: French-English, 95n1072
Chinese-English-French Kuaisu dict, 99n920
Collins-Robert French-English, English-French dict, 3d ed, 98n1024
Correctional admin vocab, 95n621
Dahl's law dict, 96n574
Dictionary of contemporary French connectors, 97n847
Dictionary of gastronomic terms, French/English, 99n1334
Dictionary of La Creole, 99n935
Electronics & telecommunications vocabulary, 95n1611
Essential French dict, 95n1077
French-English, English-French dict, unabridged ed, 95n1074
French-English, English-French practical dict, 95n1079
Informatics glossary, 95n1697

Integrated pest mgmt glossary, 95n1513
Larousse concise French/English, English/French dict, 95n1075
Larousse concise French/English, English/French dict, rev ed, 99n926
Larousse mini French-English, English-French dict, new ed, 97n848
Larousse pocket French-English/English-French dict, 95n1076
Les bon mots: how to amaze tout le monde with everyday French, 98n1025
Oxford-Hachette French desk dict, 98n1026
Oxford-Hachette French dict, 96n1100
Oxford paperback French dict, 2d ed, 95n1078
Oxford paperback French dict & grammar, 96n1101
Oxford starter French dict, 98n1027
Pockets: French dict, 98n1028
Routldege French dict of environmental tech, 98n1637
Routledge French dict of telecommunications, 99n1494
Routledge French technical dict, 96n1499
Standard French-English, English-French dict, 96n1102
Street French slang dict & thesaurus, 99n924
2001 French & English idioms, 2d ed, 97n846
Vocabulary of computer security & viruses, 96n1766
Vocabulary of enzyme engineering, 95n1618
Vocabulary of family violence, 95n850
Vocabulary of packaging, 95n1633

FRENCH LANGUAGE—DICTIONARIES—IDIOMS
Media French, 99n927
2001 French & English idioms, 2d ed, 97n846

FRENCH LANGUAGE—SYNONYMS & ANTONYMS
Cambridge French-English thesaurus, 99n925
Using French synonyms, 95n1073

FRENCH LITERATURE
Andre Malraux, 96n1253
Critical bibliog of French lit, v.5, 95n1229
Francois Rabelais: a ref gd, 1950-90, 95n1230
Guide to French lit: beginnings to 1789, 95n1231
New Oxford companion to lit in French, 96n1252

FRENCH POETRY
Lyrics of the Trouveres, 96n1251
Music & poetry in the Middle Ages, 96n1296

FRIEL, BRIAN
Brian Friel, 96n1257

FRIENDLY SOCIETIES
International ency of secret societies & fraternal orders, 98n764

FROGS
Handbook of frogs & toads of the US & Canada, 3d ed, 96n1640

FRONTIER & PIONEER LIFE
Atlas of westward expansion, 96n488
Cowboy ency, 96n510
Cowboys & the wild west, 95n541
Encyclopedia of frontier biog, v.4, 95n538
Encyclopedia of frontier biog on CD-ROM [CD-ROM], 96n497
Encyclopedia of frontier lit, 98n1130
Handbook of the American frontier, v.3, 95n440
Handbook of the American frontier, v.4: the far West, 98n357

FROST, ROBERT
Concordance to the poetry of Robert Frost, 95n1190

FRUIT
Brooks & Olmo register of fruit & nut varieties, 99n1330
Codex alimentarius, v.5a, 2d ed, 96n1534
Great citrus bk, 98n1428
Organic gardener's home ref, 96n1543
Produce ref gd to fruits & vegetables from around the world, 98n1421
Systematic treatment of fruit types, 95n1539
Taylor's gd to fruits & berries, 97n1259

FUGITIVE (TELEVISION PROGRAM)
Following The Fugitive: an episode gd & hndbk to the 1960s TV series, 97n1127
Fugitive: a complete episode gd, 1963-67, 96n1403

FULANI LANGUAGE—DICTIONARIES—ENGLISH
Hippocrene practical Fulani-English dict, 96n1103

FULLER, MARGARET
New England transcendentalists [CD-ROM], 99n1046

FUNCTION TESTS (MEDICINE)
Everything you need to know about medical tests, 97n1337

FUNDAMENTALISM
American evangelicalism 2: 1st bibliographical suppl, 1990-96, 98n1383

FUND RAISING. See also GRANTS-IN-AID; PHILANTHROPY
AIDS funding, 4th ed, 97n683
Corporate & fndn fundraising manual for Native Americans, 3d ed, 98n793
Fund-Raising regulation, 98n539
Guide to funding for intl & foreign programs, 2d ed, 96n875
National gd to funding for the environment & animal welfare, 2d ed, 96n878
National gd to funding in aging, 4th ed, 96n849
National gd to funding in arts & culture, 3d ed, 96n961
NSFRE fund-raising dict, 98n784
Philanthropic studies index, v.3, no.1, 95n868
Philanthropic studies index, 1995 cum index, 96n884

FUNERAL RITES & CEREMONIES
International hndbk of funeral customs, 99n1270
R.I.P.: the complete bk of death & dying, 98n767
Vestiges of mortality & remembrance, 95n519

FUNGI
Annotated catalogue of types of the Univ of Ill. mycological collections (ILL), 98n1451

Fungi on rhododendron, 97n1279
Hallucinogenic & poisonous mushroom field gd, 98n1452
International mycological dir, 3d ed, 96n1581
Mushrooms of N America in color, 97n1278

FURNITURE
Century of design, 99n878
Furniture assns in N America, 96n223
Upholsterer's pocket ref bk, 96n1020

FUTURE LIFE
Encyclopedia of afterlife beliefs & phenomena, 96n1445

FUTURES MARKET
Fitzroy Dearborn dir of the world's futures & options markets, 95n221

GABON
Historical dict of Gabon, 2d ed, 95n118

GABRIELI, GIOVANNI
Giovanni Gabrieli (ca.1555-1612): a thematic catalogue of his music...., 97n1034

GAMBLING
American casino gd, 1997 ed, 98n411
Casino gaming in the US, 98n724
Legalized gambling, 99n714
Legalized gambling: a ref hndbk, 95n803
Where to play in the USA: the gaming gd, 98n419

GAMES
Book of rules, 99n713
Games & entertainment on CD-ROM, 1994 ed, 95n814
Multicultural projects index, 99n856

GANDHI, MAHATMA
Comprehensive, annot bibliog on Mahatma Gandhi, 97n430
Mahatma Gandhi, 96n536

GANGS
Gangs, 97n509

GANGSTER FILMS
Gangster films, 97n1114
Guide to American silent crime films, 95n1383

GARAGE SALES
Garage sale & flea market annual, 5th ed, 98n897

GARCIA MARQUEZ, GABRIEL
Bibliographic gd to Gabriel Garcia Marquez, 1986-1992, 95n1228

GARDANO, ANTONIO
Antonio Gardano, Venetian Music Printer 1538-69, 99n1112

GARDENING. See also **LANDSCAPE GARDENING**
Adrian Bloom's yr-round garden, 99n1347
Bulbs, 99n1348
Bulbs for the rock garden, 97n1255
Container gardening through the yr, 96n1544
Eyewitness garden hndbk: annuals & biennials, 98n1436
Favorite shade plants, 96n1571
Garden trees, 97n1282
Gardener's gd to Britain, new ed, 96n1548
Gardener's gd to growing irises, 98n1454
Gardener's gd to growing ivies, 98n1455
Gardener's gd to plant diseases, 96n1547
Gardener's index, 95n1528
Gardener's Supply Co passport to gardening, 99n1350
Gardening by mail, 4th ed, 95n1525
Gardening with roses, 96n1549
Glossary of vital terms for the home gardener, 95n1529
Growing herbs, 96n1586
Index of garden plants, 95n1530
National Audubon Society bird garden, 96n1560
National Gardening Assoc dict of horticulture, 95n1531
Plantfinder's gd to ornamental grasses, 99n1351
Plantfinder's gd to tender perennials, 99n1349
Rock garden plants, 99n1353
Smaller perennials, 98n1435
Taylor's master gd to gardening, 96n1550
Taylor's dict for gardeners, 99n1345
Western garden [CD-ROM], 96n1552
What plant where, 96n1566
World weeds, 99n1368

GARFIELD, JAMES A.
James A. Garfield, 98n645

GARLAND, HAMLIN
Hamlin Garland, 99n1055

GASKELL, ELIZABETH CLEGHORN
Elizabeth Gaskell: an annot bibliog of English-lang sources 1976-91, 95n1213

GASTRONOMY
Dictionary of gastronomic terms, French/English, 99n1334

GATT (GENERAL AGREEMENT ON TARIFFS & TRADE)
NAFTA & GATT: environmental & economic issues, 98n705

GAYS. See also **LESBIANS; HOMOSEXUALITY**
Alyson almanac, 1994-95 ed, 95n852
Bent gd to gay/lesbian Canada 1994, 95n853
Cassell's queer companion, 96n864
Completely queer: the gay and lesbian ency, 99n757
Cracking the corp closet, 96n259
Ferrari's places for men, Apr 94-Apr 95, 95n854
Ferrari's places of interest, Apr 94-Apr 95, 95n856
Gay 100, 96n865
Gay almanac, 97n677
Gay & lesbian address bk, 96n53
Gay & lesbian biog, 98n782
Gay & lesbian movement, 97n681
Gay & lesbian online, 97n676
Gay & lesbian online, rev ed, 98n781
Gay & lesbian rights: a ref hndbk, 95n859

Inn places 1994, 95n857
Lesbian almanac, 97n679
Lesbian & gay liberation in Canada, 97n680
Queer theory, 99n758
St. James Press gay & lesbian almanac, 99n759
Strength in nos: a lesbian, gay, & bisexual resource, 97n703

GAY LIBERATION MOVEMENT
Lesbian & gay liberation in Canada, 97n680

GAYS IN POPULAR CULTURE
Ultimate gd to lesbian & gay film & video, 97n1126

GAYS' WRITINGS
Gay & lesbian lit, 95n1111
Gay & lesbian literary heritage, 97n888

GAZETTEERS
Cambridge gazetteer of the US & Canada, 97n381
Merriam-Webster's geographical dict, 3d ed, 98n396
Place-name changes 1900-91, 95n503
Rand McNally world facts & maps, 95n498

GEARING
Encyclopedic dict of gears & gearing, 96n1674

GEMS & PRECIOUS STONES
Colorado rockhounding, 95n1732
Fluorescence: gems & minerals under ultraviolet light, 96n1812
Gemstones, 95n1730
Gemstones of the world, rev ed, 98n1615
Minerals & gemstones of the world, rev ed, 95n1729

GENDER IDENTITY
Gender dysphoria, 95n874
Sexuality & gender in the English Renaissance, 99n776

GENEALOGY
Address bk for Germanic genealogy, 5th ed, 95n452
Address bk for German genealogy, 6th ed, 98n363
African American genealogical sourcebk, 96n429
American naturalization records 1790-1990, 2d ed, 99n402
America's best genealogy resource centers, 99n399
Ancestors: a beginner's gd to family hist & genealogy, 98n372
Ancestral trails: the complete gd to British genealogy & family hist, 99n401
Asian American genealogical sourcebk, 96n430
Biography & genealogy master index 1999, 99n404
Center: a guide to genealogical research in the natl capital area, 97n358
Collins Scottish clan & family ency, 96n435
Compendium of histl sources, rev ed, 96n431
Compendium of histl sources, rev ed, 98n364
Directory of family assns, 3d ed, 97n354
Family archive viewer [CD-ROM], 97n355
Finding your Hispanic roots, 98n368
Genealogical & local hist bks in print, 5th ed, 97n350
Genealogical & local hist bks in print: gen ref & world resources v., 5th ed, 98n359
Genealogical & local hist bks in print: US sources & resources v., 5th ed, 98n360
Genealogical research in England's public record office, 97n357
Genealogist's address bk, 3d ed, 96n428
Genealogist's companion & sourcebk, 95n458
Genealogy & local hist to 1900, 97n351
Genealogy annual, 1995, 98n361
Hispanic American genealogical sourcebk, 96n432
Hispanic surnames & family hist, 97n356
Historical register & dict of the US army, 95n693
In search of your Canadian roots, 2d ed, 95n453
In search of your European roots, 2d ed, 95n454
In search of your German roots, 3d ed, 95n455
Index to the Roll of Honor, 96n434
Index to US marriage record, 1691-1850 [CD-ROM], 99n405
Jewish roots in Poland, 99n400
Native American genealogical sourcebk, 96n433
Oxford companion to local & family hist, 97n352
Passenger & immigration lists index, 1996 suppl, 97n367
Periodical source index CD-ROM [CD-ROM], 98n373
Printed sources, 99n403
Scottish family hist, 95n462
Source: a gdbk of American genealogy, 98n370
Student's gd to African American genealogy, 97n359
Student's gd to British American genealogy, 97n360
Student's gd to Chinese American genealogy, 97n361
Student's gd to German American genealogy, 97n362
Student's gd to Irish American genealogy, 97n365
Student's gd to Italian American genealogy, 97n363
Student's gd to Jewish American genealogy, 98n369
Student's gd to Native American genealogy, 97n366
Student's gd to Scandinavian American genealogy, 97n364
Surnames of Wales, 97n353
They came in ships, 2d ed, 95n457
Touchstones: a gd to records, rights, & resources for families of American WW II casualties, 98n367
Ultimate family tree deluxe [CD-ROM], 98n371
US Catholic sources, 97n1215
Virtual roots: a gd to genealogy & local hist on the WWW, 98n366
Welsh family hist, 95n461
What did they mean by that?, 95n451
Your English ancestry, 95n459

GENERATIONS
Official gd to the generations, 96n908

GENERATION X
Complete cross-ref gd to the baby buster generations collective unconscious, 99n1187

GENETIC COUNSELING
Effects of drugs on the fetus & nursing infant, 97n1358

GENETIC ENGINEERING
Biotechnology abstracts: agricultural & environmental, 1983-Feb 1997 [CD-ROM], 98n1490
Dictionary of gene tech, 96n1657
Facts on File dict of biotech & genetic engineering, 95n1619
Human gene mapping 1994, 96n1656
Language of biotech, 2d ed, 96n1659

GENETICS
Genetics & cell biology on file, 99n1357

GEOGRAPHY
Answer atlas, 98n380
Children's atlas of natural wonders, 96n1806
Children's illus atlas, 1997 ed, 98n381
Companion ency of geography, 98n397
DK geography of the world, 97n379
Earth atlas, 95n1725
Encyclopedia of geographical features in world hist, 98n399
Exploring your world, rev ed, 95n494
Facts on File children's atlas, rev ed, 99n412
1500 Calif place names, 99n420
Geography on file, 1995 ed, 96n457
Geopedia [CD-ROM], 95n497
Hammond Citation world atlas, 97n374
Houghton Mifflin dict of geography, 98n395
Hutchinson gd to the world, 3d ed, 99n86
Junior Worldmark ency of the nations, 97n79
Lands & peoples, 98n95
Maps of the world, 98n387
Maps on file, 99n414
McGraw-Hill dict of earth sci, 98n1603
Merriam-Webster's geographical dict, 3d ed, 98n396
Merriam-Webster's pocket geographical dict, 97n380
Oxford encyclopedic world atlas, 95n481
Pockets: world atlas, 96n77
Political geography, 98n393
Spanish/English dict of human & physical geography, 95n493
World Afghanistan to Zimbabwe, 97n378
World databases in geography & geology, 96n453
World facts & maps, 98n400
World geographical ency, English lang ed, 96n456
Worldmark ency of the nations, 8th ed, 96n105

GEOGRAPHY—HISTORICAL
Atlas of human hist, 97n458
Atlas of westward expansion, 96n488
Atlas of WW I, 2d ed, 96n675
Children's atlas of civilizations, 95n572
Children's atlas of the 20th century, 96n553
Encyclopedia of intl boundaries, 96n455
First civilizations, 95n571
Four centuries of special geography, 95n492
Hammond atlas of world hist, 95n570
Historical atlas of Colo., 95n527
Historical atlas of La., 96n440
Historical atlas of SE Asia, 97n429
Historical atlas of the Holocaust, 98n493
Historical atlas of the Holocaust [CD-ROM], 98n492
Historical atlas of the Vietnam War, 97n434
Indiana: atlas of histl county boundaries, 98n379
Mapping America's past, 97n402
Naval Institute histl atlas of the US Navy, 96n701
Times atlas of European hist, 95n555

GEOLOGICAL MUSEUMS
Dinosaur safari gd, 96n1814

GEOLOGISTS
Geologists & the hist of geology, suppl 2, v.1, 97n1402

GEOLOGY. See also ROCKS
Atlas of Mesozoic & Cenozoic coastlines, 96n1807
Children's atlas of natural wonders, 96n1806
Dictionary of the Earth, 96n1805
Earth atlas, 95n1725
Field manual for the amateur geologist, rev ed, 96n1803
Geologists & the hist of geology, suppl 2, v.1, 97n1402
McGraw-Hill dict of earth sci, 98n1603
McGraw-Hill dict of geology & mineralogy, 98n1614
Multilingual thesaurus of geoscis, 97n1400
National Audubon Society 1st field gd: rocks & minerals, 99n1535
New Penguin dict of geology, 97n1401
World databases in geography & geology, 96n453

GEOPHYSICISTS
Directory of physics, astronomy, & geophysics staff, 1997 biennial ed, 99n1322

GEOPOLITICS
Dictionary of geopols, 95n708

GEORGIA
Governors of Ga., 1754-1995, rev ed, 96n496

GERMAN AMERICANS
Address bk for German genealogy, 6th ed, 98n363
Research gd to the Turner movement in the US, 97n333
Student's gd to German American genealogy, 97n362

GERMAN LANGUAGE
German loanwords in English, 95n1036

GERMAN LANGUAGE—DICTIONARIES—ENGLISH
Collins German-English, English-German dict, 2d ed, 96n1104
Collins German-English, English-German dict, unabridged 3d ed, 99n928
Elsevier's dict of European Community co/bus/financial law in English, Danish, & German, 98n517
Friendly German-English dict, 97n849
German-English dict of idioms, 97n852
Klett's modern German & English dict, 99n929
Larousse mini German-English, English-German dict, new ed, 97n850
Oxford-Duden German desk dict, new ed, 98n1030
Oxford-Duden German dict [CD-ROM], 98n1032
Oxford-Duden German dict, rev ed, 98n1031
Oxford starter German dict, 98n1033
Pocket Oxford-Duden German dict, rev ed, 99n930
Practical dict of German usage, 98n1029
Random House German-English, English-German dict, 99n931
Routledge German dict of bus commerce and finance, 98n156
Routledge German dict of construction, 98n1482
Routledge German dict of environmental tech, 99n1555
Routledge German dict of info tech, 98n1579

Routledge German dict of medicine, v.1, 99n1444
Routledge German technical dict, 97n851

GERMAN LITERATURE
Companion to 20th-century German lit, 2d ed, 99n1093
German Baroque writers, 1580-1660, 97n1006
German Baroque writers, 1661-1730, 98n1172
German writers & works of the early Middle Ages, 96n1254
Oxford companion to German lit, 3d ed, 98n1173

GERMAN LITERATURE—WOMEN
Women writers in German-speaking countries, 99n1095

GERMAN POETRY
Head-Word & rhyme-word concordances to Des Minnesangs Fruhling, 99n1094

GERMANS
Central European folk music, 97n1073
In search of your German roots, 3d ed, 95n455

GERMANY
Address bk for Germanic genealogy, 5th ed, 95n452
Berlin, 95n155
Germany's top 300: a hndbk of Germany's largest corps, 1993/94 ed, 95n281
Historical dict of Germany, 96n546
Modern Germany, 99n129
Traveler's gd to Jewish Germany, 99n438

GERMANY—EMIGRATION & IMMIGRATION
Wuerttemberg emigration index, v.6, 95n463

GERMANY—FOREIGN RELATIONS—POLAND
Polish-German borderlands: an annot bibliog, 95n554

GERMANY—HISTORY
Historical dict of Germany's Weimar Republic, 1918-33, 98n471

GERMANY—POLITICS & GOVERNMENT
Encyclopedia of German resistance to the Nazi movement, 98n470

GERONTOLOGY. *See also* **AGED**
Aging well, 96n838
Encyclopedia of aging, 96n850
Encyclopedia of gerontology, 97n667
Graying of America: an ency of aging, health, mind, & behavior, 97n668
Group work with the elderly, 98n758
Literature & gerontology, 96n845
National dir of educl programs in gerontology, 6th ed, 95n838
Older Americans almanac, 95n839
Profiles in gerontology, 96n846
Topics in gerontology, 95n832
Women & aging, 98n763

GESTURES
Dictionary of worldwide gestures, 98n711

GHANA
Family planning & reproductive health servs in Ghana, 95n849

GHOSTS
Encyclopedia of ghosts & spirits, 95n791
Ghosts & angels in Hollywood films, 95n1386
National dir of haunted places, 95n788

GHOST STORIES
St. James gd to horror, ghost, & gothic writers, 99n976

GIANTS
Giants: a ref gd from hist, the Bible, & recorded legend, 96n1346

GIFTED CHILDREN
International hndbk of research & dvlpmt of giftedness & talent, 95n352

GINSBERG, ALLEN
Response to Allen Ginsberg 1926-94, 97n972
Works of Allen Ginsberg 1941-94, 96n1210

GIRLS
National gd to funding for women & girls, 96n952

GLASS
Dictionary of glass, 97n787

GLASSWARE
Fostoria, v.2: identification & value gd to etched, carved & cut designs, 98n899

GODDESSES
Encyclopedia of mythology, 95n1321
New bk of goddesses & heroines, 3d ed, 98n1258

GODS
Encyclopedia of mythology, 95n1321

GODZILLA FILMS
Critical hist & filmography of Toho's Godzilla series, 98n1294

GOLDMAN, EMMA
Rosa Luxemburg & Emma Goldman: a bibliog, 98n637

GOLF
Complete golfer's almanac 1995, 96n821
Inside Sports Mag golf, 98n748
Official rules of golf, 99n731
Official US Open almanac, 96n820
PGA tour, 1995, 96n822
Senior PGA tour, 1995, 96n823

GOODMAN, BENNY
Benny Goodman: wrappin' it up, 97n1071

GORDIMER, NADINE
Nadine Gordimer: a bibliog of primary & secondary sources, 1937-92, 95n1240

GOSPEL MUSIC. *See also* **CHURCH MUSIC; HYMNS; SACRED MUSIC**
Blues & gospel records 1890-1943, 99n1160
Sing glory & hallelujah! histl & biogl gd to Gospel Hymns nos.1-6 Complete, 97n1086

GOTHIC LITERATURE
Ann Radcliffe, 97n998
St. James gd to horror, ghost, & gothic writers, 99n976

GOVERNMENT INFORMATION
Introduction to US govt info sources, 5th ed, 97n53
US govt dirs, 1982-95, 99n62

GOVERNMENT LEADERS
Global links: a gd to key people & insts worldwide, 99n54
Maximov's companion to who governs Moscow, 98n688
Profiles of worldwide govt leaders 1998, 4th ed, 99n649

GOVERNMENT LIBRARIES
Directory of fed libs, 3d ed, 98n573

GOVERNMENT PUBLICATIONS
Accessing US govt info, rev ed, 97n54
Bibliographic gd to govt pubs—foreign 1994, 96n57
Bibliographic gd to govt pubs—US 1994, 96n58
Complete gd to citing govt info resources, rev ed, 95n74
Government info on the Internet, 99n61
Government online, 96n1776
Guide to popular US govt pubns, 3d ed, 95n73
Guide to popular US govt pubns 1995/96, 5th ed, 99n60
Information sources in official pubns, 98n61
Introduction to US govt info sources, 5th ed, 97n53
New England in US govt pubs, 1789-1849, 99n452
NTIS ordernow [CD-ROM], 98n62
1001 free goodies & cheapies, 96n60
Subject gd to US govt ref sources, 2d ed, 98n60
US govt pers index, v.1, no.1 [CD-ROM], 95n77
Using govt info sources, 2d ed, 95n76
Washington info dir, 96n734

GOVERNMENT SPENDING POLICY
Desk ref on the fed budget, 99n687

GOVERNORS
Biographical dir of the governors of the US 1988-94, 95n717
Chief executives of Tex., 96n718
Governors of Ga., 1754-1995, rev ed, 96n496

GRAIN
Grain market, v.2, 96n1519

GRAMMAR, COMPARATIVE & GENERAL
Case, semantic roles, & grammatical relations, 96n1057
Clitics, 96n1060
Dictionary of grammatical terms in linguistics, 95n1040

GRAMOPHONE COMPANY
Berliner gramophone records, 96n1273
His master's voice/die stimme seines herrn, 95n1258

GRANDPARENTS
Grandparents, 98n780

GRANTS-IN-AID. *See also* **EDUCATION— FINANCIAL AID; PHILANTHROPY; FUNDRAISING**
Big bk of minority opportunities, 6th ed, 96n891
Chronicle financial aid gd, rev ed, 96n364
Corporate fndn profiles, 98n785
Directory of biomedical & health care grants 1995, 9th ed, 96n1685
Directory of bldg & equipment grants, 4th ed, 98n1481
Directory of computer & high tech grants, 2d ed, 96n1770
Directory of educ grants, 98n271
Directory of financial aids for minorities 1995-97, 96n880
Directory of financial aids for women 1995-97, 96n879
Directory of financial aids for women 1997-99, 99n773
Directory of grants for orgs serving people with disabilities, 10th ed, 98n774
Directory of grants in the humanities 1998/99, 12th ed, 99n812
Directory of health grants, 97n1321
Directory of intl corp giving in America & abroad 1995, 96n869
Directory of intl corp giving in America & abroad 1998, 99n764
Directory of operating grants, 3d ed, 98n786
Environmental grantmaking fndns 1996, 4th ed, 97n690
Federal grants & funding locator [CD-ROM], 99n766
Federal support for nonprofits 1994, 95n866
Financial aid for Native Americans 1997-99, 99n772
Financial aid for the disabled & their families 1994-96, 96n858
Financial resources for intl study, 2d ed, 97n309
Foundation dir suppl, 1995 ed, 96n871
Foundation grants index 1994, 95n867
Foundation grants index 1996, 24th ed, 96n883
Foundation grants to individuals, 9th ed, 96n872
Foundation reporter 1999, 30th ed, 99n767
Foundations of the 1990s, 99n768
Funding for US study, 2d ed, 97n305
Funding in aging, 98n759
Funding sources for community & economic dvlpmt 1996, 97n692
Funding sources for community & economic dvlpmt 1998, 99n770
Government assistance almanac 1996-97, 10th ed, 97n689
Grant seekers gd, 4th ed, 97n693
Grants & awards available to American writers 1996-97, 19th ed, 97n694
Grants for libs & info servs, 95n639
Grants for teachers, 95n343
Grants for the aging, 95n835
Grants on disc [CD-ROM], 97n695
Grants register 1995-97, 95n367
Grants register 1998, 16th ed, 98n300
Guide to fed funding for anti-crime programs, 95n622
Guide to fed funding for anti-crime programs, 2d ed, 98n553
Guide to fed funding for educ, 1994, 95n345
Guide to fed funding for govts & nonprofits, 1994, 95n863

Guide to fed funding for govts & nonprofits, 1995, Native American ed, 96n882
Guide to fed funding for govts & nonprofits, 19th ed, 98n792
Guide to greater Washington, DC grantmakers 1994-95, 96n876
International fndn dir 1998, 8th ed, 99n769
KR Info OnDisc grants database [CD-ROM], 96n848
National dir of corp giving, 98n790
National dir of grantmaking public charities, 97n697
National gd to funding for children, youth, & families, 3d ed, 97n698
National gd to funding for info tech, 98n583
National gd to funding for the economically disadvantaged, 95n865
National gd to funding in health, 5th ed, 99n1427
New Deal fine arts projects, 95n993
Who get grants/who gives grants, 96n877

GRAPHIC ARTS
Artist's & graphic designer's market, 1995, 96n1038
Artist's & graphic designers market, 1998, 99n875
Typography, 99n885

GRAPHIC METHODS
Information graphics, 97n1370

GRAPHIC NOVELS
Graphic novels, 96n1359

GRASSES
Manual of grasses, 96n1583
Plantfinder's gd to ornamental grasses, 99n1351

GRATEFUL DEAD
American bk of the dead: the definitive Grateful Dead ency, 99n1175
Grateful Dead & the deadheads, 98n1240

GREAT BRITAIN
Atlas of English dialects, 97n839
Blackwell hndbk of educ, 96n325
Britain 1993, 95n156
British imprints relating to N America, 1621-1760, 97n40
British sci fiction paperbacks & mags 1949-56, 96n1234
Early music dict, 96n1272
English castles, 97n394
Gardener's gd to Britain, new ed, 96n1548
Great Britain, 96n480
Handbook of copyright in British publishing practice, 3d ed, 95n655
Health & British mags in the 19th century, 99n1417
Media courses UK 1997, 4th ed, 98n860
Short stories in English: Britain & N America, 95n1165
Summer jobs Britain 1995, 26th ed, 96n279
Theses on Africa, 1976-88, 95n112
Whitaker's almanack 1995, 95n9
Willings press gd 1998, 124th ed, 99n824

GREAT BRITAIN—ANTIQUITIES
British & Irish archaeology, 95n521

GREAT BRITAIN—BIOGRAPHY
Biographies of British women, 95n910
Dictionary of natl biog, 1986-90, 97n38
Dictionary of 20th century British bus leaders, 95n282
Who's who in British hist, 99n506
Who's who in British opera, 95n1283
Who's who in the UK info world 95/96, 5th ed, 96n640
Willings press gd 1998, 124th ed, 99n824
Women & the Dict of Natl Biog, 96n26

GREAT BRITAIN—COLONIES
British empire, 97n444
Dictionary of the British Empire & Commonwealth, 97n117
French image of America, 95n531
Historical dict of the British Empire, 98n466

GREAT BRITAIN—DIRECTORIES
British dirs, 2d ed, 98n132
Directory of social research orgs in the UK, 95n97

GREAT BRITAIN—HISTORY
Agriculture in Britain & America 1660-1820, 95n1512
Atlas of British hist, 2d ed, 95n557
Bibliography of British hist 1914-89, 98n464
British archives, 3d ed, 97n440
British economic & social hist, 3d ed, 97n443
British empire, 97n444
British women's hist, 97n726
Cambridge illus hist of British theatre, 96n1422
Columbia companion to British hist, 98n465
Dangerous sky: resource gd to the Battle of Britain, 96n544
Earl Mountbatten of Burma, 1900-79, 99n505
Historical dict of Stuart England, 1603-89, 97n442
Historical dict of the UK, v.1: England & the UK, 98n467
Historical dict of the UK, v.2, 99n504
Kings of medieval England, c. 560-1485, 97n445
Larousse dict of British hist, 96n541
Late medieval England (1377-1485), 96n542
Nelson almanac, 99n642
Oxford companion to British hist, 99n503
Prostitution in Great Britain 1485-1901, 95n877
St. Martin's gd to sources in contemporary British hist, v.2, 95n558
Twentieth-Century Britain, 96n543
Victorian database on CD-ROM, 1970-95 [CD-ROM], 98n468
Wars of the roses in fiction, 96n1190
Who was who in British India, 99n485
Who's who in British hist, 99n506

GREAT BRITAIN—LIBRARY RESOURCES
Academic libs in the UK & the republic of Ireland 1994, 3d ed, 96n635
Directory of rare bk & special collections in the UK & the Republic of Ireland, 2d ed, 98n588
Libraries in the UK & Republic of Ireland 1995, 96n637
Short-Title catalogue of Hungarian bks printed before 1851 in the British Lib, 97n14

GREAT BRITAIN—POLITICS & GOVERNMENT
Anthony Eden, 1897-1977, 96n759

Art, truth, & high pols: a bibliographic study of the official lives of Queen Victoria's ministers in Cabinet, 1843-1969, 97n608
Atlas of industrial protest in Britain, 1750-1990, 97n146
British pol facts 1900-94, 7th ed, 96n758
British secret servs, 98n686
Duke of Newcastle, 1693-1768, & Henry Pelham, 1694-1754, 98n687
Edmund Burke 1729-97: a bibliog, 95n751
Joseph Chamberlain 1836-1914: a bibliog, 95n752
Lord Palmerston 1784-1865: a bibliog, 95n753
Sir Robert Peel 1788-1850: a bibliog, 97n439
William Pitt, Earl of Chatham 1708-78: a bibliog, 95n754

GREAT BRITAIN—ROYAL NAVY
Guide to British naval papers in N America, 96n679

GREAT BRITAIN—SOCIAL LIFE & CUSTOMS
Where Queen Elizabeth slept & what the butler saw, 98n1011

GREAT PLAINS
Exploring the plains states through lit, 95n1120

GREAT SMOKY MOUNTAINS (N.C. & TENN.)
Smoky Mountain voices: a lexicon of S Appalachian speech, 95n1042

GREAT ZIMBABWE (EXTINCT CITY)
Great Zimbabwe, 95n522

GREECE
Ancient civilizations of the Mediterranean [CD-ROM], 99n490
Ancient Greece & Rome, 99n491
Ancient Greeks, 98n472
Contemporary Greek artists, 95n1000
Daily life of the ancient Greeks, 99n501
Dictionary of ancient hist, 95n583
Encyclopedia of the ancient Greek world, 97n450
Fodor's exploring the Greek Islands, 98n424
Greece: Athens & the mainland, 98n425
Greek Islands, 98n426
Handbook to life in ancient Greece, 99n500
Mycenaean civilization, 97n448
Penguin histl atlas of ancient Greece, 97n449

GREEK LANGUAGE, BIBLICAL
Exhaustive concordance to the Greek N.T., 97n1199
Theological lexicon of the N.T., 96n1457

GREEK LANGUAGE—DICTIONARIES—ENGLISH
Greek-English lexicon, 97n853
Pocket Oxford Greek dict, 96n1105

GREEK LITERATURE
Companion to the Greek lyric poets, 99n1018
Hellenistic commentary to the N.T., 97n1201

GREELEY, ANDREW M.
Andrew M. Greeley: an annot bibliog, 95n1191

GREEN, ADOLPH
Betty Comden & Adolph Green: a bio-bibliog, 95n1352

GREENLAND
Synonymized checklist of the vascular flora of the US, Canada, & Greenland, 95n1555

GREEN MOVEMENT
Historical dict of the green movement, 99n1554

GREEN TECHNOLOGY
Routldege French dict of environmental tech, 98n1637
Routledge German dict of environmental tech, 99n1555

GREY LITERATURE
Information sources in grey lit, 3d ed, 95n10

GRIEF
National dir of bereavement support grps & servs, 1996, 98n769

GROUNDWATER
State groundwater regulation, 95n1771

GUAM
Historical dict of Guam & Micronesia, 96n168

GUATEMALA
Cultures of the World, 99n84

GUERRILLA WARFARE
Guerrilla warfare, 98n620
Handbook of leftist guerrilla grps in Latin America & the Caribbean, 97n609
Sendero Luminoso: an annot bibliog of the Shining Path guerrilla movement, 1980-93, 97n502

GUINEA
Guinea, 97n97

GUINEA—BISSAU
Historical dict of the Republic of Guinea-Bissau, 3d ed, 98n456

GUINEA PIGS
Guinea pig, 98n1466

GUITARISTS
1000 great guitarists, 95n1276

GUITAR MUSIC
Guitar music by women composers, 98n1218
Music for voice & classical guitar, 1945-96, 98n1219

GUITARS
Orion blue bk: guitars & musical instruments, 1998 ed, 99n1147
Orion blue bk: vintage guitars & collectibles 1998, summer ed, 99n182

GULF COAST (US)
Field gd to shells, 4th ed, 96n1595

GUN CONTROL
Gun control, 97n510

GYPSIES
Gypsies, 96n405
Historical dict of the gypsies (Romanies), 99n380

HABITAT (ECOLOGY)
Habitats, 96n1598

HAITI
Haiti, rev ed, 95n169

HAMMER FILM PRODUCTIONS
Hammer films: an exhaustive filmography, 97n1119

HANDBOOKS, VADE MECUMS, ETC.
Economist desk companion, rev ed, 95n79
Everything you pretend to know & are afraid someone will ask, 97n57
FAQ's of life, 99n67
Find it fast, 3d ed, 95n78
Numbers: how many, how far, how long, how much, 98n810
Writer's companion, 97n924

HANDICAPPED
ABC-CLIO companion to the disability rights movement, 98n776
Accent on living buyer's gd, 1994-95 ed, 96n853
ACCESS travel USA: a dir for people with disabilities, 96n856
Complete dir for people with disabilities, 1997-98, 98n771
Directory for exceptional children, 13th ed, 95n385
Directory of agencies & orgs serving individuals who are deaf-blind, rev ed, 98n772
Directory of college facilities & servs for people with disabilities, 4th ed, 98n773
Directory of grants for orgs serving people with disabilities, 8th ed, 95n846
Directory of grants for orgs serving people with disabilities, 10th ed, 98n774
Encyclopedia of disability & rehabilitation, 97n670
Financial aid for the disabled & their families 1994-96, 96n858
Financial aid for the disabled & their families 1998-2000, 99n294
Fodor's great American vacations for travelers with disabilities, 96n471
Man's gd to coping with disability, 98n775
Resources for elders with disabilities, 3d ed, 97n672
Resources for people with disabilities, 99n750
Resources for people with disabilities & chronic conditions, 3d ed, 97n673

HANDICAPPED CHILDREN
Bibliography of Va. legal hist before 1900, 2d ed, 99n548
Children's bk prizes, 99n989
Concise ency of Christianity, 99n1287
Guide to children's ref works & multimedia material, 99n994
Guide to public policy experts, 1997-98, 99n701
New England transcendentalists [CD-ROM], 99n1046
Nonprofit sector yellow bk, winter 1999 ed, 99n142
Scientists: their lives & works, v.4, 99n1302
Special-needs reading list, 99n751
Ulrich's intl pers dir 1998, 36th ed, 99n74

HANDICRAFTS
Crafts supply source bk, 3d ed, 96n1012
Crafts supply source bk, 4th ed, 98n931
Favorite hobbies & pastimes, 95n801
Index to how to do it info, 1994 suppl, 96n1014
Multicultural projects index, 99n856

HANI LANGUAGE—DICTIONARIES—ENGLISH
Hani-English/English-Hani dict, 98n1034

HANSBERRY, LORRAINE
Lorraine Hansberry: a research & production sourcebk, 98n1136

HARDWOODS
Trees of the central hardwood forests of N America, 99n1367

HARDY, THOMAS
Thomas Hardy's major novels, 99n1085

HARLEM RENAISSANCE
Harlem renaissance, 99n378

HARMONY
Harmony theory, 98n1193

HARPISTS
Nineteenth- & 20th-century harpists, 96n1287

HARPSICHORD MUSIC
History of music for harpsichord or piano & orchestra, 98n1227
Modern harpsichord music, 96n1288

HARRISON, WILLIAM HENRY
William Henry Harrison: a bibliog, 99n659

HARVARD UNIVERSITY
Anthropological lit on disc [CD-ROM], 95n391
Printed catalogues of the Harvard College Lib, 1723-90, 97n39

HAUNTED HOUSES
National dir of haunted places, 95n788

HAWAII
Exploring the Pacific states through lit, 95n1121
Historical dict of Honolulu & Hawaii, 99n459

HAWAII FIVE-O (TELEVISION PROGRAM)
Booking Hawaii Five-O: an episode gd & critical hist of the 1968-80 TV detective show, 98n1313

HAZARDOUS SUBSTANCES
Book of lists for regulated hazardous substances 1996, 97n1433
Book of lists for regulated hazardous substances, 8th ed, 99n1557

Consolidated list of products whose consumption and/or sale have been banned...., 5th ed, 96n217
Directory of hazardous waste servs, 1994-95. 5th ed, 96n1654
Encyclopedia of environmental control tech, v.7, 96n1857
Encyclopedia of environmental control tech, v.8, 96n1858
Encyclopedia of environmental control tech, v.9, 96n1859
Environmental contaminant ref databk, v.1, 97n1387
Environmental contaminant ref databk, v.2, 97n1388
Federal chemical regulation, 99n586
Hazardous chemicals & the right to know, 95n1779
Hazardous chemicals desk ref, 3d ed, 95n1781
Hazardous chemicals desk ref, 4th ed, 98n1635
Hazardous materials hndbk, 97n1436
Hazardous substances resource gd, 2d ed, 98n1642
Home health gd to poisons & antidotes, 96n1727
Resources & refs: hazardous waste & hazardous materials mgmt, 96n1852
Toxic waste sites, 99n1560
TSCA hndbk, 3d ed, 98n561

HEADS OF STATE. *See also* **POLITICIANS**
Dictators & tyrants, 96n705
Great leaders, great tyrants?, 96n706
Heads of states & govts: a worldwide ency, 95n706
Historic world leaders, 95n575
Political leaders & military figures in the 2d World War, 98n606
Political leaders of contemporary W Europe, 96n756
Profiles of worldwide govt leaders 1995, 96n708
World leaders: people who shaped the world, 95n576

HEALING
Complete home healer, 95n1674
Encyclopedia of Native American healing, 97n340

HEALTH. *See also* **MEDICINE**
ALA fingertip gd to natl health-info resources 1995-96, ref desk ed, 96n1684
Best of health, 99n1437
Complete family gd to healthy living, 97n1326
Computer health hazards, v.2, 95n1694
Consumer health info source bk, 4th ed, 95n1666
Consumer health info source bk, 5th ed, 99n1416
Dartmouth atlas of health care, 99n1414
Encyclopedia of biostats, 99n1418
Encyclopedia of family health, 99n1441
Encyclopedia of medical media & communications, 98n1529
Ethnic minority health, 98n1504
Fodor's healthy escapes, 5th ed, 98n405
Free or low cost health info, 99n1428
Health & environment in America's top-rated cities, 96n931
Health & British mags in the 19th century, 99n1417
Health & medical yrbk 1997, 98n1516
Health & medicine on the Internet, 99n1424
Health care almanac, 97n1316
Health care almanac, 99n1431
Health care bk of lists, 95n1652
Health care terms, 3d ed, 97n1319
Health industry quicksource, 97n1313
Health online, 97n1328
Health: US, 1996-97 & injury chartbk, 99n1430
HealthSpeak, 97n1315
Historical dict of the world health org, 99n1421
Human nutrition 1990-Sept 1994 [CD-ROM], 95n1643
Internet compendium: subject gds to health & sci resources, 96n1774
Key gd to electronic resources: health scis, 96n1688
Major state health care policies, 5th ed, 98n1519
Making wise medical decisions, 99n1453
Managed health care dict, 98n1510
Marshall Cavendish ency of health, rev ed, 96n1682
Medical & health info dir 1998, 9th ed, 99n1426
New A to Z of women's health, 3d ed, 96n1680
New complete medical & health ency, 95n1646
OECD health systems, 95n1651
Plunkett's health care industry almanac, 97n1329
Preventive care sourcebk 1997-98, 98n1520
Statistical record of health & medicine, 99n1436
Tobacco & health network dir 1996, 4th ed, 97n1325
Who's who in medicine & healthcare 1997-98, 98n1507
Why Eve doesn't have an Adam's apple: a dict of sex differences, 97n1318
Woman's gd to vitamins & minerals, 96n1743

HEALTH BEHAVIOR
Handbook of health behavior research, 99n1420

HEALTH CARE POLICY
Health care crisis in the US, 98n1506
Issue briefs: 1997 annual ed, 99n1432
World population monitoring 1996, 99n809

HEALTH CARE—VOCATIONAL GUIDANCE
Exploring health care careers, 99n1429

HEALTH MAINTENANCE ORGANIZATIONS
HMO/PPO dir 1996, 97n1323
Managed health care dict, 98n1510

HEALTH & RACE
Guide to ethnic health collections in the US, 97n1322

HEALTH RISK ASSESSMENT
Artist's complete health & safety gd, 2d ed, 96n1042

HEANEY, SEAMUS
Seamus Heaney: a ref gd, 97n1008

HEAT
Handbook of thermal conductivity, v.1, 96n1821
Handbook of thermal conductivity, v.2, 96n1822
Handbook of thermal conductivity, v.3, 96n1823
Handbook of thermal conductivity, v.4, 98n1622
HVAC design data sourcebk, 95n1641

HEBREW
Hebrew & Aramaic lexicon of the O.T., v.2, 97n1198

HEBREW LANGUAGE—DICTIONARIES—ENGLISH
Compact up-to-date English-Hebrew dict, 97n856

501 Hebrew verbs, 97n854
Harduf's transliterated English-Hebrew dict, 1st v., 95n1081
Harduf's transliterated English-Hebrew dict, 2d v., 95n1082
Harduf's transliterated English-Hebrew dict, 3d v., 96n1108
Harduf's transliterated English-Hebrew dict, 4th v., 98n1035
Hebrew & Aramaic lexicon of the O.T., v.1, 96n1455
My 1st 100 Hebrew words, 95n1080
Oxford English-Hebrew dict, 97n855
Theological dict of the O.T., v.7, 97n1200
Theological dict of the O.T., v.8, 98n1375

HEIDEGGER, MARTIN
Martin Heidegger (2): a bibliog, 97n1156

HELICOPTERS
Jane's all the world's aircraft 1996-97, 87th ed, 97n1440
Jane's helicopter markets & systems, 97n1442

HELLMAN, LILLIAN
Lillian Hellman: a research & production sourcebk, 99n1248

HELPING BEHAVIOR
Directory of natl helplines, 1998 ed, 99n49

HEMINGWAY, ERNEST
Reading Hemingway, 96n1211

HENRY IV
Henry IV pts 1 & 2: an annot bibliog, 95n1218

HENTY, GEORGE ALFRED
G. A. Henty 1832-1902: a bibliographical study of his British eds...., 98n1159

HEPBURN, AUDREY
Audrey Hepburn: a bio-bibliog, 95n1347

HERALDRY
Debrett's peerage & baronetage [1995], 96n426

HERBERT, GEORGE
George Herbert companion, 96n1238

HERBS
Complete family gd to natural home remedies, 98n1545
Consumer's dict of medicines, 95n1688
Dictionary of herbs, spices, seasonings, & natural flavorings, 95n1518
Encyclopedia of herbs & their uses, 96n1585
Green pharmacy, 98n1546
Growing herbs, 96n1586
Herbal home remedy bk, 99n1461
Herbs, 95n1544
Herbs of choice, 95n1545
Home herbal, 97n1281
Information sourcebk of herbal medicine, 96n1714
Naturopathic hndbk of herbal formulas, 3d ed, 96n1717
Organic gardener's home ref, 96n1543

HERESIES, CHRISTIAN
Crimes of perception: an ency of heresies & heretics, 96n1468
Dictionary of heresy trials in American Christianity, 99n1289

HEROES
Adventure heroes, 95n930
Heroes & pioneers, 99n24
Heroes of conscience: a biogl dict, 97n22
Hollywood heroes, 96n1376
Myths & hero tales, 98n1084

HERPETOLOGY
Reptile & amphibian keeper's dict, 95n1597

HIGH DEFINITION TELEVISION
High-definition TV, 95n958

HIGH INTEREST—LOW VOCABULARY BOOKS
Choices, v.3, 95n1132
Light 'n lively reads, 98n1057

HIGH TECHNOLOGY
CorpTech explore database [CD-ROM], 98n1571
CyberDictionary, 98n1575
Directory of computer & high tech grants, 2d ed, 96n1770
How the new tech works, 99n1484
International multimedia yrbk 1995-96, 96n1751
International multimedia yrbk 1995-96 on CD-ROM [CD-ROM], 96n1752

HIKING
Essential gd to wilderness camping & backpacking in the US, 96n824
Hiking trails, E US, 96n825

HINDI LANGUAGE—DICTIONARIES—ENGLISH
Hindi-English, English-Hindi practical dict, 95n1083

HINDUISM
Concise ency of Hinduism, 99n1290
Historical dict of Hinduism, 98n1392
Islam, Hinduism, & Judaism in South Africa, 98n1345
Popular dict of Hinduism, 95n1472

HINDUS
South Asian religions in the Americas, 96n1438

HISPANIC AMERICAN LIBRARIANS
Quien es quien: a who's who of Spanish-speaking librarians in the US 1994, 4th ed, 96n621

HISPANIC AMERICANS
Biographical hndbk of Hispanics & US film, 98n1277
Chronology of Hispanic-American hist, 96n550
Cuban Americans, 99n397
Dictionary of Hispanic biog, 97n334
Dictionary of 20th century culture: Hispanic culture of Mexico, Central America, & the Caribbean, 97n348
Dictionary of 20th century culture: Hispanic culture of S America, 96n406
DISCovering multicultural America [CD-ROM], 97n323

Encyclopedia of Latin American hist & culture, 97n349
Finding your Hispanic roots, 98n368
Guide to Latin American, Caribbean, & US Latino-made films & video, 99n1226
Handbook of Hispanic cultures in the US: hist, 95n421
Handbook of Hispanic cultures in the US: lit & art, 95n422
Handbook of Latin American Studies: social scis, no.55, 99n398
Hippocrene USA gd to historic Hispanic America, 95n508
Hispanic 100, 96n408
Hispanic American biog, 96n407
Hispanic American chronology, 97n335
Hispanic American genealogical sourcebk, 96n432
Hispanic databk of US cities & counties, 95n423
Hispanic firsts, 98n348
Hispanic resource dir, 3d ed, 97n336
Hispanics in Hollywood, 95n1377
Kaleidoscope: a multicultural bklst for grades K-8, 96n1182
Latinas in the US, 97n728
Latino ency, 97n337
Latinos in the US: social, economic & pol aspects, 95n424
Masterpieces of Latino lit, 95n1243
Multiethnic children's lit, 95n1136
National Hispanic media dir, 1997, 98n861
Notable Latin American women, 96n938
Notable Latino Americans, 98n349
Statistical record of Hispanic Americans, 95n425
U*X*L multicultural CD [CD-ROM], 98n333
Who's who among Hispanic Americans 1994-95, 3d ed, 96n409

HISPANIC AMERICANS IN MOTION PICTURES
Contemporary Hollywood's negative Hispanic image, 95n1387
Hispanics in Hollywood, 95n1377

HISPANIC AMERICANS IN TELEVISION
Hispanics in Hollywood, 95n1377

HISTORIANS
American women historians, 1700s-1990s, 97n411
Global ency of histl writing, 99n529
International dir of bus historians, 95n194

HISTORICAL FICTION
America in histl fiction, 98n1114
Historical figures in fiction, 95n1162
Index to histl fiction for children & young people, 96n1179
Nineteenth-Century lit criticism, v.48, 97n909
Recreating the past, 95n1161
Twentieth-Century romance & histl writers, 3d ed, 95n1163
Wars of the roses in fiction, 96n1190
What histl novel do I read next?, 99n1034

HISTORICAL FILMS
With fire & sword: Italian spectacles on American screens 1958-68, 96n1395

HISTORIC BUILDINGS
America preserved, 96n1047

Experiencing America's past: a travel gd to museum villages, 2d ed, 95n507
National Trust gd to historic bed & breakfasts, inns & small hotels, 95n511

HISTORIC PRESERVATION
Preservation yellow pages, rev ed, 98n975

HISTORIC SITES
African American historic places, 95n410
America preserved, 96n1047
American Revolutionary War sites, memorials, museums, & lib collections, 99n472
Black heritage sites, 97n330
Experiencing America's past: a travel gd to museum villages, 2d ed, 95n507
Field gd to America's historic neighborhoods & museum houses, 99n433
Guide to the Indian wars of the West, 99n474
Hippocrene USA gd to Irish America, 95n444
In their footsteps, 95n506
International dict of historic places, v.1, 96n467
International dict of historic places, v.2, 96n468
International dict of historic places, v.3, 96n469
International dict of historic places, v.4, 97n468
International dict of historic places, v.5, 97n469
Irish-American landmarks, 96n422
Landmarks of American presidents, 97n391
Masterworks of man & nature, 2d ed, 96n458
100 great cities of world hist, 96n927
Parks dir of the US, 2d ed, 95n512
Presidential sites, 99n428
What happened where, 98n500

HISTORIOGRAPHY
Annales historiography & theory, 95n573
Companion to Historiography, 99n829
Global ency of histl writing, 99n529

HISTORY
American Histl Assn's gd to histl lit, 3d ed, 96n554
Annales historiography & theory, 95n573
Chronology of the medieval world, 96n561
Dictionary of world biog, v.2: the middle ages, 99n520
DISCovering nations, states, & cultures [CD-ROM], 99n85
Encyclopedia of the hist of classical archaeology, 97n397
Fools & jesters in lit, art, & hist, 99n951
Historical abstracts on disc [CD-ROM], 99n545
History of humanity, v.1, 96n568
Hutchinson gd to the world, 3d ed, 99n86
Illustrated bk of questions & answers, 97n56
Junior Worldmark ency of the nations, 97n79
Sources of info for histl research, 95n574
They made hist, 95n35
Walford's gd to ref material, v.2: social & histl scis, 6th ed, 95n98
Worldmark ency of the nations, 8th ed, 96n105

HISTORY, ANCIENT
Ancient civilizations of the Mediterranean [CD-ROM], 99n490

Ancient Greece & Rome, 99n491
Ancient Romans, 99n518
Atlas of human hist, 97n458
Chronology of the ancient world, 96n559
Daily life in ancient Mesopotamia, 99n511
Daily life of the ancient Greeks, 99n501
Dictionary of ancient hist, 95n583
Dictionary of Judaism in the biblical period, 97n1223
Dictionary of world biog, v.1, 99n519
Encyclopedia of invasions & conquests from ancient times to the present, 97n564
From Aristotle to Zoroaster: an A to Z companion to the classical world, 99n526
Handbook to life in ancient Egypt, 99n510
Handbook to life in ancient Greece, 99n500
History of humanity, v.2, 97n479
History of the ancient & medieval world, 98n501
Hutchinson dict of ancient & medieval warfare, 99n534

HISTORY—BIBLIOGRAPHY
Bibliography for hist, hist curatorship, & museums, 98n495
Eighteenth Century, 99n516
Walford's gd to ref material, v.2, 99n83

HISTORY IN LITERATURE
Literature & its times, 98n1072

HISTORY, LOCAL
Oxford companion to local & family hist, 97n352

HISTORY MATERIALS
Genealogical & local hist bks in print, 5th ed, 97n350

HISTORY, MODERN
American decades 1980-89, 97n425
American dream: the 50s, 99n466
Annual register 1997, 99n657
Chronicle of the yr 1995, 97n465
Chronology of the expanding world, 96n560
Chronology of the modern world, 2d ed, 96n562
Current issues sourcefile [CD-ROM], 97n59
Day by day: the 80s, 96n503
Dictionary of 19th-century world hist, 95n578
Dictionary of 20th-century world hist, 98n504
Encyclopedia of invasions & conquests from ancient times to the present, 97n564
Facts on File world news CD-ROM 1997 [CD-ROM], 98n506
Founders of modern nations, 96n556
Global village companion, 97n470
Great events: the 20th century, suppl, 97n478
Heads of states & govts: a worldwide ency, 95n706
History of the world in the 20th century, 95n589
Junior chronicle of the 20th century, 98n498
Matter of fact: statements containing stats on current social, economics, & pol issues, v.24, 98n814
Miniature empires, 99n537
Our century, 95n591
Pocket factfile of 20th century people, 97n25
Sixties [CD-ROM], 98n450
Twentieth-Century America, 96n485
What everyone should know about the 20th century, 99n538
What happened where, 98n500
World War II in Europe, Africa, & the Americas, with general sources, 98n622

HOBBES, THOMAS
Hobbes dict, 97n1165

HOBBIES
Favorite hobbies & pastimes, 95n801
Index to how to do it info, 1994 suppl, 96n1014

HOCKEY
Bad boys: legends of hockey's toughest, meanest, most-feared players, 96n826
Goalies: legends from the NHL's toughest job, 96n827
Inside Sports Mag hockey, 1997 ed, 98n749
National Hockey League official gd & record bk 1997-98, 99n733
National Hockey League Stanley Cup playoffs fact gd 1998, 99n734
1997-98 hockey annual, 99n737
Official rules of ice hockey, 99n735
Professional sports team hists, 95n800
Sporting News complete hockey bk, 1995-96 ed, 96n828
Sporting News hockey gd, 1996-97 ed, 97n657
Sporting News hockey register, 1996-97 ed, 97n658
STATS hockey hndbk 1997-98, 99n736

HOCKEY—FANTASY
Official fantasy hockey gd, 99n732

HOLBEIN, HANS
Hans Holbein the younger: a gd to research, 98n943

HOLIDAYS. *See also* FESTIVALS
Chase's calendar of events 1998, 99n4
Holiday symbols 1998, 99n1189
Holidays & festivals index, 96n1358
Holidays, festivals, & celebrations dict, 2d ed, 98n1263
Holidays, festivals & celebrations of the world dict, 95n1338
International holidays, 96n1361
Religious holidays & calendars, 99n1271
Sacred celebrations: a Jewish holiday hndbk, 96n1479
Wild planet!, 96n1352
World holiday bk, 95n1335
World holiday festival & calendar bks, 99n1194

HOLINESS CHURCHES
Holiness mss, 95n1458

HOLLY
Hollies, 98n1457

HOLLYWOOD
Hollywood novel, 96n1411

HOLMES, SHERLOCK (FICTITIOUS CHARACTER)
Encyclopedia Sherlockiana, 95n1211
Good old index: the Sherlock Holmes hndbk, 98n1158
Sherlock Holmes: screen & sound gd, 95n1394

HOLOCAUST, JEWISH (1939-1945)
Atlas of the Holocaust, 95n569
Dictionary of the holocaust, 99n528
Historical atlas of the Holocaust [CD-ROM], 98n492
Historical atlas of the Holocaust, 98n493
History of the Holocaust, 95n588
Holocaust, 98n502
Holocaust, 99n540
Holocaust series, 99n533
Learning about the Holocaust, 96n1170
Medical & psychological effects of concentration camps on Holocaust survivors, v.4: genocide, 98n708
People of the Holocaust, 99n521
Understanding the Holocaust, 99n539

HOLY SPIRIT
Doctrine of the Holy Spirit, 97n1193

HOME CARE SERVICES
Encyclopedia of home care for the elderly, 96n1681

HOME ECONOMICS
Green kitchen hndbk, 98n1425
Household hints & tips, 98n180

HOME ENTERTAINMENT SYSTEMS
Games & entertainment on CD-ROM, 1994 ed, 95n814
Orion blue bk: video & TV, 1998 ed, 99n181

HOME LABOR
Telecommuters, the workforce of the 21st century, 98n212

HOMELESSNESS
American homelessness: a ref hndbk, 2d ed, 95n842
Guide to fed funding for housing & homeless programs, 3d ed, 98n765
Homelessness: a sourcebk, 95n841
Homelessness in America, 98n766
Homelessness in America, 1893-1992, 95n843

HOME OFFICES
SOHO desk ref, 99n283

HOMEOPATHY
Complete family gd to natural home remedies, 98n1545
Complete gd to homeopathy, 97n1347
Encyclopedia of homeopathy, 2d ed, 95n1673
Family homeopathy, 97n1342
Women's gd to homeopathy, 95n1672

HOME OWNERSHIP
Americans & their homes, 99n783

HOME SCHOOLING
Authentic Jane Williams' home school mrkt gd, 97n280
Authentic Jane Williams' home school market gd, 99n305
Home educ resource gd, 3d ed, 96n317

HOME SITES—PLANNING
Time-saver standards for housing & residential dvlpmt, 96n1048

HOMICIDE
Homicide: a bibliog, 2d ed, 95n617

HOMOSEXUALITY. *See also* GAYS; LESBIANS
Alyson almanac, 1994-95 ed, 95n852
Cassell's queer companion, 96n864
Gay 100, 96n865
Strength in nos: a lesbian, gay, & bisexual resource, 97n703

HOMOSEXUALITY IN MOTION PICTURES
Broadcasting it, 95n858
Images in the dark: an ency of gay & lesbian film & video, 95n1374
Ultimate gd to lesbian & gay film & video, 97n1126

HOMOSEXUALITY & LITERATURE
Gay & lesbian literary heritage, 97n888

HONDURAS
Historical dict of Honduras, 2d ed, 95n170

HONEY PLANTS
Pollen grains of Canadian honey plants, 95n1537

HONG KONG
Hong Kong bus: the portable ency for doing bus with Hong Kong, 95n262

HORN MUSIC
Discography of 78 rpm era recordings of the horn, 98n1203

HORROR FILMS
A-Z of horror films, 98n1297
Christopher Lee & Peter Cushing & horror cinema, 96n1396
Clive Barker's A Z of horror, 98n1306
Horror in silent films, 96n1391
Overlook film ency: horror, 96n1379
Science fiction, fantasy, & horror film sequels, series, & remakes, 98n1292
Science fiction, horror & fantasy film & TV credits, suppl.2, 95n1395

HORROR IN LITERATURE
Clive Barker's A-Z of horror, 98n1306

HORROR TALES
St. James gd to horror, ghost, & gothic writers, 99n976
Science fiction, fantasy, & horror writers, 96n1193
Supernatural index, 96n1194

HORROR TELEVISION PROGRAMS
Science fiction, horror & fantasy film & TV credits, suppl.2, 95n1395

HORSES
Complete horse care manual, 96n1556
Encyclopedia of the horse, 95n1582
Horse companion, 99n1383
Horse dict, 96n1555
Horse owner's veterinary hndbk, 2d ed, 99n1354
International ency of horse breeds, 97n1291

Pockets: horses, 96n70
Visual dict of the horse, 95n1583

HORTICULTURALISTS
Dictionary of British & Irish botanists & horticulturalists, rev ed, 96n1562

HORTICULTURE
Gardener's index, 95n1528
National Gardening Assoc dict of horticulture, 95n1531
Reference gd for botany & horticulture, 97n1258
Taylor's dict for gardeners, 99n1345

HOSPICE CARE
Hospice & palliative care, 98n1522

HOSPITALITY INDUSTRY
Guide to college programs in hospitality & tourism, 5th ed, 98n314

HOSPITALS
Best hospitals in America, 2d ed, 96n1693
Canadian medical dir on CD-ROM, 1996 [CD-ROM], 97n1320
Directory of hospital personnel 1994, 95n1648
Profiles of US hospitals 1995, [4th ed], 96n1690

HOSTELS
Hostelling N America, 1997, 98n403

HOTELS
America's best hotels & restaurants, 98n409
Complete gd to American bed & breakfast, 4th ed, 97n385
National Trust gd to historic bed & breakfasts, inns & small hotels, 95n511
National Trust gd to historic bed & breakfasts, inns, & small hotels, 4th ed, 97n390

HOUSE CONSTRUCTION
Taunton's fine homebldg index, issues 1-85, 96n1051

HOUSEHOLD SUPPLIES
Complete gd to household chemicals, 96n1795
Poison! how to handle the hazardous substances in your home, 98n1563
Who's buying for the home, 98n258

HOUSE PLANTS
Houseplant ency, 95n1532
House plant ency, 98n1433
Indoor garden bk, 95n1526

HOUSING
Annual bulletin of housing & bldg stats for Europe & N America 1996, 98n822
Encyclopedia of housing, 99n792
Guide to fed funding for housing & homeless programs, 3d ed, 98n765
Popular American housing, 97n1094

HUBBARD, L. RON
Fiction of L. Ron Hubbard, 95n1192

HUMAN ANATOMY
Ultimate human body version 2.0 [CD-ROM], 98n1500

HUMAN BEHAVIOR
Bibliography of human behavior, 95n770

HUMAN CAPITAL
Guide to natl professional certification programs, 96n267
Hoover's dir of human resources executives 1996, 97n255
HR words you gotta know!, 96n258
Human resources yrbk 1996/97, 98n224
State by state gd to human resources law, 1994, 96n268
State by state gd to human resources law, 1994: midyr suppl & workers' compensation laws, 96n269

HUMAN ECOLOGY
Human choice & climate change, 99n1563
Human environments, 96n1797

HUMAN GEOGRAPHY
Atlas of the environment, 95n1756
Atlas of world dvlpmt, 96n444
Spanish/English dict of human & physical geography, 95n493

HUMAN GROWTH & DEVELOPMENT
Cambridge ency of human growth & dvlpmt, 99n1465

HUMANISM
Cumulative index to vols. 1-6 of Paul Oskar Kristeller's Iter Italicum, 99n1259

HUMANITIES
American humanities index for 1995, v.21, 97n744
Benét's reader's ency, 4th ed, 98n843
Best graduate programs: humanities & social scis, 2d ed, 99n335
BHI plus [CD-ROM], 96n955
Columbia dict of modern literary & cultural criticism, 96n960
Comprehensive dissertation index, 1996 suppl, 98n844
Directory of grants in the humanities 1994/95, 95n931
Directory of grants in the humanities 1998/99, 12th ed, 99n812
Humanities: a selective gd to info sources, 4th ed, 95n921
Humanities abstracts full text [CD-ROM], 98n845
Humanities index, April 1995 to Mar 1996, 98n846
Internet compendium: subject gds to humanities resources, 96n100
World databases in humanities, 98n849

HUMAN RIGHTS
Civil rights decisions of the US Supreme Court, the 19th century, 96n607
Civil rights decisions of the US Supreme Court, the 20th century, 96n608
Constitutional law dict, v.1, 96n606
Dictionary of intl human rights law, 97n516
Encyclopedia of human rights, 2d ed, 97n517
Ethnic conflict & human rights in Sri Lanka, v.2, 95n136
Historical dict of human rights & humanitarian orgs, 98n564
Human rights bibliog, 95n630
Human rights on CD-ROM, 2d ed [CD-ROM], 96n609

Human rights orgs & pers dir 1993, 95n629
Political prisoners & trials, 96n605
United Nations ref gd in the field of human rights, 95n631
World dir of human rights research & training insts, 3d ed, 97n518
Yearbook of the Human Rights Committee 1985-86, v.2, 95n632

HUMAN SERVICES
America's top medical & human servs jobs, 2d ed, 95n310
Taxonomy of human servs, 3d ed, 95n830

HUMAN SETTLEMENTS
Compendium of human settlements stats 1995, 5th ed, 97n715

HUMOR IN LITERATURE
Taking humor seriously in children's lit, 99n998

HUMORISTS
Encyclopedia of British humorists, 97n984

HUNGARIAN LANGUAGE—DICTIONARIES—ENGLISH
Hippocrene concise Hungarian-English, English-Hungarian dict, 97n857
Oxford-Duden pictorial Hungarian-English dict, 96n1109

HUNGARY
Budapest, 98n133
Historical dict of Hungary, 98n473
Hungary, 99n131
Short-Title catalogue of Hungarian bks printed before 1851 in the British Lib, 97n14

HUNTING
Coykendall's complete gd to sporting collectibles, 98n895

HURRICANES
Encyclopedia of hurricanes, typhoons, & cyclones, 99n1532
Florida's hurricane hist, 99n1531

HUSTON, JOHN
John Huston a gd to refs & resources, 99n1207

HYDROCARBONS
Physical properties of hydrocarbons & other chemicals, v.4, 96n1793

HYDROLOGY
Rivers of the US, 99n1536

HYGIENE
Marshall Cavendish ency of health, rev ed, 96n1682
Practical ency of sex & health, 95n1647

HYMNS. *See also* CHURCH MUSIC; GOSPEL MUSIC; SACRED MUSIC
American fuging-tunes, 1770-1820, 95n1281
Christian music dirs: printed music 1997-98, 98n1244
Favorite men hymn writers, 95n1311
Hymnology, 98n1246
Hymntune index & related hymn materials, 99n1178
Musical resources for the rev common lectionary, 95n1312
Sing glory & hallelujah! histl & biogl gd to Gospel Hymns nos.1-6 Complete, 97n1086

IBM COMPUTERS. *See also* COMPUTERS; MICROCOMPUTERS
IBM mainframe programmer's desk ref, 95n1692

ICELAND
Historical dict of Iceland, 98n474
Iceland, rev ed, 97n118
Manuscript material, correspondence, & graphic material in the Fiske Icelandic Collection, 95n158

ICELANDIC PHILOLOGY
Annotated bibliog of N America doctoral dissertations on old Norse-Icelandic, 99n892

IDEA (PHILOSOPHY)
Hutchinson dict of ideas, 95n56

IDEOLOGY
Social movement theory & research, 98n690

IDIOMS
German-English dict of idioms, 97n852
Mountain range: A dict of expressions from Appalachia to the Ozarks, 98n1007
Russian idioms, 98n1043
2001 Japanese & English idioms, 97n859

IGBO LANGUAGE—DICTIONARIES—ENGLISH
Igbo English dict, 99n932

ILLINOIS
Illinois hist, 96n492

ILLUSTRATION OF BOOKS
Children's writer's & illustrator's market, 1998, 99n828
Newbery & Caldecott awards, 1998 ed, 99n995

ILLUSTRATORS
American bk & mag illustrators to 1920, v.188, 99n884
Authors & artists for YAs, v.13, 95n1144
Authors & artists for YAs, v.20, 98n1100
Authors & artists for YAs, v.21, 98n1101
Children's authors & illustrators, 5th ed, 96n1178
Contemporary Spanish-speaking writers & illustrators for children & YAs, 95n1151
Dictionary of 19th century British bk illustrators & caricaturists, rev ed, 98n944
Seventh bk of jr authors & illustrators, 97n937

IMAGE TRANSMISSION
Finding images online, 98n1592

IMAGING SYSTEMS
Digital imaging dict, 97n1368

IMMUNIZATION OF CHILDREN
Immunization resource gd, 2d ed, 97n1339

IMMUNOLOGY
Dictionary of cytokines, 96n1558
Encyclopedia of immunology, 2d ed, 99n1419

IMPERIALISM
Historical dict of the British Empire, 98n466

IMPERIAL WAR MUSEUM (GREAT BRITAIN)
Imperial War Museum film catalog, v.1, 96n557

IMPORTS
Directory of import regimes, pt.1, 96n289
Directory of import regimes, pt.2, 96n290
Directory of importers in Latin America, 1994 ed, 96n291
Importers manual USA & the dict of intl trade, 1996-97 ed [CD-ROM], 97n274
Importers manual USA, 1995-96 ed, 96n298

INCOME
American salaries & wages survey, 4th ed, 98n229
Markets of the US for bus planners, 97n276
Multistate payroll gd, 97n257
Official gd to American incomes, 2d ed, 98n225
Value of a dollar, 1860-1989, 96n198

INCUNABULA
Catalogue of the 15th-century printed bks in the Harvard Univ lib, v.3, 96n42
Catalogue of the 15th-century printed bks in the Harvard Univ Lib, v.4, 97n547
Catalogue of the 15th-century printed bks in the Harvard Univ Lib, v.5, 99n614
Rosenthal Collection of printed bks with ms annots, 98n578

INDEPENDENT REGULATORY COMMISSIONS
Directory of professional & occupational regulation in the US & Canada, 96n730

INDEXES
Alternative press index, 97n58
Annotations: a dir of pers listed in the Alternative Press Index, 1996 ed, 97n63
ASSIA plus [CD-ROM], 96n97
BHI plus [CD-ROM], 96n955
Biography index [CD-ROM], 96n24
CD-ROM bk index, 96n80
Children's song index, 1978-93, 97n1033
Essay & general lit index 1990-94, 96n81
Holidays & festivals index, 96n1358
Index to black pers 1997, 99n377
Left index, 97n61
LISA plus [CD-ROM], 96n625
Magill index to critical surveys, rev ed, 96n1161
PCI: pers contents index [CD-ROM], 98n66
Philosopher's index [CD-ROM], 96n1436
World biogl index, 3d ed, 99n32

INDEXING
Indexing bks, 95n657

INDIA
Comprehensive, annot bibliog on Mahatma Gandhi, 97n430
Cultural atlas of India, 98n113
Directory of Indian film-makers & films, 95n1364
Encyclopaedia of Indian cinema, 96n1381
Guide to Indian mss, 95n131
Historical dict of India, 97n108
India, rev ed, 96n131
India & S Asia, 3d ed, 99n104
India hndbk, 99n243
Indian social & economic dvlpmt 1993, 96n243
Mahatma Gandhi, 96n536
Reference ency: India 2001, 96n132
Who was who in British India, 99n485
Women & religion in India, 96n934

INDIANA
Indiana: atlas of histl county boundaries, 98n379
Indiana factbk 1998-99, 5th ed, 99n92

INDIANAPOLIS (IND.)
Encyclopedia of Indianapolis, 96n929

INDIAN ART
Ancient Peruvian art, 97n794

INDIAN ARTISTS
St. James gd to native N American artists, 99n865

INDIANA UNIVERSITY LIBRARIES
Portuguese lit from its origins to 1990, 95n1238

INDIAN LITERATURE
Dictionary of Native American lit, 95n1175
Native American in long fiction, 97n958
Native N American lit, 96n1259

INDIAN PEAKS WILDERNESS (COLO.)
High country names, 95n501

INDIAN RESERVATIONS
American Indian reservations & trust areas, 97n342

INDIANS
Encyclopedia of ancient Mesoamerica, 97n453
First Americans, 96n386
Indian terms of the Americas, 95n436
Indigenous langs of the Americas, 97n810

INDIANS OF CENTRAL AMERICA
Gods & symbols of ancient Mexico & the Maya, 95n1444

INDIANS OF NORTH AMERICA
A to Z of Native American women, 99n386
ABC-CLIO companion to the Native American rights movement, 97n341
American Indian: a multimedia ency [CD-ROM], 98n352
American Indian law deskbk, 2d ed, 99n561
American Indian quotations, 97n345

American Indian ref & resource bks for children & YAs, 2d ed, 96n1177
American Indian reservations & trust areas, 97n342
American Indian studies, 96n421
Archaeology of prehistoric Native America, 99n443
Atlas of Indians of N America, 96n413
Bibliographies of northern & central Calif. Indians, 95n426
Bibliography of the Indians of San Diego County, 99n383
Biographical dir of Native American painters, 97n807
Cambridge hist of the native peoples of the Americas, v.1: N America, pt.1, 99n392
Chronology of native N American hist, 95n433
Chumash & their predecessors, 99n381
Dictionary of Native American lit, 95n1175
DISCovering multicultural America [CD-ROM], 97n323
Encyclopedia of American Indian civil rights, 98n562
Encyclopedia of American Indian costume, 95n442
Encyclopedia of American Indian wars, 1942-1890, 99n460
Encyclopedia of Native American biog, 98n350
Encyclopedia of Native American healing, 97n340
Encyclopedia of Native American legal tradition, 99n388
Encyclopedia of N American Indians, 98n354
Encyclopedia of N American Indians, 98n353
Financial aid for Native Americans 1997-99, 99n772
Guide to ancient Native American sites, 96n411
Guide to fed funding for govts & nonprofits, 1995, Native American ed, 96n882
Guide to the Indian wars of the West, 99n474
Handbook of N American Indians, v.17: langs, 98n356
Handbook of the American frontier, 99n393
Handbook of the American frontier, v.3, 95n440
Handbook of the American frontier, v.4, 98n357
Health of native people of N America, 97n338
Indian slavery, labor, evangelization, & captivity in the Americas, 99n382
Indians of N & S America, 2d suppl, 99n385
Kaleidoscope: a multicultural bklst for grades K-8, 96n1182
Lumbee Indians: an annot bibliog, 95n431
Multiethnic children's lit, 95n1136
Native America in the 20th century, 95n434
Native America: portrait of the peoples, 95n438
Native American almanac, 95n441
Native American genealogical sourcebk, 96n433
Native American info dir, 2d ed, 99n391
Native American issues, 97n344
Native American painters of the 20th century, 96n1054
Native American sun dance religion & ceremony, 99n384
Native Americans, 99n390
Native Americans in fiction, 95n1118
Native Canadian anthropology & hist, rev ed, 95n430
Native educ dir 1997, 98n272
Native N American almanac, 95n443
Native N American almanac: a ref work..., 95n439
Native N American biog, 97n339
Native N American chronology, 96n415
Native N American firsts, 99n387
Native tribes of N America, 95n435
North American Indian music, 98n1191
Notable Native Americans, 96n416
Ojibwa chiefs, 1690-1890, 97n343
Performers, 96n419
Political leaders & peacemakers, 96n418
Ready ref: American Indians, 96n417
Reference ency of the American Indian, 7th ed, 96n412
Scholastic ency of the N American Indian, 98n355
Sioux & other Native American cultures of the Dakotas, 95n428
Statistical record of native N Americans, 2d ed, 96n420
Student's gd to Native American genealogy, 97n366
Timelines of Native American hist, 98n351
U*X*L multicultural CD [CD-ROM], 98n333
Word dance: the lang of Native American culture, 95n437
Writings in Indian hist, 1985-90, 96n414

INDIANS OF SOUTH AMERICA
Indians of N & S America, 2d suppl, 99n385

INDIANS OF THE WEST INDIES
Ancient Caribbean, 95n420

INDONESIA
Bibliography of the Indonesian Revolution, 99n481
Indonesia, 96n134
International dir of Indonesianists, 2d ed, 96n133
Unveiling Indonesia, 98n114

INDOOR AIR POLLUTION
Indoor pollution, 99n1565

INDUSTRIAL ARTS
Career connection for tech educ, 2d ed, 95n319

INDUSTRIAL HYGIENE. *See also* **INDUSTRIAL SAFETY**
Occupational safety & health glossary, 95n295
Patty's industrial hygiene & toxicology, v.2, 4th ed, 95n1784
Patty's industrial hygiene & toxicology, v.3, pt.B, 3d ed, 96n1875
Patty's industrial hygiene & toxicology CD-ROM [CD-ROM], 99n1566

INDUSTRIAL MANAGEMENT
Almanac of bus & industrial financial ratios 1996, 27th ed, 98n177
Field gd to bus terms, 95n185

INDUSTRIAL MUSEUMS
Company museums, industry museums & industrial tours, 95n235

INDUSTRIAL RELATIONS
Roberts' dict of industrial relations, 4th ed, 95n296
Roberts' dict of industrial relations, 4th ed, 96n257
World labour report 1997-98, 99n235

INDUSTRIAL REVOLUTION
American eras: dvlpmt of the industrial US, 1878-99, 98n445

INDUSTRIAL SAFETY. *See also* **INDUSTRIAL HYGIENE**
Directory of safety standards, lit, & servs, 98n1495

Electronic & computer industry gd to chemical safety & environmental compliance, 99n1567
Handbook of lab health & safety, 2d ed, 96n1796
Occupational safety & health glossary, 95n295
Occupational safety & health law 1997, 99n566
OSHA field inspection ref manual, 96n277
OSHA quick gd for residential builders & contractors, 99n1404
Safety & health on the Internet, 98n239
VNR dict of environmental health & safety, 95n1767

INDUSTRIAL STATISTICS
International yrbk of industrial stats 1996, 97n196

INDUSTRIAL SURVEYS
Markets of the US for bus planners, 97n276

INDUSTRIAL TOXICOLOGY
Patty's industrial hygiene & toxicology, v.2, 4th ed, 95n1784
Patty's industrial hygiene & toxicology, v.3, pt.B, 3d ed, 96n1875

INDUSTRY
Agriculture, mining, & construction USA, 99n187
America's corp families 1995, 97n158
American bus locations dir, 97n157
Business & industry [CD-ROM], 98n189
Business hist of the world, 95n242
Business orgs, agencies, & pubns dir, 8th ed, 97n160
Business stats of the US, 99n159
Business stats of the US, 1995 ed, 97n176
By the nos: emerging industries, 99n188
Elsevier's dict of industrial tech, 96n1494
Encyclopedia of American industries, 95n236
Encyclopedia of global industries, 97n204
Energy analysis of 108 industrial processes, 6th ed, 98n1494
Ernst & Young almanac & gd to US bus cities, 95n206
European regional incentives, 1996-97, 97n243
Extractives, manufacturing, & servs, 98n162
Handbook of N American industry, 99n220
How products are made, v.3, 99n189
Industrial commodity stats yrbk 1994, 97n195
Industrial commodity stats yrbk 1995, 29th ed, 99n223
International yrbk of industrial stats 1997, 98n194
Latin American markets, 1993-94 ed, 95n289
Manufacturing worldwide, 97n197
Market share reporter 1998, 8th ed, 99n190
Multimedia dir, 4th ed, 97n1363
North American industry classification system, 1997, 99n162
Ross register of Siberian industry 1995, 96n246
Thomas register of American manufacturers, 1997, 87th ed, 98n196
Thomas register on CD-ROM, 1997 [CD-ROM], 98n197
US industry & trade outlook '98, 99n191
US industry profiles, 96n224
WEFA industrial monitor 1997, 98n198
Who's who in finance & industry, 1996-97, 97n152
World databases in industry, 96n225
World engineering industries & automation, 97n199
World industrial robots 1997, 98n1581

INFANTRY. *See also* **WEAPONS**
Jane's infantry weapons 1994-95, 95n700

INFANTS. *See also* **MEDICINE—PEDIATRIC**
Complete baby & child care, 96n904
Effects of drugs on the fetus & nursing infant, 97n1358
Mayo Clinic complete bk of pregnancy & baby's 1st yr, 96n1722
New parents sourcebk, 97n709

INFORMATION NEEDS & USES
Children's nonfiction for adult info needs, 99n996

INFORMATION RESOURCES MANAGEMENT
NASIRE dir 1994, 95n728

INFORMATION RETRIEVAL
American Lib Assn gd to info access, 95n641
Business A to Z source finder, 97n147
Encyclopedia of bus info sources: Europe, 95n277
Find it fast, 4th ed, 98n575
Key gd to electronic resources: lang & lit, 98n985
Verify those credentials: do you know who you're dealing with?, 98n63

INFORMATION SCIENCE
Annual review of info sci & tech, v.28, 95n642
Annual review of info sci & tech, v.29, 1994, 96n622
ASIS thesaurus of info sci & librarianship, 95n636
Computer & info sci & tech abbrevs & acronyms dict, 95n1698
Concise dict of lib & info sci, 97n525
Dictionary of computing, 4th ed, 98n1576
Directory of Canadian lib & info sci consultants, 96n642
Encyclopedia of lib & info sci, v.57, 98n569
Encyclopedia of lib & info sci, v.58, 97n524
Encyclopedia of lib & info sci, v.59, 98n570
Encyclopedia of lib hist, 95n637
Grants for libs & info servs, 95n639
Harrod's librarians' glossary, 8th ed, 97n526
Informatics glossary, 95n1697
Information sci abstracts, v.29, no.12, 96n619
LISA plus [CD-ROM], 96n625

INFORMATION SERVICES
Burwell dir of info brokers 1994, 96n646
Burwell world dir of info brokers, 13th ed, 99n595
Directory of EU info sources 1995-96, 7th, 97n606
Find it fast, 3d ed, 95n78
Information industry dir, 1994, 95n1690
Information industry dir 1998, 18th ed, 99n602
Information sources 98, 99n202
Library systems in Europe, 96n636
Plunkett's infotech industry almanac, 97n539
Reference & info servs, 2d ed, 96n647
Research servs dir, 97n170
Scholars' gd to Washington, DC, for Russian, Central Eurasian, & Baltic studies, 95n164
Who's who in the European info world 95/96, 2d ed, 96n639
Who's who in the UK info world 95/96, 5th ed, 96n640

INFORMATION TECHNOLOGY
AEA dir, 1993-94, 95n1609
Dictionary of info tech & computer sci, 2d ed, 95n1693
Elsevier's dict of info tech in English, German, & French, 98n581
Encyclopaedic dict of info tech & systems, 95n1689
New info revolution: a ref hndbk, 97n538
Routledge German dict of info tech, 98n1579

INGE, WILLIAM
William Inge: a research & production sourcebk, 95n1193

INORGANIC COMPOUNDS
Handbook of inorganic compounds, 96n1794
Handbook of viscosity, v.4: inorganic compounds & elements, 98n1623

INSCRIPTIONS, SEMITIC
Dictionary of the NW Semitic inscriptions, 96n1129

INSECT PESTS
Agricultural entomology, 96n1625

INSECTS
Chironomidae [Diptera] of Japan, 96n1626
Indo-Australian Agaoninae (pollinators of figs), 96n1628
National Audubon Society 1st field gd: insects, 99n1389
Pockets: insects, 96n71
True bugs of the world (Hemiptera: Heteroptera), 96n1627

INSIGNIA
Encyclopedia of US Army insignia & uniforms, 98n624

INSTRUCTIONAL MATERIALS CENTERS—BIBLIOGRAPHY
Audiovisual resources for family programming, 97n313
Children's media market place, 4th ed, 96n649
Educational media & tech yrbk 1993, 95n386
Educational media & tech yrbk 1994, 95n387
Educational media & tech yrbk 1995/96, v.21, 97n312
Educational media & tech yrbk, 99n356
Recommended ref bks 1994, 95n16
Recommended ref bks for small & medium-sized libs & media centers 1997, 98n9
School lib media annual 1993, v.11, 95n663
School lib media annual 1995, v.13, 96n651

INSTRUMENTATION & ORCHESTRATION
Compendium of modern instrumental techniques, 95n1273

INSURANCE. *See also* REINSURANCE
Canadian insurance claims dir 1997, 99n246
Dictionary of insurance terms, 3d ed, 97n201
Export financing & insurance vocabulary, 97n206
Glossary of insurance & risk mgmt terms, 6th ed, 97n200
Glossary of insurance terms, 5th ed, 96n226
Insurance stats yrbk 1983-90, 95n239
Standard & Poor's insurance co ratings gd, 1995 ed, 97n202
Statistical survey of insurance & reinsurance operations in developing countries 1983-90, 96n227

INTEGRATED CIRCUITS
Master hndbk of IC circuits, 3d ed, 98n1487

INTELLECTUAL PROPERTY
Copyright laws & treaties of the world 1991-95 suppl, 98n566
International intellectual property protection for computer software, 96n638
International treaties on intellectual property, 2d ed, 98n567
McCarthy's desk ency of intellectual property, 2d ed, 97n519
Patent, copyright, & trademark, 97n520

INTELLECTUALS—GREECE—JUVENILE LITERATURE
Ancient Greeks, 98n472

INTELLIGENCE SERVICE
Dictionary of US intelligence servs, 97n597
Guinness bk of espionage, 95n761
US intelligence community, 96n716

INTENTION—RELIGIOUS ASPECTS
Communities dir, 1995 ed, 96n852

INTERDISCIPLINARY APPROACH IN EDUCATION
Interdisciplinary undergraduate programs, 2d ed, 98n289
Writing across the curriculum: an annot bibliog, 95n333

INTERIOR DECORATION
Ency of interior design, 98n935
Interior design sourcebk, 99n858
Who's who in interior design, 1994-95 ed, 95n985

INTERLIBRARY LOAN. *See also* TECHNICAL SERVICES
Interlibrary loan policies dir, 5th ed, 96n641
WLN interlib loan policies dir, 5th ed, 98n585

INTERNATIONAL AGENCIES
Directory of intl orgs, 97n617
Encyclopedia of the EU, 99n691
Europa world yrbk 1998, 39th ed, 99n66
Historical dict of aid & dvlpmt orgs, 97n615
Historical dict of European orgs, 96n139
Historical dict of human rights & humanitarian orgs, 98n564
Historical dict of intl orgs in sub-Saharan Africa, 95n755
Interinstitutional dir: European Union, 96n754
International fndn dir 1996, 7th ed, 97n696
International info docs, 98n693
International instruments of the UN, 99n696
International Washington almanac, 1994, 95n760
Major bus orgs of Eastern Europe & the Commonwealth of Independent States 1995/96, 5th ed, 97n244
Search for security: fndns in intl affairs, 97n700
Statesman's yrbk 1998-99, 135th ed, 99n82
Worldwide govt dir with intl orgs 1995, 96n709
Yearbook of intl orgs 1997/98, 98n71

INTERNATIONAL BUSINESS
Argentina co hndbk, 97n246
Asia, 2d ed, 99n240
Asian & Australasian cos, 95n240

Brazil co hndbk, 1994/95 ed, 95n286
Business One Irwin intl almanac 1993, 95n247
Canadian insurance claims dir 1997, 99n246
Cassell multilingual dict of local govt & bus, 95n750
China bus dir 1994, 95n267
China bus: the portable ency for doing bus with China, 95n261
China mktg data & stats, 99n242
Companies intl, DOS version 1.3 [CD-ROM], 95n245
Consumer Asia 1998, 99n215
Consumer China 1998, 99n216
Consumer Middle East 1998, 99n217
Consumer Europe 1994, 95n278
Consumer Europe 1998/9, 14th ed, 99n249
Cracking Latin America: a country-by-country gd to doing bus..., 95n288
Dictionary of intl bus terms, 97n203
Dictionary of intl bus terms, 99n194
Directory of American firms operating in foreign countries, 14th ed, 97n210
Directory of consumer brands & their owners 1998: Eastern Europe, 99n250
Directory of consumer brands & their owners 1998: Europe, 99n251
Directory of consumer brands & their owners 1998: Latin America, 99n260
Directory of corp affiliations 1998, 99n150
Directory of intl bus, 96n233
Directory of multinationals, 99n197
Directory of overseas catalogs, 1997, 97n212
Directory of the steel industry & the environment, 97n194
Eastern Europe, 2d ed, 99n252
European mktg data & stats 1998, 33d ed, 99n254
Europe's major cos dir 1997, 2d ed, 99n255
Europe's medium-sized cos dir, 2d ed, 99n256
Export financing & insurance vocabulary, 97n206
Fitzroy Dearborn dir of the world's banks, 11th ed, 97n190
Germany's top 300: a hndbk of Germany's largest corps, 1993/94 ed, 95n281
Globe & Mail report on bus: Canada co hndbk 1994, 96n250
Handbook of N American industry, 99n220
Handbook of world stock indices, 99n221
Hong Kong bus: the portable ency for doing bus with Hong Kong, 95n262
Hoover's hndbk of world bus 1998, 99n222
Hoover's masterlist of major intl cos 1998-99, 99n201
Industrial commodity stats yrbk 1995, 29th ed, 99n223
International advertising & mktg info sources, 96n299
International bibliog of bus hist, 98n149
International bus & trade dir, 2d ed, 99n141
International mktg data & stats 1994, 95n252
International mktg data & stats 1998, 99n224
International mktg forecasts, 99n225
International tax summaries, 1998, 99n226
International trade sources, 98n199
International trade stats yrbk, 1995, 98n252
International yrbk of industrial stats 1996, 97n196
Internet resources & servs for intl bus, 99n209
Japan bus: the portable ency for doing bus with Japan, 95n263
Korea bus: the portable ency for doing bus with Korea, 95n264
Latin America: a dir & sourcebk, 2d ed, 99n261

Major cos of Central & Eastern Europe & the Commonwealth of Independent States 1996/97, 6th ed, 97n220
Major cos of Latin America 1996, 97n247
Major cos of the Arab world 1996/97, 20th ed, 97n233
Major cos of the Far East & Australasia 1995/96, 96n245
Maxwell Espinosa shareholder dir, 95n285
Mexico bus: the portable ency for doing bus with Mexico, 95n290
Mexico co hndbk, 1995/96 ed, 96n254
North American labor markets, 99n227
OECD statl compendium 1996/1 [CD-ROM], 97n227
Ranking of world stock markets, 99n229
Singapore bus: the portable ency for doing bus with Singapore, 95n265
Statistics on occupational wages & hours of work & on food prices 1997, 99n231
Structural & ownership changes in the chemical industry of countries in transition, 99n232
Taiwan bus: the portable ency for doing bus with Taiwan, 95n266
Transnational corps: a selective bibliog 1991-92, 95n241
World bus & economic review 1994, 95n256
World database of consumer brands & their owners 1998 [CD-ROM], 99n259
World investment dir 1996, v.6: West Asia, 98n207
World investment report 1998, 99n234
World labour report 1997-98, 99n235
World mktg data & stats on CD-ROM [CD-ROM], 99n236
World retail dir 1997-98, 99n212
World retail dir & sourcebk, 2d ed, 97n222
World's major cos dir, 96n229
Worldwide branch locations of multinatl cos, 95n246
Worldwide offshore petroleum dir 1998, 30th ed, 99n213
Worldwide petrochemical dir 1998, 36th ed, 99n214
Yearbook of labor stats, 1997, 99n238

INTERNATIONAL COURTS
Historical dict of intl tribunals, 96n610

INTERNATIONAL ECONOMIC INTEGRATION
Encyclopedia of the N American Free Trade Agreement, 96n305

INTERNATIONAL ECONOMIC RELATIONS
Directory of intl economic org, 98n161
Global dvlpmt, 97n228
Glossary of industrial org economics & competition law, 95n183
Historical stats 1960-94, 1996 ed, 97n225
National accounts stats 1991, 95n254
Revenue stats of OECD member countries 1965-93, 96n772
Services: stats on intl transactions 1970/92, 96n918
World economic outlook, May 1997, 98n188

INTERNATIONALE SITUATIONNISTE
Realization & suppression of the Situationist Intl, 97n792

INTERNATIONAL FINANCE
Handbook of intl financial terms, 98n184
International financial stats locator, 96n230
McGraw-Hill dict of intl trade & finance, 95n243

INTERNATIONAL FUND FOR AGRICULTURAL DEVELOPMENT
Historical dict of the intl food agencies, 96n1529

INTERNATIONAL LAW
Glossary of industrial org economics & competition law, 95n183
Historical dict of intl tribunals, 96n610
Law of the sea: a bibliog on the law of the sea, 1968-88, 95n594
Law of the sea: a select bibliog 1993, 95n595
Recovery of internationally abducted children, 99n752
Reports required by Congress, 1995, v.2, no.1, 96n746
United Nations Commission on Intl Trade Law yrbk, v.24, 1993, 96n307
World dir of research & training insts in intl law, 3d ed, 95n600

INTERNATIONAL LEAGUE (BASEBALL)
International league, 99n724

INTERNATIONAL LIBRARIANSHIP
Library systems in Europe, 96n636

INTERNATIONAL RELATIONS
ACCESS gd to intl affairs internships in the Washington, DC, area, 95n762
African intl relations, 2d ed, 98n699
Bibliography of works on Canadian foreign relations 1986-90, 96n748
Bibliography of works on Canadian foreign relations 1991-95, 99n689
Careers in intl affairs, 6th ed, 98n698
Encyclopedia of the EU, 99n691
Encyclopedic dict of conflict & conflict resolution, 1945-96, 99n628
Fellowships in intl affairs, 95n365
Historical dict of multinatl peacekeeping, 97n616
International conflict, 98n696
International ethics, 99n698
International instruments of the UN, 99n696
International policy insts around the Pacific Rim, 99n697
International relations, 5th ed, 97n620
International relations research dir, 97n619
Whitaker's almanack world heads of govt 1998, 99n650
Whitaker's almanack world heads of state 1998, 99n651

INTERNATIONAL RELIEF
Guide to funding for intl & foreign programs, 2d ed, 96n875

INTERNATIONAL STANDARD BOOK NUMBERS
Publishers' intl ISBN dir, 20th ed, 95n676

INTERNATIONAL TRADE. See also TRADE; COMMERCE
America's intl trade, 96n239
American export register 1995, 96n286
Argentina bus, 97n245
Commodity indexes for the Standard Intl Trade Classification, revision 3, 95n258
Consumer E Europe 1998/9, 99n248
Dictionary of intl bus terms, 97n203
Dictionary of intl trade, 95n244
Directory of import regimes, pt.1, 96n289
Directory of import regimes, pt.2, 96n290
Exporting to the USA, 1995-96 ed, 96n297
Exporting to the USA & the dict of intl trade, 1996-97 ed [CD-ROM], 97n205
External trade monthly stats, 96n293
Foreign trade stats for Africa, 96n294
Handbook of intl trade & dvlpmt stats 1993, 96n234
Handbook of world mineral trade stats 1990-95, 98n251
Importers manual USA, 1995-96 ed, 96n298
Imports & exports of the Republic of China on Taiwan 1993, 95n271
International bus & trade dirs, 96n228
International dir of bus info sources & servs 1996, 2d ed, 97n213
International trade sources, 98n199
Japan trade dir 1997-98, 99n244
McGraw-Hill dict of intl trade & finance, 95n243
National accounts stats, 98n203
Philippines bus, 97n236
Retail trade intl, 1998 ed, 99n230
Thunderbird gd to intl bus resources on the WWW, 98n204
Trade data elements dir: UNTDED 1993, v.1, 96n306
Trade data elements dir v.3, 97n277
United Nations Commission on Intl Trade Law yrbk, v.24, 1993, 96n307
United States-European Community trade resources, 95n323
US & Asia statl hndbk, 1997-98 ed, 99n219
Washington almanac of intl trade & bus, 1995/96, 97n230
World bus desk ref, 95n249
World country analyst [CD-ROM], 98n205
World dir of mktg info sources, 99n211
World mktg data & stats on CD-ROM [CD-ROM], 99n236
World trade almanac 1996-97, 97n207
World trade almanac & the dict of intl trade, 1997 ed [CD-ROM], 97n208
World trade atlas: US data, Mar 1994 [CD-ROM], 95n327
World trade org dispute settlement decisions, v.1, 99n237

INTERNET (COMPUTER NETWORK). See also LISTSERVS; WORLD WIDE WEB
Adams electronic job search almanac 1998, 99n264
Best dir of recruiters on-line, 97n254
Best Web sites for teachers, 2d ed, 99n308
Business multimedia explained, 98n242
Career Xroads, 3d ed, 99n267
Catholic Internet, USA ed, 98n1390
Catholicism on the Web, 98n1391
Chemical gd to the Internet, 97n1382
Chemicals on the Internet, v.1, 98n1478
Complete "no geek-speak" gd to the Internet, 99n1499
CyberDictionary, 98n1575
CyberHound's gd to cos on the Internet, 98n1583
CyberHound's gd to Internet discussion groups, 98n1584
CyberHound's gd to people on the Internet, 98n1585
CyberHound's Internet gd to the coolest stuff out there, 97n1374
Cyberstocks, 97n182

CyberTools for bus, 98n163
Dictionary of personal computing & the internet, 98n1574
Directory of dirs on the Internet, 95n1707
Earth online, 99n1516
Essential Internet info gd, 96n1784
Film & video on the Internet, 98n1287
Finding images online, 98n1592
Free stuff from the Internet, 95n1709
Gale gd to Internet databases, 96n1779
Gay & lesbian online, rev ed, 98n781
Gay & lesbian online, 97n676
God on the Internet, 98n1365
Government info on the Internet, 99n61
Guide to Internet job searching, 1998-99 ed, 99n268
Harley Hahn's Internet & Web yellow pages 1998, 5th anniversary ed, 99n1496
Health & medicine on the Internet, 99n1424
Health online, 97n1328
High places in cyberspace, 2d ed, 99n1269
HIV/AIDS Internet info sources & resources, 99n1469
Insider's gd to mental health resources online, 98n1515
Internet: an introductory gd for UN orgs, 96n1783
Internet access providers, 95n1708
Internet & lib & info servs, 98n582
Internet compendium: subject gds to health & sci resources, 96n1774
Internet compendium: subject gds to humanities resources, 96n100
Internet compendium: subject gds to social scis, bus, & law resources, 96n101
Internet complete ref, 2d ed, 98n1594
Internet dir, 95n1702
Internet gd for the legal researcher, 2d ed, 98n535
Internet resource dir for K-12 teachers & librarians, 94/95 ed, 95n1706
Internet resource dir for K-12 teachers & librarians, 96/97 ed, 98n1590
Internet resource dir for K-12 teachers & librarians, 98/99 ed, 99n307
Internet resources & servs for intl bus, 99n209
Internet searcher's hndbk, 98n1595
Internet tools of the profession, 2d ed, 98n1586
Internet white pages 1994, 95n1705
Internet World's on Internet 94, 95n1703
Internet yellow pages, 2d ed, 96n1775
Key gd to electronic resources: lang & lit, 98n985
Mecklermedia's official Internet World Internet yellow pages, 1996 ed, 98n1587
Mecklermedia's official Internet World WWW yellow pages, 1996 ed, 98n1588
Microsoft Bkshelf Internet dir, 1996-97 ed, 98n1589
Naked in cyberspace: how to find personal info online, 98n1596
National e-mail & fax dir 1999, 99n56
Net games, 96n813
Net gd, 96n1781
Official America online yellow pages, 99n53
Official Internet dict, 99n1489
Oil & gas on the Internet, 97n1415
Online user's ency, 95n1701
Post-Soviet hndbk, 97n123
Prentice Hall dir of online bus info 1997, 97n168
Safety & health on the Internet, 98n239
Safety & health on the Internet, 2d ed, 99n281
Telecommunications, networking & Internet glossary, 95n1704
200 best aviation Web sites, 99n1576
US military online, 98n617
Virtual field trips, 98n281
Virtual musician, 98n1206
Virtual roots: a gd to genealogy & local hist on the WWW, 98n366
Wading the World Wide Web, 99n1498
Washington online: how to access the fed govt on the Internet 1995, 96n1785
Web programming lang sourcebk, 99n1487
Web site source bk 1996, 97n1377
What's on the Internet, winter 1994/95 ed, 95n1710
World Wide Web for scientists & engineers, 99n1327
Xtravaganza! the essential sourcebk for Macromedia Xtras, 99n1486

INTERNSHIP PROGRAMS
ACCESS gd to intl affairs internships in the Washington, DC, area, 95n762
America's top internships, 1998 ed, 98n221
Graduate Group's new internships for 1994-95, 96n261
Graduate Group's new internships for 1997-98, 99n322
6th annual Graduate Group's internships in state govt, 99n324
7th annual Graduate Group's internships in fed govt, 99n323
Higher educ money bk for women & minorities, 1997 ed, 97n302
Internship bible, 1998 ed, 99n270
Internships 1994, 95n299
National dir of internships, 9th ed, 95n302
Peterson's internships 1996, 16th ed, 97n256
Peterson's internships 1998, 18th ed, 99n291
Sixth bi-annual natl dir of arts internships, 1995/96, 96n1034
Student access gd to America's top 100 internships, 1995 ed, 95n303
Student sci opportunities, 95n340

INTERPERSONAL RELATIONS
Encyclopedia of relationships across the lifespan, 97n631
Focus on relationships, 95n883

INTERSTATE HIGHWAY SYSTEM
Interstate exit authority, 99n432

INVENTIONS
Eureka! scientific discoveries & inventions, 96n1496
Famous 1st facts, 99n46
Historical 1st patents, 96n1509
Illustrated almanac of sci, tech, & inventions, 99n1306
Pockets: inventions, 96n72
World of invention, 95n1496

INVENTORS
Scientists & inventors, 99n1304

INVERTEBRATES
Encyclopedia of land invertebrate behaviour, 95n1592

INVESTMENTS, FOREIGN
Australia bus, 97n237
Brazil co hndbk, 1994/95 ed, 95n286
Business One Irwin intl almanac 1993, 95n247
China bus: the portable ency for doing bus with China, 95n261
Dow Jones gd to the world stock market, 1995-96 ed, 96n212
Fitzroy Dearborn dir of the world's futures & options markets, 95n221
Fitzroy Dearborn intl dir of venture capital funds, 2d ed, 97n181
Fitzroy Dearborn intl dir of venture capital funds 1998-99, 99n198
Handbook of world stock indices, 99n221
Hong Kong bus: the portable ency for doing bus with Hong Kong, 95n262
International direct investment stats yrbk 1993, 95n250
International gd to securities market indices, 98n175
International investing with ADRs, 95n222
Japan bus: the portable ency for doing bus with Japan, 95n263
Korea bus: the portable ency for doing bus with Korea, 95n264
Mexico bus: the portable ency for doing bus with Mexico, 95n290
Russian defense bus dir 1993, 95n284
Singapore bus: the portable ency for doing bus with Singapore, 95n265
Taiwan bus: the portable ency for doing bus with Taiwan, 95n266
USA bus: the portable ency for doing bus with the US, 96n241
World investment dir, v.4: Latin America & the Caribbean, 95n291
World investment dir, v.5: Africa, 98n201
World investment report 1998, 99n234
World stock exchange fact bk, 97n186

INVESTMENTS. *See also* **FINANCE, PERSONAL**
Cyberstocks, 97n182
Directory of cos offering dividend reinvestment plans, 99n163
Directory of cos required to file annual reports with the securities & exchange commission, 1997, 99n164
Galante's venture capital & private equity dir, 1997 ed [CD-ROM], 99n199
Galante's venture capital & private equity dir, 1998 ed, 99n200
Maxwell Espinosa shareholder dir, 95n285
MFC investment hndbk 1994, 95n272
Morningstar mutual fund 500, 1997-98 ed, 99n173
100 best mutual funds you can buy, 1995, 97n185
100 best stocks to own in America, 99n166
105 best investments for the 21st century, 97n226
Plunkett's financial servs industry almanac, 98n185
Rate ref gd to the US treasury market 1984-95, 97n184
Standard & Poor's 500 gd, 1995 ed, 96n214
Standard & Poor's midcap 400 gd, 1995 ed, 96n215
Standard & Poor's smallcap 600 gd, 1996 ed, 97n171
Standard & Poor's stock & bond gd, 1998 ed, 99n174
Topline ency of histl charts, Mar 1997 ed, 98n176

US industry & trade outlook '98, 99n191
Walker's manual of penny stocks, 99n167
Walker's manual of unlisted stocks, 98n172
Wall street words, 98n170

IOWA
Atlas of histl county boundaries: Iowa, 99n447

IRAN
Armenians & Iran, 2d ed, 95n151

IRAQ
Daily life in ancient Mesopotamia, 99n511
Iraq, 2d ed, 96n135

IRAQ—KUWAIT CRISIS, 1990-1991
Operation Desert Shield/Desert Storm, 96n563

IRELAND
Academic libs in the UK & the republic of Ireland 1994, 3d ed, 96n635
Brian Friel, 96n1257
British & Irish archaeology, 95n521
Dictionary of Irish quotations, 95n445
Directory of rare bk & special collections in the UK & the Republic of Ireland, 2d ed, 98n588
Encyclopedia of Irish schools, 1500-1800, 96n315
Ireland, 96n481
Ireland: a dir 1998, 32d ed, 99n133
Ireland: an ency for the bewildered, 96n142
Irish almanac & yrbk of facts 1997, 98n134
Irish bed & breakfast bk, 96n482
Libraries in the UK & Republic of Ireland 1995, 96n637
Northern Ireland: a pol dir 1968-93, 96n761

IRELAND—BIOGRAPHY
Dictionary of Irish biog, 3d ed, 99n132
Modern Irish writers, 98n1176
Women of Ireland, 98n34

IRELAND—HISTORY
Historical dict of Ireland, 98n475

IRELAND IN LITERATURE
Dictionary of Irish lit, rev ed, 97n1007
James Joyce A to Z, 97n1009
Patrick Kavanagh: a ref gd, 98n1174

IRIGARAY, LUCE
French feminist theory 3, 98n832

IRISH
Master bk of Irish surnames, 95n464

IRISH AMERICANS
Dictionary of Irish family names, 98n376
Hippocrene USA gd to Irish America, 95n444
Irish-American landmarks, 96n422
Irish experience in NYC, 97n346
Student's gd to Irish American genealogy, 97n365

IRIS (PLANT)
Gardener's gd to growing irises, 98n1454

IRON AGE
Great Zimbabwe, 95n522

IRON INDUSTRY & TRADE
Encyclopedia of American bus hist & biog: iron & steel in the 20th century, 95n238

ISLAM
Dictionary of Islamic architecture, 97n803
Encyclopaedia of Islam, new ed, v.8, fascicules 139-40, 95n1473
Encyclopedia of apocalypticism, 99n1266
Great dates in Islamic hist, 97n137
Islam, Hinduism, & Judaism in South Africa, 98n1345
Islam in China, 95n1474
Islamic desk ref, 95n174

ISLAMIC COUNTRIES
Great dates in Islamic hist, 97n137
Islamic desk ref, 95n174
Islamic economics & finance, 97n232
Muslim almanac, 97n1219
New Islamic dynasties, 97n135
Oxford ency of the modern Islamic world, 96n1477
Year bk of the Muslim world 1996, 97n81

ISLANDS OF THE PACIFIC
Peoples of the world: Asians & Pacific Islanders, 95n127
Return to paradise: a gd to S Sea Island films, 99n1229

ISO 900 SERIES STANDARDS
Randall's practical gd to ISO 9000, 96n206

ISRAEL
Criminal justice in Israel, 96n596
History of Israel, 99n509
Israel & the Jewish world, 1948-93, 96n552
Israel & the W Bank & Gaza Strip, 2d ed, 96n163
Israeli secret servs, 98n689
New ency of Zionism & Israel, 96n164

ISRAEL—ANTIQUITIES
Jesus & his world, 97n1213

ISRAEL-ARAB CONFLICTS
Atlas of the Arab-Israeli conflict, 6th ed, 95n759
Historical ency of the Arab-Israeli conflict, 97n455

ITALIAN AMERICANS
Student's gd to Italian American genealogy, 97n363

ITALIAN LANGUAGE—DICTIONARIES—ENGLISH
Larousse mini Italian-English, English-Italian dict, new ed, 97n858
Oxford color Italian dict, 98n1036
Oxford-Duden pictorial Italian & English dict, 96n1110
Oxford Italian desk dict, 98n1037
Oxford Italian minidict, 2d ed, 98n1038

ITALIAN LITERATURE
Dictionary of Italian lit, rev ed, 97n1010
Feminist ency of Italian lit, 98n1177
Italian women writers, 95n1235

ITALIANS
Finding Italian roots, 95n456

ITALY
Ancient Greece & Rome, 99n491
Dictionary of British & Irish travellers in Italy, 1701-1800, 98n476
Dictionary of Italian cuisine, 99n1331
Italian film: a who's who, 95n1365
Italian horror films of the 1960s, 99n1205
Italy, 96n143
Italy, 97n395
Twentieth-Century Italian poets, 1st series, 95n1233

ITZA DIALECT
Itzaj Maya-Spanish-English dict, 98n1040

IVANOV, VIACHESLAV
Viacheslav Ivanov: a ref gd, 98n1181

IVORY COAST
Cote d'Ivoire, 97n96

IVY
Gardener's gd to growing ivies, 98n1455

JAINA
Pada index & reverse Pada index to early Jain canons, 97n1202

JAMES BOND FILMS
Complete James Bond movie ency, rev ed, 96n1382

JAPAN
Area bibliog of Japan, 99n111
Bibliographic gd to E Asian studies 1995, 98n109
Chironomidae [Diptera] of Japan, 96n1626
Consumer Japan 1993, 95n269
Directory of Japanese-affiliated cos in the EU, 1996-97, 97n211
Dictionary of Japanese financial terms, 96n248
Encyclopedia of Japanese pop culture, 99n112
Japan: exploring your options, 96n373
Japan & the Japanese, 97n110
Japan & the Pacific Rim, 4th ed, 99n102
Japan bus: the portable ency for doing bus with Japan, 95n263
Japan dir of professional assns, 3d ed, 96n244
Japan ency, 97n109
Japan trade dir 1997-98, 99n244
Japanese automobile industry: an annot bibliog, 95n1790
Japanese hist & culture from ancient to modern times, 2d ed, 96n537
Japanese studies in Canada: the 1990s, 98n115
MIT ency of the Japanese economy, 95n273
Modern Japan, 99n486
NTC's dict of Japan's bus code words, 99n193

Philippines in WW II & to independence (Dec. 8, 1941-July 4, 1946), 2d ed, 97n432
Pictorial ency of Japanese life & events, 95n133
Research in Japanese sources, 95n134
Student gd to Japanese sources in the humanities, 95n132

JAPANESE AMERICANS
Academic focus Japan: programs & resources in N America, 96n423
Executive order 9066 [CD-ROM], 99n470

JAPANESE LANGUAGE
Japanese psycholinguistics, 96n1059

JAPANESE LANGUAGE—DICTIONARIES—ENGLISH
Cassell English-Japanese bus dict, 95n260
Dictionary of Japanese & English idiomatic equivalents, 95n1085
Japanese-English, English-Japanese concise dict, 95n1084
Kanji dict, 97n860
Kodansha's furigana Japanese-English dict, 96n1111
Kodansha's pocket kanji gd, 96n1112
Martin's concise Japanese dict, 96n1113
New Nelson Japanese-English character dict, rev ed, 99n933
Tuttle dict of legal terms: English-Japanese, Japanese-English, 95n605
Tuttle dict of legal terms: English-Japanese, Japanese-English, rev ed, 96n613
Tuttle new dict of loanwords in Japanese, 95n1086
2001 Japanese & English idioms, 97n859

JAPANESE LITERATURE
Japanese fiction writers since WW II, 99n1096
Japanese women writers: a bio-critical sourcebk, 95n1236

JAYS
Crows & jays, 95n1569

JAZZ IN LITERATURE
Annotated bibliog of jazz fiction & jazz fiction criticism, 97n944
Bibliographic gd to jazz poetry, 99n1099

JAZZ MUSIC
All music gd to jazz, 95n1304
All music gd, 3d ed, 98n1228
Buddy DeFranco: a biogl portrait & discography, 95n1303
Command performance, USA! a discography, 97n772
Harvard biogl dict of music, 97n1024
Jazz & blues lover's gd to the US, updated ed, 96n1321
Jazz CD listener's gd, 99n1165
Jazz discography, v.9, 96n1326
Jazz discography, 99n1167
Jazz research & performance materials, 2d ed, 96n1327
Jazz: the rough gd, 97n1076
MusicHound jazz, 99n1168
New Grove dict of jazz, 96n1328
Tantalizing tingles: a discography of early ragtime, jazz...., 96n1325
Who's who of British jazz, 98n1235

JAZZ MUSICIANS
Benny Goodman: wrappin' it up, 97n1071
Dial recordings of Charlie Parker, 99n1166
Earthly recordings of Sun Ra, 96n1322
John Coltrane, 96n1324
Red Nichols story, 98n1236
Serge Chaloff, 99n1169
Straighten up & fly right: a chronology & discography of Nat "King" Cole, 96n1329
Tram: the Frank Trumbauer story, 96n1323

JEFFERSON, THOMAS
Thomas Jefferson: a biogl companion, 99n660

JEHOVAH'S WITNESSES
Jehovah's Witness lit, 95n1459

JESUS CHRIST—BIOGRAPHY
Jesus & his world, 97n1213

JEWELRY
Faberge & his works, 95n994

JEWISH-ARAB RELATIONS
Arab-Israeli dispute, 97n457
Historical dict of Palestine, 98n488
Historical ency of the Arab-Israeli conflict, 97n455

JEWS. *See also* **JUDAISM**
Atlas of Jewish hist, 95n446
Concise dict of American Jewish biog, 95n447
Contemporary Jewish-American novelists, 98n1125
Dictionary of Jewish surnames from the Kingdom of Poland, 98n375
Encyclopaedia Judaica, 98n1393
Encyclopaedia Judaica decennial bk 1983-92, 96n1478
Index to American Jewish Histl Quarterly/American Jewish Hist: vs.51-80, 97n347
Index to pubns of the American Jewish Histl Society, vs.21-50, 95n449
Jewish alcoholism & drug addiction, 95n880
Jewish info source bk, 95n1476
"Jewish question" in German-speaking countries, 1848-1914, 96n425
Jewish roots in Poland, 99n400
Jewish sports legends, 2d ed, 98n719
Jewish women in America, 99n394
Jewish writers of Latin America, 98n1180
Jewish yr bk 1997, 98n1395
Jews & Europe, 96n424
Judaica ref sources, 2d ed, 95n448
Junior Judaica: ency Judaica for youth, rev ed, 95n450
Orthodox Judaism in America, 97n1224
Princeton Review Hillel gd to Jewish life on campus, 1996 ed, 97n307
Short hist of the Jewish people, 99n395
Student's gd to Jewish American genealogy, 98n369
Travel gd to Jewish Europe, 2d ed, 97n436
Traveler's gd to Jewish Germany, 99n438
Two Jews, 3 opinions: a collection of 20th-century American Jewish quotations, 99n396
Understanding the Holocaust, 99n539

JEWS—GENEALOGY
Sourcebook for Jewish genealogies & family hists, 98n362

JOB DESCRIPTIONS
America's 50 fastest growing jobs, 2d ed, 95n308
America's top technical & trade jobs, 2d ed, 95n312
Enhanced occupational outlook hndbk, 98n226

JOB HUNTING. *See also* **CAREERS**
Adams electronic job search almanac 1998, 99n264
Adams job almanac 1995, 96n265
Adams jobs almanac 1998, 99n265
Almanac of American employers 1996-97, 97n259
American dir of job & labor market info, 95n298
America's top jobs for people without college degrees, 3d ed, 98n227
America's top office, mgmt, sales, & professional jobs, 3d ed, 98n228
Best dir of recruiters, 4th ed, 97n253
Best dir of recruiters on-line, 97n254
Career Xroads, 3d ed, 99n267
Civil serv career starter, 99n272
Cracking the corp closet, 96n259
Directory of fed jobs & employers, 97n258
DISCovering careers & jobs [CD-ROM], 96n271
Employment opportunities, USA, 99n269
Government job finder, 95n315
Government job finder, 98n234
Guide to executive recruiters, new ed, 98n218
Guide to Internet job searching, 1998-99 ed, 99n268
JIST's electronic gd for occupational exploration [CD-ROM], 96n275
JIST's multimedia occupational outlook hndbk, 2d ed [CD-ROM], 98n232
Job hotlines USA, 1994-95 ed, 95n300
Job hunter's yellow pages, 1994-95 ed, 95n301
Job hunter's sourcebk, 3d ed, 98n233
Job-Hunting on the Internet, 98n222
Job seeker's gd to socially responsible cos, 96n262
Management consulting [CD-ROM], 98n245
National job hotline dir, 1995, 95n307
National jobbank 1998, 98n237
National jobline dir, 95n305
Non-profit's job finder, 3d ed, 95n316
Non-profits & edu job finder 1997-2000, 98n235
On-line job search companion, 96n272
Peterson's hidden job market 1995, 95n304
Peterson's job opportunities in bus 1995, 96n280
Peterson's job opportunities in engineering & tech 1995, 96n1513
Peterson's job opportunities in health care 1995, 96n1689
Peterson's job opportunities in the environment 1995, 96n1876
Professional's private sector job finder 1994-95, 95n317
Professionals job finder 1997-2000, 99n273
Specialty occupational outlook: trade & technical, 97n262
State occupational outlook hndbk, 99n275
Top 100: the fastest growing careers for the 21st century, rev ed, 99n276

US employment opportunities, 98n240
World Almanac job finders gd 1997, 97n263

JOB SHARING
Job sharing: an annot bibliog, 95n293

JOHN, KING OF ENGLAND, 1167-1216
King John: an annot bibliog, 95n1217

JOHNSON, SAMUEL
Samuel Johnson ency, 97n994

JOLSON, AL
Al Jolson: a bio-bibliog, 95n1345

JOPLIN, SCOTT
Scott Joplin: a gd to research, 99n1142

JOURNALISM
Broadcast news manual of style, 2d ed, 96n992
Graduate programs in journalism & mass communications, 98n309
Journalism, 2d ed, 98n851
Sports style gd & ref manual, 97n757
Tabloid journalism, 97n747
US news coverage of racial minorities, 98n852

JOURNALISTIC ETHICS
Journalism ethics, 99n826

JOURNALISTS
American mag journalists, 1900-60: 2d series, 95n955
Biographical dict of American newspaper columnists, 96n973
Political commentators in the US in the 20th century, 98n862

JOURNALISTS IN MOTION PICTURES
From headline hunter to Superman: a journalism filmography, 98n1298
Media in the movies, 99n1228

JOYCE, JAMES
James Joyce A to Z, 97n1009

J. PAUL GETTY MUSEUM
Decorative arts: an illus summary cat of the collections of the J. Paul Getty Museum, 95n966

JUDAISM. *See also* **JEWS**
American Jewish yr bk 1996, v.96, 97n1220
Concise ency of Judaism, 99n1291
Dictionary of Judaism in the biblical period, 97n1223
Dictionary of 1000 Jewish proverbs, 98n1251
Encyclopaedia Judaica, 98n1393
Encyclopaedia Judaica decennial bk 1983-92, 96n1478
Encyclopedia of apocalypticism, 99n1266
Encyclopedia of the sayings of the Jewish people, 99n1293
Index to American Jewish Histl Quarterly/American Jewish Hist: vs.51-80, 97n347
Islam, Hinduism, & Judaism in South Africa, 98n1345
Jewish ency of moral & ethical issues, 95n1475
Jewish info source bk, 95n1476

Jewish yr bk 1997, 98n1395
Jews & Europe, 96n424
Judaica Americana, 96n1480
Judaism, 98n1394
Junior Judaica: ency Judaica for youth, rev ed, 95n450
Messengers of God: a Jewish prophets who's who, 99n1292
My 1st 100 Hebrew words, 95n1080
Orthodox Judaism in America, 97n1224
Oxford dict of the Jewish religion, 98n1396
Popular dict of Judaism, 97n1222
Princeton Review Hillel gd to Jewish life on campus, 1996 ed, 97n307
Sacred celebrations: a Jewish holiday hndbk, 96n1479
Who's who in Jewish hist, 2d ed, 96n1481

JUDGES
American leaders 1789-1994, 95n714
BNA's dir of state & fed courts, judges, & clerks, 1997 ed, 98n521
Rejected: sketches of the 26 men nominated for the Supreme Court but not confirmed by the Senate, 95n601
Supreme Court compendium, 95n612
Supreme Court justices, 96n572

JURISPRUDENCE
Feminist jurisprudence, 97n739

JUSTICE
Ready ref: American justice, 97n489

JUST WAR DOCTRINE
Encyclopedia of war & ethics, 97n1161

JUVENILE DELINQUENCY
Violent children, 96n603

KABUKI
New Kabuki ency, 98n1324

KANT, IMMANUEL
Kant dict, 96n1428

KAVANAGH, PATRICK
Patrick Kavanagh: a ref gd, 98n1174

KAY, ULYSSES
Ulysses Kay: a bio-bibliog, 95n1266

KEEL, HOWARD
Howard Keel: a bio-bibliog, 97n1078

KENNAN, GEORGE FROST
George F. Kennan: an annot bibliog, 98n700

KENNEDY, JOHN FITZGERALD
John F. Kennedy, 96n491
Who's who in the JFK assassination, 95n620

KENNERLEY, MITCHELL
Mitchell Kennerly imprint: a descriptive bibliog, 98n592

KENTUCKY
Birds of Ky., 95n1571
Kentucky: atlas of histl county boundaries, 97n371

KENYA
Kenya, rev ed, 97n98

KEYBOARD INSTRUMENTS
Encyclopedia of keyboard instruments, v.1, 95n1278

KEYNESIAN ECONOMICS
Encyclopedia of Keynesian economics, 98n152
Post Keynesian economics, 97n148

KIDNAPPING
Recovery of internationally abducted children, 99n752

KINGS & RULERS
Great leaders, great tyrants?, 96n706
Kings of medieval England, c. 560-1485, 97n445
New Islamic dynasties, 97n135
World leaders: people who shaped the world, 95n576

KNIGHTS & KNIGHTHOOD IN LITERATURE
Arthurian handbook, 2d ed, 99n1066

KNIVES. *See also* **WEAPONS**
Knives: military edged tools & weapons, 99n647
Standard knife collector's gd, 3d ed, 99n850

KODALY, ZOLTAN
Zoltan Kodaly: a gd to research, 99n1138

KOREAN AMERICANS
Korean Americans, 99n374

KOREAN WAR, 1950-1953
Guide to films on the Korean War, 98n1291
Inchon landing, Korea, 1950, 95n683
Korea [CD-ROM], 96n692
Korean War, 96n538
Korean War, 97n431
Korean war: an annot bibliog, 99n514

KOREA (SOUTH)
Korea bus: the portable ency for doing bus with Korea, 95n264

KRISTELLER, PAUL OSKAR
Cumulative index to vols. 1-6 of Paul Oskar Kristeller's Iter Italicum, 99n1259

KURDISH LANGUAGE—DICTIONARIES—ENGLISH
Kurdish-English/English-Kurdish dict, 96n1114

KURDS
Kurds & Kurdistan, 98n116

KUWAIT
Kuwait, rev ed, 97n140

KYRGYZ LANGUAGE—DICTIONARIES—ENGLISH
Kyrgyz-English/English-Kyrgyz glossary of terms, 99n934

LABOR
Almanac of American employers 1998-99, 99n266
American salaries & wages survey, 4th ed, 98n229
Directory of US labor orgs, 1997 ed, 98n219
Employment/Unemployment & earnings stats, 97n249
Handbook of US labor stats, 98n230
North American labor markets, 99n227
Sources & methods: labour stats, v.2, 97n260
Statistics on occupational wages & hours of work & on food prices 1997, 99n231
Working stiffs, union maids, reds, & riffraff: an organized gd to films about labor, 97n1141
World labour report 1997-98, 99n235
Yearbook of labor stats, 1997, 99n238
Yearbook of labour stats 1995, 54th ed, 97n261

LABOR COSTS
Employee benefits desk ency, 97n252
Multistate payroll gd, 97n257

LABOR DISPUTES
Atlas of industrial protest in Britain, 1750-1990, 97n146

LABOR LAWS & LEGISLATION
Covenants not to compete, 2d ed, 97n494
Employee duty of loyalty, 97n495
Employee duty of loyalty, 1996 suppl covering 1994, 97n496
Employment discrimination law, 3d ed, 98n530
European employment law, 96n252
International labor & employment laws, v.1, 99n564
Labor, employment, & the law, 98n515
Multistate gd to benefits law, 99n559

LABOR LEADERS
Biographical dict of European labor leaders, 97n151

LABOR MOVEMENT
ABC-CLIO companion to the American labor movement, 95n294
Historical dict of organized labor, 97n251
US labor movement, 97n250

LABOR SUPPLY
Main economic indicators: histl stats: prices, labour & wages 1962-91, 95n210
Yearbook of labour stats 1995, 54th ed, 97n261

LABOR UNIONS
ABC-CLIO companion to the American labor movement, 95n294
Directory of US labor orgs, 1994-95 ed, 96n260
Directory of US labor orgs, 1997 ed, 98n219
Historical dict of organized labor, 97n251
Profiles of American labor unions, 99n271

LAET, JEAN
Descriptive catalog of the music printed by Hubert Waelrant & Jan de Laet, 96n1266

LAKE STATES
Exploring the Great Lakes states through lit, 95n1123

LANDMARK YELLOW PAGES
Preservation yellow pages, rev ed, 98n975

LANDSCAPE GARDENING. See also GARDENING
Landscape architecture sourcebk, 98n1438
Plants that merit attention, v.2: shrubs, 97n1285
Southern gardener's bk of lists, 95n1527
Taylor's master gd to gardening, 96n1550
Time-saver standards for landscape architecture design & construction data, 99n883
Tropical look: an ency of dramatic landscape plants, 99n1344
What plant where, 96n1566

LANGUAGE DISORDERS
CHILDES/BIB: an annot bibliog of child lang & lang disorders, 1994 suppl, 95n334

LANGUAGE & LANGUAGES
Atlas of the world's langs, 95n1030
Bibliography on writing & written lang, 98n984
Cambridge ency of lang, 2d ed, 98n989
Career opportunities for bilinguals & multilinguals, 2d ed, 95n1031
Concise compendium of the world's langs, 97n813
Encyclopedia of lang & linguistics, 95n1024
Guide to world lang dicts, 99n890
Handbook of N American Indians, v.17: langs, 98n356
Key of it all, bk.1, 95n789
Key of it all, bk 2, 96n1121
Language & communication, 99n894
Languages of the world, new ed, 97n814
Linguistic cultures of the world, 98n990
Routledge dict of lang & linguistics, 97n812
Secret lang of dreams, 95n784
Southeast Asian langs & lits, 98n986
Student's dict of lang & linguistics, 98n987
World's writing systems, 97n816

LANGUAGE & LANGUAGES—COMPOSITION & EXERCISES
Encyclopedia of rhetoric & composition, 97n840

LAO LANGUAGE—DICTIONARIES—ENGLISH
Lao-English dict, 97n861

LARGE PRINT BOOKS
Complete dir of large print bks & serials 1998, 99n11
Oxford large print dict, 2d ed, 97n818
Random House Webster's large print thesaurus, 99n918

LATIN AMERICA. See also CENTRAL AMERICA; SOUTH AMERICA
Bibliographic gd to Latin American studies 1996, 98n139

Bibliography of Latin American & Caribbean bibliogs: annual report 1992-93, 95n168
Encyclopedia of Latin American hist & culture, 97n349
Encyclopedia of the inter-American system, 98n695
Handbook of leftist guerrilla grps in Latin America & the Caribbean, 97n609
Latin America on file, 96n155
Latin American classical composers, 97n1042
Latin American urbanization, 95n899
Social panorama of Latin America, 1994 ed, 96n153
South America, Central America, & the Caribbean 1997, 6th ed, 97n130
Statistical yrbk for Latin America & the Caribbean, 1994 ed, 96n154
Who's who in Latin America, 4th ed, 98n35

LATIN AMERICA—BUSINESS
Consumer Latin America 1993, 95n287
Cracking Latin America: a country-by-country gd to doing bus..., 95n288
Directory of importers in Latin America, 1994 ed, 96n291
Economic & social progress in Latin America 1995 report: overcoming volatility, 97n127
Economic panorama of Latin America 1995, 96n151
Economic survey of Latin America & the Caribbean 1995-96, 98n210
Encyclopedia of the N American Free Trade Agreement, 96n305
Hoover's masterlist of major Latin American cos 1996-97, 98n211
Latin America petroleum dir, 1995, 14th ed, 96n1834
Latin American markets, 1993-94 ed, 95n289
Major cos of Latin America 1996, 97n247

LATIN AMERICA—FOREIGN RELATIONS
Early US-Hispanic relations 1776-1860, 96n776
United States & Latin America, 98n697

LATIN AMERICA—HISTORY
Chronology of Hispanic-American hist, 96n550

LATIN AMERICAN FICTION
Index to translated short fiction by Latin American women in English lang anthologies, 98n1179

LATIN AMERICANS IN MOTION PICTURES
Contemporary Hollywood's negative Hispanic image, 95n1387

LATIN LANGUAGE—DICTIONARIES—ENGLISH
Dictionary of ecclesiastical Latin, 96n1118
Handbook of Christian Latin, 96n1115
Latin for the illiterati, 98n1039
Oxford Latin minidict, 96n1117
Pocket Oxford Latin dict, rev ed, 95n1087
Veni, vidi, vici, 96n1116

LATIN LITERATURE
Italian women writers, 95n1235

LATVIA
Historical dict of Latvia, 98n477

LAW. *See also* **LEGAL RESEARCH**
American Indian law deskbk, 2d ed, 99n561
Compilation of state & fed privacy laws, 1997 ed, 98n543
Courtroom hndbk on fed evidence, 1995 ed, 96n591
Critical legal studies, 97n492
Education & the law, 97n491
50 most influential women in American law, 98n513
Fund-Raising regulation, 98n539
Multistate gd to benefits law, 99n559
National survey of state laws, 2d ed, 99n565
Publishing law hndbk, 2d ed, 99n621
Ready ref: American justice, 97n489
Teen legal rights, 96n592

LAW—BIBLIOGRAPHY
Bibliographic gd to law 1996, 98n509
Bibliography of Va. legal hist before 1900, 2d ed, 99n548
Law & legal info dir, 9th ed, 98n523
Law bks & serials in print 1996, 97n481
Law lib ref shelf, 3d ed, 97n482
Lawyers' law bks, 3d ed, 98n512
Recommended pubs for legal research 1991, 95n596
Sport lawyer's gd to legal pers, 1995 suppl, 96n615

LAW—DICTIONARIES & ENCYCLOPEDIAS
Bieber's dict of legal abbrevs reversed, 95n592
Bieber's dict of legal citations, Prince's 5th ed, 98n516
Children, YAs, & the law, 99n551
Concise dict of medical-legal terms, 99n552
Constitutional law dict, v.2, suppl 1, 99n555
Dahl's law dict, 96n574
Dahl's law dict. an annot legal dict, Spanish-English/English-Spanish, 2d ed, 97n486
Dictionary of American & English law, 98n520
Dictionary of bus & legal terms: Russian-English/English-Russian, 96n575
Dictionary of law, 3d ed, 96n576
Dictionary of legal terms, 95n604
Dictionary of modern legal usage, 2d ed, 96n577
Elsevier's dict of European Community co/bus/financial law in English, Danish, & German, 98n517
Encyclopedia of civil rights in America, 99n588
Encyclopedia of Native American legal tradition, 99n388
Encyclopedia of words & phrases, legal maxims, 95n603
English-Russian dict of American criminal law, 99n553
Merriam-Webster's dict of law, 97n488
Modern dict for the legal profession, 1994 suppl, 96n580
Nonprofit law dict, 96n579
Real life dict of the law, 96n578
Tuttle dict of legal terms: English-Japanese, Japanese-English, 95n605
Tuttle dict of legal terms: English-Japanese, Japanese-English, rev ed, 96n613
West's ency of American law, 99n557
Wiley's English/Spanish & Spanish/English legal dict, 95n606
Wiley's English-Spanish, Spanish-English legal dict, 2d ed, 98n519

LAW—DIRECTORIES
ASTM dir of scientific & tech consultants & expert witnesses, 1997-98 ed, 99n1320
Martindale-Hubbell law dir on CD-ROM [CD-ROM], 96n584
Who's who in American law 1994-95, 95n602
Who's who in American law 1998-99, 99n550
World dir of human rights research & training insts, 3d ed, 97n518

LAW ENFORCEMENT
Applications in criminal analysis, 96n604
FBI: an annot bibliog & research gd, 95n619
Guide to fed funding for anti-crime programs, 2d ed, 98n553

LAW—EUROPE
Information sources in law, 2d ed, 98n533

LAW—INDEXES
Guide to public policy experts, 1997-98, 99n701
Index to law school theses & dissertations, 96n570
Index to legal citations & abbrevs, 2d ed, 95n593
Index to the House of Commons parliamentary papers on CD-ROM [CD-ROM], 99n571

LAW IN LITERATURE
Law in lit, 99n945

LAW—JAPAN
Japanese bus law in W langs, 99n546

LAW LIBRARIES
AALL ref bk, 96n593
Annotated catalog, S Texas College of law, special collections, 97n480

LAW OFFICES
Insider's gd to law firms, 2d ed, 96n582

LAW & POLITICS
Law & pols, 97n490
Supreme Court compendium, 95n612

LAW—POPULAR WORKS
Complete bk of personal legal forms, 2d ed, 98n541
Complete bk of small bus legal forms, 2d ed, 98n542
Consumer protection & the law, 97n487
Divorce yourself, 4th ed, 99n567
Law for the layperson, 2d ed, 98n511

LAW—QUOTATIONS
Quotable lawyer, rev ed, 99n572

LAWRENCE, D. H. (DAVID HERBERT)
D. H. Lawrence: a ref companion, 97n995

LAW REPORTS, DIGESTS, ETC.
Guide to the early reports of the Supreme Court of the US, 97n493
Noble's intl gd to the law reports, 97n483
Yearbook of the Intl Law Commission 1992, 96n614

LAW SCHOOLS
ABA official American Bar assn gd to approved law schools, 1999 ed, 99n558
Barron's gd to law schools, 11th ed, 96n581
Best law schools, 99n560
Directory of environmental law edu opportunities at American law schools, 98n558
Princeton Review student access gd to the best law schools, 96n585
REA's authoritative gd to law schools, rev ed, 96n586

LAWYERS
Insider's gd to law firms 1993-94, 95n608
Who's who in American law 1996-97, 98n514

LEAD
Lead poisoning prevention, 96n1866

LEADERSHIP
Leadership: quotations from the world's greatest motivators, 98n81

LEARNING DISABILITIES
BOSC dir: facilities for people with learning disabilities, 95n384
Complete learning disabilities dir, 1995/96, 96n374
Complete learning disabilities dir, 1998, 99n303
K & W gd to colleges for the learning disabled, 1998 ed, 98n290
Peterson's colleges with programs for students with learning disabilities, 96n341
Peterson's colleges with programs for students with learning disabilities or attention deficit disorders, 99n329

LEARNING INSTITUTIONS & SOCIETIES
Scholars' gd to humanities & social scis in the Soviet successor states, 95n165

LEBANON
Historical dict of Lebanon, 99n507
Who's who in Lebanon 1995-96, 13th ed, 96n165

LE DOEUFF, MICHELE
French feminist theory (2), 95n902

LEE, CHRISTOPHER
Christopher Lee & Peter Cushing & horror cinema, 96n1396

LEEWARD ISLANDS (WEST INDIES)
St. Kitts-Nevis, 96n172

LE FANU, JOSEPH SHERIDAN
J. Sheridan Le Fanu, 96n1256

LEFT INDEX
Left index, 97n61

LEGAL HISTORY
Bibliography of Va. legal hist before 1900, 2d ed, 99n548

LEGAL RESEARCH
Criminal justice info, 99n547
Criminal justice research in libs & on the Internet, 99n581
Critical legal studies, 97n492
Information sources in law, 2d ed, 98n533
Internet gd for the legal researcher, 2d ed, 98n535
Law & legal info dir, 9th ed, 98n523
Lawyer's research companion, 99n549
Legal info buyer's gd & ref manual 1997-98, 99n570
Legal research, 5th ed, 98n534
Legal researcher's desk ref 1996-97, 97n498
Searching the law: the states, 2d ed, 96n569
Sourcebook of local court & county record retrievers, 3d ed, 98n525

LEGENDS
Cassell dict of Norse myth & legend, 98n1259
Classical myths & legends in the Middle Ages & Renaissance, 99n1017
Goddesses, heroes, & shamans, 96n1347
Myth: myths & legends of the world explored, 97n1091

LEGISLATION
Congressional roll call 1996, 98n671
Official jl of the European Communities, v.38, English ed, 96n755
State legislative summary, 1994, 96n595

LEGISLATIVE BODIES
Encyclopedia of the American legislative system, 95n742
How to research Congress, 97n585
State legislative elections: voting patterns & demographics, 99n674
State legislative sourcebk 1996, 97n602
Women state & territorial legislators, 1895-1995, 97n601

LEGISLATIVE HISTORIES
Federal legislative hists, 96n717

LEGISLATORS
American leaders 1789-1994, 95n714
American legislative leaders in the West, 1911-94, 98n650
Committees in the US congress 1947-92, v.2, 96n733
Election results dir 1997, 98n663
Protocol: a hndbk for legislative staff, 98n677
Thaddeus Stevens papers, 95n746
Vital stats on Congress 1995-96, 98n676
Women of the US congress, 95n716

LEISURE
Favorite hobbies & pastimes, 95n801

LEPROSY
Annotated bibliog on leprosy, 99n1472

LESBIANISM IN MOTION PICTURES
Ultimate gd to lesbian & gay film & video, 97n1126

LESBIANS. See also GAYS; HOMOSEXUALITY
Alyson almanac, 1994-95 ed, 95n852
Bent gd to gay/lesbian Canada 1994, 95n853
Cassell's queer companion, 96n864
Completely queer: the gay & lesbian ency, 99n757
Ferrari's places for women, Apr 94-Apr 95, 95n855
Ferrari's places of interest, Apr 94-Apr 95, 95n856
Gay 100, 96n865
Gay almanac, 97n677
Gay & lesbian address bk, 96n53
Gay & lesbian biog, 98n782
Gay & lesbian movement, 97n681
Gay & lesbian online, 97n676
Gay & lesbian online, rev ed, 98n781
Images in the dark: an ency of gay & lesbian film & video, 95n1374
Inn places 1994, 95n857
Lesbian almanac, 97n679
Lesbian & gay liberation in Canada, 97n680
Lesbians in print, 97n678
Queer theory, 99n758
St. James Press gay & lesbian almanac, 99n759
Strength in nos: a lesbian, gay, & bisexual resource, 97n703

LESBIANS' WRITINGS
Gay & lesbian lit, 95n1111
Gay & lesbian literary heritage, 97n888
Women playwrights of diversity, 98n1106

LESOTHO
Lesotho, rev ed, 98n107

LETTER WRITING
Forms of address, 96n311

LEWIS, C.S.
C. S. Lewis readers' ency, 99n1071

LIBEL & SLANDER
Associate Pr stylebk & libel manual, 6th ed, 98n874

LIBERIA
Cultures of the World, 99n84
Liberia, 96n118

LIBRARIANS
American lib dir 1994-95, 95n638
American lib dir 1996-97, 98n572
International biog dir of natl archivists, documentalists, & librarians, 98n574
Librarian's legal companion, 95n646

LIBRARIES. See also SPECIFIC TYPES, E.G., PUBLIC LIBRARIES
American art dir 1997-98, 99n871
American lib dir 1994-95, 95n638
American lib dir 1996-97, 98n572
Articles describing archives & ms collections in the US, 98n577
Big bk of lib grant money, 95n643
Business lib & how to use it, 6th ed, 97n530
College students research companion, 99n610
Directory of medical health care libs in the UK & Republic of Ireland 1997-8, 10th ed, 99n611

Encyclopedia of lib hist, 95n637
Grants for libs & info servs, 95n639
International dir of serials specialists, 96n655
Librarian's companion, 2d ed, 97n532
Librarian's legal companion, 95n646
Library bldgs consultant list, 1993, 95n659
Symbols of American libs, 14th ed, 95n645
Whole lib hndbk 2, 96n624
World of learning 1999, 49th ed, 99n295

LIBRARIES—AUTOMATION
Browsing in info systems, 96n644
Directory of lib automation software, systems, & servs, 96n643
Directory of lib automation software, systems, & servs, 99n609

LIBRARIES, CANADA
Directory of Canadian lib & info sci consultants, 96n642
Guide to the Fonds d'Archives & collections in the holdings of the York Univ Archives, 96n653

LIBRARIES—SPECIAL COLLECTIONS
Audio bk breakthrough, 95n664
Building a popular sci lib collection for high school & adult learners, 96n660
Checklist of painters c1200-1994, 2d ed, 96n652
Directory of literary societies & author collections, 95n1106
Directory of rare bk & special collections in the UK & the Republic of Ireland, 2d ed, 98n588
Guide to collections on Paraguay in the US, 96n551
Guide to the Fonds d'Archives & collections in the holdings of the York Univ Archives, 96n653
Local hist collections in libs, 96n659
Mexican-American War of 1846-48, 96n657
Special collections in children's lit, 96n661
World dir of bus info libs, 97n548

LIBRARY CATALOGS
Science & tech: a purchase gd for libs 1995, 97n1234

LIBRARY CONSULTANTS
Directory of Canadian lib & info sci consultants, 96n642

LIBRARY OF CONGRESS
Unveiling Indonesia, 98n114

LIBRARY ORIENTATION
Business lib & how to use it, 6th ed, 97n530

LIBRARY RESOURCES
Canadiana in US repositories: a preliminary gd, 96n136
Find it fast, 3d ed, 95n78
Internet-Plus dir of express lib servs, 99n596
Library servs for off-campus & distance educ, 97n521
Scholars' gd to Washington, DC, for Russian, Central Eurasian, & Baltic studies, 95n164
Scholars' gd to Washington, D.C., media collections, 95n938

LIBRARY SCIENCE
AALL ref bk, 96n593

ARL stats 1994-95, 97n527
ASIS thesaurus of info sci & librarianship, 95n636
Bowker annual lib & bk trade almanac, 1994, 95n644
Bowker annual lib & bk trade almanac, 1995, 96n623
Bowker annual lib & bk trade almanac, 1996, 97n528
Bowker annual lib & bk trade almanac 1997, 98n576
Concise dict of lib & info sci, 97n525
Encyclopedia of lib hist, 95n637
Encyclopedia of lib & info sci, v.57, 98n569
Encyclopedia of lib & info sci, v.58, 97n524
Encyclopedia of lib & info sci, v.59, 98n570
Encyclopedia of lib & info sci, v.60, 99n593
Encyclopedia of lib & info sci, v.61, 99n594
Harrod's librarians' glossary, 8th ed, 97n526
Internet & lib & info servs, 98n582
Libraries Unltd professional collection CD 1995 [CD-ROM], 97n523
Library lit 1995, 97n529
LISA plus [CD-ROM], 96n625
National gd to funding for lib & info serv, 97n531
SUPER LCCS CD [CD-ROM], 96n633
Whole lib hndbk 2, 96n624

LIBRETTISTS
Nineteenth-Century lit criticism, v.50, 97n911
Nineteenth-Century lit criticism annual cum title index for 1996, 97n914

LIBRETTOS
Book of world-famous libretti, 95n1406

LIBYA
Historical dict of Libya, 3d ed, 99n480

LICENSES
EPM licensing letter sourcebk, 1997 ed, 97n165
National dir of state bus licensing & regulation, 96n194
State medical licensure gdlines 1998, 99n1449

LIECHTENSTEIN
Liechtenstein, 95n159

LIFE SCIENCES
Encyclopedia of life scis, 97n1268
Magill's survey of sci [CD-ROM], 95n1502
Magill's survey of sci: life sci series suppl, 99n1356
McGraw-Hill dict of biosci, 98n1440
Notable women in the life scis, 97n1231
World databases in biosci & pharmacology, 97n1241

LIFE SKILLS
Authoritative gd to self-help bks, 95n774
Finding help: a ref gd for personal concerns, 97n55
Using bibliotherapy in clinical practice, 95n772

LILIES (FLOWER)
Gardener's gd to growing lilies, 96n1572
Trilliums, 98n1448

LINCOLN, ABRAHAM
Of the people, by the people, for the people, & other quotations by Abraham Lincoln, 97n67

LINGUISTICS. *See also* **LANGUAGE & LANGUAGES**
Atlas of the langs & ethnic communities of S Asia, 99n101
Concise Oxford dict of linguistics, 99n893
Dictionary of phonetics & phonology, 97n819
Diglossia: a comprehensive bibliog 1960-90, 95n1027
Educator's word frequency gd, 97n817
Encyclopedia of lang & linguistics, 95n1024
Routledge dict of lang & linguistics, 97n812
Student's dict of lang & linguistics, 98n987

LINGUISTS
Twentieth-Century literary criticism, v.61, 97n922

LISPECTOR, CLARICE
Clarice Lispector: a bio-bibliog, 95n1225

LISTSERVS (INTERNET). *See also* **NEWSGROUPS**
CyberHound's gd to Internet discussion groups, 98n1584
Mecklermedia's official Internet World Internet yellow pages, 1996 ed, 98n1587

LITERACY
First dict of cultural literacy, 2d ed, 97n296

LITERARY AGENTS
Guide to literary agents, 1997, 98n866

LITERARY LANDMARKS
Literary gd & companion to S England, rev ed, 99n1065

LITERARY MOVEMENTS
Contemporary literary criticism, v.87, 97n896
Nineteenth-Century lit criticism, v.52, 97n913
Twentieth-Century literary criticism, v.58, 97n919

LITERARY PRIZES
Avisson bk of contests & prize competitions for poets, 98n864
Awards dir 1993-94, 95n1226
Booktalking the award winners 3, 98n1082
Booktalking the award winners: children's retrospective volume, 98n1081
Children's bks: awards & prizes, 1996 ed, 97n932
Contemporary literary criticism, v.87, 97n896
Grants & awards available to American writers, 30th ed, 99n830
Phoenix award of the children's lit assn 1990-94, 98n1092

LITERARY THEORY
Recent work in critical theory, 1989-95, 97n880

LITERATURE. *See also* **CRITICISM**
Benét's reader's ency, 4th ed, 98n843
Bibliography of sources in Christianity & the arts, 97n1206
Classical studies, 97n461
Cyclopedia of literary characters, rev ed, 99n959
Cyclopedia of world authors, 3d ed, 98n1059
Dictionary of Italian lit, rev ed, 97n1010
Dictionary of literary biog yrbk: 1995, 97n899
Dictionary of literary biog yrbk: 1996, 99n970
Directory of literary societies & author collections, 95n1106
Encyclopedia of allegorical lit, 97n890
Encyclopedia of apocalyptic lit, 97n893
Encyclopedia of satirical lit, 97n892
Essay & general lit index 1990-94, 96n81
Fools & jesters in lit, art, & hist, 99n951
Great women writers, 95n906
Illustrated dict of little-known words from literary classics, 96n1148
Larousse dict of literary characters, 95n1105
Literally entitled, 97n891
Literary criticism index, 2d ed, 95n1114
Literature & gerontology, 96n845
Literature criticism from 1400 to 1800, v.28, 97n901
Literature criticism from 1400 to 1800, v.29, 97n902
Literature criticism from 1400 to 1800, v.30, 97n903
Literature criticism from 1400 to 1800, v.31, 97n904
Lives & works in the arts from the renaissance to the 20th century, 98n847
Magill index to critical surveys, rev ed, 96n1161
Magill index to Masterplots: cum indexes, 1963-93, 95n1115
Magill's survey of world lit, 97n905
Masterplots, 2d ed, 97n906
Masterplots fiction CD-ROM, rev ed [CD-ROM], 95n1112
Merriam-Webster's ency of lit, 96n1146
New York Public Lib's bks of the century, 97n882
Nineteenth-Century lit criticism, v.46, 96n1158
Nineteenth-Century lit criticism, v.47, 97n908
Nineteenth-Century lit criticism, v.48, 97n909
Nineteenth-Century lit criticism, v.49, 97n910
Nineteenth-Century lit criticism, v.50, 97n911
Nineteenth-Century lit criticism, v.51, 97n912
Nineteenth-Century lit criticism, v.52, 97n913
Nineteenth-Century lit criticism, v.61, 99n973
Nineteenth-Century lit criticism, v.62, 99n974
Nineteenth-Century lit criticism annual cum title index for 1996, 97n914
Novels for students, v.3, 99n1013
Novels for students, v.4, 99n1014
Problems in literary research, 4th ed, 99n972
Proverbs in world lit, 98n1254
Reader's adviser on CD-ROM [CD-ROM], 97n11
Reader's catalog, 2d ed, 98n8
Recommended reading: 500 classics reviewed, 97n883
Reference gd to world lit, 2d ed, 97n917
Romantic movement, 97n884
Short stories for students, v.3, 99n1015
Short stories for students, v.4, 99n1016
Twayne's masterwork studies on CD-ROM [CD-ROM], 98n1074
Vampire readings, 99n1035

LITERATURE, BLACK AUTHORS
Modern black writers: suppl, 96n1157
Schomberg Center gd to black lit from the 18th century to the present, 97n918

LITERATURE—DICTIONARIES & ENCYCLOPEDIAS
C. S. Lewis readers' ency, 99n1071
Dictionary of literary terms & literary theory, 4th ed, 99n960
Encyclopedia of folklore & lit, 99n962

Encyclopedia of the novel, 99n963
Merriam-Webster's reader's hndbk, 99n964

LITERATURE, HISPANIC AUTHORS
Best of the Latino heritage, 98n358
Encyclopedia of Latin American lit, 98n1178
Hispanic lit criticism, 95n1242
Index to Spanish lang short stories in anthologies, 95n1241
Jewish writers of Latin America, 98n1180
Masterpieces of Latino lit, 95n1243
Modern Latin-American fiction writers, 2d series, 96n1258

LITERATURE & HISTORY
Literature & its times, 98n1072

LITERATURE—HISTORY & CRITICISM
H. L. Mencken: a descriptive bibliog, 99n1027
Literature connections to world hist, K-6, 99n512
Literature connections to world hist, 7-12, 99n513
World lit criticism suppl, 99n983

LITERATURE, MEDIEVAL
Classical & medieval lit criticism, v.14, 96n1149
Classical myths & legends in the Middle Ages & Renaissance, 99n1017
Literature criticism from 1400-1800, v.27, 96n1156

LITERATURE—MISCELLANEA
Writer's companion, 97n924

LITERATURE, MODERN
Contemporary literary criticism, v.84, 96n1152
Contemporary literary criticism, v.85, 96n1153
Contemporary literary criticism, v.86, 97n895
Contemporary literary criticism, v.87, 97n896
Contemporary literary criticism, v.88, 97n897
Contemporary literary criticism, v.89, 97n898
Contemporary literary criticism, v.90, 98n1068
Contemporary literary criticism, v.100, 99n966
Contemporary literary criticism, v.101, 99n967
Contemporary literary criticism, v.102, 99n968
Contemporary literary criticism, v.103, 99n969
Contemporary literary criticism annual cum index for 1995, 96n1151
Contemporary literary criticism yrbk 1996, v.99, 99n965
Contemporary Spanish novel, 97n1014
Guide to serial bibliogs for modern lits, 2d ed, 97n885
Literary almanac, 98n1071
Literature criticism from 1400-1800, v.27, 96n1156
Modern American lit, v.6, 4th ed, 99n1048
Modern British novel of the left, 99n1068
Modern ency of E Slavic, Baltic, & Eurasian lits, v.10, 98n1170
Modern women writers, 97n907
Oxford companion to 20th-century lit in English, 98n1073
Post-Colonial lits in English: Australia, 1970-92, 97n1002
Post-Colonial lits in English: SE Asia, New Zealand, & the Pacific, 1970-92, 97n1013
Reader's gd to 20th-century writers, 97n916
Twentieth-Century literary criticism, v.56, 96n1159
Twentieth-Century literary criticism, v.57, 96n1160
Twentieth-Century literary criticism, v.58, 97n919
Twentieth-Century literary criticism, v.59, 97n920
Twentieth-Century literary criticism, v.60, 97n921
Twentieth-Century literary criticism, v.61, 97n922
Twentieth-Century literary criticism, v.70, 99n980
Twentieth-Century literary criticism, v.71, 99n981
Twentieth-Century literary criticism, v.72, 99n982
Twentieth-Century literary criticism annual cum title index for 1996, 97n923

LITERATURE—YOUNG ADULT
Masterplots 2: juvenile & YA lit series suppl, 98n1085

LITHUANIA
Historical dict of Lithuania, 98n478

LITHUANIAN LANGUAGE—DICTIONARIES—ENGLISH
Lithuanian dict, 97n862
Lithuanian-English/English-Lithuanian concise dict, 95n1088

LITTLE BIGHORN, BATTLE OF THE
Custer & the battle of Little Bighorn, 98n441

LITURGICS
Liturgical dict of E Christianity, 95n1467

LIZARDS
Handbook of lizards, 96n1639

LLOYD, HAROLD
Harold Lloyd: a bio-bibliog, 95n1343

LOBBYING
Lobbying, PACs, & campaign finance, 96n740

LOCAL GOVERNMENT
Cassell multilingual dict of local govt & bus, 95n750
Government dir of addresses & telephone nos 1995, 3d ed, 96n732
International hndbk of local & regional govt, 95n709
Sourcebook of local court & county records retrievers, 95n611

LOCAL HISTORY
Genealogical & local hist bks in print: gen ref & world resources v., 5th ed, 98n359
Local hist collections in libs, 96n659

LOCAL LAWS
National survey of state laws, 2d ed, 99n565

LOCK, GEORGE
Victorian yellowbacks & paperbacks, 1849-1905, v.2, 96n1224

LOCOMOTIVES
Guide to N American steam locomotives, 95n1791

LOGOTYPE
Living logos, 95n322

LONDON (ENGLAND)
Biographical dict of actors, actresses, musicians, dancers, managers...v.15, 95n1411

Biographical dict of actors, actresses, musicians, dancers, managers...v.16, 95n1412
London, 97n116
Sources of London English, 97n831

LONDON PHILHARMONIC ORCHESTRA
London Philharmonic discography, 98n1204

LOS ANGELES (CALIF.)
Los Angeles A to Z, 99n91

LOS ANGELES DODGERS (BASEBALL TEAM)
Dodgers ency, 99n716

LOUISIANA
Historical atlas of La., 96n440
Louisiana almanac, 1997-98 ed, 98n100

LOUISIANA CREOLE LANGUAGE
Dictionary of La Creole, 99n935

LOVE
Sex & love quotations, 96n889

LUMBEE INDIANS
Lumbee Indians: an annot bibliog, 95n431

LUTHERAN CHURCH
Hermann Sasse: a bibliog, 97n1168

LUXEMBOURG
Historical dict of Luxembourg, 97n119
Luxembourg, rev ed, 98n135

LUXEMBURG, ROSA
Rosa Luxemburg & Emma Goldman: a bibliog, 98n637

LUX RADIO THEATRE (RADIO PROGRAM)
Lux presents Hollywood, 96n1390

LUX VIDEO THEATRE (TELEVISION PROGRAM)
Lux presents Hollywood, 96n1390

LYNCHING
Lynching & vigilantism in the US, 98n547

LYRICISTS
Songwriters: a biogl dict with discographies, 99n1117

MACARTHUR, DOUGLAS
General Douglas MacArthur, 1880-1964: historiography & annot bibliog, 95n536

MACEDONIA
Historical dict of the Republic of Macedonia, 99n495

MACHINERY
Machine design data hndbk, 95n1638
Machinists' ready ref, 8th ed, 96n1675
McGraw-Hill machining & metalworking hndbk, 95n1639
McGraw-Hill machining & metalworking hndbk, 2d ed, 99n1413

MACINTOSH (COMPUTER). *See also* **COMPUTERS; MICROCOMPUTERS**
Macintosh bible, 5th ed, 95n1696

MADAGASCAR
Madagascar, 95n119

MADISON, JAMES
James Madison & the American nation 1751-1836, 96n507

MADRID
Madrid, 98n138

MAGHREB (AFRICA)
Maghreb, 99n97

MAGIC
Encyclopaedia of Celtic wisdom, 96n788
Man, myth & magic, new ed, 96n1348
Wizards & sorcerers, 98n716

MAGNOLIAS
World of magnolias, 95n1551

MAHLER, GUSTAV
Gustav Mahler's symphonies, 98n1248

MAIL-ORDER BUSINESS
Catalog of catalogs 3, 95n226
Catalog of catalogs 5, 98n183
Catalogue of Canadian catalogues, 96n249
Directory of mail order catalogs, 1995, 9th ed, 96n219
Gardening by mail, 4th ed, 95n1525

MAINE
Connecticut, Maine, Mass., [&] R.I.,: atlas of histl county boundaries, 96n438

MAINTENANCE
Glossary of reliability & maintenance terms, 98n1497

MALAWI
Malawi, 2d ed, 96n119

MALI
Historical dict of Mali, 3d ed, 97n99
Mali, 99n98

MALRAUX, ANDRE
Andre Malraux, 96n1253

MALTA—BIBLIOGRAPHY
Malta, rev ed, 99n134

MAMMALS. *See also* **ANIMALS**
Encyclopedia of mammals, 98n1469
Encyclopedia of mammals, 2d ed, 99n1391
Handbook of mammals of the S-central states, 96n1630
Larger animals of E Africa, 98n1470

Mammals of New Guinea, rev ed, 96n1631
Mammals of the SW Pacific & Moluccan Islands, 96n1632
Mammals of Va., 99n1393
National Audubon Society field gd to N American mammals, rev ed, 97n1294
National Audubon Society 1st field gd: mammals, 99n1392

MAN
Encyclopedia plus of world problems & human potential, 4th ed [CD-ROM], 98n86
History of humanity, v.1, 96n568
History of humanity, v.2, 97n479
History of humanity, v.3, 98n507
Lands & peoples, 98n95

MANAGEMENT. *See also* TOTAL QUALITY MANAGEMENT
Business info sources, 95n179
Business pers index, v.38: Aug 1995-July 1996, 98n167
Cabell's dir of publishing opportunities in mgmt & mktg, 6th ed, 96n670
Critical gd to mgmt training videos & selected multimedia, 1996, 97n266
Dictionary of bus & mgmt, 95n187
Every manager's gd to bus processes, 97n267
Management consulting [CD-ROM], 98n245
Manager's desk ref, 2d ed, 97n265
McGraw-Hill ency of quality terms & concepts, 96n284
Nonprofit manager's resource dir, 98n244
Profiles in bus & mgmt [CD-ROM], 97n221
Ultimate bus lib, 98n148

MANAGEMENT INFORMATION SYSTEMS
Business multimedia explained, 98n242

MAN—MIGRATIONS
Penguin atlas of Diasporas, 98n807

MANNERS & CUSTOMS
Culturgrams, 95n99

MANUFACTURERS
Business stats of the US, 1995 ed, 97n176
CDs, super glue, & salsa: how everyday products are made, 96n221
CDs, super glue, & salsa, series 2, 97n193
Directory of Canadian manufacturers [BOSS 1994], 95n274
Electronic materials & processes hndbk, 2d ed, 95n1614
Encyclopedia of American industries, 95n236
European private label dir, 97n241
Extractives, manufacturing, & servs, 98n162
Guide to the best products, 1994, 95n224
How products are made, 95n237
How products are made, v.3, 99n189
How to find info about divisions, subsidiaries & products, 5th ed, 96n203
Industrial commodity stats yrbk 1994, 97n195
International yrbk of industrial stats 1996, 97n196
International yrbk of industrial stats 1997, 98n194
Jane's intl defense dir 1997, 97n218
Manufactures phone bk USA 1997, 98n195

Manufacturing worldwide, 97n197
Market share reporter 1998, 8th ed, 99n190
Thomas register of American manufacturers, 1997, 87th ed, 98n196
Thomas register on CD-ROM, 1997 [CD-ROM], 98n197
World engineering industries & automation, 97n199

MANUFACTURING PROCESSES
Manufacturing processes ref gd, 96n1670
Metalworking in Africa S of the Sahara, 96n1668

MANUSCRIPTS. *See also* LIBRARIES—SPECIAL COLLECTIONS; ARCHIVES
Articles describing archives & ms collections in the US, 98n577
Beinecke Lesser Antilles collection at Hamilton College, 95n171
Catalogue of medieval & Renaissance mss in the Houghton Lib, Harvard Univ, v.1, 97n546
Guide to British naval papers in N America, 96n679
Guide to Central American collections in the US, 96n152
Guide to collections on Paraguay in the US, 96n551
Guide to Indian mss, 95n131
Guide to mss & docs in the British Isles relating to Africa, v.1, 95n111
Guides to archives & ms collections in the US, 95n523
Holiness mss, 95n1458
Index of English literary mss, v.4, pt.3, 95n1202
Manuscript material, correspondence, & graphic material in the Fiske Icelandic Collection, 95n158
Medieval & Renaissance mss in the Walters Art Gallery, 99n600
Revealing docs: a gd to African American ms sources..., 95n414

MAORI LANGUAGE
Te Matatiki: contemporary Maori words, 97n863

MAPS—BIBLIOGRAPHY
Bibliographic gd to maps & atlases 1996, 98n391

MARBLES
Greenberg's gd to marbles, 2d ed, 97n786

MARC FORMATS
USMARC format for bibliographic data, 1994 ed, 96n634

MARCHING BANDS
Marching band hndbk, 2d ed, 96n1290

MARIJUANA
Marijuana law, 2d ed, 98n527

MARINE ANIMALS
Practical gd to the marine animals of northeastern N America, 99n1394

MARINE BIOLOGY
Oceanographic & marine resources: 1960-Jan 1997 [CD-ROM], 98n1616

MARINE FAUNA
Coral reef animals of the Indo-Pacific, 97n1295

MARINE INVERTEBRATES
Guide to marine invertebrates, 95n1594

MARINE POLLUTION
Environmental hazards: marine pollution, 95n1778

MARITIME LAW
Law of the sea: a bibliog on the law of the sea, 1968-88, 95n594
Law of the sea: a select bibliog 1993, 95n595

MARKETING
American marketplace, 3d ed, 98n246
American women, 98n247
Americans 55 & older, 99n279
Asian markets, 4th ed, 97n234
Authentic Jane Williams' home school mrkt gd, 97n280
Bond markets, 1995 ed, 96n292
Book of European forecasts, 2d ed, 97n238
Business sales leads, 1997 ed [CD-ROM], 98n248
Cabell's dir of publishing opportunities in mgmt & mktg, 6th ed, 96n670
China mktg data & stats, 99n242
Consumer Asia 1998, 99n215
Consumer Canada 1996, 97n268
Consumer China 1998, 99n216
Consumer Middle East 1998, 99n217
Consumer Europe 1994, 95n278
Consumer Europe 1998/9, 14th ed, 99n249
Consumer intl 1995, 95n248
Consumer Japan 1993, 95n269
Consumer Latin America 1997, 4th ed, 98n209
Consumer Mexico 1996, 97n269
Consumer sales leads, 1997 ed [CD-ROM], 98n249
Consumer South Africa 1995, 97n270
Consumer USA 1996, 97n271
Data sources for bus & market analysis, 4th ed, 96n296
Dictionary of mktg & advertising, 96n304
Directory of import regimes, pt.1, 96n289
Directory of import regimes, pt.2, 96n290
Directory of intl bus, 96n233
Editor & Publisher market gd 1994, 96n976
Editor & Publisher market gd 1994 [CD-ROM], 96n977
European drinks mktg dir, 4th ed, 97n240
European food mktg dir, 1994, 95n279
European mktg data & stats 1996, 31st ed, 97n273
European mktg data & stats 1998, 33d ed, 99n254
External trade monthly stats, 96n293
Fashion & merchandising fads, 95n987
Food & beverage market place, 1996, 97n1249
Foreign trade stats of Asia & the Pacific 1988-92, 96n295
Generation X: the YA market, 98n256
International advertising & mktg info sources, 96n299
International mktg data & stats 1994, 95n252
International mktg data & stats 1998, 99n224
International mktg forecasts, 99n225
Latin American advertising, mktg, & media sourcebk, 96n301
Living logos, 95n322
Market share & bus rankings worldwide [CD-ROM], 98n254
Mid-Youth market, 98n261
Rand McNally 1994 commercial atlas & mktg gd, 95n326
Shopping for a better world, 95n225
Trade data elements dir: UNTDED 1993, v.1, 96n306
Trade data elements dir v.3, 97n277
World country analyst [CD-ROM], 98n205
World dir of mktg info sources, 99n211
World econ factbk 1997/98, 5th ed, 99n233
World market share reporter 1995-96, 96n240
World mktg data & stats 1996 on CD-ROM, 2d ed [CD-ROM], 97n281
World mktg data & stats on CD-ROM [CD-ROM], 99n236
World trade almanac 1996-97, 97n207
World trade almanac & the dict of intl trade, 1997 ed [CD-ROM], 97n208
World trade atlas: US data, Mar 1994 [CD-ROM], 95n327

MARKETING RESEARCH
Dictionary of social & market research, 98n253
Handbook of mktg scales, 95n321
Market info 1995/96, 97n275

MARKET SURVEYS
Markets of the US for bus planners, 97n276

MARRIAGE
Encyclopedia of marriage & the family, 96n863
Marriage, family, & relationships, 96n862

MARRIAGE RECORDS
Index to US marriage record, 1691-1850 [CD-ROM], 99n405

MARTIAL ARTS
Encyclopedia of martial arts movies, 96n1380
Tuttle dict of the martial arts of Korea, China, & Japan, 97n659

MARTINIQUE
Martinique, 96n171

MARYLAND
Butterflies of Delmarva, 95n1579
Freshwater fishes of the Carolinas, Va., Md., & Dela., 95n1588

MASKS
Masks from antiquity to the modern era, 99n363

MASSACHUSETTS
Connecticut, Maine, Mass., [&] R.I.,: atlas of histl county boundaries, 96n438

MASS MEDIA. See also COMMUNICATIONS
ABC-CLIO companion to the media in America, 96n964
Bacon's bus media dir 1994, 95n933
Bacon's intl media dir 1996, 97n760
Dictionary of communication & media studies, 3d ed, 95n939
Dictionary of communication & media studies, 4th ed, 98n857

Dictionary of media literacy, 98n856
Graduate programs in journalism & mass communications, 98n309
History of the mass media in the US, 99n820
Hudson's Washington news media contacts dir 1994, 95n935
Mass media in the Middle East, 95n936
Media in African & Africa in the media, 98n853
National Hispanic media dir, 1997, 98n861
Plunkett's entertainment & media industry almanac, 99n827
Political commentators in the US in the 20th century, 98n862
Press freedom & dvlpmt, 98n850
Violence & the media, 97n748
Webster's new world dict of media & communications, rev ed, 98n858
Who's who in the media & communications 1998-99, 99n819
Willings press gd 1998, 124th ed, 99n824
Writer's ency, 3d ed, 97n750

MASTER OF BUSINESS ADMINISTRATION DEGREE
Peterson's gd to MBA programs 1998, 98n160

MATERIAL AGENCIES
International policy insts around the Pacific Rim, 99n697

MATERIALS SCIENCE
ASM engineered materials ref bk, 2d ed, 95n1623
ASM hndbk: comprehensive index, 95n1624
ASM hndbk: comprehensive index [CD-ROM], 95n1625
Concise metals engineering data bk, 99n1409
CRC materials sci & engineering hndbk, 2d ed, 95n1630
Encyclopedia of advanced materials, 96n1664
Encyclopedia of materials sci & engineering, v.3, 95n1631
Engineered materials hndbk, 96n1665
English-German dict of materials & process engineering, 96n1666
Fatigue data bk, 97n1308
Guide to engineering materials producers, 95n1628
Pearson's hndbk desk ed, 98n1492
Woldman's engineering alloys, 8th ed, 96n1671

MATERNAL HEALTH SERVICES
Family planning & reproductive health servs in Ghana, 95n849

MATHEMATICIANS
Combined membership list 1995-96, 96n1825
Combined membership list 1996-97, 97n1412
Mathematical scis professional dir 1997, 98n1625
Notable mathematicians, 99n1541
World dir of mathematicians 1998, 11th ed, 99n1545

MATHEMATICS
Assistantships & graduate fellowships in the mathematical scis, 1993-94, 95n1738
Assistantships & graduate fellowships in the mathematical scis, 1996-97, 98n1624
Assistantships & graduate fellowships in the mathematical scis, 1997-98, 99n1540
Companion ency of the hist & philosophy of the mathematical scis, 95n1740

CompuMath citation index 1993. 2d semiannual, 95n1739
CRC standard mathematical tables & formulae, 30th, 97n1413
Dictionary of mathematics terms, 2d ed, 96n1826
Elsevier's dict of computer sci & math in English, German, French, & Russian, 97n1366
Encyclopaedia of mathematics, v.10, 96n1827
Engineering mathematics hndbk, 99n1544
Mathematical scis professional dir 1995, 96n1828
Mathematically speaking, 99n1328
MathSci disc [CD-ROM], 97n1414
McGraw-Hill dict of mathematics, 98n1626
Memorabilia mathematica: the philomath's quotation bk, 95n1741
"Out of the mouths of mathematicians", 95n1742
Standard math interactive [CD-ROM], 99n1543
Words of mathematics, 95n1743
World databases in physics & mathematics, 96n1788

MATHIAS, WILLIAM
William Mathias, 96n1279

MATISSE, HENRI
Henri Matisse: a bio-bibliog, 95n997
Henri Matisse: a gd to research, 97n805

MAUGHAM, W. SOMERSET
Companion to the characters in the fiction & drama of W. Somerset Maugham, 97n996
William Somerset Maugham ency, 98n1160

MAURITANIA
Historical dict of Mauritania, 2d ed, 97n100

MAUSOLEUMS
Going out in style: the architecture of eternity, 98n973

MAYA LANGUAGE
Itzaj Maya-Spanish-English dict, 98n1040

MCCARTHY, JOSEPH
Encyclopedia of the McCarthy era, 97n591

MCCLELLAND & STEWART LIMITED
Bibliography of McClelland & Stewart imprints, 1909-1985, 95n677

MCDONALD'S (RESTAURANT)
McDonald's collectibles, 98n898

MEASURING INSTRUMENTS
Economist desk companion, rev ed, 95n79

MECHANICAL ENGINEERING
Dictionary of mechanical engineering, 4th ed, 97n1310
Mechanical engineering ref manual, 9th ed, 95n1637
Mechanical engineer's ref bk, 12th ed, 96n1673
Power industry abbreviator, 96n1672

MEDAL OF HONOR
Medal of honor recipients 1863-1994, 96n689

MEDIA PROGRAMS (EDUCATION)
Media review digest, v. 26, 1996, 97n9
School lib media annual 1995, v.13, 96n651

MEDICAL CARE. *See also* **HEALTH**
American health care in transition, 98n1503
Complete dir of nursing facilities for younger adults with chronic physical disabilities, 1994, 96n855
Dartmouth atlas of health care, 99n1414
Directory of health care professionals 1995, 96n1686
Health care bk of lists, 95n1652
Health care reform terms, 2d ed, 95n1657
Health care terms, healthy communities ed, 98n1511
Health industry quicksource, 97n1313
Health stats, 2d ed, 98n1505
Healthcare resource & ref gd, 95n1653
HMO/PPO dir 1996, 97n1323
Major state health care policies, 99n1433
National dir of AIDS care 1994-95, 95n1676
National health dir, 1996, 97n1324
National healthlines dir 1994, 95n1649
Plunkett's health care industry almanac, 97n1329
Plunketts health care industry almanac 1997-98, 99n1435
US health policy groups, 96n1691
Women's health concerns sourcebk, 99n1438

MEDICAL EDUCATION
Best medical schools, 99n1450
Continuing medical educ dir 1996-97, 98n1532
Directory of medical & dental schools worldwide, 6th ed, 96n1687
Directory of schools for alternative & complementary health care, 99n1448
Graduate medical educ dir 1997-98, 98n1535
Health professions educ dir 1997-98, 98n1512
Health professions educ dir, 1998-99, 99n1425
International hndbk of medical educ, 95n1667
Peterson's gd to nursing programs, 96n356
Peterson's gd to nursing programs, 99n1478
Princeton Review student access gd to the best medical schools, 96n1705
REA's authoritative gd to medical & dental schools, 96n1706

MEDICAL ETHICS
Code of medial ethics: current opinions with annots, 1996-97 ed, 98n1537
Encyclopedia of bioethics, rev ed, 96n1429

MEDICAL INSTRUMENTS & APPARATUS
Medical device register 1994: intl v, 95n1660
Szycher's dict of medical devices, 97n1332

MEDICAL LAWS & LEGISLATION
Issue briefs: 1997 annual ed, 99n1432

MEDICAL LIBRARIES
Directory of medical health care libs in the UK & Republic of Ireland 1997-8, 10th ed, 99n611

MEDICAL PERSONNEL
America's top medical & human servs jobs, 2d ed, 95n310
Bibliography of medical & biomedical biog, 2d ed, 96n1696
Peterson's job opportunities in health care 1995, 96n1689

MEDICAL POLICY
Dictionary of medical sociology, 98n1524
Encyclopedia of US biomedical policy, 97n1330
Health care crisis in the US, 98n1506
National health dir, 1996, 97n1324

MEDICAL REHABILITATION
Directory of medical rehabilitation facilities 1995, 96n1703
Living with low vision, 97n671
Resources for elders with disabilities, 3d ed, 97n672
Resources for people with disabilities & chronic conditions, 3d ed, 97n673

MEDICAL SCIENCES
Author's gd to biomedical jls, 95n1661
Chronology of medicine & related scis, 98n1541
Concise dict of biomedicine & molecular biology, 98n1439
Doody's rating serv 1997, 98n1502
National gd to funding in health, 5th ed, 99n1427

MEDICAL SCIENTISTS
Bibliography of medical & biomedical biog, 2d ed, 96n1696
Medical discoveries, 98n1530

MEDICAL STATISTICS
Cambridge dict of stats in the medical scis, 96n1699
Nursing home statl yrbk, 1995, 97n1327

MEDICARE
Medicare made easy, rev ed, 98n1539

MEDICINAL PLANTS. *See also* **HERBS**
Encyclopedia of medicinal plants, 97n1343
Handbook of African medicinal plants, 95n1546
Herbs, 95n1544

MEDICINE
Burger's medicinal chemistry & drug discovery, 5th ed, 98n1565
Cambridge world hist of human disease, 95n1662
Dr. Tom Linden's gd to online medicine, 96n1709
Health & illness, 98n1509
Health & medical yrbk 1997, 98n1516
Health care almanac, 97n1316
Health care almanac, 99n1431
Health online, 97n1328
HealthSpeak, 97n1315
Human nutrition 1990-Sept 1994 [CD-ROM], 95n1643
Introduction to ref sources in the health scis, 3d ed, 95n1644
List of serials indexed for online users 1994, 95n1668
Magill's medical gd, 96n1700
Medical discoveries, 98n1530
Mosby's primary care medicine rapid ref [CD-ROM], 99n1451
Nursing diagnosis pocket manual, 97n1353

Oxford medical companion, 96n1702
Physicians' desk ref 1995, 49th ed, 95n1684
Physician's desk ref for ophthalmology 1998, 26th ed, 99n1462
Physicians' desk ref lib, Sept 1994 [CD-ROM], 95n1685
Professional hndbk of diagnostic tests, 96n1710
PsycLit [CD-ROM], 97n625
Reference sources in sci, engineering, medicine, & agriculture, 95n1482
Remarkable lives of 100 women healers & scientists, 96n940
Statistical record of health & medicine, 99n1436
USP DI 1995, v.1, 96n1744
USP DI 1995, v.2, 96n1745
USP DI 1995, v.3, 96n1746
Who's who in medicine & healthcare 1997-98, 98n1507
Who's who in sci in Europe, 9th ed, 97n1233
World Bk health & medical annual 1997, 98n1543

MEDICINE—ABBREVIATIONS
Common medical abbrevs, 96n1695
Medical abbrevs, 8th ed, 98n1526

MEDICINE, CHINESE
Practical dict of Chinese medicine, 99n1446

MEDICINE—DICTIONARIES & ENCYCLOPEDIAS
American Heritage Stedman's medical dict, 96n1697
Companion ency of the hist of medicine, 95n1654
Concise dict of medical-legal terms, 99n552
CPT '97: physicians' current procedural terminology, 98n1525
Delmar's English/Spanish pocket dict for health professionals, 98n1527
Dictionary of medical terms, 3d ed, 95n1656
Dictionary of medicine, 2d ed, 99n1440
Dictionary of natural products, 98n1569
Dictionary of subtonics & their effects [CD-ROM], 97n1314
Encyclopedia of biostats, 99n1418
Encyclopedia of immunology, 2d ed, 99n1419
Encyclopedia of infectious diseases, 99n1445
Encyclopedia of medical media & communications, 98n1529
Encyclopedia of molecular biology & molecular medicine, v.2, 97n1270
Encyclopedia of molecular biology & molecular medicine, v.3, 97n1271
Historical dict of the world health org, 99n1421
Magill's medical gd, 1998 rev ed, 99n1443
Medical dict in 6 langs, 97n1331
Medical meanings: a glossary of word origins, 98n1528
Merriam-Webster's medical desk dict, 95n1655
Merriam-Webster's medical dict, 96n1701
Mosby's GenRx, 8th ed [CD-ROM], 95n1482
Patient's gd to medical terminology, 99n1442
Physicians' desk ref companion gd 1998, 52d ed, 99n1422
Respiratory care drug ref, 99n1481
Routledge German dict of medicine, v.1, 99n1444
Taber's cyclopedic medical dict, 18th ed, 98n1531
World Book Rush-Presbyterian-St. Luke's medical center medical ency, 7th ed, 97n1335

MEDICINE—DIRECTORIES
Complete dir for people with rare disorders, 1998/99, 99n1447
Health & medicine on the Internet, 99n1424
Medical & health info dir 1998, 9th ed, 99n1426

MEDICINE—PEDIATRICS
American Academy of Pediatrics gd to your child's symptoms, 99n1464
Columbia Univ Dept of Pediatrics children's medical gd, 98n1554
Parent's gd to medical emergencies, 98n1523
Portable pediatrician for parents, 95n1665
Practical pediatrician, 97n1354
Smart medicine for a healthier child, 96n1713
Sourcebook of pediatric psychology, 95n783

MEDICINE—POPULAR
Altitude-rated places, v.1, 2d ed, 95n1664
American Academy of Pediatrics gd to your child's symptoms, 99n1464
American Medical Assn family medical gd [CD-ROM], 96n1707
Complete bk of natural & medicinal cures, 95n1670
Complete bk of symptoms & treatments, 99n1456
Complete dir for people with rare disorders, 1998/99, 99n1447
Complete family gd to natural home remedies, 98n1545
Complete home healer, 95n1674
Complete home health advisor, 97n1344
Consumer health info source bk, 4th ed, 95n1666
Consumer health info source bk, 5th ed, 99n1416
Consumer health USA, 96n1711
Consumer health USA, v.2, 98n1538
Ear, nose, & throat disorders sourcebk, 99n1452
Encyclopedia of alternative medicine, 97n1345
Encyclopedia of bodywork, 97n1350
Encyclopedia of family health, 99n1441
Encyclopedia of healing therapies, 98n1552
Encyclopedia of medicinal plants, 97n1343
Essential gd to chronic illness, 98n1558
Everything you need to know about diseases, 97n1336
Everything you need to know about medical tests, 97n1337
Everything you need to know about medical treatments, 97n1338
Family homeopathy, 97n1342
Foot & ankle sourcebk, 97n1340
Illustrated ency of essential oils, 97n1346
Illustrated ency of healing remedies, 99n1460
Immunization resource gd, 2d ed, 97n1339
Making wise medical decisions, 99n1453
Medical advisor, 97n1348
Merck manual of medical info, home ed, 98n1540
New complete medical & health ency, 95n1646
Patient's desk ref, 95n1663
Patients gd to medical tests, 99n1454
PDR family gd to prescription drugs, 99n1483
People's gd to deadly drug interactions, 97n1359
Skin deep: an A-Z of skin disorders, treatments, & health, 97n1333
Women's complete healthbk, 97n1341

MEDICINE—PREVENTIVE
Canadian gd to clinical preventive health care, 96n1708

MEDICINE—SPECIALTIES & SPECIALISTS
Official ABMS dir of board certified medical specialists 1996, 96n1704

MEDICINE, STATE
Issue briefs: 1997 annual ed, 99n1432

MEDICINE—VOCATIONAL GUIDANCE
Career opportunities in health care, 98n1513
Exploring health care careers, 99n1429
Physician marketplace stats 1997-98, 99n1434

MEDITERRANEAN PLANTS
Plant life in the world's Mediterranean climates, 99n1359

MEDITERRANEAN REGION—CIVILIZATION
Encyclopedia of ancient civilizations of the Near East & Mediterranean, 98n487

MEETINGS
Guide to campus & non-profit meeting facilities 95, 7th ed, 95n191
International trade fairs & conferences dir 1995, 19th ed, 96n300
Robert's rules in plain English, 98n681

MELVILLE, HERMAN
Herman Melville ency, 96n1212
Melville ency: the novels, 95n1194

MEMORY
Encyclopedia of memory & memory disorders, 96n780

MENCKEN, H. L.
H. L. Mencken: a descriptive bibliog, 99n1027

MEN'S STUDIES
New men's studies, 2d ed, 96n866

MENTAL HEALTH
Depression, 96n1724
Encyclopedia of mental health, 95n780
Insider's gd to mental health resources online, 98n1515
Nurse's clinical gd to psychiatric & mental health care, 97n1355

MENTAL ILLNESS IN MOTION PICTURES
Celluloid couch, 99n1233

MERCHANDISE LICENSING
EPM licensing letter sourcebk, 1997 ed, 97n165

MERCHANT MARINE
Historical dict of the US Merchant Marine & shipping industry, 95n1794

MERCHANT SHIPS
Jane's merchant ships 1998-99, 3d ed, 99n1578

MERCURY (RECORD COMPANY)
Mercury labels: a discography, 95n1259

MESOPOTAMIA
Daily life in ancient Mesopotamia, 99n511

METALS
ASM hndbk, v.6, 95n1626
ASM metals ref bk, 95n1627
Fatigue data bk, 97n1308
Metals & alloys in unified numbering system, 6th ed, 95n1635
Worldwide gd to equivalent nonferrous metals & alloys, 3d ed, 97n1309

METAL TRADE
Annual bulletin of stats of world trade in steel 1993, 96n287
Annual bulletin of steel stats for Europe, v.21: 1991-94, 97n1307

METAL WORK
ASM hndbk, v.6, 95n1626
ASM metals ref bk, 95n1627
ASM specialty hndbk: tool materials, 96n1678
McGraw-Hill machining & metalworking hndbk, 95n1639

METAPHORS
Metaphors dict, 96n1091
Thesaurus of traditional English metaphors, 95n1045

METAPHYSICS IN LITERATURE
Metaphysical poets: a chronology, 95n1224

METCALF, JOHN
John Metcalf papers, 97n1005

METEOROLOGY. *See also* **WEATHER**
Complete weather resource, 98n1611
Elsevier's dict of climatology & meteorology, 96n1808
Encyclopedia of climate & weather, 97n1396
Glossary of weather & climate with related oceanic & hydrologic terms, 98n1612
International bibliog of meteorology, 95n1727
Weather sourcebk, 95n1728

METHODIST CHURCH
Historical dict of Methodism, 97n1214

METRIC SYSTEM
ISA gd to measurement conversions, 95n1495
Scientific unit conversion, 98n1597

METROPOLITAN AREAS
Comparative gd to American suburbs, 98n824
Gale city & metro rankings reporter, 96n930
MSA profile, 1996, 97n724

METROPOLITAN MUSEUM OF ART (NEW YORK, N.Y.)
European paintings in the Metropolitan Museum of Art by artists born before 1865, 97n804
Library cat of the Metropolitan Museum of Art. 5th suppl, 1990-92, 2d ed, 95n1015

MEXICAN WAR, 1846-1848
Historical dict of the US-Mexican war, 99n462
Mexican-American War of 1846-48, 96n657

MEXICO
Bibliographic gd to Latin American studies 1996, 98n139
Mexico environmental report, 97n224
Consumer Mexico 1996, 97n269
Dictionary of 20th century culture: Hispanic culture of Mexico, Central America, & the Caribbean, 97n348
Encyclopedia of ancient Mesoamerica, 97n453
Encyclopedia of Mexico, 98n141
Encyclopedia of world cultures, v.8: Middle America & the Caribbean, 97n318
Guide to N American steam locomotives, 95n1791
Guide to the histl geography of New Spain, rev ed, 95n567
Mexico, 95n173
Mexico bus: the portable ency for doing bus with Mexico, 95n290
Mexico co hndbk, 1995/96 ed, 96n254
Mexico data bank, 95n172
Moss flora of Mexico, 95n1547
NTC's dict of Mexican cultural code words, 97n134
Profile of western N America, 97n248

MEXICO—FOREIGN RELATIONS
US-Mexican treaties, 98n680

MEXICO—POLITICS & GOVERNMENT
Dictionary of Mexican rulers, 1325-1997, 98n485
Mexican pol biogs, 1935-93, 3d ed, 96n763

MICHENER, JAMES A.
James A. Michener, 96n1213
James A. Michener: a bibliog, 97n973

MICHIGAN
Birds of Mich., 95n1570

MICROBIOLOGY
Encyclopedia of virology plus [CD-ROM], 98n1442

MICROCOMPUTERS. *See also* COMPUTERS
CyberDictionary, 98n1575
Encyclopedia of microcomputers, v.18, 97n1371
McGraw-Hill ency of personal computing, 97n1372
PC user's essential accessible pocket dict, 96n1756
Personal computer dict, 96n1764

MICROFORMS
Guide to microforms in print 1997, 98n1580

MICRONESIA
Atlas of Micronesia, 2d ed, 95n490
Historical dict of Guam & Micronesia, 96n168
Micronesian religion & lore, 96n1439

MICROSOFT NETWORK
Microsoft Bkshelf Internet dir, 1996-97 ed, 98n1589

MIDDLE AGED PERSONS
Live better/live longer resourcebk, 95n836

MIDDLE AGES
Cambridge illus atlas of warfare: the Middle Ages, 768-1487, 97n557
Chronology of the medieval world, 96n561
Encyclopedia of the Middle Ages, 96n565
History of the ancient & medieval world, 98n501
Medieval & early modern data bank [CD-ROM], 98n165
Medieval wordbk, 97n838
Middle Ages, 97n471
Peacemaking in medieval Europe, 99n492

MIDDLE ATLANTIC STATES
Peterson's gd to middle Atlantic colleges 1995, 11th ed, 96n346

MIDDLE EAST
Arab women in ESCWA member states, 96n156
Consumer Middle East 1998, 99n217
Dictionary of modern Arab hist, 99n508
Dictionary of the Middle East, 97n138
Encyclopaedia of Middle Eastern mythology & religion, 95n1442
Encyclopedia of the modern Middle East, 97n136
Encyclopedia of world cultures, v.9: Africa & the Middle East, 97n319
External trade bulletin of the ESCWA region, 7th ed, 96n157
Folk traditions of the Arab world, 96n1342
Handbook of pol sci research on the Middle East & N Africa, 99n648
Historical dict of Syria, 97n141
Historical dict of the Gulf Arab States, 98n489
History of Israel, 99n509
Index to English per lit on the O.T. & ancient Near Eastern studies, v.6, 95n1451
International dict of historic places, v.4, 97n468
Mass media in the Middle East, 95n936
Middle East, 8th ed, 96n764
Middle East & N Africa 1995, 96n160
Middle East & N Africa 1997, 43d ed, 97n139
Middle East & N Africa 1998, 99n87
Middle East & N Africa on file, 96n459
Statistical abstract of the ESCWA region 1983-1992, 14th ed, 96n919
Who's who in the Arab world 1995-96, 12th ed, 96n161

MIDDLE EAST—ANTIQUITIES
Oxford ency of archaeology in the Near East, 98n429

MIDDLE EAST—BIBLIOGRAPHY
Bibliographic gd to Middle Eastern studies 1996, 98n143
Index to English per lit on the Old Testament & ancient Near Eastern studies, v.VII, 99n1273

MIDDLE EAST—CIVILIZATION
Civilizations of the ancient Near East, 96n159
Encyclopedia of ancient civilizations of the Near East & Mediterranean, 98n487
First civilizations, 95n571

MIDDLE EAST—ECONOMIC CONDITIONS
Survey of economic & social dvlpmts in the ESCWA region 1993, 96n129

MIDDLE EAST—FOREIGN RELATIONS
Asian states' relations with the Middle East & N Africa, 95n763
Middle East military balance 1993-94, 96n695
Middle East military balance, 1996, 99n634
National accounts studies of the ESCWA region, 96n158
1990-91 Gulf War, 97n456
Origins & dvlpmt of the Arab-Israeli conflict, 99n699
Political parties of the Middle East & N Africa, 96n765
US foreign relations with the Middle East & N Africa, 95n764

MIDDLE EAST—HISTORY
Daily life in ancient Mesopotamia, 99n511
Origins & dvlpmt of the Arab-Israeli conflict, 99n699

MIDDLE WEST (US)
Field gd to nearby nature, 95n1559
Peterson's gd to colleges in the Midwest 1995, 11th ed, 96n343
Used bk lover's gd to the Midwest, 96n1007
Who's who in the Midwest 1994-95, 95n39

MIGRATION, INTERNAL
Migration stats 1994, 96n907

MILITARISM
Militarism in Arab society, 98n609

MILITARY ART & SCIENCE
Cambridge illus atlas of warfare: Renaissance to Revolution, 1492-1792, 97n556
Dictionary of military abbrevs, 95n679
Dictionary of military hist & the art of war, 95n687
Dictionary of the modern US military, 97n566
Encyclopedic dict of conflict & conflict resolution, 1945-96, 99n628
Jane's sentinel: Central America & the Caribbean security assessment, 1996 ed, 97n129
Middle East military balance 1993-94, 96n695
Middle East military balance, 1996, 99n634
Spanish-American war, 99n626
Wars of the Americas, 99n629
World dir of defense & security, 97n567

MILITARY BASES
Carroll's military facilities dir, 96n686
Directory of US military bases worldwide, 96n687
Directory of US military bases worldwide, 99n631
Military personnel installations locator CD-ROM [CD-ROM], 99n633

MILITARY BIOGRAPHY
Generals in muddy boots: a concise ency of combat commanders, 97n562
Political leaders & military figures in the 2d World War, 98n606
They also served: military bios of uncommon Americans, 99n623

MILITARY CONTRACTS
Military contracts/procurement locator [CD-ROM], 99n632

MILITARY DECORATIONS
British Army campaign medals, 98n630

MILITARY HISTORY
Army Times bk of great land battles, 96n698
Battles of the Somme, 1916, 97n561
Brassey's ency of military hist & biog, 96n682
Cambridge illus atlas of warfare: Renaissance to Revolution, 1492-1792, 97n556
Cambridge illus atlas of warfare: the Middle Ages, 768-1487, 97n557
Dictionary of Afghan wars, revolutions, & insurgencies, 97n106
Dictionary of military hist & the art of war, 95n687
Encyclopedia of invasions & conquests from ancient times to the present, 97n564
Encyclopedia of the American military, 95n688
Encyclopedia of the Persian Gulf War, 97n454
Encyclopedia of 20th century conflict, 98n613
European powers in the 1st World War, 97n467
Guide to the sources of US military hist, suppl IV, 99n622
Handbook of American military hist, 97n569
Military hist of the Third World since 1945, 95n697
Modern campaigns, 98n615
Operation Desert Shield/Desert Storm, 96n563
Oxford companion to Australian military hist, 97n565
Oxford companion to WW II, 97n571
Pacific War atlas 1941-45, 96n676
Reader's companion to military hist, 98n616
Soviet armed forces, 1918-92, 97n558
War in N Africa, 1940-43, 97n460
West Point atlas of American wars, v.1, 96n677

MILITARY INTELLIGENCE
Dictionary of US intelligence servs, 97n597
Signals intelligence in WW II, 97n560
Spies: the secret agents who changed the course of hist, 95n765

MILITARY PERSONNEL
Great war: a gd to the serv records of all the worlds fighting men & volunteers, 99n635
Military personnel installations locator CD-ROM [CD-ROM], 99n633
Roster of Union soldiers 1861-65: US colored troops, 98n452

MILITARY POLICY
Dictionary of alternative defense, 96n683

MILITARY SUPPLIES
Jane's electro-optic systems 1996-97, 2d ed, 98n619
Jane's military communications, 1997-98, 98n618
Jane's NBC protection equipment 1996-97, 9th ed, 97n570

MILITARY UNIFORMS
Encyclopedia of US Army insignia & uniforms, 98n624

MILITARY WEAPONS
Jane's air-launched weapons image lib [CD-ROM], 98n632
Jane's land-based air defense 1998-99, 11th ed, 99n646
Knives: military edged tools & weapons, 99n647

MILITIA MOVEMENTS
Militias in America, 97n613

MILTON, JOHN
Index to the biblical refs, parallels, & allusions in the poetry & prose of John Milton, 95n1214
Milton's sonnets, 96n1214
Paradise Lost: an annot bibliog, 97n997

MIND & BODY THERAPIES
Encyclopedia of bodywork, 97n1350

MINERAL INDUSTRIES
Industrial commodity stats yrbk 1994, 97n195
World index of resources & population, 96n235

MINERALOGY
Dana's new mineralogy, 99n1537
McGraw-Hill dict of geology & mineralogy, 98n1614
National Audubon Society 1st field gd: rocks & minerals, 99n1535
Pockets: rocks & minerals, 96n73

MINERALS
Color atlas of rocks & minerals in thin section, 95n1724
Colorado rockhounding, 95n1732
Fluorescence: gems & minerals under ultraviolet light, 96n1812
Handbook of world mineral trade stats 1990-95, 98n251
Mineral investment conditions in selected countries of the Asia-Pacific region, 96n1842
Minerals & gemstones of the world, rev ed, 95n1729
Minerals industry taxation policies for Asia & the Pacific, 96n1843
Minerals: identifying, learning about, & collecting..., 95n1731

MINERALS IN HUMAN NUTRITION
Encyclopedia of nutritional suppls, 97n1349
Encyclopedia of vitamins, minerals, & suppls, 97n1265
Real vitamin & mineral bk, 98n1548

MINES & MINERAL RESOURCES
Agriculture, mining, & construction USA, 99n187
Randol mining dir 1994/95, 96n1836

MINNESOTA
Minnesota, 98n412
Radicalism in Minn. 1900-60, 96n767

MINORITES. *See also* **ETHNIC GROUPS**
American immigrant cultures, 99n365
Big bk of minority opportunities, 6th ed, 96n891
Big bk of minority opportunities, 7th ed, 99n339
Cultures of color in America, 99n367
Dictionary of race & ethnic relations, 99n366
Directory of financial aids for minorities 1995-97, 96n880
Ethnic pols in E Europe, 95n749
Ethnic studies in the US, 97n322
Guide to ethnic health collections in the US, 97n1322
Guide to multicultural resources 1997/98, 98n327
Kaleidoscope: a multicultural bklst for grades K-8, 96n1182
Minority orgs, 5th ed, 98n330
Multicultural picture bks, 95n1135
Multiethnic children's lit, 95n1136
Official gd to racial & ethnic diversity, 97n324
Race, crime, & the criminal justice system, 98n548
Research projects supported by the Canadian Ethnic Studies Program 1973-92, 95n419
Research results of projects funded by the Canadian Ethnic Studies Program 1973-88, 95n418
Voices of multicultural America, 97n967
Women of color: feminist theory, 97n729
World dir of minorities, 98n334

MINORITIES—EDUCATION
Multicultural student's gd to colleges, rev, 98n302

MINORITIES—EMPLOYMENT
Third World worker in the multinatl corp, 95n275

MINORITIES IN MOTION PICTURES
American Film Inst catalog, within our gates: ethnicity in American feature films, 1911-60, 98n1288

MINORITIES—PRESS COVERAGE
US news coverage of racial minorities, 98n852

MINORITY BUSINESS ENTERPRISES
Major studies of minority bus, 95n178
National dir of minority-owned bus firms, 7th ed, 95n200
National dir of minority-owned bus firms, 9th ed, 99n155

MINORITY WOMEN IN LITERATURE
Women playwrights of diversity, 98n1106

MINOR LEAGUE BASEBALL
Pacific Coast League: statl hist, 1903-57, 97n647
STATS minor league hndbk 1998, 99n720

MISSING PERSONS
Find anyone fast, 96n837
Using public records to find & investigate anyone, 98n703

MISSIONS
Biographical dict of Christian missions, 99n1281
Dictionary of mission, 98n1350
World gd to religious & spiritual orgs 1996, 97n1182

MISSISSIPPIAN CULTURE
Archaeology of the Mississippian culture, 97n398

MODELS (PERSONS)
Wilhelmina's modeling & acting dict, 95n1355

MOLECULAR BIOLOGY
Encyclopedia of molecular biology & molecular medicine, v.1, 97n1269
Molecular biology & biotech, 96n1561
Oxford dict of biochemistry & molecular biology, 98n1444

MONEY. *See also* **COINS**
Charlton standard catalogue of Canadian govt paper money, 11th ed, 99n843

Guide bk of US coins, 1996, 49th ed, 96n1008
Handbook of ancient Greek & Roman coins, 97n778
International encyclopaedic dict of numismatics, 98n909
Standard catalog of US paper money, 99n846
Standard catalog of US tokens 1700-1900, 98n914
Warman's coins & currency, 2d ed, 98n915

MONGOLIA
Historical dict of Mongolia, 97n111
Mongolia, 95n135

MONOGRAMS
Old masters, 98n980

MONOLOGUES
Ultimate scene & monologue sourcebk, 95n1407

MONSTERS
Monster manual: a complete gd to your favorite creatures, 95n1323

MONTANA
WPA gd to 1930s Mont., 95n513

MOON
Moon bk, rev ed, 99n1521
Who's who on the moon, 97n1394

MORE, THOMAS, SIR, SAINT
Sir Thomas More in the English Renaissance, 95n556
Thomas More: an annot bibliog of criticism, 1935-97, 99n1086

MORMON CHURCH
Comprehensive annot bk of Mormon bibliog, 98n1397
Historical atlas of Mormonism, 96n1461
Historical dict of Mormonism, 95n1464

MOROCCO
Historical dict of Morocco, new ed, 98n458
Morocco, rev ed, 96n120

MORRISON, TONI
Toni Morrison, 99n1058

MORTALITY—STATISTICS
Life & death in the US, 98n770

MOSCOW
Foreign descriptions of Muscovy, 96n147
Maximov's companion to who governs Moscow, 98n688

MOSSES
Moss flora of Mexico, 95n1547

MOTHS
Peterson 1st gd to butterflies & moths, 95n1577

MOTION PICTURE ACTORS & ACTRESSES. See also ACTORS & ACTRESSES
Al Jolson: a bio-bibliog, 95n1345
Audrey Hepburn: a bio-bibliog, 95n1347
Christopher Lee & Peter Cushing & horror cinema, 96n1396
Eleanor Powell: a bio-bibliog, 95n1353
Film actors gd, 1997, 3d ed, 97n1143
Fred Astaire: a bio-bibliog, 98n1272
From silents to sound, 99n1209
Ginger Rogers: a bio-bibliog, 95n1344
Halliwell's filmgoer's companion, 12th ed, 98n1305
Harold Lloyd: a bio-bibliog, 95n1343
Howard Keel: a bio-bibliog, 97n1078
International motion picture almanac, 1996, 67th ed, 97n770
International TV & video almanac, 1996, 41st ed, 97n771
Joan Fontaine: a bio-bibliog, 95n1341
Montgomery Clift: a bio-bibliog, 95n1348
Oscar stars from A-Z, 98n1279
Quinlan's illus dir of film character actors, new ed, 97n1106
Ronald Colman: a bio-bibliog, 98n1273
Roscoe "Fatty" Arbuckle: a bio-bibliog, 95n1354
Silent film performers, 97n1105
Some Joe you don't know: an American biogl gd to 100 British TV personalities, 97n1107
Stars in blue: movie actors in America's sea servs, 98n1281
Western & frontier film & TV credits 1903-95, 97n1130
Who's who of Victorian cinema, 98n1280
William Shatner: a bio-bibliog, 95n1346

MOTION PICTURE INDUSTRY
American film personnel & co credits, 1908-20, 97n1142
AV market place 1994, 95n965
BFI film & TV hndbk 1995, 96n1401
Biographical hndbk of Hispanics & US film, 98n1277
Chronicle of the cinema, rev ed, 98n1282
Encyclopedia of European cinema, 97n1111
Film, TV, video in Russia '94, 95n1378
First century of film, 97n1112
Footage, 99n1220
Harrison's reports & film reviews, 96n1406
International motion picture almanac, 1996, 67th ed, 97n770
Key concepts in cinema studies, 98n1284
New histl dict of the American film industry, 99n1215
Republic pictures checklist, 99n1230

MOTION PICTURE MUSIC
British cinema sheet music, 98n1195
Film composers gd, 3d ed, 97n1037
Hollywood rock, 95n1391
Hollywood song, 96n1275
Keeping score: film & TV music, 1988-97, 99n1140
Soundtracks: an intl dict of composers of music for film, 99n1131

MOTION PICTURE PRODUCERS & DIRECTORS
Contemporary literary criticism, v.89, 97n898
Directory of Indian film-makers & films, 95n1364
Encyclopedia of film directors in the USA & Europe, v.1, 95n1372
Film directors, 11th intl ed, 96n1405
George Sidney: a bio-bibliog, 95n1350
Hollywood & the foreign touch, 97n1108
Hollywood blu-bk dir 1997, 99n1221
Illustrated who's who of Hollywood directors, v.1, 96n1367

International dict of films & filmmakers, 2d ed, v.5, 95n1370
Michael Singer's film directors, 1997, 12th ed, 98n1317
Reel black talk: a sourcebk of 50 American filmmakers, 98n1278
Sub-Saharan African films & filmmakers, 1987-92, 95n1363
Tony Richardson: a bio-bibliog, 97n1096
Western & frontier film & TV credits 1903-95, 97n1130
Who's who of Victorian cinema, 98n1280
Women film directors, 96n947

MOTION PICTURE REMAKES
Science fiction, fantasy, & horror film sequels, series, & remakes, 98n1292

MOTION PICTURES. *See also* **SILENT FILMS**
A&E entertainment almanac, 1997, 98n1264
A-Z of horror films, 98n1297
Action! the action movie A-Z, 98n1293
African American films through 1959, 99n1234
American Film Inst cat of motion pictures produced in the US: feature films, 1931-40, 95n1367
American Film Inst catalog, within our gates: ethnicity in American feature films, 1911-60, 98n1288
American film personnel & co credits, 1908-20, 97n1142
Architecture on screen, 95n1012
Art directors in cinema, 99n1210
Award winning films, 95n1398
BFI film & TV hndbk 1995, 96n1401
Big bk of show bus awards, 99n1198
Billboard video yrbk 1994, 96n1402
Blacks in black & white, 2d ed, 96n1410
Brewer's cinema, 96n1373
British cinema source bk, 97n1109
British co-operative movement film catalogue, 98n1289
Canadian film & video, 98n1271
Chronicle of the cinema, 96n1371
Chronicle of the cinema, rev ed, 98n1282
Comedy quotes from the movies, 95n1402
Complete film dict, 98n1285
Complete James Bond movie ency, rev ed, 96n1382
Contemporary Hollywood's negative Hispanic image, 95n1387
Contemporary theatre, film, & TV, v.13, 96n1362
Contemporary theatre, film, & TV, v.17, 99n1195
Critical hist & filmography of Toho's Godzilla series, 98n1294
Dictionary of film quotations, 96n1374
Dictionary of 20th century culture: American culture after WW II, 95n927
Encyclopaedia of Indian cinema, 96n1381
Encyclopedia of fantasy, 98n1116
Encyclopedia of martial arts movies, 96n1380
Facets African-American video gd, 95n1392
Feature films, 1940-49: a US filmography, 95n1380
Film & TV in-jokes, 99n1239
Film & video on the Internet, 98n1287
Film anthologies index, 95n1401

Film cartoons: a gd to 20th century American animated features & shorts, 99n1231
Film distribution gd 1986-1992, v.1, 96n1384
Film ency, 2d ed, 95n1371
Film festival gd, 99n1223
Film index intl 1996 [CD-ROM], 99n1240
Film producers, studios, agents, & casting directors gd, 5th ed, 97n766
Film quotations, 95n1403
Film researcher's hndbk, 98n1309
Film superlist: motion pictures in the US public domain, 1894-1939, updated ed, 95n1368
Film writers gd, 6th ed, 97n767
Film writers gd, 7th ed, 99n1219
Filmmakers in The Moving Picture World, 98n1316
First century of film, 97n1112
Frame by frame 2: a filmography of the African American image, 1978-94, 98n1295
From headline hunter to Superman: a journalism filmography, 98n1298
Gangster films, 97n1114
Golden horrors: an illus critical filmography of terror cinema, 1931-39, 97n1122
Guide to American cinema, 1930-65, 99n1217
Guide to American cinema, 1965-95, 99n1211
Guide to American crime films of the 30s, 96n1393
Guide to American crime films of the 40s & 50s, 96n1392
Halliwell's film gd 1995, 96n1385
Hammer films: an exhaustive filmography, 97n1119
Harrison's reports & film reviews, 96n1406
Hollywood novel, 96n1411
Hollywood Reporter bk of box office hits, rev ed, 97n1128
Hollywood rock, 95n1391
Images in the dark: an ency of gay & lesbian film & video, 95n1374
International dict of broadcasting & film, 96n984
International dict of films & filmmakers, 2d ed, v.5, 95n1370
International film, TV & video acronyms, 95n1359
Italian film: a who's who, 95n1365
Jerry Lewis films, 96n1397
Key concepts in cinema studies, 98n1284
Leonard Maltin's movie & video gd, 95n1361
Leonard Maltin's movie ency, 96n1377
Magill's cinema annual 1994: a survey of the films of 1993, 95n1396
Media in the movies, 99n1228
Michael Singer's film directors, 1997, 12th ed, 98n1317
Movie list bk, 95n1389
New histl dict of the American film industry, 99n1215
Opera on screen, 99n1218
Pirates & seafaring swashbucklers on the Hollywood screen, 96n1407
Political companion to American film, 96n1409
Poverty Row studios, 1929-40: an illus hist of 53 independent film cos..., 98n1312
Reel list, 96n1400
Return to paradise: a gd to S Sea Island films, 99n1229
Shot on this site, 96n472
65 yrs of the Oscar, rev ed, 96n1372
South American cinema, 97n1124

Southern mountaineers in silent films, 95n1388
Sub-Saharan African films & filmmakers, 1987-92, 95n1363
Ultimate dir of the silent screen performers, 96n1368
Ultimate movie thesaurus, 98n1303
VideoHound's that's amore!, 96n1398
Vietnam war films, 95n1384
Wales & cinema, 96n1370
Walking shadows, 96n1399
With fire & sword: Italian spectacles on American screens 1958-68, 96n1395
Women's companion to intl film, 95n1373
Working stiffs, union maids, reds, & riffraff: an organized gd to films about labor, 97n1141

MOTION PICTURES—AUSTRALIAN
Australian film, 99n1206

MOTION PICTURES—CHINA
Chinese filmography, 98n1296

MOTION PICTURES—EUROPE
British film studios, 97n1139
Catalogue of forbidden German feature & short film productions held in Zonal Film Archives..., English lang ed, 97n764
Catalogue Russian films 1991-94, 95n1369
Charles Dickens on the screen, 97n1121
Encyclopedia of European cinema, 97n1111

MOTION PICTURES—FRANCE
French films, 1945-93, 97n1115
Paramount in Paris, 99n1236

MOTION PICTURES—ITALY
Italian horror films of the 1960s, 99n1205

MOTION PICTURES—JAPAN
Japanese filmography, 97n1117
Japanese sci fiction, fantasy & horror films, 95n1382

MOTION PICTURES—LATIN AMERICA
Latin American films, 1932-94, 98n1299

MOTION PICTURES & LITERATURE
Encyclopedia of novels into film, 99n1216
Huckleberry Finn on film, 95n1393

MOTION PICTURES—REVIEWS
Blockbuster Entertainment gd to movies & videos 1998, 99n1241
Celluloid couch, 99n1233
Guide to films on the Korean War, 98n1291
Guide to Latin American, Caribbean, & US Latino-made films & video, 99n1226
Horror & sci fiction films 4, 98n1300
Index to short & feature film reviews in the Moving Picture World, 96n1413
Leonard Maltin's movie & video gd, 1999 ed, 99n1243
Magill's cinema annual 1995, 14th ed, 97n1131
Manly movie gd, 99n1242
Motion picture gd, 98n1311
New York Times film reviews, v.19: 1993-94, 97n1133
Psychotronic video gd, 97n1140
Roger Eberts video companion, 98n1319
Science fiction serials, 99n1227
Sight & Sound film review v.: Jan. 1994 to Dec. 1994, 97n1135
Time Out film gd, 5th ed, 97n1136
TLA film & video gd 1996-97, 97n1125
Ultimate gd to lesbian & gay film & video, 97n1126
Variety's film reviews, v.23, 96n1387
VideoHound multimedia [CD-ROM], 96n1389
VideoHound's complete gd to cult flicks & trash pics, 97n1137
VideoHound's sci-fi experience, 98n1320
VideoHound's vampires on video, 98n1321

MOTION PICTURES—SPAIN
Guide to the cinema of Spain, 99n1237

MOTION PICTURE STUDIOS
British film studios, 97n1139
Poverty Row studios, 1929-40: an illus hist of 53 independent film cos...., 98n1312

MOTORCYCLES
Complete motorcycle bk, 96n1884
Encyclopedia of the motorcycle, 96n1893
Ultimate motorcycle bk, 95n1793

MOUNTAINEERING
Climbing, 96n829
World mountaineering, 99n442

MOUNTAIN PLANTS
New England's mountain flowers, 98n1450

MOUNTAIN WHITES (SOUTHERN STATES) IN MOTION PICTURES
Southern mountaineers in silent films, 95n1388

MOUNTBATTEN OF BURMA, EARL
Earl Mountbatten of Burma, 1900-79, 99n505

MOVING PICTURE WORLD
Filmmakers in The Moving Picture World, 98n1316

MOVING & RELOCATION
Moving & relocation sourcebk 1998, 2d ed, 99n781

MOZART, WOLFGANG AMADEUS
Mozart diary, 98n1213

MULTICULTURAL EDUCATION
Dictionary of multicultural educ, 98n267
Educator's gd to free multicultural materials 1998, 99n285
Multicultural educ, 97n283
Multicultural projects index, 99n856

MULTICULTURALISM. *See also* **PLURALISM (SOCIAL SCIENCES); ETHNOLOGY**
Connecting cultures, 98n1093
Culturally diverse lib collections for youth, 98n1099

Encyclopedia of multiculturalism, 95n396
Ethnic cultures of the world, 98n331
Global voices, global visions: a core collection of multicultural bks, 97n10
Guide to multicultural resources 1997/98, 98n327
Kaleidoscope: A multicultural bklist for grades K-8, 98n1087
Linguistic cultures of the world, 98n990
Multicultural dict of proverbs, 98n1250
Multicultural educ dir, 98n273
Multiculturalism, 99n369
National cultures of the world, 98n90
Official gd to racial & ethnic diversity, 97n324
Religion: a cross-cultural ency, 97n1178
Religious cultures of the world, 98n1368
Research projects supported by the Canadian Ethnic Studies Program 1973-92, 95n419
Research results of projects funded by the Canadian Ethnic Studies Program 1973-88, 95n418
What's cooking in multicultural America, 97n1254

MULTIMEDIA SYSTEMS
Business multimedia explained, 98n242
Dictionary of multimedia terms & acronyms, 98n1572
Guide to children's ref works & multimedia material, 99n994
Multimedia: the complete gd, 97n1362
Multimedia dir, 4th ed, 97n1363
Multimedia tech from A-Z, 96n1750

MULTIMEDIA SYSTEMS INDUSTRY
International multimedia yrbk 1995-96, 96n1751
International multimedia yrbk 1995-96 on CD-ROM [CD-ROM], 96n1752
Multimedia: law & practice, 95n615

MUMMIES
Encyclopedia of mummies, 99n445

MUNICIPAL GOVERNMENT
Carroll's municipal dir, 96n725
Managing your city or town, 95n768
Municipal executive dir, 96n728
Municipal yr bk 1998, v.65, 99n680

MURDOCH, IRIS
Four British women novelists, 99n1061
Iris Murdoch: a descriptive primary & annot secondary bibliog, 95n1215

MURRAY, BILLY
Billy Murray: the phonograph industry's 1st great recording artist, 98n1198

MUSEUMS
American art dir 1997-98, 56th ed, 99n871
American Revolutionary War sites, memorials, museums, & lib collections, 99n472
Art diary 97/98, 98n953
Bibliography of museum studies, 11th ed, 96n82
Cockroach hall of fame & 101 other off-the-wall museums, 95n84
Experiencing America's past: a travel gd to museum villages, 2d ed, 95n507
Field gd to America's historic neighborhoods & museum houses, 99n433
Guide to tourist railroads & railroad museums, 4th ed, 96n1886
Hall of fame museums, 99n69
Historic railroad, 97n1446
International dir of arts, 99n811
International dir of arts 1993/94, 95n1006
Keyguide to info sources in museum studies, 2d ed, 95n85
Medieval & Renaissance mss in the Walters Art Gallery, 99n600
Museum careers & training, 95n83
Museum premieres, exhibitions, & special events, 98n72
Museums of the world, 98n73
University & college museums, galleries, & related facilities, 97n62
Victoria & Albert Museum, 99n70
Volvo gd to halls of fame, 96n83

MUSEUM TECHNIQUES
Bibliography for hist, hist curatorship, & museums, 98n495

MUSHROOMS
Hallucinogenic & poisonous mushroom field gd, 98n1452
Mushroom bk, 97n1280
Mushrooms of N America in color, 97n1278

MUSIC. *See also* COMPACT DISCS; SONGS
All music gd: the best CDs, albums & tapes, 2d ed, 95n1256
Baker's biogl dict of 20th-century classical musicians, 98n1197
Baker's dict of music, 99n1123
BBC Music Mag top 1000 CDs gd, 97n1055
Berliner gramophone records, 96n1273
Bibliographic gd to music 1996, 98n1187
Billboard 1996 music yrbk, 98n1205
Chronicle of American music, 1700-1995, 97n1025
Classic FM gd to classical music, 98n1222
Compendium of modern instrumental techniques, 95n1273
Dixonia: a bio-discography of Bill Dixon, 99n1146
Film composers gd, 3d ed, 97n1037
From metal to Mozart, 96n1298
Goldmine's celebrity vocals, 96n1274
Gustav Mahler's symphonies, 98n1248
Harmony theory, 98n1193
High definition CD recordings, 95n1257
His master's voice/die stimme seines herrn, 95n1258
History of American classical music, 97n1059
Literature of American music 3, 1983-92, 97n1021
Literature of chamber music, 99n1153
Lives & works in the arts from the renaissance to the 20th century, 98n847
Music & dance of the world's religions, 97n1087
Music & poetry in the Middle Ages, 96n1296
Music, dance & theater scholarships, 96n1365
Music of the golden age, 1900-50 & beyond, 99n1139
Music of the repressed Russian avant-garde, 1900-29, 95n1261
Music since 1900, 5th ed, 95n1262
North American Indian music, 98n1191
NPR gd to bldg a classical CD collection, 95n1282
Richard Baker's companion to music, 96n1269

Schirmer pronouncing pocket manual of musical terms, 5th ed, 96n1271
Sourcebook for research in music, 95n1251
Thesaurus of abstract musical properties, 96n1277
Tudor music: a research & info gd, 95n1253
Twentieth-Century American music for the dance, 97n1103
Virtual musician, 98n1206
Women & music, 97n1020
Women in music, 2d ed, 95n1254

MUSIC—20TH CENTURY
American music in the 20th century, 99n1124
Arnold Schoenberg companion, 99n1128
Blackwell gd to recorded contemporary music, 98n1221
Conductor's gd to choral-orchestral works, 20th century, part 2, 99n1151
Songwriters: a biogl dict with discographies, 99n1117
William Schuman: a bio-bibliog, 99n1127

MUSIC—AUSTRALIA
Garland ency of world music, v.9, 99n1120
Oxford companion to Australian music, 99n1122

MUSIC—AWARDS
Big bk of show bus awards, 99n1198

MUSIC—BIBLIOGRAPHY
Basic music lib, 3d ed, 98n1186
Collected eds histl series & sets & monuments of music, 98n1190
General bibliog for music research, 3d ed, 97n1022
Music ref & research materials, 4th ed, rev, 95n1252
Music ref & research materials, 5th ed, 98n1189

MUSIC—CANADA
Canadian music & music educ, 98n1194
Guide to published Canadian violin music suitable for student performers, 95n1279
Music in Canada, 98n1192

MUSIC—CATALOGS
Descriptive catalog of the music printed by Hubert Waelrant & Jan de Laet, 96n1266
Thematic catalogues in music, 2d ed, 98n1188

MUSIC—DENMARK
Twentieth Century Danish music, 99n1154

MUSIC—DICTIONARIES
Compact music dict, 97n1026
Concise Oxford dict of music, 4th ed, 97n1027
Dictionary of 20th century culture: American culture after WW II, 95n927
Early music dict, 96n1272
Harvard biogl dict of music, 97n1024
NPR classical music companion, 98n1202
Oxford dict of music, 96n1270
Penguin dict of music, 6th ed, 97n1028

MUSIC FESTIVALS
Music festivals from Bach to blues, 97n1029

MUSIC FILMS
First Hollywood musicals, 97n1116

MUSIC—FINLAND
Historical dict of the music & musicians of Finland, 99n1121

MUSICIANS. *See also* **SINGERS**
Baker's biogl dict of 20th-century classical musicians, 98n1197
Billboard illus ency of rock, 99n1172
Contemporary musicians, v.19, 99n1115
Contemporary musicians, v.20, 99n1116
Encyclopedia of the blues, 2d ed, 99n1150
Entertainers in British films, 99n1225
International who's who in music & musicians dir, 14th ed, 96n1267
International who's who in music 1998/99, v.2, 2d ed, 99n1161
Jazz CD listener's gd, 99n1165
Jazz: the rough gd, 97n1076
Musical Americans: a biogl dict 1918-26, 98n1200
MusicHound jazz, 99n1168
Popular bands & performers, 96n1304
Portable Baker's biog dict of musicians, 96n1268
Serge Chaloff, 99n1169
Star gd, 1997-98, 98n1266

MUSIC—INDEXES
Index of songs on children's recordings, 2d ed, 95n1264
International index to music pers 1997:2 [CD-ROM], 98n1208
Keeping score: film & TV music, 1988-97, 99n1140
Song index of the Enoch Pratt Free Lib, 99n1126

MUSIC INDUSTRY
Recording industry sourcebk, 99n1199

MUSIC—LATIN AMERICA
Latin American classical composers, 97n1042

MUSIC LIBRARIES
Basic music lib, 3d ed, 98n1186
Library resources for singers, coaches, & accompanists, 99n1113

MUSIC—QUOTATIONS
Better than it sounds: a dict of humorous musical quotations, 99n1119

MUSIC—SPAIN
Bibliographical gd to Spanish music for the violin & viola, 1900-97, 99n1149

MUSIC—TERMINOLOGY
NPR classical music companion, 98n1202
Well-tempered announcer: a pronunciation gd to classical music, 97n1056

MUSIC THEORY
Form & analysis theory, 99n1114
Orchestration theory, 97n1057

MUSIC TITLE PAGES
Broadway sheet music, 97n1069

MUSIC TRADE
Career opportunities in the music industry, 3d ed, 96n1276

MUSICAL ANALYSIS
Musical anthologies for analytical study, 97n1023

MUSICAL INSTRUMENTS
Compendium of modern instrumental techniques, 95n1273
Illustrated ency of musical instruments, 97n1052
Orion blue bk: guitars & musical instruments, 1998 ed, 99n1147
Orion blue bk: vintage guitars & collectibles 1998, summer ed, 99n182

MUSICALS
American musical theatre song ency, 96n1416
American song, 2d ed, 97n1077
Broadway, movie, TV, & studio cast musicals on record, 97n1030
Broadway sheet music, 97n1069
Broadway song companion, 99n1170
Century of musicals in black & white, 95n1416
Encyclopedia of the musical theatre, 95n1415
More opening nights on Broadway: a critical quotebk of the musical theatre 1965-81, 98n1329
Musical theater synopses, 99n1244
Musicals, 2d ed, 95n1408

MUSLIMS
Muslim almanac, 97n1219
South Asian religions in the Americas, 96n1438
Year bk of the Muslim world 1996, 97n81

MUSLIM WOMEN
Muslim women throughout the world, 98n830

MYCENAE (EXTINCT CITY)
Mycenaean civilization, 97n448

MYCOLOGY
International mycological dir, 3d ed, 96n1581

MYSTERIES & MIRACLE—PLAYS
Cambridge companion to medieval English theatre, 95n1419

MYSTERY FANCIER
Mystery Fancier: an index to vs.1-13, 95n1159

MYSTICISM
Simone Weil, 96n957

MYTHOLOGY
Athena: classical mythology on CD-ROM [CD-ROM], 95n1318
Cassell dict of Norse myth & legend, 98n1259
Children's bks on ancient Greek & Roman mythology, 95n1319
Chiron dict of Greek & Roman mythology, 95n1320
Classical myths & legends in the Middle Ages & Renaissance, 99n1017
Encyclopaedia of Celtic wisdom, 96n788
Encyclopaedia of Middle Eastern mythology & religion, 95n1442
European myth & legend, 99n1185
Goddesses, heroes, & shamans, 96n1347
Gods & heroes of classical antiquity, 98n1257
Illustrated dict of mythology, 99n1186
Index to fairy tales, 1987-92, 95n1316
Legends of the earth, sea, & sky, 99n1184
Man, myth & magic, new ed, 96n1348
Myth: myths & legends of the world explored, 97n1091
Myths & hero tales, 98n1084
New bk of goddesses & heroines, 3d ed, 98n1258
Theories of myth, 98n1261
Voyages in classical mythology, 96n1349
Who's who in classical mythology, 98n1260
Who's who in Egyptian mythology, 2d ed, 96n1350
With fire & sword: Italian spectacles on American screens 1958-68, 96n1395
World mythology, 97n1092

MYXOMYCETES
Myxomycetes: a hndbk of slime molds, 96n1587

NAMES
Alphabetical gd to the lang of name studies, 97n824
Pronouncing dict of proper names, 2d ed, 99n900
Proper names master index, 95n82
What in the word? origins of words dealing with people & places, 97n823

NAMES, ETHNOLOGICAL
African ethnonyms, 97n315

NAMES, GEOGRAPHICAL
African placenames, 95n502
All over the map, 95n470
Baker ency of Bible places, 96n1450
County locator (LOCUS): ultimate place name & zip code locator, 95n69
Dictionary of Canadian place names, 99n423
High country names, 95n501
Houghton Mifflin dict of geography, 98n395
Merriam-Webster's pocket geographical dict, 97n380
Place called Peculiar, 99n421
Placenames of Russia & the former Soviet Union, 97n382
Placenames of the world, 98n401
State names, seals, flags, & symbols, rev ed, 95n499

NAMES, PERSONAL
African-American baby name bk, 99n407
Beyond Jennifer & Jason, 95n465
Bible baby names, 97n368
Celtic baby names, 98n378
Collins Scottish clan & family ency, 96n435
Dictionary of English surnames, 3d ed, 96n427
Dictionary of Irish family names, 98n376
Dictionary of Jewish surnames from the Kingdom of Poland, 98n375

Directory of family assns, 3d ed, 97n354
Encyclopedia of American family names, 96n437
Hispanic surnames & family hist, 97n356
Master bk of Irish surnames, 95n464
More names & naming, 97n370
People's names, 98n377
Well-tempered announcer: a pronunciation gd to classical music, 97n1056
What to name your African-American baby, 96n436
What's in a name, 97n369
Writer's Digest character naming sourcebk, 95n944

NAMIBIA
Namibia, rev ed, 99n99

NAPOLEON I
Impact of Napoleon, 1800-15, 98n469

NARCOTIC HABIT
Drug abuse in society, 95n882

NATIONAL AERONAUTICS & SPACE ADMINISTRATION
NASA thesaurus, 1994 ed, 95n1600

NATIONAL BASKETBALL ASSOCIATION
Sporting News official NBA gd, 95n809
Sporting News official NBA register, 95n810

NATIONAL CHARACTERISTICS
Latitudes & attitudes, 96n915

NATIONAL FOOTBALL LEAGUE
Total football, 98n747

NATIONAL GALLERY (ENGLAND)
National Gallery complete illus catalogue, 97n796

NATIONALISM
Ethnic pols in E Europe, 95n749
Nations without states: a histl dict of contemporary natl movements, 97n583

NATIONAL LEAGUE FOR NURSING
Annual gd to graduate nursing educ 1997, 99n1474
NLN gd to undergraduate RD educ, 5th ed, 99n1477

NATIONAL LIBRARY OF SCOTLAND
Library of Lord George Douglas, 99n612

NATIONAL ORGANIZATION FOR RARE DISORDERS
Complete dir for people with rare disorders, 1998/99, 99n1447

NATIONAL PARKS & RESERVES
Exploring our natl parks & monuments, 9th ed, 96n470

NATIONAL SECURITY—UNITED STATES
Index to docs of the Natl Security Council, 96n774

NATIONAL SERVICE
National serv & AmeriCorps, 98n800

NATIONAL SOCIALISM
Encyclopedia of German resistance to the Nazi movement, 98n470

NATIONAL SONGS
National anthems of the world, 8th ed, 95n1260

NATIVE RACES
Native studies collection, 95n432

NATURAL FOODS
Whole foods companion, 98n1427

NATURAL HISTORY
Atlas of wild places, 95n1558
Field gd to nearby nature, 95n1559
History of natural hist, 95n1556
Illustrated bk of questions & answers, 97n56
Masterworks of man & nature, 2d ed, 96n458
Wild New Zealand, 96n1601

NATURALISTS
Biographical dict of American & Canadian naturalists & environmentalists, 99n1552
Earthkeepers, 95n1763

NATURALIZATION RECORDS
Guide to naturalization records of the US, 98n332

NATURAL RESOURCES
Dictionary of natural resource mgmt, 98n1632
Natural resources, 99n1571
Resources of the Third World, 98n120

NATURE
Eyewitness ency of nature [CD-ROM], 97n1287
100 natural wonders of the world, 96n1602
Pockets: nature facts, 98n1458

NATURE CONSERVATION
Conservation dir, 1994, 95n1769
Wilderness preservation: a ref hndbk, 95n1785

NATURE IN LITERATURE
American nature writers, 97n965

NATURE—MYTHOLOGY
Legends of the earth, sea, & sky, 99n1184

NATUROPATHY
Complete bk of natural & medicinal cures, 95n1670
Treasury of natural 1st aid remedies from A-Z, 96n1715

NAUTICAL ALMANACS
Nautical almanac for the yr 1996, 96n1895

NAVAJO LANGUAGE—DICTIONARIES—ENGLISH
Colloquial Navaho: a dict, 95n1090
Navajo-English dict, 95n1089

NAVAL ART & SCIENCE
Encyclopedia of Naval hist, 99n639
Facts on File dict of nautical terms, 95n1795

NAVAL HISTORY
Chronology of the Cold War at sea 1945-91, 99n643
Earl Mountbatten of Burma, 1900-79, 99n505
Historical dict of the United States Navy, 99n641
Naval Institute histl atlas of the US Navy, 96n701
Nelson almanac, 99n642
Pirates!, 96n1345
Pirates & privateers of the Americas, 96n1344

NAVIGATION
Elsevier's nautical dict, 3d ed, 96n1894

NEBRASKA
Nebraska hist, 96n494

NEGOTIATION
Negotiation lit, 96n283

NEGRO DIGEST
Roots of Afrocentric thought, 99n985

NEIGHBORHOOD JUSTICE CENTERS
Resolving community disputes, 95n597

NELSON, HORATIO
Nelson almanac, 99n642

NEPTUNE (PLANET)
Atlas of Neptune, 95n1722

NETHERLANDS ANTILLES
Netherlands Antilles & Aruba, 95n167

NEUROLOGY
Brain ency, 97n1334

NEUROPSYCHOLOGY
Blackwell dict of neuropsychology, 97n626

NEW AGE MOVEMENT
Body, mind & spirit, 95n1477
New mktg opportunities, 4th ed, 96n1482

NEWBERY MEDAL
Newbery & Caldecott awards, 1998 ed, 99n995
Newbery companion, 98n1091

NEWCASTLE, THOMAS PELHAM-HOLLES, DUKE OF
Duke of Newcastle, 1693-1768, & Henry Pelham, 1694-1754, 98n687

NEW ENGLAND
New England in US govt pubs, 1789-1849, 99n452
Peterson's gd to New England colleges 1995, 11th ed, 96n347
Plant explorer's gd to New England, 96n474
Rail lines of S New England, 96n1888
Yankee talk: a dict of New England expressions, 97n835

NEW ENGLAND IN LITERATURE
New England in fiction 1787-1990, 95n1183

NEW GUINEA
Mammals of New Guinea, rev ed, 96n1631

NEW HAMPSHIRE
New Hampshire [&] Vt.: atlas of histl county boundaries, 96n439

NEW LEFT
Left gd: a gd to left-of-center orgs, 97n614
Left index, 97n61

NEWS AGENCIES
Hudson's Washington news media contacts dir 1998, 99n823

NEWSGROUPS (INTERNET). *See also* **LISTSERVS**
CyberHound's gd to Internet discussion groups, 98n1584
Mecklermedia's official Internet World Internet yellow pages, 1996 ed, 98n1587

NEWSLETTERS
College media dir 1994, 95n952
Directory of electronic journals, newsletters, & academic discussion lists, 6th ed, 97n1375
Hudson's subscription newsletter dir, 12th ed, 96n978
Hudson's subscription newsletter dir, 13th ed, 98n76
Newsletters in print 1998, 10th ed, 98n880
Oxbridge dir of newsletters 1994, 95n954

NEWSPAPERS
Bacon's bus media dir 1994, 95n933
Bacon's bus media dir 1998, 99n821
Bacon's intl media dir 1996, 97n760
Bacon's newspaper dir 1994, 95n951
Bacon's newspaper dir 1998, 46th ed, 98n877
Biographical dict of American newspaper columnists, 96n973
Burrelle's media dir, June 1994 [CD-ROM], 95n934
By the nos: publishing, 99n620
College media dir 1994, 95n952
CompuServe companion, 95n953
Editor & Publisher intl yr bk 1994, 96n980
Editor & Publisher yr bk 1994 [CD-ROM], 96n981
Gale dir of pubns & broadcast media, 131st ed, 99n822
National dir of newspaper op-ed pages, 96n979
News media yellow bk, 96n963
Newspapers online, 1995, 3d ed, 96n982
Power media selects, 9th ed, 96n988
Ulrich's intl pers dir 1998, 36th ed, 99n74

NEWSPAPERS—DATABASES
Fulltext sources online, July 1997, 98n51

NEWS SERVICES
Hudson's Washington news media contacts dir 1998, 99n823

NEW YORK
Awesome almanac—N.Y., 97n85
Cruising gd to NY waterways & Lake Champlain, 99n430
Encyclopedia of NYC, 96n107

Historical atlas of NYC, 96n487
New York, the city in more than 500 memorable quotations, 98n101
New York City in the 1980s, 95n471
Peterson's gd to NY colleges 1995, 11th ed, 96n348

NEW YORK PUBLIC LIBRARY
Dance on disc [CD-ROM], 95n1358
New York Public Lib's bks of the century, 97n882

NEW YORK STOCK EXCHANGE
New York Stock Exchange fact bk: 1993 data, 95n219

NEW YORK TIMES
Personal name index to The New York Times Index, v.5, 98n67
Personal name index to The New York Times Index, v.6, 98n68

NEW ZEALAND
Asian & Australasian cos, 95n240
Cultures of the World, 99n84
Historical dict of New Zealand, 97n144
New Zealand, rev ed, 99n114
New Zealand bks in print 1995, 23d ed, 96n23
Periodicals in print: Australia, New Zealand, & the S Pacific 1996, 13th ed, 97n64
Wild New Zealand, 96n1601

NEW ZEALAND LITERATURE
Post-Colonial lits in English: SE Asia, New Zealand, & the Pacific, 1970-92, 97n1013

NICHOLS, RED
Red Nichols story, 98n1236

NIETZSCHE, FRIEDRICH WILHELM
Nietzsche canon, 97n1157

NIGER
Historical dict of Niger, 3d ed, 98n454
Niger, 95n120

NIGERIA
Women in Nigeria, 97n725

NIXON, RICHARD M.
Nixon on stage & screen, 99n1238

NOBEL PRIZES
Nobel laureates in chemistry, 1901-92, 95n1715
Nobel prize winners 1992-96 suppl, 98n26
Who's who of Nobel prize winners 1901-95, 3d ed, 97n30
Women of peace: Nobel peace prize winners, 96n944

NONPROFIT ORGANIZATIONS. *See also* GRANTS-IN-AID
By the nos: nonprofit orgs, 99n48
Directory of grants for orgs serving people with disabilities, 10th ed, 98n774
Directory of operating grants, 3d ed, 98n786
Encyclopedia of assns, 99n50
Encyclopedia of assns: regional, state, & local orgs, 7th ed, 99n51
Guide to fed funding for govts & nonprofits, 19th ed, 98n792
Literature of the nonprofit sector, v.8, 98n783
National dir of nonprofit orgs 1995, 96n193
National dir of nonprofit orgs 1998, 99n55
Nonprofit law dict, 96n579
Nonprofit manager's resource dir, 98n244
Nonprofit sector yellow bk, winter 1999 ed, 99n142
Non-profit's job finder, 3d ed, 95n316
Non-profits & edu job finder 1997-2000, 98n235
NSFRE fund-raising dict, 98n784
Opportunities for vocational study, 96n385
Who get grants/who gives grants, 96n877
Who's who in Washington nonprofit groups 1994, 95n72

NONSEXIST LANGUAGE
Talking about people: a gd to fair & accurate lang, 99n895

NONVERBAL COMMUNICATION
Dictionary of worldwide gestures, 98n711

NONVIOLENCE
Nonviolent action, 98n496
Protest, power, & change, 98n692

NORMANDY (FRANCE)
D-Day ency, 95n686
Simon & Schuster D-Day ency: a multimedia exploration! [CD-ROM], 95n689

NORTH AFRICA
Handbook of pol sci research on the Middle East & N Africa, 99n648

NORTH AMERICA
American folklore, 97n1088
Annual bulletin of coal stats for Europe & N America, 1994, 96n1838
Annual bulletin of electric energy stats for Europe & N America, 1994, v.38, 96n1839
Arthur Andersen N American bus sourcebk, 96n288
Encyclopedia of the N American colonies, 95n540
French image of America, 95n531
Grolier lib of N American biogs, 96n27
Hammond odyssey atlas of N America, 95n466
Prices of agricultural products & selected inputs for Europe & N America 1992/93, 96n1520
Trends in Europe & N America 1995, 97n719

NORTH AMERICA—HISTORY
Bibliographic gd to N American hist 1994, 96n489
Colonial wars of N America, 1512-1763, 97n413
Great events from hist: N American series, rev ed, 98n497
Larousse dict of N American hist, 96n508

NORTH AMERICA—MAPS
Hammond road atlas America, 96n441

NORTH AMERICAN AGREEMENT ON LABOR COOPERATION
North American labor markets, 99n227

NORTH AMERICAN FREE TRADE AGREEMENT
Encyclopedia of the N American Free Trade Agreement, 96n305
Handbook of N American industry, 99n220
NAFTA & GATT: environmental & economic issues, 98n705
NAFTA bibliog, 98n255
North American labor markets, 99n227

NORTH ATLANTIC TREATY ORGANIZATION
North Atlantic Treaty Org, 96n773

NORTH CAROLINA
Atlas of histl county boundaries: N.C., 99n448
Dictionary of N.C. biog, v.5, 95n37
Freshwater fishes of the Carolinas, Va., Md., & Dela., 95n1588
North Carolina hist, 96n493

NORTHEASTERN STATES
Exploring the Northeast states through lit, 95n1122

NORWEGIAN LANGUAGE—DICTIONARIES—ENGLISH
English-Norwegian, Norwegian-English dict, 99n937
Norwegian dict, 2d ed, 96n1120

NOVUM TESTAMENTUM
Novum Testamentum, v.36a, 96n1460

NUCLEAR ARMS CONTROL
Nuclear test ban: glossary in English, French, & Arabic, 97n578

NUCLEAR WEAPONS. See also WEAPONS
Jane's NBC protection equipment 1996-97, 9th ed, 97n570
Nuclear weapons databk, v.5, 95n702

NUMBER THEORY
Key dates in no theory hist, 96n1829

NURSERY RHYMES
Oxford dict of nursery rhymes, 99n1004

NURSING
Annual gd to graduate nursing educ 1997, 99n1474
Chemotherapy hndbk, 95n1681
Delmar's A-Z NDR-97: nurse's drug ref, 98n1566
Delmar's therapeutic class drug gd for nurses 1997, 98n1567
Dictionary of nursing theory & research, 2d ed, 96n1732
Handbook of therapeutic interventions, 96n1735
NLN gd to undergraduate RD educ, 5th ed, 99n1477
Nurse's clinical gd to psychiatric & mental health care, 97n1355
Nursing diagnosis pocket manual, 97n1353
Nursing licensure gdlines, 1998, 99n1476
Nursing96 drug hndbk, 97n1360
Peterson's gd to nursing programs, 4th ed, 99n1478
PharmFacts for nurses, 97n1361
Scholarships & loans for nursing educ 1997-98, 99n1479

NURSING HOMES
Complete dir of nursing facilities for younger adults with chronic physical disabilities, 1994, 96n855
Directory of nursing homes, 1995, 96n1731
Inside gd to American nursing homes, 1988-99 ed, 99n1475
Nursing home statl yrbk, 1995, 97n1327

NUTRIBASE (COMPUTER FILE)
Nutribase nutrition facts desk ref, 96n1540

NUTRITION
Bowes & Church's food values of portions commonly used, 16th ed, 95n1520
Concise ency of foods & nutrition, 96n1524
Contemporary & histl lit of food sci & human nutrition, 96n1522
Dictionary of healthful food terms, 98n1420
Dynamic nutrition for maximum performance, 98n1514
Encyclopedia of nutrition & good health, 98n1521
Foods & nutrition ency, 2d ed, 95n1515
Green kitchen hndbk, 98n1425
Human nutrition 1990-Sept 1994 [CD-ROM], 95n1643
International dict of food & nutrition, 95n1514
Nutribase nutrition facts desk ref, 96n1540
Nutrition & diet therapy ref dict, 4th ed, 98n1422
Prescription for nutritional healing, 98n1508
Yale gd to children's nutrition, 98n1555

NUTS
Brooks & Olmo register of fruit & nut varieties, 99n1330

OBESITY
Encyclopedia of obesity & eating disorders, 95n1678

OBITUARIES
Annual obituary 1993, 95n23
Last word: The New York Times bk of obituaries & farewells, 99n34

OCCULTISM
Divining the future: prognostication from astrology to zoomancy, 96n791
Encyclopedia of afterlife beliefs & phenomena, 96n1445
Encyclopedia of occultism & parapsychology, 4th ed, 97n633
Illustrated ency of divination, 98n714
Mammoth dict of symbols, English lang ed, 97n636
Man, myth & magic, new ed, 96n1348
Tarot for beginners, 96n787
Wizards & sorcerers, 98n716
World of ghosts & the supernatural, 96n784

OCCUPATIONAL APTITUDE TESTS
ETS test collection catalog, v.2, 2d ed, 96n314

OCCUPATIONAL HEALTH & SAFETY. See also INDUSTRIAL HYGIENE
Encyclopaedia of occupational health & safety, 4th ed [CD-ROM], 99n280
Occupational safety & health law 1997, 99n566

OSHA quick gd for residential builders & contractors, 99n1404
Safety & health on the Internet, 2d ed, 99n281

OCCUPATIONAL THERAPY
Quick ref dict for occupational therapy, 99n1423

OCCUPATIONAL TRAINING
National gd to educl credit for training programs, 1997 ed, 98n315
Opportunities for vocational study, 96n385

OCCUPATIONS. *See also* CAREERS
America's top jobs for college graduates, rev ed, 95n309
America's top jobs for people without college degrees, 3d ed, 98n227
America's top medical & human servs jobs, 2d ed, 95n310
America's top office, mgmt, & sales jobs, 2d ed, 95n311
America's top office, mgmt, sales, & professional jobs, 3d ed, 98n228
Career connection for college educ, 2d ed, 95n318
Career perspectives software series [CD-ROM], 98n223
Cuts in defense jobs in US counties, metropolitan areas, & states, 1992-2003, 96n270
Dictionary of occupational terms, 95n297
DISCovering careers & jobs [CD-ROM], 96n271
Encyclopedia of careers & vocational guidance [CD-ROM], 96n382
Encyclopedia of careers & vocational guidance, 10th ed, 98n215
Enhanced occupational outlook hndbk, 98n226
Government career gds [CD-ROM], 96n256
Health professions educ dir 1997-98, 98n1512
JIST's electronic enhanced dict of occupational titles, 2d ed [CD-ROM], 98n216
JIST's electronic gd for occupational exploration [CD-ROM], 96n275
JIST's electronic occupational outlook hndbk, 2d ed [CD-ROM], 98n231
JIST's multimedia occupational outlook hndbk, 2d ed [CD-ROM], 98n232
Occupational outlook hndbk, 1996-97 ed, 98n238
Peterson's internships 1996, 16th ed, 97n256
Professional & technical careers, 99n274
Specialty occupational outlook, 96n274
Specialty occupational outlook: trade & technical, 97n262
State occupational outlook hndbk, 99n275
VGM's careers ency, 4th ed, 98n217
Vocational careers sourcebk, 99n263
Young person's occupational outlook hndbk, 97n264

OCCUPATIONS IN LITERATURE
Chaucer's pilgrims, 97n989

OCCUPATIONS—LICENSES
Professional & occupational licensure in the US, 98n704

OCEANIA
Australasia & S Pacific Islands bibliog, 98n144
Familia Gekkonidae (Reptilia, Sauria), pt.1, 96n1634
Far East & Australasia 1997, 28th ed, 97n143
International dict of historic places, v.5, 97n469
International histl stats: Africa, Asia, & Oceania, 1750-1988, 96n917
Mammals of the SW Pacific & Moluccan Islands, 96n1632

OCEANIA—LITERATURE
Indigenous lit of Oceania, 96n1260
Literature for children & YAs about Oceania, 97n142

OCEANOGRAPHY
Glossary of aquatic habitat inventory terminology, 99n1501
Library of the oceans, 99n1538
Oceanographic & marine resources: 1960-Jan 1997 [CD-ROM], 98n1616
Oceans atlas, 95n1733
Practical gd to the marine animals of northeastern N America, 99n1394

OCEAN TRAVEL
Stern's gd to the cruise vacation, 6th ed, 97n1449

OFFICE EQUIPMENT & SUPPLIES
Better buys for bus, 97n187
Essential bus buyer's gd, 98n179

OFFICE MANAGEMENT
America's top office, mgmt, & sales jobs, 2d ed, 95n311
Merriam-Webster's secretarial hndbk, 3d, 95n328
New York Public Lib bus desk ref, 99n282
Professional secretary's hndbk, 3d ed, 96n312

OFFSHORE OIL INDUSTRY
Worldwide offshore contractors & equipment dir, 1994, 95n1621
Worldwide offshore contractors & equipment dir, 1996, 97n1419

OHIO
Awesome almanac—Ohio, 97n86

OIL & GAS JOURNAL
Oil & gas jl data bk, 1995 ed, 96n1845

OLDENBURG, CLAES
Printed stuff: prints, posters, & ephemera by Claes Oldenburg, 99n867

OLD NORSE PHILOLOGY
Annotated bibliog of N America doctoral dissertations on old Norse-Icelandic, 99n892

OLYMPIC GAMES
Chronicle of the Olympics, 1896-1996, 97n660
Chronicle of the Olympics, 1896-2000, 99n738
Historical dict of the modern Olympic movement, 97n661

OMAN
Oman, rev ed, 96n166

O'NEIL, EUGENE
Proverbial Eugene O'Neill, 96n1215

ONLINE BIBLIOGRAPHIC SEARCHING. *See also* **SEARCHING, BIBLIOGRAPHICAL**
CompuServe companion, 95n953
Government online, 96n1776
List of serials indexed for online users 1994, 95n1668

ONLINE DATABASES
Fulltext sources online, July 1997, 98n51
Information industry dir 1998, 18th ed, 99n602
Net gd, 96n1781
Newspapers online, 1995, 3d ed, 96n982
ONLINE 100, 96n1777
Public records online, 1997 ed, 98n706
Sourcebook of online public record experts, 97n540

ONOMASTICS
Alphabetical gd to the lang of name studies, 97n824

OPERA
Bel Canto operas of Rossini, Donizetti, & Bellini, 96n1300
Blacks in opera, 96n1301
EJS: discography of the Edward J. Smith recordings, 95n1286
Giuseppe Verdi: a gd to research, 99n1137
Metropolitan Opera gd to recorded opera, 95n1284
Opera cos & houses of the US, 96n1302
Opera on screen, 99n1218
Opera premiere reviews & re-assessments, 99n1156
Opera: the rough gd, 99n1157
Operas in 1 act, 98n1224
Portable Kobbe's opera gd, 95n1285
Sign-off for the old Met, 99n1155
Ticket to the opera, 98n1223
Viking opera gd, 95n1287
Viking opera gd on CD-ROM [CD-ROM], 95n1288
Who's who in British opera, 95n1283

OPERATION DESERT SHIELD, MILITARY 1990-1991
Operation Desert Shield/Desert Storm, 96n563

OPERATIONS RESEARCH
CompuMath citation index 1993. 2d semiannual, 95n1739

OPHTHALMOLOGY
Dictionary of eye terminology, 3d ed, 98n1553
Physician's desk ref for ophthalmology 1998, 26th ed, 99n1462
Quick ref glossary of eye care terminology, 99n1463

ORCHESTRAL MUSIC
Cello music since 1960, 96n1286
Conductors & composers of popular orchestral music, 99n1158
Conductor's gd to choral-orchestral works, 20th century, part 2, 99n1151
London Philharmonic discography, 98n1204
Orchestra on record, 1896-1926, 98n1225
Orchestral music, 3d ed, 98n1226
Orchestration theory, 97n1057

ORCHIDS
Illustrated survey of orchid genera, 96n1578
Manual of orchids, 96n1576
Orchids for the South, 96n1574
Orchids of Brazil, 95n1543
Wild orchids across N America, 99n1363

ORGANIC COMPOUNDS
Handbook of environmental data on organic chemicals, 3d ed, 97n1389

ORGANIC GARDENING
Organic gardener's home ref, 96n1543

ORGANIC WASTES
Encyclopedia of garbage, 97n1425

ORGANIZATIONAL CHANGE
Research on professional consultation & consultation for orgl change, 98n709

ORGANIZATIONS
Buttress's world gd to abbrevs of orgs, 11th ed, 98n1

ORGANIZED CRIME
Organized crime, 96n594

ORGAN MUSIC
Musical resources for the rev common lectionary, 95n1312
Organ lit, 3d ed, 96n1289

ORIENTAL LITERATURE (ENGLISH)
Post-Colonial lits in English: SE Asia, New Zealand, & the Pacific, 1970-92, 97n1013

ORNAMENTAL CLIMBING PLANTS
Shrubs & climbers, 97n1286

ORNAMENTAL SHRUBS
Shrubs & climbers, 97n1286

ORNAMENTAL TREES
Dirr's hardy trees & shrubs, 98n1456
North American landscape trees, 97n1283
Year in trees, 96n1592

ORTHODOX EASTERN CHURCH
Historical dict of the orthodox church, 97n1212

ORWELL, GEORGE
George Orwell: a bibliog, 99n1073

OUTDOOR RECREATION
Adventure vacations, 96n473
American at play, 98n726
Attitudes toward the outdoors: an annot bibliog, 95n1759

OUTER SPACE
Eyewitness ency of space & the universe [CD-ROM], 97n1395
Frontiers of space exploration, 99n1520
Illustrated bk of questions & answers, 97n56
Kope's outer space dir, 99n1519

Outer space, 99n1522
Pockets: space facts, 96n74
Spaceflight: a Smithsonian gd, 96n1647

OUTLAWS
Lawmen & desperadoes, 96n571

OUTLINE MAPS
Outline maps on file, 98n398

OZONE LAYER
Ozone dilemma, 96n1874

PACIFIC AREA
Asia-Pacific in figures, 10th ed, 98n811
Asia-Pacific petroleum dir 1998, 14th ed, 99n195
Asia Pacific securities hndbk 1993, 95n259
Asian & Australasian cos, 95n240
Economic & social survey of Asia & the Pacific 1995, 96n128
Electric power in Asia & the Pacific, 1991 & 1992, 97n1420
Garland ency of world music, v.9, 99n1120
Japan & the Pacific Rim, 4th ed, 99n102
Mammals of the SW Pacific & Moluccan Islands, 96n1632
Source bk on ageing, 99n746
Statistical indicators for Asia & the Pacific, v.23, 95n897
Statistical indicators for Asia & the Pacific, v.27, 99n788
Statistical yrbk for Asia & the Pacific 1996, 98n815
Who's who in Australasia & the Pacific nations, 3d ed, 99n29

PACIFIC COAST (NORTH AMERICA)
Exploring the Pacific states through lit, 95n1121
Fishes of the tropical E Pacific, 96n1633
Guide to marine invertebrates, 95n1594
Pacific coast crabs & shrimps, 96n1622
Pacific NW, 98n415

PACIFIC ISLANDERS
Peoples of the world: Asians & Pacific Islanders, 95n127

PACIFIC ISLAND LITERATURE (ENGLISH)
Post-Colonial lits in English: SE Asia, New Zealand, & the Pacific, 1970-92, 97n1013

PACIFISTS
Women of peace: Nobel peace prize winners, 96n944

PACKAGING
Vocabulary of packaging, 95n1633
Wiley ency of packaging tech, 2d ed, 98n1493

PAIN
Classification of chronic pain, 2d ed, 96n1723
Pain sourcebk, 99n1473

PAINTERS. *See also* **ARTISTS**
Biographical dir of Native American painters, 97n807
Checklist of painters c1200-1994, 2d ed, 96n652
Dictionary of portrait painters in Britain up to 1920, 98n982

Hans Holbein the younger: a gd to research, 98n943
Henri Matisse: a gd to research, 97n805

PAINTING. *See also* **ART**
American paintings in the Detroit Institute of Arts, v.2, 99n887
Annotated art, 96n1052
Catalogue of paintings in the Folger Shakespeare lib, 95n1021
European paintings in the Metropolitan Museum of Art by artists born before 1865, 97n804
Gallery of her own: an annot bibliog of women in Victorian painting, 98n981
Italian paintings before 1600 in the Art Inst of Chicago, 95n1020
Les Fauves: a sourcebk, 95n1019
Native American painters of the 20th century, 96n1054
Painter's hndbk, 96n1053
Story of painting, 95n1018
3,000 yrs of Chinese painting, 99n888
World painting index, 2d suppl, 96n1056

PALEOGEOGRAPHY
Atlas of Mesozoic & Cenozoic coastlines, 96n1807

PALEONTOLOGY
Biological anomalies: humans III, 96n1559
Field gd to prehistoric life, 96n1815
Fossil atlas: fishes, 97n1404
Fossils of the Burgess Shale, 96n1813
Prehistoria [CD-ROM], 96n1816
Scholastic children's gd to dinosaurs & other prehistoric animals, 95n1735
Visual dict of prehistoric life, 96n1817

PALEOPATHOLOGY
Cambridge ency of human paleopathology, 99n1439

PALESTINE
Historical dict of Palestine, 98n488
Palestine question, 95n175

PALLADIUM
Platinum & palladium buyer's gd, 98n913

PALMERSTON, HENRY JOHN TEMPLE
Lord Palmerston 1784-1865: a bibliog, 95n753

PALMS
Palms throughout the world, 97n1284

PAN-AMERICANISM
Encyclopedia of the inter-American system, 98n695

PAPERBACKS
British sci fiction paperbacks & mags 1949-56, 96n1234
Paperbound bks in print fall 1994, 95n20
Victorian yellowbacks & paperbacks, 1849-1905, v.1, 96n1223
Victorian yellowbacks & paperbacks, 1849-1905, v.2, 96n1224

PAPER WORK
Papercutting: an intl bibliog & selected gd to US collections, 95n981

PAPUA NEW GUINEA
Cultures of the World, 99n84
Historical dict of Papua New Guinea, 95n177

PARAGUAY
Guide to collections on Paraguay in the US, 96n551

PARAMOUNT PICTURES CORP.
Paramount in Paris, 99n1236

PARAPSYCHOLOGY
Alternative realities, 96n785
Bibliographic gd to psychology 1996, 98n707
Encyclopedia of claims, frauds, & hoaxes of the occult & supernatural, 97n637
Encyclopedia of occultism & parapsychology, 4th ed, 97n633
Encyclopedia of the paranormal, 97n634
Haunted places: the natl dir, rev ed, 97n635
National dir of haunted places, 95n788
World of ghosts & the supernatural, 96n784

PARENTING. *See also* CHILD CARE
Family wisdom, 97n69
Grandparents, 98n780
Having children: the best resources to help you prepare, 99n753
Mayo Clinic complete bk of pregnancy & baby's 1st yr, 96n1722
New parents sourcebk, 97n709
Parenting A to Z, 2d ed, 98n803
Parents' resource almanac, 96n901
Sourcebook on parenting & child care, 96n899

PARIS (FRANCE)
Historical dict of Paris, 99n497
Paris, 99n127

PARKER, CHARLIE
Dial recordings of Charlie Parker, 99n1166

PARKS
Parks dir of the US, 2d ed, 95n512

PARLIAMENTARY PAPERS
Index to the House of Commons parliamentary papers on CD-ROM [CD-ROM], 99n571

PARLIAMENTARY PRACTICES
Robert's rules in plain English, 98n681

PASTERNAK, BORIS
Boris Pasternak: a ref gd, 95n1239

PASTORAL THEOLOGY
New dict of Christian ethics & pastoral theology, 97n1209

PATENT LAWS & LEGISLATION
Patent, copyright, & trademark, 97n520
Patent law index, 1997, 98n545

PATENTS
Historical 1st patents, 96n1509
McCarthy's desk ency of intellectual property, 2d ed, 97n519
Patents hndbk, 96n589
World databases in patents, 96n587

PAUL THE APOSTLE, SAINT
Dictionary of Paul & his letters, 95n1450

PEACE OFFICERS
Lawmen & desperadoes, 96n571

PEACE (PHILOSOPHY)
Peaceful peoples, 95n91
Peacemaking in medieval Europe, 99n492
Political leaders & peacemakers, 96n418
Scholars' gd to Washington, DC, for peace & intl security studies, 96n656
State of war & peace atlas, 99n700
Women of peace: Nobel peace prize winners, 96n944

PELHAM, HENRY
Duke of Newcastle, 1693-1768, & Henry Pelham, 1694-1754, 98n687

PENGUINS
Penguins of the world, 96n1616

PENNSYLVANIA
Guide to the hist of Pa., 95n530

PENTACOSTALISM
Charismatic movement, pts.1-4, 97n1205

PEONIES
Gardener's gd to growing peonies, 99n1352
Peonies, 96n1577

PERCUSSION INSTRUMENTS
Encyclopedia of percussion, 96n1291

PERENNIALS
Ball perennial manual, 97n1275
Favorite perennials, 96n1570
Perennials, 97n1274
Plantfinder's gd to tender perennials, 99n1349
Smaller perennials, 98n1435

PERESTROIKA
Gorbachev biblog, 1985-91, 98n482

PERFORMING ARTS. *See also* DANCING; MOTION PICTURES; THEATER
ARCO 100 best careers in entertainment, 96n1364
Artists & writers colonies, 97n745
Bibliographic gd to theatre arts 1996, 98n1322
Biographical dict of actors, actresses, musicians, dancers, managers...v.15, 95n1411

Black talent resource gd, 1994 ed, 95n1356
Cambridge gd to Asian theatre, 95n1414
Entertainment awards, 97n1099
Obituaries in the performing arts, 1994, 97n1097
Obituaries in the performing arts, 1995, 97n1098
Performers, 96n419
Performing arts: a gd to the ref lit, 95n1339
Performing arts bus ency, 98n1265
Peterson's professional degree programs in the visual & performing arts 1995, 96n962
Peterson's professional degree programs in the visual & performing arts, 4th ed, 99n1197

PERFORMING ARTS—AWARDS
Big bk of show bus awards, 99n1198

PERFORMING ARTS FESTIVALS
Music festivals from Bach to blues, 97n1029

PERINATAL PHARMACOLOGY
Effects of neurologic & psychiatric drugs on the fetus & nursing infant, 99n1480

PERIODICALS
ACCESS: the supplementary index to pers, 96n78
Alternative press index, 97n58
Annotations: a dir of pers listed in the Alternative Press Index, 1996 ed, 97n63
ASSIA plus [CD-ROM], 96n97
Association for Population/Family Planning Libs & Info Centers Intl (AFPLIC-I) union list of serials, 96n861
Avery index to architectural pers at Columbia Univ [CD-ROM], 95n1013
Avery index to architectural pers, 13th suppl, 95n1014
Bacon's bus media dir 1994, 95n933
Bacon's bus media dir 1998, 99n821
Bacon's dirs on disc 1995 update [CD-ROM], 96n974
Bacon's intl media dir 1996, 97n760
Bacon's mag dir 1994, 95n950
Bacon's mag dir 1998, 98n876
BHI plus [CD-ROM], 96n955
Biography index [CD-ROM], 96n24
Burrelle's media dir, June 1994 [CD-ROM], 95n934
By the nos: publishing, 99n620
CHOICE reviews on SilverPlatter [CD-ROM], 96n84
CIJE on disc, Jan 1969-Jul 1994 [CD-ROM], 95n346
College media dir 1994, 95n952
CompuMath citation index 1993. 2d semiannual, 95n1739
CompuServe companion, 95n953
Desert Mag subject index, 98n878
Directory of small pr & mag editors & publishers, 24th ed, 95n668
Earthquakes & the built environment index, 1984—July 1995 [CD-ROM], 97n1399
Free mags for libs, 4th ed, 95n647
Fulltext sources online, July 1997, 98n51
Guide to religious & inspirational mags, 95n1448
Guide to special issues & indexes of pers, 4th ed, 95n86
Health & British mags in the 19th century, 99n1417
Health industry quicksource, 97n1313

Hudson's subscription newsletter dir, 13th ed, 98n76
Index to black pers 1995, 98n345
Index to black pers 1997, 99n377
Index to dance pers: 1995, 98n1270
Index to how to do it info, 1994 suppl, 96n1014
International dir of little mags & small prs, 29th ed, 95n669
International index to music pers 1997:2 [CD-ROM], 98n1208
International relations research dir, 97n619
Latin American advertising, mktg, & media sourcebk, 96n301
Leo Burnett worldwide advertising & media fact bk, 96n302
Literary index to American mags, 1850-1900, 97n960
Magazines for kids & teens, 96n86
Magazines for libs, 8th ed, 96n85
Magazines for libs, 9th ed, 99n72
National Hispanic media dir, 1997, 98n861
News media yellow bk, 96n963
Novel & short story writer's market, 1996, 97n753
PCI: pers contents index [CD-ROM], 98n66
Periodicals in print: Australia, New Zealand, & the S Pacific 1996, 13th ed, 97n64
Philosopher's index, v.27, 95n1432
Power media selects, 9th ed, 96n988
Readers' gd abstracts full text mega ed [CD-ROM], 98n69
Readers' gd for young people [CD-ROM], 98n77
Readers' gd to per lit 1995, 98n70
Samir Husni's gd to new consumer mags, 1997 ed, 98n882
SPDCD 1995: the standard per dir [CD-ROM], 96n87
Standard per dir, 1997, 20th ed, 97n65
Standard per dir 1998, 99n73
Ulrich's intl pers dir 1994-95, 95n87
Ulrich's intl pers dir 1996, 96n88
Ulrich's intl pers dir 1997, 97n66
Ulrich's intl pers dir 1998, 99n74
Wildlife worldwide [CD-ROM], 96n1607
Women's per in the US, 97n743
World dir of trade & bus jls, 97n174

PERSIAN GULF WAR, 1991
Encyclopedia of the Persian Gulf War, 97n454
Historical dict of the Persian Gulf war 1990-91, 99n630
1990-91 Gulf War, 97n456

PERSONNEL DEPARTMENTS
American dir of job & labor market info, 95n298

PERSONNEL MANAGEMENT
Human resources yrbk 1996/97, 98n224
Manager's desk ref, 2d ed, 97n265
Mandated benefits, 98n236

PERSONNEL RECORDS
Verify those credentials: do you know who you're dealing with?, 98n63

PERU
Ancient Peruvian art, 97n794
Sendero Luminoso: an annot bibliog of the Shining Path guerrilla movement, 1980-93, 97n502

PESTS
Ball pest & disease manual, 99n1360
Integrated pest mgmt glossary, 95n1513

PETROLEUM ENGINEERING
Illustrated petroleum ref dict, 4th ed, 95n1745
International petroleum ency 1994, 95n1744
Pricing stats sourcebk, 96n1846
Refining stats sourcebk, 96n1849

PETROLEUM INDUSTRY & TRADE. *See also* OIL INDUSTRIES
Annual bulletin of gas stats for Europe & N America 1994, v.38, 96n1840
Asia-Pacific petroleum dir 1998, 14th ed, 99n195
Canadian oil industry dir, 1994, 95n1746
D & D standard oil abbreviator, 4th ed, 96n1832
European oilfield serv, supply, & manufacturers dir, 1996, 2d ed, 97n1417
Geologists & the hist of geology, suppl 2, v.1, 97n1402
Handbook of oil industry terms & phrases, 5th ed, 96n1676
International petroleum ency 1998, 99n1399
International petroleum research dir 1994, 95n1747
Latin America petroleum dir, 1995, 14th ed, 96n1834
Latin America petroleum dir, 1998, 17th ed, 99n196
Natural gas stats sourcebk, 95n1753
Oil & gas info 1992, 95n1754
Oil & gas jl data bk, 1995 ed, 96n1845
Oil & gas on the Internet, 97n1415
Pricing stats sourcebk, 99n1548
USA oil industry dir 1998, 37th ed, 99n192
Worldwide offshore contractors & equipment dir, 1996, 28th ed, 97n1419
Worldwide offshore petroleum dir 1998, 30th ed, 99n213
Worldwide petrochemical dir, 1995, 33d ed, 96n1835
Worldwide petrochemical dir, 1998, 36th ed, 99n214
Worldwide petroleum industry outlook, 99n1549

PETS
Complete bk of pet names, 98n1462
Encyclopedia of natural pet care, 99n1384
On the road with your pet, 99n424
Vacationing with your pet, 98n402

PHARMACEUTICAL INDUSTRY. *See also* DRUGS
Biotechnology in the US pharmaceutical industry 1995, 4th ed, 96n1733

PHARMACOGNOSY
Dictionary of natural products, 98n1569

PHARMACOLOGY. *See also* DRUGS
Burger's medicinal chemistry & drug discovery, 5th ed, 98n1565
Drug Topics red bk, 1995, 96n1734
European pharmaceutical technical & regulatory compendium, 96n1742
History of pharmacy, 96n1736
PharmFacts for nurses, 97n1361
Practitioner's gd to psychoactive drugs for children & adolescents, 95n1687
World databases in bioscis & pharmacology, 97n1241

PHENOMENOLOGY
Encyclopedia of phenomenology, 98n1335

PHILADELPHIA PHILLIES (BASEBALL TEAM)
New Phillies ency, 95n808

PHILANTHROPY. *See also* GRANTS-IN-AID
America's new fndns 1998, 12th ed, 99n760
Directory of social serv grants, 2d ed, 99n765
Financial aid for the disabled & their families 1998-2000, 99n294
Foundation dir 1997, 19th ed, 98n787
Foundation dir suppl, 98n788
Foundation giving, 1997 ed, 98n794
Foundation reporter 1999, 30th ed, 99n767
Foundations of the 1990s, 99n768
Fund raiser's gd to human service funding 1997, 99n774
Fund raiser's gd to religious philanthropy 1996, 9th ed, 97n691
Funding sources for community & economic dvlpmt 1998, 99n770
Guide to US fndns, their trustees, officers, & donors, 1997 ed, 98n789
National gd to funding for info tech, 98n583
National gd to funding in health, 5th ed, 99n1427
Practical gd to planned giving 1998, 98n791
PRI index, 99n771

PHILIPPINES
Historical dict of the Philippines, 99n487
Philippines bus, 97n236
Philippines in WW II & to independence (Dec. 8, 1941-July 4, 1946), 2d ed, 97n432

PHILOLOGY
English lang scholarship, 97n809
Key gd to electronic resources: lang & lit, 98n985

PHILOSOPHERS
Bibliography of Bertrand Russell, 96n1423
Biographical dict of 20th-century philosophers, 97n1158
Collaborative bibliog of women in philosophy, 98n1332
Contemporary literary criticism, v.86, 97n895
Directory of American philosophers 1994-1995, 95n1430
Directory of American philosophers 1996-97, 18th ed, 98n1340
Encyclopedia of classical philosophy, 98n1334
Encyclopedia of phenomenology, 98n1335
Georges Bataille: a bibliog, 95n1423
Great thinkers of the E world, 96n1433
Hobbes dict, 97n1165
International dir of philosophy & philosophers 1993-94, 95n1431
International dir of philosophy & philosophers 1997-98, 10th ed, 98n1342
Kant dict, 96n1428
Martin Heidegger (2): a bibliog, 97n1156
Nineteenth-Century lit criticism, v.51, 97n912

Nineteenth-Century lit criticism annual cum title index for 1996, 97n914
Oxford companion to philosophy, 97n1166
Philosopher's index [CD-ROM], 96n1436
Philosopher's phone bk, 1995, 96n1430
Roland Barthes: a bibliog, 95n1424
Routledge dict of 20th-century pol thinkers, 2d ed, 99n655
Sartre: bibliog 1980-92, 95n1426
Thirty-Five Oriental philosophers, 96n1427
Thomas Aquinas: intl bibliog 1977-90, 95n1437
Twentieth-Century literary criticism, v.59, 97n920
Twentieth-Century literary criticism, v.61, 97n922
Twentieth-Century literary criticism annual cum title index for 1996, 97n923
Wittgenstein dict, 97n1162

PHILOSOPHY
ABC-CLIO world hist companion to utopian movements, 99n1253
Aristotle's Metaphysics: annot bibliog of the 20th-century lit, 99n1250
Cambridge dict of philosophy, 97n1159
Companion to the philosophy of mind, 96n1432
Cumulative index to vols. 1-6 of Paul Oskar Kristeller's Iter Italicum, 99n1259
Dictionary of philosophy, 3d ed, 97n1164
Dictionary of philosophy & religion, new ed, 98n1337
Encyclopedia of classical philosophy, 98n1334
Encyclopedia of philosophy suppl, 97n1160
Encyclopedia of the Enlightenment, 97n475
From the beginning to Plato, 99n1255
Guidebook for publishing philosophy, 1997 ed, 98n867
Hannah Arendt 2: a bibliog, 98n636
International dir of philosophy & philosophers 1993-94, 95n1431
International dir of philosophy & philosophers 1997-98, 10th ed, 98n1342
Mikhail Bakhtin (II): a bibliog, 95n1425
Oxford companion to philosophy, 97n1166
Oxford dict of philosophy, 95n1428
Oxford hist of W philosophy, 96n1434
Philosopher's index, v.27, 95n1432
Philosophy: a gd to the ref lit, 2d ed, 98n1330
Philosophy of Cynicism, 96n1425
Story of philosophy, 99n1256
Ten yrs of classicists: dissertations & outcomes 1988-97, 99n891
Walford's gd to ref material, v.2: social & histl scis, 6th ed, 95n98
Young person's gd to philosophy, 99n1258

PHILOSOPHY, ASIAN
Companion ency of Asian philosophy, 99n1254
Encyclopedia of E philosophy & religion, 96n1483
Sourcebk for modern Japanese philosophy, 99n1257

PHILOSOPHY, INDIAN
Concise dict of Indian philosophy, rev ed, 98n1336

PHOENIX AWARD
Phoenix award of the children's lit assn 1990-94, 98n1092

PHONETICS
Dictionary of phonetics & phonology, 97n819
Phonetic symbol gd, 2d ed, 97n815

PHONOGRAPH
Berliner gramophone records, 96n1273

PHONOLOGY
Dictionary of phonetics & phonology, 97n819

PHOTOCOPYING PROCESS
Libraries & copyright, 95n656

PHOTOGRAPHERS
Biographies of Western photographers, 99n861
Contemporary photographers, 3d ed, 96n1018
Photographers on disc [CD-ROM], 98n937

PHOTOGRAPHY
A-Z of creative photography, 99n860
ARTbibliographies modern on disc, fall 1993 [CD-ROM], 95n991
Business & legal forms for photographers, rev ed, 99n859
History of photography, v.2, 96n1019
History of photography, v.3, 98n938
Index to American photographic collections, 3d ed, 97n789
Masterworks of man & nature, 2d ed, 96n458
Photographer's market, 1994, 95n989
Photographer's market, 1998, 98n936
Visual resources dir, 96n378

PHYSICAL ANTHROPOLOGY
History of physical anthropology, 98n320

PHYSICAL FITNESS
Fodor's healthy escapes, 5th ed, 98n405
Marshall Cavendish ency of health, rev ed, 96n1682

PHYSICALLY HANDICAPPED. See also HANDICAPPED
Complete dir of nursing facilities for younger adults with chronic physical disabilities, 1994, 96n855
Man's gd to coping with disability, 98n775
Resource gd for the disabled, 96n854
Woman's gd to coping with disability, 96n859
Woman's gd to coping with disability, 2d ed, 98n777

PHYSICAL MEASUREMENTS
ISA hndbk of measurement equations & tables, 95n1500
Sizes: the illus ency, 96n1787
Sizesaurus, 96n1514

PHYSICAL SCIENCES
Best graduate programs: physical & biological scis, 2d ed, 99n336
Encyclopedia of earth & physical scis, 99n1514
Magill's survey of sci [CD-ROM], 95n1502
Magill's survey of sci: earth sci series, 99n1515
Magill's survey of sci: physical sci series suppl, 99n1502

PHYSICIANS
Canadian medical dir 1994, 95n1658

Canadian medical dir on CD-ROM, 1996 [CD-ROM], 97n1320
Directory of physicians in the US, 35th ed, 98n1533
Directory of physicians in the US, 35th ed [CD-ROM], 98n1534
Official ABMS dir of board certified medical specialists 1996, 96n1704
Physician characteristics & distribution in the US, 98n1536
Physician marketplace stats 1997-98, 99n1434
State medical licensure gdlines 1998, 99n1449

PHYSICISTS
Directory of physics, astronomy, & geophysics staff, 1997 biennial ed, 99n1322

PHYSICS
CRC hndbk of chemistry & physics, 75th ed, 95n1711
Einstein dict, 97n1409
Encyclopedia of applied physics, v.15, 97n1407
Encyclopedia of applied physics, v.16, 97n1408
Handbook of physical quantities, 98n1620
Information sources in physics, 3d ed, 95n1737
Macmillan ency of physics, 97n1410
McGraw-Hill dict of physics, 2d ed, 98n1621
Physics quick ref gd, 97n1406
Popular physics & astronomy, 97n1411
Visual dict of physics, 96n1819
World databases in physics & mathematics, 96n1788

PIANISTS
Notable 20th-century pianists, 96n1293

PIANO
Encyclopedia of keyboard instruments, v.1, 95n1278
Makers of the piano, 1700-1820, 97n1050

PIANO MUSIC
International ency of violin-keyboard sonatas & composer biogs, 2d ed, 97n1043
Piano music for 1 hand, 96n1292
Piano works of Serge Prokofiev, 95n1277
Traditional world music influences in contemporary solo piano lit, 99n1148

PIANO WITH ORCHESTRA
History of music for harpsichord or piano & orchestra, 98n1227

PICTURE BOOKS FOR CHILDREN
A to zoo: subject access to children's picture bks, 99n1008
Art of children's picture bks, 2d ed, 96n1183
Dictionary of 20th century British bk illustrators, 96n1055
Multicultural picture bks, 95n1135
Picture bks to enhance the curriculum, 98n284
Picture this: picture bks for YAs, 98n1097
Seventh bk of jr authors & illustrators, 97n937
Using picture storybks to teach literary devices. v.2, 96n1164
Worth a 1,000 words: an annot gd to picture bks for older readers, 98n1090

PICTURE DICTIONARIES
Barron's jr illus dict: French-English, 95n1072
Children's visual dict, 96n43
DK illus Oxford dict, 99n44
Dorling Kindersley children's illus dict, 95n1048
Dorling Kindersley ultimate visual dict, 95n52
Kingfisher illus children's dict, 96n1087
Macmillan visual dict: multilingual ed, 95n59
Oxford-Duden pictorial English dict, 2d ed, 96n1096
Oxford-Duden pictorial Hungarian-English dict, 96n1109
Oxford-Duden pictorial Italian & English dict, 96n1110
Oxford-Duden pictorial Thai & English dict, 96n1140
Precious Moments children's Bible dict, 96n1451
Reader's Digest children's illus dict, 95n1052
Ultimate visual dict, 99n919
Visual dict of prehistoric life, 96n1817
Visual dict of the skeleton, 96n1683

PICTURES—INDEXES
Illustration index 8, 1992-96, 99n876

PIDGIN LANGUAGES
Hippocrene concise Haitian Creole-English, English-Haitian Creole dict, 96n1106

PIERCE, FRANKLIN
Franklin Pierce: a bibliog, 95n528

PIPELINES
Worldwide pipelines & contractors dir, 1995, 15th ed, 96n1837

PIRATES
Pirates!, 96n1345
Pirates & seafaring swashbucklers on the Hollywood screen, 96n1407

PITCHERS (BASEBALL)
Charmed circle: 20-game-winning pitchers in baseball's 20th century, 98n732
Cy Young award winners, 96n808
Worst baseball pitchers of all time, 95n805

PITTSBURGH
Pittsburgh bus dir, 99n152

PITT, WILLIAM
William Pitt, Earl of Chatham 1708-78: a bibliog, 95n754

PLANETS
Cambridge gd to stars & planets, 2d ed, 98n1605
NASA atlas of the solar system, 98n1609

PLANT DISEASES
Gardener's gd to plant diseases, 96n1547

PLANT ENGINEERING
Standard hndbk of plant engineering, 2d ed, 96n1677

PLANT GENETICS
Dictionary of plant genetics & molecular biology, 99n1358

PLANT MOLECULAR BIOLOGY
Dictionary of plant genetics & molecular biology, 99n1358

PLANTS. *See also* **HOUSE PLANTS**
Adrian Bloom's yr-round garden, 99n1347
American Horticultural Society A-Z ency of garden plants, 98n1432
Ball pest & disease manual, 99n1360
Ball redbk, 99n1346
Bonsai survival manual, 97n1256
Bulbs, 99n1348
Dictionary of generic names of seed plants, 96n1565
Edible plants & animals, 95n1516
Elsevier's dict of plant names, 97n1273
Flowering plants of the world, updated ed, 95n1542
Gardener's index, 95n1528
Index of garden plants, 95n1530
Manual of climbers & wall plants, 96n1575
Plant life in the world's Mediterranean climates, 99n1359
Plants & their names, 96n1563
Plants that merit attention, v.2: shrubs, 97n1285
Rock garden plants, 99n1353
Vascular plants of Russia & adjacent states (the former USSR), 96n1594

PLANTS, FOSSIL
Visual dict of prehistoric life, 96n1817

PLASTICS
Engineering plastics & composites, 2d ed, 95n1636
Glossary of plastics terminology in 6 langs, 3d ed, 97n1379
Handbook of plastic & rubber additives, 97n1385
Whittington's dict of plastics, 3d ed, 95n1601

PLATINUM
Platinum & palladium buyer's gd, 98n913

PLAY ENVIRONMENTS
Playground industry ref dir 1995, 96n800

PLAYWRIGHTS
Nineteenth-Century lit criticism, v.52, 97n913

PLURALISM (SOCIAL SCIENCES)
DISCovering multicultural America [CD-ROM], 97n323
Encyclopedia of multiculturalism, 95n396
Gale ency of multicultural America, 96n387
Multicultural children's lit, 97n933
Multiculturalism, 99n369
Official gd to racial & ethnic diversity, 97n324
Princeton hndbk of multicultural poetries, 97n1019
Writers of multicultural fiction for YAs, 97n942

POE, EDGAR ALLAN
Poe ency, 98n1137

POETRY
American & British poetry, 97n1015
Avisson bk of contests & prize competitions for poets, 98n864
Columbia Granger's gd to poetry anthologies, 2d ed, 96n1263
Columbia Granger's world of poetry [CD-ROM], 97n1017
Dictionary of literary biog, v.193, 99n1059
Directory of poetry publishers, 98n599
Exploring poetry [CD-ROM], 98n1184

Masterplots II: poetry series suppl, v.9, 99n1102
New Princeton hndbk of poetic terms, 95n1248
Poem finder 95 [CD-ROM], 97n1018
Poet's market, 1995, 95n943
Poetry criticism, v.10, 96n1265
Poetry dict, 96n1264
Poetry for students, v.1, 99n1106
Poetry for students, v.2, 99n1107
Poetry for students, v.3, 99n1108
Poetry for students, v.4, 99n1109
Poets: American & British, 99n1110
Princeton hndbk of multicultural poetries, 97n1019
Victorian poetry, 97n1000

POETRY—INDEXES
Columbia Granger's index to poetry, 10th ed, 95n1245
Columbia Granger's index to poetry in collected & selected works, 97n1016
Index of American per verse 1994, 98n1185
Index of American per verse 1995, 98n1142
Index of American per verse 1996, 99n1100
Twentieth-Century poetry from Spanish America, 99n1111

POETS
Companion to the Greek lyric poets, 99n1018
Concordance to the poetry of Robert Frost, 95n1190
Contemporary literary criticism, v.86, 97n895
Contemporary literary criticism, v.88, 97n897
Contemporary literary criticism, v.89, 97n898
DISCovering authors modules [CD-ROM], 97n900
George Gordon, Lord Byron, 98n1155
Index of American per verse: 1994, 98n1185
International who's who in poetry & poets' ency, 7th ed, 95n1246
International who's who in poetry & poets' ency 1997, 8th ed, 99n1101
Literature criticism from 1400 to 1800, v.28, 97n901
Literature criticism from 1400 to 1800, v.30, 97n903
Literature criticism from 1400 to 1800, v.31, 97n904
Nineteenth-Century lit criticism, v.47, 97n908
Nineteenth-Century lit criticism, v.49, 97n910
Nineteenth-Century lit criticism, v.50, 97n911
Nineteenth-Century lit criticism, v.51, 97n912
Nineteenth-Century lit criticism, v.52, 97n913
Nineteenth-Century lit criticism annual cum title index for 1996, 97n914
Notable poets, 99n1103
Oxford companion to 20th-century poetry in English, 95n1249
Poetry criticism, v.18, 99n1104
Poetry criticism, v.19, 99n1105
Poet's market, 1998, 98n868
Ralph Waldo Emerson: an annot bibliog of criticism, 1980-91, 95n1187
Reader's gd to 20th-century writers, 97n916
Response to Allen Ginsberg 1926-94, 97n972
Seventeenth-Century British nondramatic poets, 3d series, 95n1200
Sir Philip Sidney: an annot bibliog of texts & criticism (1554-1984), 95n1222
Twentieth-Century literary criticism, v.59, 97n920

Twentieth-Century literary criticism, v.60, 97n921
Twentieth-Century literary criticism annual cum title index for 1996, 97n923
Viacheslav Ivanov: a ref gd, 98n1181
Wallace Stevens: an annot secondary bibliog, 95n1195
William Butler Yeats ency, 98n1166

POISONS
Encyclopedia of toxicology, 99n1504
Field gd to common animal poisons, 97n1262
Field gd to venomous animals & poisonous plants, 95n1535
Home health gd to poisons & antidotes, 96n1727
Poisons & antidotes, 95n1686
TSCA hndbk, 3d ed, 98n561

POLAND
Dictionary of Jewish surnames from the Kingdom of Poland, 98n375
Historical dict of Poland, 96n144
Jewish roots in Poland, 99n400
Polish-German borderlands: an annot bibliog, 95n554
Wartime Poland, 1939-45, 98n480

POLICE
Cops, crooks, & criminologists, 97n504
Encyclopedia of police sci, 2d ed, 96n599
Jane's police & security equipment 1996-97, 9th ed, 98n555

POLICE FILMS
Guide to American silent crime films, 95n1383

POLICY SCIENCES
Information-finding & the research process, 95n769

POLISH AMERICANS
Gridiron greats: a century of Polish Americans in college football, 98n745
Who's who in Polish America, 1996-1997 ed, 97n35

POLISH LANGUAGE—DICTIONARIES—ENGLISH
Highlander Polish-English/English-Highlander Polish dict, 97n864
Polish-English, English-Polish concise dict, 95n1091

POLISH LITERATURE
Dictionary of Polish lit, 95n1237

POLITICAL ACTION COMMITTEES
Cash constituents of Congress, 2d ed, 95n735
Lobbying, PACs, & campaign finance, 96n740
Open secrets, 3d ed, 95n736

POLITICAL CONVENTIONS
Congressional Quarterly's gd to US elections, 3d ed, 95n733
National party conventions 1831-1996, 99n681

POLITICAL GEOGRAPHY
Political geography, 98n393

POLITICAL LEADERSHIP
Founders of modern nations, 96n556
Leaders from the 1960s, 95n715
Political leaders & peacemakers, 96n418

POLITICAL ORATORY
African-American orators, 98n337

POLITICAL PARTIES
Congressional Quarterly's gd to US elections, 3d ed, 95n733
Political parties of E Europe, Russia, & the successor states, 2d ed, 96n757
Political parties of the Middle East & N Africa, 96n765

POLITICAL SCIENCE
Annual report of the USA 1998, 99n673
Bibliographic gd to law 1996, 98n509
Brewer's pols, 95n707
Contemporary democracy, 98n638
Countries of the world & their leaders yrbk 1999, 99n658
Dictionary of contemporary quotations, vol.8, 3d ed, 96n90
Dictionary of govt & pol, 2d ed, 99n654
DISCovering nations, states, & cultures [CD-ROM], 99n85
Encyclopedia of student & youth movements, 99n653
European pol facts, 1900-96, 99n690
Father Charles E. Coughlin, 99n1282
Government on file, 99n684
Handbook of pol sci research on the Middle East & N Africa, 99n648
Hannah Arendt 2: a bibliog, 98n636
Illustrated dict of constitutional concepts, 97n594
International ency of public policy & admin, 99n702
Law & pols, 97n490
Political data hndbk: OECD countries, 2d ed, 98n684
Political systems of the world, 97n582
Propaganda in 20th century war & pols, 97n618
Public interest profiles 1996-97, 97n599
Reinventing govt, 98n644
Routledge dict of 20th-century pol thinkers, 2d ed, 99n655
Survey of social sci: govt & pols series, 96n741
Theories of pol processes, 98n635
United Nations dir of agencies & insts in public admin & finance, 99n703
Western pol thought, 96n704
Who's who in intl affairs 1998, 2d ed, 99n652
World factbk 1996-97, 97n80
Worldmark ency of the nations, 8th ed, 96n105

POLITICAL SCIENCE—ETHICS
International ethics, 99n698

POLITICAL SCIENCE—QUOTATIONS
Oxford dict of pol quotations, 98n641

POLITICAL SCIENTISTS
American pol scientists, 95n705

POLITICAL STATISTICS
Statesman's yr-bk, 132d ed, 96n102

POLITICIANS
Almanac of the unelected, 98n649
Beyond the hill, 97n598

Congressional dir: 105th congress, 99n669
Global links: a gd to key people & insts worldwide, 99n54
Maximov's companion to who governs Moscow, 98n688
New members of Congress almanac, 98n654
New members of Congress almanac, 99n661
Profiles of worldwide govt leaders 1998, 4th ed, 99n649
State staff dir, summer 1997, 98n667
US govt leaders, 99n663
Vice presidents, 97n590
Whitaker's almanack world heads of govt 1998, 99n650
Whitaker's almanack world heads of state 1998, 99n651
Who's who in American pols 1997-98, 99n666
Who's who in Congress 1997, 98n656
Who's who in European pols, 3d ed, 98n685
Who's who in Latin America, 4th ed, 98n35
World almanac of US pols, 1997-99 ed, 98n643

POLITICIANS—QUOTATIONS
Oxford dict of pol quotations, 98n641

POLITICIANS—UNITED STATES
Congressional Quarterly's pols in America 1996, 96n738
Cumulated indexes to the public papers of the presidents of the US: George Bush, 1989-93, 96n744
Cumulated indexes to the public papers of the presidents of the US: Ronald Reagan, 1981-89, 96n745
Who's who in American pols 1993-94, 95n719

POLITICS—LOCAL
Municipal yr bk 1998, v.65, 99n680
Utah state constitution, 99n688

POLLEN
Pollen grains of Canadian honey plants, 95n1537

POLLUTION
Earth words, 96n1861
Encyclopedia of environmental control tech, v.9, 96n1859
Encyclopedia of garbage, 97n1425
Environment & the law, 97n514
Federal chemical regulation, 99n586
Rapid gd to hazardous air pollutants, 99n1568

POLLUTION CONTROL INDUSTRY
Earth work, 96n1871

POPULAR CULTURE
American decades 1980-89, 97n425
American dream: the 50s, 99n466
American popular culture, 96n1357
American popular psychology, 95n771
Cold war culture media & the arts 1945-90, 99n1191
Complete cross-ref gd to the baby buster generations collective unconscious, 99n1187
Encyclopedia of Japanese pop culture, 99n112
Fandom dir, no.15, 1995-1996 ed, 96n1355
Fashion & costume in American popular culture, 97n1093
Handbook of Chinese popular culture, 95n1326
NTC's dict of the USA, 99n1190
Pop culture landmarks, 97n387
Rock music in American popular culture 2, 99n1173

POPULAR LITERATURE
Genreflecting: a gd to reading interests in genre fiction, 4th ed, 96n1186
Now read on: a gd to contemporary popular fiction, 2d ed, 96n1187
What to read, 96n380

POPULAR MUSIC
A&E entertainment almanac, 1997, 98n1264
All music bk of hit albums, 97n1066
All music bk of hit singles, 95n1293
All music bk of hit singles, 97n1067
All music gd, 3d ed, 98n1228
All music gd to rock, 2d ed, 98n1238
American musical theatre song ency, 96n1416
American pop from minstrel to mojo: on record, 1893-1956, 99n1162
Billboard bk of no.1 albums, 97n1060
Billboard bk of top 40 albums, 3d ed, 97n1061
Billboard bk of top 40 hits, 6th ed, 97n1062
Billboard music yrbk 1993, 95n1289
Billboard music yrbk 1994, 96n1303
Broadway sheet music, 97n1069
Broadway song companion, 99n1170
Cash Box charts for the post-modern age, 96n1312
Cash Box pop singles charts 1950-93, 95n1291
Christian music dirs, 1998, 99n1176
Christian music finder [CD-ROM], 99n1177
Cole Porter discography, 97n1068
Command performance, USA! a discography, 97n772
Contemporary musicians, v.13, 96n1305
Da Capo companion to 20th-century popular music, rev ed, 96n1306
DK ency of rock stars, 97n1081
Encyclopedia of Canadian rock, pop & folk, 95n1292
Fred Waring discography, 97n1049
Goldmine's celebrity vocals, 96n1274
Guide to popular music ref bks, 96n1311
Guinness ency of popular music, 2d ed, 96n1310
Harvard biogl dict of music, 97n1024
International who's who in music, v.2: popular music, 97n1063
International who's who in music 1998/99, v.2, 2d ed, 99n1161
Joan Baez: a bio-bibliog, 97n1074
Joel Whitburn presents Billboard's top 10 chart 1958-95, 96n1319
Joel Whitburn's pop hits 1940-54, 96n1313
Joel Whitburn's top pop albums 1955-96, 97n1070
Joel Whitburn's top pop singles 1955-93, 96n1314
Joel Whitburn's top pop singles CD gd 1955-79, 96n1316
Joel Whitburn's top R&B singles 1942-1995, 97n1079
Johnny Cash discography, 1984-93, 95n1301
Johnny Cash record catalog, 96n1317
Lissauer's ency of popular music in America, 97n1065
Moanin' low: a discography of female popular vocal recordings, 1920-33, 97n1064
Music of the golden age, 1900-50 & beyond, 99n1139
Popular bands & performers, 96n1304
Popular music, v.21, 1996, 99n1164

Popular music studies, 99n1163
Rock stars/pop stars, 96n1315
SongCite: an index to popular songs, 96n1309
Top 40 music on CD, 1955-81, 95n1290
Your hit parade & American top 10 hits, 4th ed, 96n1308

POPULAR MUSIC—WRITING & PUBLISHING
Song Writers Market, 1998, 98n1207

POPULATION
American population before the fed census of 1790, 95n891
Association for Population/Family Planning Libs & Info Centers Intl (AFPLIC-I) union list of serials, 96n861
Atlas of US economy, tech, & growth, 97n714
Handbook of population & housing censuses, pt.4, 98n805
POPLINE: through Dec 1996 [CD-ROM], 98n779
Population & dvlpmt: dir of non-govtl org in OECD countries, 96n909
Population hist of western US cities & towns, 1850-1990, 97n723
Sex & age distribution of world populations: 1994 revision, 96n912
Sex & age distribution of world populations, 99n784
Twentieth-Century hist of US population, 98n808
World population monitoring 1996, 99n809
World population prospects, 99n790
World urbanization prospects, 99n794

POPULATION FORECASTING
World index of resources & population, 96n235

PORCELAIN
Looking at European ceramics, 95n980
Pottery & porcelain ceramics price gd, 98n927

PORPOISES
Dolphins & porpoises: a worldwide gd, 95n1595
Whales, dolphins, & porpoises, 96n1629

PORTER, COLE
Cole Porter discography, 97n1068

PORTUGAL
Cultural atlas of Spain & Portugal, 96n539
Portugal with Madeira & the Azores, 98n422

PORTUGUESE LANGUAGE—DICTIONARIES—ENGLISH
HarperCollins Portuguese dict, college ed, 98n1041
Oxford pa Portuguese dict, 98n1042
Portuguese-English, English-Portuguese practical dict, 95n1092

PORTUGUESE LITERATURE
Portuguese lit from its origins to 1990, 95n1238

POSTAGE STAMPS
Brookman US, UN, & Canada stamps & postal collectibles, 98n928

POSTAL SERVICE
National 5-digit zip code & post office dir 1996, 97n52
Zip code finder, 98n59

POSTMODERNISM
Feminism & postmodern theory, 97n727

POTTERY
Charlton standard catalogue of chintz, 2d ed, 98n924
Charlton standard catalogue of Royal Doulton beswick figurines, 5th ed, 98n925
Charlton standard catalogue of Royal Doulton beswick jugs, 4th ed, 98n926
Hopi pottery symbols, 96n1015
Looking at European ceramics, 95n980
Potter's dict of materials & techniques, 4th ed, 98n932
Pottery & porcelain ceramics price gd, 98n927

POULENC, FRANCIS
Music of Francis Poulenc (1899-1963), 97n1044

POVERTY
Poverty in America: an annot bibliog, 95n869
Social indicators of dvlpmt 1994, 95n870

POWELL, ELEANOR
Eleanor Powell: a bio-bibliog, 95n1353

POWER RESOURCES
Directory of power plant equipment & processes, 1996, 97n1416
Encyclopedia of energy tech & the environment, 96n1830
Energy, 96n1833
Energy & American society, 95n1752
Energy balances for countries in transition 1993, 1994-2010, & energy prospects in CIS countries, 98n1627
Energy stats yrbk, 1992, 95n1751
Environment 2: clean air, 95n1761
Power industry abbreviator, 96n1672
UNESCO intl dir of new & renewable energy info sources & research centres, 95n1748

PRAGUE
Prague, 98n122

PREDICTIONS
Predicting the future, 98n88

PREGNANCY. See also **CHILDBIRTH; MEDICINE—PEDIATRICS**
A-to-Z of pregnancy & childbirth, 95n1645
Mayo Clinic complete bk of pregnancy & baby's 1st yr, 96n1722
Pregnancy & birth sourcebk, 98n1561

PREJUDICES
Color of words: an encyclopaedic dict of ethnic bias in the US, 98n328

PRESIDENTIAL CANDIDATES
National party conventions 1831-1996, 99n681

Presidential also-rans & running mates, 1788-1996, 99n662
US presidential candidates & the elections, 97n588

PRESIDENTIAL LIBRARIES
Presidential libs & museums, 96n519

PRESIDENTIAL MEDAL OF FREEDOM
Presidential Medal of Freedom, 98n30

PRESIDENTS—MEXICO
Dictionary of Mexican rulers, 1325-1997, 98n485

PRESIDENTS' SPOUSES—UNITED STATES
American first ladies, 97n407
Presidents, first ladies, & vice presidents, 98n653

PRESIDENTS—UNITED STATES
America at the polls, 95n737
American leaders 1789-1994, 95n714
American presidency [CD-ROM], 98n668
Encyclopedia of the American presidency, 95n542
Encyclopedia of the Reagan-Bush yrs, 97n593
Guide to the presidency, 2d ed, 98n674
How to research the presidency, 97n586
John F. Kennedy, 96n491
Landmarks of American presidents, 97n391
Presidential elections in the US, 96n742
Presidential sites, 99n428
Presidents, 98n661
Presidents: a ref hist, 2d ed, 97n589
Presidents, first ladies, & vice presidents, 98n653
Presidents of the US—their written measure, 98n648
Scholastic ency of the presidents & their times, 96n521
Scholastic ency of the presidents & their times, updated ed, 98n443
Thomas Jefferson: a biogl companion, 99n660
US presidents [CD-ROM], 96n527
William Henry Harrison: a bibliog, 99n659
World almanac of presidential quotations, 95n550
Young Oxford companion to the presidency of the US, 95n543

PRESIDENTS—UNITED STATES—ELECTIONS
Presidential elections 1789-1996, 99n682
Running for president, 95n741
US primary elections 1995-96, 98n673

PRESIDENTS—UNITED STATES—JUVENILE LITERATURE
Complete hist of our presidents, 98n658

PRESLEY, ELVIS
Elvis ency, 96n1335

PRESSURE GROUPS
Directory of Congressional voting scores & interest group ratings, 2d ed, 98n678
Greenpeace gd to anti-environmental orgs, 95n1770
Post-Soviet hndbk, 97n123
Public interest profiles 1996-97, 97n599
US religious interest groups, 95n1446

PRICE, RICHARD
Bibliography of the works of Richard Price, 95n1427

PRIMATES
International dir of primatology, 95n1593
International dir of primatology, 3d ed, 98n1471
Pictorial gd to the living primates, 98n1472

PRIME MINISTERS
Facts about the British prime ministers, 96n540

PRINTERS
British literary bk trade, 1475-1700, 98n594
Directory of printers, 1994-95 ed, 96n671

PRINTING INDUSTRY
Directory of printers, 1994-95 ed, 96n671

PRINTMAKERS
American printmakers 1880-1945, 95n1009

PRISON ADMINISTRATION
Encyclopedia of American prisons, 97n505

PRISONERS
Political prisoners & trials, 96n605

PRISONERS OF WAR
Prisoners of the Japanese in WW II, 95n549

PRISONS
American prisons, 99n574
Dictionary of American penology, rev ed, 97n506
Encyclopedia of American prisons, 97n505

PRIVACY, RIGHT OF
Compilation of state & fed privacy laws, 1997 ed, 98n543

PRIVATE COMPANIES
How to find info about private cos, 6th ed, 96n205
Ward's private co profiles, 95n213

PRIVATEERING
Pirates!, 96n1345
Pirates & privateers of the Americas, 96n1344

PRIVATE INVESTIGATORS
Whole spy catalog, 96n775

PRIVATE LIBRARIES
Private libs in Renaissance England, v.3: PLRE 67-86, 96n1006

PRIVATE PRESSES
Corvinus press: a hist & bibliog, 95n675

PROBABILITIES
Statistically speaking: a dict of quotations, 98n82

PROCESS CONTROL
Comprehensive dict of measurement & control, 3d ed, 97n1311

PROCESSING (LIBRARIES). *See also* **TECHNICAL SERVICES**
Directory of lib technical servs home pages, 98n591
Guide to technical servs resources, 95n665

PRO-CHOICE MOVEMENT
Pro-choice/pro-life issues in the 1990s, 98n757

PROFESSIONAL EDUCATION
Canadian professional schools factsheets, 95n348
Guide to natl professional certification programs, 96n267

PROFESSIONAL ETHICS
Codes of professional responsibility, 3d ed, 96n1431
Professional codes of conduct in the UK, 2d ed, 98n1341

PROFESSIONAL SPORTS
Professional sports stats, 98n722
Sporting News pro football gd, 1996 ed, 97n655
Sports phone bk USA, 1998, 99n712

PROFESSIONS. *See* **CAREERS**

PROFESSIONS—CERTIFICATION
Certification & accreditation programs dir, 98n270
Guide to natl professional certification programs, 98n313
Professional & occupational licensure in the US, 98n704

PROGRAMMING LANGUAGES (ELECTRONIC COMPUTER)
IBM mainframe programmer's desk ref, 95n1692
UNIX dict of commands, terms, & acronyms, 97n1373
Web programming lang sourcebk, 99n1487

PROGRAM-RELATED INVESTMENTS
PRI index, 99n771

PROKOFIEV, SERGE
Piano works of Serge Prokofiev, 95n1277

PRO-LIFE MOVEMENT
Anti-abortion movement, 98n756
Pro-choice/pro-life issues in the 1990s, 98n757

PROPAGANDA
Chronology & glossary of propaganda in the US, 97n595
Propaganda in 20th century war & pols, 97n618

PROPHECY
Messengers of God: a Jewish prophets who's who, 99n1292

PROSTITUTION
Prostitution in Great Britain 1485-1901, 95n877

PROTISTA
Illustrated glossary of protoctista, 95n1536

PROVENCE—COTE D'AZUR (FRANCE)
Provence & the Cote D'Azur, 96n477

PROVERBS
American proverbs about women, 99n807
Dictionary of 1000 Dutch proverbs, 99n1179
Dictionary of 1000 Jewish proverbs, 98n1251
Dictionary of 1000 Polish proverbs, 98n1252
Dictionary of 1000 Spanish proverbs with English equivalents, 97n1089
Encyclopedia of the sayings of the Jewish people, 99n1293
Multicultural dict of proverbs, 98n1250
Proverb wit & wisdom, 98n1249
Proverbial Bernard Shaw, 95n1221
Proverbial Charles Dickens, 98n1157
Proverbial Eugene O'Neill, 96n1215
Proverbs in world lit, 98n1254
Wise words & wives' tales, 95n1313

PSYCHIATRY
Encyclopedia of mental health, 95n780
Encyclopedia of psychiatry, psychology, & psychoanalysis, 97n1356
Handbook of child & adolescent psychology, v.5-7, 99n1466
Insider's gd to mental health resources online, 98n1515
Nurse's clinical gd to psychiatric & mental health care, 97n1355
Psychiatric dict, 7th ed, 98n1556
PsycLit [CD-ROM], 97n625
Wiley's English-Spanish, Spanish-English dict of psychology & psychiatry, 96n782

PSYCHOLINGUISTICS
Japanese psycholinguistics, 96n1059

PSYCHOLOGICAL TESTS
Tests in print IV, 95n787

PSYCHOLOGISTS
Biographical dict of psychology, 98n710
Twentieth-Century literary criticism, v.61, 97n922

PSYCHOLOGY. *See also* **SELF-HELP**
American popular psychology, 95n771
Bibliographic gd to psychology 1996, 98n707
Bibliography of human behavior, 95n770
Biodiversity, 99n1556
Biographical dict of psychology, 98n710
Blackwell dict of neuropsychology, 97n626
ClinPSYC: 1980-Dec 1996 [CD-ROM], 98n712
Companion ency of psychology, 95n777
Concise ency of psychology, 2d ed, 97n627
Dictionary of dvlpmtl psychology, 97n629
Encyclopedia of human behavior, 95n778
Encyclopedia of psychiatry, psychology, & psychoanalysis, 97n1356
Encyclopedia of psychology, 2d ed, 95n779
Gale ency of psychology, 97n628
Handbook of child psychology, 5th ed, 99n707
International dict of psychology, 2d ed, 97n630
Psychology: an introductory bibliog, 97n624
Psychology basics, 99n706
Psychology of aging, 96n839
PsycLit [CD-ROM], 97n625
Stress A-Z, 99n705
Survey of social sci: psychology series, 95n782

Wiley's English-Spanish, Spanish-English dict of psychology & psychiatry, 96n782

PSYCHOTHERAPY
Dictionary for psychotherapists, 95n776
Dictionary of family therapy, rev ed, 96n1718

PSYCHOTROPIC DRUGS. *See also* **DRUGS**
Effects of neurologic & psychiatric drugs on the fetus & nursing infant, 99n1480

PUBLIC ADMINISTRATION
Information-finding & the research process, 95n769
Managing your city or town, 95n768

PUBLIC HEALTH
APELL annot bibliog, 96n777
Dictionary of public health promotion & educ, 97n1317
Health stats, 2d ed, 98n1505
International hndbk of public health, 98n1518

PUBLIC LIBRARIES
Audio bk breakthrough, 95n664
Banned in the USA, 95n658
Emergency Librarian index, vs.1-20: 1973-93, 96n645
Public lib cat, 95n660

PUBLIC OFFICERS
Government affairs yellow bk, v.1, no.1, 96n187

PUBLIC OPINION
Gallup Poll, 95n92
Gallup Poll, 98n87
Index to intl public opinion, 1996-97, 99n81
Official gd to American attitudes, 97n717
Polling & survey research methods, 1935-79, 97n77

PUBLIC POLICY
Guide to public policy experts, 1997-98, 99n701
International ency of public policy & admin, 99n702

PUBLIC RECORDS
Find public records fast, 98n665
Genealogical research in England's public record office, 97n357
Guide to background investigations, 7th ed, 98n640
Land & property research in the US, 98n365
Librarian's gd to public records, special ed, 96n778
Librarian's gd to public records, rev ed, 98n666
MVR bk: motor servs gd, 1994 ed, 95n739
MVR bk: motor servs gd, 1997 ed, 98n536
MVR decoder digest, 1994, 95n740
MVR decoder digest, 1997 ed, 98n537
Printed sources, 99n403
Public records online, 1997 ed, 98n706
Sourcebook of county court records, 95n609
Sourcebook of county court records, 3d ed, 98n524
Sourcebook of fed courts: US district & bankruptcy, 95n610
Sourcebook of local court & county record retrievers, 95n611
Sourcebook of local court & county record retrievers, 3d ed, 98n525

Sourcebook of online public record experts, 97n540
Sourcebook of public record providers, 95n71
Sourcebook of state public records, 95n730
Sourcebook of state public records, 2d ed, 96n714
Using public records to find and investigate anyone, 98n703
Verify those credentials: do you know who you're dealing with?, 98n63

PUBLIC RELATIONS
National dir of corp public affairs 1994, 95n199
National dir of corp public affairs 1998, 99n154

PUBLIC SCHOOLS
Banned in the USA, 95n658

PUBLIC UTILITIES
Transportation & public utilities USA, 99n1572

PUBLISHERS & PUBLISHING
AB Bookman's yrbk, 1993-94, 95n970
Alternative publishers of bks in N America, 2d ed, 96n668
American bk publishing record, cum 1997, 99n9
Antonio Gardano, Venetian Music Printer 1538-69, 99n1112
Association of American Univ Prs dir 1996-97, 98n598
Authentic Jane Williams' home school mrkt gd, 97n280
Bibliographic hist of the bk, 96n664
Bibliography on publishing & bk dvlpmt in the Third World, 1980-93, 95n666
Book industry trends 1994: covering the yrs 1988-98, 95n667
Books from Chapel Hill 1922-97, 98n595
British literary bk trade, 1475-1700, 98n594
British literary bk trade, 1700-1820, 97n553
By the nos: publishing, 99n620
Cabell's dir of publishing opportunities in accounting, economics & finance, 6th ed, 96n669
Cabell's dir of publishing opportunities in mgmt & mktg, 6th ed, 96n670
Dictionary of literary biog documentary series, v.13, 97n963
Dictionary of literary biog documentary series, v.17, 99n955
Directory of poetry publishers, 98n599
Directory of publishers in religion, 99n619
Directory of publishing 1997, 22d ed, 98n600
Directory of publishing 1999, 24th ed, 99n618
Directory of small pr/mag editors & publishers, 24th ed, 95n668
Directory of small pr/mag editors & publishers, 28th ed, 98n601
Encyclopedia of the bk, 2d ed, 97n554
Guide to bk publishers' archives, 99n617
Harrod's librarians' glossary, 8th ed, 97n526
Information industry dir 1998, 18th ed, 99n602
Information sources 98, 99n202
International dir of little mags & small prs, 29th ed, 95n669
International literary market place 1995, 95n671
Literary market place 1995, 95n672
Managing the publishing process, 96n665
Market gd for young writers, 5th ed, 97n751
Mitchell Kennerly imprint: a descriptive bibliog, 98n592
Novel & short story writer's market, 1996, 97n753
Policies for publishers, 1995 ed, 96n674

Publishers dir, 1995, 95n673
Publishers dir, 1998, 18th ed, 98n603
Publishers, distrs, & wholesalers of the US 1994-95, 95n674
Publishers, distrs, & wholesalers of the US 1996-97, 97n555
Publishers' intl ISBN dir 1997/98, 98n604
Publishers' intl ISBN dir, 20th ed, 95n676
Publishing law hndbk, 2d ed, 99n621
Publishing market ref plus 1994-95, 2d ed [CD-ROM], 96n672
Walter Scott Publishing Co., 98n593

PUERTO RICO
Puerto Rico past & present, 99n93

PUGET SOUND SALISH LANGUAGES—DICTIONARIES—ENGLISH
Lushootseed dict, 96n1119

PUNJAB
Punjab, 97n126

PURCHASING
Essential bus buyer's gd, 98n179

PUZZLES
Antique trader's gd to games & puzzles, 98n891

PYM, BARBARA
Four British women novelists, 99n1061

QUAKERS
Quakers in fiction, 95n1157

QUALITATIVE RESEARCH
Qualitative inquiry: a dict of terms, 99n743

QUALITY CONTROL
International standards desk ref, 98n206
McGraw-Hill ency of quality terms & concepts, 96n284
Quality, TQC, TQM: a meta lit study, 98n243

QUALITY OF LIFE
Ernst & Young almanac & gd to US bus cities, 95n206
Gale city & metro rankings reporter, 96n930
Profile of western N America, 97n248
Rating gd to life in America's 50 states, 96n924

QUESTIONS & ANSWERS
FAQ's of life, 99n67
Illustrated bk of questions & answers, 97n56
New York Public Lib student's desk ref, 95n81
Top 10 of everything, 96n61

QUILTS
Award-winning quilts & their makers, v.1-4, 95n977

QUOTATIONS
African American quotations, 99n80
American Heritage dict of American quotations, 99n75
American Indian quotations, 97n345
Be reasonable, 95n1433
Better than it sounds: a dict of humorous musical quotations, 99n1119
Black woman's gumbo ya-ya, 95n920
Born this day, 97n41
Cassell companion to quotations, 99n76
Cassell dict of cynical quotations, 96n89
Cassell sex & sexuality, 95n873
Colombo's concise Canadian quotations, 99n77
Columbia dict of quotations, 95n88
Columbia world of quotations [CD-ROM], 97n68
Comedy quotes from the movies, 95n1402
Concise Oxford dict of quotations, 99n78
Criminal quotes, 98n79
Dictionary of contemporary quotations, vol.8, 3d ed, 96n90
Dictionary of film quotations, 96n1374
Dictionary of Irish quotations, 95n445
Dictionary of Scottish quotations, 98n136
Executive's bk of quotations, 95n216
Family wisdom, 97n69
Famous lines: a Columbia dict of familiar quotations, 98n80
Film quotations, 95n1403
Gale's quotations [CD-ROM], 96n91
Humorous quotations, 96n93
International educ quotations ency, 97n289
Last words: a dict of deathbed quotations, 96n95
Leadership: quotations from the world's greatest motivators, 98n81
Little Oxford dict of quotations, 96n92
Mathematically speaking, 99n1328
Memorabilia mathematica: the philomath's quotation bk, 95n1741
New Beacon bk of quotations by women, 97n70
New York, the city in more than 500 memorable quotations, 98n101
NTC's dict of quotations, 96n94
Of the people, by the people, for the people, & other quotations by Abraham Lincoln, 97n67
"Out of the mouths of mathematicians", 95n1742
Oxford dict of humorous quotations, 97n71
Oxford dict of quotations, 4th ed, 98n83
Proverbial Winston S. Churchill, 96n760
Quotable lawyer, rev ed, 99n572
Rock talk, 95n1306
Sex & love quotations, 96n889
Shakespeare quotations, 96n1239
Simpson's contemporary quotations, rev ed, 98n84
Speak the speech, 95n1220
Statistically speaking: a dict of quotations, 98n82
Talking drums: an African-American quote collection, 96n96
Two Jews, 3 opinions: a collection of 20th-century American Jewish quotations, 99n396
War & conflict quotations, 98n85
Whole world bk of quotations, 95n90
Wit: humorous quotations from Woody Allen to Oscar Wilde, 99n79
Woman to woman, 95n919
Women's words, 97n72
World almanac of presidential quotations, 95n550
Writings on writing, 95n940

RABELAIS, FRANCOIS
Francois Rabelais: a ref gd, 1950-90, 95n1230

RACE RELATIONS
Cultures of color in America, 99n367
Dictionary of race & ethnic relations, 3d ed, 95n394
Dictionary of race & ethnic relations, 99n366
Ethnic studies in the US, 97n322
Race, crime, & the criminal justice system, 98n548
Racial & ethnic diversity, 2d ed, 99n372

RACISM
Color of words: an encyclopaedic dict of ethnic bias in the US, 98n328
Environmental racism & the environmental justice movement, 97n513
Racism in contemporary America, 97n325

RADCLIFFE, ANN
Ann Radcliffe, 97n998

RADICALISM
Radicalism hndbk, 96n766
Radicalism in Minn. 1900-60, 96n767

RADICALISM IN LITERATURE
Alternative press index, 97n58

RADIO
Bacon's bus media dir 1998, 99n821
Bacon's radio dir 1994, 95n961
Bacon's radio dir 1998, 12th ed, 98n885
Big broadcast, 1920-50, 2d ed, 98n887
Burrelle's media dir, June 1994 [CD-ROM], 95n934
Burrelle's media dir, 1998 ed, 99n837
Compendium of American railroad radio frequencies, 13th ed, 96n1891
Crystal clear v.2, 96n993
Dictionary of 20th century culture: American culture after WW II, 95n927
Gale dir of pubns & broadcast media, 131st ed, 99n822
Latin American advertising, mktg, & media sourcebk, 96n301
Leo Burnett worldwide advertising & media fact bk, 96n302
National Hispanic media dir, 1997, 98n861
News media yellow bk, 96n963
North American shortwave frequency gd, v.3, 97n768
Power media selects, 9th ed, 96n988
Radio stars, 97n762
Radio's morning show personalities, 97n763
Same time ... same station: an A-Z gd to radio from Jack Benny to Howard Stern, 97n765
Talk show selects, 1995 ed, 96n989
Talk shows & hosts on radio, 3d ed, 96n975
World radio TV hndbk, 1996 ed, 97n773

RAILROADS
Compendium of American railroad radio frequencies, 13th ed, 96n1891
Eurail gd to train travel in the new Europe, 1996, 97n1443
Eurail gd to world train travel, 1996, 26th ed, 97n1444

Field gd to trains of N America, 97n1445
Guide to tourist railroads & railroad museums, 4th ed, 96n1886
Historic railroad, 97n1446
Jane's world railways, 36th ed, 96n1887
Rail lines of S New England, 96n1888
32nd annual steam passenger serv dir, 98n1649

RAIN FORESTS
Rainforest orgs, 98n1639
Rainforests of the world: a ref hndbk, 95n1777

RANKING & SELECTION (STATISTICS)
Gale city & metro rankings reporter, 96n930
Gale state rankings reporter, 95n895
Rating gd to life in America's 50 states, 96n924

RAPE
Acquaintance & date rape: an annot bibliog, 95n634
Rape in America, 96n617

RAP MUSICIANS
Rap whoz who, 98n1237

RARE BOOKS
Beinecke Lesser Antilles collection at Hamilton College, 95n171
Directory of rare bk & special collections in the UK & the Republic of Ireland, 2d ed, 98n588

RATIO ANALYSIS (STATISTICS)
Almanac of bus & industrial financial ratios 1996, 27th ed, 98n177

RATIONALISM
Be reasonable, 95n1433

RAWLINGS, MARJORIE K.
Marjorie Kinnan Rawlings: a descriptive bibliog, 97n974

RAYS (FISHES)
Sharks & rays of Australia, 96n1623

READ, GARDNER
Gardner Read: a bio-bibliog, 97n1036

READING INTERESTS
Books for the teen age 1994, 95n1119
Genreflecting: a gd to reading interests in genre fiction, 4th ed, 96n1186
Integrated curriculum: bks for reluctant readers, grades 2-5, 2d ed, 99n1006
Now read on: a gd to contemporary popular fiction, 2d ed, 96n1187
Teen genreflecting, 98n1096
What do children read next? v.2, 99n999
What else should I read?, 96n1162
What else should I read? guiding kids to good bks, v.2, 98n1076
What to read, 96n380
What Western do I read next?, 99n1028

REAGAN, RONALD
Cumulated indexes to the public papers of the presidents of the US: Ronald Reagan, 1981-89, 96n745
Reagan yrs A to Z, 97n592

REAL ESTATE BUSINESS
Dictionary of real estate, 98n263
Directory of designated members, 1996, 97n282
Language of real estate, 4th ed, 95n329

REASONING
Thinking from A to Z, 98n1339

RECORDER (MUSICAL INSTRUMENT)
Recorder: a gd to writings about the instrument, 96n1294

RECORDING & REGISTRATION
International vital records hndbk, 3d ed, 95n460

RECREATION AREAS
Attitudes toward the outdoors: an annot bibliog, 95n1759
Parks dir of the US, 2d ed, 95n512
Playground industry ref dir 1995, 96n800

RECYCLING (WASTE)
McGraw-Hill recycling hndbk, 95n1782
Recycling & waste mgmt gd to the Internet, 99n1562

REFERENCE BOOKS
American Indian ref & resource bks for children & YAs, 2d ed, 96n1177
American popular culture, 96n1357
ARBA gd to subject encys & dicts, 2d ed, 98n5
Armenian ref bks, 95n150
Basic bus lib: core resources, 3d ed, 96n173
Business info sources, 95n179
Canadian ref sources, 97n19
Dictionary of dicts & encys, 2d ed, 98n45
Fieldwork in the lib, 95n393
Global data locator, 98n812
Government ref bks 92/93, 95n75
Guide to info sources in the botanical scis, 2d ed, 97n1272
Guide to ref bks, 11th ed, 97n8
Guide to ref bks for small & medium-sized libs, 1984-94, 96n9
Guide to ref works for the study of the Spanish lang & lit & Spanish American lit, 98n1183
Guide to South African ref bks, 6th ed, 98n19
Humanities: a selective gd to info sources, 4th ed, 95n921
Information sources in sci & tech, 2d ed, 95n1481
Information sources in urban & regional planning, 96n928
Introduction to ref sources in the health scis, 3d ed, 95n1644
Journalism, 2d ed, 98n851
Law lib ref shelf, 3d ed, 97n482
Music ref & research materials, 5th ed, 98n1189
Performing arts: a gd to the ref lit, 95n1339
Problems in literary research, 4th ed, 99n972
Recent ref bks in religion, 98n1346
Recommended ref bks 1994, 95n16
Recommended ref bks for small & medium-sized libs & media centers 1995, 96n11
Recommended ref bks for small & medium-sized libs & media centers 1997, 98n9
Reference bks bulletin 1992-93, 95n14
Reference bks bulletin 1993-94, 96n12
Reference bks bulletin 1994-95, 97n12
Reference sources hndbk, 4th ed, 97n13
Reference sources in sci, engineering, medicine, & agriculture, 95n1482
Social scis, 2d ed, 97n76
Sociology: A gd to ref & info sources, 98n753
Subject gd to US govt ref sources, 2d ed, 98n60
Texas ref sources, 4th ed, 95n101
Walford's gd to ref material, v.1: sci & tech, 7th ed, 97n1229
Walford's gd to ref material, v.2: social & histl scis, 6th ed, 95n98
Writer's ultimate research gd, 97n752

REFERENCE SERVICES (LIBRARIES)
Reference & info servs, 2d ed, 96n647
Reference assessment manual, 96n648

REFORMATION
International dir of Renaissance & Reformation assns (1993), 95n553
Oxford ency of the Reformation, 97n1211

REFUGEES
Global refugee crisis, 96n895
Historical dict of refugee & disaster relief orgs, 95n829
International thesaurus of refugee terminology, 2d ed, 97n705
Refugee & immigrant resource dir, 3d ed, 95n401
Refugees in America in the 1990s, 98n801

REFUSE & REFUSE DISPOSAL
Encyclopedia of garbage, 97n1425
Handbook of solid waste mgmt, 95n1780
Recycling & waste mgmt gd to the Internet, 99n1562

REGGAE MUSIC
Reggae: the rough gd, 99n1171

REGIONALISM (INTERNATIONAL ORGANIZATION)
Historical dict of European orgs, 96n139

REGIONAL PLANNING
Information sources in urban & regional planning, 96n928

REGISTERS OF BIRTH, ETC.
International vital records hndbk, 3d ed, 95n460

REINCARNATION
Encyclopedia of afterlife beliefs & phenomena, 96n1445
Reincarnation: a selected annot bibliog, 98n715

REINSURANCE
Statistical survey of insurance & reinsurance operations in developing countries 1983-90, 96n227

RELIABILITY (ENGINEERING)
Glossary of reliability & maintenance terms, 98n1497

RELIGION
Angels A to Z, 97n1176
Anthropology of religion, 98n1359
Atlas of religious change in America, 1952-90, 96n1437
Atlas of sacred places, 95n1434
Book of Ephesians, 97n1188
Charismatic movement, pts.1-4, 97n1205
Chinese religion pubs in W langs 1981 through 1990, 95n1438
Continuum dict of religion, 95n1440
Critical review of bks in religion 1997, v.10, 99n1260
Dictionary of early Christian beliefs, 99n1285
Dictionary of philosophy & religion, new ed, 98n1337
Doctrine of the Holy Spirit, 97n1193
Encyclopaedia of Middle Eastern mythology & religion, 95n1442
Encyclopedia of American women & religion, 99n1265
Encyclopedia of apocalypticism, 99n1266
Encyclopedia of religion [CD-ROM], 98n1353
Fund raiser's gd to religious philanthropy 1996, 9th ed, 97n691
Gods & symbols of ancient Mexico & the Maya, 95n1444
Guide to religious & inspirational mags, 95n1448
High places in cyberspace, 2d ed, 99n1269
Law, religion, theology, 98n510
Man, myth & magic, new ed, 96n1348
Micronesian religion & lore, 96n1439
Modern American popular religion, 97n1171
Music & dance of the world's religions, 97n1087
Of spirituality, 97n1169
Oxford dict of the Christian Church, 3d ed, 98n1389
Oxford dict of the Jewish religion, 98n1396
Oxford dict of world religions, 98n1357
Recent ref bks in religion, 98n1346
Religion: a cross-cultural ency, 97n1178
Religion in postwar China, 95n1439
Religion in the schools, 99n300
Religious higher educ in the US, 97n301
Who's who in theology & sci, 1996 ed, 97n1175
Women & religion in Britain & Ireland, 97n1170
Women in the biblical world, v.1, 97n1186

RELIGIONS
America's religions, 98n1364
Eerdmans' hndbk to the world's religions, rev ed, 96n1446
Encyclopedia of American religious hist, 97n1180
Encyclopedia of creation myths, 96n1444
Encyclopedia of E philosophy & religion, 96n1483
God on the Internet, 98n1365
Illustrated ency of active new religions sects & cults, [rev ed], 99n1264
Illustrated ency of world religions, 98n1356
Larousse dict of beliefs & religions, 95n1443
Modern ency of religions in Russia & Eurasia, v.7, 99n1267
National gd to funding in religion, 97n1184
Native American sun dance religion & ceremony, 99n384
New dict of religions, rev ed, 97n1179
On common ground: world religions in America [CD-ROM], 98n1367
Religions of the world, 98n1348
Religious cultures of the world, 98n1368
Sects, 'cults,' & alternative religions, 98n1360
Sexuality, religion & magic, 95n875
Shambhala dict of Taoism, 97n1226
South Asian religions in the Americas, 96n1438
World religions, 98n1361
World religions [CD-ROM], 95n1447

RELIGIOUS BIOGRAPHY
Thirty-Five Oriental philosophers, 96n1427

RELIGIOUS BROADCASTING
Prime-time religion, 98n1366

RELIGIOUS EDUCATION
NCEA/Ganley's Catholic schools in America 1995, 23d ed, 97n1216

RELIGIOUS ETIQUETTE
How to be a perfect stranger, 98n1362
How to be a perfect stranger, v.2, 98n1363

RELIGIOUS FICTION
Quakers in fiction, 95n1157

RELIGIOUS INSTITUTIONS
World gd to religious & spiritual orgs 1996, 97n1182

RELIGIOUS NEWSPAPERS & PERIODICALS
History & annot bibliog of American religious pers & newspapers, 96n1447
Popular religious mags of the US, 96n1441

RENAISSANCE
Annotated catalogue of early eds of Erasmus, 96n1250
International dir of Renaissance & Reformation assns (1993), 95n553

RENEWABLE ENERGY SOURCES
Real Goods solar living sourcebk, 8th ed, 96n1847
UNESCO intl dir of new & renewable energy info sources & research centres, 95n1748

REPERTORY THEATER
Regional theatre dir 1996-97, 97n1152

REPORT WRITING
Manual for writers of term papers, theses, & dissertations, 6th ed, 97n755
100 research topic gds for students, 97n543

REPRESENTATIVE GOVERNMENT & REPRESENTATION
Canadian representatives abroad, 96n749

REPRODUCTION. See also PREGNANCY; CHILDBIRTH
World population monitoring 1996, 99n809

REPTILES
Amphibians & reptiles of Alta., 95n1596
Amphibians & reptiles of Trinidad & Tobago, 98n1474

Encyclopedia of reptiles & amphibians, 2d ed, 99n1395
Familia Gekkonidae (Reptilia, Sauria), pt.1, 96n1634
Reptile & amphibian keeper's dict, 95n1597
Reptile & amphibian problem solver, 98n1473

REPUBLICAN PARTY
Encyclopedia of the Republican Party & the ency of the Democratic Party, 98n659

REPUBLIC PICTURES
Republic pictures checklist, 99n1230

RESEARCH
Academic focus Japan: programs & resources in N America, 96n423
American Lib Assn gd to info access, 95n641
Business & economic research dir, 97n159
Directory of American research & tech 1995, 29th ed, 96n182
Directory of European research & dvlpmt 1995, 96n1504
Directory of hyphenated techniques, 96n1505
European research & dvlpmt database 1995 [CD-ROM], 96n1510
Find it fast, 4th ed, 98n575
International relations research dir, 97n619
International research centers dir 1996-97, 8th ed, 96n55
New research centers, 1996, 96n339
Profiles in bus & mgmt [CD-ROM], 97n221
Research centers dir 1996, 20th ed, 96n340
Research centers dir 1999, 24th ed, 99n333
Research servs dir, 97n170
Scholars' gd to Washington, DC, for Russian, Central Eurasian, & Baltic studies, 95n164
Technology opportunities, 2d ed, 96n1507
Who's who in European research & dvlpmt 1995, 96n1491
Writer's ultimate research gd, 97n752

RESEARCH GRANTS
Directory of grants in the humanities 1994/95, 95n931
Directory of research grants 1996, 97n687
Higher educ money bk for women & minorities, 1997 ed, 97n302

RESEARCH INSTITUTES
International dir of Renaissance & Reformation assns (1993), 95n553
Think tank dir, 97n622
UNESCO intl dir of new & renewable energy info sources & research centres, 95n1748

RESEARCH LIBRARIES
ARL stats 1994-95, 97n527

RESORTS
Super family vacations, 3d ed, 96n462

RESPIRATORY DRUGS. *See also* **DRUGS**
Respiratory care drug ref, 99n1481

RESTAURANTS
America's best hotels & restaurants, 98n409

RETAIL TRADE
European dir of retailers & wholesalers, 2d ed, 99n253
European private label dir, 97n241
Wholesale & retail trade USA, 97n279
World retail dir 1997-98, 99n212
World retail dir & sourcebk, 2d ed, 97n222

RETIREMENT
100 best retirement businesses, 95n211
365 ways...retirees' resource gd for productive lifestyles, 97n669

RETIREMENT COMMUNITIES
Directory of retirement facilities 1995, 96n847

RETIREMENT INCOMES
Quick ref to ERISA compliance, 96n285

REVOLUTIONARIES
Encyclopedia of revolutions & revolutionaries, 97n477
Who's who in democracy, 98n639
World leaders: people who shaped the world, 95n576

REVOLUTIONS
Encyclopedia of revolutions & revolutionaries, 97n477

REYNARD THE FOX (LEGENDARY CHARACTER)
Roman de Renart: a gd to scholarly work, 99n1183

RHETORIC
Eighteenth-Century British & American rhetorics & rhetoricians, 95n1113
Encyclopedia of rhetoric & composition, 97n840
New Fowler's modern English usage, 3d ed, 97n756
NTC's hndbk for writers, 96n970
Talking about people: a gd to fair & accurate lang, 99n895
Wired style, 97n758
Writing centers, 97n284

RHODE ISLAND
Connecticut, Maine, Mass., [&] R.I.,: atlas of histl county boundaries, 96n438

RHODODENDRON
Book of rhododendrons, 96n1573
Fungi on rhododendron, 97n1279

RHYMING GAMES
Neal-Schuman index to finger-plays, 95n1153

RHYTHM & BLUES MUSIC
All music gd to the blues, 97n1072
Joel Whitburn's top R&B singles 1942-1995, 97n1079

RICE, ELMER
Elmer Rice: a research & production sourcebk, 98n1326

RICHARDSON, TONY
Tony Richardson: a bio-bibliog, 97n1096

RIGHT & LEFT (POLITICAL SCIENCE)
Left gd: a gd to left-of-center orgs, 97n614
Left index, 97n61

RIGHT OF PROPERTY
Environment property & the law, 99n585
Free market environmental bibliog 1995-96, 4th ed, 98n1630

RIGHT-WING EXTREMISTS
Militias in America, 97n613

RISK MANAGEMENT
East Europe & the republics: a pol risk annual, June 1994, 95n153
Glossary of insurance & risk mgmt terms, 6th ed, 97n200

RIVERS
Rivers of the US. v.1: estuaries, 95n1726
Rivers of the US, 99n1536

RKO RADIO PICTURES, INC.
RKO features, 95n1385

ROBINSON, JOAN
Joan Robinson: a bio-bibliog, 97n150

ROBOTICS
McGraw-Hill illus ency of robotics & artificial intelligence, 96n1753
MVA/SME machine vision industry dir, 1994, 95n1640
World industrial robots 1997, 98n1581

ROCKETRY
Spaceflight & rocketry, 97n1300

ROCK FILMS
Hollywood rock, 95n1391

ROCK GARDENS
Bulbs for the rock garden, 97n1255
Cushion plants for the rock garden, 97n1257

ROCK MUSIC
All music bk of hit albums, 97n1066
All music bk of hit singles, 97n1067
All music gd, 3d ed, 98n1228
All music gd to rock, 96n1330
All music gd to rock, 2d ed, 98n1238
American bk of the dead: the definitive Grateful Dead ency, 99n1175
Beatles: the ultimate recording gd, 3d ed, 96n1338
Billboard illus ency of rock, 99n1172
Billboard music yrbk 1994, 96n1303
Billboard's American rock 'n' roll in review, 98n1239
Billboard's hottest hot 100 hits, rev ed, 97n1080
Bob Dylan, 96n1334
Elvis ency, 96n1335
Encyclopedia of Canadian rock, pop & folk, 95n1292
Great rock discography, 97n1085
Illustrated discography of surf music, 1961-65, 3d ed, 96n1332
It's only rock 'n' roll: the ultimate gd to the Rolling Stones, 98n1241
Joel Whitburn's rock tracks, 96n1337
Literature of rock, 3, 96n1333
MusicHound rock: the essential album gd, 97n1084
Pioneers of rock & roll, 95n1307
Rock & roll reader's gd, 98n1242
Rock music in American popular culture 2, 99n1173
Rock music scholarship, 97n1082
Rock song index, 98n1243
Rock stars/pop stars, 96n1315
Rock talk, 95n1306
Rock who's who, 2d ed, 97n1083
Rocket man: the ency of Elton John, 96n1331
Singer-songwriters, 96n1307
Story of rock'n'roll, 96n1336
Ultimate ency of rock, 95n1305

ROCK MUSIC—COLLECTIBLES
Goldmine price gd to rock 'n' roll memorabilia, 99n851

ROCK PLANTS
Cushion plants for the rock garden, 97n1257
Rock garden plants, 99n1353

ROCK & ROLL HALL OF FAME & MUSEUM
Unofficial ency of the rock & roll hall of fame, 99n1174

ROCKS. *See also* **GEOLOGY**
Color atlas of rocks & minerals in thin section, 95n1724
National Audubon Society 1st field gd: rocks & minerals, 99n1535
Pockets: rocks & minerals, 96n73

ROCKY MOUNTAINS REGION
Exploring the mountain states through lit, 95n1125
High country names, 95n501

ROGERS, GINGER
Ginger Rogers: a bio-bibliog, 95n1344

ROGERS, ROY
Roy Rogers, 96n1408

ROLLING STONES
It's only rock 'n' roll: the ultimate gd to the Rolling Stones, 98n1241

ROMANCE LITERATURE
Romance writer's pink pages, 95n942
Romance writer's sourcebk, 97n754
Twentieth-Century romance & histl writers, 3d ed, 95n1163
What do I read next?, 1994, 95n1158

ROMAN DE RENART
Roman de Renart: a gd to scholarly work, 99n1183

ROMANIA
Ceausescu's Romania: an annot bibliog, 95n160
Historical dict of Romania, 97n120
Romania, rev ed, 99n136
Who was who in 20th century Romania, 95n30

ROMANIAN LANGUAGE—DICTIONARIES— ENGLISH
NTC's Romanian & English dict, 97n865

ROMANTICISM
Romantic movement, 97n884

ROMANTICISM—GREAT BRITAIN— BIO-BIBLIOGRAPHY
British short-fiction writers, 1880-1914, 97n979

ROMANTIC LITERATURE
Romantic hearts: a personal ref for romance readers, 3d ed, 98n1115

ROME
Ancient civilizations of the Mediterranean [CD-ROM], 99n490
Ancient Rome chronology, 264-27 BC, 99n523
Dictionary of ancient hist, 95n583
Encyclopedia of the Roman Empire, 95n579
Guide to the aqueducts of ancient Rome, 96n1046
Handbook to life in ancient Rome, 95n586
Handbook to life in ancient Rome, 96n547
Pockets: ancient Rome, 96n64

ROOSEVELT, ELEANOR
Eleanor Roosevelt: a comprehensive bibliog, 95n532

ROSES
Gardening with roses, 96n1549
Graham Stuart Thomas rose bk, rev ed, 96n1551
Roses, 97n1277

ROUTLEDGE, GEORGE
Victorian yellowbacks & paperbacks, 1849-1905, v.1, 96n1223

ROYAL DOULTON FIGURINES
Charlton standard catalogue of Royal Doulton beswick figurines, 5th ed, 98n925
Charlton standard catalogue of Royal Doulton beswick jugs, 4th ed, 98n926

RUBBER
Handbook of plastic & rubber additives, 97n1385

RUBINSTEIN, ANTON
Anton Rubinstein, 99n1144

RUGBY FOOTBALL
Rugby catalogue of info sources, 96n830

RUGGLES, CARL
Carl Ruggles, 96n1280

RUGS, ORIENTAL
Oriental rugs: a bibliog, 95n973

RUNNING
National road race ency, 98n751

RURAL CONDITIONS
Encyclopedia of rural America, 98n98

RURAL DEVELOPMENT
Rural economic dvlpmt, 1975-93: an annot bibliog, 95n180

RUSH, BENJAMIN
Benjamin Rush, M.D.: a bibliographic gd, 97n403

RUSSELL, BERTRAND
Bibliography of Bertrand Russell, 96n1423

RUSSELL, LILLIAN
Lillian Russell: a bio-bibliog, 98n1275

RUSSIA. *See also* **FORMER SOVIET REPUBLICS; SOVIET UNION**
Atlas of Russian hist, 2d ed, 95n562
Cambridge ency of Russia & the former Soviet Union, 2d ed, 95n152
Catalogue Russian films 1991-94, 95n1369
Collapse of communism in the Soviet Union, 99n693
Cultural atlas of Russia & the Former Soviet Union, rev ed, 99n125
Dictionary of Russian & Soviet artists 1420-1970, 95n1001
Encyclopedia of world cultures, v.6: Russia & Eurasia/China, 95n397
Ethnohistorical dict of the Russian & Soviet empires, 95n400
Faberge & his works, 95n994
Film, TV, video in Russia '94, 95n1378
Great dates in Russian & Soviet hist, 95n561
Historical dict of Russia, 99n502
Longman biogl dir of decision-makers in Russia & the successor states, 96n145
Maximov's companion to who governs the Russian Federation, summer 96, v.2, no.1, 97n610
Military ency of Russia & Eurasia, v.5, 96n146
Modern ency of religions in Russia & Eurasia, v.7, 99n1267
Placenames of Russia & the former Soviet Union, 97n382
Russia, rev ed, 99n124
Russia & Eurasia facts & figures annual, v.21, 98n128
Russia & Eurasia facts & figures annual, v.22, 98n129
Russia & Eurasia facts & figures, v.24, 99n126
Russia & the former Soviet Union: a bibliographic gd to English lang pubs, 1986-91, 95n162
Russia survival gd, 5th ed, 95n283
Russia/USSR, 2d ed, 95n161
Russian defense bus dir 1993, 95n284
Russian far east: an economic hndbk, 96n247
Russian revolution, 1905-21, 96n548
Supplement to The Modern Ency of Russian, Soviet, & Eurasian Hist, v.1, 97n476
Vascular plants of Russia & adjacent states (the former USSR), 96n1594
Warships of the USSR & Russia, 1945-95, 98n629

RUSSIAN LANGUAGE—DICTIONARIES— ENGLISH
Barron's Russian dict, 98n1044
Comparative Russian-English dict of Russian proverbs & sayings, 96n1125

Concise Oxford Russian dict, 97n866
Dictionary of bus & legal terms: Russian-English/English-Russian, 96n575
Dictionary of Russian slang & colloquial expressions, 96n1128
Elsevier's dict of agriculture & food production, 96n1516
English-Russian dict of American criminal law, 99n553
English-Russian economics glossary, 97n154
English-Russian, Russian-English dict, rev ed, 96n1124
HarperCollins Russian dict: Russian-English, English-Russian, college ed, 96n1123
NTC's compact Russian & English dict, 95n1093
NTC's new college Russian & English dict, 98n1045
Oxford Russian minidict, 96n1126
Oxford starter Russian dict, 98n1046
Pocket Oxford Russian dict, 2d ed, 96n1127
Russian-English collocational dict of the human body, 97n867
Russian-English comprehensive dict, 98n1047
Russian idioms, 98n1043

RUSSIAN LITERATURE
Early modern Russian writers, late 17th & 18th centuries, 96n1261
Reference gd to Russian lit, 99n1097

RWANDA
Historical dict of Rwanda, 95n121
Rwanda, 95n122

RYGA, GEORGE
George Ryga papers, 96n1249

SACRED MUSIC. *See also* HYMNS; CHURCH MUSIC; GOSPEL MUSIC
Chamber music for solo voice & instruments 1960-89, 96n1299
Handbook to Bach's sacred cantata texts, 98n1247
Hymntune index & related hymn materials, 99n1178
Music & dance of the world's religions, 97n1087
Sacred dramas of J. S. Bach, 96n1284
Songs for bass voice, 96n1295
Tomas Luis de Victoria: a gd to research, 99n1132

SACRED SPACE
Atlas of holy places & sacred sites, 97n1167
Atlas of sacred places, 95n1434
Encyclopedia of sacred places, 98n1349

SAFETY EDUCATION
CRC hndbk of lab safety, 4th ed, 97n1386
Injury prevention for young children, 97n710
Preventive care sourcebk 1997-98, 98n1520

SAFETY REGULATIONS
Artist's complete health & safety gd, 2d ed, 96n1042
Directory of safety standards, lit, & servs, 98n1495

SAGE
Book of salvias, 98n1434

SAILBOATS
Field gd to sailboats of N America, 95n1796

SAILORS
Stars in blue: movie actors in America's sea servs, 98n1281

SAINT HELENA
St. Helena, Ascension, & Tristan da Cunha, 98n146

SAINTS
Bible & the saints, 96n1448
Book of saints, 6th ed, 95n1460
Book of saints, 99n1263
Fifty-seven saints, 2d ed, 96n1464
Our Sunday Visitor's ency of saints, 99n1261
Oxford dict of saints, 99n1262
Penguin dict of saints, 3d ed, 97n1174
Post-Biblical saints art index, 95n1010

SALAMANDERS
Handbook of salamanders, 96n1635
Salamanders of the US & Canada, 99n1396

SALES PERSONNEL
America's top office, mgmt, & sales jobs, 2d ed, 95n311

SALTWATER FISHING
Northeast gd to saltwater fishing & boating, 95n817
Southeast gd to saltwater fishing & boating, 95n818

SALVIA
Book of salvias, 98n1434

SAMARITANS
Bibliography of the Samaritans, 2d ed, 95n1435

SAMOAN ISLANDS
Samoa (American Samoa, Western Samoa, Samoans abroad), 98n145

SAN FRANCISCO (CALIFORNIA)
San Francisco almanac, rev ed, 97n83

SANITARY ENGINEERING
Dictionary of environmental sci & tech, 2d ed, 98n1636

SAN MARINO
San Marino, 97n121

SANSKRIT LANGUAGE—DICTIONARIES—ENGLISH
Concise dict of Indian philosophy, rev ed, 98n1336
Hippocrene concise Sanskrit-English dict, 97n868

SAO TOME & PRINCIPE
Sao Tome & Principe, 96n121

SAPP, ALLEN
Allen Sapp: a bio-bibliog, 97n1038

SARTRE, JEAN-PAUL
Sartre: bibliog 1980-92, 95n1426

SASSE, HERMANN
Hermann Sasse: a bibliog, 97n1168

SATELLITES
International satellite dir, 1995, 10th ed, 96n1780
International satellite dir 1998, 99n1497
Space satellite hndbk, 3d ed, 95n1720
World satellite almanac, 1995, 7th ed, 96n1648
WRTH satellite broadcasting gd, 1995 ed, 96n997

SATIRE
Encyclopedia of satirical lit, 97n892

SAUDI ARABIA
Historical dict of Saudi Arabia, 95n176

SAVINGS & LOAN ASSOCIATIONS
Savings & loan crisis: an annot bibliog, 95n234

SAXOPHONISTS
Tram: the Frank Trumbauer story, 96n1323

SCANDINAVIA
Cultural atlas of the Viking world, 95n563

SCANDINAVIAN AMERICANS
Student's gd to Scandinavian American genealogy, 97n364

SCHOENBERG, ARNOLD
Arnold Schoenberg companion, 99n1128

SCHOOL FIELD TRIPS
Virtual field trips, 98n281

SCHOOL INTEGRATION
Historical dict of school segregation & desegregation, 99n301

SCHOOL MEDIA CENTERS. *See also*
INSTRUCTIONAL MEDIA CENTERS
Best bks for children, 5th ed, 95n1130
Cataloging nonbk materials with AACR2R & MARC, 96n631
Children's catalog, 17th ed, 98n586
Children's media market place, 4th ed, 96n649
Elementary school lib collection, 19th ed, 95n661
Elementary school lib collection, 19th ed [CD-ROM], 95n662
Elementary school lib collection, 20th ed, 97n544
Elementary school lib collection, 20th ed [CD-ROM], 97n545
Emergency Librarian index, vs.1-20: 1973-93, 96n645
Middle & jr high school lib catalog, 7th ed, 96n650
School lib media annual 1993, v.11, 95n663
School lib media annual 1995, v.13, 96n651
Senior high school lib catalog, 15th ed, 98n587
Wading the World Wide Web, 99n1498

SCHOOL PSYCHOLOGY
Historical ency of school psychology, 97n286

SCHOOL VIOLENCE
School violence, 98n278

SCHUMAN, WILLIAM
William Schuman: a bio-bibliog, 99n1127

SCIENCE
Applied sci & tech index 1996, 98n1418
Bibliographic gd to tech 1996, 98n1398
Building a popular sci lib collection for high school & adult learners, 96n660
DISCovering sci [CD-ROM], 98n1413
Environmental acronyms, 96n1850
Eureka! scientific discoveries & inventions, 96n1496
European research & dvlpmt database 1995 [CD-ROM], 96n1510
Great scientific achievements: the 20th century, 95n1489
History of sci in the US, 97n1235
Illustrated almanac of sci, tech, & inventions, 99n1306
Illustrated bk of questions & answers, 97n56
Information sources in sci & tech, 2d ed, 95n1481
Internet compendium: subject gds to health & sci resources, 96n1774
Magill's survey of sci, v.7, 99n1315
Magill's survey of sci [CD-ROM], 95n1502
Magill's survey of sci CD-ROM [CD-ROM], 99n1324
MathSci disc [CD-ROM], 97n1414
Milestones in sci & tech, 2d ed, 95n1503
New bk of popular sci, 1998 ed, 99n1317
New York Public Lib sci desk ref, 96n1512
Peterson's top colleges for sci, 97n306
Questions & answers bk of sci facts, 98n1404
Reader's adviser on CD-ROM [CD-ROM], 97n11
Reference sources in sci, engineering, medicine, & agriculture, 95n1482
Science & tech: a purchase gd for libs 1995, 97n1234
Science & tech breakthroughs, 99n1308
Science & tech firsts, 98n1402
Science navigator [CD-ROM], 96n1500
Science on file [CD-ROM], 98n1415
Scientific & technical bks & serials in print 1995, 22d ed, 96n1484
Scientific revolution, 97n1227
SciTech ref plus 1995-96 [CD-ROM], 97n1228
Student sci opportunities, 95n340
U*X*L sci fact finder, 99n1319
Walford's gd to ref material, v.1: sci & tech, 7th ed, 97n1229
Wilson chronology of sci & tech, 99n1307
Women & sci, 97n730
World Book's young scientist, 98n1410
World of scientific discovery, 95n1497

SCIENCE—DICTIONARIES & ENCYCLOPEDIAS
Callaham's Russian-English dict of sci & tech, 4th ed, 97n1237
Dictionary of sci, 95n1490
Dictionary of sci, 96n1493
DK nature ency, 99n1309
DK sci ency, rev ed, 99n1310
DK ultimate visual dict of sci, 99n1311
Encyclopedia of analytical sci, 96n1495
Encyclopedia of life scis, 97n1268
Encyclopedia of sci, 95n1487
Eyewitness ency of sci [CD-ROM], 98n1403
Gale ency of sci, 97n1238
Grolier student ency of sci, tech, & the environment, 97n1239

Illustrated dict of sci, rev ed, 96n1497
Illustrated sci ency, 98n1405
Interactive sci ency [CD-ROM], 99n1313
Kingfisher 1st sci ency, 99n1314
Larousse dict of sci & tech, 97n1240
Macmillan ency of earth scis, 97n1391
Macmillan ency of sci, rev ed, 98n1406
McGraw-Hill concise ency of sci & tech, 3d ed, 95n1492
McGraw-Hill dict of scientific & technical terms, 5th ed, 95n1493
McGraw-Hill ency of sci & tech, 8th ed, 98n1407
McGraw-Hill multimedia ency of sci & tech [CD-ROM], 95n1494
McGraw-Hill multimedia ency of sci & tech [CD-ROM], 99n1316
My 1st sci dict, 96n1498
Routledge German technical dict, 97n851
Science dict, 96n1501
Van Nostrand's scientific ency, 8th ed, 96n1502
Visual ency of sci, 96n1503
World Bk ency of sci, 98n1409

SCIENCE—DIRECTORIES
ASTM dir of scientific & technical consultants & expert witnesses, 1994 ed, 95n1498
ASTM intl dir of testing laboratories, 1998 ed, 99n1321
Directory of hyphenated techniques, 96n1505
Guide to American scientific & technical dirs, 3d ed, 95n1499
World gd to scientific assns & learned societies, 7th ed, 99n1323

SCIENCE FICTION
Aliens, robots, & spaceships, 96n1360
American sci fiction TV series of the 1950s, 99n1213
Anatomy of wonder 4, 96n1191
Barlowe's gd to fantasy, 98n979
Best in sci fiction, 95n1164
British sci fiction paperbacks & mags 1949-56, 96n1234
Burroughs cyclopaedia, 97n969
Dystopian lit, 95n1109
Encyclopedia of TV sci fiction, 98n1283
Jules Verne ency, 97n952
Magill's gd to sci fiction & fantasy lit, 97n948
St. James gd to fantasy writers, 97n950
St. James gd to sci fiction writers, 4th ed, 97n951
Science fiction: the illus ency, 96n1192
Science fiction & fantasy ref index 1992-95, 98n1117
Science fiction, fantasy, & horror writers, 96n1193
Science fiction serials, 99n1227
Ultimate gd to sci fiction, 2d ed, 97n949
VideoHound's sci-fi experience, 98n1320
What do I read next?, 1994, 95n1158
What fantastic fiction do I read next?, 99n1036
Work of Jack Vance, 96n1218

SCIENCE FICTION FILMS
Dystopian lit, 95n1109
Horror & sci fiction films 4, 98n1300
Japanese sci fiction, fantasy & horror films, 95n1382
Overlook film ency: sci fic, 95n1375
Science fiction, fantasy, & horror film sequels, series, & remakes, 98n1292
Science fiction, horror & fantasy film & TV credits, suppl.2, 95n1395
Sci-Fi on tape, 98n1318

SCIENCE FICTION TELEVISION PROGRAMS
Science fiction TV series, 98n1286
Science fiction, horror & fantasy film & TV credits, suppl.2, 95n1395

SCIENCE—HANDBOOKS & YEARBOOKS
Addison-Wesley sci hndbk, 98n1412
Handbook of current sci & tech, [2d ed], 97n1242
Handbook of research on sci teaching & learning, 95n344
Handbooks & tables in sci & tech, 3d ed, 95n1483
Handy sci answer bk, 2d ed, 98n1414
McGraw-Hill yrbk of sci & tech 1996, 97n1243
McGraw-Hill yrbk of sci & tech 1999, 99n1325
Science yr 1997, 98n1416
Science yr 1998, 98n1417
World Wide Web for scientists & engineers, 99n1327

SCIENCE—PERIODICALS
Directory of bus per special issues, 96n209

SCIENCE PROJECTS
Junior sci experiments on file, 95n1501
Science experiments & projects index, 95n1506
Science experiments index for young people, 2d ed, 97n1244
Science projects for all students, 99n1326

SCIENCE & STATE
Science, tech, & society in the 3d World, 96n138

SCIENCE—STUDY & TEACHING
Educator's gd to free sci materials, 35th ed, 95n1480
Educator's gd to free sci materials 1998-99, 39th ed, 99n286
Resources for teaching middle school scis, 99n1296

SCIENTIFIC APPARATUS & INSTRUMENTS
Instruments of sci, 99n1312
Scientific instruments 1500-1900, 99n1318

SCIENTISTS
American men & women of sci 1995-96, 19th ed, 96n1485
American women in sci, 1950 to the present, 99n1299
ASTM dir of scientific & tech consultants & expert witnesses, 1997-98 ed, 99n1320
Biographical dict of scientists, 95n1485
Biographical ency of scientists, 95n1484
Biographical ency of scientists, 99n1300
Biographies of scientists, 99n1298
Cambridge dict of scientists, 98n1399
Directory of hyphenated techniques, 96n1505
Distinguished African American scientists of the 20th century, 97n1230
Scientists: their lives & works, v.5, 99n1303
Grolier lib of sci biogs, 98n1400
Larousse dict of scientists, 96n1487
Mathematical scis professional dir 1997, 98n1625

Notable 20th-century scientists, 96n1490
Notable women in the physical scis, 98n1598
Prominent scientists: an index to collective biogs, 3d ed, 95n1505
Remarkable lives of 100 women healers & scientists, 96n940
Scientists, 98n1401
Scientists & inventors, 99n1304
Scientists since 1660, 99n1297
Scientists: their lives & works, v.4, 99n1302
Who's who in European research & dvlpmt 1995, 96n1491
Who's who in sci & engineering 1996-97, 3d ed, 97n1232
Who's who in sci & engineering 1998-99, 99n1305
Who's who in sci in Europe, 9th ed, 97n1233
Who's who in theology & sci, 1996 ed, 97n1175
World of scientific discovery, 95n1497

SCOTLAND
Collins ency of Scotland, 96n148
Dictionary of Scottish art & architecture, 96n1025
Dictionary of Scottish church hist & theology, 95n1466
Dictionary of Scottish quotations, 98n136
Scotland in the 19th century, 95n564

SCOTS
Scottish family hist, 95n462

SCOTTISH LITERATURE
Literature criticism from 1400 to 1800, v.29, 97n902

SCOTTISH POETRY
Literature criticism from 1400 to 1800, v.29, 97n902

SCREENWRITERS
Betty Comden & Adolph Green: a bio-bibliog, 95n1352
Contemporary literary criticism, v.86, 97n895
Film writers gd, 6th ed, 97n767
Film writers gd, 7th ed, 99n1219

SCRIBNER (PUBLISHER)
Dictionary of literary biog documentary series, v.16, 99n954
Nineteenth-Century American western writers, 99n957

SCULPTURE
Looking at European sculpture, 98n983
Sculpture, 95n1023

SEARCHING, BIBLIOGRAPHICAL. See also ONLINE BIBLIOGRAPHICAL SEARCHING
American Lib Assn gd to info access, 95n641
College students research companion, 99n610
100 research topic gds for students, 97n543

SEASHORE
National seashores, rev ed, 96n475

SECRET SERVICE—GREAT BRITAIN
British secret servs, 98n686

SECRET SERVICE—ISRAEL
Israeli secret servs, 98n689

SECRET SOCIETIES
International ency of secret societies & fraternal orders, 98n764

SECTS (RELIGIOUS)
New religious movements in Western Europe, 98n1343
Sects, 'cults,' & alternative religions, 98n1360

SECURITIES
American Stock Exchange 1994 fact bk, 95n218
Asia Pacific securities hndbk 1993, 95n259
Directory of cos required to file annual reports with the SEC, 96n183
Directory of listed derivative contracts 1996/97, 98n171
International gd to securities market indices, 98n175
Rate ref gd to the US treasury market 1984-95, 97n184
Topline ency of histl charts, Mar 1997 ed, 98n176
Wall street words, 98n170
World stock exchange fact bk, 97n186

SECURITY, INTERNATIONAL. See also PEACE
Scholars' gd to Washington, DC, for peace & intl security studies, 96n656

SEGREGATION IN EDUCATION
Historical dict of school segregation & desegregation, 99n301

SELF-CULTURE
Adventures in Video, 97n314

SELF-EMPLOYED
Working solo sourcebk, 96n263

SELF-HELP TECHNIQUES
Authoritative gd to self-help bks, 95n774
Finding help: a ref gd for personal concerns, 97n55
Law for the layperson, 2d ed, 98n511
National dir of bereavement support grps & servs, 1996, 98n769
Self-help dir, 95n827
Using bibliotherapy in clinical practice, 95n772

SELF-PUBLISHING
Business & legal forms for authors & self-publishers, 98n605

SEMANTICS
Case, semantic roles, & grammatical relations, 96n1057

SEMITIC LANGUAGES, DICTIONARIES
Dictionary of the NW Semitic inscriptions, 96n1129
Hamito-Semitic etymological dict, 96n1107

SENECA INDIANS
Seneca & Tuscarora Indians: an annot bibliog, 95n427

SENEGAL
Historical dict of Senegal, 2d ed, 95n123

SEPARATION (PSYCHOLOGY)
Books to help children cope with separation & loss, 4th ed, 95n773

SEQUELS (LITERATURE)
Sequels: an annot gd to novels in series, 99n1029
To be continued: an annot gd to sequels, 97n946

SERIAL PUBLICATIONS
ACCESS: the supplementary index to pers, 96n78
Association for Population/Family Planning Libs & Info Centers Intl (AFPLIC-I) union list of serials, 96n861
CIJE on disc, Jan 1969-Jul 1994 [CD-ROM], 95n346
El-Hi textbks & serials in print 1994, 95n350
Guide to special issues & indexes of pers, 4th ed, 95n86
Sequels: an annot gd to novels in series, 99n1029
Serious about series, 99n1012
Standard per dir, 1997, 20th ed, 97n65
Ulrich's intl pers dir 1997, 35th ed, 97n66

SERIALS SUBSCRIPTION AGENCIES
International subscription agents, 6th ed, 95n648

SERVICE INDUSTRIES
Encyclopedia of American industries, 95n236
Services—the export of the 21st century: a gdbk of US serv exporters, 98n262
Services: stats on intl transactions 1970/92, 96n918

SET DESIGNERS
Oliver Smith: a bio-bibliog, 95n1349

SEX
And Adam knew Eve: a dict of sex in the Bible, 96n1452
Black bk, 4th ed, 98n796
Cassell sex & sexuality, 95n873
Complete dict of sexology, new expanded ed, 96n885
Dr. Ruth's ency of sex, 95n878
Fetishes, Florentine girdles, & other explorations into the sexual imagination, 96n886
Human sexuality, 95n872
International ency of sexuality, 98n797
Research gd to human sexuality, 95n876
Sex & love quotations, 96n889
Sexual behavior in modern China, English-lang ed, 99n775
Sexuality & gender in the English Renaissance, 99n776
Sexuality & the elderly, 98n798
Sexuality, religion & magic, 95n875
Studies in human sexuality, 2d ed, 96n887

SEX CRIMES
Childhood sexual abuse, 96n618

SEX DIFFERENCES
Why Eve doesn't have an Adam's apple: a dict of sex differences, 97n1318

SEX DISCRIMINATION
Gender equity in educ, 96n313

SEX DISTRIBUTION (DEMOGRAPHY)
Sex & age distribution of world populations: 1994 revision, 96n912
Women's atlas of the US, rev ed, 96n933

SEX & LAW
Guide to America's sex laws, 97n499

SEX ROLES
International hndbk on gender roles, 95n871

SEXUAL HARASSMENT
Sexual harassment, 96n888
Sexual harassment, 97n702
Sexual harassment, 2d ed, 99n563
Sexual harassment: a ref hndbk, 95n633

SEXUALLY TRANSMITTED DISEASES
World population monitoring 1996, 99n809

SHADE-TOLERANT PLANTS
Favorite shade plants, 96n1571

SHAKESPEARE, WILLIAM
Auditions & scenes from Shakespeare, 95n1216
Catalogue of paintings in the Folger Shakespeare lib, 95n1021
Coined by Shakespeare, 99n1078
Dictionary of sexual lang & imagery in Shakespearean & Stuart lit, 96n1243
Dictionary of Shakespeare's semantic wordplay, 99n1084
Dictionary of who, what, & where in Shakespeare, 98n1161
Exploring Shakespeare [CD-ROM], 98n1162
Hamlet: a gd to the play, 99n1077
Henry IV pts 1 & 2: an annot bibliog, 95n1218
King John: an annot bibliog, 95n1217
Pronouncing Shakespeare's words, 99n1076
Shakespeare, 99n1079
Shakespeare cos & festivals, 96n1420
Shakespeare dict, 96n1241
Shakespeare films in the classroom, 95n1397
Shakespeare for students, bk 2, 98n1163
Shakespeare interactive [CD-ROM], 99n1080
Shakespeare interactive [CD-ROM], 99n1081
Shakespeare quotations, 96n1239
Shakespearean criticism, v.26, 96n1242
Shakespearean criticism, v.38, 99n1082
Shakespearean criticism yrbk 1996, v.37, 99n1083
Shakespeare's characters for students, 98n1164
Shakespeare's lang, 97n999
Speak the speech, 95n1220
Taming of the Shrew: an annot bibliog, 95n1219
Walking shadows, 96n1399
Who's who in Shakespeare, 96n1240
World Shakespeare biblog on CD-ROM 1990-93 [CD-ROM], 98n1165

SHAMANISM
Encyclopedia of Native American healing, 97n340

SHAN LANGUAGE—DICTIONARIES—ENGLISH
Shan-English dict, 97n869

SHARKS
Sharks & rays of Australia, 96n1623

SHATNER, WILLIAM
William Shatner: a bio-bibliog, 95n1346

SHAW, GEORGE BERNARD
Proverbial Bernard Shaw, 95n1221

SHELLS
Field gd to shells, 4th ed, 96n1595

SHERIDAN, ANN
Ann Sheridan: a bio-bibliog, 98n1274

SHINING PATH (GUERILLA MOVEMENT)
Sendero Luminoso: an annot bibliog of the Shining Path guerrilla movement, 1980-93, 97n502
Sendero Luminoso in context, 99n573

SHIPPING
Historical dict of the US Merchant Marine & shipping industry, 95n1794
Review of maritime transport 1993, 96n1897
Review of maritime transport 1997, 98n260

SHIP REGISTERS
Way's packet dir, 1848-1994, rev ed, 96n1898

SHIPS. *See also* **WARSHIPS**
Ships of the world, 98n1651

SHIPWRECKS
Atlas of shipwrecks & treasure, 96n1896
Shipwrecks, 97n1448

SHOPPING
Shopping for a better world, 95n225

SHORT STORIES
American short-story writers since WW II, 95n1179
British short-fiction writers, 1880-1914, 95n1209
British short-fiction writers, 1915-45, 97n980
British short-fiction writers, 1945-80, 96n1228
Index to Spanish lang short stories in anthologies, 95n1241
Index to translated short fiction by Latin American women in English lang anthologies, 98n1179
Masterplots 2: short story series suppl, 97n953
Reader's gd to the short stories of Eudora Welty, 98n1138
Reader's gd to the short stories of Sherwood Anderson, 95n1184
Reader's gd to the short stories of Stephen Crane, 98n1133
Reader's gd to the short stories of William Faulkner, 95n1189
Reference gd to short fiction, 95n1167
Short fiction: a critical companion, 98n1119
Short stories for students, v.1, 98n1120
Short stories for students, v.2, 98n1121
Short stories for students, v.3, 99n1015
Short stories for students, v.4, 99n1016
Short stories in English: Britain & N America, 95n1165
Short story criticism, v.17, 96n1196
Short story criticism, v.18, 97n954
Short story criticism, v.19, 97n955
Short story criticism, v.20, 97n956
Short story criticism, v.21, 97n957
Short story criticism, v.26, 99n1037
Short story criticism, v.27, 99n1038
Short story index 1989-93, 95n1166
Short story index 1995, 98n1122
Short story writers, 98n1123
Twentieth-Century short story explication, v.2, 96n1195
Twentieth-Century short story explication: new series, v.3: 1993-94, 98n1118

SHORTWAVE RADIO
Shortwave listening on the road, 97n774

SHRIKES
Shrikes: a gd to the shrikes of the world, 99n1380

SHRIMPS
Pacific coast crabs & shrimps, 96n1622

SHRINES
Atlas of holy places & sacred sites, 97n1167

SHRUBS
Dirr's hardy trees & shrubs, 98n1456
Field gd to the trees & shrubs of the S Appalachians, 95n1553
Pruning of trees, shrubs, & conifers, [rev ed], 96n1588
Virus diseases of trees & shrubs, 2d ed, 95n1552

SIBELIUS, JEAN
Jean Sibelius: a gd to research, 99n1135

SIBERIA
Ross register of Siberian industry 1995, 96n246

SICK CHILDREN
Sourcebook of pediatric psychology, 95n783

SIDNEY, GEORGE
George Sidney: a bio-bibliog, 95n1350

SIDNEY, PHILIP
Sir Philip Sidney: an annot bibliog of texts & criticism (1554-1984), 95n1222

SIGNS & SYMBOLS
Abbreviations dict, 9th ed, 96n2
Continuum ency of symbols, 95n1441
Dictionary of symbols, 99n886
Elsevier's dict of acronyms, initialisms, abbrevs, & symbols, 99n1
Mammoth dict of symbols, English lang ed, 97n636
Phonetic symbol gd, 2d ed, 97n815
Symbols of nationhood, 95n142

SIKHISM
Encyclopaedia of Sikh religion & culture, 97n1225
South Asian religions in the Americas, 96n1438

SIKSIKA LANGUAGE—DICTIONARIES— ENGLISH
Blackfoot dict of stems, roots, & affixes, 2d ed, 97n872

SILENT FILMS
American silent film comedies, 96n1378
Guide to American silent crime films, 95n1383
Horror in silent films, 96n1391
Silent film necrology, 96n1369
Silent film performers, 97n1105
Silent films on video, 97n1120
Southern mountaineers in silent films, 95n1388
Ultimate dir of the silent screen performers, 96n1368

SILVERWORK
Catalogue of American silver, 96n999

SINATRA, FRANK
Ol' blue eyes: a Frank Sinatra ency, 99n1118

SINGAPORE
Singapore bus: the portable ency for doing bus with Singapore, 95n265

SINGERS
Billy Murray: the phonograph industry's 1st great recording artist, 98n1198
Classical singers of the opera & recital stages, 95n1250
Contemporary musicians, v.19, 99n1115
Contemporary musicians, v.20, 99n1116
Lillian Russell: a bio-bibliog, 98n1275
Moanin' low: a discography of female popular vocal recordings, 1920-33, 97n1064
Singers of the century, 98n1201

SINGLE-PARENT FAMILY
Children of separation, 95n851

SIR ROBERT PEEL
Sir Robert Peel 1788-1850: a bibliog, 97n439

SITSKY, LARRY
Larry Sitsky: a bio-bibliog, 98n1214

SITUATIONIST INTERNATIONAL
Realization & suppression of the Situationist Intl, 97n792

SKATING
Encyclopedia of figure skating, 99n739

SKELETON
Visual dict of the skeleton, 96n1683

SKIING
Good skiing & snowboarding gd 1998, 99n740
Good skiing gd 1997, 97n662

SKIN
Illustrated dict of dermatologic syndromes, 96n1728
Skin deep: an A-Z of skin disorders, treatments, & health, 97n1333

SLAVERY
Comprehensive name index for The American Slave, 98n341
Dictionary of Afro-American slavery, updated ed, 98n438
Historical ency of world slavery, 99n531
Historical gd to world slavery, 99n542
Indian slavery, labor, evangelization, & captivity in the Americas, 99n382
Macmillan ency of world slavery, 99n535
Pan-African chronology, 97n426

SLAVIC COUNTRIES
American bibliog of Slavic & E European studies for 1993, 97n114
Bibliographic gd to Slavic, Baltic, & Eurasian studies 1996, 98n126

SLAVIC LITERATURE
South Slavic writers before WW II, 96n1262
South Slavic writers since WW II, 99n1091

SLIDES (PHOTOGRAPHY)
Visual resources dir, 96n378

SLOVENIA
Slovenia, 97n122

SMALL BUSINESS
Bond's franchise gd, 1996, 97n180
Encyclopedia of small bus, 99n277
Free money from the fed govt for small businesses & entrepreneurs, 2d ed, 97n189
Language of small bus, 95n188
Major studies of minority bus, 95n178
MoneyFind bkware dir of small bus investors, 95n197
100 best retirement businesses, 95n211
Small bus profiles, v.1, 95n212
Small bus profiles, v.2, 96n196
Small bus sourcebk, 10th ed, 98n166
SOHO desk ref, 99n283
StartSmart small bus advisor [CD-ROM], 96n207
Working solo sourcebk, 96n263

SMALL LIBRARIES—COLLECTION DEVELOPMENT
Guide to ref bks for small & medium-sized libs, 1984-94, 96n9

SMITH, OLIVER LEMUEL
Oliver Smith: a bio-bibliog, 95n1349

SMITHSONIAN INSTITUTION
Catalog of the Cooper-Hewitt Museum of Design lib of the Smithsonian Inst libs, 95n924
150 yrs of America's Smithsonian [CD-ROM], 98n74
Smithsonian on disc [CD-ROM], 95n635
Smithsonian on disc, 4th ed [CD-ROM], 99n613

SNAKES
Coral snakes of the Americas, 98n1475
Encyclopedia of snakes, 96n1637
Handbook of snakes of the US & Canada, 95n1598
Snakes of the US & Canada, v.2, 96n1638

SNOWBOARDING
Good skiing & snowboarding gd 1998, 99n740

SOAP OPERAS
Prime time network serials, 98n1310

SOCCER
Encyclopedia of World Cup soccer, 95n822
Soccer stars, 96n831
United States & World Cup soccer competition, 95n823
World ency of soccer, 95n824

SOCIAL ACTION
Building a new South, 96n98

SOCIAL CONFLICT
Aggression & conflict, 96n835

SOCIAL HISTORY
Atlas of world dvlpmt, 96n444
Columbia chronicles of American life, 1910-92, 96n501
Encyclopedia of social hist, 95n96
Handbook to life in ancient Rome, 96n547
Women writers in the US, 97n738

SOCIAL INDICATORS
Illustrated bk of world rankings, rev ed, 98n813

SOCIAL INSTITUTIONS
Directory of social research orgs in the UK, 95n97
Family studies database [CD-ROM], 97n674

SOCIAL INTERACTIONS
Encyclopedia of relationships across the lifespan, 97n631

SOCIALISM
Historical dict of socialism, 99n695
Rosa Luxemburg & Emma Goldman: a bibliog, 98n637

SOCIALIZATION
Growing up: a cross-cultural ency, 97n708

SOCIAL JUSTICE
Building a new South, 96n98

SOCIAL MEDICINE
Dictionary of medical sociology, 98n1524

SOCIAL MOVEMENTS
ABC-CLIO companion to the Native American rights movement, 97n341
Social movement theory & research, 98n690

SOCIAL NORMS
Don't do it: a dict of the forbidden, 99n1193
Learning to behave: a gd to American conduct bks before 1900, 95n1422

SOCIAL PROBLEMS
Encyclopedia of social work, 19th ed, 96n893
Encyclopedia of world problems & human potential, 4th ed, 95n828
Encyclopedia plus of world problems & human potential, 4th ed [CD-ROM], 98n86

SOCIAL PSYCHOLOGY
Sociology of emotions: an annot bibliog, 95n826

SOCIAL REFORMERS
American reform & reformers, 97n408
British reform writers, 1789-1832, 97n977
Jane Addams papers, 97n706
Leaders from the 1960s, 95n715
Radicalism hndbk, 96n766
Radicalism in Minn. 1900-60, 96n767

SOCIAL RESPONSIBILITY OF BUSINESS
Shopping for a better world, 95n225
Shopping with a conscience, 98n178

SOCIAL SCIENCES
ASSIA plus [CD-ROM], 96n97
Best graduate programs: humanities & social scis, 2d ed, 99n335
Comprehensive dissertation index, 1996 suppl, 98n844
Contemporary thesaurus of social sci terms & synonyms, 95n94
Education index, July 1995 to June 1996, 98n279
Multilevel design, 96n99
PAIS select [CD-ROM], 98n89
Reader's adviser on CD-ROM [CD-ROM], 97n11
Selective inventory of social sci info & doc 1993, 95n95
Social sci ency, 2d ed, 97n75
Social scis, 2d ed, 97n76
Social scis abstracts full text [CD-ROM], 98n92
Social scis index, April 1995 to Mar 1996, 98n93
Sociofile: 1974-Dec 1996 [CD-ROM], 98n94
Sociology: A gd to ref & info sources, 98n753
Survey of social sci: govt & pols series, 96n741
Survey of social sci: sociology series, 96n836
Walford's gd to ref material, v.2, 6th ed, 95n98
Walford's gd to ref material, v.2, 7th ed, 99n83
World databases in social scis, 97n78

SOCIAL SCIENCES—RESEARCH
Dictionary of social & market research, 98n253
Qualitative inquiry: a dict of terms, 99n743

SOCIAL SCIENCES—STATISTICS
National cultures of the world, 98n90

SOCIAL SERVICES
Carroll's fed assistance dir, 96n892
Directory of social serv grants, 97n688
Directory of social serv grants, 2d ed, 99n765
Post-release assistance programs for prisoners, 2d ed, 96n600
Social work almanac, 2d ed, 96n894
Social work dict, 3d ed, 96n890

SOCIAL STUDIES—TEACHING
Educator's gd to free social studies materials 1998-99, 38th ed, 99n287

SOCIAL SURVEYS
Polling & survey research methods, 1935-79, 97n77

SOCIAL WELFARE
Encyclopedia of modern American social issues, 99n742
Historical dict of the welfare state, 99n777

SOCIAL WORK
International hndbk on social work educ, 97n704
NASW register of clinical social workers 1993, 95n879
Women's info exchange natl dir, 95n915

SOCIOLOGICAL JURISPRUDENCE
Sociology of law, 95n598

SOCIOLOGY
Concise Oxford dict of sociology, 96n834
Dictionary of ethics, theology, & society, 97n73
Encyclopedia of world problems & human potential, 4th ed, 95n828
Sociology: A gd to ref & info sources, 98n753
Survey of social sci: sociology series, 96n836

SOCIOLOGY, CHRISTIAN (CATHOLIC)
New dict of Catholic social thought, 96n1470

SOCIOLOGY, RURAL
Encyclopedia of rural America, 98n98

SOFTBALL
Official rules of softball, 99n741

SOFTWARE ENGINEERING
Encyclopedia of sftwr engineering, 95n1607
Software engineering standards & specifications, 95n1608

SOFTWARE MANUALS
Xtravaganza! the essential sourcebk for Macromedia Xtras, 99n1486

SOIL MECHANICS
Compendium of soil clean-up technologies & soil remediation cos, 98n1496
Literature of soil sci, 95n1509

SOLAR ENERGY
Real Goods solar living sourcebk, 8th ed, 96n1847

SOLAR SYSTEM
NASA atlas of the solar system, 98n1609
Solar system, 99n1524

SOMALI LANGUAGE—DICTIONARIES—ENGLISH
English-Somali, Somali-English Dict, 96n1134

SOMME, FIRST BATTLE OF THE, FRANCE, 1916
Battles of the Somme, 1916, 97n561

SONATAS
International ency of violin-keyboard sonatas & composer biogs, 2d ed, 97n1043

SONGS
American song, 2d ed, 97n1077
Americana song reader, 99n1125
Children's song index, 1978-93, 97n1033
Hollywood song, 96n1275
Music & poetry in the Middle Ages, 96n1296
Singer's gd to the American art song 1870-1980, 95n1272
Song finder, 96n1318

SONGS, GERMAN
German poetry in song, 97n1032

SONGS (LOW VOICE)
Songs for bass voice, 96n1295

SONGS, OLD FRENCH
Lyrics of the Trouveres, 96n1251

SONGS WITH GUITAR
Music for voice & classical guitar, 1945-96, 98n1219

SONGS WITH INSTRUMENTAL ENSEMBLE
Chamber music for solo voice & instruments 1960-89, 96n1299

SONNETS
Milton's sonnets, 96n1214

SOTHO LANGUAGE
Understanding everyday Sesotho, 96n1135

SOUL MUSIC
Blackwell gd to soul recordings, 95n1308
Soul music A-Z, rev ed, 96n1339

SOUND
Encyclopedia of acoustics, 98n1619

SOUND—EQUIPMENT & SUPPLIES
Orion blue bk: audio 1997, 99n177

SOUND RECORDING INDUSTRY
Billboard bk of top 40 albums, 3d ed, 97n1061
Directory of American disc record brands & manufacturers, 1891-1943, 95n1255
Recording industry sourcebk, 99n1199

SOUND RECORDINGS
All music bk of hit singles, 95n1293
All music gd: the best CDs, albums & tapes, 2d ed, 95n1256
All music gd to rock, 96n1330
Blackwell gd to recorded contemporary music, 98n1221
Christian music dirs: recorded music 1994, 95n1310
Decca lables: a discography, 97n1031
Directory of American disc record brands & manufacturers, 1891-1943, 95n1255
Ethnic & vernacular music, 1898-1960, 97n1075

Fred Waring discography, 97n1049
Golden age of Walt Disney records 1933-88, 98n1209
His master's voice/die stimme seines herrn, 95n1258
Joel Whitburn's top pop singles 1955-93, 96n1314
Mercury labels: a discography, 95n1259
Metropolitan Opera gd to recorded opera, 95n1284
World dir of moving image & sound archives, 95n963

SOUND RECORDINGS IN EDUCATION
Audio bk breakthrough, 95n664

SOUTH AFRICA
Atlas of apartheid, 95n395
Consumer South Africa 1995, 97n270
Dictionary of South African English on histl principles, 97n830
Gasterias of South Africa, 95n1550
Lesotho, rev ed, 98n107
South Africa, rev ed, 96n122
Who's who in South African pols, no.5, 97n611

SOUTH AFRICA—BIBLIOGRAPHY
Guide to South African ref bks, 6th ed, 98n19
Nadine Gordimer: a bibliog of primary & secondary sources, 1937-92, 95n1240
South Africa as apartheid ends: an annot bibliog..., 95n124
South African bibliog, 3d ed, 97n551

SOUTH AFRICA—RELIGION
African traditional religion in South Africa, 98n1344
Christianity in South Africa, 98n1382
Islam, Hinduism, & Judaism in South Africa, 98n1345

SOUTH AMERICA
Africa, Asia, & S America since 1800, 96n555
Birds of S America, v.2, 95n1573
Dictionary of 20th century culture: Hispanic culture of S America, 96n406
Encyclopedia of world cultures, v.7: S America, 95n398
Handbook of Latin American Studies: social scis, no.55, 99n398
South America, Central America, & the Caribbean 1997, 6th ed, 97n130
South America, Central America, & the Caribbean 1999, 7th ed, 99n138
South American cinema, 97n1124
Wars of the Americas, 99n629

SOUTH AMERICA—BUSINESS
Directory of consumer brands & their owners 1998: Latin America, 99n260
Latin America: a dir & sourcebk, 2d ed, 99n261
Latin America petroleum dir 1998, 17th ed, 99n196

SOUTH AMERICA—MOTION PICTURES
Guide to Latin American, Caribbean, & US Latino-made films & video, 99n1226

SOUTH ASIA
Atlas & survey of S Asian hist, 96n534
Bibliography of S Asia, 95n128
India & S Asia, 3d ed, 99n104
South Asian religions in the Americas, 96n1438

SOUTH ASIA—LANGUAGE
Atlas of the langs & ethnic communities of S Asia, 99n101

SOUTH CAROLINA
Freshwater fishes of the Carolinas, Va., Md., & Dela., 95n1588

SOUTH DAKOTA
South Dakota hist, 95n429

SOUTHEAST ASIA
Southeast Asian langs & lits, 98n986

SOUTHERN STATES
Building a new South, 96n98
Garden bulbs for the South, 96n1546
Handbook of mammals of the S-central states, 96n1630
Illustrated glossary of early S architecture & landscape, 95n1016
Orchids for the South, 96n1574
Peterson's gd to colleges in the South 1995, 10th ed, 96n344
Southeast gd to saltwater fishing & boating, 95n818
Southern gardener's bk of lists, 95n1527
Who's who in the South & Southwest 1995-96, 97n36

SOUTHERN STATES—LITERATURE
Contemporary poets, dramatists, essayists, & novelists of the South, 96n1199
Contemporary Southern men fiction writers, 99n1039
Contemporary Southern women fiction writers, 95n1181
Dictionary of literary biog documentary series, v.12, 96n1201
Encyclopedia of southern lit, 99n1047
Exploring the SE states through lit, 95n1126

SOUTHWESTERN STATES
Exploring the SW states through lit, 95n1124
Who's who in the South & Southwest 1995-96, 97n36

SOVIET UNION. *See also* **FORMER SOVIET REPUBLICS; RUSSIA**
ACCESS gd to ethnic conflicts in Europe & the former Soviet Union, 95n146
Atlas of Russian hist, 2d ed, 95n562
Bibliography of the Soviet Union, its predecessors & successors, 97n124
Cambridge ency of Russia & the former Soviet Union, 2d ed, 95n152
Collapse of communism in the Soviet Union, 99n693
Critical companion to the Russian revolution 1914-21, 98n481
Dictionary of Russian & Soviet artists 1420-1970, 95n1001
East Europe & the republics: a pol risk annual, June 1994, 95n153
Ethnohistorical dict of the Russian & Soviet empires, 95n400
Evangelical sectarianism in the Russian Empire & the USSR, 97n1173
Gorbachev bibliog, 1985-91, 98n482
Great dates in Russian & Soviet hist, 95n561
Guide to the republics of the former Soviet Union, 95n166
Newly independent states of Eurasia, 95n163

Russia & the former Soviet Union: a bibliographic gd to English lang pubs, 1986-91, 95n162
Russia/USSR, 2d ed, 95n161
Russian revolution, 1905-21, 96n548
Scholars' gd to humanities & social scis in the Soviet successor states, 95n165
Scholars' gd to Washington, DC, for Russian, Central Eurasian, & Baltic studies, 95n164
Soviet armed forces, 1918-92, 97n558
Stalin: an annot gd to bks in English, 95n565
Statistical hndbk of social & economic indicators for the former Soviet Union, 97n125
USSR population census, 1989 [CD-ROM], 98n130
Vascular plants of Russia & adjacent states (the former USSR), 96n1594
Warships of the USSR & Russia, 1945-95, 98n629
Women in Russia & the Soviet Union, 95n903

SPACE FLIGHT
Jane's space dir 1996-97, 12th ed, 97n1301
Spaceflight: a Smithsonian gd, 96n1647
Spaceflight & rocketry, 97n1300
USA in space, 97n1302

SPACE SCIENCES
Eyewitness ency of space & the universe [CD-ROM], 97n1395
Space scis dict 2, 96n1645
Space scis dict 3, 96n1646

SPACE & TIME
Time & space, 96n1820

SPAIN
Cultural atlas of Spain & Portugal, 96n539
Historical dict of Spain, 97n432
Maxwell Espinosa shareholder dir, 95n285
Pilgrimage to Santiago de Compostela, 96n1462
Regions of Spain, 97n451
Spain, 97n396
Spain, 2d ed, 96n149
Spanish civil war in lit, film, & art, 95n566

SPANISH AMERICAN LITERATURE
Best of the Latino heritage, 98n358
Guide to ref works for the study of the Spanish lang & lit & Spanish American lit, 98n1183
Spanish American lit, 99n1098

SPANISH AMERICANS
Contemporary Spanish-speaking writers & illustrators for children & YAs, 95n1151

SPANISH-AMERICAN WAR, 1898
War of 1898 & US interventions 1898-1934, 95n685

SPANISH DRAMA
Spanish dramatists of the golden age, 99n1026

SPANISH FICTION
Contemporary Spanish novel, 97n1014

SPANISH LANGUAGE
Dictionary of 1000 Spanish proverbs with English equivalents, 97n1089

SPANISH LANGUAGE—COGNATE WORDS—ENGLISH
NTC's dict of Spanish cognates thematically organized, 98n1048

SPANISH LANGUAGE—DICTIONARIES—ENGLISH
Collins Spanish-English, English-Spanish dict, unabridged 5th ed, 99n939
Dahl's law dict: an annot legal dict, Spanish-English/English-Spanish, 2d ed, 97n486
Delmar's English/Spanish pocket dict for health professionals, 98n1527
Dictionary of bus, English-Spanish, Spanish-English, [repr ed], 99n147
Dictionary of Chicano Spanish, 2d ed, 96n1136
Dictionary of contemporary Spain, 99n943
Economics, trade, & dvlpmt: English-Spanish general terminology, 97n272
Elsevier's dict of financial & economic terms, 97n153
English-Spanish, Spanish-English electrical & computer engineering dict, 97n1297
Larousse concise Spanish-English/English-Spanish dict, 95n1095
Larousse concise Spanish-English/English-Spanish dict, rev ed, 99n940
Larousse English-Spanish/Spanish-English dict, new, 97n873
Larousse mini Spanish-English/English-Spanish dict, new ed, 97n874
Larousse pocket Spanish-English/English-Spanish dict, 95n1096
Mastering Spanish vocabulary, 97n875
NTC's dict of common mistakes in Spanish, 96n1137
NTC's dict of Latin American Spanish, 98n1049
NTC's dict of Spanish false cognates, 95n1094
Oxford paperback Spanish dict & grammar, 98n1050
Oxford Spanish desk dict, 99n941
Oxford starter Spanish dict, 98n1051
Pockets: Spanish dict, 98n1052
Random House Latin-American Spanish dict, 99n942
Routledge Spanish dict of bus, commerce, & finance, 99n146
Routledge Spanish technical dict, 98n1408
Spanish verbs, 99n938
Spanish-English/English-Spanish concise dict (Latin America), 95n1098
Spanish-English/English-Spanish dict, unabridged ed, 95n1097
Spanish/English dict of human & physical geography, 95n493
Wiley dict of civil engineering & construction: English-Spanish, Spanish-English, 97n1304
Wiley's English-Spanish, Spanish-English dict of psychology & psychiatry, 96n782
Wiley's English-Spanish, Spanish-English bus dict, 98n157
Wiley's English-Spanish, Spanish-English dict, 99n1506
Wiley's English-Spanish, Spanish-English legal dict, 95n606
Wiley's English-Spanish, Spanish-English legal dict, 2d ed, 98n519

SPANISH LANGUAGE—PROVINCIALISM
NTC's dict of Mexican cultural code words, 97n134

SPANISH LITERATURE
Index to Spanish lang short stories in anthologies, 95n1241
Twentieth-Century poetry from Spanish America, 99n1111
Twentieth-Century Spanish poets: 2d series, 95n1244

SPANISH SUCCESSION, WAR OF
Treaties of the War of the Spanish Succession, 96n762
War of the Spanish Succession, 1702-13, 97n435

SPARKLING WINES
Millennium champagne & sparkling wine gd, 99n1342

SPARROWS
Sparrows & buntings, 97n1288

SPECIAL LIBRARIES
American Revolutionary War sites, memorials, museums, & lib collections, 99n472
Directory of special libs & info centers, v.1, 21st ed, 98n589
Directory of special libs & info centers, v.2, 21st ed, 98n590
Guide to the Sol Feinstone collection of the David Lib of the American Revolution, 96n654
University of London Lib catalogue of the Goldsmiths' Lib of Economic Lit, v.5, 96n662
World dir of bus info libs, 3d ed, 99n615

SPEECHES, ADDRESSES, ETC.
African American voices, 97n328
Representative American speeches, 1937-97, 99n975
Representative American speeches, 1995-96, 98n1131
Voices of multicultural America, 97n967

SPELLERS
Scholastic dict of spelling, 99n912

SPICES
Dictionary of herbs, spices, seasonings, & natural flavorings, 95n1518

SPICE TRADE
Spice trade, 96n308

SPIES
Spies, 98n701

SPIRITS
Encyclopedia of ghosts & spirits, 95n791
Spirits, fairies, gnomes, & goblins, 97n1090

SPIRITUALISM
Angels A to Z, 97n1176
Consulting spirits, 99n708
Encyclopedia of afterlife beliefs & phenomena, 96n1445

SPIRITUALS
Choral arrangements of the African-American spirituals, 99n1152

SPORTS
Athletes, 96n410
Biographical dict of American sports, 1992-95 suppl, 96n793
Book of rules, 99n713
Chase's sports calendar of events 1997, 97n639
Chronicle of the Olympics, 1896-1996, 97n660
Chronicle of the Olympics, 1896-2000, 99n738
Encyclopedia of sports sci, 98n720
Encyclopedia of women & sports, 97n644
Encyclopedia of world sport, 98n721
Lincoln lib of sports champions, 6th, 95n793
National sports policies, 98n725
Professional sports team hists, 95n800
Social issues in contemporary sport, 95n792
Sport lawyer's gd to legal pers, 95n599
Sport lawyer's gd to legal pers, 1995 suppl, 96n615
Sport on film & video, 95n798
Sport thesaurus, 1994 ed, 96n802
Sporting News pro football gd, 1996 ed, 97n655
Sporting News this day in sports, 95n802
Sports ethics, 96n801
Sports in N America, v.1, 99n711
Sports in N America, v.4, 96n798
Sports in N America, v.5, 97n642
Sports phone bk USA, 1998, 99n712
Sports stars, 95n794
Sports stars: series 2, 97n641
Sportspeak: an ency of sport, 97n643
Track & field record holders, 97n663
Ultimate bk of sports lists 1998, 98n727
Winning edge, 3d ed, 95n799

SPORTS CARDS
Standard catalog of football cards, 98n900

SPORTSCASTERS
Sports style gd & ref manual, 97n757

SPORTS JOURNALISM
Sports style gd & ref manual, 97n757

SPORTS MEDICINE
Dictionary of sports injuries & disorders, 97n1357
Sports medicine bible, 96n1729

SPORTS MUSEUMS
Hall of fame museums, 99n69

SPORTS—SCHOLARSHIPS, FELLOWSHIPS, ETC.
Athletic scholarships, 95n795
Peterson's sports scholarships & college athletic programs, 95n797

SPORTSWRITERS
Twentieth-Century American sportswriters, 98n883

SPY STORIES
Mystery & suspense writers, 99n1032

SQUARE DANCING
Square dance & contra dance hndbk, 97n1101

SRI LANKA
Ethnic conflict & human rights in Sri Lanka, v.2, 95n136
Historical dict of Sri Lanka, 99n484

STALIN, JOSEPH
Stalin: an annot gd to bks in English, 95n565

STANDARDIZATION
Index & dir of industry standards, 95n1504

STANDARDS, ENGINEERING
ASTM standards source [CD-ROM], 96n1663

STARS
Cambridge gd to stars & planets, 2d ed, 98n1605
Cambridge star atlas, 2d ed, 97n1393
Photographic atlas of the stars, 98n1604

STATE GOVERNMENTS
Almanac of state legislatures, 95n710
Carroll's state dir, 96n726
Facts about the states, 2d ed, 95n102
Government dir of addresses & telephone nos 1995, 3d ed, 96n732
How to find co intelligence in state docs, 15th ed, 96n202
NASIRE dir 1994, 95n728
Sourcebook of state public records, 95n730
State executive dir, 96n729
State legislative sourcebk 1996, 97n602
State legislative summary, 1994, 96n595
Teacher educ policy in the states, 95n375
Teacher educ policy in the states, 96n329
USA state factbk [CD-ROM], 95n107

STATESMEN. See also POLITICIANS
Anthony Eden, 1897-1977, 96n759
Heads of states & govts: a worldwide ency, 95n706
Political leaders of contemporary W Europe, 96n756
US govt leaders, 99n663
Who's who in democracy, 98n639
World leaders: people who shaped the world, 95n576

STATISTICS
Agriculture, mining, & construction USA, 99n187
America's top-rated smaller cities, 1994-95 ed, 96n926
Atlas of US economy, tech, & growth, 97n714
Baseball ratings, 2d ed, 96n804
Business stats of the US, 1995 ed, 97n176
City crime rankings, 3d ed, 98n552
Compendium of human settlements stats 1995, 5th ed, 97n715
Compendium of social stats & indicators, 4th issue, 99n787
CompuMath citation index 1993. 2d semiannual, 95n1739
Consumer China 1994, 95n268
County & city extra, 1995, 4th ed, 97n712
Datapedia of the US, 1790-2000, 95n896
Encyclopedia of statl scis: update v.1, 98n809
Energy stats yrbk, 1992, 95n1751
Florida statl abstract, 1994, 28th ed, 96n916
Gale bk of averages, 95n894
Gale country & world rankings reporter, 96n905
Geographic database for US economy, tech, & growth [CD-ROM], 98n818
Global data locator, 98n812
Handbook of US labor stats, 98n230
Historical stats 1960-94, 1996 ed, 97n225
Illustrated bk of world rankings, rev ed, 98n813
Instat: intl stats sources, 97n716
International histl stats: Africa, Asia, & Oceania, 1750-1988, 96n917
Key indicators of county growth 1970-2025, 1996 ed, 98n806
Matter of fact: statements containing stats on current social, economics, & pol issues, v.24, 98n814
Mexico data bank, 95n172
National accounts stats 1991, 95n254
OECD statl compendium 1996/1 [CD-ROM], 97n227
Official gd to the American marketplace, 2d ed, 96n911
Peoplepedia: the ultimate ref on the American people, 97n74
Projections of educ stats to 2008, 99n299
Services: stats on intl transactions 1970/92, 96n918
Social indicators of dvlpmt 1994, 95n870
Statistical abstract of the ESCWA region 1983-1992, 14th ed, 96n919
Statistical abstract of the US 1995, 115th ed, 96n920
Statistical abstract of the world, 96n921
Statistical hndbk of working America, 96n922
Statistical hndbk on adolescents in America, 97n718
Statistical hndbk on women in America, 2d ed, 97n740
Statistical indicators for Asia & the Pacific, v.23, 95n897
Statistical indicators for Asia & the Pacific, v.27, 99n788
Statistical record of native N Americans, 2d ed, 96n420
Statistical record of women worldwide, 96n953
Statistical yrbk, 1992, 95n898
Statistical yrbk, 1994, 98n816
Statistical yrbk for Asia & the Pacific 1996, 98n815
Statistically speaking: a dict of quotations, 98n82
Statistics on occupational wages & hours of work & on food prices 1997, 99n231
Statistics sources 1996, 19th ed, 96n923
Trends in Europe & N America 1995, 97n719
UNCTAD statl pocket bk, 96n925
Women & men in Europe & N America 1995, 97n720
Women in China, 99n808
World dir of non-official statl sources, 2d ed, 99n789
World population prospects, 99n790
World stats pocketbk, 97n721
World tables 1994, 95n257
World urbanization prospects, 99n794
World's women 1995, [2d ed], 96n954

STATLER BROTHERS—DISCOGRAPHY
Statler Brothers discography, 98n1232

STEELE, RICHARD, SIR
Joseph Addison & Richard Steele, 96n1237

STEEL INDUSTRY & TRADE
Annual bulletin of steel stats for Europe, v.21: 1991-94, 97n1307
Directory of the steel industry & the environment, 97n194

Encyclopedia of American bus hist & biog: iron & steel in the 20th century, 95n238
Steel market in 1995 & prospects for 1996, 97n198

STEEL, STAINLESS
ASM specialty hndbk: stainless steels, 96n1662

STEEL, STRUCTURAL
Structural steel designer's hndbk, 2d ed, 95n1603

STEINBECK, JOHN
John Steinbeck, 96n1216
John Steinbeck: an annot gd to biogl sources, 97n975

STERNE, LAWRENCE
Critical essays on Laurence Sterne, 99n1074

STEVENS, THADDEUS
Thaddeus Stevens papers, 95n746

STEVENS, WALLACE
Wallace Stevens: an annot secondary bibliog, 95n1195

STILL, WILLIAM GRANT
William Grant Still: a bio-bibliog, 97n1046

ST. KITTS-NEVIS
St. Kitts-Nevis, 96n172

ST. LUCIA
St. Lucia, 97n145

STOCK EXCHANGES
American Stock Exchange, 96n211
American Stock Exchange 1994 fact bk, 95n218
Dow Jones gd to the world stock market, 1995-96 ed, 96n212
Handbook of world stock indices, 99n221
New York Stock Exchange fact bk: 1993 data, 95n219
Ranking of world stock markets, 99n229
Standard & Poor's smallcap 600 gd, 1996 ed, 97n171
World stock exchange fact bk, 97n186

STOCKHOLM (SWEDEN)
Historical dict of Stockholm, 98n483

STOCKS. *See also* **INVESTMENTS**
Dow Jones averages, 1885-1995, 97n183
Handbook of N American stock exchanges, 99n168
100 best stocks to own in America, 3d ed, 95n223
100 best stocks to own in America, 99n166
Standard & Poor's stock & bond gd, 1998 ed, 99n174
Topline ency of histl charts, Mar 1997 ed, 98n176
Walker's manual of penny stocks, 99n167
Walker's manual of unlisted stocks, 98n172

STORES, RETAIL
Plunkett's retail industry almanac, 98n259

STORYTELLERS
Storytellers: a biogl dir of 120 English-speaking performers worldwide, 99n1182

STORYTELLING
Great new nonfiction reads, 96n1184
Latest & greatest read-alouds, 95n1137
National storytelling dir, 1996, 97n549
Storytelling ency, 98n1256

STRATEGY
Keyguide to info sources in strategic studies, 95n690

STREET ADDRESSES
National dir of addresses & telephone nos, 1995 ed, 96n56

STRESS—PHYSIOLOGICAL & PSYCHOLOGICAL
Stress A-Z, 99n705

STRUCTURAL ENGINEERING
Handbook of construction tolerances, 95n1602

STUDENT EXCHANGE PROGRAMS
Youth exchanges, 96n371

STUDENT MOVEMENTS
Encyclopedia of student & youth movements, 99n653

STYLE, LITERARY
Using picture storybks to teach literary devices. v.2, 96n1164

SUBCULTURE—UNITED STATES
ABC-CLIO companion to the 1960s counterculture in America, 98n437

SUBJECT HEADINGS
Art & architecture thesaurus, 2d ed, 95n650
BHA: bibliog of the hist of art: subject headings/English, 97n790
Classification plus [CD-ROM], 97n533
HIV/AIDS & HIV/AIDS-related terminology, 97n537
Libraries Unltd professional collection CD 1995 [CD-ROM], 97n523
Sears list of subject headings, 15th ed, 95n652
Sears list of subject headings, 16th ed, 98n580
Sport thesaurus, 1994 ed, 96n802
Subject headings for African American materials, 96n626
Subject headings for children 1994, 96n632

SUBJECT HEADINGS, LIBRARY OF CONGRESS
Free-floating subdivisions, 6th ed, 95n651
LC period subdivisions under names of places, 5th ed, 96n630
Library of Congress subject headings: principles & application, 3d ed, 96n627
Library of Congress subject headings, 19th ed, 97n534

SUBMARINES
Jane's fighting ships 1996-97, 99th ed, 97n573

SUBSIDIARY CORPORATIONS
America's corp families 1995, 97n158
How to find info about divisions, subsidiaries & products, 5th ed, 96n203

SUBSIDIES
European regional incentives, 1996-97, 97n243

SUBSTANCE ABUSE
Dictionary of street alcohol & drug terms, 4th ed, 95n881
Drug abuse in society, 95n882
Encyclopedia of drugs & alcohol, 97n707
Jewish alcoholism & drug addiction, 95n880
National gd to funding in substance abuse, 96n896

SUBURBS
Comparative gd to American suburbs, 98n824

SUBVERSIVE ACTIVITIES
Encyclopedia of the McCarthy era, 97n591

SUCCULENT PLANTS
Cacti & succulents, 95n1548
Complete bk of cacti & succulents, 95n1549
Gasterias of South Africa, 95n1550

SUICIDE
Encyclopedia of famous suicides, 98n768

SULLIVAN, ARTHUR, SIR
Sir Arthur Sullivan: a resource bk, 98n1212

SUMMER EMPLOYMENT
Overseas summer jobs 1995, 26th ed, 96n278
Peterson's summer opportunities for kids & teenagers 1996, 13th ed, 97n167
Summer jobs 1994, 43d ed, 95n306
Summer jobs Britain 1995, 26th ed, 96n279
Summer theatre dir 1996, 97n1153
Work your way around the world, 7th ed, 96n273

SUMMER SCHOOLS
Guide to summer camps & summer schools 1995/96, 27th ed, 96n326
Peterson's summer study abroad, 96n367

SUN DANCE—GREAT PLAINS
Native American sun dance religion & ceremony, 99n384

SUN RA (SONNY BLOUNT)
Earthly recordings of Sun Ra, 96n1322

SUPERNATURAL
Encyclopedia of claims, frauds, & hoaxes of the occult & supernatural, 97n637
Haunted places: the natl dir, rev ed, 97n635
Strange & unexplained happenings, 97n638
Supernatural index, 96n1194
World of ghosts & the supernatural, 96n784

SURGEONS
Canadian medical dir 1994, 95n1658

SURGERY
Surgeons' ref for minimally invasive surgery products, 96n1730

SURVEYORS
Dictionary of land surveyors & local map-makers of Great Britain & Ireland, 1530-1850, 98n394

SUSTAINABLE DEVELOPMENT
Dictionary of environment & sustainable dvlpmt, 98n1633
Gale environmental almanac, 95n1776
Human dvlpmt report 1994, 95n93
International hndbk of environmental sociology, 99n1564
Real Goods solar living sourcebk, 8th ed, 96n1847
What works, 95n276

SVOBODA
Select index to Svoboda, v.3, 95n956
Select index to Svoboda, v.4, 95n957

SWAZILAND
Swaziland, rev ed, 96n123

SWEDEN
Historical dict of Sweden, 96n150

SWEDISH LANGUAGE—DICTIONARIES—ENGLISH
NTC's compact Swedish & English dict, 98n1053
Prisma's abridged English-Swedish & Swedish-English dict, 96n1138

SWINDLERS & SWINDLING
Scams, shams, & flimflams, 95n1337

SWORDS
Encyclopedia of the sword, 96n816

SYDNEY
Sydney, 97n392

SYMBOLISM
Mammoth dict of symbols, English lang ed, 97n636

SYMBOLISM (ART MOVEMENT)
Four French symbolists, 97n806

SYMBOLISM IN ART
Dictionary of symbols in western art, 96n1030
Hopi pottery symbols, 96n1015
Illustrated dict of symbols in E & W art, 96n1031

SYMBOLISM OF NUMBERS
Key of it all, bk.1, 95n789
Key of it all, bk.2, 96n1121

SYMBOLISM (PSYCHOLOGY)
Encyclopedia of archetypal symbolism, v.1, 98n1351
Encyclopedia of archetypal symbolism, v.2: the body, 98n1352
Secret lang of dreams, 95n784
Secret lang of symbols, 95n785

SYMPHONIES
Gustav Mahler's symphonies, 98n1248

SYMPTOMATOLOGY
Columbia Univ Dept of Pediatrics children's medical gd, 98n1554

SYNAGOGUES
American synagogue, 97n1221
National dir of churches, synagogues, & other houses of worship, 95n1445

SYNTHETIC TRAINING DEVICES
Jane's simulation & training systems 1996-97, 9th ed, 98n1573

SYRIA
Bibliography of Syrian archaeological sites to 1980, 96n484
Historical dict of Syria, 97n141

SYSTEM FAILURE (ENGINEERING)
When tech fails, 95n1642

TABLOID NEWSPAPERS
Tabloid journalism, 97n747

TABOR—DICTIONARIES
Don't do it: a dict of the forbidden, 99n1193

TAILLEFERRE, GERMAINE
Germaine Tailleferre: a bio-bibliog, 95n1271

TAILORING
Cutting for all! the satorial arts, related crafts, & the commercial paper pattern, 98n934

TAIWAN
Historical dict of Taiwan, 95n137
Imports & exports of the Republic of China on Taiwan 1993, 95n271
Taiwan bus: the portable ency for doing bus with Taiwan, 95n266

TALKING BOOKS
Kliatt audiobk gd, 95n12

TALK SHOWS
Talk shows & hosts on radio, 3d ed, 96n975

TALLYRAND, CHARLES-MAURICE DE
Charles-Maurice de Talleyrand 1754-1838, 97n447

TALMUD
Dictionary of Judaism in the biblical period, 97n1223

TAMIL LITERATURE
Lexicon of Tamil lit, 96n1255

TAMING OF THE SHREW
Taming of the Shrew: an annot bibliog, 95n1219

TANKS (MILITARY)
Armored forces: hist & sourcebk, 96n702
Jane's tank & combat vehicle recognition gd, 97n576
Standard gd to US WW II tanks & artillery, 95n703
Tanks, 98n631

TANZANIA
Cultures of the World, 99n84
Historical dict of Tanzania, 2d ed, 98n457
Tanzania, rev ed, 97n102

TAOISM
Historical dict of Taoism, 99n1294
Shambhala dict of Taoism, 97n1226

TAP DANCING
Tap dance dict, 99n1203

TAPESTRY
French tapestries & textiles in the J. Paul Getty Museum, 98n946

TARIFF
NAFTA bibliog, 98n255

TARZAN FILMS
Kings of the jungle, 95n1381

TASMANIA
Tasmania, 98n118

TATAR LANGUAGE—DICTIONARIES—ENGLISH
Tatar-English/English-Tatar dict, 96n1139

TAXATION
Desk ref on the fed budget, 99n687
Dictionary of tax terms, 95n330
International tax summaries, 1998, 99n226
State & local taxation answer bk, 98n264
State tax actions 1997, 99n284
US master tax gd, 1994, 95n332

TEACHER EDUCATORS
AACTE dir of members, 1994, 95n338

TEACHERS
Alternative paths to teaching, 95n360
American Assn of Colleges for Teacher Educ dir of members 1995, 96n316
International ency of teaching & teacher educ, 2d ed, 97n298
Teacher educ policy in the states, 95n375
Teacher educ policy in the states, 96n329

TEACHING—AIDS & DEVICES
Educators gd to free films, filmstrips, & slides 1995, 55th ed, 96n375
Educators gd to free videotapes 1995, 42d ed, 96n376
Educators grade gd to free teaching aids 1995, 41st ed, 96n322
Elementary teachers gd to free curriculum materials 1995, 52d ed, 96n323
Encyclopedia of educ info, 1994/95, 96n324
Film & video finder, 5th ed, 98n310

Media review digest, v. 26, 1996, 97n9
Teaching children's lit, 96n379

TECHNICAL EDUCATION
Career connection for tech educ, 2d ed, 95n319

TECHNICAL INSTITUTES
Peterson's vocational & technical schools, 95n389
Peterson's vocational & technical schools & programs, 99n360

TECHNICAL LITERATURE
Information sources in grey lit, 3d ed, 95n10

TECHNICAL WRITING
How to write & publish a scientific paper, 4th ed, 95n941
Scientific style & format, 6th ed, 95n947

TECHNOLOGY
Annual review of info sci & tech, v.29, 1994, 96n622
Applied sci & tech index 1996, 98n1418
ASTM dir of scientific & technical consultants & expert witnesses, 1994 ed, 95n1498
Atlas of US economy, tech, & growth, 97n714
Bibliographic gd to tech 1996, 98n1398
Biographical dict of the hist of tech, 97n1236
Callaham's Russian-English dict of sci & tech, 4th ed, 97n1237
Career connection for tech educ, 2d ed, 95n319
Concise engineering & tech index 1987-May 1994 [CD-ROM], 95n1479
CorpTech dir of tech cos 1996, 10th US ed, 96n1749
Dictionary of communications tech, 3d ed, 99n1492
Dictionary of multimedia terms & acronyms, 98n1572
Dictionary of sci, 96n1493
Directory of bus per special issues, 96n209
Elsevier's dict of industrial tech, 96n1494
Encyclopedia of computer sci & tech, v.34, suppl 19, 97n1367
Encyclopedia of sci, 95n1487
Failed tech, 96n1511
Gale 5 lang tech dict, 95n1488
Great scientific achievements: the 20th century, 95n1489
Grolier student ency of sci, tech, & the environment, 97n1239
Guide to American scientific & technical dirs, 3d ed, 95n1499
Handbook of current sci & tech, [2d ed], 97n1242
Handbooks & tables in sci & tech, 3d ed, 95n1483
Handy sci answer bk, 2d ed, 98n1414
Illustrated almanac of sci, tech, & inventions, 99n1306
Illustrated bk of questions & answers, 97n56
Information sources in sci & tech, 2d ed, 95n1481
Larousse dict of sci & tech, 97n1240
Macmillan ency of sci, rev ed, 98n1406
Magill's survey of sci [CD-ROM], 95n1502
McGraw-Hill concise ency of sci & tech, 3d ed, 95n1492
McGraw-Hill dict of scientific & technical terms, 5th ed, 95n1493
McGraw-Hill ency of sci & tech, 8th ed, 98n1407
McGraw-Hill multimedia ency of sci & tech [CD-ROM], 95n1494
McGraw-Hill multimedia ency of sci & tech [CD-ROM], 99n1316
McGraw-Hill yrbk of sci & tech 1999, 99n1325
McGraw-Hill yrbk of sci & tech 1996, 97n1243
Milestones in sci & tech, 2d ed, 95n1503
Peterson's job opportunities in engineering & tech 1995, 96n1513
Questions & answers bk of sci facts, 98n1404
Routledge French technical dict, 96n1499
Routledge German technical dict, 97n851
Routledge Spanish technical dict, 98n1408
Science & tech: a purchase gd for libs 1995, 97n1234
Science & tech breakthroughs, 99n1308
Science & tech firsts, 98n1402
Science navigator [CD-ROM], 96n1500
Science yr 1997, 98n1416
Science yr 1998, 98n1417
Science, tech, & society in the 3d World, 96n138
Scientific & technical bks & serials in print 1995, 22d ed, 96n1484
Scientific revolution, 97n1227
SciTech ref plus 1995-96 [CD-ROM], 97n1228
Technological capacity-bldg & tech partnership, 96n1515
Technology, 96n1508
Technology opportunities, 2d ed, 96n1507
Walford's gd to ref material, v.1: sci & tech, 7th ed, 97n1229
Who's who in sci in Europe, 9th ed, 97n1233
Who's who in tech, 7th ed, 96n1492
Wilson chronology of sci & tech, 99n1307
World Book's young scientist, 98n1410

TEDDY BEARS
Teddy bear ency, 95n974

TEENAGERS
Adolescence: the survival gd for parents & teenagers, 98n802
Adolescents at risk, 95n1134
Best bks for YAs, 95n1127
Statistical hndbk on adolescents in America, 97n718
Young adult lit & nonprint materials, 95n654

TELECOMMUNICATIONS
Comprehensive networking glossary & acronym gd, 96n1759
Desktop ency of telecommunications, 99n1493
Dictionary of communications tech, 3d ed, 99n1492
Electronics & telecommunications vocabulary, 95n1611
Informatics hndbk, 98n1593
International satellite dir, 1995, 10th ed, 96n1780
International satellite dir 1998, 99n1497
McGraw-Hill illus telecom dict, 99n1491
Net gd, 96n1781
Plunkett's entertainment & media industry almanac, 99n827
Reference manual for telecommunications engineering, 2d ed, 95n1612
Routledge French dict of telecommunications, 99n1494
Telecommunications dir 1995-96, 7th ed, 96n1782
Telecommunications: key contacts & info sources, 99n1500
Telecommunications research resources, 96n1778
Telecommunications, networking & Internet glossary, 95n1704

TELECOMMUNICATIONS IN EDUCATION
College degrees by mail & modem 1998, 99n302

TELECOMMUTING
Telecommuters, the workforce of the 21st century, 98n212

TELEPHONE DIRECTORIES
Business: name & bus type index [CD-ROM], 98n158
Business sales leads, 1997 ed [CD-ROM], 98n248
Consumer sales leads, 1997 ed [CD-ROM], 98n249
FaxUSA, 1998, 99n151
Government phone bk USA 1997, 5th ed, 98n52
Instant natl locator gd, 3d ed, 98n53
Krupin's toll-free environmental dir, 96n1867
National consumer phone bk USA 1998, 99n153
PhoneDisc powerfinder [CD-ROM], 98n54
Toll-Free phone bk USA 1997, 98n55
US homes [CD-ROM], 98n56
US homes & bus [CD-ROM], 98n57

TELEVISION
Bacon's TV/cable dir 1994, 95n962
BFI film & TV hndbk 1995, 96n1401
Broadcast news [CD-ROM], 96n991
Burrelle's media dir, June 1994 [CD-ROM], 95n934
Collector's gd to TV memorabilia, 1960s & 1970s, 98n922
Contemporary theatre, film, & TV, v.13, 96n1362
Contemporary theatre, film, & TV, v.17, 99n1195
Dictionary of 20th century culture: American culture after WW II, 95n927
Dictionary of TV & AV terminology, 99n838
Early TV, 98n889
Encyclopedia of TV, 98n888
Facts on File dict of TV, cable, & video, 95n959
Film & TV in-jokes, 99n1239
Latin American advertising, mktg, & media sourcebk, 96n301
Leo Burnett worldwide advertising & media fact bk, 96n302
National Hispanic media dir, 1997, 98n861
News media yellow bk, 96n963
Power media selects, 9th ed, 96n988
Tabloid journalism, 97n747
Television & cable factbk, 1994 ed, 95n964
Television research, 96n987
Television writers gd, 4th ed, 97n769
World radio TV hndbk, 1996 ed, 97n773

TELEVISION ACTORS & ACTRESSES. See also ACTORS & ACTRESSES
Quinlan's illus dir of film character actors, new ed, 97n1106
Some Joe you don't know: an American biogl gd to 100 British TV personalities, 97n1107
Star gd, 1997-98, 98n1266
Television guest stars, 95n1366
Television program master index, 97n1144
Television western players of the 50s, 98n1276
Western & frontier film & TV credits 1903-95, 97n1130
Written out of TV, 97n1129

TELEVISION BROADCASTING
Bacon's bus media dir 1998, 99n821
Bacon's TV/cable dir 1998, 12th ed, 98n886
Facts on File dict of TV, cable, & video, 95n959
Film, TV, video in Russia '94, 95n1378
Gale dir of pubns & broadcast media, 131st ed, 99n822
International film, TV & video acronyms, 95n1359
International TV & video almanac, 1996, 41st ed, 97n771

TELEVISION EQUIPMENT
Orion blue bk: video & TV, 1998 ed, 99n181

TELEVISION MUSICALS
Broadway, movie, TV, & studio cast musicals on record, 97n1030
Television musicals, 98n1301

TELEVISION—PRODUCTION & DIRECTION
Hollywood blu-bk dir 1997, 99n1221
Western & frontier film & TV credits 1903-95, 97n1130

TELEVISION PROGRAMS
American sci fiction TV series of the 1950s, 99n1213
Big bk of show bus awards, 99n1198
Booking Hawaii Five-O: an episode gd & critical hist of the 1968-80 TV detective show, 98n1313
Charles Dickens on the screen, 97n1121
Children's TV, 1947-90, 96n1404
Complete dir to sci fiction, fantasy, & horror TV series, 99n1224
Critical hist of TVs The Twilight Zone, 1959-64, 99n1232
Definitive Andy Griffith show ref, 97n1134
Dictionary of teleliteracy, 97n1110
Encyclopedia of daytime TV, 99n1212
Encyclopedia of TV game shows, 2d ed, 97n1113
Encyclopedia of TV sci fiction, 98n1283
Experimental TV, test films, pilots, & trial series, 1925-95, 98n1314
Following The Fugitive: an episode gd & hndbk to the 1960s TV series, 97n1127
Fugitive: a complete episode gd, 1963-67, 96n1403
Prime time network serials, 98n1310
Science fiction TV series, 98n1286
Serials on British TV 1950-94, 97n1104
Shot on this site, 96n472
Talk show selects, 1995 ed, 96n989
Television program master index, 97n1144
Television westerns episode gd, 98n1308
This is a Thriller: an episode gd, hist, & analysis of the classic 1960s TV series, 97n1138
Toasting Cheers: an episode gd to the 1982-93 comedy series...., 98n1302
Total TV, 4th ed, 97n1132
Variety & Daily Variety TV reviews, v.18: 1993-94, 98n1315
VideoHound multimedia [CD-ROM], 96n1389
Walking shadows, 96n1399
Written out of TV, 97n1129

TELEVISION PROGRAMS—JAPAN
Complete anime gd, 98n1307

TELEVISION SPECIALS
Special ed: a gd to network TV documentary series & special news reports, 1980-89, 98n1304
Television specials, 96n1412

TENNESSEE
Fishes of Tenn., 95n1584

TENNIS
Bud Collins' modern ency of tennis, 95n825
Bud Collins' tennis ency, [3d ed], 98n750
WTA Tour, 96n832

TERATOGENIC AGENTS
Reproductive effects of chemical, physical, & biological agents REPROTOX, 96n1712
Teratogenic effects of drugs, 95n1682

TERMS & PHRASES
CPT '97: physicians' current procedural terminology, 98n1525

TERRORISM
Encyclopedia of world terrorism, 98n551
Historical dict of terrorism, 96n597
Shadow of death: an analytic bibliog on pol violence, terrorism, & low-intensity conflict, 97n501
Terrorism, 1992-95, 98n556
Terrorism in the US, 98n557
Terrorist group profiles [CD-ROM], 96n601

TERRORISM IN MASS MEDIA
Terrorism & the news media, 95n616

TEXAS
Art for hist's sake, 95n1008
Awesome almanac—Tex., 97n89
Chief executives of Tex., 96n718
Texas ref sources, 4th ed, 95n101

TEXTBOOKS
El-Hi textbks & serials in print 1994, 95n350
El-Hi textbks & serials in print 1997, 98n283

TEXTILE INDUSTRY
Garment & textile dict, 98n933
Historical dir of trade unions, v.4, 96n264

TEXTILES
French tapestries & textiles in the J. Paul Getty Museum, 98n946

THAILAND
MFC investment hndbk 1994, 95n272
Thailand, 99n435

THAI LANGUAGE—DICTIONARIES—ENGLISH
Oxford-Duden pictorial Thai & English dict, 96n1140

THEATER. See also DRAMA
American drama criticism: suppl 4 to the 2d ed, 97n1146
American playwrights, 1880-1945, 96n1202
American theatre, 97n1150
American theatre: a chronicle of comedy & drama, 1869-1914, 95n1418
Annotated dict of technical, histl, & stylistic terms relating to Theatre & Drama, 96n1417
Best plays of 1996-97, 99n1246
Bibliographic gd to theatre arts 1996, 98n1322
Bibliography of theatre hist in Canada, 95n1404
Big bk of show bus awards, 99n1198
Brewer's theater, 96n1414
British playwrights, 1880-1956, 97n985
British playwrights, 1956-95, 97n986
Cambridge companion to medieval English theatre, 95n1419
Cambridge gd to African & Caribbean theatre, 95n1420
Cambridge gd to American theatre, updated ed, 97n1151
Cambridge gd to Asian theatre, 95n1414
Cambridge gd to theatre, new ed, 96n1415
Cambridge hist of American theatre, v.1, 99n1247
Cambridge illus hist of British theatre, 96n1422
Contemporary theatre, film, & TV, v.13, 96n1362
Contemporary theatre, film, & TV, v.17, 99n1195
Dictionary of traditional S-E Asian theatre, 96n1418
Directory of theatre training programs 1997-99, 6th ed, 98n1325
Directory of theatre training programs, 5th ed, 96n1419
German theatre, 98n1323
International biblog of theatre, 97n1148
International dict of theatre-3: actors, directors, & designers, 97n1149
Lillian Hellman: a research & production sourcebk, 99n1248
Maxwell Anderson on the European stage 1929-92, 97n1147
More opening nights on Broadway: a critical quotebk of the musical theatre 1965-81, 98n1329
Music, dance & theater scholarships, 96n1365
Musical theater synopses, 99n1244
New Kabuki ency, 98n1324
New York Times theater reviews, v.28: 1993-94, 97n1154
Regional theatre dir 1996-97, 97n1152
Students' gd to playwriting opportunities, 96n1421
Summer theatre dir 1996, 97n1153
Theatregoer's almanac, 98n1327
Theatrical design in the 20th century, 97n1155

THEATERS
Opera cos & houses of the US, 96n1302

THEATRICAL PRODUCERS & DIRECTORS
Biographical dict of actors, actresses, musicians, dancers, managers...v.15, 95n1411
Biographical dict of actors, actresses, musicians, dancers, managers...v.16, 95n1412
Great stage directors, 95n1413
International dict of theatre-3: actors, directors, & designers, 97n1149
Margaret Webster: a bio-bibliog, 95n1340
Theatrical directors, 95n1410
Tony Richardson: a bio-bibliog, 97n1096

THEOLOGIANS
Jonathan Edwards, 96n1440
Who's who in theology & sci, 1996 ed, 97n1175

THEOLOGY
Blackwell ency of modern Christian thought, 95n1465
Collegeville pastoral dict of biblical theology, 97n1196
Confessions of Saint Augustine, 97n1207

Dictionary of ethics, theology, & society, 97n73
Dictionary of feminist theologies, 97n1177
Dictionary of fundamental theology, 95n1470
Dictionary of mission, 98n1350
Dictionary of Scottish church hist & theology, 95n1466
Emil Brunner: a bibliog, 97n1172
Evangelical dict of biblical theology, 97n1197
Handbook of Catholic theology [rev ed], 96n1475
Handbook of evangelical theologians, 95n1461
Hermann Sasse: a bibliog, 97n1168
New intl dict of O.T. theology & exegesis, 98n1374
Oxford dict of world religions, 98n1357
Westminster dict of theological terms, 98n1358

THEOSOPHY
Theosophy in the 19th century, 95n1436

THERAPEUTICS
Complete bk of natural & medicinal cures, 95n1670
Handbook of therapeutic interventions, 96n1735

THERMODYNAMICS
Handbook of thermal conductivity, v.1, 96n1821
Handbook of thermal conductivity, v.2, 96n1822
Handbook of thermal conductivity, v.3, 96n1823
Handbook of transport property data, 96n1824

THIN SECTIONS (GEOLOGY)
Color atlas of rocks & minerals in thin section, 95n1724

THOREAU, HENRY DAVID
New England transcendentalists [CD-ROM], 99n1046

THOUGHT & THINKING—HISTORY
Wilson chronology of ideas, 99n525

THRILLER (TELEVISION PROGRAM)
This is a Thriller: an episode gd, hist, & analysis of the classic 1960s TV series, 97n1138

TIME
Encyclopedia of time, 95n58

TITANIUM ALLOYS
Materials properties hndbk: titanium alloys, 96n1669

TITLES OF BOOKS
Literally entitled, 97n891

TOADS
Handbook of frogs & toads of the US & Canada, 3d ed, 96n1640

TOBACCO
Smoking: the health consequences of tobacco use, 96n1721
Tobacco & health network dir 1996, 4th ed, 97n1325

TOGO
Historical dict of Togo, 3d ed, 97n103
Togo, 96n124

TOILETS
Handbook of cosmetic & personal care additives, 95n1712
Thunder, flush, & Thomas Cooper, 99n1188

TOKENS
Standard catalog of US tokens 1700-1900, 98n914

TOKYO (JAPAN)
Historical dict of Tokyo, 98n461

TOLERANCE (ENGINEERING)
Handbook of construction tolerances, 95n1602

TOMBS
Vestiges of mortality & remembrance, 95n519

TOTALITARIANISM
Dictators & tyrants, 96n705

TOTAL QUALITY MANAGEMENT
Bibliography of bus/competitive intelligence & benchmarking lit, 96n175
McGraw-Hill ency of quality terms & concepts, 96n284
Quality mgmt sourcebk, 98n241
Quality, TQC, TQM: a meta lit study, 98n243

TOURIST TRADE
Career opportunities in travel & tourism, 96n461
Guide to college programs in hospitality & tourism, 5th ed, 98n314
Yearbook of tourism stats, 46th ed, 96n463

TOXICOLOGY
Effects of neurologic & psychiatric drugs on the fetus & nursing infant, 99n1480
Encyclopedia of environmental control tech, v.7, 96n1857
Encyclopedia of toxicology, 99n1504
Poison! how to handle the hazardous substances in your home, 98n1563
Poisons & antidotes, 95n1686

TOXIC TORTS
TSCA hndbk, 3d ed, 98n561

TOYS
America's Standard Gauge electric trains, 99n852
Beanie family album & collectors gd, 99n853
Best toys, bks & videos for kids, 96n1010
Matchbox toys 1947-96, 2d ed, 98n929

TRACK & FIELD ATHLETICS
American women's track & field, 97n664
Track & field record holders, 97n663

TRADEMARKS
McCarthy's desk ency of intellectual property, 2d ed, 97n519
Patent, copyright, & trademark, 97n520

TRADE & PROFESSIONAL ASSOCIATIONS
Business orgs, agencies, & pubns dir, 8th ed, 97n160
Directory of designated members, 1996, 97n282

Directory of trade & investment related orgs of developing countries & areas in Asia & the Pacific, 7th ed, 97n235
Gale ency of bus & professional assns, 96n185
Gale's ready ref shelf [CD-ROM], 97n50
Historical dir of trade unions, v.4, 96n264
Japan dir of professional assns, 3d ed, 96n244
Professional codes of conduct in the UK, 2d ed, 98n1341
Trade shows worldwide 1998, 12th ed, 99n210
World dir of trade & bus assns, 97n173
World gd to trade assns, 4th ed, 97n175

TRADE REGULATION
National dir of state bus licensing & regulation, 96n194

TRADE SECRETS
Employee duty of loyalty, 97n495
Employee duty of loyalty, 1996 suppl covering 1994, 97n496
Trade secrets: a state-by-state survey, 99n589

TRADE. *See also* **COMMERCE; INTERNATIONAL TRADE**
Economic survey of Latin America & the Caribbean 1995-96, 98n210
International bus & trade dir, 2d ed, 99n141
Japan trade dir 1997-98, 99n244
US industry & trade outlook '98, 99n191
World dir of trade & bus jls, 97n174

TRAFFIC ACCIDENTS
Statistics of road traffic accidents in Europe & N America 1995, 96n1890

TRAILS
Hiking trails, E US, 96n825

TRAINS, ELECTRIC
America's Standard Gauge electric trains, 99n852

TRANSCENDENTALISM
Biographical dict of transcendentalism, 97n962
Encyclopedia of transcendentalism, 97n964

TRANSLATING & INTERPRETING
Routledge ency of translation studies, 99n896
Translation & interpreting schools, 99n897
Translator's hndbk 1997, 98n991

TRANSPORTATION
ABC-CLIO companion to transportation in America, 97n1437
Annual bulletin for transport stats for Europe, 1995, v.45, 96n1877
Annual bulletin of transport stats for Europe & N America 1996, v.46, 98n1644
Dorling Kindersley visual timeline of transportation, 96n1878
Handbook of transport property data, 96n1824
Jane's merchant ships 1998-99, 3d ed, 99n1578
On the move, 95n1786
Transportation & public utilities USA, 99n1572
Travel dict, new ed, 99n425
Trilingual vocabulary of road transport vehicles, 97n229
200 best aviation Web sites, 99n1576

TRAVEL. *See also* **FAMILY RECREATION**
ACCESS travel USA: a dir for people with disabilities, 96n856
Alternative travel dir 1998, 4th ed, 99n439
Altitude-rated places, v.1, 2d ed, 95n1664
American at play, 98n726
Americans traveling abroad, 95n515
America's best bed & breakfasts, 2d ed, 98n408
Anderson's travel companion: a gd to the best non-fiction & fiction for travelling, 97n383
Australia, 99n436
Best places to go, 95n505
Business traveler's world gd, 99n441
California, 98n413
City profiles USA 1996, 97n388
Coasting: an expanded gd to the N gulf coast, 3d ed, 99n427
Complete gd to American bed & breakfast, 4th ed, 97n385
Complete gd to America's natl parks, 10th ed, 99n429
Cruising gd to NY waterways & Lake Champlain, 99n430
Eurail gd to world train travel, 1996, 26th ed, 97n1444
Everything Civil War, 98n447
Ferrari's places for men, Apr 94-Apr 95, 95n854
Ferrari's places for women, Apr 94-Apr 95, 95n855
Ferrari's places of interest, Apr 94-Apr 95, 95n856
Field gd to America's historic neighborhoods & museum houses, 99n433
Fodor's ballpark vacations, 98n731
Fodor's exploring Canada, 98n421
Fodor's exploring the Greek Islands, 98n424
Fodor's great American vacations for travelers with disabilities, 96n471
Fodor's healthy escapes, 5th ed, 98n405
Fodor's upclose Europe, 99n437
Frommer's comprehensive travel gd: Caribbean '95, 96n483
Great escapes: the spring breaker's gd to beaches & beyond, 98n417
Greece: Athens & the mainland, 98n425
Greek Islands, 98n426
Haunted places: the natl dir, rev ed, 97n635
Historic festivals, 97n386
Hostels USA, 99n431
Inn places 1994, 95n857
Interstate exit authority, 99n432
Italy, 97n395
Jazz & blues lover's gd to the US, updated ed, 96n1321
Landmarks of American presidents, 97n391
Milepost: trip planner for Ala. & Western Canada, 49th ed, 98n406
Official baseball atlas, 1994 ed, 95n807
On the road with your pet, 99n424
Pop culture landmarks, 97n387
Presidential sites, 99n428
Travel & vacation phone bk USA, 98n404
Travel dict, 95n504
Travel dict, new ed, 97n384
Travel dict, new ed, 99n425
Travel gd to Jewish Europe, 2d ed, 97n436
Traveler's atlas, 99n440
Traveler's hndbk, 7th ed, 99n426
Traveler's sourcebk 1997, 98n418

Vacationing with your pet, 98n402
Weissmann travel planner for W & E Europe 1994-95, 95n518
Wild planet!, 96n1352
World mountaineering, 99n442
World tourism dir '95/96, pt.1, 3d ed, 96n464
World tourism dir '95/96, pt.2, 3d ed, 96n465
World tourism dir '95/96, pt.3, 3d ed, 96n466

TRAVELERS
Dictionary of British & Irish travellers in Italy, 1701-1800, 98n476

TRAVELERS' WRITINGS
American travel writers, 1776-1864, 99n1044
British travel writers, 1837-75, 97n981

TREADWELL, SOPHIE
Sophie Treadwell: a research & production sourcebk, 98n1132

TREASURE-TROVE
Atlas of shipwrecks & treasure, 96n1896

TREATIES
Copyright laws & treaties of the world 1991-95 suppl, 98n566
International treaties on intellectual property, 2d ed, 98n567
Multilateral treaties deposited with the secretary-general, 96n612
Treaties of the War of the Spanish Succession, 96n762

TREES. *See also* **FLOWERING TREES; SHRUBS**
Field gd to the palms of the Americas, 96n1589
Field gd to the trees & shrubs of the S Appalachians, 95n1553
Garden trees, 97n1282
Maples of the world, 95n1554
Palms throughout the world, 97n1284
Pockets: trees, 96n75
Pruning of trees, shrubs, & conifers, [rev ed], 96n1588
Trees of the central hardwood forests of N America, 99n1367
Virus diseases of trees & shrubs, 2d ed, 95n1552
Year in trees, 96n1592

TRIALS
Civil trial practice deskbk, 98n528
Courtroom drama: 120 of the world's most notable trials, 99n556
Great American trials, 95n613
Great world trials, 98n532
Political prisoners & trials, 96n605
Women's rights on trial, 98n563

TRILLIUMS
Trilliums, 98n1448

TRINIDAD & TOBAGO
Historical dict of Trinidad & Tobago, 98n484

TRISTAN DA CUNHA ISLANDS
St. Helena, Ascension, & Tristan da Cunha, 98n146

TROPICAL PLANTS
Tropical look: an ency of dramatic landscape plants, 99n1344

TROUVERES
Lyrics of the Trouveres, 96n1251

TRUCKING
Trilingual vocabulary of road transport vehicles, 97n229

TRUMBAUER, FRANK
Tram: the Frank Trumbauer story, 96n1323

TUNISIA
Historical dict of Tunisia, 2d ed, 98n459

TURKISH LANGUAGE—DICTIONARIES—ENGLISH
Dictionary of the Turkic langs, 97n876

TURTLES
Turtles of the US & Canada, 96n1636

TUSCARORA INDIANS
Seneca & Tuscarora Indians: an annot bibliog, 95n427

TUTORS
Writing centers, 97n284

TWAIN, MARK
Huckleberry Finn on film, 95n1393
Mark Twain A to Z, 96n1217

TWENTIETH CENTURY
American decades 1980-89, 97n425
Chronicle of the 20th century, 96n558
Encyclopedia of the US in the 20th century, 97n416
Larousse dict of 20th century hist, 96n566

TWILIGHT ZONE (TELEVISION PROGRAM)
Critical hist of TVs The Twilight Zone, 1959-64, 99n1232

TYLER, ANNE
Anne Tyler: a critical companion, 99n1051

TYPE-SETTING
Glossary of typesetting terms, 96n667

TYPE & TYPE-FOUNDING
Type foundries of America & their catalogs, rev ed, 96n666

TYPHOONS
Encyclopedia of hurricanes, typhoons, & cyclones, 99n1532

TYPOGRAPHY
Typography, 99n885

UGANDA
Historical dict of Uganda, 96n125
Uganda, rev ed, 97n104

UKRAINIAN LANGUAGE—DICTIONARIES—ENGLISH
Ukrainian-English, English-Ukrainian practical dict, 95n1099

UKRAINIAN NEWSPAPERS
Select index to Svoboda, v.3, 95n956
Select index to Svoboda, v.4, 95n957

UNDERGROUND PRESS
APT for libs 1995: alternative pr titles for the general reader, 96n79

UNDERTAKERS & UNDERTAKING
Mortuary sci, 95n845

UNDERWATER ARCHAEOLOGY
Encyclopedia of underwater & maritime archaeology, 99n446

UNEMPLOYMENT
Employment/Unemployment & earnings stats, 97n249

UNESCO
Historical dict of the UNESCO, 98n694

UNIDENTIFIED FLYING OBJECTS
Haunted places: the natl dir, rev ed, 97n635
High strangeness: UFOs from 1960 through 1979, 97n632
Strange & unexplained happenings, 97n638
UFO: the definitive gd to unidentified flying objects & related phenomena, 96n789
UFOs & ufology, 99n709

UNITED NATIONS
Directory of UN info sources, 5th ed, 96n769
Guide to info at the UN, 96n770
Historical dict of multinatl peacekeeping, 97n616
Historical dict of the UNESCO, 98n694
Human rights bibliog, 95n630
Index to proceedings of the economic & social council, 96n771
Index to proceedings of the General Assembly: 47th session, 95n756
Index to proceedings of the Security Council, 48th yr, 95n757
Index to resolutions of the security council, 1946-91, 95n758
International instruments of the UN, 99n696
Multilateral treaties deposited with the secretary-general, 96n612
United Nations Commission on Intl Trade Law yrbk, v.24, 1993, 96n307
United Nations disarmament yrbk, v.18: 1993, 95n767
United Nations ref gd in the field of human rights, 95n631
Worldmark ency of the nations, 8th ed, 96n105
Yearbook of the Intl Law Commission 1992, 96n614

UNITED STATES
Peoplepedia: the ultimate ref on the American people, 97n74
Puerto Rico past & present, 99n93
USA & Canada 1994, 95n106
USA & Canada 1998, 99n88
Worldmark ency of the states, 96n106

UNITED STATES—ARMED FORCES
Biographical dict of WWII generals & flag officers: the US armed forces, 97n409
Dictionary of the modern US military, 97n566
Directory of US military bases worldwide, 96n687
Guide to the evaluation of educl experiences in the armed servs, 1996, v.1: Army, 98n275
Guide to the evaluation of educl experiences in the armed servs, 1996, v.2: Navy, 98n276
Guide to the evaluation of educl experiences in the armed servs, 1996, v.3: Air Force, Coast Guard, Dept of Defense, Marine Corps, 98n277
How to locate anyone who is or has been in the military, rev ed, 96n688
Medal of honor recipients 1863-1994, 96n689
Women in the US military, 1901-95, 97n559

UNITED STATES—ARMED FORCES RADIO SERVICE
Command performance, USA! a discography, 97n772

UNITED STATES—ARMY
Historical register & dict of the US army, 95n693
On the trail of the buffalo soldier, 96n699
Roster of Union soldiers 1861-65: US colored troops, 98n452
US Army patches, 98n625

UNITED STATES—BIOGRAPHY
Cambridge dict of American biog, 96n35
Dictionary of American biog, comprehensive index, 97n32
Encyclopedia of American biog, 2d ed, 97n33
Presidential Medal of Freedom, 98n30
Who's who in Polish America, 1996-1997 ed, 97n35

UNITED STATES—CENSUS
Dubester's US census bibliog with SuDocs class nos & indexes, 97n711
Historical stats of the US, bicentennial ed [CD-ROM], 98n819
State atlas of pol & cultural diversity, 98n329
Understanding the census, lib ed, 97n713

UNITED STATES—CIVILIZATION
America: hist & life on disc [CD-ROM], 96n512
American eras: civil war & reconstruction, 1850-77, 98n444
American eras: dvlpmt of the industrial US, 1878-99, 98n445
American eras: the reform era & E US dvlpmt, 99n468
Cold war culture media & the arts 1945-90, 99n1191
Columbia chronicles of American life, 1910-92, 96n501
Encyclopedia USA, v.22, 97n417
Guide to American studies resources, 1994, 96n338
Hispanic 100, 96n408
Revolutionary America 1763-1800, 97n399

UNITED STATES—CLIMATE
Weather of US cities, 5th ed, 97n1398

UNITED STATES—COMMERCE
United States-European Community trade resources, 95n323

UNITED STATES—CONGRESS
Accessing US govt info, rev ed, 97n54
Almanac of the unelected, 98n649
Almanac of the unelected 1994, 95n713

Beyond the hill, 97n598
Biographical dir of the American Congress, 1774-1996, 98n651
Cash constituents of Congress, 2d ed, 95n735
Clinton 500, 95n744
Committees in the US congress 1947-92, v.2, 96n733
Congress & the nation, v.8, 95n731
Congress & the nation, 1993-96, 99n675
Congress at your fingertips: 103d Congress, 2d session, 1994: alpha ed, 95n720
Congress at your fingertips: 103d Congress, 2d session, 1994: condensed ed, 95n721
Congress at your fingertips: 103d Congress, 2d session, 1994: standard ed, 95n722
Congressional dir: 105th congress, 99n669
Congressional elections 1946-96, 99n676
Congressional Quarterly almanac, v.49, 95n732
Congressional Quarterly almanac, v.52, 98n670
Congressional Quarterly's pols in America 1996, 96n738
Congressional roll call 1996, 98n671
Congressional staff dir fall 1997, 98n652
Congressional voting gd, 5th ed, 96n736
Congressional yrbk 1993, 96n739
Congressional yrbk 1996, 104th Congress, 2nd session, 98n672
Congressional yellow bk. fall 1994, 95n734
CQ's pocket gd to the lang of Congress, 95n723
Directory of Congressional voting scores & interest group ratings, 2d ed, 98n678
Encyclopedia of the US congress, 96n720
Facts about the Congress, 97n600
Handbook of campaign spending: money in the 1992 Congressional races, 95n738
Heritage Foundation Congressional dir, 99n671
How to research Congress, 97n585
Members of Congress, 97n584
New members of Congress almanac: 103rd Congress, 95n718
New members of Congress almanac: 105th US Congress, 98n654
New members of Congress almanac, 99n661
Open secrets, 3d ed, 95n736
Open secrets: the ency of congressional money & pols, 4th ed, 98n675
United States Congress, 96n715
Vital stats on Congress 1995-96, 98n676
Who's who in Congress 1997, 98n656
Women of Congress, 98n833
Women of the US congress, 95n716

UNITED STATES—CONSTITUTION
Companion to the US Constitution & its amendments, 2d ed, 99n685
Complete bill of rights, 98n669
Constitutional law & YAs, 2d ed, 98n540
Constitutional law dict, v.1, 96n606
Constitutional law dict, v.2, suppl 1, 99n555
Encyclopedia of constitutional amendments, proposed amendments, & amending issues, 1789-1995, 97n596

Encyclopedia of the American Constitution [CD-ROM], 98n518
United States constitution, 99n686

UNITED STATES—DECLARATION OF INDEPENDENCE
Roots of the Republic, 97n410
Signers of the Declaration of Independence, 98n434

UNITED STATES—DEFENSES
Cuts in defense jobs in US counties, metropolitan areas, & states, 1992-2003, 96n270

UNITED STATES—DEPARTMENT OF COMMERCE
NTIS ordernow [CD-ROM], 98n62

UNITED STATES—DEPARTMENT OF DEFENSE
US military online, 98n617

UNITED STATES—DEPARTMENT OF TREASURY
Biographical dict of the US Secretaries of the Treasury, 1789-1995, 97n587

UNITED STATES—ECONOMIC CONDITIONS
Almanac of state legislatures, 95n710
Annual report of the USA 1998, 99n673
Atlas of contemporary America, 95n890
Economic indicators hndbk, 95n204
Economic integration in Europe & N America, 96n232
Markets of the US for bus planners, 97n276
Statistical hndbk of working America, 96n922
US & Asia statl hndbk, 1997-98 ed, 99n219
USA bus: the portable ency for doing bus with the US, 96n241
Women in the US: economic conditions, 96n937

UNITED STATES—EMIGRATION & IMMIGRATION
United States immigration, 97n621

UNITED STATES—EXECUTIVE DEPARTMENTS
Federal executive dir: May/June 1994, 95n725
Federal regional executive dir, Mar/Aug 1994, 95n726
Federal yellow bk, fall 1994, 95n727

UNITED STATES—FEDERAL BUREAU OF INVESTIGATION
FBI: an annot bibliog & research gd, 95n619

UNITED STATES—FOREIGN RELATIONS
American foreign policy during the French Revolution-Napoleonic period 1789-1815, 95n712
American foreign policy index 1995, v.3, no.2, 96n743
Early US-Hispanic relations 1776-1860, 96n776
Encyclopedia of the inter-American system, 98n695
Encyclopedia of US foreign relations, 98n660
George F. Kennan: an annot bibliog, 98n700
Notable US Ambassadors Since 1775, 98n655
United States & Latin America, 98n697
US foreign relations with the Middle East & N Africa, 95n764
US-Mexican treaties, 98n680

UNITED STATES—GAZETTEERS
American places dict, 95n500

UNITED STATES—GENEALOGY
Land & property research in the US, 98n365
Source: a gdbk of American genealogy, 98n370
US military records, 95n695

UNITED STATES—GUIDE BOOKS
Complete gd to American bed & breakfast, 4th ed, 97n385
Experiencing America's past: a travel gd to museum villages, 2d ed, 95n507
Hostelling USA, 1996, 97n389

UNITED STATES—HISTORICAL GEOGRAPHY
Atlas of American hist, updated ed, 95n524
Atlas of westward expansion, 96n488
Hammond US hist atlas, 95n468
Historical atlas of the congresses of the Confederate States of America 1861-65, 95n526
Historical atlas of the US, rev ed, 95n525

UNITED STATES—HISTORY
ABC-CLIO companion to American reconstruction, 1862-77, 97n420
America: hist & life on disc [CD-ROM], 96n512
American dream: the 50s, 99n466
American eras: dvlpmt of a nation 1783-1815, 99n467
American eras: the revolutionary era 1754-83, 99n469
American Heritage ency of American hist, 99n458
Atlas of histl county boundaries: Iowa, 99n447
Atlas of histl county boundaries: N.C., 99n448
Dictionary of American hist, 97n419
Dictionary of American hist suppl, 97n414
DISCovering US hist [CD-ROM], 98n446
Encyclopedia of frontier biog on CD-ROM [CD-ROM], 96n497
Encyclopedia of frontier biog, v.4, 95n538
Encyclopedia of the American presidency, 95n542
Encyclopedia of women's hist in America, 97n736
Encyclopedia USA, v.23, 97n418
Encyclopedia USA, v.24, 98n440
Encyclopedia USA, v.25, 99n461
Encyclopedia USA, suppl v.1, 98n439
Events that changed America in the 18th century, 99n456
Facts about the states, 2d ed, 95n102
French image of America, 95n531
Handbook of Hispanic cultures in the US: hist, 95n421
Historic docs of 1997, 99n679
Historic festivals, 97n386
Historical dict of Honolulu & Hawaii, 99n459
Historical stats of the US, bicentennial ed [CD-ROM], 98n819
Landmark docs in American hist [CD-ROM], 96n498
Larousse dict of N American hist, 96n508
Operation Desert Shield/Desert Storm, 96n563
Outlaws, mobsters, & crooks, 99n578
Profiles in American hist, 95n537
Profiles in American hist, 96n509
Scholastic ency of the presidents & their times, updated ed, 98n443
Scribner's American hist & culture [CD-ROM], 99n465
Tree of liberty: a documentary hist of rebellion & pol crime in America, rev ed, 99n476
United States hist, 97n406
USA state factbk [CD-ROM], 95n107
Victorian America, 1876 to 1913, 97n400
World's Colombian Exposition, 97n404
Young reader's companion to American hist, 96n528

UNITED STATES—HISTORY—19TH CENTURY
ABC-CLIO companion to American reconstruction, 1862-77, 97n420
American eras: the reform era & E US dvlpmt, 99n468
Freedom's lawmakers: a dir of black officeholders during Reconstruction, rev ed, 98n344
James Madison & the American nation 1751-1836, 96n507

UNITED STATES—HISTORY—20TH CENTURY
America in the 20th century, 96n499
Encyclopedia of the US in the 20th century, 97n416
Korean War, 97n431
Longman companion to America in the era of the 2 world wars, 1910-45, 98n449
Modern America 1914-45, 96n518
Sixties [CD-ROM], 98n450
Twentieth-Century America, 96n485

UNITED STATES—HISTORY—BIBLIOGRAPHY
Bibliographic gd to N American hist 1994, 96n489
Biographical dir of the American Congress, 1774-1996, 98n651
Black/White relations in American hist, 99n454
Guides to archives & ms collections in the US, 95n523
Handbook for research in American hist, 2d ed, 95n535
Literature connections to American hist, 7-12, 99n450
New England in US govt pubs, 1789-1849, 99n452
Readers gd to American hist, 98n442
United States hist: a selective gd to info sources, 95n529

UNITED STATES—HISTORY—CHRONOLOGY
African American hist in the press 1851-99, 97n412
American decades 1900-09, 97n422
American decades 1910-19, 97n423
American decades 1920-29, 97n424
American decades 1930-39, 96n513
American decades 1940-49, 96n514
American decades 1950-59, 95n544
American decades 1960-69, 96n515
American decades 1970-79, 96n516
American decades on CD [CD-ROM], 99n457
Chronicle of America, 96n500
Chronicle of America, rev ed, 98n435
Datapedia of the US, 1790-2000, 95n896
Great dates in US hist, 95n539
Great events from hist: N American series, rev ed, 98n497
Unites States in the 19th century, 98n436

UNITED STATES—HISTORY—CIVIL WAR, 1861-1865
American Civil War, 96n504
American Civil War, 97n421

Atlas of the Civil War, 96n486
Biographical dict of the Union, 96n495
Civil War [CD-ROM], 96n691
Civil War 100, 99n625
Civil War battlefields, 96n517
Civil War bks: a critical bibliog, 98n432
Civil War CD-ROM [CD-ROM], 97n401
Civil War in bks, 98n433
Civil War sites, memorials, museums, & lib collections, 98n448
Compendium of the Confederate armies: Ky., Md., Mo., Confederate units & Indian units, 96n522
Compendium of the Confederate armies: La., 96n523
Compendium of the Confederate armies: Miss., 96n524
Compendium of the Confederate armies: S.C. & Ga., 96n525
Compendium of the Confederate armies: Tex., 96n526
Everything Civil War, 98n447
Historical atlas of the congresses of the Confederate States of America 1861-65, 95n526
Index to the Roll of Honor, 96n434
Learning about...the Civil War, 99n453
Roster of Confederate soldiers 1861-65, 98n451
Southern loyalists in the Civil War, 95n546
Supplement to the official records of the Union & Confederate armies, 99n475

UNITED STATES—HISTORY—COLONIAL ERA
American Revolutionary War sites, memorials, museums, & lib collections, 99n472
Colonial wars of N America, 1512-1763, 97n413
North America in colonial times, 99n464

UNITED STATES—HISTORY—JUVENILE LITERATURE
Literature connections to American hist, K-6: resources to enhance & entice, 99n449

UNITED STATES—HISTORY—MILITARY
American military hist, 96n678
Facts about the American wars, 99n471
Guide to the Indian wars of the West, 99n474
Handbook of American military hist, 97n569
Historical dict of the US Marine Corps, 99n638
Historical dict of the United States Navy, 99n641
Naval Institute histl atlas of the US Navy, 96n701
Reference gd to US military hist 1919-45, 95n548
Reference gd to US military hist: 1945 to the present, 96n520
US military records, 95n695
War of 1898 & US interventions 1898-1934, 95n685
Wars of the Americas, 99n629

UNITED STATES—HISTORY—REVOLUTIONARY ERA
American eras: the revolutionary era 1754-83, 99n469
Bibliography of the works of Richard Price, 95n1427
Encyclopedia of the American Revolution, 3d ed, 96n506
Guide to the Sol Feinstone collection of the David Lib of the American Revolution, 96n654
James Madison & the American nation 1751-1836, 96n507
Revolutionary America 1763-1800, 97n399

UNITED STATES—HISTORY—WAR OF 1812
Encyclopedia of the war of 1812, 98n612
War of 1812 eyewitness accounts, 98n608

UNITED STATES—HISTORY—WEST
New ency of the American west, 99n463

UNITED STATES—HISTORY—WORLD WAR, 1914-1918
United States in the 1st world war, 96n685

UNITED STATES—IMPRINTS
Books from Chapel Hill 1922-97, 98n595
Checklist of American imprints for 1846, 99n13

UNITED STATES—IN LITERATURE
America in histl fiction, 98n1114

UNITED STATES—JUDICIARY
Judicial staff dir, 1997, 98n522

UNITED STATES—JUVENILE LITERATURE
Scholastic ency of the US, 99n1005

UNITED STATES—MAPS
All over the map, 95n470
Atlas of contemporary America, 95n890
Big bk of America, 95n469
Hammond road atlas & vacation gd, 96n442
Hammond US atlas, Gemini ed, 95n467
Macmillan color atlas of the states, 97n82

UNITED STATES—MARINE CORPS
Historical dict of the US Marine Corps, 99n638

UNITED STATES—MILITIA
Militia & the Natl Guard in America since colonial times, 95n682

UNITED STATES—NATIONAL GUARD
Militia & the Natl Guard in America since colonial times, 95n682

UNITED STATES—NATIONAL PARKS
Complete gd to America's natl parks, 10th ed, 99n429

UNITED STATES—NAVY
Historical dict of the United States Navy, 99n641

UNITED STATES—OFFICIALS & EMPLOYEES
Freedom's lawmakers: a dir of black officeholders during Reconstruction, rev ed, 98n344

UNITED STATES—POLITICS & GOVERNMENT
Almanac of state legislatures, 95n710
America votes 21, 96n735
American first ladies, 97n407
American govt & pols, 98n646
Annual report of the USA 1998, 99n673
Carroll's fed advisory dir 1995, 96n722
Carroll's fed dir, 96n723

Carroll's fed regional dir, 96n724
Chronology & glossary of propaganda in the US, 97n595
Clinton 500, 95n744
Congress & the nation, 1993-96, 99n675
Congressional Quarterly almanac, v.52, 98n670
Congressional Quarterly's desk ref on American govt, 96n737
Congressional voting gd, 5th ed, 96n736
Election results dir 1997, 98n663
Encyclopedia of American govt, 99n667
Encyclopedia of American pol reform, 98n657
Encyclopedia of modern American social issues, 99n742
Encyclopedia of the Reagan-Bush yrs, 97n593
Events that changed America in the 18th century, 99n456
Government on file, 99n684
Historic docs index, 1972-95, 98n682
Historic docs of 1997, 99n679
Historical gd to the US govt, 99n668
Illustrated dict of constitutional concepts, 97n594
Introduction to US govt info sources, 5th ed, 97n53
John Adams: a bibliog, 95n533
Presidents: a ref hist, 2d ed, 97n589
Protocol: a hndbk for legislative staff, 98n677
Reagan yrs A to Z, 97n592
Religious right, 97n1218
Running for president, 95n741
Safire's new pol dict, 95n729
Staff dirs on CD-ROM [CD-ROM], 99n672
State budget actions 1997, 99n678
Thaddeus Stevens papers, 95n746
United States govt manual 1996/97, 97n604
US govt dirs, 1982-95, 99n62
Vital stats on American pols, 4th ed, 95n743
Vital stats on American pols, 6th ed, 99n683
Washington representatives 1998, 22d ed, 99n665
Who's who in American pols 1993-94, 95n719
Words in the news, 95n724
World almanac of US pols, 1993-95 ed, 95n711
World almanac of US pols, 1997-99 ed, 98n643

UNITED STATES—POPULATION
Bibliography of American demographic hist, 96n906
Historical stats of the states of the US, 95n893
Social work almanac, 2d ed, 96n894
State atlas of pol & cultural diversity, 98n329
Twentieth-Century hist of US population, 98n808

UNITED STATES—RELIGION
America's religions, 98n1364
Encyclopedia of religious controversies in the US, 98n1354
History & annot bibliog of American religious pers & newspapers, 96n1447
Modern American popular religion, 97n1171
Religion & the American experience, the 20th century, 96n1442

UNITED STATES—SOCIAL CONDITIONS
American attitudes, 2d ed, 99n90
Atlas of contemporary America, 95n890
Encyclopedia of modern American social issues, 99n742
Radicalism hndbk, 96n766
Social work almanac, 2d ed, 96n894

UNITED STATES—SOCIAL LIFE & CUSTOMS
ABC-CLIO companion to the 1960s counterculture in America, 98n437
America in the 20th century, 96n499
Learning to behave: a gd to American conduct bks before 1900, 95n1422
Modern America 1914-45, 96n518
Victorian America, 1876 to 1913, 97n400
World almanac of the USA, 95n108

UNITED STATES—SPANISH-AMERICAN WAR, 1898
Spanish-American war, 99n626

UNITED STATES—STATISTICS
American attitudes, 2d ed, 99n90
American salaries & wages survey, 3d ed, 96n266
CQ's state fact finder 1997, 98n817
Datapedia of the US, 1790-2000, 95n896
Gale state rankings reporter, 95n895
Health: US, 1996-97 & injury chartbk, 99n1430
Historical stats of the US, bicentennial ed [CD-ROM], 98n819
Historical stats of the states of the US, 95n893
Indiana factbk 1998-99, 5th ed, 99n92
New view almanac, 97n7
Rating gd to life in America's 50 states, 96n924
Sourcebk of county demographics, 11th ed, 99n785
Sourcebk of ZIP code demographics, 13th ed, 99n786
Statistical abstract of the US 1995, 115th ed, 96n920
Statistical hndbk on adolescents in America, 97n718
Statistical hndbk on women in America, 2d ed, 97n740
Statistical portrait of the US, 99n791
World almanac of the USA, rev ed, 99n89

UNITED STATES—STUDY & TEACHING
American studies in China: a dir, 95n109
Guide to American studies resources, 1994, 96n338

UNITED STATES—SUPREME COURT
Citizen's companion to US Supreme Court opinions, 1996-97 term, 99n562
Congressional Quarterly's gd to the US Supreme Court, 3d ed, 98n529
Facts about the Supreme Court of the US, 98n538
Freedom of religion decisions of the US Supreme Court, 97n1183
Freedom of speech decisions of the US Supreme Court, 97n541
Freedom of the press decisions of the US Supreme Court, 97n761
Guide to the early reports of the Supreme Court of the US, 97n493
Guide to the US supreme court, 98n526
Rejected: sketches of the 26 men nominated for the Supreme Court but not confirmed by the Senate, 95n601
Supreme Court compendium, 95n612
Supreme Court compendium, 2d ed, 97n497
Supreme Court justices, 96n572
Supreme Court rules: the 1997 revisions, 99n569
Supreme Court yrbk 1995-96, 97n603

Young Oxford companion to the Supreme Court of the US, 95n607

UNITED STATES—TERRITORIAL EXPANSION
Trans-Mississippi west 1804-1912, pt.1, 95n545

UNITS
Sizes: the illus ency, 96n1787

UNITS—CONVERSION TABLES
Scientific unit conversion, 98n1597

UNIVERSITY OF CALGARY
Mapping the territory, 96n658

UNIVERSITY OF CAMBRIDGE
Central Cambridge, 95n374

UNIX
UNIX & X command compendium, 96n1762
UNIX dict of commands, terms, & acronyms, 97n1373

UPDIKE, JOHN
John Updike: a bibliog, 1967-93, 95n1196

UPHOLSTERY
Upholsterer's pocket ref bk, 96n1020

URANIUM
Uranium: resources, production & demand, 1993, 95n1755

URBAN CLIMATOLOGY
Weather of US cities, 5th ed, 97n1398

URBAN FAUNA
Peterson 1st gd to urban wildlife, 95n1560

URBAN STUDIES
Challenge of urbanization, 97n722
Encyclopedia of urban America, 99n793
Latin American urbanization, 95n899
World urbanizations prospects: the 1994 revision, 96n932
World urbanization prospects, 99n794

URBAN TRANSPORTATION
Jane's urban transport systems 1994-95, 95n1792

USED CARS
Used car reliability & safety gd, 96n1885

UTAH
Utah hist ency, 96n511
Utah state constitution, 99n688

UTOPIAS
ABC-CLIO world hist companion to utopian movements, 99n1253
Dystopian lit, 95n1109
Encyclopedia of utopian lit, 96n1147
Utopian/dystopian lit, 95n1101

UZBEK LANGUAGE—DICTIONARIES—ENGLISH
Uzbek-English, English-Uzbek concise dict, 96n1141

VACATIONS. *See also* **TRAVEL; HOLIDAYS; FESTIVALS**
Adventure holidays 1995, 18th ed, 96n460
Adventure vacations, 96n473
Great escapes: the spring breaker's gd to beaches & beyond, 98n417
Stern's gd to the cruise vacation, 6th ed, 97n1449

VAMPIRES
Complete vampire companion, 95n1327
Vampire bk: the ency of the undead, 95n1328
Vampire ency, 95n1325
Vampire gallery: a who's who of the undead, 99n1214
Vampire readings, 99n1035
VideoHound's vampires on video, 98n1321

VANCE, JACK
Work of Jack Vance, 96n1218

VAN CLEEF, LEE
Lee Van Cleef: a bibliog, film, & TV ref, 99n1208

VAUDEVILLE
Encyclopedia of vaudeville, 95n1417

VEGETABLE GARDENING
Knott's hndbk for vegetable growers, 4th ed, 98n1437
Organic gardener's home ref, 96n1543
Taylor's gd to heirloom vegetables, 97n1260

VEGETABLES
Codex alimentarius, v.5a, 2d ed, 96n1534
Produce ref gd to fruits & vegetables from around the world, 98n1421

VEGETARIAN RESTAURANTS
Vegetarian Journal's gd to natural foods restaurants in the US & Canada, 3d ed, 99n434

VENDORS & PURCHASERS
Peterson's contract servs for higher educ, 96n342

VENEZUELA
Historical dict of Venezuela, 2d ed, 98n142

VENICE (ITALY)
Venice & the Veneto, 96n478

VENTILATION
HVAC design data sourcebk, 95n1641

VENTURE CAPITAL
Fitzroy Dearborn dir of venture capital funds, 96n184
Fitzroy Dearborn intl dir of venture capital funds, 2d ed, 97n181
Fitzroy Dearborn intl dir of venture capital funds 1998-99, 99n198

Galante's venture capital & private equity dir, 1997 ed [CD-ROM], 99n199
Galante's venture capital & private equity dir, 1998 ed, 99n200
MoneyFind bkware dir of small bus investors, 95n197

VERDI, GIUSEPPE
Giuseppe Verdi: a gd to research, 99n1137

VERMONT
New Hampshire [&] Vt.: atlas of histl county boundaries, 96n439

VERNE, JULES
Jules Verne ency, 97n952

VETERANS
Financial aid for vets, military personnel, & their dependents 1994-96, 96n690
How to locate anyone who is or has been in the military, rev ed, 96n688
Veterans benefits: the complete gd, 95n696

VETERINARY MEDICINE
Animal health yrbk 1993, 96n1553
Complete horse care manual, 96n1556
Literature of animal sci & health, 95n1533
Veterinarian's ency of animal behavior, 96n1554
Veterinary drug hndbk, 2d ed, 97n1263

VICE-PRESIDENTIAL CANDIDATES
Presidential also-rans & running mates, 1788-1996, 99n662

VICE-PRESIDENTS — UNITED STATES
American leaders 1789-1994, 95n714
Presidents, first ladies, & vice presidents, 98n653
Vice presidents, 97n590
Vice presidents, 99n664
Young Oxford companion to the presidency of the US, 95n543

VICO, GIAMBATTISTA
Vico: a bibliog of works in English from 1884-1984, 96n1426

VICTIMS OF CRIMES
Crime victim compensation programs, 95n625
Victims rights, 99n590

VICTORIA & ALBERT MUSEUM
Victoria & Albert Museum, 99n70

VICTORIANA
Illustrated ency of Victoriana, 96n1016

VICTORIA, TOMAS LUISDE
Tomas Luis de Victoria: a gd to research, 99n1132

VIDEO RECORDINGS
Adventures in Video, 97n314
Best toys, bks & videos for kids, 96n1010
Billboard 1996 music yrbk, 98n1205
Billboard video yrbk 1993, 95n1390
Billboard video yrbk 1994, 96n1402
Blockbuster Entertainment gd to movies & videos 1998, 99n1241
Bowker's complete video dir 1995, 96n986
Bowker's dir of videocassettes for children 1998, 99n10
Canadian film & video, 98n1271
Charles Dickens on the screen, 97n1121
Complete gd to special interest videos [CD-ROM], 95n1360
Critical gd to mgmt training videos & selected multimedia, 1996, 97n266
Educators gd to free videotapes 1995, 42d ed, 96n376
Educators gd to free videotapes 1998, 45th ed, 99n357
Facets African-American video gd, 95n1392
Facts on File dict of TV, cable, & video, 95n959
Field gd to current training videos, 96n282
Film & video finder, 5th ed, 98n310
Film & video on the Internet, 98n1287
International dict of broadcasting & film, 96n984
International film, TV & video acronyms, 95n1359
International TV & video almanac, 1996, 41st ed, 97n771
Leonard Maltin's movie & video gd, 95n1361
Leonard Maltin's movie & video gd, 1999 ed, 99n1243
Manly movie gd, 99n1242
Media review digest, v. 26, 1996, 97n9
Psychotronic video gd, 97n1140
Roger Ebert's video companion, 1994 ed, 95n1362
Roger Eberts video companion, 98n1319
Sci-Fi on tape, 98n1318
Silent films on video, 97n1120
Spencer's complete gd to special interest videos, 4th ed, 99n1245
Time Out film gd, 5th ed, 97n1136
TLA film & video gd 1996-97, 97n1125
Variety's video dir plus [CD-ROM], 96n1388
Video annual 1994, 96n994
Video rating gd for libs on CD-ROM 1990-94 [CD-ROM], 96n995
Video source bk 1996, 17th ed, 96n996
VideoHound multimedia [CD-ROM], 96n1389
VideoHound's golden movie retriever 1994, 95n1399
VideoHound's sci-fi experience, 98n1320
VideoHound's vampires on video, 98n1321
Videos of African & African-related performance, 97n1145

VIDEO RECORDINGS FOR CHILDREN
Parent's gd to the best children's videos & where to find them, 96n1386

VIDEO RECORDINGS—PRODUCTION & DIRECTION
Hollywood blu-bk dir 1997, 99n1221

VIDEO TAPE INDUSTRY
AV market place 1994, 95n965
Film, TV, video in Russia '94, 95n1378

VIENNA (AUSTRIA)
Vienna, 96n479
Vienna, 99n119

VIETNAM
Historical dict of Vietnam, 99n488
Vietnam studies, 98n117
Who's who in Vietnam, 99n113

VIETNAMESE CONFLICT, 1961-1975
Encyclopedia of the Vietnam War, 97n433
Encyclopedia of the Vietnam War, 99n527
Historical atlas of the Vietnam War, 97n434
Vietnam [CD-ROM], 96n694
Vietnam experience, 99n1041
Vietnam war films, 95n1384
Vietnam War lit, 3d ed, 98n1056

VIETNAMESE LANGUAGE
NTC's Vietnamese-English dict, 97n877

VIGILANTES
Lynching & vigilantism in the US, 98n547

VIKINGS
Cultural atlas of the Viking world, 95n563

VIOLA MUSIC
Bibliographical gd to Spanish music for the violin & viola, 1900-97, 99n1149

VIOLENCE
Shadow of death: an analytic bibliog on pol violence, terrorism, & low-intensity conflict, 97n501
Statistical hndbk on violence in America, 97n507
Statistics on weapons & violence, 97n512
Violence & the media, 97n748
Violence in American society, 95n618
Violence in American society, 99n583

VIOLIN MUSIC
Bibliographical gd to Spanish music for the violin & viola, 1900-97, 99n1149
Guide to published Canadian violin music suitable for student performers, 95n1279
International ency of violin-keyboard sonatas & composer biogs, 2d ed, 97n1043

VIOLONCELLO MUSIC
Cello music since 1960, 96n1286

VIRGINIA
Bibliography of Va. legal hist before 1900, 2d ed, 99n548
Butterflies of Delmarva, 95n1579
Freshwater fishes of the Carolinas, Va., Md., & Dela., 95n1588

VIROLOGY
Encyclopedia of virology, 95n1680
Encyclopedia of virology plus [CD-ROM], 98n1442

VIRTUAL REALITY
Virtual Reality World's virtual reality market place 1994, 95n1700

VIRUS DISEASES OF PLANTS
Virus diseases of trees & shrubs, 2d ed, 95n1552

VISCOSITY
Handbook of viscosity, v.4: inorganic compounds & elements, 98n1623

VISION DISORDERS
Living with low vision, 97n671

VITAMINS
Encyclopedia of nutritional suppls, 97n1349
Encyclopedia of vitamins, minerals, & suppls, 97n1265
Real vitamin & mineral bk, 98n1548
Woman's gd to vitamins & minerals, 96n1743

VOCABULARY
Basic word list, 3d ed, 98n992
English vocabulary quick ref, 99n901
Sisson's word & expression locator, 2d ed, 96n1092

VOCAL MUSIC
Giovanni Gabrieli (ca.1555-1612): a thematic catalogue of his music...., 97n1034

VOCATIONAL EDUCATION
Chronicle 2-yr college databk, rev ed, 96n335
Chronicle vocational school manual, rev ed, 96n381
Continuing medical educ dir 1996-97, 98n1532
Ferguson's gd to apprenticeship programs, 2d ed, 99n359
National gd to educl credit for training programs, 1997 ed, 98n315
Peterson's vocational & technical schools, 95n389
Peterson's vocational & technical schools & programs, 99n360

VOCATIONAL GUIDANCE. *See also* CAREERS
America's 50 fastest growing jobs, 2d ed, 95n308
America's top jobs for college graduates, rev ed, 95n309
America's top jobs for people without college degrees, 3d ed, 98n227
America's top medical & human servs jobs, 2d ed, 95n310
America's top office, mgmt, & sales jobs, 2d ed, 95n311
America's top office, mgmt, sales, & professional jobs, 3d ed, 98n228
America's top technical & trade jobs, 2d ed, 95n312
Career connection for college educ, 2d ed, 95n318
Career discovery ency, 98n213
Career opportunities for bilinguals & multilinguals, 2d ed, 95n1031
Career perspectives software series [CD-ROM], 98n223
Careers in intl affairs, 6th ed, 98n698
College Board gd to jobs & career planning, 2d ed, 95n388
College majors & careers, 3d ed, 98n316
Cracking the corp closet, 96n259
Dictionary of occupational terms, 95n297
Earth work, 96n1871
Encyclopedia of careers & vocational guidance [CD-ROM], 96n382
Encyclopedia of careers & vocational guidance, 2d ed [CD-ROM], 98n214

Encyclopedia of careers & vocational guidance, 10th ed, 98n215
Enhanced occupational outlook hndbk, 98n226
Exploring health care careers, 99n1429
Free & inexpensive career materials, 96n383
Gale's career guidance system, expanded ed [CD-ROM], 96n384
Health professions educ dir 1997-98, 98n1512
JIST's electronic enhanced dict of occupational titles, 2d ed [CD-ROM], 98n216
JIST's electronic gd for occupational exploration [CD-ROM], 96n275
JIST's electronic occupational outlook hndbk, 2d ed [CD-ROM], 98n231
JIST's multimedia occupational outlook hndbk, 2d ed [CD-ROM], 98n232
Job hunter's sourcebk, 3d ed, 98n233
Occupational outlook hndbk, 1996-97 ed, 98n238
On-line job search companion, 96n272
Professional & technical careers, 99n274
Professional careers sourcebk, 3d ed, 95n390
Professional careers sourcebk, 5th ed, 99n361
US employment opportunities, 98n240
VGM's careers ency, 4th ed, 98n217
Vocational careers sourcebk, 99n263
Young person's occupational outlook hndbk, 97n264

VOLCANOES
Encyclopedia of earthquakes & volcanoes, 95n496
Volcanoes of the world, 2d ed, 96n1818

VOLUNTARISM
Alternatives to the Peace Corps, 96n868
Christian voluntarism in Britain & N America, 96n867
Philanthropic studies index, 1995 cum index, 96n884
Philanthropic studies index, v.3, no.1, 95n868
Volunteer America, 4th ed, 98n795

VONNEGUT, KURT
Vonnegut ency, 96n1219

VOTING
Congressional voting gd, 5th ed, 96n736

WAELRANT, HUBERT
Descriptive catalog of the music printed by Hubert Waelrant & Jan de Laet, 96n1266

WAGES
American salaries & wages survey, 3d ed, 96n266
American salaries & wages survey, 4th ed, 98n229
Employment/Unemployment & earnings stats, 97n249
Main economic indicators: histl stats: prices, labour & wages 1962-91, 95n210

WALES
Surnames of Wales, 97n353
Wales & cinema, 96n1370
Welsh family hist, 95n461

WAR
Cambridge illus atlas of warfare: Renaissance to Revolution, 1492-1792, 97n556
Dictionary of Afghan wars, revolutions, & insurgencies, 97n106
Encyclopedia of the Vietnam War, 99n527
Hutchinson dict of ancient & medieval warfare, 99n534
International conflict, 98n696
Propaganda in 20th century war & pols, 97n618
State of war & peace atlas, 99n700
War & conflict quotations, 98n85
War of the Spanish Succession, 1702-13, 97n435
Wars in the Third World since 1945, 2d ed, 97n568

WAR CORRESPONDENTS
Historical dict of war journalism, 98n881

WARD, EBENEZER
Victorian yellowbacks & paperbacks, 1849-1905, v.2, 96n1224

WAR FILMS
Hollywood war films, 1937-45, 97n1123

WARING, FRED
Fred Waring discography, 97n1049

WAR IN LITERATURE
Vietnam War lit, 3d ed, 98n1056

WAR IN THE PRESS
Historical dict of war journalism, 98n881

WAR—MORAL & ETHICAL ASPECTS
Encyclopedia of war & ethics, 97n1161

WARSAW (POLAND)
Historical dict of Warsaw, 98n479
Warsaw, 98n423

WARSHIPS. *See also* **SHIPS**
Battleships of the world, 98n626
Battleships: US battleships, 1935-92, rev ed, 96n700
Cruisers of WW II, 97n574
Jane's fighting ships 1994-95, 95n698
Jane's fighting ships 1996-97, 99th ed, 97n573
Jane's major warships 1997, 99n640
Jane's warship recognition gd, 97n577
Jane's warships image lib [CD-ROM], 98n627
Naval Institute gd to the ships & aircraft of the US Fleet, 16th ed, 98n628
Warships of the USSR & Russia, 1945-95, 98n629

WAR SONGS
World War I songs, 96n696

WASHINGTON (D.C.)
AIA gd to the architecture of Washington, DC, 3d ed, 96n1049
Buildings of the District of Columbia, 95n1017
Guide to greater Washington, DC grantmakers 1994-95, 96n876
Hudson's Washington news media contacts dir 1994, 95n935

Hudson's Washington news media contacts dir 1998, 99n823
International Washington almanac, 1994, 95n760
Scholars' gd to Washington, D.C., media collections, 95n938
Washington '97, 14th ed, 98n58
Washington info dir, 96n734
Who's who in Washington nonprofit groups 1994, 95n72

WASPS
Indo-Australian Agaoninae (pollinators of figs), 96n1628

WATER
Agrochemicals desk ref: environmental data, 95n1510
Environment 1: clean water, 95n1760
State groundwater regulation, 95n1771

WATERCOLOR PAINTING
Index of American watercolor exhibitions 1900-45, 95n1022

WEALTH
New fortunes 1994, 96n176
Who's wealthy in America, 1998, 99n59

WEAPONS. *See also* **FIREARMS; NUCLEAR WEAPONS**
Jane's ammunition hndbk 1996-97, 5th ed, 98n633
Jane's armour & artillery 1995-96, 16th ed, 97n575
Jane's infantry weapons 1994-95, 95n700
Jane's infantry weapons 1998-99, 24th ed, 99n645
Jane's land-based air defense 1998-99, 11th ed, 99n646
Jane's police & security equipment 1996-97, 9th ed, 98n555
Jane's simulation & training systems 1996-97, 9th ed, 98n1573
Naval Institute gd to world naval weapons systems, 1994 update, 95n701
Naval Institute gd to world naval weapons systems 1997-98, 98n634
Statistics on weapons & violence, 97n512
Vital gd to combat guns & infantry weapons, 97n579

WEATHER. *See also* **METEOROLOGY**
Associated Press lib of disasters, 99n64
Blizzards, 99n1525
Chronology of weather, 99n1526
Complete weather resource, 98n1611
Droughts, 99n1527
Encyclopedia of climate & weather, 97n1396
Floods, 99n1528
Florida's hurricane hist, 99n1531
Glossary of weather & climate with related oceanic & hydrologic terms, 98n1612
Handy weather answer bk, 98n1613
Hurricanes, 99n1529
National Audubon Society 1st field gd: weather, 99n1533
Pockets: weather facts, 96n76
Tornadoes, 99n1530
USA Today weather almanac 1995, 96n1809
Weather almanac, 99n1534
Weather America, 97n1397
Weather hndbk, 96n1810
Weather of US cities, 5th ed, 97n1398
Weather sourcebk, 95n1728
World weatherdisc, 1994 ed [CD-ROM], 96n1811

WEBSTER, MARGARET
Margaret Webster: a bio-bibliog, 95n1340

WEEDS
Weed flora of Egypt, rev ed, 96n1582
Weeds of the NE, 98n1453
World weeds, 99n1368

WEIGHTS & MEASURES
Economist desk companion, rev ed, 95n79
Macmillan dict of measurement, 95n1491
Numbers: how many, how far, how long, how much, 98n810

WEIL, SIMONE
Simone Weil, 96n957

WELDING
Jefferson's welding ency, 18th ed, 98n1491
Welding codes standards & specifications, 99n1411

WELFARE
Welfare reform, 98n799

WELLERISMS
Dictionary of wellerisms, 95n1314

WELTY, EUDORA
Eudora Welty: a bibliog of her work, 95n1197
Reader's gd to the short stories of Eudora Welty, 98n1138

WESTERN FILMS
Overlook film ency: the western, 95n1376
Western & frontier film & TV credits 1903-95, 97n1130

WESTERN SAHARA
Historical dict of W Sahara, 2d ed, 95n110
Western Sahara, 97n105

WESTERNS (TELEVISION PROGRAMS)
Television western players of the 50s, 98n1276
Television westerns episode gd, 98n1308

WESTERN STORIES
What do I read next?, 1994, 95n1158
What Western do I read next?, 99n1028
Work of William Eastlake, 96n1209

WEST INDIES
Ancient Caribbean, 95n420
Butterflies of the W Indies & S Fla., 95n1578
Field gd to shells, 4th ed, 96n1595
St. Kitts-Nevis, 96n172
St. Lucia, 97n145

WEST, JESSAMYN
Jessamyn West: a descriptive & annot bibliog, 99n1056

WEST (US)
American West: a multicultural ency, 96n505

Bibliographical gd to the study of Western American lit, 2d ed, 97n959
Cowboy dict, 95n1041
Cowboy ency, 96n510
Cowboys & the wild west, 95n541
Encyclopedia of the American West, 97n415
Happy trails: a dict of W expressions, 95n1043
Narrative bibliog of the African American frontier, 97n405
Old West: day by day, 96n502
Peterson's gd to colleges in the West 1995, 9th ed, 96n345
Population hist of western US cities & towns, 1850-1990, 97n723
Profile of western N America, 97n248
Trans-Mississippi west 1804-1912, pt.1, 95n545
Western American novelists, 96n1205
Western lore & lang, 97n841
Who's who in the west 1994-95, 95n40
Who's who in the west 1998-99, 26th ed, 98n32

WETLANDS
Wetland economics, 1989-93, 96n1600
Wetlands in danger, 95n1773

WHALES
Whales, dolphins, & porpoises, 96n1629

WHISKEY
Bourbon companion, 99n1337
Complete gd to whiskey, 98n1426

WHIST
Bidding dict, 98n744

WHOLESALE TRADE
European dir of retailers & wholesalers, 2d ed, 99n253
Wholesale & retail trade USA, 97n279

WILD ANIMAL TRADE
International wildlife trade, 96n1599

WILDE, OSCAR
Oscar Wilde ency, 99n1075

WILDER, LAURA INGALLS
Laura Ingalls Wilder: an annot bibliog of critical, biogl, & teaching studies, 98n1139

WILDERNESS AREAS
Atlas of wild places, 95n1558
Essential gd to wilderness camping & backpacking in the US, 96n824
Wilderness preservation: a ref hndbk, 95n1785

WILDERNESS SURVIVAL
Survival, 96n812

WILD FLOWERS
Desert wildflowers of N America, 99n1365
Field gd to wild flowers of S Europe, 95n1541
Guide to wildflowers in winter, 96n1584
New England's mountain flowers, 98n1450

Sierra Nev. Wildflowers, 99n1362
Wild flowers of the Pacific NW, 99n1366

WILDLIFE CONSERVATIONISTS
Portraits in conservation: E & S Africa, 96n1596

WILDLIFE MANAGEMENT
Attitudes toward the outdoors: an annot bibliog, 95n1759

WILLIAMS, TENNESSEE
Tennessee Williams, 96n1220
Tennessee Williams, 99n1057

WILSON, AUGUST
August Wilson: a research & production sourcebk, 99n1249

WILSON, WOODROW
Woodrow Wilson, 98n647

WIND ENSEMBLES
Wind ensemble sourcebk & biogl gd, 98n1220

WIND QUINTETS
Wind chamber music, 97n1058

WINE & WINE MAKING
Best wines! 1999, 3d ed, 99n1335
Champagne companion, 96n1354
Connoisseurs' hndbk of the wines of Calif. & the Pacific Northwest, 4th ed, 99n1341
Good wine gd 1999, 99n1340
Larousse ency of wine, 96n1527
New Sotheby's wine ency, 98n1424
Oxford companion to wine, 96n1528
Wine Spectator Mag's gd to great wine values, 99n1338

WISTERIA
Wisterias, 96n1579

WIT & HUMOR
Animation, caricature, & gag & pol cartoons in the US & Canada, 95n1331
Comic art of Europe, 95n1332
Film & TV in-jokes, 99n1239
Humor in 18th- & 19th-century British lit, 99n1060
Humorous quotations, 96n93
Oxford dict of humorous quotations, 97n71
Robert Benchley, 96n1207
Ultimate ref bk, 95n89
Wit: humorous quotations from Woody Allen to Oscar Wilde, 99n79

WITTGENSTEIN, LUDWIG
Wittgenstein dict, 97n1162

WITTIG, MONIQUE
French feminist theory (2), 95n902

WOLFE, THOMAS
Thomas Wolfe: an annot critical bibliog, 97n976

WOMEN
ABC-CLIO companion to women's progress in America, 95n914
American women, 98n247
Arab women in ESCWA member states, 96n156
Big bk of opportunities for women, 98n269
Black woman's gumbo ya-ya, 95n920
Collaborative bibliog of women in philosophy, 98n1332
Contemporary Australian women 1996/97, 97n734
Contemporary women's issues 1992-July 1997 [CD-ROM], 98n838
Dictionary of feminist theory, 2d ed, 96n948
Directory of financial aids for women 1995-97, 96n879
Facts on File ency of black women in America, 98n343
Feminist chronicles 1953-93, 95n917
Information please women's sourcebk, 1995, 96n951
Larousse dict of women, 98n24
Latinas in the US, 97n728
Muslim women throughout the world, 98n830
National gd to funding for women & girls, 96n952
New Beacon bk of quotations by women, 97n70
Northwest women: an annot bibliog of sources on the hist of Oreg. & Washington women, 1787-1970, 98n828
Statistical record of women worldwide, 96n953
Subject gd to women of the world, 97n741
US women's interest groups, 97n737
Woman to woman, 95n919
Women & aging, 96n936
Women & men in Europe & N America 1995, 97n720
Women & religion in Britain & Ireland, 97n1170
Women in Nigeria, 97n725
Women in Russia & the Soviet Union, 95n903
Women in the US: economic conditions, 96n937
Women of color: feminist theory, 97n729
Women of Ireland, 98n34
Women of strength, 97n733
Women's almanac, 98n827
Women's atlas of the US, rev ed, 96n933
Women's desk ref, 95n918
Women's firsts, 99n806
Women's info exchange natl dir, 95n915
Women's issues, 98n837
Women's per in the US, 97n743
Women's voices, 98n840
Women's words, 97n72
World's women 1995, [2d ed], 96n954

WOMEN ARTISTS
Dictionary of women artists, 98n948
Encyclopedia of women artists of the American west, 99n869
Latin American women artists, 97n793
North American women artists of the 20th century, 96n1026
Remarkable lives of 100 women artists, 96n939
Women artists, 2d ed, 96n1021
Women artists & designers in Europe since 1800, 99n864

WOMEN ATHLETES
American women's track & field, 97n664
Encyclopedia of women & sports, 97n644
NCAA basketball: the official 1997 women's college basketball records bk, 98n740
Outstanding women athletes, 2d ed, 99n710
Women of the All-American Girls Professional Baseball League, 98n734

WOMEN—BIOGRAPHY
A to Z of Native American women, 99n386
Biographical dict of Chinese women, 99n798
Biographies of British women, 95n910
50 most influential women in American law, 98n513
Great lives from hist: American women series, 96n942
Grolier lib of women's biogs, 99n799
International who's who of women, 99n26
Notable black American women, bk.2, 97n34
Notable Latin American women, 96n938
Notable women in the life scis, 97n1231
Notable women in world hist, 99n797
100 women who shaped world hist, 96n32
Prominent women of the 20th century, 97n26
Susan B. Anthony: a biogl companion, 99n800
Who's who of American women 1995-96, 19th ed, 96n38
Women & the Dict of Natl Biog, 96n26
Women in context, 99n39
Women of peace: Nobel peace prize winners, 96n944
Women who reformed pols, 96n943

WOMEN COMPOSERS
Guitar music by women composers, 98n1218
Women composers, v.1, 97n1047
Women composers, v.2, 97n1048
Women composers, v.3, 99n1145
Women composers, 2d ed, 95n1267
Women composers & songwriters, 97n1035

WOMEN—DEVELOPING COUNTRIES
Women in the Third World, 98n839
Women in the Third World, 99n805

WOMEN—DISEASES
Woman's ency of natural healing, 98n1550

WOMEN DRAMATISTS
Contemporary African-American female playwrights, 99n1050
Female dramatist, 99n1025
Women playwrights of diversity, 98n1106

WOMEN—EDUCATION
Gender equity in educ, 96n313
Gender gap in higher educ, 95n372
Historical dict of women's educ in the US, 99n803
Women educators in the US, 1820-1993: a bio-bibliog sourcebk, 95n335

WOMEN—EMPLOYMENT
Women workers, 97n732

WOMEN—HEALTH & HYGIENE
EveryWoman's gd to prescription & nonprescription drugs, 98n1564

Family planning & reproductive health servs in Ghana, 95n849
History of women & sci, health, & tech, 2d ed, 95n904
New A to Z of women's health, 3d ed, 96n1680
Woman's body, 96n1692
Woman's ency of natural healing, 98n1550
Woman's gd to vitamins & minerals, 96n1743
Women & health, 98n1501
Women's complete healthbk, 97n1341
Women's gd to homeopathy, 95n1672
Women's health concerns sourcebk, 99n1438

WOMEN HISTORIANS
American women historians, 1700s-1990s, 97n411

WOMEN—HISTORY
American women's almanac, 98n826
Asian American woman, 99n795
British women's hist, 97n726
Chronology of women's hist, 95n911
Encyclopedia of women's hist in America, 97n736
Grolier lib of women's biogs, 99n799
Reader's companion to US women's hist, 99n804
Scholastic ency of women in the US, 98n836
Statistical hndbk on women in America, 2d ed, 97n740
Wilson chronology of women's achievements, 99n802
Women's chronology, 95n912
Women's chronology, 98n834
Women's firsts, 98n835
Women's hist, 99n801
Women's world: a timeline of women in hist, 96n945

WOMEN IN AGRICULTURE
Women in agriculture, 97n1245

WOMEN IN ART
Encyclopedia of women in religious art, 97n797

WOMEN IN BUSINESS
ABC-CLIO companion to women in the workplace, 95n913
National dir of woman-owned bus firms, 95n201
National dir of woman-owned bus firm, 9th ed, 99n156
Women & work in developing countries, 95n292
Womens' bus resource gd, 95n208

WOMEN IN CHRISTIANITY
Women in Christian hist, 97n731
Women in the biblical world, v.1, 97n1186

WOMEN IN MOTION PICTURES
Women film directors, 96n947
Women's companion to intl film, 95n1373

WOMEN IN POLITICS
Women in modern American pols, 98n829

WOMEN IN SCIENCE
American women in sci, 96n1486
American women in sci, 1950 to the present, 99n1299
Contemporary women scientists, 95n1486
History of women & sci, health, & tech, 2d ed, 95n904

Ladies in the lab? American & British women in sci, 1800-1900, 99n1301
Notable women in the physical scis, 98n1598
Remarkable lives of 100 women healers & scientists, 96n940
Women & sci, 97n730

WOMEN IN TECHNOLOGY
History of women & sci, health, & tech, 2d ed, 95n904

WOMEN INTELLIGENCE OFFICERS
Women in espionage, 95n907

WOMEN JOURNALISTS
Remarkable lives of 100 women writers & journalists, 96n941

WOMEN JUDGES
Women in law, 97n485

WOMEN LAWYERS
Women in law, 97n485

WOMEN—LEGAL STATUS
Women's legal gd, 98n544

WOMEN LEGISLATORS
Women of Congress, 98n833
Women of the US congress, 95n716
Women state & territorial legislators, 1895-1995, 97n601

WOMEN & LITERATURE
American women writers, v.5, 95n1168
Anne Tyler: a critical companion, 99n1051
British women writers, 1700-1850, 98n1144
Contemporary Southern women fiction writers, 95n1181
Detecting women 2, 1996-97 ed, 97n947
Dictionary of literary biog documentary series, v.12, 96n1201
Eighteenth-Century Anglo-American women novelists, 98n1111
Emily Dickinson ency, 99n1052
Encyclopedia of feminist literary theory, 99n961
Feminist criticism of American women poets, 96n1222
Feminist ency of Italian lit, 98n1177
Four British women novelists, 99n1061
French women playwrights before the 20th century, 95n1405
French women playwrights of the 20th century, 97n943
Great women writers, 95n906
Italian women writers, 95n1235
Japanese women writers: a bio-critical sourcebk, 95n1236
Jessamyn West: a descriptive & annot bibliog, 99n1056
Laura Ingalls Wilder: an annot bibliog of critical, biogl, & teaching studies, 98n1139
Literature criticism from 1400 to 1800, v.30, 97n903
Lorraine Hansberry: a research & production sourcebk, 98n1136
Marjorie Kinnan Rawlings: a descriptive bibliog, 97n974
Masterplots II: women's lit series, 96n949
Modern women writers, 95n1174
Modern women writers, 97n907
Nineteenth-Century American women writers, 98n1126
One hundred yrs of American women writing, 1848-1948, 98n1124

Oxford companion to women's writing in the US, 96n1200
Oxford gd to British women writers, 95n1203
Remarkable lives of 100 women writers & journalists, 96n941
Romantic poetry by women: a bibliog, 1770-1835, 95n1247
Silk stalkings: more women write of murder, 99n1033
Third world women's lits, 96n946
Toni Morrison, 99n1058
Virginia Woolf A to Z, 96n1221
Women playwrights in England, Ireland, & Scotland 1660-1823, 98n1151
Women writers in German-speaking countries, 99n1095
Women writers in the US, 97n738
Women writers of Gt Brit & Europe, 98n1067

WOMEN MATHEMATICIANS
Notable women in math, 99n1542

WOMEN MUSICIANS
Extraordinary women in support of music, 98n1199
Women & music, 97n1020
Women in music, 2d ed, 95n1254

WOMEN ORATORS
Women public speakers in the US, 1925-93, 95n905

WOMEN PAINTERS
Abstract expressionist women painters, 97n808
Gallery of her own: an annot bibliog of women in Victorian painting, 98n981

WOMEN PRISONERS
Female offenders, 98n549

WOMEN—QUOTATION, MAXIMS, ETC.
American proverbs about women, 99n807

WOMEN & RELIGION
Encyclopedia of American women & religion, 99n1265
Of spirituality, 97n1169
Women & religion in India, 96n934

WOMEN—SCHOLARSHIPS, FELLOWSHIPS, ETC
Directory of financial aids for women 1997-99, 99n773

WOMEN—SEXUAL BEHAVIOR
Fetishes, Florentine girdles, & other explorations into the sexual imagination, 96n886

WOMEN SOCIAL REFORMERS
Women who reformed pols, 96n943

WOMEN—SOCIETIES & CLUBS
US women's interest groups, 97n737

WOMEN'S PERIODICALS
Women's pers in the US: consumer mags, 96n950
Women's per in the US, 97n743

WOMEN SPIES
Women in espionage, 95n907

WOMEN'S RIGHTS
ABC-CLIO companion to women's progress in America, 95n914
US women's interest groups, 97n737
Women in the Third World, 98n839
Women in the Third World, 99n805
Women's desk ref, 95n918
Women's rights on trial, 98n563
Women's voices, 98n840
World population monitoring 1996, 99n809

WOMEN'S STUDIES
Asian American woman, 99n795
Index to women's studies anthologies, 98n841
Reader's gd to women's studies, 99n796
Resourceful woman, 95n916
Women in China, 99n808

WOMEN'S STUDIES INDEX
Women's studies index 1995, 98n842
Women's studies on disc [CD-ROM], 97n742

WOMEN & THE MILITARY
Women & the military, 96n680
Women & the military, 97n563
Women in the US military, 1901-95, 97n559

WOOD PRODUCTS. *See also* FORESTS & FORESTRY
Directory of the wood products industry, 1998, 99n1343
Guide to useful woods of the world, 95n1524
North American factbk, 1994-95, 96n1541

WOOD WARBLERS
Warblers of the Americas, 96n1613

WOODWORKING TOOLS
Complete gd to sharpening, 96n1679

WOOLF, VIRGINIA
Major authors on CD-ROM: Virginia Woolf [CD-ROM], 99n1087
Virginia Woolf A to Z, 96n1221

WORDS, NEW
Barnhart dict companion, v.10, no.1, summer 1997, 98n1010
Barnhart new-words concordance, 95n1025

WORDSWORTH, WILLIAM
Wordsworth's reading 1770-99, 95n1223

WORK ENVIRONMENT
Encyclopedia of environmental control tech, v.8, 96n1858

WORK & FAMILY
110 Canadian stats on work & family, 95n848
Work-Family research, 98n778

WORKING CLASS
Working stiffs, union maids, reds, & riffraff: an organized gd to films about labor, 97n1141

WORLD BANK
Historical dict of the World Bank, 98n186

WORLD CUP (SOCCER)
Encyclopedia of World Cup soccer, 95n822
United States & World Cup soccer competition, 95n823

WORLD GOVERNMENT
Dictionary of govt & pol, 2d ed, 99n654
Statesman's yrbk 1998-99, 135th ed, 99n82

WORLD HEALTH
International hndbk of public health, 98n1518

WORLD HEALTH ORGANIZATION
Historical dict of the world health org, 99n1421

WORLD HISTORY
Chronicle of the 20th century, 96n558
Chronicle of the world, rev ed, 97n464
Chronology of world hist, compact ed, 96n564
Classical studies, 97n461
Columbia gd to the Cold War, 99n543
Complete atlas of world hist, 98n491
DISCovering world hist [CD-ROM], 98n505
Dorling Kindersley hist of the world, 95n587
Eighteenth Century, 99n515
Eighteenth Century, 99n516
Europa world yrbk 1998, 39th ed, 99n66
Eyewitness hist of the world [CD-ROM], 96n567
Great misadventures, 99n522
Hammond atlas of the 20th century, 97n459
Historical gd to world slavery, 99n542
History of humanity, v.3, 98n507
History of the world in the 20th century, 95n589
Kingfisher illus hist of the world, 95n590
Literature connections to world hist, K-6, 99n512
Literature connections to world hist, 7-12, 99n513
Miniature empires, 99n537
Pocket factfile of 20th century events, 97n466
Timelines of world hist, 99n524

WORLD HISTORY—DICTIONARIES & ENCYCLOPEDIAS
Dead countries of the 19th & 20th centuries, 99n530
Dictionary of 19th-century world hist, 95n578
Dictionary of 20th-century world hist, 98n504
Dictionary of world biog, v.1, 99n519
Dictionary of world biog, v.2: the middle ages, 99n520
Encyclopedia of geographical features in world hist, 98n399
Encyclopedia of great civilizations, 95n580
From Aristotle to Zoroaster: an A to Z companion to the classical world, 99n526
Hutchinson dict of ancient & medieval warfare, 99n534
Hutchinson dict of world hist, 95n581
Illustrated ency of world hist, 98n503
Larousse dict of 20th century hist, 96n566
Larousse dict of world hist, 95n582
Macmillan ency of world slavery, 99n535
World hist: a dict of important people, places, & events..., 95n585

WORLD LEADERS
Countries of the world & their leaders yrbk 1999, 99n658
Profiles in world hist, 97n472
Whitaker's almanack world heads of govt 1998, 99n650
Whitaker's almanack world heads of state 1998, 99n651

WORLD MUSIC
Traditional world music influences in contemporary solo piano lit, 99n1148
World music CD listener's gd, 99n1159

WORLD POLITICS
Annual register 1995, 97n581
Cold War, 99n544
Cold War ency, 97n473
Cold War ref gd, 98n508
Countries of the world & their leaders yrbk 1995: suppl, 96n710
Countries of the world & their leaders yrbk 1999, 99n658
Encyclopedia of revolutions & revolutionaries, 97n477
Encyclopedia of the Cold War, 95n577
Europa world yrbk 1998, 39th ed, 99n66
Facts on File world pol almanac, 3d ed, 96n711
Federal systems of the world, [2d ed], 96n712
Handbook of the nations, 14th ed, 96n713
International dir of govt 1995, 2d ed, 96n707
Nations without states: a histl dict of contemporary natl movements, 97n583
Political systems of the world, 97n582
Profiles of worldwide govt leaders 1995, 96n708
Profiles of worldwide govt leaders 1998, 4th ed, 99n649
Statesman's yrbk 1998-99, 135th ed, 99n82
Wars in the Third World since 1945, 2d ed, 97n568
World dir of defense & security, 97n567
World factbk 1996-97, 97n80
World facts & maps, 98n400
World gd 1997/98, 10th ed, 98n97
Worldwide govt dir with intl orgs 1995, 96n709

WORLD RECORDS
Book of mosts, 99n65
Guinness bk of records 1995, 95n1329
Guinness multimedia disc of records, 1994: Windows 2.0 [CD-ROM], 95n1330
Top 10 of everything 1999, 99n63
Women's firsts, 98n835

WORLD'S COLOMBIAN EXPOSITION
World's Colombian Exposition, 97n404

WORLD SERIES (BASEBALL)
Inside Sports world series factbk, 97n645

WORLD TRADE ORGANIZATION
World trade org dispute settlement decisions, v.1, 99n237

WORLD WAR, 1914-1918
Atlas of WW I, 2d ed, 96n675
Dardanelles campaign, 1915, 98n494
Dictionary of the 1st World War, 97n474
European powers in the 1st World War, 97n467

Great war: a gd to the serv records of all the worlds fighting men & volunteers, 99n635
Grolier lib of WW I, 98n614
Historical atlas of WW I, 95n681
Historical dict of WW I, 99n532
Imperial War Museum film catalog, v.1, 96n557
United States in the 1st world war, 96n685
World War I, 99n541
World War I aviation, rev ed, 98n610
World War I songs, 96n696

WORLD WAR, 1939-1945
Biographical dict of WW II, 97n463
Biographical dict of WWII generals & flag officers: the US armed forces, 97n409
China-Burma-India campaign, 1931-45, 99n517
Cruisers of WW II, 97n574
D-Day ency, 95n686
Dangerous sky: resource gd to the Battle of Britain, 96n544
Executive order 9066 [CD-ROM], 99n470
Facts on File D-Day atlas, 95n680
Hollywood war films, 1937-45, 97n1123
Holocaust, 99n540
Juvenile novels of WW II, 95n1140
Medical & psychological effects of concentration camps on Holocaust survivors, v.4: genocide, 98n708
New Grolier ency of WW II, 96n684
Normandy [CD-ROM], 96n693
Oxford companion to WW II, 97n571
Pacific War atlas 1941-45, 96n676
Pacific War ency, 99n627
Philippines in WW II & to independence (Dec. 8, 1941-July 4, 1946), 2d ed, 97n432
Political leaders & military figures in the 2d World War, 98n606
Prisoners of the Japanese in WW II, 95n549
Signals intelligence in WW II, 97n560
Simon & Schuster D-Day ency: a multimedia exploration! [CD-ROM], 95n689
Solomon Islands campaign, Guadalcanal to Rabaul, 98n611
Southwest Pacific campaign, 1941-45, 97n462
Standard gd to US WW II tanks & artillery, 95n703
Touchstones: a gd to records, rights, & resources for families of American WW II casualties, 98n367
Understanding the Holocaust, 99n539
Vital gd to fighting aircraft of WW II, 97n580
War in N Africa, 1940-43, 97n460
Wartime Poland, 1939-45, 98n480
Ways of war: the era of WW II in children's & YA fiction, 96n1165
Who's who in WW II, 96n681
World War II: a statl survey, 95n691
World War II in Europe, Africa, & the Americas, with general sources, 98n622
World War II in the N Pacific, 95n684

WORLD WIDE WEB. *See also* **LISTSERVS; NEWSGROUPS; INTERNET**
Catholic Internet, USA ed, 98n1390
Chemicals on the Internet, v.1, 98n1478
Collecting in cyberspace, 98n893
College.edu: on-line resources for the cyber-savvy, 98n301
CyberTools for bus, 98n163
Directory of lib technical servs home pages, 98n591
Finding images online, 98n1592
God on the Internet, 98n1365
Internet complete ref, 2d ed, 98n1594
Internet gd for the legal researcher, 2d ed, 98n535
Job-Hunting on the Internet, 98n222
Key gd to electronic resources: art & art hist, 98n942
Mecklermedia's official Internet World WWW yellow pages, 1996 ed, 98n1588
Naked in cyberspace: how to find personal info online, 98n1596
Net jl dir, vol. 1, no. 2, 98n1591
Thunderbird gd to intl bus resources on the WWW, 98n204
Virtual field trips, 98n281
Virtual musician, 98n1206
Virtual roots: a gd to genealogy & local hist on the WWW, 98n366
Web site source bk 1998, 99n58

WOUNDS & INJURIES
Injury prevention for young children, 97n710

WRESTLERS
Biographical dict of professional wrestling, 98n752

WRITING
Bibliography on writing & written lang, 98n984
Blackwell ency of writing systems, 97n811
Theorizing composition, 99n831

WRITING CENTERS
Writing centers, 97n284

WRITTEN COMMUNICATION
World's writing systems, 97n816

WUORINEN, CHARLES
Charles Wuorinen: a bio-bibliog, 95n1265

X WINDOW SYSTEM (COMPUTER SYSTEM)
UNIX & X command compendium, 96n1762

YEARBOOKS
A&E entertainment almanac, 1997, 98n1264
American Jewish yr bk 1996, v.96, 97n1220
Annual register 1997, 99n657
Congressional yrbk 1996, 104th Congress, 2nd session, 98n672
Health & medical yrbk 1997, 98n1516
Industrial commodity stats yrbk 1994, 97n195
International yrbk 1997, 98n44
International yrbk of industrial stats 1996, 97n196
Library lit 1995, 97n529
Magill's cinema annual 1995, 14th ed, 97n1131
McGraw-Hill yrbk of sci & tech 1996, 97n1243
Popular music, v.21, 1996, 99n1164

Reference bks bulletin 1994-95, 97n12
Science yr 1997, 98n1416
Science yr 1998, 98n1417
Sources & methods: labour stats, v.2, 97n260
Yearbook of labour stats 1995, 54th ed, 97n261
United States govt manual 1996/97, 97n604
World Bk health & medical annual 1997, 98n1543
World Bk yr bk, 1997, 98n64

YEATS, W. B. (WILLIAM BUTLER)
William Butler Yeats ency, 98n1166

YELLOWBACK BOOKS
Victorian yellowbacks & paperbacks, 1849-1905, v.1, 96n1223
Victorian yellowbacks & paperbacks, 1849-1905, v.2, 96n1224

YEMEN
Yemen, rev ed, 99n139

YIDDISH LANGUAGE
Yiddish linguistics, 95n1026

YIDDISH LANGUAGE—DICTIONARIES—ENGLISH
English-Yiddish/Yiddish-English dict, [rev ed], 98n1054
English-Yiddish/Yiddish-English practical dict, 95n1100
Harduf's transliterated English-Yiddish/Yiddish-English dict, [rev ed], 98n1055
Hippocrene practical English-Yiddish/Yiddish-English dict, expanded ed, 97n878

YOGA
Shambhala ency of yoga, 98n1338

YORUBA LANGUAGE—DICTIONARIES—ENGLISH
Hippocrene concise Yoruba-English, English-Yoruba dict, 97n879

YOUNG ADULT LITERATURE
Adolescents at risk, 95n1134
Africa in lit for children & YAs, 96n1166
American Indian ref & resource bks for children & YAs, 2d ed, 96n1177
Authors & artists for YAs, v.13, 95n1144
Authors & artists for YAs, v.14, 96n1171
Authors & artists for YAs, v.20, 98n1100
Authors & artists for YAs, v.21, 98n1101
Best bks for YA readers, 98n1094
Biography today, 1993 annual cum, 96n25
Best bks for YAs, 95n1127
Books for the teen age 1994, 95n1119
Books for you, 98n1095
Booktalking the award winners 3, 98n1082
Booktalking the award winners: children's retrospective volume, 98n1081
Characters in YA lit, 98n1103
Culturally diverse lib collections for youth, 98n1099
Fantasy lit for children & YAs, 4th ed, 96n1167
Fiction sequels for readers 10 to 16, 2d ed, 99n1010
Focus on relationships, 95n883
Horn Bk gd to children's & YA bks, v.7, no.2, 98n1078
Index to histl fiction for children & young people, 96n1179
Junior DISCovering authors [CD-ROM], 95n1145
Juvenile novels of WW II, 95n1140
Learning about...the Civil War, 99n453
Learning about the Holocaust, 96n1170
Magazines for kids & teens, 96n86
Middle & jr high school lib catalog, 7th ed, 96n650
Middleplots 4, 95n1131
Novels for students, v.3, 99n1013
Novels for students, v.4, 99n1014
100 most popular YA authors, 97n941
100 most popular YA authors, rev ed, 98n1102
Outstanding bks for the college bound, 99n1011
Picture this: picture bks for YAs, 98n1097
Recreating the past, 95n1161
Serious about series, 99n1012
Short stories for students, v.3, 99n1015
Short stories for students, v.4, 99n1016
Something about the author, v.94, 99n988
Something about the author, v.95, 99n986
Something about the author autobiog series, v.24, 98n1080
Something about the author autobiog series, v.25, 99n987
Supplementing lit programs, 95n1129
Teen genreflecting, 98n1096
This land is our land: a gd to multicultural lit for children & YAs, 95n1133
Twentieth-Century YA writers, 95n1147
Ways of war: the era of WW II in children's & YA fiction, 96n1165
What do YAs read next?, 95n1139
What do YAs read next? v.2, 98n1098
What else should I read? guiding kids to good bks, v.2, 98n1076
Writers for YAs, 98n1104
Writers of multicultural fiction for YAs, 97n942
Young adult lit & nonprint materials, 95n654
Your reading, 1995-96 ed, 97n925

YOUNG ADULT LITERATURE, SPANISH
Recommended bks in Spanish for children & YAs, 1991-95, 98n1079

YOUNG ADULTS—LAW
Children, YAs, & the law, 99n551

YOUTH
National gd to funding for children, youth, & families, 3d ed, 97n698
State legislative summary, 1994, 96n595

YOUTH—EMPLOYMENT
Peterson's summer opportunities for kids & teenagers 1996, 13th ed, 97n167

YOUTH HOSTELS
Hostelling N America, 1997, 98n403
Hostelling USA, 1996, 97n389
Hostels USA, 99n431

YOUTH MOVEMENTS
Encyclopedia of student & youth movements, 99n653

YOUTH ORGANIZATIONS
Directory of American youth orgs 1994-95, 5th ed, 96n902
Directory of American youth orgs 1998-99, 7th ed, 99n52

YUGOSLAVIA. *See also* **FORMER YUGOSLAV REPUBLICS**
Breakup of Yugoslavia & the war in Bosnia, 99n116
Slovenia, 97n122

ZAIRE
Zaire, 96n126

ZAMBIA
Historical dict of Zambia, 2d ed, 99n477

ZIMBABWE
Zimbabwe, rev ed, 95n125

ZIONISM
New ency of Zionism & Israel, 96n164

ZIP CODES. *See also* **STREET ADDRESSES**
County locator (LOCUS): ultimate place name & zip code locator, 95n69
Instant natl locator gd, 3d ed, 98n53
National 5-digit zip code & post office dir 1996, 97n52
Sourcebook of zip code demographics, 10th ed, 96n913
Zip code finder, 98n59

ZODIAC
Signs of the zodiac, 98n717

ZONAL FILM ARCHIVES
Catalogue of forbidden German feature & short film productions held in Zonal Film Archives..., English lang ed, 97n764

ZOOLOGY
Animal life, 96n1604
Guide to the zoological lit: the animal kingdom, 95n1562
Species info lib [CD-ROM], 96n1606
Wildlife worldwide [CD-ROM], 96n1607
World alive [CD-ROM], 96n1609